VBA for Modelers

Developing Decision Support
Systems with Microsoft® Excel

VBA for Modelers

Developing Decision Support
Systems with Microsoft® Excel

S. Christian Albright

Kelley School of Business, Indiana University

DUXBURY

THOMSON LEARNING

Australia • Canada • Mexico • Singapore • Spain • United Kingdom • United States

DUXBURY

THOMSON LEARNING

Sponsoring Editor: *Curt Hinrichs*
Marketing Representative: *Chris Kelly*
Production Editor: *Janet Hill*
Production Service: *Susan L. Reiland*
Cover Design: *Denise Davidson*

Editorial Assistant: *Nathan Day*
Print Buyer: *Kris Waller*
Typesetting: *Scratchgravel Publishing Services*
Printing and Binding: *Webcom*

For more information about this or any other Duxbury product, contact:
DUXBURY
511 Forest Lodge Road
Pacific Grove, CA 93950 USA
www.duxbury.com
1-800-423-0563 Thomson Learning Academic Resource Center

Printed in Canada

10   9   8   7   6   5   4   3   2

Library of Congress Cataloging-in-Publication Data
Albright, S. Christian.
     VBA for modelers: developing decision support systems with Microsoft Excel/S.
   Christian Albright
         p. cm.
     ISBN 0-534-38012-3 (alk. paper)
        1. Decision support systems. 2. Microsoft Visual Basic for applications. 3. Microsoft
     Excel (Computer file). I. Title.

T58.62.A43 2001
658.4'03'02855369—dc21   00-064357

To Mary, my wonderful wife, best friend, and constant companion.

*And to Charlie, the dearest and funniest cocker spaniel of all—
may she live another 12 years.*

Contents

9 Arrays 125

10 More on Variables and Subroutines 147

11 Working with the Solver Add-In in VBA 171

12 User Forms 187

18 A Production Scheduling Application   307

19 A Minimum-Cost Network Flow Application   333

20 A Stock Trading Simulation   353

21 A Capital Budgeting Application   367

22 An Application for Estimating the Relationship Between Two Variables   381

23 An Exponential Utility Application   395

24 Simulation of a Multiserver Queue   409

Preface

I wrote *VBA for Modelers* for students and professionals who wish to create decision support systems using Microsoft Excel-based spreadsheet models. The book assumes the reader is either familiar with spreadsheet modeling or is taking a concurrent course in management science or operations research. It does not assume any prior programming experience. The book contains two parts. Part I covers the essentials of VBA (Visual Basic for Applications) programming, and Part II covers many applications with their associated programming code.

There are many excellent books available for VBA programming, many others covering decision support systems, and still others for spreadsheet modeling methodologies. However, I have not found a book that attempts to unify these subjects in a practical way. *VBA for Modelers* is designed for this purpose, and I hope you find *VBA for Modelers* to be an important resource and reference in your own work.

Why This Book?

The original impetus for this book began about five years ago. Wayne Winston and I were experimenting with the spreadsheet approach to teaching management as we were writing the first edition of our *Practical Management Science* (*PMS*) book. Because I have always had an interest in computer programming, I decided to learn VBA, the relatively new macro language for Excel, and use it to a limited extent in my undergraduate management science modeling course. My intent was to teach the students how to "wrap" a given spreadsheet model, such as a product mix model, into an *application* with a "front end" and a "back end" by using VBA. The front end would enable a user to provide inputs to the model, usually through one or more dialog boxes, and the back end would present the user with a nontechnical report of the results. I found it to be an exciting addition to the usual modeling course, and my students overwhelmingly agreed. The primary problem with teaching this type of course has been the lack of an appropriate VBA textbook. Although there are many good VBA "trade books" available, they usually go into much more technical VBA detail than I have time to cover, and their objective usually is to teach VBA programming as an end in itself. Over the years, several colleagues have suggested that I write the appropriate book, and this year I finally decided to do it. The timing is perfect because it coincides with the publication of the second edition of *PMS*. I expect that many adopters of *PMS* will decide to use parts of *VBA for Modelers* to supplement their management science courses, just I have been doing. For readers who have taken a management science course, there is more than enough material in this book to fill an entire elective course or to be used for self-study.

Objectives of the Book

VBA for Modelers shows how the power of spreadsheet modeling can be extended to the masses. Through VBA, complex management science models can be made accessible to nonexperts by providing them with simplified input screens and output reports. The book will illustrate, in complete detail, how such applications can be developed for a wide variety of business problems.

In writing the book, I have always concerned myself with the following question: How much will the readers be able to do on their own? Is it enough for the students to see the completed applications, marvel at how powerful they are, and possibly take a look at the code that runs in the background? Or should they be taken to the point where they can develop their *own* applications, code and all? I am still not sure what the correct answer is, and I suspect it will vary, depending on the audience, but I know I *can* get readers to the point where they can develop modest applications on their own and, importantly, experience the thrill of programming success.

With these thoughts in mind, I have written this book so that it can be used at several levels. For the reader who wants to learn VBA from scratch and then apply it, I have provided a "VBA primer" in the first 13 chapters. It is admittedly not as complete as some of the thick Excel VBA books available, but I believe it covers the basics of VBA quite adequately. Importantly, it covers coding methods for working with Excel ranges in Chapter 6 (and uses these methods extensively in later chapters), so that readers will not have to use trial and error or wade through online help, as I had to do when I was learning the language. Readers can then proceed to the applications chapters, 14–30, and apply their skills. In contrast, there are probably many readers who do not have time to learn all of the details. They can still use the applications in the second part of the book for illustration purposes. Indeed, the applications have been developed for generality. For example, the minimum-cost network flow model in Chapter 19 is perfectly general and can be used to solve *any* of the minimum-cost network flow models in Chapter 5 of (the revised) *PMS* or similar text by providing the appropriate input data.

Approach

My philosophy in this book is similar to that in *PMS*—I like to teach (and learn) through examples. I have found that I can learn a programming language only if I have a strong motivation to learn it. I doubt that readers of this book are any different. The applications in the latter chapters are based on many of the most interesting examples from *PMS*. They provide the motivation for the reader to learn the material. The examples illustrate that this book is not about programming for the sake of programming, but is instead about developing useful applications for business. Students and professionals already realize that Excel modeling skills make them more valuable in the workplace. This book will help them realize that VBA skills can make them even *more* valuable.

Contents of the Book

The book is written in two parts. Part I, Chapters 1–13, is a VBA primer for students with little or no programming experience in VBA (or any other language). Although all of these chapters are geared to VBA, some are more about general programming concepts, whereas others deal with the unique aspects of programming for Excel. Specifically, Chapters 7, 9, and 10 discuss control logic (If–Then–Else constructions), loops, arrays, and subroutines, topics that are common to all programming languages. In contrast, Chapters 6 and 8 explain how to work with some of the most common Excel objects (ranges, workbooks, worksheets, and charts) in VBA. In addition, several chapters discuss aspects of VBA that can be used with Excel or any other applications (Access, Word, Powerpoint, etc.) that use VBA as their programming language. Specifically, Chapter 3 explains the Visual Basic Editor (VBE), Chapter 5 illustrates how to record macros, Chapter 11 explains how to run Excel's Solver add-in with VBA code, Chapter 12 explains how to build user forms (dialog boxes), and Chapter 13 discusses the important topics of debugging and error handling.

The material in Part I is reasonably complete, but it is available, in greater detail and with a somewhat different emphasis, in several other books.[1] The unique aspect of *this* book is Part II, Chapters 14–30. Each chapter in this part discusses a specific application. Most of these are optimization and simulation applications, and many are quite general. For example, Chapter 16 discusses a general product mix application, Chapter 18 discusses a general production scheduling application, Chapter 19 discusses a general minimum-cost network flow application, Chapter 20 discusses a stock market trading simulation, Chapter 24 discusses a multiple-server queue simulation, Chapter 25 discusses a general application for pricing European and American options, and Chapter 27 discusses a general portfolio optimization application. (Almost all of the underlying models for these applications are discussed in *PMS* though I have attempted to make these applications standalone.) The applications can be used as they stand to solve real problems, or they can be used as examples of VBA application development. All of the steps in the development of these applications are explained, and all of the VBA source code is included. Using an analogy to a car, readers can simply get in and drive, or they can open the hood and see how everything works.

Chapter 14 gets the process started in a "gentle" way. It provides a general introduction to application development, with a list of guidelines. It then illustrates

---

[1] My favorite is *Microsoft Excel 2000 Power Programming with VBA* by John Walkenbach, IDG Books, 1999.

these guidelines in a car loan application. This application should be within the grasp of most readers, even if they are not great programmers. By tackling this application first, readers get to develop a simple model, dialog boxes, reports, and charts, and then tie everything together. This car loan application illustrates an important concept that I stress throughout the book. Specifically, applications that really *do* something are often long and have a lot of details. But this does not mean that they are *difficult*. With perseverance (a word I use frequently), readers can fill in the details one step at a time and ultimately experience the thrill of finishing an application that works correctly.

Virtually all management science applications require input data. An extremely important issue for VBA application development is how to get the required model data into the spreadsheet model. I illustrate a number of possibilities in Part II. If only a small amount of data is required, then dialog boxes work well. These are used for data input in many of the applications. However, there are many times when the data requirements are much too large for dialog boxes. In these cases, the data are usually stored in some type of database. I illustrate some common possibilities. In Chapter 16, the input data for a product mix model are stored in a separate worksheet. In Chapter 26, the stock price data for finding the betas of stocks are stored in a separate Excel workbook. In Chapter 28, the data for a DEA model are stored in a text (.txt) file. In Chapter 19, the data for a minimum cost network flow model are stored in an Access database (.mdb) file. Finally, in Chapter 27, the stock price data required for a portfolio optimization model are located on a Web site and are imported into Excel, *at runtime*! In each case, I explain the VBA statements that are necessary to retrieve the data into the Excel application.

How to Use the Book

I have already discussed several approaches to using this book, depending on how much VBA one wishes to learn. For readers with very little or no computer programming background who want to learn the fundamentals of VBA, Chapters 1–13 should be covered first, in approximately that order. (I should point out that it is practically impossible to avoid "later" programming concepts while covering "early" ones. For example, I admit to using a few If constructions and For Each loops in early chapters, *before* discussing them formally in Chapter 7. I don't believe this should cause problems. I use plenty of comments, and readers can always look ahead if they need to.) Once the VBA fundamentals are covered in the first 13 chapters, Chapter 14 should be covered next. Beyond that, the applications in the remaining chapters can be covered in practically any order, depending on the interests of the reader. However, note that some of the details in certain applications will not make much sense unless one has had the appropriate training in the management science *models*. For example, Chapter 29 discusses an AHP application for choosing a job. The VBA code is fairly straightforward, but it will not make much sense without knowledge of AHP. I assume that the knowledge of the models comes from a separate source, such as *PMS*; I cover it only briefly here.

At the other extreme, readers can simply use the Excel application files to solve problems. Indeed, the applications have been written specifically for non-technical end users, so that readers at all levels should have no difficulty opening the application files and using them appropriately. In short, readers can decide how much of the material "under the hood" is worth their time.

Exercises

To our *PMS* users who are accustomed to 60 or more exercises per chapter, I admit that there is no such abundance here, at least not yet. However, at the end of each chapter (starting with Chapter 3), there is a collection of programming exercises that either practice or extend the programming concepts in the chapter. These exercises should keep readers plenty interested and busy. Some have been marked "More difficult" for the obvious reason. As I develop more exercises in the future, I will place them on my Web site, www.indiana.edu/~mgtsci, where they will be available for downloading. Solutions to all exercises will be available to instructors by contacting Duxbury Thomson Learning.

In addition, each of Chapters 6–13 presents an exercise immediately after the introductory section. (This idea was suggested by one of the reviewers. In his words, these exercises provide the "dramatic tension.") The material in these chapters, necessary as it is, can be tough going for beginning programmers, especially if they are not sufficiently motivated. These exercises are intended to provide the motivation. I expect that readers will see these exercises, say to themselves, "I'll be able to do that?", and read on with increased interest. Each of these exercises has an accompanying "finished" version that contains the solution, but I urge readers to try the exercises on their own before looking at the solutions. By the way, I have found in my current course that these exercises provide excellent ready-made hands-on demos for use in a classroom setting, assuming the class is being delivered in a computer lab. After a brief explanation of the concepts in the chapter, I get my students to open the template, and then I lead them through to the finished solution.

CD-ROM

The CD-ROM that accompanies this book contains all of the Excel (.xls) and other files mentioned in the chapters, including those in the exercises. The Excel files require Excel 97 or a more recent version; they will not work with Excel 95 or an earlier version. In addition, many of the files have a "reference" to Excel's Solver. *They will not work unless the Solver add-in is loaded.* Finally, the application in Chapter 19 uses Microsoft's new ActiveX Data Object (ADO) model to import the data from an Access file into Excel. This will work only in Excel 2000 or a more recent version.

Web Site

The book is accompanied by a Web site that was mentioned earlier. The Web site contains detailed descriptions and comments on the programs used in Part II. These comments break down individual coding elements of each completed application. Throughout the book, Web resources are identified with the icon shown in the margin. Additionally, the Web site will post additional exercises and other updates as they become available in the future. You can access the site from www.duxbury.com (select Online Book Companions) or directly at www.indiana.edu/~mgtsci.

Acknowledgments

I would like to thank several groups. First, I want to thank all of the students who have taken my management science course since I began using VBA in it. Special thanks go to the *first* such class in Spring 1996. In those days, I was about two days ahead of the students in terms of learning VBA, and I realize now that the code I was using was, to say the least, not very elegant. However, they gave me better teaching evaluations than I could ever have expected (probably because I was taking the risk of teaching something new and useful), and this encouraged me to keep at it.

Second, I want to thank all of my colleagues at Duxbury Thomson Learning. Foremost among them is my editor, Curt Hinrichs. When he first suggested that I write a VBA book, my reaction was, "Not another book—I thought I was finally going to have some time to play some golf in the summer!" However, I eventually agreed to write a short, no-frills book to accompany the second edition of *PMS*. Once the project gained momentum and we started hearing positive things from reviewers, Curt persuaded me to expand the book into one that could be used as a stand-alone textbook for an entire course. As always, I believe he made the right decision, and, now that the writing is behind me, I thank him for it. Thanks also go to the professionals at Duxbury and Brooks/Cole including Susan Reiland, Janet Hill, Samantha Cabaluna, Tom Ziolkowski, Nathan Day, and Seema Atwal.

Third, I want to thank the reviewers of the manuscript. The reviewing process for this book was not as extensive as for some books, but the reviews I received were very insightful and prompted a number of changes that have made the book much better. Thanks go to:

Donald Byrkett, Miami University
Kostis Christodoulou, London School of Economics
Charles Franz, University of Missouri
Larry LeBlanc, Vanderbilt University
Jerrold May, University of Pittsburgh
James Morris, University of Wisconsin
Tom Schriber, University of Michigan

Finally, I want to thank my wife, Mary. Throughout this summer, she has never once complained when I've retreated to "my hole" to write chapters and

VBA code. She has always had the coffee brewing, a sandwich made at lunch time, and a great dinner by the time my brain was no longer functioning. She will receive her reward at royalty check time!

S. Christian Albright
e-mail: albright@indiana.edu
Web site: www.indiana.edu/~mgtsci

Part I

VBA Fundamentals

This part of the book is for readers who need a fairly quick introduction to programming in general, and to Visual Basic for Applications (VBA) for Excel in particular. It discusses programming topics that are common to practically all programming languages, including variable types and declarations, control logic, looping, arrays, subroutines, and error handling. It also discusses many topics that are specific to VBA and its use with Excel, including the Excel object model, recording macros, working with ranges, workbooks, worksheets, charts, and other Excel objects, developing user forms (dialog boxes), and running Excel's Solver add-in with VBA code.

Starting with Chapter 6, each chapter in Part I presents a business-related exercise immediately after the introductory section. The objective of each such exercise is to motivate readers to work through the details of the chapter, knowing that many of these details will be required to solve the exercise. The solutions are provided in "finished" files, but we urge readers to try the exercises on their own, before looking at the solutions.

The chapters in this part should be read in (at least approximately) the order they are written. Programming is a skill that builds upon itself. Although it is not always possible to avoid referring to a concept from a later chapter in an early chapter, we have attempted to refrain from doing this as much as possible.

Introduction to VBA Development in Excel

1.1 Introduction

Our book *Practical Management Science* illustrates how to solve a wide variety of business problems by developing appropriate Excel models. If you are familiar with this modeling process, you probably do not need to be convinced of the power and applicability of Excel. You realize that Excel modeling skills will make you valuable to virtually any company you choose to work for. This book takes the process one *giant* step farther. It teaches you how to develop *applications* in Excel by using Excel's programming language, Visual Basic for Applications (VBA).

In *Practical Management Science* (and all other management science books written around Excel), you learn how to model a particular problem. You enter given inputs in a worksheet, you relate them with appropriate formulas, and you eventually calculate required outputs. You might also optimize a particular output with Solver, and you might create one or more charts to show outputs graphically. You do all of this through the Excel interface, using its menus and toolbars, entering formulas into its cells, using the Chart Wizard, using the Solver dialog box, and so on. If you are conscientious, you document your work so that another person in your company can use your completed model. For example, you clearly indicate the input cells so that other users will know which cells they should enter their own inputs in, and which they should leave alone.

Now suppose that your position in a company is to *develop* applications for other, less technical people in the organization to use. Part of your job is still to develop spreadsheet models, as described in *Practical Management Science*, but the details of these models will probably be incomprehensible to many users. These users might know that they have, say, a product mix problem, where they will have to supply certain inputs and then some computer magic will eventually determine an optimal mix of products. However, the part in between is more than they want to deal with. Your job, therefore, is to develop a user-friendly application with a model (probably hidden from the user) surrounded by a "front end" and a "back end." The front end will present the user with dialog boxes or some other means for allowing them to "define" their problem. Here they will be able to specify input parameters and possibly other choices. Your application will take these choices, build the appropriate model, optimize it if necessary, and eventually present the back end to the user: a nontechnical report of the results, possibly with accompanying charts.

This application development is possible with VBA, as this book will demonstrate. There is no claim that it is easy, or that it can be done quickly, but it is within the realm of possibility for people other than "professional programmers." It requires a logical mind, a willingness to experiment and take full advantage of online help, plenty of practice, and, above all, perseverance. Even professional programmers seldom accomplish their tasks without difficulty and plenty of errors; this is the nature of programming. However, they learn from their errors, and they refuse to quit until they figure out how to make their programs work. Computer programming is essentially a process of getting by one small hurdle after another. This is where perseverance is so important. However, if you are not easily discouraged, and if you love the feeling of accomplishment that comes from finally getting something to work, you will love the challenge of application development described in this book.

1.2 Example Applications

If you have used *Practical Management Science*, you probably have a good idea of what a spreadsheet model is. However, you might not understand what is meant by spreadsheet *applications*, with "front ends" and "back ends." In other words, you might not understand what this book intends to teach you. The best way to find out is to run some of the applications that will be explained later. At this point, *you* can become the nontechnical user by opening any of the following files that accompany this book: **ProductMix.xls**, **Scheduling.xls**, **StockOptions.xls**, **NetworkFlow.xls**, **StockBeta.xls**, or **StockQuery.xls**. (For the latter file, you will need an open Internet connection.) Simply open any of these files and follow instructions. It should be easy. After all, the purpose of writing these applications is to make it easy for a nontechnical user to run them and get results they can understand. Now step back and imagine what must be happening in the background to enable these applications to do what they are doing. This is what you will be learning in this book. Hopefully, by running a few applications, you will become anxious to learn how to do it yourself. If nothing else, these sample applications will illustrate just how powerful a tool VBA for Excel can be.

1.3 Required Background

The readers of this book probably vary widely in their programming experience. At one extreme, there are undoubtedly many of you who have never programmed in VBA or any other language. At the other extreme, there are probably a few of you who have programmed in VBA, but have never attempted application development as it is defined here. In the middle, some of you have probably had some programming experience in another language such as C, COBOL, FORTRAN, Pascal, or Visual Basic, but have never learned any VBA. This book is intended to appeal to all of these audiences. Therefore, a simplified answer to the question, "What programming background do I need?" is, "None; you need only a willingness to learn and practice."

If you ran some of the applications discussed in Section 1.2, you are probably anxious to get started developing similar applications. If you already know the fundamentals of VBA for Excel (which definitely means that you are in the minority!), you can jump ahead to chapters in Part II of this book that describe these applications. But most of you will have to learn how to walk before you can run. Therefore, the chapters in Part I go through the basics of the VBA language, especially as it applies to Excel. The coverage of this basic material will provide you with enough explanations and examples of VBA's important features to enable you to understand the applications in Part II—and to do some Excel development on your own.

If you want more detailed guidance in VBA for Excel, refer to *Excel 2000 Power Programming with VBA* by John Walkenbach, an excellent 800-page book with enough information and insights to meet practically any developer's needs. (Walkenbach has also published a scaled-down version of this book in the popular *Dummies* series, and it is also excellent, especially for a beginning programmer.) In addition, once you master some of the basic concepts, you can learn from online help. Indeed, this is perhaps the best way to learn, especially in the middle of a development project. If you need to know one specific detail to get you past a hurdle in the program you are writing, you can look it up quickly in online help. A good way to do this will be demonstrated shortly.

This book does assume some modeling ability and general business background. For example, if you ran the **ProductMix.xls** application, you probably realize that it develops and optimizes a product mix model, one of the best-known linear programming models. One (but not the only) step in developing this application is to develop a product mix model, exactly as in Chapter 3 of *Practical Management Science*. As another example, if you ran the **StockOptions.xls** application, you realize the need to understand option pricing (explained in Chapter 12 of *Practical Management Science*). Many of the applications in this book are based on examples (product mix, scheduling, network flow, and so on) from *Practical Management Science*. You can refer to those examples if necessary.

1.4 Visual Basic Versus VBA

Before going any further, we should clear up one common misconception. Visual Basic and VBA are *not* the same thing. Visual Basic is a software development package that you can buy and run separately, without the need for Excel (or Office). It is a stand-alone package, in Version 6 at the time of this writing. On the other hand, VBA comes with Office. If you own Microsoft Office, you own VBA. The Visual Basic language is very similar to VBA, but it is not the same. No attempt will be made here to detail the differences. However, the main difference you should understand is that VBA is the language you need to manipulate Excel, as we will do here. Think of it as follows. The VBA language consists of a "backbone" programming language, with typical programming elements you find in all programming languages: looping, logical If–Then–Else constructions, arrays, subroutines, variable types, and others. In this respect, VBA and Visual Basic are essentially identical. However, the "for Applications" in Visual Basic for Applications means that any application software package, such as Excel, Access, Word, or even a non-Microsoft software package, can "expose" its "objects" to VBA, so that VBA can manipulate them programmatically. In short, VBA can be used to develop applications for any of these software packages.

Excel objects will be discussed in some depth in later chapters, but a few typical Excel objects you will recognize right away are ranges, worksheets, and charts. VBA for Excel knows about these Excel objects, and it is capable of manipulating them with code. For example, it can change the font of a cell, it can name a range, it can add or delete a worksheet, and it can change the title of a chart. Part of learning VBA for Excel is learning the "backbone" language, the elements that have nothing to do with Excel specifically. But another part, and possibly the more difficult part, involves learning how to manipulate Excel's objects in code. That is, it involves learning how to write computer programs to do what you are used to doing through the familiar Excel interface. If you ever take a course in Visual Basic (meaning the stand-alone package), you will learn the "backbone" elements of VBA, but you will not learn how to manipulate objects in Excel. This requires VBA, and you *will* learn it in this book.

By the way, there are also VBA for Access, VBA for Word, VBA for PowerPoint, and others. The only difference between them is that each has its own specific objects. To list just a few, Access has tables, queries, and forms, Word has paragraphs and footnotes, and PowerPoint has slides. Each version of VBA shares the same "backbone" language, but each requires you to learn how to manipulate the objects in the specific application. There is undoubtedly a learning curve in moving, say, from VBA for Excel to VBA for Access, but it is not nearly as steep as if they were totally separate languages. In fact, the power of VBA (and the relative ease of programming in it) is prompting many third-party software developers to license VBA from Microsoft, so that they can use VBA as the programming language for their applications. In short, once you know VBA, even if it is just VBA for Excel, you know a lot about what is happening in the programming world—and you can very possibly use this knowledge to obtain a valuable job in business.

1.5 Summary

VBA is becoming the programming language of choice for an increasingly wide range of application developers. As this chapter has discussed, the main reason for this is that VBA provides a "backbone" programming language that can then be adapted to many Microsoft and non-Microsoft application software packages, including Excel. In addition, VBA is a relatively easy programming language to master. This makes it accessible to a large number of "nonprofessional" programmers in the business world—including you! By learning how to program in VBA, you will greatly magnify your value as an employee.

The Excel Object Model

2.1 Introduction

Perhaps the best place to start when learning VBA for Excel is the Excel object model—the concept behind it and how it is implemented. Even if you have programmed in another language, this will probably be new material, even a new way of thinking, for you. However, without understanding Excel objects, you will not be able to proceed very far with VBA for Excel. This chapter provides a very brief introduction to the Excel object model, just enough to get us started. Later chapters will focus on many of the most important Excel objects and how they can be manipulated with VBA code.

2.2 Objects, Properties, and Methods

Consider the many "things" you see in the everyday world. To name a few, there are cars, houses, computers, people, and so on. We might consider all of these as **objects**. For example, let's focus on a particular car. This car has attributes, and there are things you can do to (or with) a car. Some of its attributes are its weight, its horsepower, its color, and the number of doors. Some of the things you can do to (or with) a car are drive it, park it, accelerate it, crash it, and sell it. In VBA, the attributes of an object are called **properties**: the size property, the horsepower property, the color property, the number of doors property, and so on. In addition, each property has a **value** for any *particular* car. For example, the car might be white and it might have four doors. In contrast, the things you can do to an object are called **methods**: the drive method, the park method, the accelerate method, the crash method, the sell method, and so on. Methods can also have "qualifiers," called **arguments**, which indicate *how* a method is carried out. For example, an argument of the crash method might be speed—how fast the car was going when it crashed.

The following analogy to parts of speech might be useful. Objects correspond to *nouns*, properties correspond to *adjectives*, methods correspond to *verbs*, and arguments of methods correspond to *adverbs*. You might want to keep this analogy in mind as the discussion proceeds.

Now let's move from cars to Excel. Imagine all of the things—objects—you work with in Excel. Some of the most common are ranges, worksheets, charts, and workbooks. (A workbook is a synonym for an Excel file.) Each of these is an object in the Excel object model. For example, consider the single-cell range B5.

This range is considered a **Range** object. [1] Like a car, it has properties. It has a **Value** property: the value (either text or numeric) in the cell. It has a **HorizontalAlignment** property: left, center, or right aligned. It has a **Formula** property: the formula (if any) in the cell. These are just a few of the properties of a range. We will see others later on.

A Range object also has methods. For example, you can copy a range, so **Copy** is a method of a Range object. You can probably guess the argument of the Copy method: the **Destination** argument (that is, the paste range). Another range method is the **ClearContents** method, which is equivalent to highlighting the range and pressing the Delete key. It deletes the contents of the range, but it does not change the formatting. If you want to clear the formatting as well, there is also a **Clear** method. Neither the ClearContents method nor the Clear method has any arguments.

Learning the various objects in Excel, along with their properties and methods, is a lot like learning vocabulary in English—especially if English is not your native language. You learn a little at a time and generally broaden your vocabulary through practice and experience. Some objects, properties, and methods are naturally used most often, and you will probably pick them up quickly. Others you will never need, and you will probably remain unaware that they even exist. However, there are many times when you *will* need to use a particular object or one of its properties or methods that you have not yet learned. Fortunately, there is excellent online help available—a dictionary of sorts—for learning about objects, properties, and methods. It is called the **Object Browser** and will be discussed in the next chapter.

2.3 Collections as Objects

Continuing the car analogy, imagine that you enter a large used car lot. Each car in the lot is a particular object, but it also makes sense to consider the *collection* of all cars in the lot as an object. We call this a **collection** object. Clearly, the collection of cars is not conceptually the same as an individual car. Rather, it is an object that includes all of the individual cars.

Collection objects also have properties and methods, but they are not the same as the properties and methods of the objects they contain. Generally, there are many fewer properties and methods for collections. Probably the two most common are the **Count** property and the **Add** method. The Count property indicates how many objects are in the collection (how many cars are in the lot), whereas the Add method adds a new object to a collection (a new car joins the lot).

It is easy to spot collections and the objects they contain in the Excel object model. Collection objects are plural, whereas a typical object contained in a collection is singular. A good example involves worksheets (of a given workbook). The **Worksheets** collection (note the plural) is the collection of all worksheets in the

---

[1] From here on, "proper" case, such as Range or HorizontalAlignment, will be used for objects, properties, and methods. This is in preparation for the proper case conventions used in VBA.

workbook. Any one of these worksheets is a **Worksheet** object (note the singular). Again, these must be treated differently. You can count worksheets in the Worksheets collection, or you can add another worksheet to the collection. In contrast, typical properties of a Worksheet are its **Name** (the name on the sheet tab) and **Visible** (True or False) properties, and a typical method of a Worksheet is the **Delete** method.

The main exception to this plural/singular characterization is the **Range** object. There is no "Ranges" collection object. A Range object cannot really be considered singular *or* plural; it is essentially some of each. A Range object can be a single cell, a rectangular range, a "union" of several rectangular ranges, an entire column, or an entire row. Range objects are probably the most difficult to master in all of their varied forms. This is unfortunate because they are probably the most frequently used objects in Excel. Think of your own experience in Excel, and you will realize that you are almost always doing something with ranges. An entire chapter (Chapter 6) is devoted to Range objects, so that you can master some of the techniques for manipulating these important objects.

2.4 The Hierarchy of Objects

Returning one last time to cars, we have agreed that a car is an object with methods and properties. But what is the status of a car's hood, a car's trunk, or a car's set of wheels? These are also objects, with their own properties and methods. In fact, the set of wheels is a collection object that contains individual wheel objects. The point, however, is that there is a natural hierarchy, as illustrated in Figure 2.1. The Cars collection is at the top of the hierarchy. It contains a set of individual cars. The notation Cars (Car) indicates that the collection object is called Cars and that each member of this collection is called a Car object. Each car "contains" a number of objects: a Wheels collection of individual Wheel objects, a Trunk object, a Hood object, and others not shown. Each of these can have its own properties and methods. Also, some can contain objects farther down the hierarchy. For example, the figure indicates that an object down the hierarchy from Hood is the HoodOrnament object. Note that each of the rectangles in this figure represents an *object*. Each object has properties and methods that we could show emanating from its rectangle, but this would greatly complicate the figure.

Figure 2.1 Object model for cars

Part of the object model for cars

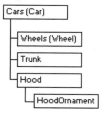

Figure 2.2 Excel object model

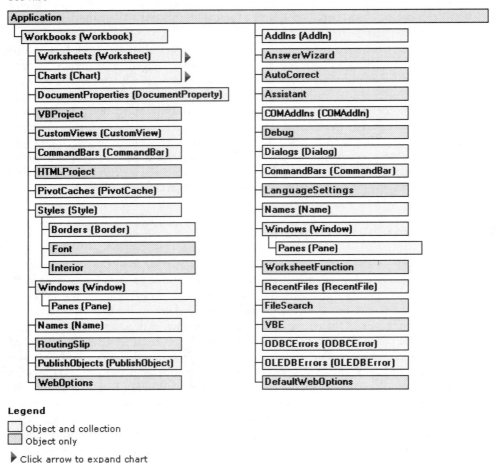

Microsoft Excel Objects

See Also

Application	
Workbooks (Workbook)	AddIns (AddIn)
Worksheets (Worksheet) ▶	AnswerWizard
Charts (Chart) ▶	AutoCorrect
DocumentProperties (DocumentProperty)	Assistant
VBProject	COMAddIns (COMAddIn)
CustomViews (CustomView)	Debug
CommandBars (CommandBar)	Dialogs (Dialog)
HTMLProject	CommandBars (CommandBar)
PivotCaches (PivotCache)	LanguageSettings
Styles (Style)	Names (Name)
Borders (Border)	Windows (Window)
Font	Panes (Pane)
Interior	WorksheetFunction
Windows (Window)	RecentFiles (RecentFile)
Panes (Pane)	FileSearch
Names (Name)	VBE
RoutingSlip	ODBCErrors (ODBCError)
PublishObjects (PublishObject)	OLEDBErrors (OLEDBError)
WebOptions	DefaultWebOptions

Legend

☐ Object and collection
☐ Object only

▶ Click arrow to expand chart

The same situation occurs in Excel. The full diagram of the Excel object model appears in Figure 2.2. This figure shows how all objects, including collection objects, are arranged in a hierarchy. At the top of the hierarchy is the **Application** object. This refers to Excel itself.[2] One object (of several) one step down from Application is the **Workbooks** collection, the collection of all open **Workbook** objects. From any particular Workbook object in this collection, we can go one step down the hierarchy to the **Worksheets** collection, the collection of all worksheets in this workbook.

---

[2]If we were discussing VBA for Access, say, there would also be an Application object at the top of the hierarchy, but it would be Access.

Figure 2.3   Excel object model for worksheets

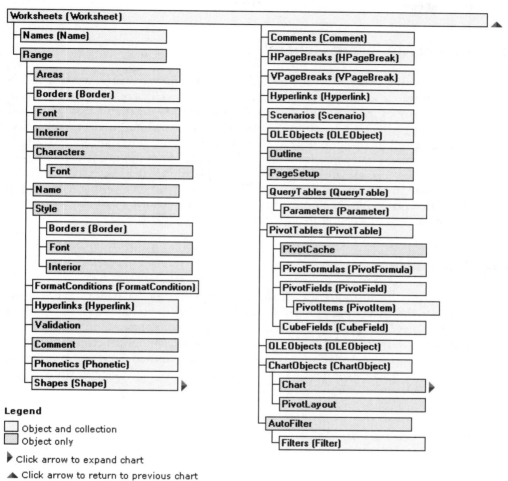

Microsoft Excel Objects (Worksheet)

See Also

Legend

☐ Object and collection
☐ Object only

▶ Click arrow to expand chart
▲ Click arrow to return to previous chart

If you are viewing this figure in online help and you want to see the hierarchy below the Worksheets (Worksheet) rectangle, you can click on the arrow next to it to create the expanded view in Figure 2.3. Here you see that from any particular worksheet in the collection, you can go one step down to any of its Range objects. You can even go down below Range objects, to Font objects and Comment objects, for example.

At this point, you do not need to worry about this object model and all of its details. However, once you get more familiar with Excel's objects in the context of VBA programming, these diagrams can be very useful for reference. (They can be found in online help. To access them, get into the Visual Basic Editor by pressing

Alt-F11, click on Help, search for the key word Object under the Index tab, and click on the Microsoft Excel Object topic. You not only get the diagram, but you can also click on any of the rectangles in the diagram for further help on the corresponding object.)

2.5 Object Models in General

We will use the Excel object model in this book because we will be working in Excel. However, you should now have a reasonably good idea of what it takes to use VBA for any other applications such as Word, Access, or even a non-Microsoft product—you must learn *its* object model. You can think of each application "plugging in" its object model to the underlying VBA language. Indeed, third-party software developers who want to license VBA from Microsoft often need to *create* an object model appropriate for their application. Then they can use VBA to manipulate the objects in this model. This is a powerful idea, and it is the reason that VBA is becoming the programming language of choice for so many developers—regardless of whether they are doing any work in Excel!

2.6 Summary

This chapter has introduced the concept of an object model, and it has briefly introduced the Excel object model we will be focusing on in the rest of this book. If you have never programmed in an object-oriented environment, it is a whole new experience. However, the more you do it, the more natural it becomes. It is certainly the direction today's programming world is headed, so if you want to be part of this world, you have to start thinking in terms of objects. You will get plenty of chances to do so throughout the book.

The Visual Basic Editor

3

3.1 Introduction

At this point, you might be asking where VBA lives. We claimed in Chapter 1 that if you own Excel, you also own VBA, but most of you have probably never seen it. The answer to your question is that you do your VBA work in the **Visual Basic Editor** (**VBE**), which you can access easily from Excel by pressing the **Alt-F11** key combination. (The Tools/Macro/Visual Basic Editor menu item also gets you there, but Alt-F11 is quicker.) The VBE provides a very user-friendly environment for writing your VBA programs. This chapter will walk you through the VBE and show you its most important features. It will also help you write your first VBA program.

3.2 Important Features of the VBE

To understand this section most easily, you should follow along at your PC. Open Excel and press **Alt-F11** to get into the VBE. It should look something like Figure 3.1, although the configuration you see might be somewhat different. By the time this discussion is completed, you will be able to make your screen look like Figure 3.1 or change it according to your own preferences. This is your programming workspace, and you have quite a lot of control over how it appears. This chapter provides some guidance, but the best way to learn is by experimenting.

The large blank pane on the right is the **Code** window. It is where you write your code. The rest of the VBE consists of the top menu, one or more toolbars, and one or more optional windows. Let's start with the windows. The **Project Explorer** window, repeated in Figure 3.2, shows an Explorer-type list of all open projects. (Your list will probably be different from the one shown here.) For example, the active project shown here has the generic name VBAProject and corresponds to the workbook Book2, that is, the file Book2.xls.[3] Below a given project, the Project Explorer window shows its "elements." These include any worksheets or chart sheets in the Excel file, an element called ThisWorkbook, and any modules (for VBA code), user forms (for dialog boxes), or references (for links to other

---

[3]What is the difference between a project and a workbook? For our purposes, there is no difference. However, VBA allows them to have separate names: VBAProject and Book2, for example. If you save Book2 as Practice.xls, say, the project name will still be VBAProject. Admittedly, it is confusing, but just think of projects as Excel files and don't worry too much about project names.

Figure 3.1 Visual Basic Editor (VBE)

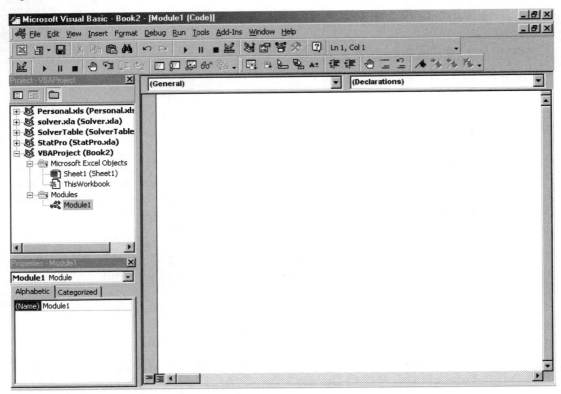

Figure 3.2 Project Explorer window

Figure 3.3 Properties window

files that have code you need) associated with the project. (Modules, forms, and references will be discussed in detail in later chapters.)

The **Properties** window, shown in Figure 3.3, lists a set of properties. This list depends on what is currently selected. For example, the property list in Figure 3.3 is relevant for the selection in Figure 3.2, namely, the project itself. It indicates a single property only—the project's name. Therefore, if you want to change the name of the project from the generic VBAProject to something more meaningful like MyFirstVBA, here is the place to do it. Chapter 12 will discuss the use of the Properties window in more detail. For now, since you won't need the Properties window, you can close it by clicking on its close button (the upper right X).

The VBE also has at least three toolbars that are very useful: the **Standard**, **Edit**, and **Debug** toolbars. They appear in Figures 3.4, 3.5, and 3.6, where some of the most useful buttons are pointed out. (If any of these toolbars are not visible on your PC, you can make them visible through the View menu.) From the Standard toolbar, you can run, pause, or stop a program you have written. You can also display the Project or Properties window (if it is hidden), and you can display the Object Browser or the Control Toolbox (more about these later). From the Edit toolbar, you can perform useful editing tasks, such as indenting or outdenting (the opposite of indenting), and you can comment or uncomment blocks of code, as will be discussed later. Finally, although the Debug toolbar will probably not mean much at this point, it is invaluable when you need to debug your programs—as you will undoubtedly need to do! It will be discussed in more detail in Chapter 13.

Figure 3.4 Standard toolbar

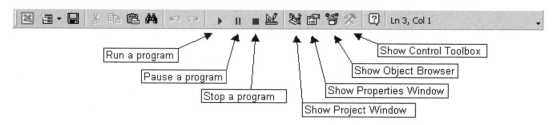

Figure 3.5 Edit toolbar

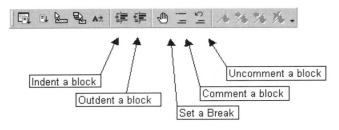

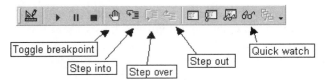

Figure 3.6 Debug toolbar

For future reference, here are a few menu items of particular importance.

- You need at least one module in a project if you want to write any code. To insert a module, use the **Insert/Module** menu item. If you ever have a module you do not need, highlight the module in the Project window and use the File/Remove Module menu item.
- Chapter 12 will show you how to build your own dialog boxes. VBA calls these **user forms**. To insert a new user form into a project, use the **Insert/UserForm** menu item. You can delete an unwanted user form in the same way that you delete a module.
- Under the Insert menu, you will also see a Class Module item. Ignore this for now. It is considerably more advanced and will not be discussed in this book.
- The Tools/Options menu item is a lot like the Tools/Options menu item in Excel. It allows you to change the look and feel of the VBE in a variety of ways. You should probably leave the default settings alone—with one exception. Try it now. Select Tools/Options, and make sure the Require Variable Declarations box under the Editor tab *is* checked. The effect of this will be explained in Section 4.3 of the next chapter.
- If you ever want to password-protect your project so that other people cannot see your code, use the Tools/VBA Properties menu item and click on the Protection tab. This gives you a chance to enter a password. (Just don't forget it, or you will not be able to see your *own* code.)
- If you click on the familiar Save button (or use the File/Save menu item), this will save the project currently highlighted in the Project window. It saves your code *and* anything in the underlying Excel spreadsheet. (It is all saved in the .xls file.) You can achieve the same objective by switching back to Excel and saving in the usual way from there.

3.3 The Object Browser

VBA's **Object Browser** is a wonderful online help tool. To get to it, open the VBE and click on the Object Browser button on the Standard toolbar (see Figure 3.4).[4] This opens a window as in Figure 3.7. At the top left, there is a list of object model "libraries" that you can get help on. Our main interest is in the Excel library and the VBA library. The Excel library provides help on all of the objects and their properties and methods in the Excel object model. The VBA library provides help on the VBA elements that are common to *all* applications that can use VBA: Excel, Access, Word, and others. For now, select the Excel library. In the bottom left pane, you see a list of all objects in the Excel object model, and in the right pane, you see a list of all properties and methods for any object selected in the left pane. (A property is designated by a hand icon, whereas a method is designated by a green rectangular icon.)

To get help on any of these items, simply select it and then click on the question mark icon. It is too early in our VBA discussion to be asking for online help, but you should not forget about the Object Browser. It can be invaluable as you develop your projects. Use it!

Figure 3.7 Object browser

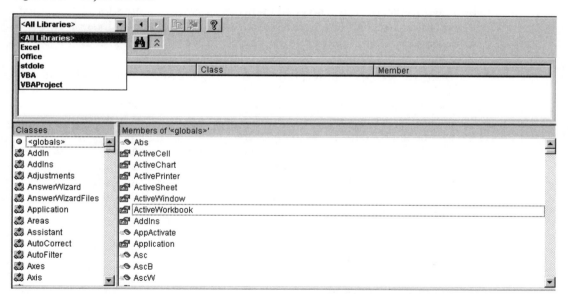

---

[4]This assumes you installed VBA help when you installed Microsoft Office. If you cannot get any help, you will have to go through the Setup program on the Office CD-ROM and install VBA help.

Figure 3.8   Immediate window

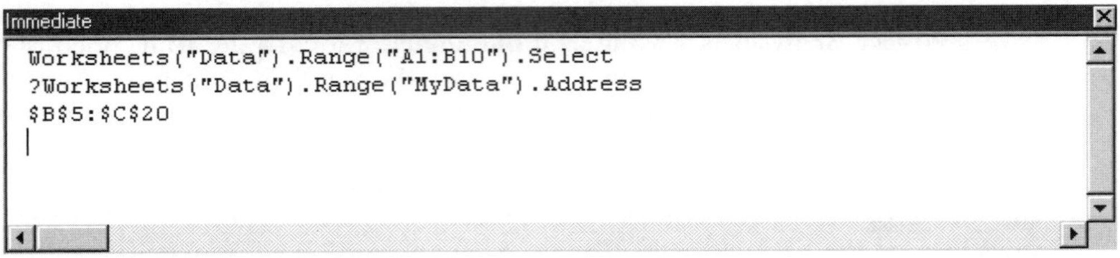

```
Immediate                                                            ×
Worksheets("Data").Range("A1:B10").Select
?Worksheets("Data").Range("MyData").Address
$B$5:$C$20
|
```

3.4   The Immediate and Watch Windows

There are two other windows in the VBE that you should be aware of: the **Immediate** and **Watch** windows. Each can be opened through the View menu or the Debug toolbar. (The Immediate window can also be opened quickly with the **Ctrl-g** key combination.) The Immediate window, shown in Figure 3.8, is useful for issuing one-line VBA commands. If you type a command and press Enter, the command takes effect immediately. For example, the first line in Figure 3.8 selects the range A1:B10 of the Data worksheet (assuming there is a Data worksheet in the active workbook). If you type this, press Enter, and switch back to Excel, you will see that the range A1:B10 has been highlighted. If you precede the command by a question mark, you can get an immediate answer to a question. For example, if you type the second line in the figure (which asks for the address of the range named MyData) and then press Enter, you immediately get the answer on the third line.

Many programmers send information to the Immediate window through their code. If you see the command **Debug.Print**, followed by something to be printed, the programmer is asking for this to be printed to the Immediate window. This is not a "permanent copy" of the printed information. It is usually done to see whether a program is working properly.

The Watch window is used for debugging. Programs typically include several variables that change value as the program runs. If the program does not appear to be working as it should, you can put a "watch" on one or more key variables to see how they change as the program progresses. Debugging will be discussed in detail in Chapter 13.

3.5   A First Program

Although you do not yet know much about VBA programming, you know enough to write a simple program and run it. Besides, sooner or later you will have to stop reading and do some programming on your own. Now is a good time to get started. Although the example in this section is very simple, there are a few details you probably won't understand completely, at least not yet. Don't worry

Figure 3.9 Sales by region and month

	A	B	C	D	E	F	G
1	*Month*	*Region 1*	*Region 2*	*Region 3*	*Region 4*	*Region 5*	*Region 6*
2	Jan-98	144770	111200	163140	118110	105010	167350
3	Feb-98	155180	155100	129850	133940	140880	104110
4	Mar-98	86230	162310	142950	131490	150160	158720
5	Apr-98	148800	165160	123840	141050	175870	108100
6	May-98	157140	130300	114990	128220	147790	167470
7	Jun-98	126150	163240	149360	152240	167320	181070
8	Jul-98	174010	183360	122120	149730	134220	135530
9	Aug-98	171780	130050	124130	134510	175590	122230
10	Sep-98	126260	162690	123960	128260	172570	121300
11	Oct-98	150250	150070	97140	165670	111570	159440
12	Nov-98	180720	146370	122200	148150	106310	124800
13	Dec-98	130140	167210	179220	116150	193620	124550
14	Jan-99	145900	124890	97160	139640	156140	180100
15	Feb-99	123470	127730	159030	148450	158130	117560
16	Mar-99	120950	149830	127550	204700	161240	156710
35	Oct-00	124160	148560	120190	155600	132590	155510
36	Nov-00	109840	189790	127460	135160	149470	163330
37	Dec-00	127100	108640	145300	127920	151130	122900

about that. Later chapters will clarify the details. For now, just follow the directions and realize the thrill of getting a program to work!

This example is based on a simple data set in the file **FirstProgram.xls**. It shows sales of some company by region and by month for a 3-year period. (See Figure 3.9, where some rows have been hidden. The range B2:G37 has been named SalesRange.) Your boss wants you to write a program that will scan the sales of each region and, for each, display a message that indicates the number of months sales in that region are above a user-selected value such as $150,000. To do this, go through the following steps.

Step 1   **Open the file.** Get into Excel and open the **FirstProgram.xls** file.

Step 2   **Get into the VBE.** Press Alt-F11 to open the VBE. Make sure the Project Explorer Window is visible. If it isn't, open it with the View/Project Explorer menu item.

Step 3   **Add a module.** In the Project Explorer window, make sure the **FirstProgram.xls** project is highlighted (click on it if necessary), and use the Insert/Module menu item to add a module (which will automatically be named Module1) to this project. This module will hold your VBA code.

Step 4   **Start a sub.** Click anywhere in the Code window, type **Sub CountHighSales**, and press Enter. You should immediately see the contents in Figure 3.10. You have started a program called CountHighSales. (Any other descriptive name could be used instead.) Including the keyword **Sub** informs VBA that you want to write a "subroutine," so it adds empty parentheses next to the name CountHighSales and adds the keywords **End Sub** at the bottom—two necessary elements of any subroutine. The rest of your code will be placed between the Sub and End Sub lines. Chapters 4 and 10 discuss subroutines in more detail, but for now, just think of a subroutine as a section of code that performs a particular task. For this simple example, there will be only *one* subroutine.

Figure 3.10 Beginning lines of a subroutine

Step 5 **Type the code.** Type the code exactly as shown in Figure 3.11 between the Sub and End Sub lines. It is important to indent properly for readability. To indent as shown, press the Tab key. Also, note that there is no "word wrap" in the VBE. To finish a line and go to the next line, you need to press the Enter key. Other than this, the Code window is essentially like a word processor. Be sure to check your spelling carefully and fix any errors before proceeding. (You'll note that keywords such as Sub and End Sub are automatically colored blue by the VBE. This is a great feature for helping the programmer.)

Figure 3.11 VBA code

```
FirstProgram.xls - Module1 (Code)
(General)                                        CountHighSales

Sub CountHighSales()
    Dim i As Integer, j As Integer, NumberHigh As Integer, SalesCutoff As Currency
    SalesCutoff = InputBox("What sales value do you want to check for?")
    For j = 1 To 6
        NumberHigh = 0
        For i = 1 To 36
            If Range("SalesRange").Cells(i, j) >= SalesCutoff Then _
                NumberHigh = NumberHigh + 1
        Next i
        MsgBox "For region " & j & ", sales were above " & Format(SalesCutoff, "$0,000") _
            & " on " & NumberHigh & " of the 36 months."
    Next j
End Sub
```

Step 6 **Run the program from the VBE.** Your program is now finished. The next step is to run it. There are several ways to do so, two of which will be demonstrated here. For the first method, make sure the cursor is *anywhere* within your subroutine and select the Run/Run Sub/UserForm menu item. (Alternatively, click on the "blue triangle" button on the Standard toolbar or press the F5 key.) If all goes well, you should see the input box in Figure 3.12, where you can enter a value such as 150000. (The program will then search for all values greater than or equal to

$150,000 in the data set.) Next, you will see a series of message boxes such as the one in Figure 3.13, each of which tells you how many months sales in some region are above the sales cutoff value you entered. This is exactly what you want the program to do!

Figure 3.12 Input box for sales cutoff value

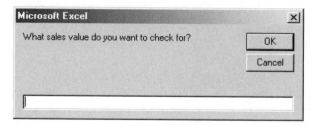

Figure 3.13 Message box for region 2

Step 7 **Run the program with a button.** The method of running the program in the previous step is fine for you, the programmer, but your boss won't want to get into the VBE to run the program. She probably doesn't even want to *see* the VBE. She will instead want to run the program directly from the Excel worksheet that contains the data. You can make this easy for her. First, switch back to Excel (click on its button on the bottom taskbar of your screen). Then right-click on any toolbar to show a list of Excel toolbars, and check the Forms toolbar's box to make this toolbar visible. The fourth item on the Forms toolbar is for creating buttons to run macros (that is, subroutines). To create such a button, click on the toolbar's button item and then drag a rectangular button somewhere on your worksheet, as shown in Figure 3.14. You will immediately be asked to assign a macro to this button—this is asked immediately because the *only* purpose of a button is to run a macro. Of course, you want to assign the CountHighSales macro you just wrote to the button. Then you can type a more meaningful caption on the button itself. (Again, see Figure 3.14 for a suggested caption.) At this point, the button is "selected" (there is a dotted border around it). To deselect it, click anywhere else on the worksheet. Now your button is ready to go. To run your program, just click on the button.

Step 8 **Save the file.** In case you haven't done so already, save the file under the original (or a new) name. This will save your code and the button you created.

Figure 3.14 Button on the worksheet

	A	B	C	D	E	F	G	H	I	J	K	L	M
1	**Month**	**Region 1**	**Region 2**	**Region 3**	**Region 4**	**Region 5**	**Region 6**						
2	Jan-98	144770	111200	163140	118110	105010	167350						
3	Feb-98	155180	155100	129850	133940	140880	104110						
4	Mar-98	86230	162310	142950	131490	150160	158720						
5	Apr-98	148800	165160	123840	141050	175870	108100						
6	May-98	157140	130300	114990	128220	147790	167470						
7	Jun-98	126150	163240	149360	152240	167320	181070						
8	Jul-98	174010	183360	122120	149730	134220	135530						
9	Aug-98	171780	130050	124130	134510	175590	122230						
10	Sep-98	126260	162690	123960	128260	172570	121300						
11	Oct-98	150250	150070	97140	165670	111570	159440						
12	Nov-98	180720	146370	122200	148150	106310	124800						
13	Dec-98	130140	167210	179220	116150	193620	124550						
14	Jan-99	145900	124890	97160	139640	156140	180100						
15	Feb-99	123470	127730	159030	148450	158130	117560						
16	Mar-99	120950	149830	127550	204700	161240	156710						
35	Oct-00	124160	148560	120190	155600	132590	155510						
36	Nov-00	109840	189790	127480	135160	149470	163330						
37	Dec-00	127100	108640	145300	127920	151130	122900						

> Count High Sales Values

A note on saving. You have undoubtedly been told to save frequently in all of your computer-related courses. Frequent saving is at least as important in a programming environment as anywhere else. After you slave to get a program working correctly, you don't want that sinking feeling that comes from having your unsaved work wiped out by a sudden power outage or the dreaded "An unexpected error has occurred and this program cannot continue" message. So we will say it, too: save, save, save!

Troubleshooting

What if you try to run your program and you get an error message? First, read your program carefully and make sure it is exactly like the one in Figure 3.11. In particular, the characters at the ends of the If and MsgBox lines are underscore (_) characters. They must be preceded by a space. (Their purpose is to extend long lines of code over to the next line.) Similarly, the ampersand (&) characters in the MsgBox line should have a space on each side of them. If you have any lines colored red, this is a sure sign you have typed something incorrectly. (This is another feature of the VBE designed to help programmers.) In any case, if you get some version of the dialog box in Figure 3.15, click on the End button. This stops a buggy program and lets you fix any errors.

Figure 3.15 A typical error dialog box

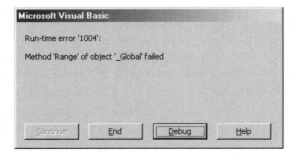

If your typing is correct and you still get an error, check steps 6 and 7. If you are using step 6 to run the program, make sure your cursor is somewhere *inside* the subroutine. If you are using the button method in step 7, make sure you have assigned the CountHighSales macro to the button. (Right-click on the button and select the Assign Macro menu item.) There are not that many things that can go wrong with this small program, so you should eventually get it to work. Remember, perseverance!

Brief Analysis of the Program

We could not expect you to write this program without our help at this point. But you can probably understand the gist of it. The first line (after the Sub line) "declares" variables that will be used later on. The second line displays an "input box" (see Figure 3.12) that gets a user's input. The section starting with **For j = 1 To 6** and ending with **Next j** is a "loop" that performs a similar task for each sales region. As you will learn in later chapters, loops are among the most powerful tools in a programmer's arsenal. For example, if there were 600 regions rather than 6, the only required change would be to change 6 to 600 in the third line. Computers are excellent at performing repetitive tasks!

Within the loop on regions, there is another loop on months, starting with **For i = 1 To 36** and ending with **Next i**. Within this loop there is an If statement that checks whether the sales value for the region in that month is at least as large as the sales cutoff value. If it is, the "counter" variable NumberHighSales is increased by 1. Once this inner loop has been completed, the results for the region are reported in a "message box" (see Figure 3.13).

Again, the details are undoubtedly a bit unclear at this point, but you can probably understand the overall method. And if you typed everything correctly and ran the program as instructed, you now know the thrill of getting a program to work as planned. We hope you will experience this feeling frequently as you work through the book.

3.6 Summary

This chapter has introduced the Visual Basic Editor (VBE)—its toolbars, some of its menu items, and its windows. We have also briefly discussed online VBA help and the Object Browser. You will be doing most of your development work in the VBE, so you should become familiar with it right away. We believe you will come to appreciate what a friendly and helpful programming environment it provides.

PROGRAMMING EXERCISES

1. Open Excel and open two new workbooks, which will probably be called Book1 and Book2 (or some such generic names). Get into the VBE and make sure the Project Explorer window is visible. Insert a module into Book1, and click on the

plus sign next to Modules for Book1 to see the module you just inserted. Now type the following sub in the code window for this module, and then run it. It should display the name of the workbook.

```
Sub ShowName()
    MsgBox "The name of this workbook is " & ThisWorkbook.Name
End Sub
```

Finally, go to the Project Explorer window and drag the module you inserted down to Book2. This should create a copy of the module in Book2. Run the sub in the copied module. It should display the name of the second workbook. The point of this exercise is that you can copy code from one workbook to another by copying the module containing the code, and copying a module is as simple as dragging in the Project Explorer window.

2. Open the **FirstProgram.xls** file you created in Section 3.5, and get into the VBE so that you can look at the code. Use the Debug/Add Watch menu item, and type NumberHigh in the text box. You are adding a "watch" for the variable NumberHigh, so that you can see how it changes as the program runs. Next, place the cursor *anywhere* inside the code, and press the F8 key repeatedly. This "steps" you through the program one line at a time. Every time the program sees a sales figure greater than the cutoff value you specify, NumberHigh will increase by 1, which you should see in the Watch window. (You'll probably get tired of pressing F8. You can stop the program prematurely at any time by clicking on the "blue square" Reset button on the Standard toolbar.)

3. Get into the VBE and open the Immediate window. Then type the following lines, pressing the Enter key after each line. Now do you see why it is called the *Immediate* window?

```
?Application.Name
?Application.DefaultFilePath
?Application.Path
?Application.Version
?Application.UserName
?IsDate("February 29, 1999")
?IsDate("February 29, 2000")
?Workbooks.Count
?ActiveWorkbook.Name
```

4. Open a new workbook in Excel, get into the VBE, and insert a module into this new workbook. Type the following code in the code window. Make sure there is no Option Explicit line at the top of the code window. (If there is one, delete it.)

```
Sub EnterUserNameSlowly()
    Range("A1") = "The user of this copy is Excel is listed below."
    YourName = Application.UserName
    NChars = Len(YourName)
    For i = 1 To NChars
        Range("A3") = Left(YourName, i)
        newHour = Hour(Now())
```

```
            newMinute = Minute(Now())
            newSecond = Second(Now()) + 1
            waitTime = TimeSerial(newHour, newMinute, newSecond)
            Application.Wait waitTime
        Next
    End Sub
```

Next, return to Sheet1 of this workbook, add a button and assign the EnterUserNameSlowly sub to it, and then run the sub by clicking on the button. Can you now explain what the code is doing? (If you like, look up the Wait method of the Application object in the Object Browser for online help.)

5. Open the **FirstPrograms.xls** file you created in Section 3.5, and get into the VBE. Use the Tools/VBAProject Properties menu item, and click on the Protection tab. Check the Lock project for viewing box, enter a password in the other two boxes, and click on OK. Get back to Excel, save the file, and close it. Now reopen the file and try to look at the code. You have just learned how to password-protect your code. Of course, you have to remember the password. Otherwise, not even you, the author, can look at the code! (If you ever want to remove the protection, just uncheck the Lock project for viewing box and delete the passwords from the boxes.)

Getting Started with VBA

4

4.1 Introduction

Now that you know about the VBE, you can start doing some *real* programming in VBA—not just copying what's in the book but writing some of your own code. This chapter will get you started with the most basic elements—how to create a "sub," how to declare variables with a Dim statement, how to get information from a user with an "input box," how to display information in a "message box," and how to document your work with comments. It will also briefly discuss "strings," and it will explain how to specify objects, properties, and methods in VBA code. Finally, it will introduce VBA's extremely useful With construction and provide several other VBA tips.

4.2 Subroutines

The logical section of code that performs a particular task is called a **subroutine**, or simply a **sub**. Right away, there is a chance for confusion. Subroutines are also called **macros**, and they are also called **procedures**. There is also a particular type of subroutine called a **function subroutine** that will be discussed in Chapter 10. There is no need to make any fine distinctions among subs, macros, and procedures. We will simply call them all subs. A sub is any set of code that performs a particular task. It can contain one line of code or it can contain hundreds of lines. However, it is not good programming practice to let subs get too long. If the purpose of your application is to perform several related tasks, it is a good idea to break it up into several relatively short subs, each of which performs a specific task. Then, as we will see, there can be a "main" sub that acts as the control center—it "calls" the other subs one at a time. In this case, the collection of subs that fit together is called a **program**. In other words, a program is a collection of subs that achieves an overall objective.

Each sub has a name, which must be a single word. This word, which can be a concatenation of several words such as GetUserInputs, should indicate the purpose of the sub. You can use names such as Sub1 or MySub, but this is a bad practice. You will have no idea in a week what Sub1 or MySub is intended to do, whereas GetUserInputs clearly indicates the sub's purpose.

All subs must begin with the keyword **Sub** and then the name of the sub followed by parentheses, as in:

```
Sub GetUserInputs()
```

You can type this line directly into a module in the VBE, or you can use the Insert/Procedure menu item, which will prompt you for a name. (If there is no module for the current project, you must insert one.) The editor will immediately insert the following line for you:

```
End Sub
```

Every sub must start with the Sub line, and it must end with the **End Sub** line. You will notice that the editor also colors the reserved words Sub and End Sub blue. In fact, it colors all reserved words blue, just as an aid to the programmer. Now that your sub is "bracketed" by the Sub and End Sub statements, you can start typing code in between.

Why are there parentheses next to the sub's name? As we will see in Chapter 10, a sub can take "arguments," and these arguments must be placed inside the parentheses. If there are no arguments, which is often the case, then there is nothing inside the parentheses, but they still must be present.

If a program contains several logically related subs, it is common to place all of them in a single module, although some programmers put some subs in one module and some in another, primarily for organizational purposes. The subs in a particular module can be arranged in any order. If there is a "main" sub that calls other subs to perform certain tasks, it is customary to place the main sub at the top of the module and then place the other subs below it, in the order they are called. But even this is not necessary; any order is accepted by VBA.

Succeeding sections will instruct you to "run" a sub. There are several ways to do this, as we saw in the previous chapter. For now, the easiest way is to place the cursor *anywhere* within the sub and click on the **Run** button (the blue triangle) on the VBE Standard toolbar. Alternatively, you can press the **F5** key, or you can use the **Run/Run Sub/UserForm** menu item.

4.3   Understanding and Declaring Variables

Virtually all programs use variables. Variables contain values, much like the variables x and y you use in algebra. For example, the next three lines illustrate a simple use of variables. The first line sets the UnitCost variable equal to 1.20, the second line sets the UnitsSold variable to 20, and the third line calculates the variable TotalCost as the product of UnitCost and UnitsSold. Of course, the value of TotalCost here will be 24.0.

```
UnitCost = 1.20
UnitsSold = 20
TotalCost = UnitCost * UnitsSold
```

Unlike algebra, you can also have a line such as the following:

```
TotalCost = TotalCost + 20
```

To understand this, you must understand that each variable has a location in memory, where its value is stored. If a variable appears to the left of an equals sign, then its new value in memory becomes whatever is on the right side of the equals sign. For example, if the previous value of TotalCost was 260, then the new value will be 280, and it will replace the old value in memory.

Although it is not absolutely required, you should *always* declare all of your variables at the beginning of each sub with the keyword **Dim**.[5] (Dim is an abbreviation of dimension, a holdover from the old Basic language. It would make more sense to use the word Declare, but we are stuck with Dim.) Declaring variables has two advantages. First, it helps catch spelling mistakes. Suppose you use the variable UnitCost several times in a sub, but in one case you misspell it as UnitsCost. If you have already declared UnitCost in a Dim statement, VBA will catch your spelling error, reasoning that UnitsCost is not on the list of declared variables.

The second reason for declaring variables is that you can then specify the *types* of variables you have. Each type requires a certain amount of computer memory, and each is handled in a certain way by VBA. It is much better for you, the programmer, to tell VBA what types of variables you have than to let it try to figure this out from context. The variable types used most often are the following:

- **String** (for names like "Bob")
- **Integer** (for integer values in the range -32,768 to 32,767)
- **Long** (for really large integers beyond the Integer range)
- **Boolean** (for variables that can be True or False)
- **Single** (for numbers with decimals)
- **Double** (for numbers with decimals where you require more accuracy than with Single)
- **Currency** (for monetary values)
- **Variant** (a catchall, where you let VBA decide how to deal with the variable)

Variable declarations can be placed anywhere within a sub, but it is customary to include them right after the Sub line, as in the following:

```
Sub Test()
    Dim i As Integer, UnitCost As Currency, Found As Boolean
    Other statements
End Sub
```

Some programmers prefer a separate Dim line for each variable. This can lead to a long list of Dim statements if there are a lot of variables. Others tend to prefer a single Dim, followed by a list of declarations separated by commas. You can take your pick (or mix them). However, you *must* follow each variable with the

---

[5]If you declare a variable inside a sub, it is called a *local* variable. It is also possible to declare a variable outside of subs, in which case it is a *module-level* variable. This issue is discussed in more detail in Chapter 10.

keyword **As** and then the variable type. Otherwise, the variable will be declared as the default **Variant** type, which is not considered good programming practice. For example, variables i and j in the following line are (implicitly) declared as Variant, not as Integer. Only k is declared as Integer.

```
Dim i, j, k As Integer
```

If you want all of them to be Integer, the following declaration is necessary:

```
Dim i As Integer, j As Integer, k As Integer
```

Using Option Explicit

You can *force* yourself to adopt the good habit of declaring all variables by using the tip mentioned in the previous chapter. Specifically, use the Tools/Options menu item in the VBE and check the Require Variable Declarations box under the Editor tab. (By default, it is *not* checked.) From that point on, every time you open a new module, the line **Option Explicit** will be at the top. This simply means that VBA will force you to declare your variables. If you forget to declare a variable, it will remind you with an error message when you run the program. If you ever see the message in Figure 4.1, you will know that you forgot to declare a variable (or misspelled one). If you *never* see this error, you will know that you are the most careful programmer in the world—we all forget from time to time.

Figure 4.1 Error message for undeclared variable

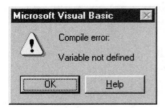

Object Variables

Before leaving this section, we introduce one other type of variable. This is an **object variable**, which "points" to an object. For example, suppose you have a Range object, specified by the range name Scores on a worksheet named Data, that you intend to reference several times in your program. To save yourself a lot of typing, you can "Set" a range object variable named, say, SRange to this range with the lines

```
Dim SRange As Range
Set SRange = ActiveWorkbook.Worksheets("Data").Range("Scores")
```

From then on, you can refer simply to SRange. For example, you could change its font size with the line

```
SRange.Font.Size = 12
```

This is a lot easier than typing

```
ActiveWorkbook.Worksheets("Data").Range("Scores").Font.Size = 12
```

There are two fundamental things to remember about object variables.

- They must be declared just like any other variables in a Dim statement. The type can be the generic **Object** type, as in

```
Dim SRange as Object
```

or it can be more specific, as in

```
Dim SRange as Range
```

The latter is much preferred because VBA does not then have to figure out what *type* of object you want SRange to be. (It is *not* enough to include Range in the name of the variable.)
- When you define an object variable—that is, put it to the left of an equals sign—you must use the keyword **Set**. In fact, this is the only time you use the keyword Set. The following line will produce an error message because the keyword Set is missing:

```
SRange = ActiveWorkbook.Worksheets("Data").Range("Scores")
```

In contrast, assuming that TotalCost is a variable of type Single (or any non-object variable type), the following line will produce an error message because the keyword Set should *not* be there:

```
Set TotalCost = 24.0
```

Therefore, the moral is always to use the keyword Set when defining object variables, but never to use it when defining other variables.

4.4 Input Boxes and Message Boxes

Two of the most common tasks in VBA programs are to get inputs from users and to display messages or results in some way. There are many ways to perform both tasks, and many of them will be illustrated in the applications in later chapters, but for now, we illustrate a very simple way to perform these tasks. This takes advantage of two built-in VBA functions: the **InputBox** and **MsgBox** functions. They are not complex or fancy, but they are very useful.

The **InputBox** function takes at least one argument: a prompt to the user. A second argument that is often used is the title that appears at the top of the dialog box. An example is the following:

```
InputBox "Enter the product's unit price.","Selling price"
```

If you type this line in a sub and run the sub, the dialog box in Figure 4.2 will appear:

Figure 4.2 Typical input box

This generic dialog box has OK and Cancel buttons, a title (which would be Microsoft Excel if you didn't supply one), a prompt, and a text box for the user's input.

The **MsgBox** function takes at least one argument: a message that you want to display. Two other optional arguments often used are a button indication and a title. A typical example is the following:

```
MsgBox "The product's unit price is $2.40.", vbInformation, "Selling price"
```

The first argument is the text "The product's unit price is $2.40." The second argument is vbInformation, a built-in VBA constant that asks for an "i" icon in the message box. The third argument is the title, "Selling price". If you type this line in a sub and run the sub, the message box in Figure 4.3 will appear.

Figure 4.3 Typical message box

Message Boxes with Yes and No buttons

The previous example illustrates the most common use of a message box: to display a message. However, message boxes can be used for simple logic by including the appropriate buttons. For example, the following line not only displays the message with Yes and No buttons (see Figure 4.4), but it also captures the button pressed in the Result variable. In this case, the second argument, vbYesNo, indicates that Yes and No buttons should be included. The value of Result will be vbYes or vbNo, two built-in VBA constants. Then we could use a logical If statement to proceed appropriately, depending on whether Result is vbYes or vbNo.

```
Result = MsgBox("Do you want to continue?", vbYesNo, "Chance to quit")
```

Figure 4.4 Message box with yes and no buttons

You can even use the InputBox and MsgBox functions in the same line, as in:

```
MsgBox InputBox("Type your name.", "User's name"), vbInformation, "User's Name"
```

The first argument of the MsgBox function is now the *result* of the InputBox function. When I ran this, I first saw the input box and typed my name, as in Figure 4.5. I then saw the message box in Figure 4.6, the "message" being my name.

Figure 4.5 Input box

Figure 4.6 Message box

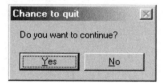

Here are a couple of other points that apply to input boxes and message boxes, as well as to other VBA statements.

- **Continuing statements on more than one line.** Lines of code can often get long and run past the right side of the screen. You can continue them on another line by using the **underscore** character (_) preceded by a space. For example, you can write

```
MsgBox InputBox("Type your full address, including city and state.", _
        "User's address"), vbInformation, "User's Address"
```

This is treated as a *single* line of code. Actually, a line can be broken as many times as you like with the underscore character.

- **Whether to use parentheses.** If you have been paying close attention, you have noticed that sometimes the arguments of InputBox and MsgBox are included in parentheses and sometimes they are not. For example, compare the line

```
MsgBox "Thank you for supplying your name.", vbExclamation, "Name accepted"
```

with the line

```
Result = MsgBox("Do you want to continue?", vbYesNo, "Chance to quit")
```

The first simply displays a message. The second also captures the result of the message box (vbYes or vbNo) in the Result variable. The rule for parentheses, for the InputBox function, the MsgBox function, and other VBA functions, is that parentheses are *required* when the result is captured in a variable or used in some way. In contrast, parentheses are *optional* (and are usually omitted) when no result is being captured or used in some way. This rule of when to use parentheses is difficult to understand until you become more proficient in VBA. However, if your program fails to work and you cannot find anything else wrong, check whether you might have violated this rule. Then remove the parentheses or add them, and see whether the bug disappears.

Exercise 4.1   Displaying a Message

Before proceeding, try the following simple exercise. Open a new workbook and save it as **Ex4_01.xls**. Then create a sub called RevenueCalc that does the following: (1) It asks the user for the unit price of some product and stores this in the variable UnitPrice, defined as Currency type; (2) it asks the user for the number of items sold of this product and stores this in the variable QuantitySold, defined as Integer type; (3) it calculates the revenue from this product and stores this in the variable Revenue, defined as Currency type; and (4) it displays a message such as "The revenue from this product was $380."

Try to do as much of this as you can without help. Then consult the file **Ex4_01Finished.xls** for a solution. You will probably have trouble with the

MsgBox line. The message consists of two parts: a literal part ("The revenue from this product was") and a variable part (the calculated revenue).[6] These two parts need to be **concatenated** with the **ampersand** (&) symbol, an operation that is explained later in this chapter. The solution also contains a **Format** function to display the revenue as, say, $380 rather than 380. This will also be explained in a later section. ■

4.5 Comments

You might think that once you get your program to run correctly, your job is finished. This is not the case. Sometime in the future, either you or someone else might have to modify your program as new objectives arise. Therefore, it is extremely important that you *document* your work. There are several ways to document a program, including the use of meaningful names for subs and variables. However, the best means of documentation is the liberal use of **comments**. A comment is simply text that you type anywhere in your program to indicate to yourself or someone else what your code means. It is very easy to insert a comment anywhere in the program, inside a sub or outside of a sub. You start the line with a single quote. That line is then colored green (to distinguish it from the program itself), and it is ignored by VBA. Of course, comments will *not* be ignored by those who read your program. For them, the comments are often the most interesting part!

It is also possible to include a comment in the same line as a line of code. To do so, type the code, follow it with one or more spaces, then a single quote, then the comment, as in:

Range("A1").Value = "March Sales" ' This is the title cell for the sheet.

There is a tendency on the part of programmers to wait until the last minute, after the code has been written, to insert comments—if they insert them at all. Try instead to get into the good habit of inserting comments as you write your code. Admittedly, it takes time, but it also aids your logical thought process if you force yourself to explain what you are doing as you are doing it. Of course, comments can also be overdone. There is usually no point in documenting every single line of code. Use your discretion on what *really* needs to be documented.

4.6 Strings

The InputBox function takes at least one argument, a prompt such as "Enter your name." Similarly, the MsgBox function takes at least one argument, a message such as "Thank you for the name." Technically, each of these is called a **string**. A string is simply text, surrounded by double quotes. Strings are sometimes arguments to InputBox, MsgBox, and other functions, and they are also used in many

---

[6] It also has a third part if you want to end the sentence with a period.

other ways in VBA. For example, because a string corresponds (loosely) to a label in Excel, if you want to use VBA to enter a label into a cell in Excel, you set the Value property of the Range object representing the cell to a string. We will see more of this later. The point now is that strings are used in practically all VBA programs.

Often a string is a literal set of text, such as "The user's name is Chris Albright." (Again, remember that the double quotes are part of the string and cannot be omitted.) Many times, however, a string cannot be written literally and must be pieced together in sections. We call this **string concatenation**. As an example, suppose the following InputBox statement is used to get a product name:

```
Product = InputBox("Enter the product's name.")
```

The user types the product's name into the text box, and it is stored as a string, "LaserJet 1100" for example, in the Product variable. Now suppose you want to display a message in a message box such as "The product's name is LaserJet 1100." What should the first argument of the MsgBox be? It cannot be the literal "The product's name is LaserJet 1100." This is because you, the programmer, do not know what product name will be supplied in the input box. Therefore, you must "build" the message string by concatenating three strings: the literal "The product's name is ", the *variable* string Product, and the literal period ".". To concatenate these, you use the concatenation character, the **ampersand** (&), surrounded on both sides by a space. (More than one space on either side is accepted, but at least one is required.) The resulting MsgBox statement is

```
MsgBox "The product's name is " & Product & "."
```

Note how the ampersand is used twice to separate the *variable* information from the literal parts of the string. String concatenation—the alternation of literal and variable parts of a string—is extremely important and is used in practically all programs.

A completed sub that gets a product's name and then displays it in a message box appears below, along with the results from running it, in Figures 4.7 and 4.8.

```
Sub GetProductName()
    Product = InputBox("Enter the product's name.")
    MsgBox "The product's name is " & Product & ".", vbInformation
End Sub
```

Figure 4.7 Input box

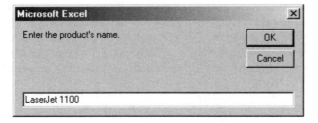

Figure 4.8 Message box

One tricky aspect of string concatenation occurs when you use the underscore character to break a string into two lines. You might think that the following should work:

```
MsgBox "This is a long string, so it is broken up into _
        two lines."
```

However, this will produce an error message. If you break a string across two lines, you *must* concatenate it, as in

```
MsgBox "This is a long string, so it is broken up into " & _
        "two lines."
```

(Note that there is a space after the word *into*, so that *into* and *two* will not run together in the message. There is also a space on each side of the ampersand, as required by VBA.) Alternatively, you could place the ampersand on the second line, as in

```
MsgBox "This is a long string, so it is broken up into " _
        & "two lines."
```

The point is that an ampersand is required *somewhere* when you break strings across lines.

Exercise 4.2   Displaying a Message

Return to Exercise 4.1 from Section 4.4. There you obtained a unit price and a quantity sold from input boxes, calculated the revenue, and then displayed a message such as "The revenue from this product was $380." You should now understand that the last part of this message, the actual revenue, requires string concatenation. (Look again at the **Ex4_01Finished.xls** file.) Now try expanding your program slightly (and save your results in the file **Ex4_02.xls**). Start by using an input box to get the product's name. Then use input boxes to get this product's unit price and the quantity sold, but include the product's name in the prompts for these input boxes. For example, a prompt might be "Enter the unit price for LaserJet 1100." Next, calculate the revenue. Finally, display a message that contains all of the information, something like "For the LaserJet 1100, the unit price is $500, the quantity sold is 25, and the revenue is $12,500." Do as much as you can on your own. If you need help, look at the solution in the file **Ex4_02Finished.xls.** ∎

A note on formatting in message boxes. If the revenue is 12500, how do you get it to appear as $12,500 in a message? This can be done with VBA's **Format** function. This function takes two arguments: the number to be formatted, and a string that indicates how to format the number. To format 12500 in the usual currency format (with a dollar sign and comma separators), you can use **Format(12500,"$#,##0")**. If the variable Revenue holds the actual revenue, then you would use **Format(Revenue,"$#,##0")**. Using the Format function is tricky. Rather than memorizing a lot of formatting "codes," it is best to consult online help on the Format function when you get stuck. This online help contains several examples that you can mimic.

Useful String Functions

String concatenation is useful when you need to "piece together" several small strings to create one long string. You might also need to get *part* of a string. There are three useful VBA string functions for doing this: **Right**, **Left**, and **Mid**. These are illustrated in the following lines.

```
ShortString1 = Right("S. Christian Albright", 8)
ShortString2 = Left("S. Christian Albright", 12)
ShortString3 = Mid("S. Christian Albright", 4, 5)
```

The first line returns "Albright". In general, the **Right** function takes two arguments, a string and an integer n, and it returns the rightmost n characters of the string. The **Left** function is similar; it returns the leftmost n characters. In the second line, it returns "S. Christian". (The space after "S." is considered a character.) Finally, the **Mid** function takes a string and two integer arguments. The first integer specifies the starting character and the second specifies the number of characters to return. Therefore, the third line above returns "Chris". Starting at the fourth character, "C", it returns the next five characters. Note that the third argument of Mid can be omitted, in which case it is 1 by default.

One other useful string function is the **Len** function. It takes a single argument, a string, and returns the number of characters in the string. For example, the line

```
NCharacters = Len("S. Christian Albright")
```

returns 21. (Again, remember that spaces count!)

These functions can be used in many combinations. Suppose you want all but the last two characters of some string called ThisString, but you don't know the number of characters in ThisString. Then the following combination of Len and Left will do the job:

```
AllBut2 = Left(ThisString, Len(ThisString) - 2)
```

For example, if ThisString turns out to have 25 characters, AllBut2 will be the leftmost 23 characters.

4.7 Specifying Objects, Properties, and Methods

Objects, properties, and methods were introduced in Chapter 2. Now it is time to see how they are implemented in VBA code. This is important material. Virtually nothing can be done in VBA for Excel without knowing how to manipulate its objects in code. The basic rules are as follows.

- **Specifying a member of a collection.** To specify a particular member of a collection, use the *plural* name of the collection, with the particular member specified in parentheses and enclosed inside quotes, as in Worksheets("Data"). In the special case of the Range object, where there is no plural, just write Range, followed by a specification of the range inside parentheses. (We will devote an entire chapter, Chapter 6, to Range objects because they are so important.) You can generally specify any particular member of a collection in one of two ways: by index (a number) or by name (a string). For example, you can specify Worksheets(2) or Worksheets("Data"). The name method is *much* preferred. After all, how would anyone know for sure which worksheet the *second* one is? It is much easier to understand the reference to the worksheet's name.
- **Specifying objects down a hierarchy.** To specify objects down a hierarchy, separate them with a period, with objects farther down the hierarchy to the right, as in

```
Workbooks("Sales").Worksheets("March").Range("Midwest")
```

This line is essentially read backwards. It specifies the range named Midwest from the March worksheet of the Sales workbook. We say that an object to the right is **qualified** by any objects listed to its left.

This rule has a number of variations. For example, if you refer simply to Range("Midwest"), do you need to qualify it with a specification of the particular workbook and worksheet this range is in? The answer is sometimes "yes" and sometimes "no." It depends on the context. Specifically, there are built-in VBA objects called **ActiveWorkbook** and **ActiveSheet** (but no ActiveWorksheet). They refer to the workbook and sheet currently selected. If you refer simply to Range("Midwest"), this is equivalent to

```
ActiveWorkbook.ActiveSheet.Range("Midwest")
```

Since this is probably what you want, the shorter Range("Midwest") is perfectly acceptable. However, if you specify Range("A1"), be sure that the *active* worksheet contains the cell A1 you are interested in. That is, if you do not qualify Range("A1"), VBA will guess which A1 cell you mean, and it might not guess correctly. You are safer to qualify it, as in Worksheets("Data").Range("A1"), for example.

- **Specifying a property.** To specify a property of an object, list the property name to the right of the object, separated by a period, as in

```
Range("A1").Value
```

This refers to the Value property of the range A1—that is, the contents of cell A1. A property can be set or returned. For example, the following line puts the string "Sales for March" in cell A1:

```
Range("A1").Value = "Sales for March"
```

In contrast, the following line gets the label in range A1 and stores it as a string in the variable Title:

```
Title = Range("A1").Value
```

- **Specifying a method.** To specify a method for an object, list the method name to the right of the object, separated by a period, as in

```
Range("Midwest").ClearContents
```

- **Specifying arguments of a method.** If a method has arguments, list them, separated by commas, next to the method's name. Each argument should have the name of the argument (which can be found from online help), followed by :=, followed by the value of the argument. For example, the following copies the range A1:B10 to the range D1:E10. Here, Destination is the name of the argument of the Copy method.

```
Range("A1:B10").Copy Destination:=Range("D1:E10")
```

It is possible to omit the argument name and the :=, and to write

```
Range("A1:B10").Copy Range("D1:E10")
```

However, this can be dangerous and can lead to errors unless you know the rules well. It is better to supply the argument name and the :=. Even if you are an experienced programmer, this practice makes your code more readable for others.

These are the rules, and you can return to this section as often as you like to refresh your memory. They will not be discussed any further here, but they will continually be reinforced with examples in later chapters.

Exercise 4.3 Calculating Ordering Costs

The file **Ex4_03.xls** is a "template" for calculating the total order cost for ordering a product with quantity discounts. The table (range named LTable) in the range A4:C8 contains unit costs for various order quantity intervals. Then the range B11:B13 contains a typical order cost calculation, where the input is the order quantity in cell B11 and the ultimate output is the total cost in cell B13. Take a look at this file to see how a VLOOKUP function is used to calculate the appropriate unit cost in cell B12.

The file **Ex4_03Finished.xls** indicates what the exercise is supposed to accomplish. Open it now and click on the "Create table" button. It asks for three possible order quantities. Then it fills in the table in the range D12:E14 with these order quantities and the corresponding total costs. Basically, it plugs each potential order quantity into cell B11 and transfers the corresponding total cost from cell B13 to column E of the table. If you then click on the "Clear table" button, the information in this table is deleted.

Now that you see what the finished application should do, go back to the **Ex4_03.xls** file and attempt to write two subs, CreateTable and ClearTable, that will eventually be attached to buttons. Go as far as you can on your own. If you need help, look at the code in the **Ex4_03Finished.xls** file.

This exercise will undoubtedly leave you wishing for more. First, even with only three order quantities, there is a lot of repetitive code. Copying and pasting your code (and then making suitable modifications) can cut down on the amount of typing required, but still, there must be a more efficient approach. Second, the program ought to allow *any* number of entries in the table, not just three. To see how these issues can be addressed, open the file **Ex4_03Advanced.xls**, click on its buttons, and look at its code. There is probably a lot you will not understand yet, but at least this gives you something to strive for. You will eventually understand all of the code in this file. Just wait a few chapters! ■

4.8 The With Construction

There is an extremely useful shortcut you can take when working with objects and their properties and methods. It is the **With** construction, and unless you have ever programmed in VBA, you have probably never seen it. The easiest way to explain it is with an example. Suppose you want to set a number of properties for the range A1 in the March worksheet of the Sales workbook. You could use the following code.

```
Workbooks("Sales").Worksheets("March").Range("A1").Value = "Sales for March"
Workbooks("Sales").Worksheets("March").Range("A1").HorizontalAlignment = xlLeft
Workbooks("Sales").Worksheets("March").Range("A1").Font.Name = "Times New Roman"
Workbooks("Sales").Worksheets("March").Range("A1").Font.Bold = True
Workbooks("Sales").Worksheets("March").Range("A1").Font.Size = 14
```

As you can see, there is a lot of repetition in these five lines, which means a lot of unnecessary typing. The **With** construction allows you to do it much more easily:

```
With Workbooks("Sales").Worksheets("March").Range("A1")
  .Value = "Sales for March"
  .HorizontalAlignment = xlLeft
```

```
   With .Font
      .Name = "Times New Roman"
      .Bold = True
      .Size = 14
   End With
End With
```

The first line has the keyword **With**, followed by an object reference. The last line brackets it with the keywords **End With**. In between, any object, property, or method that starts with a period "tacks on" the object following the With. For example, .Value in the second line is equivalent to

```
Workbooks("Sales").Worksheets("March").Range("A1").Value
```

This example also illustrates how With constructions can be *nested*. The line With .Font is equivalent to

```
With Workbooks("Sales").Worksheets("March").Range("A1").Font
```

Then, for example, the .Name reference inside this second With is equivalent to

```
Workbooks("Sales").Worksheets("March").Range("A1").Font.Name
```

The use of With (and nested With) constructions can save a lot of typing. (It also speeds up the execution of your programs.) However, make sure you do the following two things:

- **Remember End With.** Remember the End With that must accompany each With. A good habit is to write the End With line immediately after typing the With line. That way, you don't forget.
- **Indent appropriately.** Indenting is not required—your programs will run perfectly well without it—but errors are much easier to catch (and avoid) if you indent, and your programs are *much* easier to read. Compare the above code to the version below:

```
With Workbooks("Sales").Worksheets("March").Range("A1")
.Value = "Sales for March"
.HorizontalAlignment = xlLeft
With .Font
.Name = "Times New Roman"
.Bold = True
.Size = 14
End With
End With
```

This version without indenting is certainly harder to read. By the way, do *not* indent by pressing the Space key repeatedly. This usually does not get things lined up properly. Instead, use the Tab key (or the Shift-Tab key combination for outdenting, the opposite of indenting). To indent or outdent an entire block of code, use the VBE toolbar buttons for this purpose on the Edit toolbar.

Exercise 4.4   Using With Constructions

Open the file **Ex4_03Finished.xls** (or your own version in **Ex4_03.xls**) from the previous exercise and save it as **Ex4_04.xls**. Then use the With construction wherever possible. For one possible solution, see the file **Ex4_04Finished.xls**. ∎

4.9   Other Useful VBA Tips

This section illustrates a few miscellaneous features of VBA that are frequently useful.

Screen Updating

A VBA program for Excel sometimes makes many changes in one or more worksheets before eventually showing results. During this time the screen can flicker, which wastes time and can be annoying. The following line "turns off" screen updating. It essentially says, "Do the work and just show me the results at the end."

```
Application.ScreenUpdating = False
```

To appreciate how this works, open the file **ScreenUpdating.xls**. It has two buttons, each attached to a sub. Each sub performs the same operations, but one turns off screen updating and the other leaves it on. You will notice the difference!

Display Alerts

If you use the Excel interface to delete a worksheet, you get a warning, as shown in Figure 4.9. In some applications you don't want this warning; you just want the worksheet to be deleted. In this case (and other cases where you don't want an Excel warning), you can use the following line:

```
Application.DisplayAlerts = False
```

This can actually be a bit dangerous—you might *want* a warning later on—so it is a good idea to turn display alerts back on immediately, as in the following lines:

```
Application.DisplayAlerts = False
Worksheets("Report").Delete
Application.DisplayAlerts = True
```

Figure 4.9 Excel warning message

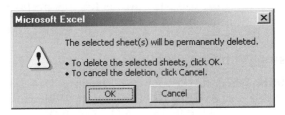

Timer Function

Programmers often like to see how long their programs (or parts of their programs) take to run. This is easy to do with the VBA **Timer** function. It returns the current clock time. If it is used twice, once at the beginning of some code and once later on, then the difference in the two times is the elapsed run time. The following lines illustrate how it can be used. The start time is captured in the variable StartTime. This is followed by any number of programming lines. Finally, the variable ElapsedTime captures the current time (from Timer) minus the start time. Note that these times are measured in *seconds*.

```
StartTime = Timer
Statements
ElapsedTime = Timer - StartTime
MsgBox "This section took " & ElapsedTime & " seconds to run."
```

4.10 Summary

This chapter has covered a lot of VBA programming fundamentals, including subroutines ("subs"), variables, input boxes and message boxes, comments, string operations, specification of objects, properties, and methods, With constructions, and a few other VBA elements. All of these will be used repeatedly in later chapters, especially in the applications in Part II of the book. Don't worry if they are not completely clear yet. It takes plenty of practice to master these VBA fundamentals.

PROGRAMMING EXERCISES

1. Open a new workbook, get into the VBE, insert a module, and type the following code in the code window.

```
Sub CalcExpenses()
  CustName = InputBox("Enter the name of a customer.")
  NPurchases = InputBox("Enter the number of purchases made by " & CustName _
```

```
      & " during the month.")
   TotalSpent = 0
   For i = 1 To NPurchases
      AmtSpent = InputBox("Enter the amount spent by " & CustName & " on purchase " & i)
      TotalSpent = TotalSpent + AmtSpent
   Next
   MsgBox CustName & " spent a total of " & Format(TotalSpent, "$#,##0.00") & _
      " during the month.", vbInformation
End Sub
```

a. Make sure there is no Option Explicit line at the top of the module. (If there is, delete it.) Then run the program. It should work fine. (If it doesn't, check your spelling.)

b. Enter an Option Explicit line at the top of the module. Now run the program. It should produce an error message. The problem is that the Option Explicit statement forces you to declare variables, and none of the variables in this sub have been declared. Declare them appropriately with a Dim statement and re-run the program. It should now work.

2. Write a program, and store it in a file called **TravExpenses.xls**, that does the following: (1) It asks for a person's first name and stores is it in FName, (2) it asks for a person's last name and stores it in LName, (3) it asks for the number of miles the person traveled on a recent trip and stores it in NMiles, (4) it asks for the average miles per gallon the person got on the trip and stores it in MPG, (5) it asks for the average price per gallon paid for gas on the trip and stores it in AvgPrice, (6) it calculates the cost of the trip and stores it in TripCost, and (7) it displays a message such as "Bob Jones traveled 800 miles, got 31.3 miles per gallon on average, paid $1.46 per gallon on average, and paid a total of $37.32 for gas." Make sure there is an Option Explicit line at the top of the module and that you declare all of your variables appropriately.

3. Write a program, and store it in a file called **StringFns.xls**, that does the following: (1) It asks the user for a word with at least 10 characters and stores it in MyWord, (2) it displays a message indicating the number of characters in the word, (3) it displays a message showing the first four characters of the word, (4) it displays a message showing the last six characters of the word, (5) it displays a message showing the fifth character in the word, and (6) it displays a message showing all but the first two and last two characters in the word.

4. The file **Formatting1.xls** contains the following code for formatting some data. It is all correct. Rewrite the code so that there are no With constructions. Then run the modified program to make sure it still works. Can you see how With constructions reduce "code bloat"?

```
Sub Formatting()
   With ActiveWorkbook.Worksheets("Sheet1")
      With .Range("A1")
         .Value = "Expenses for March"
         With .Font
            .Name = "Arial"
            .Bold = True
```

```
          .ColorIndex = 5
          .Size = 14
        End With
        .HorizontalAlignment = xlLeft
      End With
      With Range("A3:A6")
        .InsertIndent 1
        With .Font
          .Italic = True
          .Bold = True
        End With
      End With
      With .Range("B3:B6")
        .Interior.ColorIndex = 37
        .NumberFormat = "$#,##0"
      End With
    End With
  End Sub
```

5. The file **Formatting2.xls** contains the following code for formatting some data. This code works perfectly well, but (to say the least) it is a bit repetitive. Rewrite it by using as many With constructions as make sense, using appropriate indentation. Then run your modified code to make sure it still works.

```
Sub Formatting()
  ActiveWorkbook.Worksheets("Sheet1").Range("A1").Font.Bold = True
  ActiveWorkbook.Worksheets("Sheet1").Range("A1").Font.Size = 14
  ActiveWorkbook.Worksheets("Sheet1").Range("A1").HorizontalAlignment = xlLeft
  ActiveWorkbook.Worksheets("Sheet1").Range("A3:A6").Font.Bold = True
  ActiveWorkbook.Worksheets("Sheet1").Range("A3:A6").Font.Italic = True
  ActiveWorkbook.Worksheets("Sheet1").Range("A3:A6").Font.ColorIndex = 5
  ActiveWorkbook.Worksheets("Sheet1").Range("A3:A6").InsertIndent 1
  ActiveWorkbook.Worksheets("Sheet1").Range("B2:D2").Font.Bold = True
  ActiveWorkbook.Worksheets("Sheet1").Range("B2:D2").Font.Italic = True
  ActiveWorkbook.Worksheets("Sheet1").Range("B2:D2").Font.ColorIndex = 5
  ActiveWorkbook.Worksheets("Sheet1").Range("B2:D2").HorizontalAlignment = xlRight
  ActiveWorkbook.Worksheets("Sheet1").Range("B3:D6").Font.ColorIndex = 3
  ActiveWorkbook.Worksheets("Sheet1").Range("B3:D6").NumberFormat = "$#,##0"
End Sub
```

6. The **CountLarge.xls** file has quantities sold for 1000 products for each of 60 months, for a total of 60,000 values. The following code counts the number of these that are greater than 100. Check how long it takes to do this by inserting the Timer function appropriately in the code and displaying the elapsed time in a message box.

```
Sub CountLarge()
  Dim cell As Range, NLarge As Long
  For Each cell In Range("Sales")
    If cell.Value > 100 Then NLarge = NLarge + 1
  Next
  MsgBox NLarge & " cells in the Sales range have a quantity larger than 100.", vbInformation
End Sub
```

7. Write single lines of code for each of the following.
   a. Set the value of cell A17 in the Sales sheet of the active workbook to 1325.
   b. Capture the value of cell B25 in the Quantities sheet of the workbook Sales.xls in the variable MarchSales.
   c. Clear the contents of the range named Sales.
   d. Copy the range A1:A10 on the Sheet1 sheet of the active workbook to the range A1:A10 of the MarchSales sheet in the Sales.xls workbook. (You can assume that Sales.xls is *not* the active workbook.)
   e. Assume there is a table of some type in the range named Sales of the active workbook. Autoformat this table as "Classic 2". (*Hint:* Go to the Object Browser, and look at the methods of the Range object. You should find one that has to do with autoformatting.)

5

Recording Macros

5.1 Introduction

This chapter illustrates a very quick way to start programming—by *recording* while you perform a task in Excel. Just as you can record yourself singing or playing the piano, you can record your keystrokes as you work in Excel. As the recorder records what you are doing, it generates VBA code in a module. If this sounds too good to be true, it is—at least to an extent. There are certain things you cannot record (loops and control logic, for example), and the recorded code, even though correct, is usually not very "stylish." Still, there are two reasons why recording can be useful. First, it is helpful for beginners. A beginning programmer can immediately generate code, then look at it and probably learn a few things. Second, it is useful even for experienced programmers who need to learn one particular detail of VBA code. For example, what is the VBA code for entering a comment in a cell? You could look it up in online help, but you could also record the process of entering a comment in a cell and then examine the resulting code. It might provide just the clue you need to get past a particular coding hurdle.

5.2 How to Record a Macro

Recording is easy. You use the **Tools/Macro/Record New Macro** menu item to display the dialog box in Figure 5.1. This allows you to give the macro a descriptive name, provide a description of the macro, give it a shortcut key, and tell Excel where to store the recorded code.[7]

The storage location for the macro is particularly important. As Figure 5.1 indicates, you can store the macro in the current workbook, in a new workbook, or in a special workbook called **Personal.xls**. If you store it in the current workbook, you can use the macro in that workbook but not in others (at least not without some extra work). This is sometimes acceptable, but suppose you want to record macros for tasks you do repeatedly. In fact, suppose your whole purpose in recording these macros is to have them available *all the time* as you are working in Excel.

---

[7]A shortcut key is useful if you want to be able to run the macro with a Ctrl-key combination. For example, if you enter the letter k in the box, then the macro will run when you press the Ctrl-k key combination. Just be aware that if there is already a Ctrl-key combination, especially one that you use frequently, your new one will override it. For example, many people like to use Ctrl-s to save a file, so it would not be wise to override this with your own use of Ctrl-s.

Figure 5.1 Record Macro dialog box

Record Macro   ? X

Macro name:
RedOutline

Shortcut key: Store macro in:
      Ctrl+   This Workbook   ▼

Description: Personal Macro Workbook
                     New Workbook
Macro recorded 4/4/2 This Workbook

                        OK   Cancel

Then the **Personal.xls** file should be your choice. It is a special file that Excel stores in its **XLStart** folder, so that it is opened every time Excel is opened.[8] It is actually opened as a hidden file, so that you are not even aware of its presence—but its macros are always available.

Take a look at your own XLStart directory to see if you have a **Personal.xls** file. If you do not, record a macro and specify the Personal Macro Workbook option in Figure 5.1. This will create a **Personal.xls** file on your computer, which you can then add to as often as you like. (By the way, you can either *record* macros to the **Personal.xls** file, or you can type code directly into it in the VBE.)

After you complete the dialog box in Figure 5.1 and click on OK, you should see the **Stop Recording** toolbar in Figure 5.2. (If it is not visible, right-click on any toolbar and check the Stop Recording box to make this toolbar visible. Actually, this action will be recorded!) There are two buttons on this toolbar. The one on the left (the blue square) is of primary interest. It stops the recorder. Therefore, perform your task and then click on this button to stop the recording. Just remember that the recorder will record virtually *everything* you do until you click the Stop Recording button, so be careful—and don't forget to stop recording when you are finished.

Figure 5.2 Stop recording toolbar

Suppose you already have a module in your current workbook (or your **Personal.xls** file, if that is where you are saving the recorded macro). Then the chances are that Excel will create a *new* module and place the recorded macro in it.

---

[8] The XLStart folder is in the path C:\Program Files\Microsoft Office\Office\XLStart if you used the default paths when you installed Office. Any .xls file in this folder is launched automatically when Excel is launched.

Actually, the rules for whether it opens a new module or uses an existing module are somewhat obscure, but the point is that you might have to search through your modules to find the newly recorded code.

5.3 Recorded Macro Examples

We have included two files, **Recording.xls** and **RecordingFinished.xls**, to give you some practice in recording macros. The **Recording.xls** file includes six worksheets, each with a simple task to perform—with the recorder on. The tasks selected are tasks that most spreadsheet users perform frequently. This section goes through these tasks and presents the recorded code. Although this recorded code gets the job done, it is not, at least from a perfectionist's point of view, very elegant code. Therefore, the **RecordingFinished.xls** file contains the recorded code and modifications of it. This is the usual practice when using the recorder. You usually record a macro to get one key detail. Then you modify the recorded code to fit your specific purposes and discard any excess you do not need.

For the rest of this section, it is best to open the **Recording.xls** file and work through each example with the recorder on. Your recorded code might be slightly different from the code in the file because you might do the exercises slightly differently.

EXAMPLE 5.1 Entering a Formula

This example, shown in Figure 5.3, asks you to name a range and enter a formula to sum the values in this range.

Figure 5.3 Example 5.1 worksheet

	A	B	C	D	E	F	G	H
1	**Naming a range and entering a formula**							
2								
3	Turn the recorder on, name the range with the numbers MonthlyCosts, then enter							
4	the formula =SUM(MonthlyCosts) at the bottom of the column, then turn the recorder off.							
5								
6	Month	Cost						
7	Jan-00	$14,581						
8	Feb-00	$11,002						
9	Mar-00	$13,065						
10	Apr-00	$11,877						
11	May-00	$12,785						
12	Jun-00	$10,061						
13	Jul-00	$14,561						
14	Aug-00	$12,391						
15	Total cost							

The recorded code and modifications of it appear below in the **SumFormula** and **SumFormula1** subs. If you think about range operations in Excel, you will realize that you usually *select* a range—that is, highlight it—and then do something to it. Therefore, when you record a macro involving a range, you typically see the **Select** method in the recorded code. This is actually not necessary. When you want to do something to a range with VBA, you do *not* need to select it first. As you see in the modified version, the **Select** method is never used. However, there is a reference to the Exercise1 sheet, just to clarify that the ranges referred to are in the Exercise1 sheet.

Note how the recorded macro names a range. It uses the **Add** method of the **Names** collection of the **ActiveWorkbook**. This Add method requires two arguments: the name to be given and the range being named. The latter is done in **R1C1 notation**. For example, R7C2 refers to row 7, column 2, that is, cell B7. This is a typical example of recorded code being difficult to read. The modified code shown below uses a much easier way of naming a range (by setting the **Name** property of the range).

Recorded Code

```
Sub SumFormula()
' SumFormula Macro
' Macro recorded 4/5/2000 by Chris Albright
    Range("B7:B14").Select
    ActiveWorkbook.Names.Add Name:="MonthlyCosts", RefersToR1C1:= _
        "=Exercise1!R7C2:R14C2"
    Range("B15").Select
    ActiveCell.FormulaR1C1 = "=SUM(MonthlyCosts)"
    Range("B16").Select
End Sub
```

Modified Code

```
Sub SumFormula1()
    With Worksheets("Exercise1")
        .Range("B7:B14").Name = "MonthlyCosts"
        .Range("B15").Formula = "=SUM(MonthlyCosts)"
    End With
End Sub
```

EXAMPLE 5.2   Copying and Pasting

This example, shown in Figure 5.4, asks you to copy a formula down a column.

The recorded code and modifications of it are shown below in the **CopyPaste** and **CopyPaste1** subs. Here again, you see **Select** and **Selection** several times in the recorded code. The recorded code also contains the strange line

Figure 5.4 Example 5.2 worksheet

	A	B	C	D	E	F	G
1	Copying and pasting a formula						
2							
3	Column D is the sum of columns B and C. The typical formula is shown in cell D7.						
4	Turn on the recorder, copy this formula down column D, and turn the recorder off.						
5							
6	Month	Region 1 sales	Region 2 sales	Total sales			
7	Jan-00	$14,583	$10,531	$25,114			
8	Feb-00	$10,030	$12,861				
9	Mar-00	$14,369	$11,172				
10	Apr-00	$13,108	$14,957				
11	May-00	$14,410	$13,395				
12	Jun-00	$11,439	$12,306				
13	Jul-00	$12,753	$12,593				
14	Aug-00	$13,074	$11,631				
15	Sep-00	$10,957	$11,651				

ActiveSheet.Paste. (Why does it paste to the ActiveSheet and not to a particular range? We still find this hard to understand.) The modified version is much simpler and easier to read.

Recorded Code

```
Sub CopyPaste()
' CopyPaste Macro
' Macro recorded 4/5/2000 by Chris Albright
    Range("D7").Select
    Selection.Copy
    Range("D7:D15").Select
    ActiveSheet.Paste
    Application.CutCopyMode = False
End Sub
```

Modified Code

```
Sub CopyPaste1()
    With Worksheets("Exercise2")
        .Range("D7").Copy Destination:=.Range("D7:D15")
    End With
' The next line is equivalent to pressing the Esc key to get
' rid of the dotted line around the copy range.
    Application.CutCopyMode = False
End Sub
```

This example indicates how you can learn something fairly obscure by recording. Remember that when you copy and then paste in Excel, the copy range retains a dotted border around it. You can get rid of this dotted border in Excel by pressing the **Esc** key. How do you get rid of it in VBA? The answer appears in the recorded code—you finish with the line **Application.CutCopyMode = False**.

EXAMPLE 5.3 Copying and Pasting Special as Values

This example, in Figure 5.5, asks you to copy a range of formulas and then use the PasteSpecial/Values option to paste it onto itself.

Figure 5.5 Example 5.3 worksheet

	A	B	C	D	E	F	G	H	I
1	Copying a range of formulas and pasting onto itself with the PasteSpecial Values option								
2									
3	Column D is the sum of columns B and C. Replace the formulas in column D with values.								
4									
5	Turn on the recorder, Edit/Copy and Edit/Paste Special (with the Values option), then turn off the recorder.								
6									
7	Month	Region 1 sales	Region 2 sales	Total sales					
8	Jan-00	$14,583	$10,531	$25,114					
9	Feb-00	$10,030	$12,861	$22,891					
10	Mar-00	$14,369	$11,172	$25,541					
11	Apr-00	$13,108	$14,957	$28,065					
12	May-00	$14,410	$13,395	$27,805					
13	Jun-00	$11,439	$12,306	$23,745					
14	Jul-00	$12,753	$12,593	$25,346					
15	Aug-00	$13,074	$11,631	$24,705					
16	Sep-00	$10,957	$11,651	$22,608					

The recorded code and its modifications are listed below in the **PasteValues** and **PasteValues1** subs. This time the recorded code is used as a guide to make a slightly more general version of the macro. Instead of copying a *specific* range (D8:D16), the modification copies the current *selection*, whatever it might be. Also, note that when recorded code contains a method, such as the **PasteSpecial** method of a **Range** object, it includes *all* of the arguments of that method. Typically, many of these use the default values of the arguments, so they do not really need to be included in the code. The modified code has dropped the Operation, SkipBlanks, and Transpose arguments because the actions performed in Excel did not change any of these.

Recorded Code

```
Sub PasteValues()
' PasteValues Macro
' Macro recorded 4/5/2000 by Chris Albright
    Range("D8:D16").Select
    Selection.Copy
    Selection.PasteSpecial Paste:=xlValues, Operation:=xlNone, _
        SkipBlanks:=False, Transpose:=False
    Application.CutCopyMode = False
End Sub
```

Modified Code

```
Sub PasteValues1()
' Note: This macro is somewhat more general. It copies and pastes to the
' current selection, whatever range it happens to be.
  With Selection
    .Copy
    .PasteSpecial Paste:=xlValues
  End With
  Application.CutCopyMode = False
End Sub
```

EXAMPLE 5.4   Formatting Cells

This example, shown in Figure 5.6, asks you to format a range of labels in several ways.

Figure 5.6 Example 5.4 worksheet

	A	B	C	D	E	F	G	H
1	Formatting the cells in a range							
2								
3	Format the following cells so that the font is Times New Roman, size 12, bold, and red.							
4								
5	Select the range *before* turning on the recorder.							
6								
7		Jan	Feb	Mar	Apr	May	Jun	

The recorded code and its modifications appear below in the **Formatting** and **Formatting1** subs. This is a typical example of "junk code" generated by the recorder. The exercise changes a few properties of the **Font** object, but the recorded code shows *all* of the Font's properties, whether changed or not. The modified code lists only the properties that are changed.

Recorded Code

```
Sub Formatting()
' Formatting Macro
' Macro recorded 4/5/2000 by Chris Albright
    With Selection.Font
      .Name = "Roman"
      .Size = 10
      .Strikethrough = False
      .Superscript = False
      .Subscript = False
      .OutlineFont = False
      .Shadow = False
      .Underline = xlNone
```

```
         .ColorIndex = xlAutomatic
      End With
      With Selection.Font
         .Name = "Times New Roman"
         .Size = 12
         .Strikethrough = False
         .Superscript = False
         .Subscript = False
         .OutlineFont = False
         .Shadow = False
         .Underline = xlNone
         .ColorIndex = xlAutomatic
      End With
      Selection.Font.Bold = True
      Selection.Font.ColorIndex = 3
  End Sub
```

Modified Code

```
Sub Formatting1()
    With Selection.Font
       .Name = "Times New Roman"
       .Size = 12
       .Bold = True
       .ColorIndex = 3
    End With
End Sub
```

EXAMPLE 5.5   Creating a Chart

This example, shown in Figure 5.7, asks you to create a chart (as shown in Figure 5.8) on the same sheet as the data for the chart.

Figure 5.7   Example 5.5 worksheet

	A	B	C	D	E	F
1	**Creating a chart**					
2						
3	Create a bar chart on this sheet for the following grade distribution.					
4						
5	Grade	Number				
6	A	25				
7	B	57				
8	C	43				
9	D	10				
10	F	4				

Figure 5.8 Example 5.5 chart

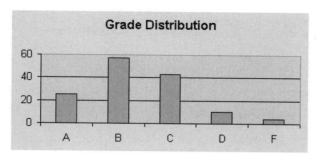

The recorded code and its modifications are listed in the **ChartOnSheet** and **ChartOnSheet1** subs. It is helpful to use the recorder when you want to use VBA to create or modify a chart. There are too many objects, properties, and methods for charts to remember, so you might as well let the recorder help you out. Note that the modified version leaves most of the recorded code alone. It simply inserts some With constructions to avoid repetitive references to the same object.

Recorded Code

```
Sub ChartOnSheet()
' ChartOnSheet Macro
' Macro recorded 4/5/2000 by Chris Albright
    Charts.Add
    ActiveChart.ChartType = xlColumnClustered
    ActiveChart.SetSourceData Source:=Sheets("Exercise5").Range("A5:B10"), _
        PlotBy:=xlColumns
    ActiveChart.Location Where:=xlLocationAsObject, Name:="Exercise5"
    With ActiveChart
        .HasTitle = True
        .ChartTitle.Characters.Text = "Grade Distribution"
        .Axes(xlCategory, xlPrimary).HasTitle = False
        .Axes(xlValue, xlPrimary).HasTitle = False
    End With
    ActiveChart.HasLegend = False
    ActiveSheet.Shapes("Chart 3").IncrementLeft 67.5
    ActiveSheet.Shapes("Chart 3").IncrementTop 10.5
    ActiveWindow.Visible = False
    Windows("RecordingFinished.xls").Activate
    Range("A2").Select
End Sub
```

Modified Code

```
Sub ChartOnSheet1()
    Charts.Add
    With ActiveChart
```

```
        .ChartType = xlColumnClustered
        .SetSourceData Source:=Sheets("Exercise5").Range("A5:B10"), _
            PlotBy:=xlColumns
        .Location Where:=xlLocationAsObject, Name:="Exercise5"
        .HasTitle = True
        .ChartTitle.Characters.Text = "Grade Distribution"
        .Axes(xlCategory, xlPrimary).HasTitle = False
        .Axes(xlValue, xlPrimary).HasTitle = False
        .HasLegend = False
    End With
    With ActiveSheet.Shapes("Chart 3")
        .IncrementLeft 67.5
        .IncrementTop 10.5
    End With
    ActiveWindow.Visible = False
    Windows("RecordingFinished.xls").Activate
    Range("A2").Select
End Sub
```

EXAMPLE 5.6   Sorting

This final example, in Figure 5.9, asks you to sort a range in descending order based on the Total column.

Figure 5.9 Example 5.6 worksheet

	A	B	C	D
1	Sorting a range			
2				
3	Sort on the Total column, from highest to lowest			
4				
5	Sales rep	January sales	February sales	Total
6	Adams	$3,843	$3,848	$7,691
7	Jones	$2,895	$3,223	$6,118
8	Miller	$3,707	$2,788	$6,495
9	Nixon	$3,544	$2,745	$6,289
10	Roberts	$3,672	$2,360	$6,032
11	Smith	$2,825	$2,369	$5,194
12	Thomas	$2,270	$2,035	$4,305
13	Wilson	$2,740	$2,625	$5,365

The recorded code and its modifications are listed in the **Sorting** and **Sorting1** subs. This again illustrates how you do not need to select a range before doing something to it. It also shows how the recorded code lists *all* arguments of the **Sort** method. The ones that have not been changed from their default values are deleted in the modified code.

Recorded Code

```
Sub Sorting()
' Sorting Macro
' Macro recorded 4/5/2000 by Chris Albright
  Range("D6").Select
  Selection.Sort Key1:=Range("D6"), Order1:=xlDescending, Header:=xlGuess, _
    OrderCustom:=1, MatchCase:=False, Orientation:=xlTopToBottom
End Sub
```

Modified Code

```
Sub Sorting1()
  Range("D6").Sort Key1:=Range("D6"), Order1:=xlDescending, _
    Header:=xlYes
End Sub
```

As these examples illustrate, you can learn a lot by recording Excel tasks and then examining the recorded code. However, you usually need to modify the code to make it more readable and possibly to make it fit your specific needs. Also, be aware that there are many things you cannot record. Specifically, there is no way to record If logic and loops, two of the most important programming constructs available to a programmer. You have to program these manually—the recorder cannot help you out.

The following exercise allows you to try some recording on your own.

Exercise 5.1

One convention used consistently in *Practical Management Science* is to enclose model inputs within a blue border. It is not difficult to use Excel's Format/Cells menu item to create a blue border around a range, but it does take a few keystrokes. It is much more efficient, especially if you are going to do it many times, to record a macro that creates a blue border around a selected range. Then you can attach this macro to a toolbar button that is always handy. This exercise leads you through the process of creating the macro and the button.

Open a blank workbook and select any range. Because you might not be familiar with creating a border around a cell, practice doing it first, *before* turning on the recorder. (Use the Format/Cells menu item, click on the Border tab, select a line style and a color, and finally click on the Outline button.) Once you are comfortable creating a blue outline, select some other range, turn the recorder on, name your macro BlueBorder, and save it to your **Personal.xls** file. Then go through the steps you just practiced to create a blue border, and turn off the recorder when you are finished.

Now create a new toolbar and put a button on it to run the BlueBorder macro. Here are the steps to do this.

Step 1 Right-click on any Excel toolbar to see a list of all toolbars, and select **Customize** at the bottom of the list. You are now in **customize mode**, where you will stay through the rest of the steps. In fact, any time you want to modify toolbars, you must get into customize mode first.

Step 2 Click on the Toolbars tab (if necessary), click on the New button, and name your new toolbar something like MyStuff (or any other name you prefer). A new toolbar will appear with no buttons on it. You can "dock" it wherever you like.

Step 3 Click on the Commands tab of the Customize dialog box and then scroll down the Categories list and select the Macros item. In the right pane you will see a generic happy-face button. Drag it to your new toolbar.

Step 4 Right-click on your new happy-face button to bring up the dialog box in Figure 5.10. The most important menu item is the Assign Macro item. Select it and then select the BlueBorder macro from the resulting list.

Figure 5.10 Menu for modifying toolbar buttons

Step 5 The menu in Figure 5.10 also lets you change the "tool tip" you see (when you rest your cursor over a toolbar button) by changing the Name property. Change it to Blue Outline.

Step 6 Finally, this menu allows you to change the happy-face icon to something more suggestive. To do this, select the Edit Button Image item. This brings up a "paint" program where you can draw your own icon. Be as creative as you like.

Step 7 After you have finished editing the toolbar button image, close the Customize dialog box. Then try out your button by selecting any range (or even multiple ranges) and clicking on the button. You should immediately see a blue border!

This process of recording a macro, saving it to your **Personal.xls** file, and creating a toolbar button to run the macro makes you an instant programmer. You will be amazed at how useful simple little macros like this can be if you design them to automate tasks you perform frequently. By the way, if you have created toolbar buttons that you no longer need, just get into customize mode and drag any unneeded button off its toolbar. It will immediately disappear.

5.4 Summary

The macro recorder serves two basic purposes: (1) It provides a great way for beginning programmers to learn how common Excel operations translate into VBA code, and (2) it allows even seasoned programmers to discover the one detail they might need to get a program working. However, there are also two drawbacks to the recorder that you should realize: (1) The recorded code is often far from elegant and "bloated" with unnecessary lines, and (2) it is incapable of capturing logic or loops, two of the most powerful aspects of VBA. In short, the recorder can be very useful, but it has its limits.

PROGRAMMING EXERCISES

1. VBA can be used to format worksheet ranges in a variety of ways—the font, the interior (background of the cells), the alignment, and others. The recorder can be useful for learning the appropriate properties and syntax. Try the following. Open a new workbook and type some labels or numbers into various cells. Then turn on the recorder and format the cells in any ways you think might be appropriate. Examine the recorded code. You will probably find that it sets many properties that you never intended to set. Delete the code that does not appear to be necessary and run your modified macro.

2. The ColorIndex property of the Font object (or the Interior object) determines the color of the font (or the background of a cell). For example, index 3 means red. However, it is hard to remember which color goes with which index. Try the following. Open a new workbook and type a label in some cell. Highlight this cell, turn the recorder on, and change the color of the font (or the cell's background) repeatedly, choosing any colors you like from the color palettes. As you do so, write down the colors you've selected. Then examine the recorded code. You should be able to match colors to indexes. (You can either keep this list handy for future reference, or you can repeat this exercise any time you want to discover the index for a particular color.)

3. Using the recorder can be particularly useful for learning how to use VBA to modify charts. The file **ChartPractice.xls** contains a small database and a chart that is based on it. Open this file, turn the recorder on, and change any of the elements of the chart—the type of chart, the chart title, the axis labels, and so on. (You might be surprised at how many things you can change in a chart.) As you do this, write down the list of changes you make. Then examine the recorded code and try to match the sections of code with the changes you made. (If you want more information on any particular chart property you see in the code, place the

cursor on it and press the F1 key. This will provide immediate online help for the element you selected. Alternatively, look it up in the Object Browser.)

4. The previous exercise shows how to use the recorder to learn about properties of an *existing* chart. You can also use the recorder to learn how to create a chart from scratch. Try the following. Open the **ChartPractice.xls** file, delete the chart, and then recreate it with the recorder on. Examine the recorded code to learn even more about how VBA deals with charts. (As with many recording sessions, you might want to practice building a chart *before* turning the recorder on. You don't want the recorder to record your mistakes!)

5. An operation we often perform is to highlight a range of cells that contain numbers and format them as integers, that is, as numbers with no decimals. Although this is easy to do with the Format/Cells menu item, it takes a few steps. Record a general macro for performing this operation, store it in your **Personal.xls** file, and create a button on a new or existing toolbar to run this macro. Once you are finished, you will always be a click away from formatting a range as integer. (*Hint:* Select a range of numbers *before* turning the recorder on. Then your macro will always work on the current selection.)

6. Many (most?) spreadsheets in the business world contain tables of various types. To dress them up, people often use Excel's autoformat feature. Using the Excel interface, this is easy: Highlight the table, use the Format/AutoFormat menu item, and choose one of many available formatting options. Try it now with code. Create a table in a worksheet, highlight it, turn the recorder on, and use the menu item to autoformat the table. Then examine the code. You'll see that it uses the **AutoFormat** method of a Range object, and that one of the arguments of this method specifies the particular formatting option through a built-in constant such as **xlRangeAutoFormatClassic1**. (If you ever need to learn the name of one of these constants, just repeat this exercise. This is a perfect example of how the recorder can be used to learn one critical detail of a program.)

7. Continuing the previous exercise, record a macro that formats a table with your favorite autoformatting option, and store the macro in your **Personal.xls** file. Then create a button on a new or existing toolbar that runs this macro. When you are finished, you will be a click away from autoformatting any table with your favorite option.

Working with Ranges

6.1 Introduction

This chapter focuses on ways to work with ranges in VBA. This is a particularly important topic because the majority of operations in Excel are *range* operations. You select ranges, you enter values and formulas in ranges, you format ranges in various ways, you copy ranges, and so on. Therefore, it is important to be able to perform these common tasks with VBA code. Unfortunately, it can be difficult to do even the easiest tasks unless you know the correct techniques. This chapter will show you sample VBA code that accomplishes many common tasks. You can then adapt this code to your own programs, sometimes with little or no change.

6.2 Exercise

Most of this chapter is rather detailed and can be tedious reading without having some purpose in mind. You can be assured that the material in this chapter *will* be used extensively in almost all of the succeeding chapters, but it is useful to introduce a rather simple exercise right away. You should probably not try this exercise yet, but you should keep it in mind as you read through the rest of the chapter. By the end, you should have more than enough tools to solve it—one way or another.

Exercise 6.1

The file **CalcNPV.xls** contains a model for calculating the net present value (NPV) from an investment. Five inputs are listed in the range B4:B8 (see Figure 6.1). These are used to implement the calculations for cash inflows in row 12, and the NPV is then calculated with the formula **=NPV(B8,B12:K12)-B4** in cell B14. All of the logic to this point is incorporated into the worksheet and does not need to be changed at all. When you enter different inputs in the B4:B8 range, the NPV in cell B14 will automatically recalculate.

The rows 18–22 contain possible values of the inputs, where each row is sorted in increasing order. The values shown are for illustration only—you can change them if you like. The goal of the exercise is to ask the user for any *two* of the five inputs. Then the application should find the minimum and maximum values for these two inputs from the corresponding 18–22 rows, substitute each combination (min of first and min of second, min of first and max of second, max

Figure 6.1 Setup for exercise

	A	B	C	D	E	F	G	H	I	J	K	L
1	Calculating the net present value of a stream of cash flows											
2												
3	**Inputs**											
4	1. Cash outflow, beginning of year 1	$40,000										
5	2. Cash inflow, end of year 1	$12,000										
6	3. Pct increase in cash inflow per year	12%										
7	4. Number of years of cash inflows	10										
8	5. Discount rate	16%										
9												
10	**Model of cash inflows (all occur at the ends of years)**											
11	Year	1	2	3	4	5	6	7	8	9	10	
12	Cash inflow	$12,000	$13,440	$15,053	$16,859	$18,882	$21,148	$23,686	$26,528	$29,712	$33,277	
13												
14	Net present value (NPV)	$48,787			Note that the values in each of rows 18-22 are in increasing order, so that the minimum value is at the left and the maximum value is at the right. Even if more values are added, you can assume that they will always be placed in increasing order.							
15												
16	**Possible values of the inputs to test**											
17												
18	1. Cash outflow, beginning of year 1	$10,000	$15,000	$20,000	$25,000	$30,000	$35,000	$40,000				
19	2. Cash inflow, end of year 1	$4,000	$5,000	$6,000	$7,000	$8,000	$9,000	$10,000	$11,000	$12,000		
20	3. Pct increase in cash inflow per year	2%	3%	4%	5%	6%	7%	8%	9%	10%	11%	12%
21	4. Number of years of cash inflows	5	6	7	8	9	10					
22	5. Discount rate	8%	9%	10%	11%	12%	13%	14%	15%	16%		
23												
24	**Sensitivity table (NPV for combinations of min and max of two selected inputs)**											
25			NPV									
26												
27												

of first and min of second, and max of first and max of second) into the appropriate cells in the B4:B8 range, and report the input values and corresponding NPVs in a table, starting in row 25. As an example, if the user selects inputs 3 and 5, the final result will appear as in Figure 6.2. Note that the values for the third input go from 2% to 12%, whereas the values for the fifth input go from 8% to 16%. Of course, these limits could change if the values in rows 18–22 are changed. The VBA should be written to respond correctly, regardless of the values in rows 18–22 (assuming they are always listed in increasing order from left to right).

The screen shot in Figure 16.2 is taken from the file **CalcNPVFinished.xls**. You can open this file and click on the Run Sensitivity Analysis button to see more exactly how the application should work. However, try not to look at the code in this file until you have tried developing the application on your own, starting with the file **CalcNPV.xls**. ■

6.3   Important Properties and Methods of Ranges

This section lists several of the more important and frequently used properties and methods of **Range** objects. You can skim over it on first reading, as it is more for reference purposes. However, you should find it handy as you work through the exercises and examples in this chapter and later chapters. Of course, you can find all of this information (and much more) in the online Object Browser in the VBE.

Figure 6.2 Completed solution

	A	B	C	D	E	F	G	H	I	J	K	L
1	Calculating the net present value of a stream of cash flows											
2												
3	Inputs											
4	1. Cash outflow, beginning of year 1	$40,000										
5	2. Cash inflow, end of year 1	$12,000				Run Sensitivity Analysis						
6	3. Pct increase in cash inflow per year	12%										
7	4. Number of years of cash inflows	10										
8	5. Discount rate	16%										
9												
10	Model of cash inflows (all occur at the ends of years)											
11	Year	1	2	3	4	5	6	7	8	9	10	
12	Cash inflow	$12,000	$13,440	$15,053	$16,859	$18,882	$21,148	$23,686	$26,528	$29,712	$33,277	
13												
14	Net present value (NPV)	$48,787			Note that the values in each of rows 18-22 are in increasing order, so that the							
15					minimum value is at the left and the maximum value is at the right. Even if more							
16	Possible values of the inputs to test				values are added, you can assume that they will always be placed in increasing order.							
17												
18	1. Cash outflow, beginning of year 1	$10,000	$15,000	$20,000	$25,000	$30,000	$35,000	$40,000				
19	2. Cash inflow, end of year 1	$4,000	$5,000	$6,000	$7,000	$8,000	$9,000	$10,000	$11,000	$12,000		
20	3. Pct increase in cash inflow per year	2%	3%	4%	5%	6%	7%	8%	9%	10%	11%	12%
21	4. Number of years of cash inflows	5	6	7	8	9	10					
22	5. Discount rate	8%	9%	10%	11%	12%	13%	14%	15%	16%		
23												
24	Sensitivity table (NPV for combinations of min and max of two selected inputs)											
25		Input 3	Input 5	NPV								
26		0.02	0.08	$47,074								
27		0.02	0.16	$22,029								
28		0.12	0.08	$91,583								
29		0.12	0.16	$48,787								

Properties

- **Address.** This property returns the address of a range as a string, such as "B2:C6".
- **Cells.** This returns a reference to a Range object and is usually used to refer to a particular cell. For example, Range("A1:A10").Cells(3) refers to the third cell in the range, A3, whereas Range("A1:C10").Cells(3,2) refers to the cell in the third row and second column of the range—that is, cell B3. If the range has more than a single row and column, that is, if it is "rectangular," then it is customary to use two arguments in Cells, where the first is the row and the second is the column. However, if the range is only part of a single column or a single row, then a single argument of Cells suffices.

A technical note. We hate to get overly technical, but there is one aspect of the Excel object model that should be discussed, at least once. Many objects, including the Range object, have *properties* that are in fact references to *objects* down the hierarchy. The Cells property is an example (as are EntireColumn, Font, and other properties in the list shown in this section). If you look up the **Range** object in the Object Browser, you will indeed see that **Cells** is classified as a *property*. However, the purpose of this property is to return an *object*. For example, consider the code **Range("A1: G10").Cells(3,5).Value**. Cells(3,5) is a property of the Range("A1:G10") object, but it returns an *object*, the range (cell) E3. The Value property then returns the contents of cell E3. This distinction between objects and properties can be confusing, especially for beginners. Fortunately, it will have little to do with how you do your actual programming.

- **Column.** This returns the number of the first column in the range, where column A has number 1, column B has number 2, and so on.

- **CurrentRegion.** This returns a reference to a range bounded by any combination of blank rows and blank columns. For example, if the range consists of A1:B10 and C5:D8, then the current region is essentially the smallest rectangular region enclosing all of this, A1:D10. (If you have ever used Excel's pivot tables, the CurrentRegion is how Excel "guesses" where your data set lives, assuming your cursor is somewhere within the data set. It returns the CurrentRegion of your cursor location.)

- **EntireColumn.** This returns a reference to the range consisting of the entire columns in the range. For example, Range("A1:C3").EntireColumn returns the entire columns A, B, and C.

- **Font.** This returns a reference to the font of the range. Then the properties (such as Size, Name, Bold, Italic, and so on) of this font can be changed, as in **Range("A1:D1").Font.Bold = True**.

- **Formula.** This returns the formula in the range as a string.

- **FormulaR1C1.** This returns the formula in a range as a string in R1C1 notation. This is particularly useful for formulas that are copied down or across. For example, suppose each cell in the range C3:C10 is the sum of the corresponding cells in columns A and B. Then the FormulaR1C1 property of the range C3:C10 would be **"=RC[-2]+RC[-1]"**. The R by itself means to stay in the *same* row. The [-2] and [-1] next to C reference two cells to the left and one cell to the left, respectively. To get some experience with R1C1 notation, try the following. Enter some numbers in the range A1:D10 and calculate row sums and column sums with the SUM function in column E and row 11, respectively. Then use the Tools/Options menu item, click on the General tab, and check the R1C1 reference style box. You might be surprised at how your formulas now appear.

- **HorizontalAlignment.** This returns the horizontal alignment of the cells in the range. The three possible values are **xlRight**, **xlLeft**, and **xlCenter**.

- **Interior.** This returns a reference to the interior of the cells in a range. It is often used to color the "background" of the cells, as in **Range("A1"). Interior.ColorIndex = 3**. (This would color cell A1 red, because 3 is the color index for red.)

- **Name.** This returns the name of the range (if any has been specified). If it is used in a line such as **Range("B3:E20").Name = "Sales"**, it creates a range name for the specified range.

- **NumberFormat.** This returns the format code (as a string) for the range. This is usually used to specify the number format for a range, as in **Range("C3:C10").NumberFormat = "#,##0.00"**. However, it is difficult to learn (or remember) these format codes. One way is to format a cell such as A1 manually in some way and then use the line **Debug.Print Range("A1"). NumberFormat**. This will print the number format of cell A1 to the Immediate window in the VBE (which you can open, if it isn't already open, with Ctrl-G). You can then see the appropriate format code.

- **Offset.** This returns a reference relative to a range, where the range is usually a single cell. This property is *very* useful and is used constantly in the applications in later chapters. It will be explained in more detail in the next section.
- **Row, EntireRow.** These are similar to the Column and EntireColumn properties.
- **Value.** This is usually used for a single-cell range, in which case it returns the value in the cell (which could be a label, a number, or the result of a formula). Note that the syntax Range("A1").Value can be shortened to Range("A1"). That is, if .Value is omitted, it is taken for granted. Most programmers take frequent advantage of this shortcut.

Methods

- **Clear.** This deletes everything from the range—the values *and* the formatting.
- **ClearContents.** This can be used instead of **Clear** to delete only the values and leave the formatting in place.
- **Copy.** This copies a range. It usually has a single argument named **Destination**, which is the paste range. For example, the line **Range("A1:B10"). Copy Destination:=Range("E1:F10")** copies the range A1:B10 to the range E1:F10.
- **PasteSpecial.** This pastes the contents of the clipboard to the range according to various specifications spelled out by its arguments. A frequently used option is the following. Suppose we want to copy the range C3:D10, which contains formulas, to the range F3:G10 as *values.* The required code is as follows.

```
Range("C3:D10").Copy
Range("F3:G10").PasteSpecial Paste:=xlPasteValues
```

- **Select.** This selects the range, which is equivalent to highlighting the range in Excel.
- **Sort.** This sorts the range. The specific way it sorts depends on the arguments used. For a typical example, suppose we want to sort the data set in Figure 6.3 (see Section 6.5) in ascending order on Score 2 (column C). Then the following line does the job. The **Key1** argument specifies which column to sort on, and the **Header** argument specifies that there are column headings at the top of the range that should *not* be sorted.

```
Range("A1:F19").Sort Key1:=Range("C2"), Order1:=xlAscending, Header:=xlYes
```

Again, this is only a small subset of the properties and methods of the Range object, but it is the subset we use most frequently in applications. If you want to learn more, or if you want to look up any specific property or method, the best way is to open the Object Browser in the VBA, select the Excel library, scroll down the left pane for the Range object, select any property or method in the right pane, and click on the question mark button for help.

6.4 Specifying Ranges with VBA

Once a range is referenced properly in VBA code, it is relatively easy to set (or return) properties of the range or use methods of the range. The hard part is usually referencing the range in the first place. Part of the reason is that there are so many ways to do it. This section describes the basic syntax for several of these methods. Then the next section presents a number of small subs that implement the methods. Like the previous section, the material here is mostly for reference. However, keep the exercise in Section 6.2 in mind as you read this section and the next. You will need to implement some of these ideas to do the exercise.

The most common ways to reference a range are as follows:

- **Use an address.** Follow Range with an address in double quotes, such as Range("A1") or Range("A1:B10").
- **Use a range name.** Follow Range with the name of a range in double quotes, such as Range("Sales"). This assumes there is a range with the name Sales in the active workbook.
- **Use a variable for a range name.** Declare a string variable, such as SalesName, and set it equal to the name of the range. This would be done with a line such as

```
SalesName = Range("Sales").Name
```

Then follow Range with this variable, as in **Range(SalesName).** Note that there are now no double quotes. They are essentially included in the variable SalesName (because it is a string variable).

- **Use a Range object variable.** Declare a variable, such as SalesRange, as a Range *object* and define it with the keyword **Set**. This can be done with the following two lines:

```
Dim SalesRange as Range
Set SalesRange = Range("Sales")
```

Then simply refer to SalesRange from then on. For example, to change the font size of the range, we could write **SalesRange.Font = 12.** (This method might be a bit advanced for now, but it is usually the method of choice for professional programmers.)

- **Use the Cells property.** Follow Range with the **Cells** property, which takes one or two arguments. For example,

```
Range("B5:B14").Cells(3)
```

refers to the third cell in the range B5:B14—that is, cell B7. In contrast,

```
Range("C5:E15").Cells(4,2)
```

refers to the cell in the fourth row and second column of the range C5:E15—that is, cell D8. In the first case, B5:B14 is a single-column range, so it suffices to use a single argument for the Cells property. (The same is true for a single-row range.) However, in the second case, where C5:E15 spans multiple rows and columns, it is more natural to use two arguments for the Cells property. The first argument refers to the row, the second to the column.

- **Use the Offset property.** Follow Range with the Offset property, which takes two arguments. For example, the reference

```
Range("A5").Offset(2,3)
```

says to start in cell A5, then go 2 rows down and 3 columns to the right. This takes you to cell D7. The first argument of Offset indicates the *row* offset. You use a positive offset to go down and a negative offset to go up. The second argument indicates the *column* offset. You use a positive offset to go to the right and a negative offset to go to the left. Either argument can be 0, as in

```
Range("A5").Offset(0,3)
```

This refers to cell D5.

- **Use top left and bottom right arguments.** Follow Range with two arguments, a top left cell and a bottom right cell, separated by commas. This corresponds to the way you often select a range in Excel. You click on the top left cell, hold down the Shift key, and click on the bottom right cell. For example,

```
Range(Range("C1"),Range("D10"))
```

returns the range C1:D10. Another example, which uses a With construction to save typing, is as follows:

```
With Range("A1")
    Range(.Offset(1, 1), .Offset(3, 3)).Select
End With
```

This code selects the range B2:D4. The top left cell is the cell offset by 1 row and 1 column from A1, namely, B2. Similarly, the bottom right cell is the cell offset by 3 rows and 3 columns from A1, namely, D4. Note, for example, that .Offset(1,1) is equivalent to Range("A1").Offset(1,1) because it is inside the With construction.

- **Use the End property.** You have probably used the **End-Arrow** key combination to select ranges in Excel, particularly if they are large ranges. For example, if the range A1:M100·is filled with values and you want to select it, you can click on cell A1, hold down the Shift key, then press the End and down arrow keys in succession, and finally press the End and right arrow keys in succession. It beats scrolling! The question is how to do this in VBA. It is easy once you know the **End** property. This takes one argument to determine the direction. It can be any of the built-in constants **xlDown**, **xlUp**, **xlToRight**, or **xlToLeft**. The following example is typical:

```
With Range("A1")
    Range(.Cells(1, 1), .End(xlDown).End(xlToRight)).Select
End With
```

The middle line selects a range that is specified by a top left cell and a bottom right cell. The first argument, .Cells(1,1), which is equivalent to Range("A1").Cells(1,1) because it is inside a With, is simply cell A1. The second argument, .End(xlDown).End(xlToRight), which is equivalent to Range("A1").End(xlDown).End(xlToRight), again because it is inside a With, is at the bottom right of the rectangular range that begins up in cell A1. The advantage of using the End property is that you do not need to know the *size* of the range. The above code specifies the correct range regardless of whether the data live in A1:B10 or A1:M500.

6.5   Examples of Ranges with VBA

It is one thing to know the information in the previous two sections in an abstract sense. It is another to use this information correctly to perform some task. This section presents a number of small subs for illustration. (All of these subs are listed in Module1 of the file **Ranges.xls**.) When presenting example subs that actually *do* something, it is always difficult to avoid aspects of VBA that have not yet been covered. Whenever this occurs, there is a brief explanation of anything new.

Watching your sub run. It is very informative to run these subs and watch what they do. Here is a useful strategy. First, make sure that only Excel and the VBE are open. (No other program icons should appear on your taskbar at the bottom of the screen.) Then right-click on any blank gray part of this taskbar to bring up a menu, and select **Tile Windows Vertically**. You should see the VBE code on one side and the Excel worksheet on the other. Next, put your cursor anywhere within a sub you want to run, and press the **F8** key repeatedly. This "steps" through your sub one line at a time. By having the Excel window visible, you can immediately see the effect of each line of code.

Most of the examples in this section are based on a small database of performance scores on various activities for a company's employees. These data are in the **Ranges.xls** file and are listed in Figure 6.3. The subs in this section all do something with this data set—perhaps not earthshaking, but illustrative of the methods you can use to work with ranges. (The labels in cells A21 and H1 are used only to indicate that the data set is separated by a blank row and a blank column from other data that might be on the worksheet.)

Figure 6.3 Employee performance scores

	A	B	C	D	E	F	G	H	I	J	K
1	Employee	Score1	Score2	Score3	Score4	Score5		Some extra junk might be over here.			
2	1	90	87	76	95	86					
3	2	78	90	99	84	84					
4	3	72	60	84	58	69					
5	4	82	66	81	69	72					
6	5	95	85	82	77	93					
7	6	90	93	66	88	93					
8	7	90	100	57	70	89					
9	8	90	98	61	56	83					
10	9	96	67	85	56	97					
11	10	87	69	77	78	76					
12	11	81	68	61	66	93					
13	12	58	57	72	75	77					
14	13	70	92	59	99	85					
15	14	69	71	89	68	72					
16	15	85	94	66	78	67					
17	16	55	79	99	98	76					
18	17	60	75	63	67	90					
19	18	83	93	88	58	56					
20											
21	Some extra junk might be down here.										

EXAMPLE 6.1   Using Addresses

The **Range1** sub refers to ranges by their literal addresses. This type of program is useful if you know that the location and size of a data range are not going to change. For several ranges, this sub displays the address of the range in a message box by using the **Address** property of a **Range** object. For example, the line

```
MsgBox Range("A2:A19").Address
```

displays the address of the range "A1:F19" in a message box.

```
Sub Range1()
' This sub refers to ranges literally. It would be used if you know the
' location and size of a data range are not going to change.
    MsgBox Range("A1").Address
    MsgBox Range("B1:F1").Address
    MsgBox Range("A2:A19").Address
    MsgBox Range("B2:F19").Address

' The following two lines are equivalent because the Value property is the
' default property of a Rangeobject. Note how string concatenation is used
' in the message.
    MsgBox "The first score for the first employee is " & Range("B2").Value
    MsgBox "The first score for the first employee is " & Range("B2")
End Sub
```

At the end of this sub, note how .Value can be used but is not necessary. Most programmers take advantage of this shortcut.

EXAMPLE 6.2 Creating and Deleting Range Names

The **Range2** sub first uses the **Name** property of a **Range** object to create several ranges names. Then (to restore the workbook to its original condition, which is done for illustration purposes only) these range names are deleted. To delete a range name, you first set a reference to a particular name in the **Names** collection of the ActiveWorkbook. Then you use the **Delete** method.

```
Sub Range2()
' This sub creates range names for various ranges, again assuming the
' location and size of the data range are not going to change.
    Range("B1:F1").Name = "ScoreNames"
    Range("A2:A19").Name = "EmployeeNumbers"
    Range("B2:F19").Name = "ScoreData"

' Delete these range names if you don't really want them.
    ActiveWorkbook.Names("ScoreNames").Delete
    ActiveWorkbook.Names("EmployeeNumbers").Delete
    ActiveWorkbook.Names("ScoreData").Delete

' Alternatively, delete them all at once with the following lines.
    Dim nm As Object
    For Each nm In ActiveWorkbook.Names
        nm.Delete
    Next
End Sub
```

If there were, say, 50 names in the Names collection, it would be tedious to write 50 similar lines of code to delete each one. The **For Each** construction at the bottom of the sub illustrates a much quicker way. For Each loops will not be discussed formally until the next chapter, but you can probably see what this one is doing. It goes through each member of the Names collection, using a generic variable name (nm) for a typical member. Then nm.Delete deletes this range name from the collection.

EXAMPLE 6.3 Formatting Ranges

The **Range3** sub first names a range, then it uses the range name to turn the **Bold** property of the font of this range to True. For illustration (and to restore the sheet to its original condition), it then sets the Bold property to False. Note that the Bold property of a Font object is one of many **Boolean** properties in Excel. A Boolean property has only two possible values: True and False.

```
Sub Range3()
' If a range has a range name, you can refer to it by its name.
    Range("B2:F19").Name = "ScoreData"
    Range("ScoreData").Font.Bold = True
' Now turn bold off, and delete the range name.
    Range("ScoreData").Font.Bold = False
```

```
        ActiveWorkbook.Names("ScoreData").Delete
End Sub
```

Note the object hierarchy in the line

```
Range("ScoreData").Font.Bold = True
```

Each **Range** object has a **Font** object down the hierarchy from it, and the **Font** object then has a **Bold** property. This line shows the proper syntax for referring to this property.

EXAMPLE 6.4   Using a String Variable for a Range Name

The **Range4** sub is almost identical to the **Range3** sub, except that it uses the string variable RName to capture and then use the name of a range.

```
Sub Range4()
    Dim RName As String
    RName = "ScoreData"
    Range("B2:F19").Name = RName
    Range(RName).Font.Bold = True
' Now turn bold off, and delete the range name.
    Range(RName).Font.Bold = False
    ActiveWorkbook.Names(RName).Delete
End Sub
```

Note the lack of double quotes around RName in the line

```
Range(RName).Font.Bold = True
```

Because RName is a string variable, it essentially includes the double quotes, so they shouldn't be repeated here.

EXAMPLE 6.5   Using the Cells Property and the Top Left, Bottom Right Combination

The **Range5** sub refers to ranges with the **Cells** property. Remember that if the Cells property uses two arguments, the first refers to the row and the second to the column. This sub also shows how to refer to a range by its top left and bottom right cells. As explained in the comments, a With construction can be used here to save typing.

```
Sub Range5()
  Range("B2:F19").Name = "ScoreData"
```

```
' The following displays the address of the 2nd row, 3rd column cell (cell D3) of the
' ScoreData range.
   MsgBox Range("ScoreData").Cells(2, 3).Address
' The following shows how to specify a range in the format Range(TopLeft,BottomRight).
' Here TopLeft refers to the top left cell in the range, BottomRight refers to the
' bottom right cell in the range. The top left in the following is cell C3, and the
' bottom right is cell E4.
   MsgBox Range(Range("ScoreData").Cells(2, 2), Range("ScoreData").Cells(3, 4)).Address
' This is cumbersome (having to spell out Range("ScoreData") twice). A more efficient
' method uses the following With construction.
   With Range("ScoreData")
       MsgBox Range(.Cells(2, 2), .Cells(3, 4)).Address
   End With
End Sub
```

EXAMPLE 6.6 Using the End Property and the Offset Property

The **Range6** sub uses the **End** property to specify the bottom right cell of a range that might expand or contract as data are added to, or deleted from, a worksheet. It also uses the **Offset** property as a convenient way to specify other ranges relative to some "anchor" cell. In the middle of the sub, the **Count** property of the **Columns** collection is used to count the columns in a range. Similarly, **.Rows.Count** counts the rows. Finally, note how string concatenation is used in the MsgBox statements.

```
Sub Range6()
    Dim NScores As Integer, NEmployees As Integer
' Up to now, we have made the implicit assumption that the range of the data will not
' change, so that we can refer to it literally (e.g., B2:F19). But a more general
' approach is to assume the number of rows and/or columns could change. This sub shows
' how to specify the range. Think of the With Range("A1") statement as setting an
' "anchor" that everything else is offset relative to.
    With Range("A1")
       Range(.Offset(0, 1), .End(xlToRight)).Name = "ScoreNames"
       Range(.Offset(1, 0), .End(xlDown)).Name = "EmployeeNumbers"
       Range(.Offset(1, 1), .End(xlDown).End(xlToRight)).Name = "ScoreData"
    End With
' Alternatively, we could find the number of columns and the number of rows in the
' data set, then use these.
    With Range("A1")
       NScores = Range(.Offset(0, 1), .End(xlToRight)).Columns.Count
       MsgBox "There are " & NScores & " scores for each employee.", vbInformation, _
          "Number of scores"
       NEmployees = Range(.Offset(1, 0), .End(xlDown)).Rows.Count
       MsgBox "There are " & NEmployees & " employees in the data set.", _
          vbInformation, "Number of employees"
' Now (just for variety) include row 1, column A in the range.
       Range(.Offset(0, 0), .Offset(NEmployees, NScores)).Name = "EntireDataSet"
       MsgBox "The entire data set is in the range " & Range("EntireDataSet").Address, _
          vbInformation, "Data set address"
    End With
' Delete all range names.
    Dim nm As Object
```

```
    For Each nm In ActiveWorkbook.Names
        nm.Delete
    Next
End Sub
```

EXAMPLE 6.7   Referring to Rows and Columns

It is often necessary to refer to a row or column of a range. It might also be necessary to refer to an *entire* row or column, as you do when you click on a row number of a column label in the margin. The **Range7** sub shows how to do either. For example, **.Rows(12)** refers to the 12th row of a range, whereas **.Columns(4)** **.EntireColumn** refers to the entire column corresponding to the 4th column in the range (in this case, column D).

```
Sub Range7()
' This sub shows how to select rows or columns.
    With Range("A1:F19")
        .Rows(12).Select
        MsgBox "12th row of data range has been selected."
        .Rows(12).EntireRow.Select
        MsgBox "Entire 12th row has been selected."
        .Columns(4).Select
        MsgBox "4th column of data range has been selected."
        .Columns(4).EntireColumn.Select
        MsgBox "Entire 4th column has been selected."
    End With
' Here is another way to refer to rows in a worksheet.
    Rows("4:5").Select
    MsgBox "Rows 4 and 5 should now be selected."
' Here is another way to refer to columns in a worksheet.
    Columns("D:E").Select
    MsgBox "Columns D and E should now be selected."
' The following line does NOT work — it produces an error.
'   Columns("4:5").Select
End Sub
```

EXAMPLE 6.8   Formatting Cells in a Range

One of the most useful things you can do with VBA is format cells in a range. The **Range8** sub illustrates how to apply various formats to a range. Note in particular the **ColorIndex** property of the **Font** or the **Interior** of a Range. The integer value of ColorIndex indicates the color. For example, 1 is black, 3 is red, and 5 is blue. (How do you know which number goes with which color? It is undoubtedly buried somewhere in online help. An easier way to learn how to color something light gray, for example, is to turn the recorder on, color something light gray, and look at the recorded code. The magic color index number will be there!)

This is a particularly good example for tiling the Excel and VBE windows vertically and then stepping through the code one line at a time (with the F8 key).

You can then see the code in one window and the effect of the formatting in the other window.

```
Sub Range8()
' Here are some common ways to format data in ranges.
    With Range("A1")
        Range(.Offset(0, 1), .End(xlToRight)).Name = "ScoreNames"
        Range(.Offset(1, 0), .End(xlDown)).Name = "EmployeeNumbers"
        Range(.Offset(1, 1), .End(xlDown).End(xlToRight)).Name = "ScoreData"
    End With
' Do some formatting.
    With Range("ScoreNames")
        .HorizontalAlignment = xlRight
        With .Font
          .Bold = True
          .ColorIndex = 3 ' 3 is red.
          .Size = 16
        End With
        .EntireColumn.AutoFit
    End With
    With Range("EmployeeNumbers").Font
        .Italic = True
        .ColorIndex = 5 ' 5 is blue.
        .Size = 12
    End With
    With Range("ScoreData")
        .Interior.ColorIndex = 15 ' 15 is light gray.
        .Font.Name = "Times Roman"
        .NumberFormat = "0.0"
    End With
    MsgBox "Formatting has been applied"
' Restore the original style. ("Normal" is a name for the default style.)
    Range("ScoreNames").Style = "Normal"
    Range("EmployeeNumbers").Style = "Normal"
    Range("ScoreData").Style = "Normal"
    MsgBox "Original formatting restored"
' Apply an autoformat (you could pick from many choices).
    With Range("A1")
        Range(.Offset(0, 0), .End(xlDown).End(xlToRight)).AutoFormat _
          xlRangeAutoFormatClassic3
    End With
    MsgBox "Classic 3 autoformatting has been applied."
' Restore the original style.
    Range("A1").Style = "Normal"
    Range("ScoreNames").Style = "Normal"
    Range("EmployeeNumbers").Style = "Normal"
    Range("ScoreData").Style = "Normal"
    MsgBox "Original formatting restored"
End Sub
```

EXAMPLE 6.9   Entering Formulas

The **Range9** sub illustrates how to enter formulas in cells through VBA. There are two properties you can use: the **Formula** property and the **FormulaR1C1** property. The **Formula** property requires a string that matches what you would type if you were entering the formula directly into Excel. For example, to enter the formula =Average(Score1), you set the Formula property equal to the string **"=Average(Score1)"**.

The **FormulaR1C1** property is harder to learn, but it is sometimes the natural way to go, given how relative addresses work in Excel. For example, suppose you have two columns of numbers and you want to form a third column to their right where each cell in this third column is the sum of the two numbers to its left. Then you would set the FormulaR1C1 property of this range equal to **"=Sum(RC[-2]:RC[-1])"**. The R with no brackets next to it means to stay in the *same* row. The C with brackets next to it means, in this case, to go from 2 columns to the left to 1 column to the left. (Remember that for rows, plus means down, minus means up. For columns, plus means to the right, minus means to the left.)

Note that this sub uses a couple of **For** loops in the middle. For loops will be discussed in detail in the next chapter. All you need to know here is that the variable i goes from 1 to the number of scores. First, it is 1, then 2, then 3, and so on. You should study this sub carefully. It is probably the most difficult example so far. Also, it is another excellent candidate for tiling the Excel and VBE windows vertically and then using the F8 key to step through the code one line at a time.

```
Sub Range9()
' This sub shows how to enter formulas in cells. You do this with the Formula property
' or the FormulaR1C1 property of a range. Either property takes a string value that
' must start with an equals sign, just as you enter a formula in Excel. It first names
' a range for each column of scores, then it uses the Formula property to get the
' average of each column right below the scores in that column.
    Dim NScores As Integer, NEmployees As Integer, i As Integer
' Determine the number of score columns and the number of employees. Then name the
' score ranges Score1, Score2, etc.
    With Range("A1")
        NScores = Range(.Offset(0, 1), .End(xlToRight)).Columns.Count
        NEmployees = Range(.Offset(1, 0), .End(xlDown)).Rows.Count
        For i = 1 To NScores
            Range(.Offset(1, i), .Offset(1, i).End(xlDown)).Name = "Score" & i
        Next
    End With
' For each score column, enter the average formula just below the last score. Note how
' string concatenation is used. For i = 1, for example, the string on the right will be
' "=Average(Score1)".
    For i = 1 To NScores
        Range("A1").Offset(NEmployees + 1, i).Formula = "=Average(Score" & i & ")"
    Next
' Now use the FormulaR1C1 property to find the average score for each employee. Note
' how each cell in the column of averages has the SAME formula in R1C1 notation. It is
' the average of the range from NScores cells to the left to 1 cell to the left. For
' example, if NScores is 4, this is RC[-4]:RC[-1]. The lack of brackets next to R mean
' that these scores all come from the same row as the cell where the formula is
' being placed.
    With Range("A1").Offset(0, NScores + 1)
        Range(.Offset(1, 0), .Offset(NEmployees, 0)).FormulaR1C1 = "=Average(RC[-" & _
            NScores & "]:RC[-1])"
    End With
End Sub
```

EXAMPLE 6.10   Referring to Other Range Objects[9]

The **Range10** sub introduces the **CurrentRegion** and **UsedRange** properties, as explained in the comments. It also demonstrates how to refer to a **Union** of possibly noncontiguous ranges. Finally, it illustrates the **Areas** property of a range.

```
Sub Range10()
' Here are some other useful range properties. The CurrentRegion and UsedRange
' properties are rectangular ranges. The former is the range "surrounding" a given
' range. The latter is a property of a worksheet. It indicates the smallest rectangular
' range containing all nonempty cells.
    Dim URange As Range
      MsgBox "The range holding the dataset is " & Range("A1").CurrentRegion.Address, _
    vbInformation, "Current region"
      MsgBox "The range holding everything is " & ActiveSheet.UsedRange.Address, _
    vbInformation, "Used range"
' It is sometimes useful to take the union of ranges that are not necessarily
' contiguous.
    Set URange = Union(Range("A1").CurrentRegion, Range("A21"), Range("H1"))
    With URange
       .Name = "UnionOfRanges"
       MsgBox "The address of the union is " & .Address, vbInformation, _
          "Address of union"
' The Areas property returns the "pieces" in the union.
       MsgBox "The union is composed of " & .Areas.Count & " distinct areas.", _
          vbInformation, "Number of areas"
    End With
End Sub
```

6.6 Summary

The examples in this chapter present a lot of material, more than you can probably digest on first reading. However, they should give you the clues you need to complete Exercise 6.1 and to understand the applications in later chapters. Indeed, you can feel free to "borrow" any parts of these examples for your own work, either for the exercise or for later development projects. As we stated in the introduction, most of the operations you perform in Excel are done to ranges, and our primary objective in this book is to show you how to perform these operations with VBA. Therefore, we expect that you will frequently revisit the examples in this chapter as you attempt to manipulate ranges in your own VBA programs.

PROGRAMMING EXERCISES

1. The file **EmployeeScores.xls** contains the same data set as in the **Ranges.xls** file (the file that was used for the examples in Section 6.5). However, the VBA code

---

[9] This example is more advanced and can be considered optional, especially on a first reading of this chapter.

has been deleted. Also, there is now a heading in cell A1, and the data begin in row 3. Save a copy of this file as **EmployeeScores1.xls** and work with the copy to do the following with VBA. (Place the code for all of the parts in a single sub.)

  a. Boldface the font of the label in cell A1, and change its font size to 14.
  b. Boldface and italicize the headings in row 3, and change their horizontal alignment to the right.
  c. Change the color of the font for the employee numbers in column A to blue.
  d. Change the background (the Interior property) of the range with scores to light gray.
  e. Enter the label Averages in cell A22 and boldface it.
  f. Enter a formula in cell B22 that averages the scores above it. Then copy this formula to the range C22:F22.

2. Repeat the previous exercise, starting with a fresh copy, **EmployeeScores2.xls**, of the original **EmployeeScores.xls** file. Now, however, use VBA to name the following ranges with the range names specified: cell A1 as Title, the headings in row 3 as Headings, the employee numbers in column A as EmpNumbers, and the range of scores as Scores. Then refer to these range names as you do parts **a** to **f**.

3. Repeat Exercise 1 once more, starting with a fresh copy, **EmployeeScores3.xls**, of the original **EmployeeScores.xls** file. Instead of naming ranges as in Exercise 2, declare Range object variables called TitleCell, HeadingRange, EmpNumbersRange, and ScoresRange, and "set" them to the ranges described in Exercise 2. Then refer to these object variables as you do parts **a** to **f**.

4. Repeat the previous three exercises. However, write your code so that it will work even if more data are added to the data set—new scores, new employees, or both. Try your programs on the original data. Then add an extra column of scores and some extra employees, and see if it still works properly.

5. Write a reference (in VBA code) to each of the following ranges. (You can assume that each of these ranges is in the active worksheet of the active workbook, so that you don't have to qualify the references by worksheet or workbook.)

  a. The third element of the range from A1 to A10.
  b. The cell at the intersection of the 24th row and 10th column of the range that begins in cell A1 and extends across and down to cell Z500.
  c. The cell at the intersection of the 24th row and 10th column of a range that has the range name Sales.
  d. The cell at the intersection of the 24th row and 10th column of a range that has been "set" to the Range object variable SalesRange.
  e. The entire column corresponding to cell D7.
  f. The set of entire columns from column D through column K.
  g. A range of employee names, assuming the first is in cell A3 and they extend down column A (although you don't know how many there are).
  h. A range of sales figures in a rectangular block, assuming that region labels are to their left in column A (starting in cell A4), and month labels are above them in row 3 (starting in cell B3). You don't know how many regions or months there are, and you want the range to include only sales figures, not labels.

     i. The cell that is two rows down from, and five columns to the right of, the active cell. (The active cell is where the cursor is. It can always be referred to in VBA as **ActiveCell**.)

6. The file **ProductSales.xls** has sales totals for 12 months and 10 different products in the range B4:M13. Write a VBA sub to enter formulas for the totals in column N and row 14. Use the **FormulaR1C1** property to do so. (You should set this property for two ranges: the one in column N and the one in row 14.)

7. (More difficult) Repeat the previous exercise, but now assume the data set could change, either by adding more months, more products, or both. Using the **FormulaR1C1** property, fill the row below the data and the column to the right of the data with formulas for totals. (*Hint:* First find the number of months and the number of products, and store these numbers in variables. Then use string concatenation to build a string for each FormulaR1C1 property.)

8. See if you can do the previous two exercises by using the **Formula** property rather than the **FormulaR1C1** property. (*Hint:* Enter a formula in cell N4 and then use the Copy method to copy down. Proceed similarly in row 14.)

9. The file **ExamScores.xls** has four exam scores, in columns B through E, for each of the students listed in column A. Write a VBA sub that sorts the scores in increasing order on exam 3.

10. (More difficult) Repeat the previous exercise, but now give the user some choices. Specifically, write a VBA sub that (1) uses an input box to ask for an exam from 1 to 4, (2) uses an input box to ask whether the user wants to sort scores in ascending or descending order (you can ask the user to enter A or D), and (3) sorts the data on the exam requested and the order requested. Make sure the headings in row 3 are *not* sorted.

Control Logic and Loops

7

7.1 Introduction

All programming languages contain logical constructions for controlling the sequence of statements through a program, and VBA is no exception. This chapter describes the two constructions used most often: the **If** and **Case** constructions. The If construction has already been used in previous chapters—it is practically impossible to avoid in any but the most trivial programs—but this chapter will discuss it in more detail. The Case construction is an attractive alternative to a complex If construction when each of several cases requires its own code.

This chapter also discusses the extremely important concept of loops. Have you ever had to stuff hundreds of envelopes? If you have ever had to perform this or any similar mind-numbing task over and over, you will appreciate loops. Perhaps the single most useful feature of computer programs is their ability to loop, that is, to repeat the same type of task any number of times—10 times, 100 times, even 10,000 or more times. All programming languages have this looping ability, the only difference among them being the way they implement looping. VBA does it with **For** loops and **Do** loops, as this chapter will illustrate. Fortunately, it is quite easy. It is amazing how much work you can make the computer perform by writing just a few lines of code.

The material in this chapter represents the essential elements of almost all programming languages, including VBA. Without control logic and loops, computer programs would lose much of their power. Therefore, it is extremely important that you master the material in this chapter. You will get a chance to do this with the exercise in the next section and the programming exercises at the end of the chapter. Beyond this, you will continue to see control logic and loops in virtually all later chapters.

7.2 Exercise

The following exercise is typical in its need for control logic and loops. You can be thinking about it as you read through this chapter. It is not difficult, but it will keep you busy for a while. Even more important, it will give you that wonderful feeling of accomplishment once you solve it. It is a great example of the power of the tools in this chapter.

Exercise 7.1   Finding Record Highs and Lows for Stock Prices

The file **Records.xls** contains two worksheets. The Prices sheet contains monthly adjusted closing prices (adjusted for dividends and stock splits) for several large companies from 1992 until the beginning of the year 2000. The Records sheet is a template for calculating the record highs and lows for any one of these companies. It is shown in Figure 7.1 (with a number of hidden rows). The Wal-Mart prices in column B have been copied from the WMT column of the Prices sheet.

Figure 7.1   Template for record highs and lows for Wal-Mart

	A	B	C	D	E	F	G	H	I	J
1	**Adjusted closing prices**			**Record values from 1995 on, based on data back through 1992**						
2	Date	WMT		Date	Price	High or Low				
3	Jan-92	12.804								
4	Feb-92	12.834								
5	Mar-92	12.668								
6	Apr-92	12.430								
7	May-92	12.609								
8	Jun-92	12.800								
9	Jul-92	13.306								
10	Aug-92	13.603								
95	Sep-99	47.416								
96	Oct-99	56.139								
97	Nov-99	57.447								
98	Dec-99	68.963								
99	Jan-00	54.622								
100	Feb-00	48.636								

The purpose of the exercise is to scan column B from top to bottom. If you see a price that is higher than any price so far, then it is called a "record high." Similarly, if a price is lower than any price so far, then it is called a "record low." Each record high and record low that occurs from January 1995 on should be recorded in columns D, E, and F. Column D records the date, column E records the price, and column F records whether it is a record high or low. Note that the record highs and lows are based on the data from 1992 through 1994, as well as more recent dates. For example, for a price in March 1996 to be a record high, it must beat all prices from January 1992 through February 1996. We just do not tabulate record highs and lows during the period from 1992 to 1994.

The file **RecordsFinished1.xls** contains the finished application. You can open it, copy (manually) any stock's price data from the Prices sheet to the Records sheet, and then click on the button. Figures 7.2 and 7.3 indicate the results you should obtain for Wal-Mart. The message box in Figure 7.2 summarizes the results, whereas columns D, E, and F show the details of the record prices. Feel free to run the program on other stocks' prices, but do *not* look at the VBA code in the file until you have given it your best effort.

If you like, you can extend this exercise in a natural direction. Modify your code so that there is now a loop over all stocks in the Prices sheet. For each stock, your modified program should copy the prices from the Prices sheet to the Records sheet and *then* continue as in the first part of the exercise. Essentially, the code from the first part of the exercise should be placed inside a loop on the stocks. The fin-

Figure 7.2 Summary of results

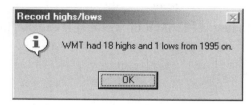

Figure 7.3 Detailed results

	A	B	C	D	E	F	G	H	I	J	K	L
1	**Adjusted closing prices**			**Record values from 1995 on, based on data back through 1992**								
2	Date	WMT		Date	Price	High or Low						
3	Jan-92	12.804		Jan-96	9.910	Low						
4	Feb-92	12.834		Jun-97	16.655	High						
5	Mar-92	12.668		Jul-97	18.471	High						
6	Apr-92	12.430		Nov-97	19.768	High						
7	May-92	12.609		Feb-98	22.891	High						
8	Jun-92	12.800		Mar-98	25.153	High						
9	Jul-92	13.306		May-98	27.288	High		Find record highs and lows				
10	Aug-92	13.603		Jun-98	30.113	High						
11	Sep-92	14.092		Jul-98	31.291	High						
12	Oct-92	14.509		Oct-98	34.276	High						
13	Nov-92	15.344		Nov-98	37.378	High						
14	Dec-92	15.267		Dec-98	40.460	High						
15	Jan-93	15.535		Jan-99	42.727	High						
16	Feb-93	15.505		Feb-99	42.789	High						
17	Mar-93	15.162		Mar-99	45.848	High						
18	Apr-93	12.774		Jun-99	48.050	High						
19	May-93	13.312		Oct-99	56.139	High						
20	Jun-93	12.551		Nov-99	57.447	High						
21	Jul-93	12.132		Dec-99	68.963	High						
22	Aug-93	12.327										
23	Sep-93	11.788										
24	Oct-93	12.626										
25	Nov-93	13.718										
26	Dec-93	11.981										

ished version of this part of the exercise is in the file **RecordsFinished2.xls**. Again, feel free to open the file and click on the button to see the sorts of results you should obtain, but do not look at the code until you have attempted it yourself.[10]

7.3 If Constructions

An If construction is useful when there are one or more possible conditions, each of which requires its own code. Here, a **condition** is any expression that is either true or false. Typical conditions are **Total <= 200**, **SheetName = "Data"**, and **FoundIt = True** (where FoundIt is a Boolean variable). We often need to check whether a condition is true or false, and then proceed accordingly. This is the typical situation where an If construction is useful.

---

[10] The results from this exercise indicate how bullish the stock market was in the late 1990s. There were numerous record highs and almost no record lows!

There are several "versions" of the If construction, in increasing order of complexity.

- **Single-line If.** The simplest version can be written on a single line. It has the form

```
If condition Then statement
```

Here, *condition* is any condition and *statement* is any single statement. This simple form requires only a single line of code (and there is no End If). An example is

```
If NumberOrdered <= 200 Then UnitCost = 1.30
```

- **If-Then-Else-End If.** A more common version of the If construction requires several lines and has the form:

```
If condition Then
    Statements1
[Else
    Statements2]
End If
```

(The square brackets denote that the lines within them are optional. You do *not* actually type the square brackets. In other words, the Else part of this construction is optional.) In this form, the condition is first tested. If it is true, then the statements denoted by *Statements1* are executed. You might also want to execute another set of statements, denoted by *Statements2*, in case the condition does not hold. If so, you must insert these after the keyword **Else**. In fact, there are four keywords in this form: **If**, **Then**, **Else**, and **End If**. (Note the required space between "End" and "If".) An example of this construction is the following:

```
If NumberOrdered <= 200 Then
    UnitCost = 1.30
    MsgBox "The unit cost is " & UnitCost
Else
    UnitCost = 1.25
    MsgBox "The unit cost is " & UnitCost
End If
```

- **If-Then-ElseIf-Else-End If.** The most general version of the If construction allows more than a single condition to be tested by using one or more **ElseIf** keywords. (Note that there is *no* space between "Else" and "If".) The general form is

```
If condition1 Then
    Statements1
```

```
[ElseIf condition2 Then
    Statements2
ElseIf condition3 Then
    Statements3
...
Else
    OtherStatements]
End If
```

(Again, the square brackets indicate optional parts. They are not actually typed in the program.) This construction performs exactly as it reads. There can be as many ElseIf lines as needed (denoted by the ...), and the Else part is not required. It is used only if you want to execute other statements in case all of the above conditions are false. An example of this version is the following:

```
If NumberOrdered <= 200 Then
    UnitCost = 1.30
ElseIf NumberOrdered <= 300 Then
    UnitCost = 1.25
ElseIf NumberOrdered <= 400 Then
    UnitCost = 1.20
Else
    UnitCost = 1.15
End If
```

In this construction, the program goes through the conditions until it finds one that is true. Then it executes the corresponding statement(s) and jumps down to the End If line. If none of the conditions holds and there is an Else line, the statement(s) following it are executed.

- **Nested If statements.** It is also possible to *nest* If constructions, in which case proper indentation is required for ease of reading. Here is an example:

```
If Product = "Widgets" Then
    If NumberOrdered <= 200 Then
        UnitCost = 1.30
    Else
        UnitCost = 1.20
    End If
ElseIf Product = "Gadgets" Then
    If NumberOrdered <= 500 Then
        UnitCost = 2.70
    ElseIf NumberOrdered <= 600 Then
        UnitCost = 2.60
    Else
        UnitCost = 2.50
    End If
Else
    UnitCost = 2.00
End If
```

The meaning of this code should be self-evident, but only because the lines are indented properly. Just try to imagine these lines without any indentation, and you will understand why the indentation is necessary! Besides indentation, make sure you follow every **If** with an eventual **End If** (unless the If construction is of the simple one-line version). In fact, it is a good practice to type the End If right after you type the If, just so you don't forget. Also, every condition must be followed by the keyword **Then**.

The file **IfExamples.xls** contains several examples to illustrate If constructions. They are all based on the small data set shown in Figure 7.4. Each example changes the formatting of the data in some way. The Restore button is attached to a sub that restores the data to its original "plain vanilla" formatting. In each example there is a For Each loop that goes through all of the cells in some range. (For Each loops will be discussed in detail in Section 7.6.) There is then at least one If construction that decides how to format cells in the range.

Figure 7.4 Data set for If examples

	A	B	C	D
1	**Sample database to use for If examples**			
2		Restore		
3	Employee	Score1	Score2	Score3
4	1	90	87	76
5	2	78	90	99
6	3	72	60	84
7	4	82	66	81
8	5	95	85	82
9	6	90	93	66
10	7	90	100	57
11	8	90	98	61
12	9	96	67	85
13	10	87	69	77
14	11	81	68	61
15	12	58	57	72
16	13	70	92	59
17	14	69	71	89
18	15	85	94	66
19	16	55	79	99
20	17	60	75	63
21	18	83	93	88

EXAMPLE 7.1 Single-Line If Construction

The **If1** sub illustrates a one-line If construction. If an employee's first score (in column B) is greater than 80, the corresponding employee number is boldfaced. Note that the range A4:A21 has been range-named Employee.

```
Sub If1()
    Dim cell As Range
    For Each cell In Range("Employee")
        If cell.Offset(0, 1) > 80 Then cell.Font.Bold = True
    Next
End Sub
```

EXAMPLE 7.2　If-ElseIf-End If Construction

The **If2** sub illustrates an If with a single ElseIf (and no Else). If an employee's first score is less than 70, the sub colors the corresponding employee number red (color index 3). Otherwise, if it is greater than 85, the sub colors the employee number blue (color index 5). If the score is from 70 to 85, no action is taken. Hence, there is no need for an Else.

```
Sub If2()
    Dim cell As Range
    For Each cell In Range("Employee")
        If cell.Offset(0, 1) < 70 Then
            cell.Font.ColorIndex = 3
        ElseIf cell.Offset(0, 1) > 85 Then
            cell.Font.ColorIndex = 5
        End If
    Next
End Sub
```

EXAMPLE 7.3　If-ElseIf-Else-End If Construction

The **If3** sub extends the **If2** sub. Now there is an Else part to handle scores from 70 to 85. All such scores are colored yellow (color index 4).

```
Sub If3()
    Dim cell As Range
    For Each cell In Range("Employee")
        If cell.Offset(0, 1) < 70 Then
            cell.Font.ColorIndex = 3
        ElseIf cell.Offset(0, 1) > 85 Then
            cell.Font.ColorIndex = 5
        Else
            cell.Font.ColorIndex = 4
        End If
    Next
End Sub
```

EXAMPLE 7.4　Nested If Constructions

The **If4** sub illustrates how a nested If construction allows us to test whether all three of the employees' scores are greater than 80 (in which case the employee's number is boldfaced). Note that the statement setting Bold to True is executed only if *each* of the three If conditions is true.

```
Sub If4()
    Dim cell As Range, RowCt As Integer, MinScore As Single
```

```
        For Each cell In Range("Employee")
            If cell.Offset(0, 1) > 80 Then
                If cell.Offset(0, 2) > 80 Then
                    If cell.Offset(0, 3) > 80 Then
                        cell.Font.Bold = True
                    End If
                End If
            End If
        Next
    End Sub
```

EXAMPLE 7.5 Compound (And, Or) Conditions

Conditions can be of the *compound* variety, using the key words **And** and **Or**. It is often useful to group the conditions in parentheses to eliminate any ambiguity. For example, the compound condition in the line

```
If condition1 And (condition2 Or condition3) Then
```

is true if *condition1* is true and at least one of *condition2* and *condition3* is true. Note that the individual conditions must be spelled out completely. For example, it is tempting to write

```
If Color = "red" Or "blue" Then
```

However, this will generate an error message. The corrected line is

```
If Color = "red" Or Color = "blue" Then
```

The **If5** sub illustrates a typical compound condition. It first checks whether an employee's first score is greater than 80 *and* at least one of the employee's last two scores is greater than 85. If this compound condition is true, then it boldfaces the employee's number, it colors the first score red, and it colors blue any second or third score that is greater than 85.

```
Sub If5()
    Dim cell As Range
    For Each cell In Range("Employee")
' Boldface student numbers who did well on the first score and even better on at least
' one of the last two scores.
        If cell.Offset(0, 1) > 80 And (cell.Offset(0, 2) > 85 Or cell.Offset(0, 3) > _
            85) Then
            cell.Font.Bold = True
            cell.Offset(0, 1).Font.ColorIndex = 3
            If cell.Offset(0, 2) > 85 Then cell.Offset(0, 2).Font.ColorIndex = 5
            If cell.Offset(0, 3) > 85 Then cell.Offset(0, 3).Font.ColorIndex = 5
        End If
    Next
End Sub
```

7.4 Case Constructions

If constructions can become fairly complex, especially when there are multiple ElseIf parts. The **Case** construction discussed here is often used by programmers as a less complex alternative. Suppose the action you take depends on the value of some variable. For example, you might have a product index that can have values from 1 to 10, and for each product index, you need to take a different action. This could be accomplished with an If construction with multiple ElseIf lines. However, the Case construction provides an alternative. The general form of this construction is

```
Select Case Variable
    Case Value1
        Statements1
    Case Value2
        Statements2
    ...
    [Case Else
        Other Statements]
End Select
```

(As usual, the square brackets are not typed. They indicate only that the Else part is optional.) Here, the keywords are **Select Case**, **Case**, and **End Select**, and *Variable* is any variable on which the various cases are based. Then *Value1*, *Value2*, and so on, are mutually exclusive values of *Variable* that require different actions, as specified by *Statements1*, *Statements2*, and so on. Actually, these values can be single values or ranges of values. For example, if *Variable* is ProductIndex, then you might need to do one thing if ProductIndex is from 1 to 5, another thing if ProductIndex is 6, and still another if ProductIndex is from 7 to 10. You can also include the Case Else, although it is not required. It specifies the action(s) to take if none of the other cases hold.

The following is a typical example of how the cases can be specified.

```
Select Case ProductIndex
    Case Is <= 3
        UnitPrice = 1.2 * UnitCost
    Case 4 To 6
        UnitPrice = 1.3 * UnitCost
    Case 7
        UnitPrice = 1.4 * UnitCost
    Case Else
        UnitPrice = 1.1 * UnitCost
End Select
```

Note the three ways the values are specified after the keyword Case: **Is <= 3**, **4 To 6**, and **7** (where **Is** and **To** are keywords). What are the rules? VBA's online help tells us that the following can come after the keyword Case:

"Delimited list of one or more of the following forms: *expression, expression* **To** *expression*, **Is** *comparisonoperator expression*. The **To** keyword specifies a range of values. If you use the **To** keyword, the smaller value must appear before **To**. Use the **Is** keyword with comparison operators (except **Is** and

Like) to specify a range of values. If not supplied, the **Is** keyword is automatically inserted."

As is often the case with VBA's online help, this gives the *precise* rules, but it is not easy to read. The alternative is to mimic the examples you see here or in other sources. Alternatively, there is nothing you can accomplish with Case constructions that you cannot also accomplish with (somewhat complex) If constructions. The construction that is used is often a matter of programming taste more than anything else.

The file **CaseExamples.xls** illustrates Case constructions. It is based on the small data set in Figure 7.5. As with the If examples, the examples here change the formatting of the data, so the Restore button is attached to a macro that restores the formatting to its original form. Note that the range A4:A21 has been range-named Family.

Figure 7.5   Data set for case examples

	A	B	C	D	E
1	Sample database to illustrate Case constructions				
2		Restore			
3	Family	Income			
4	1	$43,800			
5	2	$40,200			
6	3	$23,100			
7	4	$47,400			
8	5	$39,700			
9	6	$27,700			
10	7	$43,600			
11	8	$51,300			
12	9	$37,600			
13	10	$37,200			
14	11	$74,800			
15	12	$57,400			
16	13	$38,000			
17	14	$55,400			
18	15	$44,800			
19	16	$55,400			
20	17	$41,400			
21	18	$54,500			

EXAMPLE 7.6   Single Statement After Each Case

The **Case1** sub uses a For Each loop to go through each cell in the Family range. The Case construction is then based on the family's income, that is, the value in cell.Offset(0,1). Depending on which of four income ranges the family's income is in, the income is colored red, green, blue, or magenta. Then the data are sorted according to Income, so that all of the incomes of a particular color are adjacent to one another.

```
Sub Case1()
    Dim cell As Range
    For Each cell In Range("Family")
        With cell
```

```
                    Select Case .Offset(0, 1)
                        Case Is < 35000
                            .Offset(0, 1).Font.ColorIndex = 3
                        Case 35001 To 50000
                            .Offset(0, 1).Font.ColorIndex = 4
                        Case 50001 To 65000
                            .Offset(0, 1).Font.ColorIndex = 5
                        Case Else
                            .Offset(0, 1).Font.ColorIndex = 7
                    End Select
                End With
            Next
            Range("B3").Sort Key1:=Range("B4"), Order1:=xlAscending, Header:=xlYes
    End Sub
```

EXAMPLE 7.7 Multiple Statements After Cases

The **Case2** sub is very similar to the **Case1** sub. The main difference is that it shows how multiple statements can follow any particular case. Here, the incomes less than 35,000 are colored red. In addition, if they are less than 30,000, they are also italicized. Similarly, incomes greater than 65,000 are colored magenta, and if they are greater than 70,000, they are boldfaced.

```
Sub Case2()
    Dim cell As Range
    For Each cell In Range("Family")
        With cell
            Select Case .Offset(0, 1)
                Case Is < 35000
                    .Offset(0, 1).Font.ColorIndex = 3
                    If .Offset(0, 1) < 30000 Then .Offset(0, 1).Font.Italic = True
                Case 35001 To 50000
                    .Offset(0, 1).Font.ColorIndex = 4
                Case 50001 To 65000
                    .Offset(0, 1).Font.ColorIndex = 5
                Case Else ' above 65000
                    .Offset(0, 1).Font.ColorIndex = 7
                    If .Offset(0, 1) > 70000 Then .Offset(0, 1).Font.Bold = True
            End Select
        End With
    Next
    Range("B3").Sort Key1:=Range("B4"), Order1:=xlAscending, Header:=xlYes
End Sub
```

If you find that you favor Case constructions to If constructions in situations like these, just remember the following: The construction must begin with **Select Case**, and it must end with **End Select**.

7.5 For Loops

As we stated in the introduction, loops allow computers to do what they do best: repetitive tasks. There are actually two basic types of loops in VBA: **For** loops and

Do loops. Of these two types, For loops are usually the easier to write, so we will discuss them first.

For loops take the following general form, where the keywords are **For**, **To**, **Step**, and **Next**.

```
For i = First To Last [Step Increment]
    Statements
Next [i]
```

(As usual, square brackets indicate optional elements. You should not type the brackets.) There is always a "counter" variable, here i. (Typical variable names used for counters are i, j, k, m, and n, although any variable names can be used.) The first line states that i goes from *First* to *Last* in steps of *Increment*. For each of these values, the *Statements* in the body of the loop are executed. The default value of the Step parameter is 1, in which case the Step part can be omitted. The loop always ends with the keyword Next. It is possible, but not required, to write the counter variable in the Next line. This is sometimes useful when you have several For loops and there could be some confusion about which Next goes with which For.

The following is a simple example of a For loop that sums the first 1000 positive integers and reports their sum. This is actually a very common operation, where you accumulate some type of total within a loop. It is always a good idea to *initialize* the total to 0 just before starting the loop, as is done here.

```
Sum = 0
For i = 1 to 1000
    Sum = Sum + i
Next
MsgBox "The sum of the first 1000 positive integers is " & Sum
```

Virtually any types of statements can be used in the body of the loop. The following example illustrates how If logic can be used inside a loop. Here, you can assume that the worksheet Salaries has 500 employee names in column A (starting in row 2) and that their corresponding salaries are in column B. This code counts the number of employees with salaries greater than $50,000. The loop finds this number, TotalHigh, by adding 1 to the current value of TotalHigh each time it finds a salary greater than $50,000. Note how the counter variable i is used in the Offset to find the salary for employee i.

```
TotalHigh = 0
With Worksheets("Salaries").Range("A1")
    For i = 1 to 500
        If .Offset(i,1) > 50000 Then TotalHigh = TotalHigh + 1
    Next
End With
MsgBox "The number of employees with salaries greater than $50,000 is " _
    & TotalHigh
```

Exiting a For Loop Prematurely

Sometimes you need to exit a For loop prematurely. This is possible with the **Exit For** statement. It immediately takes you out of the loop. For example, suppose again that 500 employee names are in column A, starting in row 2, and you want to know whether there is an employee named James Snyder. The following code illustrates one way to do this. It uses a Boolean variable Found that is initially set to False. The program then loops through all employees. If it finds James Snyder, it sets Found to True, exits the loop, and reports that James Snyder has been found. However, if it gets through the loop *without* finding James Snyder, then Found is still False, so it then displays a message to this effect.

```
Found = False
With Worksheets("Salaries").Range("A1")
    For i = 1 to 500
        If .Offset(i,0) = "James Snyder" Then
            Found = True
            Exit For
        End If
    Next
End With
If Found = True Then
    MsgBox "James Snyder is in the employee list."
Else
    MsgBox "James Snyder is not in the employee list."
End If
```

Nested For Loops

It is also common to **nest** For loops. This is particularly useful in Excel if you want to loop through all of the cells in a *rectangular* range. Then there is one counter such as i for the rows and another counter such as j for the columns. The following example illustrates nested loops.

EXAMPLE 7.8 Nested For Loops

Consider the worksheet named Sales with the data in Figure 7.6. (This data set and accompanying code are in the file **ForExamples.xls**.) Each row corresponds to a sales region, and each column corresponds to a month. The numbers in the body of the table are sales figures for various regions and months, and we want the total sales over all regions and months. Then the nested For loops in the following **GetGrandTotal** sub do the job. Note how the sales figure for region i and month j is captured by the offset relative to cell A3. Note also how the counter variables are included in the Next lines (Next i and Next j) for clarity. Actually, the indentation achieves the same effect—easy readability.

```
Sub GetGrandTotal()
    Dim Total As Single, i As Integer, j As Integer
```

```
        Total = 0
        With Worksheets("Sales").Range("A3")
            For i = 1 To 13
                For j = 1 To 9
                    Total = Total + .Offset(i, j)
                Next j
            Next i
        End With
        MsgBox "Total sales for the 13 regions during this 9-month period is " & Total
    End Sub
```

Figure 7.6 Monthly sales by region

	A	B	C	D	E	F	G	H	I	J
1	Sales by region and month									
2										
3		Jan-99	Feb-99	Mar-99	Apr-99	May-99	Jun-99	Jul-99	Aug-99	Sep-99
4	Region 1	2270	1290	1600	2100	1170	1920	1110	2060	3130
5	Region 2	1730	3150	1180	740	1650	900	1830	1220	1620
6	Region 3	1840	1700	2170	3300	1390	1660	1720	2090	880
7	Region 4	3280	1920	2000	1270	1510	2280	2730	2160	1380
8	Region 5	2090	2110	2040	2270	1650	1910	2220	3380	1850
9	Region 6	1820	2570	2060	2190	1840	3310	1920	1080	940
10	Region 7	2400	1880	2980	2370	1910	2580	3470	2220	2200
11	Region 8	1680	1680	3120	1010	1550	2880	1410	2800	1520
12	Region 9	2230	2960	2240	2120	1870	2790	1390	2290	1620
13	Region 10	2040	2310	2120	2750	1220	1270	2080	2150	2650
14	Region 11	1430	2970	1800	2510	1660	1900	2910	770	2740
15	Region 12	1760	1590	1610	1550	1730	1150	3660	1670	3440
16	Region 13	1870	1330	1930	2080	2210	1850	3360	1930	1100

Continuing this example, suppose you want to append a "Totals" row to the bottom, where you sum sales across regions for each month, and a "Totals" column to the right, where you sum sales across months for each region. The following GetTotals sub accomplishes this. It is actually quite general. It first finds the number of months and number of regions in the data set, so that it will work for any numbers of months and regions, not just those in Figure 7.6. For example, the following line, inside the With Range("A3"), shows how to count the number of month labels to the right of cell A3.

```
NMonths = Range(.Offset(0, 1), .Offset(0, 1).End(xlToRight)).Columns.Count
```

This is a very common operation for counting columns (or rows), so you should get used to it.

```
Sub GetTotals()
    Dim i As Integer, j As Integer, RegionTotal As Single, _
        MonthTotal As Single, NMonths As Integer, NRegions As Integer
    With Worksheets("Sales").Range("A3")
' Capture the number of months and number of regions.
```

```
        With Range("A3")
            NMonths = Range(.Offset(0, 1), .Offset(0, 1).End(xlToRight)).Columns.Count
            NRegions = Range(.Offset(1, 0), .Offset(1, 0).End(xlDown)).Rows.Count
        End With
' Insert labels.
        .Offset(0, NMonths + 1) = "Totals"
        .Offset(NRegions + 1, 0) = "Totals"
' Get totals in right column.
        For i = 1 To NRegions
            RegionTotal = 0
            For j = 1 To NMonths
                RegionTotal = RegionTotal + .Offset(i, j)
            Next j
            .Offset(i, NMonths + 1) = RegionTotal
        Next i
' Get totals in bottom row.
        For j = 1 To NMonths
            MonthTotal = 0
            For i = 1 To NRegions
                MonthTotal = MonthTotal + .Offset(i, j)
            Next i
            .Offset(NRegions + 1, j) = MonthTotal
        Next j
    End With
End Sub
```

Pay particular attention in this sub to the initialization statements for RegionTotal and MonthTotal. For example, in the first pair of loops (where the totals in the right column are calculated), the outer loop goes through all of the rows for the regions. For a particular region, we must first reinitialize RegionTotal to 0, and *then* loop through all of the months, adding each month's sales value to the current RegionTotal value. Make sure you understand why the RegionTotal = 0 and MonthTotal = 0 statements are not only necessary, but must be placed exactly where they have been placed for the program to work properly.

The For loop examples to this point have had the counter variable going from 1 to some fixed number, in steps of 1. Other variations are possible, including the following:

- **Variable upper limit.** It is possible for the upper limit to be a variable that has been defined earlier. In the following lines, the number of customers is first captured in the variable NCustomers (as the number of rows in the Data range). Then NCustomers is used as the upper limit of the loop.

```
NCustomers = Range("Data").Rows.Count
For i = 1 to NCustomers
    Statements
Next
```

- **Lower limit other than 1.** It is possible for the lower limit to be an integer other than 1, or even a variable that has been defined earlier, as in the following lines. Here, the minimum and maximum scores in the Scores range are first captured in the MinScore and MaxScore variables. Then a loop uses these as the lower and upper limits for its counter.

```
MinScore = Application.Min(Range("Scores"))
MaxScore = Application.Max(Range("Scores"))
For i = MinScore to MaxScore
    Statements
Next
```

- **Counting backwards.** It is possible to let the counter go backwards by using a negative value for the Step parameter, as in the following lines. Admittedly, this is not common, but there are times when it is very useful.

```
For i = 500 to 1 Step -1
    Statements
Next
```

- **Lower limit greater than upper limit.** Another relatively uncommon situation, but one that *can* occur, is when the lower limit of the counter is greater than the upper limit (and the Step parameter is positive). This occurs in the following lines. What does the program do? It never enters the body of the loop at all; it just skips over the loop entirely. And, unlike what you might expect, there is no error message!

```
LowLimit = 10
HighLimit = 5
For i = LowLimit to HighLimit
    Statements
Next
```

7.6 For Each Loops

There is another type of For loop in VBA that is not found in most other programming languages: the **For Each** loop. Actually, this type of loop has been used a few times in this and previous chapters, so you are probably somewhat familiar with it by now. It is used whenever you want to loop through all objects in a collection, such as all cells in a Range or all worksheets in a workbook's Worksheets collection. Unlike the For loops in the previous section, you (the programmer) might have no idea how many objects are in the collection, so you don't know how many times to go through the loop. Fortunately, you don't need to know. The For Each loop figures it out for you. If there are three worksheets, say, then it goes through the loop three times. If there are 15 worksheets, then it goes through the loop 15 times. The burden is not on you, the programmer, to figure out the number of objects in the collection.

The typical form of a For Each loop is the following.

```
Dim itm as Object
For Each itm in Collection
    Statements
Next
```

Here, we show the declaration of the object variable *itm* explicitly. Also, *itm*, *Object*, and *Collection* have been italicized to indicate that they will vary depending on the type of collection. In any case, *itm* is a generic name for a particular item in the collection. Programmers generally use a short variable name, depending on the type of item. For example, if you are looping through all worksheets, you might use the variable name wsht, or even ws. Actually, any name will do. In this case, *Object* should be replaced by Worksheet, and *Collection* should be replaced by Worksheets (or ActiveWorkbook.Worksheets). The following code illustrates how you could search through all worksheets of the active workbook for a sheet named Data. If you find one, you can exit the loop immediately. Note that you must declare the generic ws variable as an object—specifically, a Worksheet object.

```
Dim ws as Worksheet, Found as Boolean
Found = False
For Each ws in ActiveWorkbook.Worksheets
    If ws.Name = "Data" Then
        Found = True
        Exit For
    End If
Next
If Found = True Then
    MsgBox "There is a worksheet named Data."
Else
    MsgBox "There is no worksheet named Data."
End If
```

The important thing to remember about For Each loops is that the generic item, such as ws in the above code, is an *object* in a collection. Therefore, it has the same properties and methods as any object in that collection, and they can be referred to in the usual way, such as ws.Name. Also, there is no built-in loop counter unless you want to create one—and there *are* situations where you will want to do so. As an example, the code below generalizes the previous code slightly. It counts the number of worksheets with a name that starts with "Sheet". (To do this, it uses the string function **Left**. For example, Left("Sheet17",5) returns the leftmost 5 characters in "Sheet17", namely, "Sheet".)

```
Dim ws as Worksheet, Counter as Integer
Counter = 0
For Each ws in ActiveWorkbook.Worksheets
    If Left(ws.Name, 5) = "Sheet" Then
        Counter = Counter + 1
    End If
Next
MsgBox "There are " & Counter & " sheets with a name starting with Sheet."
```

For Each with Ranges

One particular type of "collection" is a Range object. Remember that there is no "Ranges" collection, but the singular Range acts like a collection, and you can use it in a For Each loop. Then the individual items in the collection are the cells in the range. The following is a typical example. It counts the number of cells in a range that contain formulas. (To do so, it uses the **HasFormula** property, which returns True or False.) Note that **cell** is *not* a keyword in VBA. It is used here to denote a typical member of the Range collection—that is, a typical cell. Instead of **cell**, any other name (such as cl) for this generic object could have been used. In any case, this generic member must first be declared as a Range object.

```
Dim cell as Range, Counter as Integer
Counter = 0
For Each cell in Range("Data")
    If cell.HasFormula = True Then Counter = Counter + 1
Next
MsgBox "There are " & Counter & " cells in the Data range that contain formulas."
```

If you have programmed in another language, but not in VBA, it might take you a while to get comfortable with For Each loops. They simply do not exist in programming languages that do not have objects and collections. However, don't shy away from them—they can be extremely useful. For examples, refer back to any of Examples 7.1 through 7.7 in this chapter. They all use a For Each loop to loop through all cells in a range.

7.7 Do Loops

The For loops in Section 7.5 are perfect for looping a fixed number of times. However, there are many times when you need to loop *while* some condition holds or *until* some condition holds. Then you can use a **Do** loop. Do loops are somewhat more difficult to master than For loops, partly because you have to think through the logic more carefully, and partly because there are four variations of Do loops available. Usually, any of these variations can be used, and you have to decide which one is most natural.

The four variations are as follows. In each variation, the keyword **Do** appears in the first line of the loop, and the keyword **Loop** begins the last line of the loop. The first two variations check a condition at the top of the loop, whereas the last two variations check a condition at the bottom of the loop.

Variation 1: Do Until...Loop

```
Do Until condition
    Statements
Loop
```

Variation 2: Do While...Loop

```
Do While condition
    Statements
Loop
```

Variation 3: Do...Loop Until

```
Do
    Statements
Loop Until condition
```

Variation 4: Do...Loop While

```
Do
    Statements
Loop While condition
```

Here are some general comments that should help your understanding of Do loops.

- **Conditions at the top.** In the first two variations, the program checks the condition just before going through the body of the loop. In an Until loop, the statements in the body of the loop are executed only if the condition is *false*; in a While loop, the statements are executed only if the condition is *true*.
- **Conditions at the bottom.** The same holds in variations 3 and 4. The difference here is that the program decides whether to go through the loop *again*. The effect is that the statements in the loop might *never* be executed in the first two variations, but they will certainly be executed *at least once* in the last two variations.
- **Exit Do statement.** As with a For loop, you can exit a Do loop prematurely. To do so, you now use an **Exit Do** statement inside the loop.
- **Possibility of infinite loops.** A Do loop has no built-in counter as in a For loop. Therefore, you as a programmer *must* change something within the loop to give it a chance of eventually exiting. Otherwise, it is easy to be caught in an **infinite loop** from which the program can never exit. The following is a simple example. It shows that it is easy to get into an infinite loop. It happens to all of us. You can assume that Valid has been declared as a Boolean variable—it is either True or False.

```
Valid = False
Do Until Valid
    Password = InputBox("Enter a valid password.")
Loop
```

Go through the logic in these statements to see if you can locate the problem. Here it is. The Boolean variable Valid is never changed inside the loop. It is initialized to False, and it never changes. But the loop continues until Valid is True, which will never occur. If you type this code into a sub and then run it, the sub will never stop!

Breaking out of an infinite loop. This might not sound too bad, but suppose you have spent the last hour writing a program, you have not saved your work (shame on you!), and you decide to test your program by running it. All of a sudden, you realize that you are in an infinite loop that you cannot get out of, and panic sets in. How can you save your work? Fortunately, there is a way to break out of an infinite loop—use the **Ctrl-Break** key combination. (The **Break** key is at the top of most keyboards.) This allows you to exit the program and save your work. This brush with disaster also reminds you to save more often!

How do you avoid the infinite loop in the above example? Let's suppose that any password of the form "VBAPass" followed by an integer from 1 to 9 will be accepted. In this case the following code will do the job. It checks whether the user enters one of the valid passwords, and if so, it sets Valid to True, allowing an exit from the loop. But there is still a problem. What if the poor user just doesn't know the password? She might try several invalid passwords and eventually give up, either by entering nothing in the input box or by clicking on the Cancel button. The program checks for this by seeing whether Password, the string returned from the InputBox statement, is the empty string, "". (Clicking on the **Cancel** button of an input box returns the empty string.) In this case, the program not only exits the loop, but it ends abruptly because of the keyword **End**. After all, you don't want the user to be able to continue if she doesn't know the password.

```
Valid = False
Do Until Valid
    Password = InputBox("Enter a valid password.")
    If Password = "" Then
        MsgBox "Sorry, but you cannot continue."
        End
    Else
        For i = 1 to 9
            If Password = "VBAPass" & i Then
                    Valid = True
                    Exit For
            End If
        Next
    End If
Loop
```

Study this code carefully. Note that the **Exit For** statement provides an exit from the For loop, because the program has found that the user entered a valid password such as VBAPass3. In this case there is no need to check whether she entered VBAPass4, VBAPass5, and so on. In addition, by this time, Valid has just been set to True. Therefore, when control passes back to the top of the Do loop, the condition will be true, and the Do loop will be exited.

EXAMPLE 7.9   Locating a Name in a List

The file **DoExamples.xls** illustrates a typical use of Do loops. It starts with a database of customers in a Data worksheet, as shown in Figure 7.7 (with several hidden rows). Column A contains a company's customers for 1999, and column B contains the customers for 2000. The year 2001 has not yet occurred, so the company doesn't know its customers for 2001—hence the empty list in column C. We want the user to select a column from 1 to the number of columns (here 3, but the program is written more generally for any number of columns). Then the goal of the program is to check whether a customer with name Kreuger is in the selected column. (The blank Cust2001 column has been included here for illustration. It shows what happens if you try to locate a particular name in a *blank* list.)

Figure 7.7 Customer lists

	A	B	C
1	Cust1999	Cust2000	Cust2001
2	Barlog	Aghimien	
3	Barnett	Bang	
4	Bedrick	Barnett	
5	Brulez	Bedrick	
6	Cadigan	Brulez	
7	Castleman	Cadigan	
8	Chandler	Castleman	
9	Chen	Chandler	
10	Cheung	Cheung	
11	Chong	Chong	
12	Chou	Cochran	
92	Yablonka	Tracy	
93	Zick	Ubelhor	
94	Ziegler	Usman	
95		Vicars	
96		Villard	
97		Wendel	
98		Wier	
99		Wise	
100		Yablonka	
101		Yeiter	
102		Zakrzacki	
103		Zhou	

The **DoLoop1** sub shows how to perform the search with a **Do Until** loop. It searches down the selected column until it runs into a blank cell, signifying that it has checked the entire customer list for that column. If it finds a match to Kreuger along the way, it exits the loop prematurely with an **Exit Do** statement. Note that the program works even if column C is chosen. You should reason for yourself exactly what the program does in this case—and why it works properly.

```
Sub DoLoop1()
    Dim SelectedCol As Integer, NColumns As Integer, RowCount As Integer, Match As Boolean
    With Range("A1")
        NColumns = Range(.Offset(0, 0), .End(xlToRight)).Columns.Count
    End With
    SelectedCol = InputBox("Enter a column number from 1 to " & NColumns)
' Go to the top of the selected column.
    With Range("A1").Offset(0, SelectedCol - 1)
        RowCount = 1
        Match = False
' Keep going until a blank cell is encountered. Note that if there are no names at all in the
' selected column, the body of this loop will never be executed.
        Do Until .Offset(RowCount, 0) = ""
            If UCase(.Offset(RowCount, 0)) = "KREUGER" Then
                Match = True
                MsgBox "Kreuger was found as name " & RowCount & " in column " & _
                    SelectedCol & ".", vbInformation, "Match found"
```

```
' Exit the loop prematurely as soon as a match is found.
                Exit Do
            Else
' Unlike a For loop, the counter must be updated manually in a Do loop.
                RowCount = RowCount + 1
            End If
        Loop
    End With
    If Match = False Then MsgBox "No match for Kreuger was found.", vbInformation, "No match"
End Sub
```

Probably the most important parts of this loop are the row counter variable, RowCount, and the "updating" statement RowCount = RowCount + 1. Without these, there would be an infinite loop. But because RowCount increases by 1 every time through the loop, the condition following Do Until is always based on a *new* cell. Eventually, the program will find Kreuger or it will run out of customers in the selected column. That is, it will eventually end.

A note on VBA's UCase and LCase functions. Note the condition that checks for Kreuger uses VBA's **UCase** (uppercase) function. This function transforms any string into one with all uppercase characters. This is often useful when you are not sure whether names are capitalized fully, partially, or not at all. By checking for uppercase only, you take all guesswork out of the search. Of course, you could also use VBA's **LCase** (lowercase) function to search for all lowercase characters.

Changing Do Until to Do While. It is easy to change a Do Until loop to a Do While loop or vice versa. You just change the condition to its opposite. The **DoExamples.xls** file contains a **DoLoop2** sub that uses Do While instead of Do Until. The only change is that the Do Until line becomes the following. (Note that <> means "not equal to.")

```
Do While .Offset(RowCount, 0) <> ""
```

Putting conditions at the bottom of the loop. It is also possible to perform the search for Kreuger using variation 3 or 4 of a Do loop—that is, to put the conditions at the *bottom* of the loop. The **DoLoop3** and **DoLoop4** subs of the **DoExamples.xls** file illustrate these possibilities. However, for this particular task (of finding Kreuger), it is probably more natural to place the condition at the top of the loop. This way, if the first element of the selected column's list is blank, as for the year 2001, the body of the loop is never executed at all.

7.8 Summary

The programming tools discussed in this chapter are arguably the most important tools in VBA or any other programming language. It is hard to imagine many interesting, large-scale applications that do not require some control logic and loops. They appear everywhere. Fortunately, they are not difficult to master, and your knowledge of them will be reinforced by numerous examples in later chapters.

PROGRAMMING EXERCISES

1. Write a sub that displays a message box. The message should ask whether the total receipt for a sale is greater than $100, and it should display Yes and No buttons. If the result of the message box is **vbYes** (the built-in VBA constant that results from clicking on the Yes button), a second message box should inform the user that she gets a 10% discount.

2. Write a sub that asks for the unit cost of a product with an input box. Embed this within a Do loop so that the user keeps being asked until she enters a positive numeric value. (*Hint:* Use VBA's **IsNumeric** function. Also, note that if the user clicks on the **Cancel** button, an empty string is returned.)

3. Write a sub that asks for a product index from 1 to 100. Embed this within a Do loop so that the user keeps being asked until he enters an integer from 1 to 100. (*Hint:* Use a For loop for checking.)

4. All passwords in your company's system must be eight characters long, must start with an uppercase letter, and must consist only of uppercase letters and digits—no spaces. Employees are issued a password, but then they are allowed to change it to one of their own choice.
   a. Write a sub to get a user's new password. It should use an input box, embedded within a Do loop, to get the password. The purpose of the loop is to check that they indeed enter a valid password.
   b. Expand your sub in part **a** to include a second input box that asks the user to verify the password in the first input box (which by then is known to be valid). Embed the whole procedure within an "outer" Do loop. This outer loop keeps repeating until the user provides a valid password in the first input box and enters the same password in the second input box.

5. Repeat the previous exercise, but now assume that, in addition to the other restrictions on valid passwords, passwords can have at most two digits—the rest must be uppercase letters.

6. Repeat Exercise 4, but now perform a second check. Use the file **Passwords.xls,** which has a single sheet called Passwords. This sheet has a list of all passwords currently being used by employees in column A, starting in cell A1. If the new employee selects one of these passwords, an appropriate message is displayed, and the user has to choose another password. When the user finally chooses a valid password that is not being used, a "Congratulations" message should be displayed, and the new password should be added to the list.

7. Write a sub that asks the user for three things in three successive input boxes: (1) a "first" name (which can actually be their middle name if they go by their middle name), (2) a last name, and (3) an initial. Use Do loops to ensure that the first name and last name are all letters—no digits, spaces, or other characters. Also, check that the initial is a single letter or is blank (since some people don't like to use an initial). If an initial is given, ask the user in a message box with Yes and No buttons whether the initial is a *middle* initial. (The alternative is that it is a *first* initial.) Then display a message box listing the user's full name, such as "Your full name is F. Robert Jacobs", "Your name is Stephen E. Lee", or "Your name is "George Washington".

8. Assume you have a mailing list file. This file is currently the active workbook, and the active sheet of this workbook has full names in column A, starting in cell A1, with last name last and everything in uppercase letters (such as STEPHEN E. LEE). Write a sub that counts the number of names in the list with last name LEE and then displays this count in a message box. Note that there might be last names such as KLEE.

9. The file **PriceData.xls** has a single sheet that lists your products (by product code). For each product, it lists the unit price and a discount percentage that customers get if they purchase at least a minimum quantity of the product. For example, the discount for the first product is 7%, and it is obtained if the customer purchases at least 20 units of the product. Write a sub that asks for a product code with an input box. This should be placed inside a Do loop that checks whether the code is one in the list. Then it should ask for the number of units purchased, which must be a positive number. (You don't have to check that the input is an *integer*. We'll assume the user doesn't enter something like 2.73.) Finally, it should display a message something like the following: "You purchased _ units of product _. The total cost is _. Because you purchased at least _ units, you got a discount of _ on each unit." Of course, your code will fill in the blanks. Also, the last sentence will not be displayed if the user didn't purchase enough units to get a discount. (*Note:* You should write this sub, and the subs in the next two exercises, so that they are valid even if the list of products expands in the future.)

10. Continuing the previous exercise, write a sub that first asks the user for the number of different products purchased. Then use a For loop that goes from 1 to this number, and place the code from the previous exercise (modified if necessary) inside this loop. That is, each time through the loop you should get and display information about a particular product purchased. At the end of the sub, display a message that shows the total amount spent on all purchases.

11. Again, use the **PriceData.xls** file described in Exercise 9. Write a sub that asks the user for a purchase quantity that can be any multiple of 5 units, up to 50 units. Then enter a label in cell E3 something like "Cost of _ units", where the blank is filled in by the user's input. Below this, enter the total cost of this many units for each product. For example, cell E4 will contain the purchase cost of this many units of the first product in the list. Enter these as values, not formulas. Then sort on column E in descending order.

12. The file **CustAccts.xls** has account information on a company's customers. For each customer, listed by customer ID, Sheet1 has the amount the customer has purchased during the current year and the amount the customer has paid on these purchases so far. For example, the first customer purchased an amount worth $2466 and has paid up in full. In contrast, the second customer purchased an amount worth $1494 and has paid only $598 of this. Write a sub to create a list on Sheet2 of all customers who still owe more than $1000. (It should first clear the contents of any previous list on this sheet.) The list should show customer IDs and the amounts owed. This sub should work even if the data change, including the possibility of more or fewer customer accounts.

13. (More difficult) The file **CustOrders.xls** shows orders by date for a company's customers on Sheet1. Many customers have ordered more than once, so they have

multiple entries in the list. Write a sub that finds the total amount spent by each customer on the list and reports those whose total is more than $2000 on Sheet2. As part of your sub, sort the list on Sheet2 in descending order by total amount spent. (*Hint:* The data on Sheet1 are currently sorted by date. It might be helpful to use VBA to sort them by Customer ID. Then at the end of the sub, restore the list to its original condition by sorting on date.)

14. You are a rather paranoid business executive, always afraid that a competitor might be snooping on your sensitive e-mail messages. Therefore, you decide to use a very simple form of encryption. The table in the file **Scramble.xls** shows your scheme. For example, all instances of the letter "a" are changed to the letter "e", all instances of "b" are changed to "v". Note at the bottom of the table that uppercase letters are scrambled differently than lowercase letters. For example, all instances of "A" are changed to "D". (Spaces, periods, and other nonalphabetic characters are not changed.) Write two subs, Scramble and Unscramble. In each, ask the user for a message in an input box. In the Scramble sub, this will be an original message; in the Unscramble sub, it will be a scrambled message. Then in the Scramble sub, scramble the message and display it. Similarly, in the Unscramble sub, unscramble the message and display it. (Of course, in a real situation we would assume that you and the person you are e-mailing each have the **Scramble.xls** file. You would use the Scramble sub, and the person you are e-mailing would use the Unscramble sub.)

15. (More difficult) A prime number is one that is divisible only by itself and 1. The first few prime numbers are 2, 3, 5, 7, 11, and 13. Note that 2 is the only *even* prime number.

    a. Write a sub that finds the first n prime numbers, where you can choose n, and lists them in column B of Sheet1 of the **Prime.xls** file. The first few are already listed for illustration. (*Hint:* You might want to use VBA's **Mod** function. It returns the remainder when one number is divided by another. For example, **45 Mod** 7 returns 3.)

    b. Change the sub in part **a** slightly so that it now finds all prime numbers less than or equal to some number m, where you can choose m, and lists them in Sheet2 of the **Prime.xls** file.

Working with Other Excel Objects

8

8.1 Introduction

This chapter extends Chapters 6 and 7. Chapter 6 focused on Range objects. This chapter illustrates how to work with three other common objects in Excel: workbooks, worksheets, and charts. In doing so, it naturally illustrates further uses of control logic and loops. Workbooks, worksheets, and charts are certainly not the only objects you will encounter in Excel, but if you know how to work with these objects and ranges, you will be well along the way. All of the objects in this chapter have many properties and methods, and only a small fraction of them will be illustrated. As usual, you can learn much more from online help, particularly the Object Browser.

8.2 Exercise

The exercise in this section illustrates the manipulation of multiple workbooks, worksheets, and ranges. It is fairly straightforward, although you have to be careful to "keep your bearings" as you move from one workbook or worksheet to another. Work on this exercise as you read through the rest of this chapter. All of the tools required to solve it will be explained in the chapter (unless they were already explained in a previous chapter). When you finally get it working, you will feel like a real Excel "power programmer."

Exercise 8.1 Consolidating Data from Multiple Sheets

Consider a company that sells several of its products to five large customers. The company currently has a file with two sheets, Revenues and Costs, for each customer. These files are named **Customer1.xls** through **Customer5.xls**. Each sheet shows the revenues or costs by day for all products sold to that customer. For example, a sample of the revenue data for customer 1 appears in Figure 8.1. Each of the customer files has data for the *same* dates (currently, all weekdays from January 25, 2000, through June 9, 2000, although new data could be added in the future). In contrast, different customers have data for *different* numbers of products. For example, customer 1 purchases products 1 to 4, customer 2 purchases products 1 to 6, and so on.

Figure 8.1 Sample revenue data for customer 1

	A	B	C	D	E
1	Date	Product 1	Product 2	Product 3	Product 4
2	25-Jan-00	1890	2010	1150	2480
3	26-Jan-00	2880	2670	2280	3520
4	27-Jan-00	1520	2400	3430	1710
5	28-Jan-00	2270	2530	3220	2050
6	31-Jan-00	3280	2730	2080	2670
7	01-Feb-00	2630	1970	2900	1930
8	02-Feb-00	3030	3250	2410	3260
9	03-Feb-00	1990	1600	2360	2220
10	04-Feb-00	2800	1970	2650	2450
11	07-Feb-00	2360	2640	3280	2120
12	08-Feb-00	2680	2370	2600	1600
13	09-Feb-00	3260	2500	2550	2010
14	10-Feb-00	3130	1920	2440	2460
15	11-Feb-00	3090	3160	1830	2560

The purpose of the exercise is to consolidate the data from these five workbooks into a single Summary sheet in a workbook named **Consolidated.xls**. This file already exists, but it includes only headings, as shown in Figure 8.2. When it is finished, the dates will go down column A, the revenues and costs for customer 1 will go down columns B and C, those for customer 2 will go down columns D and E, and so on. The revenues and costs for all customers combined will go down columns L and M. Note that the revenues and costs in columns B and C, for example, are totals over all products purchased by customer 1.

Figure 8.2 Template for consolidated file

	A	B	C	D	E	F	G	H	I	J	K	L	M
1		Customer 1		Customer 2		Customer 3		Customer 4		Customer 5		Total all customers	
2	Date	Revenues	Costs	Revenues	Costs	Revenues	Costs	Revenues	Costs	Revenues	Costs	Revenues	Costs
3													

Figure 8.3 shows part of the results for the finished application. The button on the right runs the program. It should have a loop over the customers that successively opens each customer's file, sums the revenues and costs for that customer and places the totals in the consolidated file, and then closes the customer's file. Finally, after entering all of the information in Figure 8.3 up through column K, the program should enter *formulas* in columns L and M to obtain the totals.

To see how this application works, make sure none of the individual customers' files are open, open the **ConsolidatedFinished.xls** file, and click on the button. Although you will have to watch closely to notice that anything is happening, each of the customers' files will be opened for a fraction of a second before being closed, and the results in Figure 8.3 will appear. As usual, you can "cheat" by looking at the VBA code in the finished file, but you should resist doing so until you have given it your best effort.

Figure 8.3 Results from finished application

	A	B	C	D	E	F	G	H	I	J	K	L	M	N	O
1		Customer 1		Customer 2		Customer 3		Customer 4		Customer 5		Total all customers			
2	Date	Revenues	Costs	Revenues	Costs	Revenues	Costs	Revenues	Costs	Revenues	Costs	Revenues	Costs		
3	25-Jan-00	7530	5730	13810	8740	5290	2960	6520	5400	13310	7470	46460	30300		Consolidate
4	26-Jan-00	11350	5500	15860	9080	5510	3100	7100	4290	12610	7380	52430	29350		
5	27-Jan-00	9060	5770	14840	9190	5000	3410	7250	4990	12570	7570	48720	30930		
6	28-Jan-00	10070	5750	14910	9270	4800	2770	8500	4650	12900	7900	51180	30340		
7	31-Jan-00	10760	6180	13540	9180	4050	2700	7650	3550	12880	7050	48880	28660		
8	1-Feb-00	9430	5750	18810	9410	4770	2510	8830	3960	12000	7890	53840	29520		
9	2-Feb-00	11950	6010	16550	9760	4150	2690	8540	4720	11390	7010	52580	30190		
10	3-Feb-00	8170	5830	15040	8960	4300	2830	7610	5180	11900	8490	47020	31290		
11	4-Feb-00	9870	6240	17660	9120	5750	2720	7220	4070	12460	6800	52960	28950		
12	7-Feb-00	10400	5630	14560	9390	3990	2730	6560	4780	12560	7900	48070	30430		
13	8-Feb-00	9250	5820	13690	8960	4300	2820	7330	4320	10920	7620	45490	29540		
14	9-Feb-00	10320	7030	17180	9070	3470	2800	6640	4410	11230	8350	48840	31660		
15	10-Feb-00	9950	5950	14940	9240	4350	3330	6120	4120	12870	7520	48230	30160		
16	11-Feb-00	10640	5700	12850	9170	5340	2860	7150	4260	12740	6880	48720	28870		
17	14-Feb-00	9250	6010	13320	8650	5090	2990	7040	4700	12420	7590	47120	29940		
18	15-Feb-00	9100	6190	13560	8340	4430	3690	7670	4980	13310	7060	48070	30260		

8.3 Collections and Specific Members of Collections

Collections and members of collections (remember, plural and singular?) were already discussed in Chapter 4, but these ideas bear repeating here as we discuss workbooks, worksheets, and charts. There are actually two ideas you need to master: (1) specifying a member of a collection, and (2) specifying a hierarchy in the object model.

The three collections required for this chapter are the **Workbooks**, **Worksheets**, and **Charts** collections.[11] The Workbooks collection is the collection of all open workbooks. Any member of this collection—a particular workbook—can be specified with its name, such as **Workbooks("Customers.xls")**. This refers to the Customers.xls file (assumed to be open in Excel). Similarly, a particular worksheet such as the Data worksheet can be referenced as **Worksheets("Data")**, and a particular chart sheet such as the Sales chart sheet can be referenced as **Charts("Sales")**. The point is that if you want to reference any particular member of a collection, you must spell out the plural collection name and then follow it in parentheses with the name of the member in double quotes.[12]

As for hierarchy, it works as follows. The Workbooks collection consists of individual workbooks. Any particular workbook *contains* a Worksheets collection and a Charts collection. If a particular worksheet, such as the Data worksheet, belongs to the *active* workbook, you can refer to it simply as **Worksheets("Data")**. You could also refer to it as **ActiveWorkbook.Worksheets("Data")**. However, there are times when you need to spell out the workbook, as in **Workbooks ("Customers.xls").Worksheets("Data")**. This indicates explicitly that you want the Data worksheet from the Customers workbook.

---

[11] The **ChartObjects** collection is also mentioned in Section 8.6.

[12] It is also possible to refer to a member with a numeric index, such as Worksheets(3), but this method should generally not be used. (How would you or anyone else remember what the *third* worksheet is?)

In a similar way, you can specify the Sales chart sheet as **Charts("Sales")** or, if the Sales sheet is in the active workbook, as **ActiveWorkbook.Charts("Sales")**. Alternatively, to designate the Sales chart sheet in the Customers workbook, you can write **Workbooks("Customers.xls").Charts("Sales")**.

The Worksheets collection is one step down the hierarchy from the Workbooks collection. Range objects are one step farther down the hierarchy. Suppose you want to refer to the range A3:C10. If this is in the active sheet, you can refer to it as **Range("A3:C10")** or as **ActiveSheet.Range("A3:C10")**. If you want to indicate explicitly that this range is in the Data sheet, then you should write **Worksheets("Data").Range("A3:C10")**. But even this assumes that the Data sheet is in the *active* workbook. If you want to indicate explicitly that this sheet is in the Customers file, then you should write **Workbooks("Customers.xls").Worksheets("Data").Range("A3:C10")**. You always read this type of reference from right to left—the range A3:C10 of the Data sheet in the Customers file.

Once you know how to refer to these objects, you can easily refer to their properties by adding a dot and then a property or method after the reference. Some examples are:

```
ActiveWorkbook.Worksheets("Data").Range("C4").Value = "Sales for 1999"
```

and

```
Charts("Sales").Delete
```

Many other examples will appear throughout this chapter.

One final concept mentioned briefly in Chapter 2 is that the Workbooks, Worksheets, and Charts collections are also objects and therefore have properties and methods. Probably the most commonly used property of each of these collections is the **Count** property. For example, **ActiveWorkbook.Worksheets.Count** returns the number of worksheets in the active workbook. Probably the most commonly used method of each of these collections is the **Add** method. This adds a new member to the collection (which then becomes the *active* member). For example, consider the following lines:

```
ActiveWorkbook.Worksheets.Add
ActiveSheet.Name = "NewData"
```

The first line adds a new worksheet to the active workbook, and the second line names this new sheet NewData.

8.4   Examples of Workbooks in VBA

The file **Workbooks.xls** illustrates how to open and close workbooks, how to save them, how to specify the paths where they are stored, and how to display several of their properties, all with VBA. It is the basis for the following examples.

EXAMPLE 8.1 Opening and Closing Workbooks

The **Workbooks1** sub shows how to open and close a workbook. It also uses the **Count** property of the Worksheets collection to return the number of worksheets in a workbook, and it uses the **Name** property of a Workbook to return the name of the workbook. As illustrated in the sub, the opening and closing operations are done slightly differently. To open a workbook, you use the **Open** method of the Workbooks collection, followed by the **Filename** argument. This argument specifies the name (and path) of the workbook file. To close a workbook, you use the **Close** method of that workbook without any arguments.[13] Note that the file you are trying to open must exist in the location you specify. Otherwise, you will obtain an error message. Similarly, the file you are trying to close must currently be open.

```
Sub Workbooks1()
    Workbooks.Open Filename:="C:\My Documents\Test.xls"
    MsgBox "There are " & ActiveWorkbook.Worksheets.Count & " worksheets in " _
        & "the " & ActiveWorkbook.Name & " file."
    Workbooks("Test.xls").Close
End Sub
```

If this sub is run, then assuming the Test.xls file exists in the C:\My Documents folder and has three worksheets, the message in Figure 8.4 will be displayed.

Figure 8.4 Information about opened file

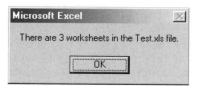

EXAMPLE 8.2 Saving a Workbook

The **Workbooks2** sub illustrates how to save an open workbook. This requires either the **Save** method or the **SaveAs** method, both of which mimic the similar operations in Excel. The Save method requires no arguments—it simply saves the file under its current name—whereas the SaveAs method typically has arguments that specify how to perform the save. There are quite a few optional arguments for the SaveAs method. The code below illustrates two of the more common arguments: **Filename** (the name and path of the file) and **FileFormat** (the type of format, such as the normal .xls format, to save the file as). You can look up other arguments in online help.

---

[13]This is not precisely true. The Open and Close methods both have optional arguments we have not mentioned here. You can find full details in online help.

```
Sub Workbooks2()
    With ActiveWorkbook
' This saves the active workbook under the same name - no questions asked.
        .Save
' The SaveAs method requires as arguments information you would normally fill out in
' the SaveAs dialog box.
        .SaveAs Filename:="C:\My Documents\NewWorkbook", FileFormat:=xlWorkbookNormal
' Check the name of the active workbook now.
        MsgBox "The name of the active workbook is " & .Name
    End With
End Sub
```

If you run this sub from the Workbooks.xls file, the SaveAs method will save a copy of this file in the C:\My Documents folder as NewWorkbook.xls and the message in Figure 8.5 will be displayed.

Figure 8.5 Confirmation of saved name

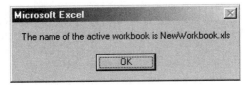

EXAMPLE 8.3 Locating the Path of a Workbook

When you open a workbook in Excel through the usual menu interface, you often need to search through folders to find the file you want to open. This example illustrates how the path to a file can be specified in VBA. Suppose, as in Exercise 8.1, that you are writing a sub in one workbook that opens another workbook. Also, suppose that both of these workbooks are in the *same* folder on your hard drive. Then you can use **ThisWorkbook.Path** to specify the path of the workbook to be opened. VBA always uses the **ThisWorkbook** object to refer to the workbook containing the VBA code. Then it uses the **Path** property to specify the path to this workbook. For example, if the workbook containing the code is in the folder C:\VBAExamples\Chapter 8, then ThisWorkbook.Path returns the string "C:\VBAExamples\Chapter 8". If another file in this same folder has file name Test.xls, then you can refer to it with the concatenated string

```
ThisWorkbook.Path & "\Test.xls"
```

Note how the second part of this string starts with a backslash. The Path property does not end with a backslash, so the backslash required for separating the folder from the filename must begin the literal part of the string.

The **Workbooks3** sub illustrates the entire procedure. It assumes that the code is in one file and that another file named Customer.xls exists in the same folder.

```
Sub Workbooks3()
' This sub assumes a file named Customer.xls exists in the same folder as the file
' containing this code. Otherwise, an error message will be displayed.
    Workbooks.Open ThisWorkbook.Path & "\Customer.xls"
    MsgBox "The Customer.xls file is now open.", vbInformation
    Workbooks("Customer.xls").Close
    MsgBox "The Customer.xls file is now closed.", vbInformation
End Sub
```

EXAMPLE 8.4   Checking Properties of a Workbook

The **Workbooks4** sub illustrates a few properties you can check for an open workbook. These include its name, its file format, whether it is password-protected, whether it is an add-in, its path, whether it is read only, and whether it has been changed since the last time it was saved. Most of these properties would be used only in more advanced applications, but it nice to know that they are available.

```
Sub Workbooks4()
' This sub shows some properties you can obtain from an open workbook.
    With ActiveWorkbook
' Display the file's name.
        MsgBox "The active workbook is named " & .Name
' Check the file format (.xls, .csv, .xla, and many others). Actually, this will display
' an obscure number, such as -4143 for .xls. You have to search online help to decipher
' the number!
        MsgBox "The file format is " & .FileFormat
' Check whether the file is password protected (True or False).
        MsgBox "Is the file password protected? " & .HasPassword
' Check whether the file is an add-in, with an .xla extension (True or False).
        MsgBox "Is the file an add-in? " & .IsAddin
' Check the file's path.
        MsgBox "The path to the file is " & .Path
' Check whether the file is ReadOnly (True or False).
        MsgBox "Is the file read only? " & .ReadOnly
' Check whether the file has been saved since the last changed (True or False).
        MsgBox "Has the file been changed since the last save? " & .Saved
    End With
End Sub
```

8.5   Examples of Worksheets in VBA

This section presents several examples to illustrate typical operations with worksheets. Each example is based on the file **Worksheets.xls**. It contains an AllStates sheet that lists states in column A where a company has offices, as shown in Figure 8.6. Then for each state in the list, there is a sheet for that state that shows where the company's headquarters are located, how many branch offices it has, and what its 1999 sales were. For example, there is a sheet named Texas, and it contains the information in Figure 8.7.

Figure 8.6 State list

	A	B	C
1	States where the company has offices		
2	Texas		
3	Ohio		
4	Indiana		
5	New York		
6	Pennsylvania		
7	California		
8	Michigan		
9	Massachusetts		

Figure 8.7 Information for a typical state

	A	B
1	Headquarters	Dallas
2	Branch offices	4
3	Sales in 1999	$17,500

EXAMPLE 8.5   Displaying Information on All States

The **Worksheets1** sub loops through all sheets other than the AllStates sheet and displays information about each state in a separate message box. A typical state's sheet is referred to as **ws** (any other generic variable name could be used). The loop excludes the AllStates sheet by using an If statement to check whether the sheet's name is not AllStates. If this condition is true—the sheet's name is not AllStates—then the message is displayed. (Again, remember that <> means "not equal to.")

```
Sub Worksheets1()
    Dim ws As Worksheet
' Go through each state (however many there are) and display info for that state.
    For Each ws In ActiveWorkbook.Worksheets
        With ws
            If.Name <> "AllStates" Then MsgBox "The headquarters of " _
                & .Name & " is & .Range("B1") & ", there are " _
                    & .Range("B2") & " branch offices, and sales in 1999 were " & _
                    Format(.Range("B3"), "$#,##0") & ".", vbInformation, .Name & " info"
            End If
        End With
    Next
End Sub
```

If you run this sub, you will see a message such as the one in Figure 8.8 for each state.

Figure 8.8 Information about a typical state

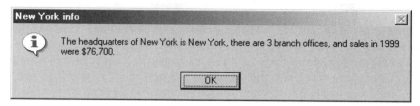

EXAMPLE 8.6 Displaying States and Headquarters

The **Worksheets2** sub is similar to the **Worksheets1** sub. It lists all states in the workbook and their headquarters in a *single* message box, with each state on a different line. The new line is accomplished with the built-in constant **vbCrLf** (short for carriage return and line feed), and string concatenation is used heavily to "build" a long message in the Msg variable.

```
Sub Worksheets2()
' This sub lists all of the states and their headquarters from
' the state sheets. It uses the built-in constant vbCrLf to format
' the message box nicely.
    Dim ws As Worksheet, Msg As String
    Msg = "The states and their headquarters listed in this workbook are:"
    For Each ws In ActiveWorkbook.Worksheets
        If ws.Name <> "AllStates" Then _
            Msg = Msg & vbCrLf & ws.Name & ": " & ws.Range("B1")
    Next
    MsgBox Msg, vbInformation, "State info"
End Sub
```

When this sub is run, the message box in Figure 8.9 is displayed.

Figure 8.9 State and headquarters information

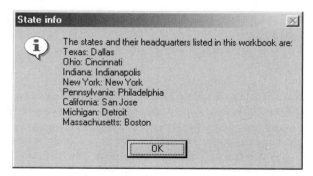

EXAMPLE 8.7   Adding a New State

The **Worksheets3** sub allows a new state to be added. It first asks the user to specify a new state not already in the list and then asks the user for information about this new state. The sub then copies an existing state's sheet to create a new sheet (essentially a template), and then it names the new sheet appropriately and puts its information in cells B2, B3, and B4. Note how the Do loop is used to keep asking the user for a new state until one not already on the current list is provided.

```
Sub Worksheets3()
' This sub asks the user for a new state and its information, then creates a new sheet
' for the new state.
    Dim IsNew As Boolean, NewState As String, HQ As String, NBranches As Integer, _
        Sales99 As Currency, ws As Worksheet

' Keep asking for a new state until the user provides one that is really new.
    Do
        NewState = InputBox("Enter a new state.", "New state")
        IsNew = True
        For Each ws In ActiveWorkbook.Worksheets
            If NewState = ws.Name Then
                MsgBox "This state already has a worksheet. Enter another state.", _
                    vbExclamation, "Duplicate state"
                IsNew = False
                Exit For
            End If
        Next
    Loop Until IsNew
' Get the required information for the new state.
    HQ = InputBox("Enter the headquarters of " & NewState, "Headquarters")
    NBranches = InputBox("Enter the number branch offices in " & NewState, _
        "Branch offices")
    Sales99 = InputBox("Enter sales in 1999 in " & NewState, "1999 Sales")
' Add the name of the new state to the list in the AllStates sheet.
    Worksheets("AllStates").Range("A1").End(xlDown).Offset(1, 0) = NewState
' Copy the Indiana sheet (or it could be any other state's sheet) to obtain a new
' sheet, which becomes the active sheet. Then change its name and information.
    Worksheets("Indiana").Copy after:=Worksheets(Worksheets.Count)
    With ActiveSheet
        .Name = NewState
        .Range("B1") = HQ
        .Range("B2") = NBranches
        .Range("B3") = Sales99
    End With
End Sub
```

Note the line

```
Worksheets("AllStates").Range("A1").End(xlDown).Offset(1,0) = NewState
```

Starting in cell A1, this line uses **.End(xlDown)** to go to the bottom of the current list. Then it uses **.Offset(1,0)** to go one more row down. This is the first blank cell, where the name of the new state is placed.

Note also the line

```
Worksheets("Indiana").Copy after:=Worksheets(Worksheets.Count)
```

This line makes a copy of the Indiana sheet, and it places the copy after the worksheet referred to as Worksheets(Worksheets.Count). To see the effect of this, assume there are currently 8 worksheets. Then Worksheets.Count is 8, so the copy is placed after Worksheets(8). This means it is placed just after (to right of) all existing worksheets. This provides an example where it *is* useful to refer to a worksheet by number rather than by name.

EXAMPLE 8.8 Sorting Worksheets

The **Worksheets4** sub illustrates how to sort the worksheets for the individual states in alphabetical order. The trick is to use VBA's **Sort** method to sort the states in column A of the AllStates sheet. Then it uses the **Move** method of a worksheet, with the **After** argument, to move the sheets around according to the sorted list in the AllStates sheet.

```
Sub Worksheets4()
' This sub puts the state sheets (not including the AllStates sheet) in alphabetical
' order. It first sorts the states in the AllStates sheet, then uses this order.
    Dim Sht1 As String, Sht2 As String, cell As Range
    With Worksheets("AllStates")
        .Range("A1").Sort Key1:=.Range("A1"), Order1:=xlAscending, Header:=xlYes
        With .Range("A1")
            Range(.Offset(1, 0), .End(xlDown)).Name = "States"
        End With
    End With
    Sht1 = "AllStates"
    For Each cell In Range("States")
        Sht2 = cell.Value
        Worksheets(Sht2).Move after:=Worksheets(Sht1)
        Sht1 = Sht2
    Next
    MsgBox "State sheets are now in alphabetical order."
End Sub
```

Pay very close attention to how the For Each loop works. Sht1 is initially the AllStates sheet. After that, Sht1 is always the current sheet in alphabetical order, and Sht2 is the name of the *next* sheet in alphabetical order, which is moved to the right of Sht1. After the move, the value of the variable Sht1 is replaced by the value of Sht2 to get ready for the *next* move.

A note on using the Watch window. This logic is a bit tricky. To understand it better, try the following. Open the **Worksheets.xls** file, get into the VBE, and create watches for the Sht1 and Sht2 variables. (You do this with the Debug/Add Watch menu item.) Then put your cursor anywhere inside the Worksheets4 sub and step through the program one line at a time by repeatedly pressing the F8 key. Once you get toward the bottom of the sub, you can see in the Watch window how the values of Sht1 and Sht2 keep changing.

8.6 Examples of Charts in VBA

A Chart object is one of the trickiest Excel objects to manipulate with VBA. The reason is that a chart has so many objects associated with it, and each has a large number of properties and methods. If you need to create charts in VBA, it is probably best to record most of the code and then modify the recorded code as necessary, making frequent visits to online help. Alternatively, you can use the Chart Wizard to create the chart, and then use VBA only to modify the existing chart in some way.

The following subs indicate some of the possibilities. They are listed in the file **Charts.xls**. This file has monthly sales for several products; a portion is shown in Figure 8.10. We first used the Chart Wizard manually (no VBA) to create a line chart on the same sheet as the data. This chart shows the monthly time series movement of two of the products, as illustrated in Figure 8.11. Although VBA could be used to build the chart from scratch, it is much easier to build a chart first with the Chart Wizard and then use VBA to fine-tune it.

Figure 8.10 Monthly product sales data

	A	B	C	D	E	F	G	H
1	Month	Product1	Product2	Product3	Product4	Product5	Product6	Product7
2	Jan-98	791	613	450	434	488	400	559
3	Feb-98	781	649	646	548	442	652	423
4	Mar-98	520	631	488	622	513	545	726
5	Apr-98	635	615	568	709	686	461	629
6	May-98	418	463	433	523	548	655	420
7	Jun-98	431	504	580	540	767	487	631
8	Jul-98	786	534	490	408	653	704	708
9	Aug-98	695	734	618	564	620	453	553
10	Sep-98	547	671	699	721	657	448	760
11	Oct-98	703	580	441	459	617	436	472
12	Nov-98	579	658	419	523	424	720	529
13	Dec-98	601	592	408	666	800	691	723
14	Jan-99	522	724	410	764	504	481	657

Location of a Chart

The first issue is the location of the chart. As you might know, a chart can be placed on a separate chart sheet (a special type of sheet reserved only for charts, with no rows and columns), or it can be embedded in a worksheet, as in Figure 8.11. The choice is usually a matter of taste. (If you are using the Chart Wizard, you can make this choice in the last step of the wizard.) In the first case, assuming the name of the chart sheet is SalesChart, you would refer to it in VBA as

Figure 8.11 Sales chart of two selected products

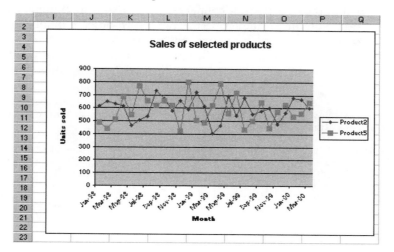

Charts("SalesChart"). Here, **Charts** is the collection of all chart sheets, and it is followed by the name of the particular chart sheet.

In the second case, assuming this chart is the *only* embedded chart on a worksheet called Sales, you must first refer to the object "containing" the chart as **Worksheets("Sales").ChartObjects(1)**. Then the Chart object itself is one step down the hierarchy from the **ChartObject** object. Admittedly, it is confusing and probably sounds like double-talk, but just think of **ChartObject** objects as floating above a worksheet's cells. These objects have no other purpose than to "hold" **Chart** objects. You can resize and move the ChartObject containers, and then you can manipulate the properties of the underlying chart, such as its axes and its legend. Finally, just to make sure the point is clear, remember that the ChartObject object is relevant only for charts placed on a worksheet. It is not relevant for chart sheets.

EXAMPLE 8.9   Displaying Properties of a Chart

The **Charts1** sub works with the chart contained in the first (only) ChartObject container of the Sales sheet of the **Charts.xls** file. Remember that the chart itself was *not* created with VBA. The VBA below simply displays properties of the chart that already exists. It first refers to the **ChartObject** container and displays its **Left, Top, Height**, and **Width** properties. These are properties of many objects in Excel that can be moved and resized. **Top** is the distance (in **points**, where a point is 1/72 of an inch) from the top of the container to the top of row 1, **Left** is the distance from the left of the container to the left of column A, and **Height** and **Width** are the height and width of the container.

The sub then uses the **With .Chart** statement to refer to the **Chart** object contained in the ChartObject container and proceeds to examine a number of its properties. Note that some properties can return obscure numbers. For example, the **ChartType** property in this example returns 65, evidently the index for a line chart of the type shown. The other properties should be fairly self-explanatory. You should run this sub to see what the message boxes display.

```
Sub Charts1()
' This sub illustrates some of the properties of a chart. The chart already exists (was
' built with the Chart Wizard) on the Sales sheet.
    With Worksheets("Sales").ChartObjects(1)
        MsgBox "The next four messages indicate the position of the chart."
        MsgBox "Left property: " & .Left
        MsgBox "Top property: " & .Top
        MsgBox "Height property: " & .Height
        MsgBox "Width property: " & .Width
        MsgBox "The next few messages indicate some properties of the chart."

        With .Chart
            MsgBox "Chart name: " & .Name
            MsgBox "Chart type: " & .ChartType
            MsgBox "HasLegend property: " & .HasLegend
            MsgBox "HasTitle property: " & .HasTitle
            MsgBox "Title: " & .ChartTitle.Text
            MsgBox "Number of series plotted: " & .SeriesCollection.Count
            MsgBox "Some properties of the horizontal axis (there are many!):"
            With .Axes(xlCategory)
                MsgBox "Format of tick labels: " & .TickLabels.NumberFormat
                MsgBox "Title: " & .AxisTitle.Caption
                MsgBox "Font size of title: " & .AxisTitle.Font.Size
            End With
            MsgBox "Some properties of the vertical axis:"
            With .Axes(xlValue)
                MsgBox "Title: " & .AxisTitle.Caption
                MsgBox "Font size of title: " & .AxisTitle.Font.Size
                MsgBox "Minimum scale: " & .MinimumScale
                MsgBox "Maximum scale: " & .MaximumScale
            End With
        End With
    End With
End Sub
```

EXAMPLE 8.10 Changing Properties of a Chart

The previous sub simply *displays* the current values of various chart properties. The **Charts2** sub *modifies* the chart. Specifically, it allows the user to choose which two products (out of the seven available) to plot. It uses the **SeriesCollection** object, which is one step down the hierarchy from the **Chart** object. In general, a chart plots a number of **Series** objects, labeled **SeriesCollection(1)**, **SeriesCollection(2)**, and so on. The properties of each series can be changed, as described in the comments in the sub, to plot different data. Specifically, the **Values** property designates the data range for the series, the **XValues** property designates the range for the values on the horizontal axis, and the **Name** property is a descriptive name for the series that is used in the legend. Note that the data ranges in the Sales sheet have already been range-named Product1 through Product7. These range names are used in the sub. Also, note how the line

```
.Name = Range("Product" & Prod1).Cells(1).Offset(-1, 0)
```

uses **.Cells(1)** to go to the first sales figure in a product range and then uses **.Offset(–1,0)** to go one row above to find the product's name (such as Product1).

```
Sub Charts2()
' This sub allows you to change the product columns (two of them) that are charted.
    Dim Prod1 As Integer, Prod2 As Integer
    MsgBox "You can choose any two of the products to plot versus time."
    Prod1 = InputBox("Enter the index of the first product to plot (1 to 7)")
    Prod2 = InputBox("Enter the index of the second product to plot (1 to 7, not " _
        & Prod1 & ")")
' Note that the columns of data already have the range names Product1, Product2, etc.
    With Worksheets("Sales").ChartObjects(1).Chart
        With .SeriesCollection(1)
' The Values property indicates the range of the data being plotted. The XValues
' property indicates the values on the X-axis (in this case, months). The Name property
' is the name of the series (which is shown in the legend). This name is in row 1,
' right above the first cell in the corresponding Product range.
            .Values = Range("Product" & Prod1)
            .XValues = Range("Month")
            .Name = Range("Product" & Prod1).Cells(1).Offset(-1, 0)
        End With
        With .SeriesCollection(2)
            .Values = Range("Product" & Prod2)
            .Name = Range("Product" & Prod2).Cells(1).Offset(-1, 0)
        End With
    End With
End Sub
```

EXAMPLE 8.11   More Properties and Methods of Charts

The **Charts3** sub indicates some further possibilities when working with charts.[14] Try running it to see the effects on the chart. (Does anyone memorize all of these properties and methods? We doubt it, but some experimentation with the recorder on and a few visits to online help will enable you to create this same level of code—if and when you really need it.)

```
Sub Charts3()
' This sub shows some other things you can do to fine-tune charts.
    Dim Color1 As Integer, Color2 As Integer
' Use this next statement so that the random colors chosen later on will be
' different from run to run.
    Randomize
    Worksheets("Sales").ChartObjects(1).Activate
```

---

[14] This sub is more advanced and can be skipped on a first reading.

```
    With ActiveChart
        With .PlotArea
            MsgBox "The plot area will be changed from gray to blank."
            .ClearFormats
            MsgBox "It will now be restored to light gray."
            .Interior.ColorIndex = 15
        End With
        With .Axes(xlValue)
            MsgBox "The horizontal grid lines will be deleted."
            .HasMajorGridlines = False
            MsgBox "They will now be restored."
            .HasMajorGridlines = True
        End With
        MsgBox "The two series will now change to some random colors."
' Generate two random colors (that aren't the same).
        Color1 = Int(Rnd * 40) + 1
        Do
            Color2 = Int(Rnd * 40) + 1
        Loop Until Color2 <> Color1
        With .SeriesCollection(1)
            .Border.ColorIndex = Color1
            .MarkerBackgroundColorIndex = Color1
            .MarkerForegroundColorIndex = Color1
        End With
        With .SeriesCollection(2)
            .Border.ColorIndex = Color2
            .MarkerBackgroundColorIndex = Color2
            .MarkerForegroundColorIndex = Color2
        End With
        .Deselect
    End With
End Sub
```

8.7 Summary

This chapter builds upon your knowledge of Range objects from Chapter 6. It is necessary to be able to manipulate workbooks, worksheets, and charts with VBA code in many applications, and this chapter has illustrated some of the most useful techniques for doing so. At this point, it is not terribly important that you memorize all the properties and methods of these objects. It is more important that you have some feeling for what is *possible* and that you know how to find help when you need it. You can always revisit the examples in this chapter to search for key details, and you can always visit the Object Browser for excellent online help.

PROGRAMMING EXERCISES

1. Open a new workbook and insert a module in this workbook. Then write a sub that does the following: (1) It opens some workbook that you know exists on your PC (you can choose which one), (2) it displays a message indicating the number of

worksheets in this workbook, (3) it closes the workbook, and (4) it tries to open a workbook that you know does not exist on your PC. What happens when it tries to open this latter workbook?

2. Open a new workbook and save it under any name you like. Then write a sub that displays a message something as follows: "The name of this workbook is _, and it was created by _." The blanks should be filled in by appropriate properties of the ActiveWorkbook (or the Application) object.

3. Suppose you have a folder on your hard drive that contains a number of Excel files with the names Customer1.xls, Customer2.xls, and so on. You're not sure how many such files there are, but they are named this way, with consecutive integers. Write a sub to open each file, one at a time, save it under a new name, and then close it. The new names should be CustOrders1.xls, CustOrders2.xls, and so on.

4. Continuing the previous exercise, suppose you want to check whether the Customer files are "read only." Write a sub that (1) counts the number of Customer files in the folder and the number of them that are read only and (2) displays this information in a message box.

5. The file **Cities.xls** contains an AllCities sheet that lists all cities where a company has offices. Write a sub that does the following: (1) It sorts the list of cities in alphabetical order, (2) for each city in the list, it checks whether there is a sheet with the name of that city in the workbook, and if there isn't one, it adds one, and (3) it deletes any city sheet if the sheet's name is not in the current AllCities list. The sub should be written so that it can be run at any time and will always respond with the current list of cities in the AllCities sheet.

6. The AllProducts sheet in the file **ProductInfo.xls** lists information on various software packages a company sells. Each product has an associated category listed in column B. Write a sub that creates a sheet for each category represented in the list, with the name of the sheet being the category (such as Business). For each category sheet, it should enter the product names and their prices in columns A and B, starting in row 4. Each category sheet should have an appropriate label, such as "Products in the Business category", in cell A1, it should have labels "Product" and "Price" in cells A3 and B3, and the column-width for its column A should be the same as the column-width of column A in the AllProducts sheet. (Note that there are only three categories represented in the current data. However, the program should be written so that it works for any number of categories—and any number of products—that might be present.)

7. The AllProducts sheet in the file **ProductPurchases.xls** has unit prices for all software packages a mail-order company sells. It also has an Invoice sheet. Whenever the company takes an order from a customer, the order taker gets the customer's name, the date, and the quantity of each product the customer wants to purchase. These quantities are written in column C of the AllProducts sheet. The information on this sheet is then used to create an invoice for the customer on the Invoice sheet. The current Invoice sheet is a "template" for a general invoice. The manager wants you to write two subs, ClearOld and CreateInvoice, and attach them to the buttons at the top of the AllProducts sheet. They should do the following.

a. The ClearOld sub should clear any quantities from a previous order from column C of the AllProducts sheet. It should also clear any old data from row 5 down of the Invoice sheet.

b. The CreateInvoice sub should be run right after the order taker has gotten the information from the customer and has entered quantities in column C of the AllProducts sheet. First, it should use input boxes to ask for the customer's name and the date, and it should use these to complete the labels in cells A1 and A2 of the Invoice sheet. Then it should transfer the relevant data about products (only those ordered) to the Invoice sheet, it should calculate the prices for each product ordered (unit price times quantity ordered), and it should calculate the tax on the order (5% sales tax) and the total cost of the order, including tax, in column D, right below the prices of individual products, with appropriate labels in column C (such as "5% sales tax" and "Total Cost").

c. As a finishing touch, add some code to the CreateInvoice sub to print the finished invoice. (Although the chapter didn't discuss printing, you should be able to discover how to do it, either by using the recorder or by looking up online help.)

8. The file **SalesChartFinished.xls** has monthly data on two products, a corresponding chart and four buttons. The ranges of the product data in columns B and C are range-named Product1 and Product2. To understand what you are supposed to do, open this file and click on the buttons. It should be clear what's going on. Unfortunately (for you), the code behind the buttons is password-protected. Your job is to create similar code yourself in the file **SalesChart.xls**. This file has the same chart and same buttons, but there is no code yet (which means that the buttons aren't attached to any macros yet). This code is tricky, and you'll probably have to look through the code in the examples a few times, as well as online help, to get everything working correctly. (We did!)

9

Arrays

9.1 Introduction

Chapter 7 emphasized the benefits of loops for performing repeated tasks. Loops are often accompanied by the topic of this chapter, arrays. Arrays are basically lists, where each element of the list is an indexed element of the array. To get the idea, suppose you need to capture the names and salaries of your employees, which are currently listed in columns A and B of a worksheet. Later on in the program, you plan to analyze them in some way. Then you might use a loop (either a For loop or a Do loop) to go through each employee in the worksheet. But how do you store the employee information in memory for later processing? The answer is that you store it in Employee and Salary arrays. The name and salary of employee 1 are stored in Employee(1) and Salary(1), those for employee 2 are stored in Employee(2) and Salary(2), and so on.

A useful analogy is to the small mailboxes you see at a post office. An array is analogous to a group of mailboxes, numbered 1, 2, and so on. You can put something into a particular mailbox—that is, an array element—in a statement like **Employee(5) = "Bob Jones"**. Similarly, you can see the contents of a particular mail box with a statement like **MsgBox "The fifth employee is " & Employee(5)**. In other words, array elements work just like normal variables, except that you have an indexed list of them. This indexing makes them particularly amenable to looping, as this chapter will illustrate.

9.2 Exercise

Arrays are used primarily to deal with lists. The following exercise is typical in its use of arrays. Although there are certainly ways to do the exercise *without* arrays, they make the job much easier. Actually, this exercise is simpler than the examples discussed later in this chapter, but you might want to study the examples before attempting this exercise.

Exercise 9.1   Aggregating Sales Data

Consider a large appliance/electronics store with a number of salespeople. The company keeps a spreadsheet listing the names of the salespeople and the dollar amounts of individual sales transactions. This information is in the file **Transactions.xls**, as illustrated in Figure 9.1. (Note the many hidden rows.) Periodically,

Figure 9.1 Salespeople and transaction data

	A	B	C	D	E	F	G	H	I
1	**Data on sales people**			**Individual sales**				**Aggregated sales**	
2	Name	SS#		Salesperson SS#	Date	Dollar amount		Salesperson	Dollar amount
3	Adams	776-61-4492		640-34-5749	1-Mar-00	323			
4	Barnes	640-34-5749		365-99-1247	1-Mar-00	260			
5	Cummings	115-12-5882		365-99-1247	1-Mar-00	305			
6	Davis	736-95-5401		932-62-4204	1-Mar-00	366			
7	Edwards	880-52-9379		986-38-6372	1-Mar-00	217			
8	Falks	348-79-3515		449-44-7141	1-Mar-00	294			
9	Gregory	546-44-7576		640-34-5749	1-Mar-00	289			
10	Highsmith	467-86-5786		769-79-9580	1-Mar-00	460			
11	Invery	765-85-7850		932-62-4204	1-Mar-00	567			
12	Jacobs	986-38-6372		449-44-7141	1-Mar-00	970			
13	Ketchings	769-79-9580		919-58-6925	1-Mar-00	426			
14	Leonard	468-38-8871		115-12-5882	1-Mar-00	214			
15	Moore	919-58-6925		546-44-7576	1-Mar-00	306			
16	Nixon	126-27-9832		467-86-5786	1-Mar-00	258			
17	Price	631-55-5579		546-44-7576	1-Mar-00	287			
18	Reynolds	529-61-3561		765-85-7850	2-Mar-00	183			
19	Stimson	474-60-8847		640-34-5749	2-Mar-00	196			
20	Travis	449-44-7141		365-99-1247	2-Mar-00	322			
21	Vexley	539-55-4012		640-34-5749	3-Mar-00	180			
22	Wheaton	833-44-9683		474-60-8847	3-Mar-00	205			
23	Zimmerman	932-62-4204		126-96-8510	3-Mar-00	286			
24				126-96-8510	3-Mar-00	264			
781				348-79-3515	23-Jul-00	333			
782				932-62-4204	23-Jul-00	167			
783				952-12-3694	24-Jul-00	253			
784				776-61-4492	24-Jul-00	211			
785				952-12-3694	24-Jul-00	56			

salespeople are hired and fired. The list in column A is always the most current list, and it is always shown in alphabetical order. Column B lists the corresponding Social Security numbers. The sales data in columns D to F are sorted by date. Also, some of these sales are for salespeople no longer with the company. That is, some of the Social Security numbers in column D have no corresponding values in column B.

The purpose of the exercise is to write a program to fill columns H and I with aggregate dollar amounts for each salesperson currently employed. You can open the file **TransactionsFinished.xls** and click on its button to see the results, which should appear as in Figure 9.2. However, do not look at the VBA code until you have tried writing the program yourself. Make sure you think through a solution method before you begin programming. Most important, think about what arrays you will need, and how they will be used.

9.3 The Need for Arrays

Many beginning programmers find arrays difficult to master, and they react by arguing that arrays are not worth the trouble. They are wrong on both counts. First, arrays are not that difficult. If you understand the mailbox analogy and keep it in mind, you should catch on to arrays quite easily. Second, arrays are definitely not just a "luxury" for computer programmers. They are absolutely necessary for dealing with lists. Consider a slightly different version of the employee salary example

Figure 9.2 Results

	H	I	J	K	L
1	**Aggregated sales**				
2	Salesperson	Dollar amount			
3	Adams	12429			
4	Barnes	11308		Aggregate	
5	Cummings	8117			
6	Davis	9831			
7	Edwards	7602			
8	Falks	9223			
9	Gregory	7112			
10	Highsmith	7234			
11	Invery	9436			
12	Jacobs	12012			
13	Ketchings	10935			
14	Leonard	8765			
15	Moore	8551			
16	Nixon	11374			
17	Price	8055			
18	Reynolds	9246			
19	Stimson	10161			
20	Travis	8202			
21	Vexley	8594			
22	Wheaton	9030			
23	Zimmerman	10224			

from the introduction. Now suppose you would like to go through the list of employees in columns A and B (again inside a loop) and keep track of the names and salaries of all employees who make a salary greater than $50,000. Later on, you might want to analyze these employees in some way, such as finding their average salary.

The easiest way to proceed is to go through the employee list, with a counter initially equal to 0. Each time you encounter a salary greater than $50,000, you add 1 to the counter and store the employee's name and salary in HiPaidEmp and HiSalary arrays. Here is how the code might look (assuming the employees start in row 2 and that the number of employees in the data set is known to be NEmployees).

```
Counter = 0
With Range("A1")
    For i = 1 to NEmployees
        If .Offset(i,1) > 50000 Then
            Counter = Counter + 1
            HiPaidEmp(Counter) = .Offset(i,0)
            HiSalary(Counter) = .Offset(i,1)
        End If
    Next
End If
```

After this loop is completed, you will know the number of highly paid employees—it is the final value of Counter. More important, you will know the identities and salaries of these employees. The information for the first highly-paid employee is stored in HiPaidEmp(1) and HiSalary(1), the information for the second is stored in HiPaidEmp(2) and HiSalary(2), and so on. You are now free to analyze the data in these newly created lists in any way you like.

All right, there is admittedly a non-array solution for this example. Each time you find a highly paid employee, you could immediately transfer the information on this employee to another section of the worksheet (columns D and E, say) rather than storing it in arrays. Then you could analyze the data in columns D and E later on if you like. In other words, there is usually a way around using arrays if you search long enough—especially if you are working in Excel where you can store information easily. However, most programmers agree that arrays represent the best method for working with lists, not only in VBA but in all other programming languages. They offer power and flexibility that simply cannot be achieved without them.

9.4 Rules for Working with Arrays

When you declare a variable with a Dim statement, VBA knows from the variable's type how much memory to set aside for it. The situation is slightly different for arrays. Now, VBA must know how many elements are in the array, as well as their variable type, so that it can set aside the right amount of memory for the entire array. Therefore, when you declare an array, you must indicate to VBA that you are declaring an *array* of a certain type, not just a single variable. You must also tell VBA how many elements are in the array. You can do this in the declaration line or later in the program. Finally, you must indicate what index you want the array to begin with. Unlike what you might expect, the default first index is *not* 1; it is 0. However, you can override this if you like.

Here is a typical declaration of two arrays named Employee and Salary:

```
Dim Employee(100) As String, Salary(100) As Currency
```

This declaration indicates that (1) each element of the Employee array is a string variable, (2) each element of the Salary array is a currency variable, and (3) each array has 100 elements.

The Option Base Statement

Surprisingly, unless you add a certain line to your code, the first employee will *not* be Employee(1) and the last employee will not be Employee(100); they will be Employee(0) and Employee(99). This is because the default in VBA is called **0-based indexing**. This means that the indexes of an array are 0, 1, 2, and so on. Evidently, technical computer people think most naturally this way, even though most of the rest of us do not. Most of us prefer **1-based indexing**, where the indexes are 1, 2, 3, and so on. If you want your arrays to be 1-based, you can use the following **Option Base** line:

```
Option Base 1
```

This line should be placed at the top of each of your modules, probably right below the **Option Explicit** line (which, if you remember, forces you to declare your variables).

Even if 0-based indexing is in effect, you can override it by indicating explicitly how you want a particular array to be indexed. The following line shows how you can do this for the Employee and Salary arrays.

```
Dim Employee(1 To 100) As String, Salary(1 To 100) As Currency
```

Now the first employee will be Employee(1) and the last will be Employee(100), regardless of any Option Base line at the top of the module.

Dynamic Indexing and Redim

There are many times where you know you need an array. However, when you are writing the code, you have no way of knowing how many elements it will contain. For example, you might have an input box statement near the top of your sub asking the user for the number of employees at her company. Once she tells you that there are 150 employees, then (but not until then) you will know you need an array of size 150. So how should you declare the array in this case? You do it in two steps. First, you declare that you need an *array*, as opposed to a single variable, in the Dim statement by putting empty parentheses next to the variable name, as in

```
Dim Employee() as String
```

Then in the body of the sub, once you learn how many elements the array should have, you use the **Redim** statement to set aside the appropriate amount of memory for the array. The following two lines illustrate a typical example.

```
NEmployees = InputBox("How many employees are in your company?")
Redim Employee(NEmployees)
```

If the user enters 10, then the Employee array will be of size 10. If she enters 1000, it will be of size 1000. The Redim statement enables the array to adjust to the precise size you need.

You can actually use the Redim statement as many times as you like in a sub to readjust the size of the array. (The examples later in the chapter will illustrate why you might want to do this. It is actually not at all uncommon.) The only problem is that when you use the Redim statement to change the size of an array, all of the previous *contents* of the array are deleted. This is often not what you want. Fortunately, you can override this default behavior with the keyword **Preserve**, as in the following lines.

```
NEmployees = NEmployees + 1
Redim Preserve Employee(NEmployees)
```

These lines would be appropriate if you just discovered that you have one extra employee, so that you need one extra element in the Employee array. To keep from deleting the names of the previous employees when you redimension the array, you insert the keyword Preserve in the Redim line. This gives you an extra array element, but the previous elements retain their current values.

Multiple Dimensions

Arrays can have more than one dimension. (The arrays so far have been one-dimensional.) For example, a two-dimensional array has two indexes, as in Employee(2,18). This might be appropriate if you want to index your employees by location and by number, so that this refers to employee 18 at location 2. The main difference in working with multidimensional arrays is that you must indicate the number of elements for *each* dimension. As an example, the following line indicates that the Employee array requires 10 elements for the first dimension and 100 for the second dimension.

```
Dim Employee(10,100) As String
```

Therefore, VBA will set aside 10(100) = 1000 locations in memory for this array.

Note that this *could* be quite wasteful. If the first dimension is the employee location and the second is the employee number at a location, suppose there are 100 employees at location 1 but only 5 at location 2. Then the array elements Employee(2,6) through Employee(2,100) are essentially wasted. Even though today's computer memory is cheap and abundant, computer programmers worry about this sort of thing. Therefore, they warn against using multidimensional arrays unless it is really necessary. You will frequently see code with two-dimensional arrays, but you will almost never see arrays with three or more dimensions.

9.5 Examples of Arrays in VBA

The best way to understand arrays—and to appreciate the need for them—is to study some examples. The first example is a fairly simple one. The next three are more challenging and interesting. They are typical of the examples that really *require* arrays.

EXAMPLE 9.1 Looking Up a Price

The VLookup and HLookup functions in Excel are very useful for looking up information in a table. This example illustrates how we can accomplish the same thing with VBA and arrays. The file **UnitPrices.xls** contains a table of product codes and unit prices, as shown in Figure 9.3 (with many hidden rows). We want to write a program that asks the user for a product code. It then searches the list of

Figure 9.3 Table of product information

	A	B	C
1	Table of unit prices for products		
2			
3	Product code	Unit price	
4	L2201	50.99	
5	N1351	34.99	
6	N7622	10.95	
7	B7118	99.95	
8	R1314	105.99	
9	W6734	42.95	
10	T4463	72.99	
11	G9196	62.95	
12	B3850	101.99	
1211	F5012	80.95	
1212	D8665	51.95	
1213	R7932	93.95	
1214	R8509	14.95	
1215	L4701	3.95	

Figure 9.4 Unit price of requested product

product codes for a matching product code. If it finds one, it displays an appropriate message, such as in Figure 9.4. If it does not find a match, it displays a message to that effect.

Although there are many ways to write the required program, the **LookupPrice** sub listed below illustrates how to do it with arrays. The number of products is found first, then the ProdCode and UnitPrice are redimensioned appropriately, and a For loop is used to populate these arrays with the data in columns A and B of the worksheet. Next, after a user specifies a product code, another For loop searches the ProdCode array for a match to the requested code. If one is found, the corresponding element of the UnitPrice array is stored in the RequestedPrice variable, and an appropriate message is displayed at the end.

```
Option Explicit
Option Base 1
Sub LookupPrice()
    Dim ProdCode() As String, UnitPrice() As Currency, i As Integer, Found As Boolean, _
        RequestedCode As String, RequestedPrice As Currency, NProducts As Integer
```

```
' Find the number of products, redimension the arrays, and fill them with the
' data in the lists.
   With Range("A3")
        NProducts = Range(.Offset(1, 0), .End(xlDown)).Rows.Count
        ReDim ProdCode(NProducts)
        ReDim UnitPrice(NProducts)
        For i = 1 To NProducts
            ProdCode(i) = .Offset(i, 0)
            UnitPrice(i) = .Offset(i, 1)
        Next
   End With
' Get a product code from the user.
   RequestedCode = InputBox("Enter a product code (a uppercase letter followed by four " _
        & "digits).")
' Look for the code in the list. Record its unit price if it is found.
   Found = False
   For i = 1 To NProducts
        If ProdCode(i) = RequestedCode Then
            Found = True
            RequestedPrice = UnitPrice(i)
            Exit For
        End If
   Next
' Display an appropriate message.
   If Found Then
        MsgBox "The unit price of product code " & RequestedCode & " is " & _
            Format(RequestedPrice, "$0.00"), vbInformation, "Product found"
   Else
        MsgBox "The product code " & RequestedCode & " is not on the list.", vbInformation, _
            "Product not found"
   End If
End Sub
```

EXAMPLE 9.2   Keeping Track of Products Sold

A company keeps a spreadsheet of each sales transaction it makes. These transaction data, sorted by date, are listed in columns A to C of the **ProdSales.xls** file. (See Figure 9.5, which has many hidden rows.) Each row shows the 4-digit code of the product sold, plus the date and dollar amount of the transaction. Periodically, the company wants to know how many separate products have been sold, and it wants a list of all products sold, the number of transactions for each product sold, and the total dollar amount for each product sold. It wants this list to be placed in columns E to G, and it wants the list to be sorted in descending order by dollar amount.

The **ProdSales** sub listed below does the job. When a button is clicked to run this sub, the message box in Figure 9.6 appears, and the list in Figure 9.7 is created. (This figure does not show all 49 products sold. Some rows have been hidden.)

The idea behind the program is to loop through the product codes in column A, which are stored in an array called ProdCodesData, one at a time. We use these to "build" an array called ProdCodesFound. It eventually contains the *distinct* product codes in column A. At each step of the loop, we compare a product code in column A to all product codes already found. If this product code has already

Figure 9.5 Transaction data

	A	B	C
1	**Individual sales data**		
2	Product Code	Date	Amount ($)
3	2508	1/2/2000	469
4	1111	1/5/2000	481
5	1107	1/6/2000	434
6	1119	1/6/2000	596
7	2502	1/10/2000	552
8	2523	1/11/2000	401
9	2515	1/13/2000	533
10	1107	1/15/2000	375
11	1108	1/15/2000	528
12	1118	1/15/2000	628
13	2513	1/23/2000	465
188	2515	12/21/2000	454
189	1111	12/23/2000	463
190	2515	12/23/2000	532
191	1104	12/25/2000	524
192	1111	12/26/2000	535
193	2510	12/30/2000	512

Figure 9.6 Number of products sold

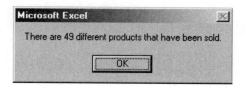

Microsoft Excel

There are 49 different products that have been sold.

OK

Figure 9.7 Details of products sold

	E	F	G	H	I	J	K
1	**Summary data**						
2	Product Code	Quantity	Amount ($)				
3	1118	7	3818			List the products sold	
4	1106	8	3764				
5	2520	7	3696				
6	1120	6	3415				
7	2505	6	3306				
8	2516	6	3296				
9	2501	6	3270				
10	1101	7	3129				
11	2525	5	2979				
12	1104	6	2919				
13	2508	5	2878				
14	2519	6	2830				
49	2510	1	512				
50	1109	1	451				
51	2514	1	342				

been found, we add 1 to its number of transactions and we add the dollar amount of the current transaction to the total dollar amount for this product. Otherwise, if the product code is one we have not already found, we add an item to the ProdCodesFound array, and we set the number of transactions for this new product to 1 and its total dollar amount to the dollar amount of the current transaction. Three other arrays facilitate the bookkeeping. The DollarsData array stores the data in column C, and the Quantity and DollarsTotal arrays store the numbers of transactions and total dollar amounts for all product codes found.

Once all product codes in column A have been examined, we enter the data from the ProdCodesFound, Quantity, and DollarsTotal arrays in columns E to G, and we sort them on column G in descending order.

```
Option Explicit
Option Base 1
Sub ProdSales()
    Dim NSales As Integer, ProdCodesData() As Integer, ProdCodesFound() As Integer, _
        Quantity() As Integer, DollarsData() As Single, DollarsTotal() As Single, _
        i As Integer, j As Integer, NewProduct As Boolean, NFound As Integer
' Clear any old results in columns E to G.
    With Range("E2")
        Range(.Offset(1, 0), .Offset(0, 2).End(xlDown)).ClearContents
    End With
' Find the number of sales in the data set, redimension the ProdCodesData and
' DollarsData arrays, and fill them with the data in columns A and C.
    With Range("A2")
        NSales = Range(.Offset(1, 0), .End(xlDown)).Rows.Count
        ReDim ProdCodesData(NSales)
        ReDim DollarsData(NSales)
        For i = 1 To NSales
            ProdCodesData(i) = .Offset(i, 0)
            DollarsData(i) = .Offset(i, 2)
        Next
    End With
' Initialize the number of product codes found to 0.
    NFound = 0
' Loop through all transactions.
    For i = 1 To NSales
' Set the Boolean NewProduct to True, and change it to False only if the current product
' code is one already found.
        NewProduct = True
        If NFound > 0 Then
' Loop through all product codes already found and compare them to the current product
' code.
            For j = 1 To NFound
                If ProdCodesData(i) = ProdCodesFound(j) Then
' The current product code is not a new one, so update its Quantity and DollarsTotal
' values appropriately.
                    NewProduct = False
                    Quantity(j) = Quantity(j) + 1
                    DollarsTotal(j) = DollarsTotal(j) + DollarsData(i)
                    Exit For
                End If
            Next
        End If
        If NewProduct Then
' The current product code is a new one, so update the list of codes found so far, and
' initialize the Quantity and DollarsTotal values for this new product.
            NFound = NFound + 1
            ReDim Preserve ProdCodesFound(NFound)
            ReDim Preserve Quantity(NFound)
            ReDim Preserve DollarsTotal(NFound)
            ProdCodesFound(NFound) = ProdCodesData(i)
            Quantity(NFound) = 1
            DollarsTotal(NFound) = DollarsData(i)
        End If
    Next
```

```
' Place the results in columns E to G.
    For j = 1 To NFound
        With Range("E2")
            .Offset(j, 0) = ProdCodesFound(j)
            .Offset(j, 1) = Quantity(j)
            .Offset(j, 2) = DollarsTotal(j)
        End With
    Next
' Sort on column G in descending order, and display a message about the number of
' distinct products found.
    Range("E3").Sort Key1:=Range("G3"), Order1:=xlDescending, Header:=xlYes
    MsgBox "There are " & NFound & " different products that have been sold."
End Sub
```

Although there are plenty of comments in the above code, some further explanation might be useful.

- The ProdCodeData and DollarsData arrays are redimensioned *without* the keyword **Preserve**, whereas the ProdCodesFound, Quantity, and DollarsTotal arrays are redimensioned with it. The reason is that the former two arrays are redimensioned only once, so there is no need to worry about deleting previous contents—there aren't any. However, the latter three arrays are redimensioned every time a new product code is found, and when this happens, we do *not* want to delete previous contents.

- When we find a new product code, we increase NFound by 1 and redimension the ProdCodesFound, Quantity, and DollarsTotal arrays by adding an extra element to each. After doing this, we place the appropriate values in the newly created elements of these arrays. For example, if NFound goes from 34 to 35, we must specify the 35th element of these arrays.

- To specify a range that is to be sorted, it suffices to specify any cell within this range. Similarly, to specify the column to sort on (in the Key1 argument), it suffices to specify any cell within this column.

EXAMPLE 9.3   Traveling Salesperson Heuristic

This example deals with a famous problem in management science: the traveling salesperson problem. A salesperson must start in a certain city, visit each other city exactly once, and return to the original city. The problem is to find the route with the minimum total distance. Although this problem is easy to state, it is extremely difficult to solve optimally, even for a moderately small number of cities such as 25. Therefore, management scientists have discovered **heuristics** that usually give "good" but not necessarily optimal solutions. The advantage of the heuristics is that they are quick and easy to implement. This example illustrates the **nearest neighbor** heuristic. It is very easy to state: The salesperson should always go next to the closest city not yet visited. Of course, he must return to the original city (labeled here as city 1) at the end.

The **TravSales.xls** file implements this heuristic for 15 cities. (It could easily be extended for many more than 15.) There are actually two subs in this file. The first, **GenDistances**, generates random distances between the cities. It doesn't use any arrays, but it provides a good illustration of For loops. By running this sub repeatedly, you can generate many 15-city problems, each with a *different* set of distances. Figure 9.8 shows a matrix of distances generated by the GenDistances sub. Note that the distances are symmetric. For example, the distance from city 5 to city 10 is the same as the distance from city 10 to city 5. This is guaranteed by the way GenDistances is written.

Figure 9.8 Distances for traveling salesperson problem

	City 1	City 2	City 3	City 4	City 5	City 6	City 7	City 8	City 9	City 10	City 11	City 12	City 13	City 14	City 15
City 1		66	66	26	13	22	79	80	5	15	21	11	59	27	82
City 2	66		60	42	19	10	89	42	79	74	95	52	88	55	42
City 3	66	60		64	24	61	14	2	71	63	5	69	74	60	20
City 4	26	42	64		29	4	70	14	100	55	43	44	91	64	98
City 5	13	19	24	29		57	44	57	90	93	17	17	99	23	82
City 6	22	10	61	4	57		83	42	2	55	67	11	53	42	1
City 7	79	89	14	70	44	83		43	79	23	7	3	90	47	93
City 8	80	42	2	14	57	42	43		100	63	61	71	26	27	64
City 9	5	79	71	100	90	2	79	100		5	23	67	79	79	66
City 10	15	74	63	55	93	55	23	63	5		60	57	96	83	31
City 11	21	95	5	43	17	67	7	61	23	60		5	94	90	37
City 12	11	52	69	44	17	11	3	71	67	57	5		35	92	57
City 13	59	88	74	91	99	53	90	26	79	96	94	35		72	41
City 14	27	55	60	64	23	42	47	27	79	83	90	92	72		64
City 15	82	42	20	98	82	1	93	64	66	31	37	57	41	64	

(Spreadsheet notes: Traveling salesperson model. A salesperson starts in city 1, must visit each other city exactly once, and must end by returning to city 1. The distance matrix below shows distances between all pairs of cities. A famous problem in management science is to find the sequence of cities the salesperson should follow to minimize the total distance traveled. This is a VERY difficult problem. We'll investigate a reasonably good *heuristic* (educated guess) solution: always go next to the nearest city not yet visited. We want to write VBA code to find the associated route from this "nearest neighbor" heuristic and its total distance. Buttons: Generate distance matrix; Run nearest neighbor heuristic. Distance matrix (symmetric, so values above the diagonal are the same as values below).)

The GenDistances sub appears below, with plenty of comments.

```
Sub GenDistances()
' This sub enters random integers from 1 to 100 above the diagonal and then enters
' values below the diagonal to make the matrix symmetric.
    Dim i As Integer, j As Integer, NCities As Integer

' The following statement ensures that different random numbers will be used each time
' the procedure is run.
    Randomize
    With Range("DistMatrix")
        NCities = .Rows.Count

        For i = 1 To NCities - 1
' Note that Rnd is a built-in VBA function.  It generates random numbers from 0 to 1.
' Int is another VBA function that chops off the decimal and returns an integer.
            For j = i + 1 To NCities
                .Cells(i, j) = Int(Rnd * 100) + 1
            Next
        Next
        For i = 2 To NCities
            For j = 1 To i - 1
                .Cells(i, j) = .Cells(j, i)
            Next
        Next
    End With
End Sub
```

Here are a few notes about the GenDistances sub.

- VBA's **Randomize** and **Rnd** functions are used in tandem. The **Rnd** function generates a random number uniformly distributed between 0 and 1 each time it is called. To get a random *integer* from 1 to 15, we multiply Rnd by 15 and "chop off" its decimal with the **Int** function. This generates an integer from 0 to 14, so we add 1 to it. The **Randomize** function is used so that *different* random numbers are generated each time the sub is run.
- The range name DistMatrix refers to the range B13:P27. We find the number of cities, NCities, as the count of the rows of this range.
- The first set of nested For loops fills up the matrix *above* the diagonal, and the second set creates a mirror image *below* the diagonal.

The second sub, **NearestNeighbor**, uses arrays to implement the nearest neighbor heuristic. Once the distances are known, the NearestNeighbor sub can be run (by clicking on the second button in Figure 9.8) to generate the nearest neighbor route. When it is run (for the distances in Figure 9.8), the message box in Figure 9.9 displays the total distance traveled, and the route is specified in the worksheet, as shown in Figure 9.10. The traveler first goes from city 1 to city 8, then to city 11, and so on. (For this small problem, you can check manually, using Figure 9.8 as a guide, that this is indeed the solution to the nearest neighbor heuristic.)

Figure 9.9 Total distance

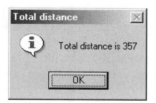

Figure 9.10 Route information

	A	B
29	Nearest neighbor route	
30	Stop #	City
31	1	1
32	2	8
33	3	11
34	4	14
35	5	4
36	6	13
37	7	7
38	8	9
39	9	3
40	10	2
41	11	6
42	12	15
43	13	5
44	14	10
45	15	12
46	16	1

The NearestNeighbor code is listed below. Although there are plenty of comments, a few explanations should be helpful.

- The **Option Base 1** statement is placed at the top of the module, so that all arrays begin with index 1.
- There are two arrays, the Boolean array Visited and the integer array Route. If Visited(6) is True, for example, this means that city 6 has been visited, so it cannot be visited again. Otherwise, if Visited(6) is False, then city 6 is a candidate for the next visit. The Route array identifies the cities on the different stops of the route. For example, if Route(8) equals 3, this means that city 3 is the eighth city to be visited.
- Visited and Route are declared initially with empty parentheses, just to make the sub more general. (As it is written, it will work for any number of cities, not just 15.) Once the number of cities is known (from the count of the rows in the DistMatrix array), the arrays are redimensioned appropriately. Note that the **Preserve** keyword is not necessary because the arrays are empty anyway at the time they are redimensioned.
- Several variables need to be initialized appropriately before the real work can be done. They include Route(1), Route(NCities+1), NowAt, TotDist, and the Visited array.
- The heuristic is performed with two nested For loops. The outer loop goes over the "steps" of the route. Its purpose is to discover which city will be the second visited, which will be third, and so on. The inner loop finds the nearest neighbor city for that step. It does this with a "running minimum" where it finds the smallest distance to all cities from the current city (NowAt) among all those not yet visited. The best of these is labeled NextAt. Then after this inner loop is completed, NowAt becomes NextAt in preparation for the next pass through the inner loop.
- After the loops are completed, the distance back to city 1 is added to the TotDist variable, the contents of the Route array are placed in the worksheet (below cell B30), and the total distance is displayed in a message box.
- We fibbed earlier when we said that this same sub will work for *any* number of cities. The problem is that if there are too many cities, then the display of the Route array below cell B30 will write over part of the distance matrix! There are ways around this. How would you do it?

```
Option Explicit
Option Base 1
Sub NearestNeighbor()
' This sub runs the nearest neighbor heuristic.
' Definition of variables:
'   NCities - number of cities in the problem
'   Visited - a Boolean array: True if a city has been visited, False otherwise
'   Step - a counter for the number of cities visited so far
'   Route - an array where element i is the i-th city visited
'       Note that Route(1) and Route(NCities+1) must both be 1.
'   NowAt - city current at
'   NextAt - city to visit next
'   TotDist - total distance traveled
```

```
'     MinDist - the minimum distance to the nearest (yet unvisited) neighbor
'     i - integer loop index
    Dim NCities As Integer, Visited() As Boolean, Step As Integer, _
        Route() As Integer, NowAt As Integer, NextAt As Integer, _
        TotDist As Integer, MinDist As Integer, i As Integer
' Get the size of the problem (number of nodes) and redimension the Visited and
' Route arrays appropriately.
    NCities = Range("DistMatrix").Rows.Count
    ReDim Visited(NCities)
    ReDim Route(NCities + 1)
' Initialize variables.
    Route(1) = 1
    Route(NCities + 1) = 1
    Visited(1) = True
    For i = 2 To NCities
        Visited(i) = False
    Next
    NowAt = 1
    TotDist = 0
' Go through the steps on the route, one at a time, to see which cities should be
' visited in which order.
    For Step = 2 To NCities
' Find which city should be visited next by finding a 'running minimum' of distances
' from the current city to all other cities.  The next city is a candidate only if it
' is not the current city and it has not yet been visited.  Start the running minimum
' (MinDist) at a LARGE value, so that anything will beat its initial value.
        MinDist = 10000
        For i = 2 To NCities
            If i <> NowAt And Visited(i) = False Then
                If Range("DistMatrix").Cells(NowAt, i) < MinDist Then
' Capture the best candidate so far and its associated distance from the current city.
                    NextAt = i
                    MinDist = Range("DistMatrix").Cells(NowAt, NextAt)
                End If
            End If
        Next i
' Store the city to visit next in Route, record that it has been visited, and update
' the total distance.
        Route(Step) = NextAt
        Visited(NextAt) = True
        TotDist = TotDist + MinDist
' Get ready for the next time through the loop.
        NowAt = NextAt
    Next Step
' Update the total distance to include the return to city 1.
    TotDist = TotDist + Range("DistMatrix").Cells(NowAt, 1)
' Record the route from city 1 back to city 1 in the spreadsheet, starting in cell B30.
    For Step = 1 To NCities + 1
        Range("B30").Offset(Step, 0) = Route(Step)
    Next Step
' Show the total distance in a message box.
    MsgBox "Total distance is " & TotDist, vbInformation, "Total distance"
End Sub
```

You should go through this code line by line until you understand how it
works. It is structured to do exactly what you would do if you had to perform the
nearest neighbor heuristic manually. Of course, its advantage is that it is extremely
fast—and it doesn't make mistakes.

EXAMPLE 9.4 Merging Lists

This example is also easy to describe but no less challenging to implement. It is an example of merging two lists and is contained in the file **MergingLists.xls**. As in all applications in Part II of the book, there is an Explanation sheet (see Figure 9.11) that users see when they open the file. It explains the purpose of the application, and it has a button that runs a simple macro to take them to the Lists worksheet (the one with the data). The code attached to this button is very simple:

```
Sub GoToLists()
    Worksheets("Lists").Activate
    Range("A2").Select
End Sub
```

Figure 9.11 Explanation of merging example

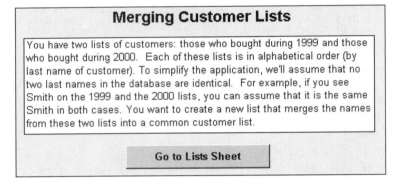

The lists (with some hidden rows) in the Lists sheet are already sorted in alphabetical order and appear in Figure 9.12. Note that some customers are in the 1999 list only, some are in the 2000 list only, and some are in both. The merged list in column D should include each customer in either list exactly once.

A Conceptual Method

Before discussing any VBA code, you must have a mental picture of how you would do the merging manually. After all, it is pointless to try to write code for a procedure unless you thoroughly understand the steps you would take to perform it manually. Here is one reasonable approach.

1. Start at the top of each of the existing lists and compare the names.
    - If they are the same, transfer this common name to column D and move down one row in both column A and column B for the next comparison.
    - If the name in column A comes before the name in column B in alphabetical order, transfer the name in column A to column D and move

Figure 9.12 Lists to be merged

	A	B	C	D
1	**Existing lists**	Merge Lists		**Merged list**
2				
3	Customers 1999	Customers 2000		Customers
4	Barlog	Aghimien		
5	Barnett	Bang		
6	Bedrick	Barnett		
7	Brulez	Bedrick		
8	Cadigan	Brulez		
9	Castleman	Cadigan		
93	Wyatt	Theodas		
94	Yablonka	Tracy		
95	Zick	Ubelhor		
96	Ziegler	Usman		
97		Vicars		
98		Villard		
99		Wendel		
100		Wier		
101		Wise		
102		Yablonka		
103		Yeiter		
104		Zakrzacki		
105		Zhou		

down one row in column A (but *not* in column B) for the next comparison. Proceed similarly if the name in column B comes before the name in column A in alphabetical order. For example, the second comparison in the above lists will be between Barlog and Bang.

2. Continue as in step 1, always making a comparison between a name in column A and a name in column B, until you have transferred all of the names from at least one of the column A and column B lists. Then if there are names left in one of the lists, transfer all of them to column D.

Try this procedure on the lists in Figure 9.12, and you will see that it works perfectly. Even though the list in column B is longer, you will finish transferring the names from column B first, with Zick and Ziegler left in the column A list. The last step of the procedure is to move these two names to the bottom of the merged list in column D.

Coding the Method

Now it is a matter of coding this procedure. The **MergeLists** sub listed below contains the relevant code. It is written to work for *any* two lists in columns A and B, not just the ones shown in Figure 9.12. (The only restriction is that the names should be unique, in the sense that there should be only one Smith, say, in either list, and if Smith appears in both lists, it should be the same Smith. Duplicated names raise other issues that are not addressed here.) Again, there are plenty of comments, but a few explanations should help.

- There are three arrays, List1, List2, and List3, with sizes LS1, LS2, and LS3. The first two are filled with the two known customer lists. The third is filled by the merging procedure.

- The array sizes LS1 and LS2 can be obtained immediately by looking at the existing customer lists. The array size LS3 will be known only at the end of the procedure. We could redimension LSize3 right away with size LS1+LS2 (that will certainly be large enough—do you see why?), but instead we redimension List3 with one extra element every time we add a new customer to the merged list. To keep from deleting previous customers from the merged list, the **Preserve** keyword is necessary.
- The "flow" of the sub is that any previous merged list is first deleted from column D with the **ClearContents** method. Next, the list sizes of the existing lists are found, and the List1 and List2 arrays are filled with existing customer names. Finally, the merging procedure is used to fill the List3 array, which is eventually written to column D.
- Note how the conceptual method described earlier is implemented in VBA. The sub uses the Index1 and Index2 integer variables to indicate how far down the existing customer lists the procedure is. The corresponding customer names are Name1 and Name2. A comparison between them indicates which to add to the merged list, as well as which of Index1 and Index2 to increment by 1. A **Do While** loop is (arguably) the more natural here. It says to keep going through the lists as long as there is at least one name remaining in each list.
- After the Do loop is completed, the contents of the list not yet completed (if either) are transferred to the merged list. Then the contents of List3 are written to column D of the worksheet.

```
Option Explicit
Option Base 1
Sub MergeLists()
' The LSx variables are list sizes for the various lists (x from 1 to 3).  The Listx
' arrays contain the members of the lists (again, x from 1 to 3). The lists are indexed
' from 1 to 3 as follows:
'    List1 - customers from 1999 (given data)
'    List2 - customers from 2000 (given data)
'    List3 - customers who bought in either or both years (to be found)
    Dim i As Integer, j As Integer
    Dim LS1 As Integer, LS2 As Integer, List1() As String, List2() As String
    Dim LS3 As Integer, Index1 As Integer, Index2 As Integer, _
        Name1 As String, Name2 As String, List3() As String
' Delete the old merged list (if any) in column D.
    With Range("D3")
        Range(.Offset(1, 0),.Offset(1, 0).End(xlDown)).ClearContents
    End With
' Get the list sizes and the members of the lists for the given data in columns A, B.
    With Range("A3")
        LS1 = Range(.Offset(1, 0), .End(xlDown)).Rows.Count
        ReDim List1(LS1)
        For i = 1 To LS1
            List1(i) = .Offset(i, 0)
        Next
        LS2 = Range(.Offset(1, 1), .Offset(0, 1).End(xlDown)).Rows.Count
        ReDim List2(LS2)
        For i = 1 To LS2
            List2(i) = .Offset(i, 1)
        Next
    End With
```

```
' Create the merged list.
' Initialize new list size to be 0.
    LS3 = 0
' Go through List1 and List2 simultaneously. Index1 and Index2 indicate how far down
' each list we currently are, and Name1 and Name2 are the corresponding customer names.
    Index1 = 1
    Index2 = 1
' Keep going until we get past at least one of the lists.
    Do While Index1 <= LS1 And Index2 <= LS2
        Name1 = List1(Index1)
        Name2 = List2(Index2)
' Each step through the loop we'll add one customer name to the merged list, so update
' the list size and redimension List3.
        LS3 = LS3 + 1
        ReDim Preserve List3(LS3)
' See which of the two names being compared is first in alphabetical order.  It becomes
' the new member of the merged list. Once it's added, go to the next name (by updating
' the Index) in the appropriate list. If there's a tie, update both Indexes.
        If Name1 < Name2 Then
            List3(LS3) = Name1
            Index1 = Index1 + 1
        ElseIf Name1 > Name2 Then
            List3(LS3) = Name2
            Index2 = Index2 + 1
        ElseIf Name1 = Name2 Then
            List3(LS3) = Name2
            Index1 = Index1 + 1
            Index2 = Index2 + 1
        End If
    Loop
' By this time, we're through at least one of the lists (List1 or List2). Therefore,
' add all leftover names from the OTHER list to the merged list.
    If Index1 > LS1 And Index2 <= LS2 Then
        For i = Index2 To LS2
            LS3 = LS3 + 1
            ReDim Preserve List3(LS3)
            List3(LS3) = List2(i)
        Next
    ElseIf Index1 <= LS1 And Index2 > LS2 Then
        For i = Index1 To LS1
            LS3 = LS3 + 1
            ReDim Preserve List3(LS3)
            List3(LS3) = List1(i)
        Next
    End If
' Record the merged list in column D of the worksheet.
    With Range("D3")
        For i = 1 To LS3
            .Offset(i, 0) = List3(i)
        Next
    End With
' End with the cursor in cell A2.
    Range("A2").Select
End Sub
```

The introduction to this chapter claimed that arrays are useful for working with lists. This merging example is a perfect example of this claim. The merging could certainly be done without arrays, but arrays provide the perfect means for accomplishing the job.

9.6 Array Functions

This chapter concludes with a brief description of a rather curious construct in VBA: the **Array function**. The following code illustrates how Array functions work.

```
Option Base 1
Sub ArrayFunctionExample()
    Dim Days as Variant
    Days = Array("Mon","Tues","Wed","Thurs","Fri","Sat","Sun")
    MsgBox "The first day in the array is " & Days(1)
End Sub
```

The keyword **Array**, followed by a list inside parentheses, is used to "populate" the variable Days. Then Days acts like a typical array. For example, Days(1) in the message box statement will be "Mon". (It would be "Tues" if the **Option Base 1** statement were not included. Remember, the default is **0-based indexing**.) However, Days is not *declared* like a typical array. It must be declared as a Variant, with no empty parentheses in the Dim statement. VBA figures out that you want Days to be an array only after you set Days equal to the Array function in the third line of the sub.

You might not use Array functions very often, but as this example code shows, they provide a convenient way to populate an array.

9.7 Summary

We already know from previous chapters how powerful looping can be in computer programs. Arrays increase this power tremendously, especially when processing lists in some way. We have attempted to illustrate this power by a variety of examples, and we will continue to illustrate the power of arrays in later chapters. Arrays are not necessarily the easiest aspect of VBA programming, but they are well worth the effort required to master them.

PROGRAMMING EXERCISES

1. Write a sub that does the following: (1) It declares an array called PracticeArray of size 100, (2) it stores the value i in element i (for i from 1 to 100), and it uses a For loop to switch the contents of the elements i and i+1 for each i from 1 to 99. At the end, transfer the contents of PracticeArray to column A of a worksheet. The effect of all the switching should be to push the 1 down to the bottom of the list. Is that what you got? (*Hint:* When you switch two array elements, you need a third "temporary" variable.)

2. The file **HiSpenders.xls** contains a list of customers and the amounts they spent during the past month. Write a sub that captures the existing lists in two arrays

and then creates two new arrays of customer names and amounts spent for customers who spent at least $500. After these new arrays have been filled, transfer their contents to columns D and E of the worksheet.

3. The file **CustomerLists.xls** contains two lists of customers: those who purchased from our company in 1999 and those who purchased in 2000. Write a sub that captures the existing lists in two arrays and then creates three new arrays of customers who purchased only in 1999, customers who purchased only in 2000, and customers who purchased in both years. After these new arrays have been filled, transfer their contents to columns D, E, and F of the worksheet.

4. The file **Flights.xls** has a list of flights flown by EastWest Airlines in columns A, B, and C. The list includes the flight number, the origin, and the destination of each flight. You are interested in flights that leave from any city in column E and end up at any city in column F. You need to list such flights in columns H, I, and J. Write a VBA program to do so, using arrays. Your program should work even if the lists in columns A-C and in E-F change. To see how it should work, look at the **FlightsFinished.xls** file. Its code is password-protected.

5. The VBA expression **Int(Rnd * N) + 1**, where N is an integer variable, can be used to generate a random integer from 1 to N. Suppose we have a list of customers, labeled from 1 to N, and we want to choose a random subset of them of size M (where M < N). Write a sub to do this. It should first ask the user for N and M, using two input boxes. It should then fill an array of size M called Chosen, where Chosen(1) is the index of the first person chosen, Chosen (2) is the index of the second person chosen, and so on. No person can be chosen more than once, so no two elements of the Chosen array should have the same value. Finally, the sub should list the values of the array in column A of a worksheet.

6. The file **Incomes.xls** has annual incomes for many households in a particular town. As in the previous problem, choose a random subset of M households. Then report the average of *all* incomes in the file, and the average of the incomes in the subset, in a message box. Unlike the previous problem, the user cannot select N; it is the number of households listed in the file. However, the user should be allowed to choose the sample size M.

7. Consider the following state lottery. Five random digits are selected. This is the "winning number." You can buy as many lottery cards as you like at $1 per card. Each card contains five random digits. If you get a card that matches the winning number, you win $100,000. Write a sub that does the following. It first generates a random winning number and stores it in a string variable (so that you can use string concatenation), and it asks the user how many cards he wants to buy. Then it uses a For loop to generate this many cards and store their numbers in a Card array (which should be a *string* array). Next, it uses a Do loop to keep checking cards until a winner has been found or no more cards remain. Finally, it displays a message stating whether you are a winner and your net gain or loss. Note that you can generate a single random digit from 0 to 9 with the expression **Int(Rnd * 10)**.

8. The previous problem is realistic because a lottery player must commit to the number of cards purchased *before* learning the winning number. However, suppose we want to see how many cards you would have to buy, on average, before getting a card with the winning number. Write a sub that does the following. It

has an "outer" For loop that goes from 1 to 100, so that we can repeat the whole process 100 times, each with a different winning number. Each time you go through this loop, you will generate a winning card, you will use a Do loop to keep generating cards until you get a winner, and you will keep track of the number of cards required in an element of the ReqdCards array (of size 100). At the end of the program, you will display summary measures of ReqdCards in a message box: the average of its elements, the smallest of its elements, and the largest of its elements. For example, the latter is the most cards you ever had to buy in any of the 100 lotteries. (*Note:* Although you will be working with integers, they will likely be very *large* integers. Therefore, declare them as Long, not Integer, types. Also, don't be surprised if this program takes a while to run. It took ours about 5–10 minutes.)

9. If you have ever studied relational databases, you have heard of "joins." This exercise illustrates what a join is. The file **MusicCDs1.xls** contains data on a person's classical music CD collection. There are three sheets. The Labels sheet lists all music labels (such as Philips), where they are indexed with consecutive integers. The CDs sheet lists the person's CDs. Specifically, it shows, for each CD, the index of the music label, the composer, and the piece(s) on the CD. We say that the tables on these two sheets are "related" through the label indexes. Write a sub, using arrays, to "join" the information on these two sheets. The joined information should be placed on the Join sheet. As the headings show, it should show, for each CD, the music label (its name, not its index), the composer, and the piece(s).

10. The previous problem demonstrated a "one-to-many" relationship. This means that each CD has only one music label, but many CDs can have the same label. Relationships can also be "many-to-many," as this exercise illustrates. The file **MusicCDs2.xls** contains four sheets. The Works sheet lists works of music, along with the composers, and they are indexed by consecutive integers. The Conductors sheet lists conductors, which are also indexed by consecutive integers. The CDs sheet has an entry for each CD owned. For each entry, it shows the index of the work and the index of the conductor. The relationship is now "many-to-many" because it is possible to have more than one CD of a given work, each conducted by a different conductor, and it is possible to have more than one CD with a given conductor, each conducting a different work. Write a sub, using arrays, to fill the Join sheet, which currently has only headings. As these headings indicate, each row should list the composer, the work, and the conductor for a particular CD. (This sheet should end up with as many rows as the CDs sheet.) Finally, the sub should keep track of any works on the Works sheet that you do not own, and it should display these in some way (you can decide how).

11. (More difficult) Your company makes steel rods of a fixed diameter and length 50 inches. Your customers request rods of the following lengths (all in inches): 5, 8, 12, 15, 20, and 25. Write a sub to find all ways to cut the rods so that any leftovers are unusable. For example, one way to do it is with one 5-inch rod, one 8-inch rod, and three 12-inch rods. This uses 49 inches of the rod, and the other inch is unusable. As you find usable patterns, list them in the **Patterns.xls** file. (One possible pattern is already shown in row 5 for illustration.)

More on Variables and Subroutines

10

10.1 Introduction

To this point, all of the programs we have discussed have been single, self-contained subs. This chapter illustrates how individual subs can be part of a bigger picture, which will be very important for the applications discussed in the second part of the book. A typical application can have many subs in one or more modules, and they can be related. First, they can share the same variables. For example, one sub might use an input box to capture an employee's salary in the variable Salary. Then another sub might use this variable in some way. Both subs need to know about the Salary variable. In technical terms, the Salary variable must have the appropriate **scope**.

Subs can also **call** one another, and they can **pass arguments** (share information) when they make the call. As programs become longer and more complex, it is common to break them down into smaller subs, where each sub performs a specific task. Then there is often a "main" sub that calls the other subs. In effect, the main sub acts as a control center. "Modularizing" programs in this way makes them easier to read (and to debug). In addition, there is a better chance that the smaller subs will be *reusable* in other programs. In fact, one of the most important ideas in computer programming today is the idea of reusable code. Professional programmers attempt to make their subs as general and self-contained as possible so that other programmers will not have to reinvent the wheel every time they write a program.

Finally, this chapter introduces a particular type of subroutine called a **function subroutine**. Unlike the subroutines discussed so far, the primary purpose of a function subroutine is to return a value. Actually, all of the Excel functions you use in formulas, such as Sum, Max, and so on, are really function subroutines. This chapter illustrates how you can develop your *own* custom functions and then use them in VBA programs or in Excel worksheets.

10.2 Exercise

The emphasis in this chapter is on dividing an overall program into several subroutines, each of which performs a particular task. The following exercise is typical. It could be written in one fairly long sub, but a much better way is to modularize it. By the time you have finished reading this chapter, you should be able to solve this exercise, according to the specific instructions, without much difficulty.

Exercise 10.1   Updating Customer Accounts

Consider a company that services air conditioners and heaters. It currently has 30 residential customers in a certain region, and it keeps track of service charges for these customers in the file **CustAccts.xls**. This file contains a sheet called NewCharges. Each week the company deletes the charges from the previous week and adds charges for the current week to this sheet. Figure 10.1 shows the charges for the most recent week.

Figure 10.1 New charges

	A	B	C	D
1	Information on new charges			
2				
3	Date	Customer	Account #	Charge
4	17-Dec-00	Astrid	A1865	89.42
5	18-Dec-00	Bricker	B1808	70.94
6	18-Dec-00	Allenby	A1151	87.11
7	19-Dec-00	Argos	A1225	71.15
8	19-Dec-00	Exley	E3597	96.15
9	19-Dec-00	Owens	O2752	77.94
10	20-Dec-00	Stevens	S3211	133.12
11	20-Dec-00	Spinaker	S2378	81.17
12	20-Dec-00	West	W3967	152.77

The file also contains a separate sheet for each customer, where the sheet name is the customer's account number. For example, the sheet for customer Stevens (account number S3211) appears in Figure 10.2. Columns A and B list all of Stevens's charges since the account was opened, and columns D to G summarize the yearly totals. The totals in column E are sums of charges for the various years. The discounts in column F are based on the company's discount policy: no discount on the first $100 (for any year), 5% discount on the next $100, and 7.5% discount on all charges over $200. The net in column G is the total minus the discount.

The purpose of the exercise is to update the customer account sheets with the charges on the NewCharges sheet. This includes new entries in columns A and B, plus updates of the total and discount for the year 2000 in columns E and F. As an example, after running the program, the Stevens account sheet should appear as in Figure 10.3. Of course, if a customer has no charge in the NewCharges sheet, this customer's account sheet does not need to be updated.

This exercise can be done in many ways, but to get the most benefit from it, it should be done as follows. There should be a Main sub that loops through all of the charges in the NewCharges sheet. For each charge, an Update sub should be called that takes three arguments: the customer's account number, the date of the charge, and the amount of the charge. This Update sub should add the new charge to the end of the customer's charges (as in cells A21 and B21 in Figure 10.3 for Stevens), and it should update the Total and Discount cells for the year 2000. To find the discount, it should call a function subroutine that calculates the discount for any yearly total passed to it.

Figure 10.2 Typical customer account sheet

	A	B	C	D	E	F	G
1	**Stevens account**						
2							
3	**All charges**			**Summary by year**			
4	Date	Charge		Year	Total	Discount	Net
5	26-Feb-95	$112.02		1995	$427.65	$22.07	$405.58
6	25-Mar-95	$104.69		1996	$399.75	$19.98	$379.77
7	16-Sep-95	$210.94		1997	$321.89	$14.14	$307.75
8	20-Jan-96	$176.75		1998	$350.31	$16.27	$334.04
9	6-Mar-96	$127.82		1999	$433.30	$22.50	$410.80
10	31-Dec-96	$95.18		2000	$113.02	$0.65	$112.37
11	26-Mar-97	$113.82					
12	17-Aug-97	$208.07					
13	4-Jan-98	$111.35					
14	17-Oct-98	$134.91					
15	11-Dec-98	$104.05					
16	27-Mar-99	$103.38					
17	26-Jul-99	$137.46					
18	18-Aug-99	$92.23					
19	8-Dec-99	$100.23					
20	31-Aug-00	$113.02					

Figure 10.3 Updated account sheet

	A	B	C	D	E	F	G
1	**Stevens account**						
2							
3	**All charges**			**Summary by year**			
4	Date	Charge		Year	Total	Discount	Net
5	26-Feb-95	$112.02		1995	$427.65	$22.07	$405.58
6	25-Mar-95	$104.69		1996	$399.75	$19.98	$379.77
7	16-Sep-95	$210.94		1997	$321.89	$14.14	$307.75
8	20-Jan-96	$176.75		1998	$350.31	$16.27	$334.04
9	6-Mar-96	$127.82		1999	$433.30	$22.50	$410.80
10	31-Dec-96	$95.18		2000	$246.14	$8.46	$237.68
11	26-Mar-97	$113.82					
12	17-Aug-97	$208.07					
13	4-Jan-98	$111.35					
14	17-Oct-98	$134.91					
15	11-Dec-98	$104.05					
16	27-Mar-99	$103.38					
17	26-Jul-99	$137.46					
18	18-Aug-99	$92.23					
19	8-Dec-99	$100.23					
20	31-Aug-00	$113.02					
21	20-Dec-00	$133.12					

As usual, you can try running the program in the completed file **CustAcctsFinished.xls**, but you should not look at the code until you have tried writing the VBA code yourself.

10.3   Scope of Variables and Subroutines

This section discusses the important concept of **scope**, or "Which parts of a program have access to which other parts?" Variables and subroutines both have scope. We will discuss each.

Scope of Variables

You already know how to declare a variable with a **Dim** statement. Here is a typical example:

```
Sub Test1()
    Dim Salary As Currency
    Salary = 50000
    OtherStatements
End Sub
```

When a variable such as Salary is declared *inside* a sub in this way, it is called a **procedure-level** variable, or a **local** variable. The only sub that recognizes this variable is the sub that contains it. Suppose there is another sub with the following lines:

```
Sub Test2()
    MsgBox "The value of salary is " & Salary
    OtherStatements
End Sub
```

If you run Test1 and then Test2, the message box in Test2 will *not* display "The value of salary is 50000". This is because Test2 does not know the value of the Salary variable; only Test1 knows it. In fact, Test2 can have its own Salary variable, as in

```
Sub Test2()
    Dim Salary As Currency
    Salary = 40000
    MsgBox "The value of salary is " & Salary
    OtherStatements
End Sub
```

If you run Test1 and then Test2, then Test2 will have no memory that Salary was 50000 in Test1. It knows only about *its* version of Salary, defined as 40000. In other words, local variables in different subs can have the same names, but they lead independent existences. (Technically, they have different memory locations.)

What if you want different subs to have access to common variables? Then you can declare these variables at the *top* of a module, before any subs. Actually, you have two options. First, you can declare a variable at the top of a module with the usual **Dim** keyword, as in

```
Dim Salary As Currency
```

This variable is then a **module-level** variable, which means that every sub in the module has access to Salary. (An alternative to the keyword Dim is the keyword **Private**. A Private variable also has module-level scope.) The second possibility is to declare a variable at the top of a module with the keyword **Public**, as in

```
Public Salary As Currency
```

Then Salary has **project-level** scope, which means that *all* modules in the entire project have access to it.[15] This is often useful when you have two or more modules in your project. (It is also useful when you have "event code" for **user forms**, as explained in Chapter 12. Then Public variables are also recognized by the event code.)

   If you declare a variable to have module-level or project-level scope, then you almost surely do *not* want to declare the same variable inside a sub with a Dim statement. For example, consider the following code:

```
Public Salary As Currency

Sub Test1()
    Salary = 50000
End Sub

Sub Test2()
    Dim Salary As Currency
    MsgBox "Salary is " & Salary
End Sub
```

If you run Test1 and then Test2, then the message box in Test2 will *not* display "Salary is 50000" as you might expect—it will display "Salary is 0". The reason is that the Dim statement in Test2 creates a local version of Salary that *overrides* the public version. This local version is initialized to 0 by default. Hence the message says that Salary is 0, which is probably not what you want.

Scope of Subroutines

Subroutines also have scope. As discussed in the next section, one sub can **call** another inside a program. Scope then determines which subs can call which others. The default is that all subs have **public** scope unless specified otherwise. This means that when you define a sub as in

```
Sub Test()
```

---

[15]Some programmers use the term **global variable** rather than **public variable**. This is the term used in many other programming languages.

any other sub in the entire project can call this Test sub. To make this more explicit, you can precede Sub with the keyword **Public**, as in

```
Public Sub Test()
```

However, this is not really necessary because a sub's scope is public by default.

Now suppose that you want Test to be callable only by subs within its module. Then you *must* precede Sub with the keyword **Private**, as in

```
Private Sub Test()
```

Then any sub in the same module as Test can call Test, but subs outside of its module have no access to Test. By the way, the scoping rules for subs are exactly the same for function subroutines, the topic of Section 10.6.

10.4 Modularizing Programs

There is a tendency among beginning programmers to write one long sub in a program—a sub that does it all. This is a bad habit for at least three reasons:

- **Hard to read.** Long subs are hard to read. Would you like to read a book with a single long chapter or a chapter with a single long paragraph? (If you've read much William Faulkner, you know what we mean.)
- **Hard to debug.** Long subs are hard to debug.
- **Hard to reuse.** It is difficult to reuse the code from long subs in other programs.

A preferred approach is to modularize programs so that they become a sequence of relatively short subs, each with a very specific task to perform. These short subs then overcome the three criticisms above: (1) their brevity and focus make them easier to read, (2) they can be tested independently, or at least in sequence, so that bugs are easier to detect and fix, and (3) there is a much greater chance that they can be reused in other programs.

The question, then, is how to tie the subs together in an overall program. Fortunately, this is quite easy. You allow one sub to **call** another sub. Here is a typical setup:

```
Sub Main()
    Call Task1
    Call Task2
End Sub

Sub Task1()
    Call Task3
    OtherStatements
End Sub
```

```
Sub Task2()
    Statements
End Sub

Sub Task3
    Statements
End Sub
```

The Main sub does nothing but call the Task1 sub and then the Task2 sub. The Task1 sub in turn calls the Task3 sub, and it then executes some other statements. We say that Main **passes control** to Task1, which then passes control to Task3. When Task3 is completed, it passes control back to Task1. When Task1 is completed, it passes control back to Main, which immediately passes control to Task2. Finally, when Task2 is completed, it passes control back to Main. At this point, the program ends. This code also indicates how easy it is to call another sub. You simply type the keyword **Call**, followed by the name of the sub being called.[16]

There is a trade-off when modularizing a program. At one extreme, you can have a single long sub. At the other extreme, you can create a separate sub for every small task your program performs. You typically need to find a middle ground that breaks an overall program into reasonable "chunks." Different programmers argue about the term "reasonable." For example, some say they don't like subs with more than 10 lines, which we believe is a bit restrictive. However, they all agree that some modularizing is appropriate in long programs.

EXAMPLE 10.1 Traveling Salesperson Model Revisited

To see how modularizing works, we rewrote the code for the traveling salesperson nearest-neighbor heuristic from the previous chapter. (See the file **TravSalesMod.xls**.) Now instead of one long NearestNeighbor sub, there is a short **NearestNeighbor** "main" sub that calls four other subs, **GetProblemSize**, **Initialize**, **PerformHeuristic**, and **DisplayResults**, to do the work. The code appears below. (The comments have been omitted to emphasize the overall structure.) Note how the names of the subs indicate the basic tasks to be performed. This is always good programming practice.

Compare the code below with the one-sub code in the original **TravSales.xls** file. You will probably agree that the "divide and conquer" strategy used here makes the program easier to understand. It not only helps you see the big picture, but it also helps you to understand the details by presenting them in bite-sized doses.

---

[16]It is also possible to omit the keyword **Call**. Then instead of writing, say, **Call Test1**, you simply write **Test1**. However, we prefer using the keyword **Call**, to remind us that a sub is being called.

```
Dim NCities As Integer, Visited() As Boolean, Route() As Integer, TotDist As Integer

Sub NearestNeighbor()
    Call GetProblemSize
    Call Initialize
    Call PerformHeuristic
    Call DisplayResults
End Sub

Sub GetProblemSize()
    NCities = Range("DistMatrix").Rows.Count
    ReDim Visited(NCities)
    ReDim Route(NCities + 1)
End Sub

Sub Initialize()
    Dim i As Integer
    Route(1) = 1
    Route(NCities + 1) = 1
    Visited(1) = True
    For i = 2 To NCities
        Visited(i) = False
    Next
    TotDist = 0
End Sub

Sub PerformHeuristic()
    Dim Step As Integer, i As Integer, NowAt As Integer, NextAt As Integer, MinDist As Integer
    NowAt = 1
    For Step = 2 To NCities
        MinDist = 10000
        For i = 2 To NCities
            If i <> NowAt And Visited(i) = False Then
                If Range("DistMatrix").Cells(NowAt, i) < MinDist Then
                    NextAt = i
                    MinDist = Range("DistMatrix").Cells(NowAt, NextAt)
                End If
            End If
        Next i
        Route(Step) = NextAt
        Visited(NextAt) = True
        TotDist = TotDist + MinDist
        NowAt = NextAt
    Next Step
    TotDist = TotDist + Range("DistMatrix").Cells(NowAt, 1)
End Sub

Sub DisplayResults()
    Dim Step As Integer
    For Step = 1 To NCities + 1
        Range("B30").Offset(Step, 0) = Route(Step)
    Next Step
    MsgBox "Total distance is " & TotDist, vbInformation, "Total distance"
End Sub
```

When you divide a program into multiple subs, you have to be careful with variable declarations. If a particular variable is required by more than one of the subs, it should be declared at the top of the module. The **module-level** variables above are NCities, TotDist, and the Visited and Route arrays. Other variables that are needed only in a specific sub, such as the Step variable in the DisplayResults sub, should be declared locally. In general, this forces you to examine your variables (and the logical structure of your program) carefully to see what belongs where. You *could* take the easy way out by declaring *all* variables at the top as module-level variables, but this is considered very poor programming practice. It signals that you haven't thought very carefully about the overall structure of your program.

10.5 Passing Arguments

In a typical modularized program, a particular sub can be called several times. Each time it is called, the sub performs the same basic task, but possibly with different inputs. As a very simple example, suppose a "main" sub calls a "display" sub to display a customer's name in a message box. We want the display sub to be very general, so that it will display any name given to it. The question is how we get the customer's name from the main sub to the display sub. There are two ways: (1) by using module-level variables and (2) by **passing arguments**. We compare these two methods below.

Module-level Variables Method

The following program illustrates the use of module-level variables. We assume there is a range called Names that contains the last names and first names of 10 customers. We want to display each customer's full name in a message box. To do so, we declare module-level variables LastName and FirstName in the first line. Then the Main sub loops through the rows of the Names range, stores the last and first names of the current customer in the LastName and FirstName variables, and calls the DisplayName sub to display the customer's full name. The DisplayName sub knows the current values of LastName and FirstName because they are module-level variables.

```
Dim LastName As String, FirstName As String

Sub Main()
    Dim i as Integer
    For i = 1 to 10
        LastName = Range("Names").Cells(i,1)
        FirstName = Range("Names").Cells(i,2)
    Next
    Call DisplayName
End Sub

Sub DisplayName()
    Dim CustName As String
    CustName = FirstName & " " & LastName
    MsgBox "The customer's full name is " & CustName
End Sub
```

Passing Arguments Method

Alternatively, we can **pass arguments** (in this case, names) from the Main sub to the DisplayNames sub. In this context, we refer to the Main sub as the **calling** sub and the DisplayNames sub as the **called** sub. To implement the method, the variables LastName and FirstName are no longer declared as module-level variables. They are now declared locally in the Main sub, and they are passed to the DisplayName sub as arguments in the next-to-last line of Main. Specifically, to pass arguments, we type the name of the called sub (DisplayName) and then list the variables being passed, separated by commas and included within parentheses. The first line of the called sub then indicates the arguments it expects to receive.

```
Sub Main()
    Dim i as Integer
    For i = 1 to 10
        LastName = Range("Names").Cells(i,1)
        FirstName = Range("Names").Cells(i,2)
    Next
    Call DisplayName(LastName, FirstName)
End Sub

Sub DisplayName(LName As String, FName As String)
    Dim CustName As String
    CustName = FName & " " & LName
    MsgBox "The customer's full name is " & CustName
End Sub
```

Note that the arguments in the first line of the DisplayName sub are LName and FName. They are *not* the same as the names passed to it, LastName and FirstName. This is perfectly legal. The variables being passed from the calling sub and the arguments in the called sub do not need to have the same names, although they often do. The only requirements are that they must match in number, type, and order. If Main passes two string variables to DisplayName, then DisplayName must have two arguments declared as string type. Otherwise, VBA will display an error message. Also, if the last name is the first variable in the passing statement, it should be the first argument in the argument list of the called sub.[17]

Summarizing, we have the following rules for passing arguments:

- To call a sub with arguments, type its name and follow it with arguments separated by commas and included within parentheses. An example is

```
Call DisplayName(LastName, FirstName)
```

- The called sub should declare its arguments inside parentheses next to the name of the sub. An example is

```
Sub DisplayName(LName As String, FName As String)
```

---

[17]Actually, this is not quite true. It is possible to include the *names* of the arguments when calling the sub, in which case the arguments can come in a different order, but we will not use this variation here.

- The names of the variables in the calling sub do not need to be the same as the names of the arguments in the called sub, but they should match in number, type, and order.

Now you have two ways to deal with shared variables. You can declare them as module-level (or project-level) variables at the top of a module, or you can pass them as arguments from one sub to another. Which method is better? Most professional programmers favor passing arguments whenever possible. The reason is that this makes a sub such as DisplayName totally self-contained. It can be reused, exactly as it stands, in a different program, because it is not dependent on a list of module-level variables that might or might not exist. However, passing variables is a somewhat more difficult concept, and it is sometimes more awkward to implement than the "global variable" approach. Therefore, both methods can be used, and you will see both in the applications in the second part of the book.

EXAMPLE 10.2 Formatting Extremes

The file **FormatExtremes.xls** contains monthly sales values for a company's sales regions. For each month, the smallest and largest of these values are shown below the monthly data. (See Figure 10.4.) The company wants to highlight the extreme sales in each month. Specifically, it wants to color the minimum sale in each month red and italicize it, and it wants to color the maximum sale in each month blue and boldface it. For convenience, the range names Sales, Minimums, and Maximums have been given to the ranges B4:M19, B21:M21, and B22:M22, respectively.

Figure 10.4 Sales data

	A	B	C	D	E	F	G	H	I	J	K	L	M
1	Sales by region and month												
2													
3		Jan	Feb	Mar	Apr	May	Jun	Jul	Aug	Sep	Oct	Nov	Dec
4	Region 1	25630	19660	15270	33810	19360	15770	22490	8350	18310	18160	14040	10680
5	Region 2	18490	10060	13150	17350	12120	16940	24120	4550	13920	11020	10370	8590
6	Region 3	13360	12630	20350	10850	17650	20570	18500	36460	7530	11880	18110	18760
7	Region 4	17280	22930	19310	12230	16490	6760	12850	18930	16640	13590	8180	10830
8	Region 5	10970	10550	11780	7210	23280	7320	15840	19690	19280	8690	9810	10540
9	Region 6	7990	14690	20680	17130	12620	7400	8420	13810	7090	8990	12570	15260
10	Region 7	40310	10820	18310	13900	6390	13290	12980	28440	15530	25940	16600	18160
11	Region 8	10770	18250	29580	21020	10200	9380	15210	5750	13710	11770	10820	23160
12	Region 9	10530	14170	24630	16910	21670	11750	10470	19150	20170	13370	20600	26180
13	Region 10	8600	22950	14080	16760	17270	16670	18650	10370	12040	13810	8000	11690
14	Region 11	11510	15660	16870	17930	15110	7760	12090	10260	23240	14760	15430	16540
15	Region 12	10360	11490	15000	14060	9770	13110	24320	24500	13300	15610	21040	12620
16	Region 13	18670	12350	20450	9860	16730	10100	12870	11390	16220	11760	18480	13330
17	Region 14	16360	18640	17050	24230	10760	14420	16730	17260	22470	11980	10710	19640
18	Region 15	20760	13610	6340	12510	14570	11930	26490	21130	21530	20390	24960	16100
19	Region 16	18690	23710	10530	18050	17730	7230	20750	23370	18070	10490	18980	12390
20													
21	Minimum	7990	10060	6340	7210	6390	6760	8420	4550	7090	8690	8000	8590
22	Maximum	40310	23710	29580	33810	23280	20570	26490	36460	23240	25940	24960	26180
23													
24													
25					Format Extremes								
26													

This task is accomplished with the **FormatExtremes** and **ChangeFont** subs listed below. The FormatExtremes sub is the "main" sub. (It is attached to the button on the sheet.) It loops through all of the cells in the Sales range with a pair of nested For loops. For each cell, it calls the ChangeFont sub to change the font of the cell appropriately (if the sales value in this cell is an extreme for the month). Four arguments are passed to ChangeFont sub: the address of the cell, the sales value in the cell, the minimum sales value for the month, and the maximum sales value for the month. All of these arguments have the same names in the called sub as in the calling sub, but they could be different and the program would still work correctly.

```
Sub FormatExtremes()
    Dim NMonths As Integer, NRegions As Integer, i As Integer, j As Integer, _
        MinVal As Single, MaxVal As Single, Addr As String, SalesVal As Single
    NMonths = Range("Sales").Columns.Count
    NRegions = Range("Sales").Rows.Count
    For j = 1 To NMonths
        MinVal = Range("Minimums").Cells(j)
        MaxVal = Range("Maximums").Cells(j)
        For i = 1 To NRegions
            Addr = Range("Sales").Cells(i, j).Address
            SalesVal = Range("Sales").Cells(i, j)
            Call ChangeFont(Addr, SalesVal, MinVal, MaxVal)
        Next
    Next
End Sub

Sub ChangeFont(Addr As String, SalesVal As Single, MinVal As Single, MaxVal As Single)
    With ActiveSheet.Range(Addr)
        If SalesVal = MinVal Then
            .Font.ColorIndex = 3
            .Font.Italic = True
        ElseIf SalesVal = MaxVal Then
            .Font.ColorIndex = 5
            .Font.Bold = True
        End If
    End With
End Sub
```

Note how general the ChangeFont sub is. It could easily be used in any other program that needs to change the font of particular cells. All we need to pass to it are the address of a cell, a sales value, and minimum and maximum sales values to compare to. By the way, if you run this program (by clicking on the button), the results will appear as in Figure 10.5.

Passing by Reference and by Value (Optional)

When you pass a variable such as LastName from one sub to another, the default method is **by reference**. This means that the variables in the calling and the called subs share the same memory location, so that any changes to LName in the called sub will be reflected in the calling sub. For example, suppose LastName has value "Jones" when it is passed, and then the called sub changes it in a line such as

```
LName = "Smith"
```

Figure 10.5 Formatted cells

	Jan	Feb	Mar	Apr	May	Jun	Jul	Aug	Sep	Oct	Nov	Dec
Sales by region and month												
Region 1	25630	19660	15270	**33810**	19360	15770	22490	8350	18310	18160	14040	10680
Region 2	18490	*10060*	13150	17350	12120	16940	24120	*4550*	13920	11020	10370	*8590*
Region 3	13360	12630	20350	10850	17650	**20570**	18500	36460	7530	11880	18110	18760
Region 4	17280	22930	19310	12230	16490	*6760*	12850	18930	16640	13590	8180	10830
Region 5	10970	10550	11780	*7210*	**23280**	7320	15840	19690	19280	*8690*	9810	10540
Region 6	*7990*	14690	20680	17130	12620	7400	*8420*	13810	*7090*	8990	12570	15260
Region 7	**40310**	10820	18310	13900	*6390*	13290	12980	28440	15530	**25940**	16600	18160
Region 8	10770	18250	**29580**	21020	10200	9380	15210	5750	13710	11770	10820	23160
Region 9	10530	14170	24630	16910	21670	11750	10470	19150	20170	13370	20600	**26180**
Region 10	8600	22950	14080	16760	17270	16670	18650	10370	12040	13810	*8000*	11690
Region 11	11510	15660	16870	17930	15110	7760	12090	10260	**23240**	14760	15430	16540
Region 12	10360	11490	15000	14060	9770	13110	24320	24500	13300	15610	21040	12620
Region 13	18670	12350	20450	9860	16730	10100	12870	11390	16220	11760	18480	13330
Region 14	16360	18640	17050	24230	10760	14420	16730	17260	22470	11980	10710	19640
Region 15	20760	13610	*6340*	12510	14570	11930	**26490**	21130	21530	20390	**24960**	16100
Region 16	18690	**23710**	10530	18050	17730	7230	20750	23370	18070	10490	18980	12390
Minimum	7990	10060	6340	7210	6390	6760	8420	4550	7090	8690	8000	8590
Maximum	40310	23710	29580	33810	23280	20570	26490	36460	23240	25940	24960	26180

[Format Extremes]

Then the value of LastName will be "Smith" when control passes back to the calling sub.

If this is *not* the behavior you want, you can pass the variable **by value**. This sends a *copy* of LastName to the called sub, so that any changes made there to LName are *not* reflected in the calling sub. In the above example, LastName would remain "Jones" in the calling sub. If you want to pass by value, the called sub must have the keyword **ByVal** next to the argument, as in

```
Sub DisplayName(ByVal LName As String, ByVal FName As String)
```

On the other hand, if you want to emphasize that you are passing by reference, you can write

```
Sub DisplayName(ByRef LName As String, ByRef FName As String)
```

However, the keyword **ByRef** is never really necessary because passing by reference is the default method. Because it is the method we use in all later examples, you will never see either keyword, **ByRef** or **ByVal**.

Passing Arrays (Optional)

Consider the following scenario. You have written a general-purpose sub called SortNames that takes any array of last names and sorts them in alphabetical order. (The details of how it does this are irrelevant for now.) You would like to be able to call SortNames from any sub by passing any array of last names to it. In particular, you want this to work regardless of the *size* of the array being passed. That is, it should work for a 10-element array, a 1000-element array, or an array of any other size. What is the appropriate way to proceed?[18]

The following code will do the job. (The *OtherStatements* line indicates the detailed code for sorting. It is not relevant for the point we're making here.)

```
Sub CallingSub()
    Dim Names(100) As String
    For i = 1 To 100
        Names(i) = Range("Names").Cells(i)
    Next
    Call SortNames(Names)
End Sub

Sub SortNames(Names() As String)
    Dim NNames As Integer
    NNames = UBound(Names)
    OtherStatements
End Sub
```

The calling sub stores 100 names in an array of size 100. (It populates this array by pulling the names from a worksheet range, which we assume is filled with 100 last names.) It then passes the Names array to the SortNames sub with the line

```
Call SortNames(Names)
```

Note that there are no parentheses next to Names in this line. We know Names is an array only because it was declared earlier to be an array. On the other end, the first line of the SortNames sub uses empty parentheses next to the Names argument to indicate that it is expecting an array. It will know how large an array to work with only when an array of a specific size is passed to it.

If desired, you can determine the size of the array that has been passed to SortNames by writing the line

```
NNames = UBound(Names)
```

somewhere inside the SortNames sub. The VBA **UBound** function returns the largest index in the array.[19] Therefore, when an array of size 100 is passed to SortNames, NNames becomes 100. If an array of size 1000 were passed instead, NNames would be 1000. The point is that this procedure works regardless of the size of the array that is passed.

10.6 Function Subroutines

The subroutines to this point—the things we have called subs—can perform virtually any task. They can sort numbers in a worksheet, they can create and manipu-

---

[18]This section is included because passing arrays is a common operation, and most VBA books don't tell you how to do it!

[19]This assumes 1-based indexing. If the default 0-based indexing is in effect, **UBound** returns 1 less than the number of array elements. In this case it would return 99.

late charts, they can add or delete worksheets, and so on. This section discusses a special type of subroutine called a **function subroutine** that has a much more specific objective—to return a value. The following simple example illustrates one possibility. It returns the larger of two numbers passed to it (Number1 and Number2) in the variable Larger.

```
Function Larger(Number1 As Single, Number2 as Single) As Single
    If Number1 >= Number2 Then
        Larger = Number1
    Else
        Larger = Number2
    End If
End Function
```

This function subroutine looks a lot like a normal sub. For example, it can take arguments, in this case Number1 and Number2, both of String type. However, it has some important differences:

- Instead of beginning with Sub and ending with End Sub, it begins with **Function** and ends with **End Function**.
- It returns a certain *type* of variable, in this case Single. This type is specified in the first line, after the argument list.
- It returns the value assigned to its name. In the example, the return value will come from one of the two lines that start **Larger =**. For example, if the numbers 3 and 5 are passed to this function, it will return 5.

A function subroutine can be used in one of two ways. It can be called by another sub (or even another function subroutine), or it can be used as a new spreadsheet function. Here is an example of the first method, where the calling sub calls Larger in the next-to-last line.

```
Sub CallingSub()
    Dim FirstNumber As Single, SecondNumber As Single
    FirstNumber = 3
    SecondNumber = 5
    MsgBox "The larger of the two numbers is " & Larger(FirstNumber, _
        SecondNumber)
End Sub
```

The message box will report that the larger number is 5. (Note once again that the variables being passed can have different names from the arguments of the function, but they should agree in number, type, and order.)

To illustrate the second method, open a new workbook in Excel, get into the VBE, insert a new module, and type the code for the Larger function exactly as above. Now enter the *formula* **=Larger(5,3)** in any cell. It will recognize your new function, and it will correctly enter 5 in the cell.

This creates a whole new realm of possibilities for you as a programmer. You can define your own functions and then use them in Excel formulas! You might not need to do this very often because Excel already includes so many of its own functions. However, there will undoubtedly be a *few* times when you want to take advantage of functions. Here are some things you should know.

- If you write the code for a function in Workbook1 and then try to use this function in a formula in Workbook2, it won't be recognized. The problem is that Workbook2 recognizes only the functions written in *its* modules. There are at least two solutions to this problem. First, you can set a **reference** to Workbook1 in Workbook2. To do so, make sure Workbook1 is open. Then activate Workbook2, get into the VBE, select the Tools/References menu item, and check the Workbook1 box. The only problem with this method is that Workbook1 must be open. A better method is to put all of your favorite functions in your **Personal.xls** file (recall Chapter 5). Then set a reference to it in any workbook where you want to use these functions. The advantage of this method is that the Personal.xls file is always open (unless you deliberately close it).

- Suppose you want to write a function that accepts one or more *lists* as arguments. In particular, these lists might come from worksheet ranges. For example, suppose you want to emulate Excel's Sum function. Then the following code will work:

```
Function MySum(Values As Variant) As Single
    Dim v As Variant, Total As Single
    For Each v In Values
        Total = Total + v
    Next
    MySum = Total
End Function
```

The point here is that the Values argument, which contains the list of values to be summed, must be declared as a Variant, even though it acts like a collection. This enables us to use the For Each loop inside the function. Importantly, this list could come from a worksheet range, as illustrated in Figure 10.6. The gray cells contain row and column sums, indicated by the typical formula in the text box. It is even possible to copy this formula across and down, just like any other Excel formula.

Figure 10.6 Using the MySum function in a worksheet

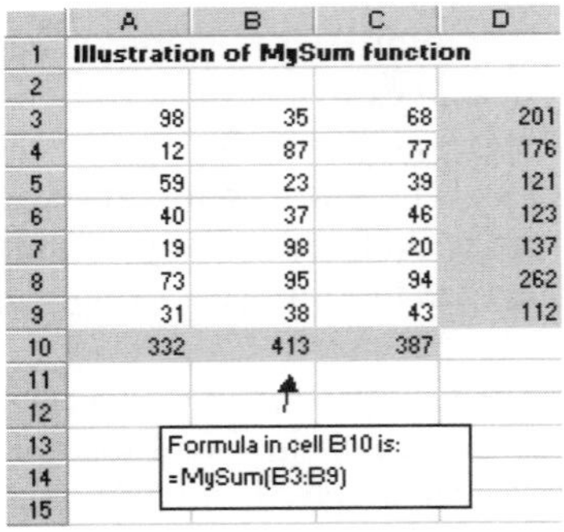

EXAMPLE 10.3   Concatenating Names

This example illustrates a useful string function called FullName. It is *not* a built-in Excel function. Instead, it is a function written by us, not Microsoft, and is defined by the code listed below. (You can find this code in the **Functions.xls** file.) The function takes four arguments: a person's first name, last name, initial (if any), and a Boolean variable. The Boolean variable is True if the initial is the person's *middle* initial, and it is False if the initial is really the initial of the person's first name (in which case, the "first name" argument is really the person's middle name). The "initial" argument can have a period after it, or it can have no period. (The code uses VBA's **Left** function, with last argument 1, to chop off the period in case there is one. Then the code adds a period, just to ensure that there is one after the initial.) Also, the "initial" argument can be an empty string (no initial in the name), in which case the Boolean value is irrelevant.

```
Function FullName(FName As String, LName As String, Initial As String, Middle As Boolean) _
    As String
    If Initial = "" Then
        FullName = FName & " " & LName
    ElseIf Middle Then
        FullName = FName & " " & Left(Initial, 1) & ". " & LName
    Else
        FullName = Left(Initial, 1) & ". " & FName & " " & LName
    End If
End Function
```

Figure 10.7 illustrates the use of this function. The "inputs" to the function are in rows 1 to 3. The formulas in cells A5 to C5 are

=FullName(A2,A3,A1,FALSE)

=FullName(B1,B3,B2,TRUE)

and

=FullName(C1,C3,C2,TRUE)

Note that the arguments after FullName must be in the correct order: first name, last name, initial, and Boolean. However, they could come from any cells in the spreadsheet. Also, note that Abraham Lincoln has no middle initial. Therefore, the Boolean value in the cell C5 formula is irrelevant—it could be TRUE or FALSE.

Figure 10.7   FullName examples

	A	B	C
1	S.	Wayne	Abraham
2	Christian	L	
3	Albright	Winston	Lincoln
4			
5	S. Christian Albright	Wayne L. Winston	Abraham Lincoln

EXAMPLE 10.4   Generating Random Numbers

If you have done any spreadsheet simulation, you know the need for random numbers from various probability distributions. Some simulation add-ins such as @Risk have their own collections of random number functions. This example illustrates a simple function you can write and use in your own simulations, *without* the need for an add-in like @Risk. It generates random integers that are equally likely to be anywhere within a given range, such as 1 to 100. The name of the function, DUniform, stands for "discrete uniform." Its code is listed below. (It is stored in the file **Functions.xls**.)

```
Function DUniform(LoLim As Integer, HiLim As Integer) As Integer
    Application.Volatile
    Randomize
    DUniform = Int((HiLim - LoLim + 1) * Rnd) + LoLim
End Function
```

Several points might require some explanation:

- The **Application.Volatile** line ensures that if this function is entered in a worksheet, it will recalculate (and thereby generate a *different* random number) each time the worksheet recalculates.
- The **Randomize** line ensures that you won't get the *same* random number each time this function is called. (This would certainly destroy the function's usefulness in simulation.)
- The **Rnd** function is a built-in VBA function similar to Excel's RAND function. It generates random numbers uniformly distributed between 0 and 1. The **Int** function then chops off the decimal so that the result in the next-to-last line is an integer. The rest of this line ensures that the integer is between LoLim and HiLim (inclusive).

This function is illustrated in Figure 10.8, where several random numbers from 100 to 500 are generated. (See the RandomNumbers sheet in the **Functions.xls** file.) The formula in cell A7, which is then copied down, is

=DUniform($B$3,$B$4)

If you open this file and recalculate (by pressing the F9 key, for example), you will see that all of the random numbers change.

If you want to use this function or develop your own random number functions, you will probably want it to be available regardless of which files are open. As discussed earlier, a good option is to place the code in your **Personal.xls** file. Then set a reference to the Personal.xls file in any file where you want to use the function. (Remember, you set a reference in the VBE from the Tools/References menu item.)

Figure 10.8 Discrete uniform random numbers

	A	B	C	D
1	Discrete Uniform random numbers			
2				
3	Lower limit	100		
4	Upper limit	500		
5				
6	Random numbers			
7	166			
8	361			
9	318			
10	236			
11	480			
12	149			
13	153			
14	140			
15	179			
16	464			
17	410			
18	115			
19	349			
20	449			
21	443			

10.7 The Workbook_Open Subroutine

All subroutines we have discussed to this point have been created, from scratch, by the programmer. VBA also includes a number of subroutines that can be used by a programmer to respond to various "events." These subroutines, called **event handlers**, will be discussed in much more detail in Chapter 12 when we introduce user forms. However, there is one simple event handler that we introduce here. It responds to the event where a workbook is opened. In short, if you want anything to occur when you open an Excel workbook, you can write the appropriate code in this subroutine.

Event handlers have built-in names—you have no control over the names given to these subroutines. The particular event handler discussed here has the name **Workbook_Open**. Also, it is a **Private** sub by default. Therefore, its first line is always the following:

```
Private Sub Workbook_Open()
```

Another distinguishing feature of this subroutine is that it is *not* placed in a module. Instead, it is stored in the **ThisWorkbook** code window. To get to this window, double-click on the ThisWorkbook item in the Project Explorer (see Figure 10.9). This opens a code window that looks just like a module code window, except that it is reserved for event handlers having to do with workbook events.

Figure 10.9 ThisWorkbook item in the Project Explorer

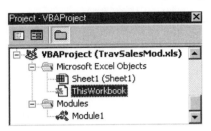

The code in a Workbook_Open sub is usually not very elaborate. A typical use of this sub is to ensure that a worksheet named Explanation is activated when a user opens a workbook. (We use it for this purpose in all of the applications in the second half of the book.) The following sub is all that is required:

```
Private Sub Workbook_Open()
    Worksheets("Explanation").Activate
End Sub
```

Of course, you could place other statements in this sub—to hide certain worksheets, for example. Again, if there are any actions you want to occur when a workbook opens, the Workbook_Open sub is the place to put them.

As you might guess, there is also a built-in event handler for the event where a workbook is *closed*. It is named **Workbook_BeforeClose**. Because this subroutine is somewhat more complex (it takes a rather obscure argument, for example) and is not used in later applications, we will not discuss it here. However, if you are interested, you can find online help for it in the Object Browser.

10.8 Summary

Long programs should not be written in a single long sub; this is considered bad style. In this chapter we have illustrated how to organize long programs into a sequence of shorter subs, each of which performs a specific task. The resulting code is easier to read and debug, and pieces of it are more likely to be reusable in other programs. We discussed how it is a good programming practice to pass arguments from one sub to another whenever possible. When this is done, the called subs can often be written in a totally self-contained manner, which allows them to be reused in other programs. We also introduced function subroutines. These perform the specific task of returning a value, and they can be called by other subs (even other function subroutines), or they can be used as new spreadsheet functions. Finally, we briefly introduced event handlers. Specifically, we illustrated how the Workbook_Open sub can be used to perform any desired actions when a workbook is opened.

PROGRAMMING EXERCISES

1. Open a new file with a single worksheet, and enter some numbers in the range A1:B10. (Any numbers will do.) Write a Main sub that has a For loop from i=1 to i=10. Each time through this loop, a sub Process should be called with three arguments: i and the two numbers in columns A and B of row i. The Process sub should enter the larger of the two numbers in column C of row i, and it should color its font red if the number in row A is the larger. Otherwise, it should color the font blue.

2. The file **CustLists.xls** contains lists of customers from 1999 and 2000 in columns A and B. Write a sub called FindMatch that takes a single argument CustName (a string variable). It checks whether this customer is in both lists. If it is, it displays a message to this effect, and it boldfaces both instances of the customer's name. Otherwise, it displays a message that the customer's name is *not* on both lists. Next, write a Main sub that uses an input box to ask for a customer name. Then it calls FindMatch with this customer's name as the argument.

3. The file **Wal-Mart.xls** contains monthly adjusted closing prices (adjusted for dividends and stock splits) for Wal-Mart stock from 1992 to early 2000.

    a. Write a sub called RecordHigh1 that takes a single argument called Price. This sub searches down the list of prices for the first price that exceeds the Price argument. If it finds one, it displays the corresponding date in a message, something as in "The first date Wal-Mart stock price exceeded _ was _." If the price never exceeded the argument Price, it displays a message to this effect. Next, write a Main sub that uses an input box to ask the user for a price and then calls RecordHigh1 with this price as the argument.

    b. Write another sub called RecordHigh2 that takes a single argument called SpecifiedMonth. This sub searches down the list of prices for the last time up until (and including) the specified month where the stock reached a record high (that is, it was larger than all prices before it, going back to the beginning of 1992). It then displays a message such as, "The most recent record, up until _, was in _, when the price reached _." (Note that Jan-92 is a record high by default, so at least one record high will always be found.) Change the Main sub from part **a** so that the input box now asks for a month and then calls RecordHigh2 with this month as an argument.

4. The file **BoyGirlFinished.xls** contains a sheet with scores for boys and girls. Open the file and click on the button. You'll see that it asks the user for 1 (boys) or 2 (girls). It then names the range of the scores for the chosen gender as DataRange, it enters a label and the average score for the chosen gender (as a *formula*) in cells D9 and E9, and it formats the D9:E9 range appropriately (blue font for boys, red font for girls). The code in this file is password-protected. Now open the **BoyGirl.xls** file, which contains only the data, and write your own code to perform the same tasks. It should contain a Main sub that calls the following subs: (1) GetResponse (to show the input box and get the user's response), (2) NameGenderRange (to name the appropriate range as DataRange), (3) FormatOutputRange (to format the output range D9:E9 appropriately), and

(4) EnterOutput (to enter a label in D9 and a formula in E9). Write your subs so that there are no module-level variables. Instead, a string variable Gender should be an argument of each called sub, where Gender can be "boys" or "girls". Also, write the program so that it will work even if more data are added to the data set.

5. Open a new workbook and write a sub called GetWorkbookInfo that takes an argument called FileName (a string). This sub attempts to open the file called FileName. Assuming that it is successful (the file exists), a message box displays the creator of the file and the number of worksheets in the file. It then closes the file. Next, write a Main sub that use an input box to ask for the name of a file, including its path information, and then calls GetWorkbookInfo with this file name as the argument. (Your GetWorkbookInfo will have one serious deficiency—it will bomb if the requested file doesn't exist, at least not in the specified path. Don't worry about this for now. We will see how to check for it in Chapter 13.)

6. The program in the **MergeLists.xls** file from the previous chapter (see Example 9.4) is written as a single sub.
   a. Break it into several shorter subs, all called from a Main sub. The called subs should be (1) ClearOld (to clear the old merged list in column D, if any), (2) GetData (to put the data in the current lists in arrays), and (3) CreateMergedList (to create the merged list in column D). Don't pass any variables; use all module-level variables for any shared variables.
   b. Repeat part **a**, but pass variables. In particular, the variables LS1 and LS2, and the arrays List1 and List2, should be arguments of both GetData and CreateMergedList. (*Hint*: Refer to the section in the chapter dealing with passing arrays as arguments.)

7. The program in the **ProdSales.xls** file from the previous chapter (see Example 9.2) is written as a single sub. Break it into at least three shorter subs, all called from a Main sub. You can decide how to break it up and whether you want to use module-level variables or pass arguments.

8. The file **RecentSalesFinished.xls** contains a list of a company's sales reps in the SalesReps sheet. For each of several midwest states, there is a sheet showing recent sales by the sales reps in that state. Open this file and click on the button on the SalesReps sheet. You'll see it asks for a sales rep and then a state, and it summarizes sales by that rep in that state in a message box. Run this several times (including queries for reps and states not in the company's list) to see all the functionality built in to it. The code in this file is password-protected. Now open the file **RecentSales.xls**, which contains only the data and a Main sub that calls some yet-to-be-written subs. Your job is to write the subs, using the arguments indicated in the Main sub, to achieve the same functionality.

9. The file **TransactionsFinished.xls** contains two sheets. The CustomersProducts sheet lists a company's customers and its products. The Transactions sheet lists information about recent transactions involving these customers and products. Open this file and click on the button on the CustomersProducts sheet. You'll be asked for a last name and a first name of a customer. If this customer is found on the list, you'll be asked for the name of a product. If this product is found on the list, a message will be displayed summarizing the sales of this product to this customer. Try it a few times (including queries for customers or products not in the

lists) to see how it works. The code in this file is password-protected. Now open the file **Transactions.xls**, which contains only the data and a Main sub that calls some yet-to-be-written subs. Your job is to write the subs, using the arguments indicated in the Main sub, to achieve the same functionality.

10. The file **Errors1.xls** contains a list of forecasting errors in column A made by some forecasting method. Write a function subroutine called MAE that finds the mean absolute error, that is, the average of the absolute values of the errors. It should be written to work on *any* range of errors such as the one in column A. Then try it out by entering the appropriate formula in cell E1.

11. The file **Errors2.xls** contains a time series of monthly sales in column A and a series of forecasts of these sales in column B. Write a function subroutine called MAPE that finds the mean absolute percentage error of the forecasts, that is, the average of the absolute percentage errors. For example, the absolute percentage error in row 2 is $|713 - 738| / 713 = 0.035$, or 3.5%. Write this function so that it will work with *any* two ranges of observations and corresponding forecasts. Then try it out by entering the appropriate formula in cell E1.

12. The **triangular** distribution is a probability distribution that is commonly used in business simulations. It is literally triangularly shaped. There are three parameters to this distribution, which we'll label a, b, and c. The parameters a and c are the minimum and maximum possible values, and the parameter b is the most likely value (where you see the high point of the triangle). This is a simple distribution for people to understand, but it is a bit complex to generate random numbers from this distribution. The method is as follows:

- Calculate $d = (b - a)/(c - a)$.
- Generate a uniformly distributed random number U between 0 and 1 (with VBA's Rnd function).
- If $U \le d$, then $a + (c - a)\sqrt{dU}$ is the required random number.
- If $U > d$, then $a + (c - a)[1 - \sqrt{(1 - d)(1 - U)}]$ is the required random number.

(VBA has a built-in Sqr function for taking square roots.) Write a function subroutine called Triangular that takes three arguments, corresponding to a, b, and c, and returns a triangularly distributed random number. (Use the Application.Volatile and Randomize statements that were used in Example 10.4.) Then try out your random number generator in a worksheet by entering the formula and copying it down to generate a large number of these random numbers. You might also want to create a histogram of these random numbers, just to see if it has an approximate triangle shape.

Working with the Solver Add-In in VBA

11.1 Introduction

There are many add-ins for Excel that have been developed by third-party software companies. Many of these companies have provided VBA capabilities that programmers can use to manipulate the add-ins. Specifically, this is true of the Solver optimization add-in that is part of Microsoft Office. The Solver can be manipulated not only through the familiar menu interface (with the Tools/Solver menu item), but it can also be manipulated "behind the scenes" with VBA code. This chapter will explain how to do it.

Although this chapter discusses the Solver add-in only, you should be aware that many other add-ins can also be manipulated with VBA—and the number will certainly continue to grow. Two examples are the Analysis ToolPak that is part of Microsoft Office and the @Risk simulation add-in.[20] In each case, programmers must search for help (hopefully online help) that specifies the VBA functions available with the add-in. These functions are *not* part of Excel VBA, and they are not always well documented by the companies that have developed them. However, as this chapter will indicate, they can be very powerful tools for VBA development.

11.2 Exercise

This exercise requires you to run the Solver on an existing model with VBA code. Because the size of the problem can change, based on the value of a user input, the VBA code must respecify the Solver settings before running the Solver.

Exercise 11.1 Scheduling Production

Consider a company that must plan its monthly production of footballs. It begins month 1 with a given number of footballs on hand, and at the beginning of each month, it must decide how many footballs to produce. There are three constraints: (1) The quantity on hand after production must be at least as large as that month's (known) demand, (2) production in a month can never exceed production capacity, and (3) the ending inventory in any month can never exceed the

---

[20]If you have ever loaded the Analysis ToolPak with the Tools/Add-Ins menu item, you have probably noticed that there is an "Analysis ToolPak – VBA" box you can check. This gives you access to the VBA functions that accompany the Analysis ToolPak.

storage capacity. We assume that production and storage capacity remain constant through the planning period. There are two costs: (1) the unit production cost, which increases gradually through the planning period, and (2) the unit holding cost, which is a percentage of the unit production cost and is charged on each month's ending inventory.

The file **Production.xls** contains a model for finding the company's minimum-cost production schedule for any planning period up to 12 months. (See Figure 11.1.) The inputs are in shaded cells, the decision variables (changing cells) are in row 12, and row 28 shows the cumulative total costs up through any month. The current model uses a planning period of 12 months, and the solution shown in Figure 11.1 is optimal for this planning period. The Solver settings appear in Figures 11.2 and 11.3. Note that rows 12, 14, 16, 18, 20, and 22 (columns B to M) have been range-named Produced, ProdCap, Onhand, Demand, EndInv, and StorCap, respectively. Also, cell M28 has range name TotCost. These range names are provided to make the Solver setup in Figure 11.2 easier to read.

The purpose of the exercise is to develop a sub that asks the user for a planning period from 4 to 12 months. (You can also have it ask for other inputs, such as the initial inventory and the holding cost percentage, if you like.) Based on the length of the planning period, the sub should then rename the ranges in rows 14 to 22 and row 28 appropriately (using only the months in the planning period), it should reset the Solver (the VBA equivalent of clicking on the Reset All button in Figure 11.2) and then respecify the Solver settings in Figures 11.2 and 11.3, and finally it should run the Solver. Note that if you rename the ranges appropriately, the Solver window will always end up looking like the one in Figure 11.2, but it *is* necessary to reset and then respecify the settings when the physical ranges change. As an added touch, you might try "hiding" the columns in Figure 11.1 that are not used—for example, columns L and M for a 10-month model.

Figure 11.1 Production model

	A	B	C	D	E	F	G	H	I	J	K	L	M
1	**Multiperiod production model**												
2													
3	**Input data**												
4	Initial inventory (100s)	50											
5	Holding cost (% of prod cost)	5%											
6													
7	Month	1	2	3	4	5	6	7	8	9	10	11	12
8	Production cost/unit	$12.50	$12.55	$12.70	$12.80	$12.85	$12.95	$12.95	$13.00	$13.00	$13.10	$13.10	$13.20
9													
10	**Production plan (all quantities are in 100s of footballs)**												
11	Month	1	2	3	4	5	6	7	8	9	10	11	12
12	Units produced	50	200	300	300	250	100	150	300	300	300	300	250
13		<=	<=	<=	<=	<=	<=	<=	<=	<=	<=	<=	<=
14	Production capacity (100s)	300	300	300	300	300	300	300	300	300	300	300	300
15													
16	On hand after production	100	200	350	350	250	100	150	330	320	370	310	250
17		>=	>=	>=	>=	>=	>=						
18	Demand	100	150	300	350	250	100	120	310	250	360	310	250
19													
20	Ending inventory	0	50	50	0	0	0	30	20	70	10	0	0
21		<=	<=	<=	<=	<=	<=	<=	<=	<=	<=	<=	<=
22	Storage capacity	100	100	100	100	100	100	100	100	100	100	100	100
23													
24	**Summary of costs (all costs are in hundreds of dollars)**												
25	Month	1	2	3	4	5	6	7	8	9	10	11	12
26	Production costs	$625	$2,510	$3,810	$3,840	$3,213	$1,295	$1,943	$3,900	$3,900	$3,930	$3,930	$3,300
27	Holding costs	$0	$31	$32	$0	$0	$0	$19	$13	$46	$7	$0	$0
28	Cumulative total	$625	$3,166	$7,008	$10,848	$14,061	$15,356	$17,318	$21,231	$25,176	$29,113	$33,043	$36,343

Figure 11.2 Solver setup

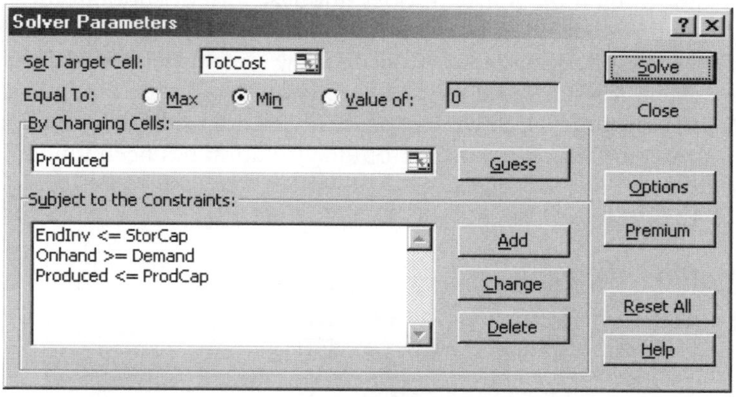

Figure 11.3 Solver Options window

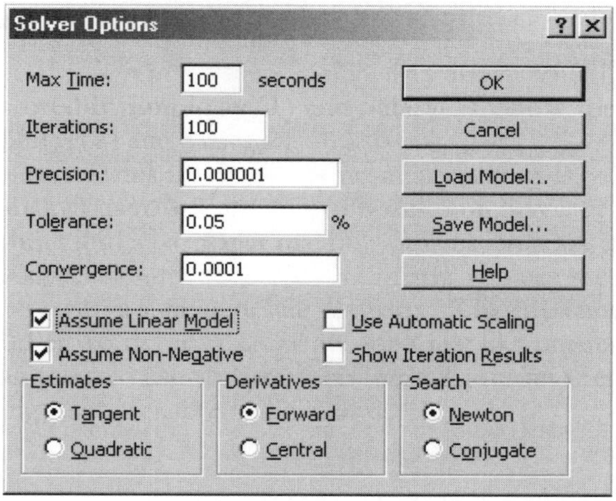

The file **ProductionFinished.xls** contains one possible solution. Feel free to open it and click on its button to run it. However, do not look at the VBA code until you have tried writing it yourself.

11.3   Invoking the Solver in VBA

Many of the applications in the remaining chapters are optimization models, where Excel's Solver is invoked to obtain an optimal solution. This section explains briefly how to do this. It makes two important assumptions. First, it assumes that you have some familiarity with the Solver and know how to use it in the usual menu-driven way. Second, it assumes that an optimization model already exists. That is, the inputs and the formulas relating all quantities must already have been entered in a worksheet. This section deals only with specifying the Solver settings and running the Solver; it does not deal with the optimization model itself.

As you probably know, the Solver is an add-in written by Frontline Systems, *not* by Microsoft. It has a very user-friendly Excel interface, shown by the dialog boxes in Figures 11.4 and 11.5, where you describe the model, set options, and eventually click on the Solve button.[21] If all goes well, you obtain the dialog box in Figure 11.6, indicating that an optimal solution has been found.

Figure 11.4 Solver Parameters dialog box

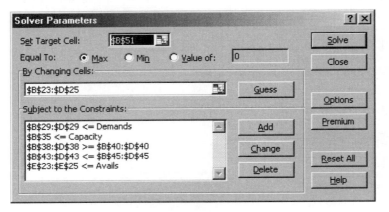

Figure 11.5 Solver Options dialog box

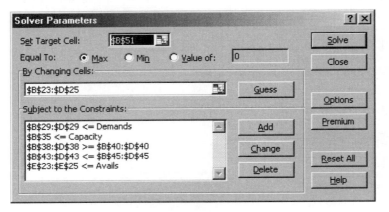

---

[21]If you have the version of Solver that comes with Excel, the Premium button in Figure 11.4 will not appear. The dialog box we show here is for the Premium Solver, a special version that is included in *Practical Management Science.* However, this has no effect on the discussion in this chapter.

Figure 11.6 Solver Results dialog box

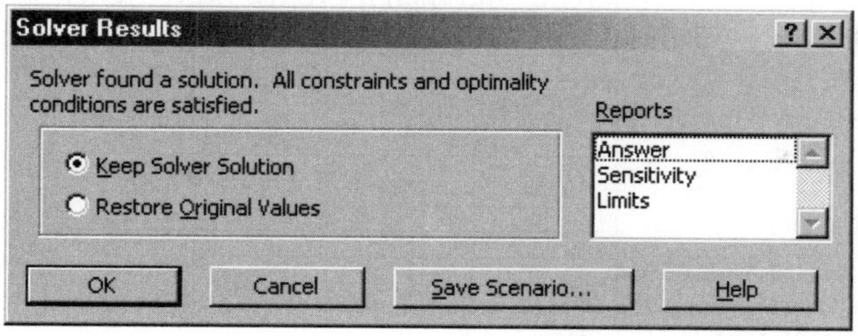

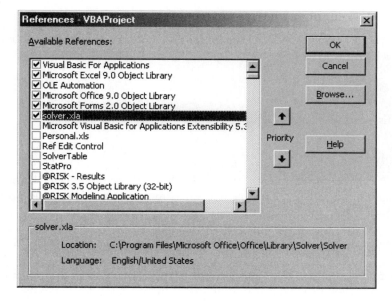

Fortunately, Frontline Systems has written several VBA functions that allow developers to operate Solver "behind the scenes" with code. These functions enable you to specify the model (target cell, changing cells, and constraints), set options, optimize, and even capture the message in Figure 11.6 (which might be that there is no feasible solution, for example).

Setting a Reference

To use these functions in an application, the first step is to set a **reference** to the Solver add-in in the VBE. Otherwise, VBA will not recognize the Solver functions and you will get a "Sub or function not defined" error message. You set the reference with the Tools/References menu item in the VBE. This brings up a long list of possible "libraries" of code to choose from. One of these should be **Solver.xla**, as shown in Figure 11.7. To add the reference, simply check its box. The reference

Figure 11.7 List of potential references

will then appear in the Project Explorer window, as shown in Figure 11.8. Again, if you forget to set this reference and then try to use Solver functions in your code, you will get an error message.

Figure 11.8 Reference in Project Explorer window

Solver Functions

All of the Solver functions begin with the word Solver. The ones used most often are SolverReset, SolverOk, SolverAdd, SolverOptions, and SolverSolve. This section explains each of these briefly. More detailed help on these and other Solver functions can be obtained from Frontline Systems' Web site at www.frontsys.com/mlvbaref.htm. (Keep this address handy; it is difficult to find help on the Solver functions anywhere else.) The information you will need is the following.

SolverReset Function

To reset the Solver (which is equivalent to clicking on the Reset All button in Figure 11.4), use the line

```
SolverReset
```

This clears all previous settings and lets you start with a clean slate.

SolverOk Function

This function does three things: (1) It identifies the target cell (the objective), (2) it specifies whether the problem is a maximization or minimization problem, and (3) it identifies the changing cells. The following line is typical:

```
SolverOk SetCell:=Range("Profit"), MaxMinVal:=1, ByChange:=Range("Quantities")
```

Note that the **MaxMinVal** argument is 1 for a maximization problem and 2 for a minimization problem. Also, note that if there are several changing cell ranges (so that you would enter them, separated by commas, in the usual Solver dialog box), you can use **Union** in the **ByChange** argument. For example, you could write the following to indicate that there are two ranges of changing cells: the Quantities range and the Prices range.

```
SolverOk SetCell:=Range("Profit"), MaxMinVal:=1, _
    ByChange:=Union(Range("Quantities"),Range("Prices"))
```

SolverAdd Function

This function adds a new constraint each time it is called. It takes three arguments: a left-hand side, a relation index, and a right-hand side. The relation index is 1 for "<=", 2 for "=", 3 for ">=", 4 for "integer", and 5 for "binary". (This is the same order in which they appear in the Solver Add Constraint dialog box. Also, note that there is no right-hand-side argument for the latter two options.) The first and third arguments are specified differently. The left-hand side must be specified as a range, whereas the right-hand side must be specified as a string or a number. Here are several possibilities:

```
SolverAdd CellRef:=Range("Used"), Relation:=1, FormulaText:="Available"
SolverAdd CellRef:=Range("EndInventory"), Relation:=3, FormulaText:=0
SolverAdd CellRef:=Range("Investments"), Relation:=5
```

The first states that the Used range must be less than or equal to the Available range. The second states that the EndInventory range must be greater than or equal to 0. The third states that the Investments range must be binary.

SolverOptions Function

This function allows you to set any of the options in Figure 11.5. The two you will probably set most frequently are the Assume Linear Model and Assume Non-Negative options. They can be set as follows.

```
SolverOptions AssumeLinear:=True, AssumeNonneg:=True
```

This is equivalent to checking the Assume Linear Model and Assume Non-Negative boxes in Figure 11.5. In general, *any* number of options can follow the SolverOptions function (all separated by commas).

SolverSolve Function

This function is equivalent to clicking the Solve button in the usual Solver dialog box—it performs the optimization. There are two things you should know about SolverSolve. First, if it is used with the argument **UserFinish:=True**, then the dialog box in Figure 11.6 will *not* appear. This dialog box could be a nuisance to a nontechnical user, so it is often convenient to keep it from appearing with the line

```
SolverSolve UserFinish:=True
```

If you *want* the dialog box in Figure 11.6 to appear, just delete the UserFinish:
=True part (or use UserFinish:=False, the default value).

Second, the SolverSolve function returns an integer value that indicates
Solver's "success." If this integer is 0, it means that Solver was successful, with the
message in Figure 11.6. Actually, the integers 1 and 2 also indicate success, with
slightly different messages. In contrast, the integer 4 means that Solver did not
converge, and the integer 5 means that there are no feasible solutions. (More details are on the Web site given earlier.) You can check for any of these and proceed
accordingly. For example, the following lines are common. They run Solver, check
for feasibility, and display an appropriate message if there are no feasible solutions.

```
Dim Result As Integer
Result = SolverSolve(UserFinish:=True)
If Result = 5 Then
    MsgBox "There are no feasible solutions."
    End
Else
    Worksheets("Report").Activate
End If
```

Actually, the Result variable is not really necessary in this code; it could be shortened to the following:

```
If SolverSolve(UserFinish:=True) = 5 Then
    MsgBox "There are no feasible solutions."
    End
Else
    Worksheets("Report").Activate
End If
```

Note the syntax. The UserFinish:=True is inside parentheses if the integer result of
this function is used. If it is not used, then the argument is usually *not* put in parentheses, as in

```
SolverSolve UserFinish:=True
```

This syntax is common to all functions in VBA, not just to Solver functions. Parentheses are required if the function's value is used; otherwise, parentheses are
typically omitted.

Some applications require *only* the SolverSolve function. Their Solver dialog
boxes can be set up manually (with the Solver dialog box, not with VBA) at design
time. Then all that is required at run time is to optimize. Other applications, such
as Exercise 11.1, require a SolverReset line, and then SolverOk, SolverAdd, and
SolverOptions lines, before SolverSolve can be called. That is, they must set up the
model completely—at run time—before they can optimize. This is usually the case
when the *size* of the model changes from run to run.

EXAMPLE 11.1 Optimal Product Mix

The file **ProductMix.xls** contains a typical product mix linear programming model. (It is the same as the product mix model in Chapter 3 of *Practical Management Science*.) A company must decide how many frames of four different types to produce to maximize profit. There are two types of constraints: (1) resources used (labor hours, glass, and metal) must not exceed resources available, and (2) production must not exceed maximum quantities that can be sold. The model appears in Figure 11.9 with an optimal solution. (You can open the file and examine the various formulas. They are all quite straightforward.) The Solver dialog box, filled in manually, appears in Figure 11.10.

The purpose of the example is to generate a sensitivity table in the range G4:L12, as indicated in Figure 11.9. Specifically, for each multiple in column G, we want to replace the original maximum sales values in row 18 by the multiple of these values, run Solver, and report the numbers of frames produced and the corresponding profit in the sensitivity table. Note that when the multiple is "unlimited," there is no maximum sales constraint at all. In that case, there should be only one constraint in the Solver dialog box. The results will appear as in Figure 11.11.

Figure 11.9 Model with optimal solution

	A	B	C	D	E	F	G	H	I	J	K	L
1	**Product mix model**											
2												
3	**Input data**						**Sensitivity to multiples of maximum sales**					
4	Hourly wage rate	$8.00		Run sensitivity analysis			Multiple	Frame1	Frame2	Frame3	Frame4	Profit
5	Cost per oz of metal	$0.50					0.50					
6	Cost per oz of glass	$0.75					0.75					
7							1.00					
8	Frame type	1	2	3	4		1.25					
9	Labor hours per frame	2	1	3	2		1.50					
10	Metal (oz.) per frame	4	2	1	2		1.75					
11	Glass (oz.) per frame	6	2	1	2		2.00					
12	Unit selling price	$28.50	$12.50	$29.25	$21.50		Unlimited					
13												
14	**Production plan**											
15	Frame type	1	2	3	4		**Range names used:**					
16	Frames produced	1000	800	400	0		Produced - B16:E16					
17		<=	<=	<=	<=		MaxSales - B18:E18					
18	Maximum sales	1000	2000	500	1000		Used - B21:B23					
19							Available - D21:D23					
20	**Resource constraints**	Used		Available			TotProfit - F32					
21	Labor hours	4000	<=	4000			Multiples - G5:G12					
22	Metal (oz.)	6000	<=	6000								
23	Glass (oz.)	8000	<=	10000								
24												
25	**Revenue, cost summary**											
26	Frame type	1	2	3	4	Totals						
27	Revenue	$28,500	$10,000	$11,700	$0	$50,200						
28	Costs of inputs											
29	Labor	$16,000	$6,400	$9,600	$0	$32,000						
30	Metal	$2,000	$800	$200	$0	$3,000						
31	Glass	$4,500	$1,200	$300	$0	$6,000						
32	Profit	$6,000	$1,600	$1,600	$0	$9,200						

Figure 11.10 Solver dialog box

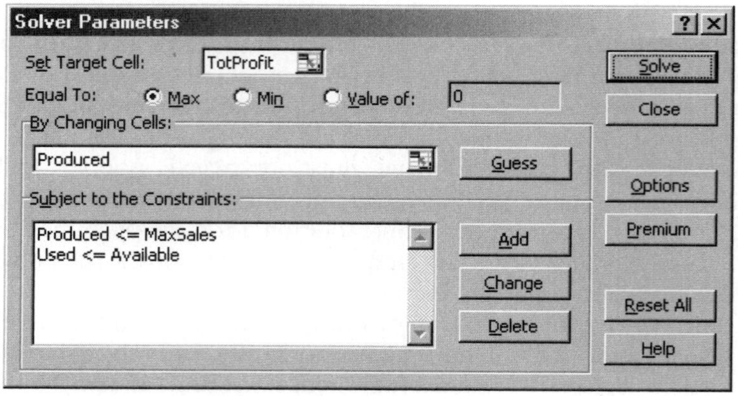

Figure 11.11 Completed sensitivity table

	G	H	I	J	K	L
3	Sensitivity to multiples of maximum sales					
4	Multiple	Frame1	Frame2	Frame3	Frame4	Profit
5	0.50	500	1000	250	500	$7,500
6	0.75	750	1250	375	63	$8,688
7	1.00	1000	800	400	0	$9,200
8	1.25	1250	300	400	0	$9,700
9	1.50	1400	0	400	0	$10,000
10	1.75	1400	0	400	0	$10,000
11	2.00	1400	0	400	0	$10,000
12	Unlimited	1400	0	400	0	$10,000

To develop this project, the first step is to open the VBE and add a reference to Solver.xla. Then the following VBA code does the job. The "main" sub, called **Sensitivity**, is attached to the button in Figure 11.9. Its basic function is to call a number of other subs to perform the various tasks. Note that three of these subs, **ChangeModel**, **RunSolver**, and **StoreResults**, are called within a For Each loop that loops over all cells in the Multiples range. Also, note how an argument is passed to each of these subs. More explanation on the various subs is provided below.

```
Option Explicit
Option Base 1

Dim MaxSales(4) As Single

Sub Sensitivity()
    Dim cell As Range, Mult As Variant, ModelCounter As Integer, IncludeConstraint As Boolean
    Application.ScreenUpdating = False
    Call SaveOriginalValues
    ModelCounter = 0
    For Each cell In Range("Multiples")
        ModelCounter = ModelCounter + 1
        Mult = cell.Value
        If IsNumeric(Mult) Then IncludeConstraint = True
```

```
        Call ChangeModel(Mult)
        Call RunSolver(IncludeConstraint)
        Call StoreResults(ModelCounter)
    Next
    Call RestoreOriginalValues
End Sub
```

The first sub called, **SaveOriginalValues**, stores the original maximum sales values in the MaxSales array for later use.

```
Sub SaveOriginalValues()
    Dim i As Integer
    For i = 1 To 4
        MaxSales(i) = Range("MaxSales").Cells(i)
    Next
End Sub
```

The **ChangeModel** sub takes the Mult argument and checks whether it is numeric with VBA's handy **IsNumeric** function. If it is, the sub multiplies the original maximum sales values by Mult and places these multiples in the MaxSales range.

```
Sub ChangeModel(Mult As Variant)
    Dim i As Integer
    If IsNumeric(Mult) Then
        For i = 1 To 4
            Range("MaxSales").Cells(i) = Mult * MaxSales(i)
        Next
    End If
End Sub
```

The **RunSolver** sub first resets the Solver and then sets it up from scratch. It takes a Boolean argument, IncludeConstraint. If this value is True (because Mult is numeric), then the maximum sales constraint is included; otherwise, it is not included. Note that if *all* values of Mult in column G were numeric, then only the SolverSolve line of this sub would be required. This is because the Solver setup, developed manually as in Figure 11.10, would never change. You might argue that with only one possible change (the inclusion or exclusion of the maximum sales constraint), it should not be necessary to reset and then respecify the Solver setup *entirely*. This argument is correct. It is indeed possible to delete or add a single constraint to an existing Solver setup, but we have taken the "reset" route here, primarily to illustrate the various Solver functions.

```
Sub RunSolver(IncludeConstraint As Boolean)
    SolverReset
    SolverOk SetCell:=Range("TotProfit"), MaxMinVal:=1, ByChange:=Range("Produced")
    SolverAdd CellRef:=Range("Used"), Relation:=1, FormulaText:="Available"
    If IncludeConstraint Then _
        SolverAdd CellRef:=Range("Produced"), Relation:=1, FormulaText:="MaxSales"
    SolverOptions AssumeLinear:=True, AssumeNonNeg:=True
    SolverSolve UserFinish:=True
End Sub
```

The **StoreResults** sub takes the Solver results in the Produced and TotProfit ranges and transfers them to the sensitivity table. It takes a single argument, ModelCounter, that specifies how far down the table to place the results. Note that ModelCounter is increased by 1 each time through the For Each loop in the Sensitivity sub.

```
Sub StoreResults(ModelCounter As Integer)
    Dim i As Integer
    With Range("G4")
        For i = 1 To 4
            .Offset(ModelCounter, i) = Range("Produced").Cells(i)
        Next
        .Offset(ModelCounter, 5) = Range("TotProfit")
    End With
End Sub
```

Finally, the **RestoreOriginalResults** sub places the original maximum sales values back in the MaxSales range and runs the Solver one last time. This is not absolutely necessary—by the time this sub is called, the sensitivity table is complete—but it is a nice touch. This way, the final thing the user sees is the solution to the original problem.

```
Sub RestoreOriginalValues()
    Dim i As Integer
    For i = 1 To 4
        Range("MaxSales").Cells(i) = MaxSales(i)
    Next
    Call RunSolver(True)
End Sub
```

11.4 A Solver VBA Bug

We have discovered one minor bug in the Solver VBA functions.[22] Suppose you have a model of varying size. On one run it might have 10 changing cells, whereas on another run it might have 20 changing cells. Therefore, a SolverReset is required, and all of the Solver dialog box settings must be respecified. Now suppose that at least one of the constraints is an integer or a binary constraint. Unfortunately, there are situations where the Solver will *ignore* such constraints, even though you specify them in your VBA code. A simple fix (which admittedly makes little sense, but it works) is to repeat a couple of lines of code: the SolverReset and SolverOK lines.

For example, suppose the changing cell range (InvLevel) in the following lines can change size from one run to the next. Then the Solver might ignore the fifth line, which makes the changing cells binary. (This example is from Chapter 21 of this book.)

---

[22] The technical support staff at Frontline Systems had not been aware of this bug until we called it to their attention, but they acknowledge that it *is* a bug, and they agree that the fix described here is as good as any.

```
SolverReset
SolverOK SetCell:=Range("TotNPV"), MaxMinVal:=1, ByChange:=Range("InvLevel")
SolverOptions IntTolerance:=0, AssumeLinear:=True
SolverAdd CellRef:=Range("TotCost"), Relation:=1, FormulaText:="Budget"
SolverAdd CellRef:=Range("InvLevel"), Relation:=5
SolverSolve UserFinish:=True
```

However, when the first two lines are repeated, as listed below, everything works fine—the binary constraint is *not* ignored.

```
SolverReset
SolverOK SetCell:=Range("TotNPV"), MaxMinVal:=1, ByChange:=Range("InvLevel")
' The two previous lines are repeated because of a bug in the Solver VBA functions.
' If they aren't repeated, the binary constraint might not be added!
SolverReset
SolverOK SetCell:=Range("TotNPV"), MaxMinVal:=1, ByChange:=Range("InvLevel")
SolverOptions IntTolerance:=0, AssumeLinear:=True
SolverAdd CellRef:=Range("TotCost"), Relation:=1, FormulaText:="Budget"
SolverAdd CellRef:=Range("InvLevel"), Relation:=5
SolverSolve UserFinish:=True
```

11.5 Summary

This chapter has illustrated how we can take advantage of VBA functions written by a third-party developer to run its add-in. Specifically, we have discussed Solver functions that can be used to perform optimization of an existing optimization model. These functions allow us to set up and run the Solver, completely with VBA. We will take advantage of this ability in several of the applications in the second half of the book.

PROGRAMMING EXERCISES

1. The file **ProdMix.xls** contains a typical product mix model. A company needs to decide how many of each type of picture frames to produce, subject to constraints on resource availabilities and upper bounds on production quantities. The objective is to maximize profit. The model is set up appropriately, although the current solution is not optimal. The cells in blue are inputs, and the cells in red are changing cells. The text box indicates ranges names being used. Write a sub that sets up the Solver and then runs it.

2. The file **ProdSched.xls** contains a multiperiod production scheduling model. A company has to schedule its production over the next several months to meet known demands on time. There are also production capacity and storage capacity constraints, and the objective is to minimize the total cost. The model is currently set up (correctly) for a 6-month planning horizon. The cells in blue are inputs, and the cells in red are changing cells. The text box indicates range names currently being used. This model can easily be changed, by deleting columns or copying across to the right, to make the planning horizon longer or shorter. Suppose

someone else does this. Your job is to write a sub that renames ranges appropriately, sets up the Solver correctly, and then runs it. That is, your sub should optimize the model in the worksheet, regardless of how many months its planning horizon is.

3. The file **FacilityLoc.xls** contains a model for locating a central warehouse. There are four customers that send shipments to this warehouse. Their coordinates are given, as well as their numbers of annual shipments. The objective is to minimize the annual distance traveled, and there are no constraints. The cells in blue are inputs, and the cells in red are changing cells. The text box indicates range names being used. This is a nonlinear model, so it is conceivable that there is a local minimum in addition to the global minimum. If there is, then it is possible that the Solver solution could depend on the initial solution used (in the red cells). To test this, write two short subs and attach them to the buttons. The first should generate "reasonable" random initial solutions. (Use VBA's **Rnd** function, which generates a uniformly distributed random number from 0 to 1, in an appropriate way. Make sure to put a **Randomize** statement at the top of the sub so that you get different random numbers each time you run the sub.) The second sub should then run the Solver. (It doesn't need to set up the Solver. You can do that manually.) Then repeatedly click the left button and then the right button. Do you always get the same Solver solution?

4. The file **Transport.xls** contains a transportation model where a product must be shipped from three plants to four cities at minimal shipping cost. The constraints are that no plant can ship more than its capacity, and each city must receive at least what it demands. The model has been developed (correctly) on the Model sheet. The company involved wants to run this model on five scenarios. Each of these scenarios, shown on the Scenarios sheet, has a particular set of capacities and demands. Write a sub that uses a For loop over the scenarios to do the following: (1) It copies the data for a particular scenario to the relevant parts of the Model sheet, (2) it runs the Solver, and (3) it copies selected results to the Results sheet. To get you started, the Results sheet currently shows the results for scenario 1. This is the format you should use for all scenarios.

5. The file **Pricing.xls** contains a model for finding the optimal price of a product. The product is American-made and sold in Germany. The company wants to set the price, in DM, so that its profit, in dollars, is maximized. The demand for the product is a function of price, and it is assumed that the elasticity of demand is constant. This leads to the formula for demand in cell B14, which depends on the parameters in row 10. (These parameters are assumed to be known.) The revenue, in dollars, is then price times demand. Of course, this depends on the exchange rate in cell B4. The company wants to perform a sensitivity analysis on the exchange rate. The results will be placed in the Sensitivity sheet, which already lists the exchange rates the company wants to test. Do the following: (1) Enter *any* data in columns B, C, and D of the Sensitivity sheet and use them to create three line charts (to the right of the data) that show price, demand, and profit versus the exchange rate, and (2) write a sub that substitutes each exchange rate into the model, runs the Solver, and transfers the results to the Sensitivity sheet. When you run your sub, the charts should update automatically with the new data.

6. The file **Stocks.xls** contains stock price returns for many large companies for a 5-year period. Each company has its own sheet, with the stock's ticker symbol as the name of the sheet. There is also an S&P500 sheet with the "market" returns. The Model sheet uses the market returns and the returns from a given stock to estimate the equation **Market = Alpha + Beta * Stock**, where Market and Stock are the returns, and Alpha and Beta are parameters to be estimated. The estimated Beta is especially useful to financial analysts. It is a measure of the volatility of the stock. The model is set up correctly (currently with data from American Express). The Alpha and Beta parameters are found by minimizing the sum of squared errors in cell E4. Write a sub that does the following: (1) It uses a For Each loop to go through all sheets except the Results, Model, and S&P500 sheets, that is, all stock sheets, (2) it copies the stock's returns to column C of the Model sheet, (3) it runs the Solver, and (4) it reports the results in a new line in the Results sheet. At the end, the Results sheet should have the ticker symbol and the Alpha and Beta for each stock. (*Note*: Your sub doesn't need to set up the Solver. You can do that once and for all at design time manually.)

7. (This exercise requires user forms, the topic of the next chapter.) The file **Planting.xls** contains a very simple model that a farmer could use to plant his crops optimally. The inputs are in blue, and the changing cells are in red. The purpose of this exercise is to develop a VBA application that allows the user to (1) choose any of the input cells as the cell to vary in a sensitivity analysis, (2) choose a range to vary this cell over, (3) run the Solver over this range, and (4) report the results in the Sensitivity sheet. Here are some guidelines. For (1), you should develop a user form that has a list box with descriptive names of all input cells, such as Profit per acre of wheat, Workers used per acre of wheat, and so on. The user should be allowed to choose only one item from this list. For (2), you should develop a second user form where the user can enter a minimum value, a maximum value, and an increment. For example, the user might specify that she wants to vary the profit per acre of wheat from $150 to $350 in increments of $50. Perform error checks to ensure that numerical values are entered, the minimum value is less than the maximum value, and the increment is positive. For (3), store the current values of the selected input in a variable, run the sensitivity analysis, and then restore the current value. For (4), make sure you adjust the labels in cells A1 and A3 of the Sensitivity sheet for the particular input chosen.

8. The Solver add-in contains some hidden secrets that can come in handy if you know them. (You might have to develop a friendship with someone in Frontline Systems' technical support group to learn them!) Here is one such secret. The changing cells in any Solver model are given the range name "solver_adj". This name won't appear in the list of range names when you use the Insert/Name/Define menu item, but it's there. You can use it as follows. Open the file **PlantLoc.xls**. This is a fairly large Solver model that can be used to find optimal locations of plants and warehouses. It is currently set up correctly, but it might be difficult to look at the model and know where the changing cells are. (We have deleted the red border we usually place around changing cells.) You could peek at the Solver dialog box to find the changing cells, but don't do so. Instead, write a sub that displays, in a message box, the address of the range with name "solver_adj".

9. Continuing the previous problem, you might wonder whether there are any other "hidden" Solver range names. Open the **PlantLoc.xls** file again. You'll notice some headings out in columns AA and AB. Enter the following sub and run it. It finds all range names that start with "Model!solver". You'll see that Solver has stored quite a lot of information! What range name is given to the objective cell? (The part of the code that deals with errors is necessary because some of the Solver's defined "names" do not refer to *ranges*. We'll see how these error statements work in Chapter 13.)

```
Sub ShowSolverRangeNames()
    Dim nm As Object, Counter As Integer
    Counter = 1
    With Range("AA1")
        For Each nm In ActiveWorkbook.Names
            On Error Resume Next
            If Left(nm.Name, 12) = "Model!solver" And Range(nm.Name).Address <> "" Then
                If Err = 0 Then
                    .Offset(Counter, 0) = nm.Name
                    .Offset(Counter, 1) = Range(nm.Name).Address
                    Counter = Counter + 1
                End If
            End If
        Next
    End With
End Sub
```

User Forms

12.1 Introduction

This chapter introduces user forms, or what you know as dialog boxes. Everyone who has ever used a Windows program is familiar with dialog boxes. They are the primary means for getting users' inputs. In fact, they are so familiar that you probably take them for granted, never stopping to think how they actually work. This chapter explains how to create user forms for your own applications.[23] This entails two distinct operations. First, you have to *design* the user form to have the required functionality and look attractive. Second, you have to write **event code** that sits behind the user form waiting to respond appropriately to whatever the user does. For example, most user forms have OK and Cancel buttons. During the design stage, you have to place and resize these buttons on the form. Then you have to write VBA code to respond appropriately when a user clicks on one of these buttons. Specifically, if the user clicks on the Cancel button, the dialog box should disappear and probably no other action should be taken. If the user clicks on the OK button, the user's inputs should be captured in some way, and the dialog box should disappear.

Working with user forms is arguably the most fun part of VBA application development. You can use your creative and artistic talents to design the dialog boxes that users will interact with. You can then use your logical skills to ensure that everything works properly when users click on buttons, select items from a list box, check "radio" buttons, fill in text boxes, and so on. In short, you get to *create* what you have been using for years—dialog boxes—and you start to see why there is a "V" in VBA.

12.2 Exercise

Working with user forms is not difficult, but there are many small steps to master, and practice is the key to mastering these. The following exercise is typical. It requires very little in the way of calculation, but you must put all of the pieces of the

---

[23]Throughout this chapter, the terms "dialog box" and "user form" are used interchangeably. The former term is used by most users, whereas the latter term is used by programmers. In fact, many programmers spell "user form" as UserForm, all one word with capital letters. We will use the less formal spelling here. Also, if you ever hear a reference to a "form," it is really to a "user form."

application together in just the right way. By the time you have read through the rest of this chapter and have studied its examples, this exercise should be fairly straightforward—but it is exactly the type your boss will appreciate!

Exercise 12.1   Summarizing Monthly Sales

Consider a company that has regional stores in Atlanta, Charlotte, and Memphis. Each region sells a variety of products, although the products vary from region to region. The file **SummSales.xls** contains a separate sheet for each region that shows monthly sales for a 3-year period for each product the region sells. Part of the Atlanta sheet appears in Figure 12.1. Note that the product codes sold in any region always appear in row 4.

Figure 12.1 Sample data for Atlanta

	A	B	C	D	E	F	G	H
1	Sales for Atlanta							
2								
3		Product code						
4	Month	U394K71	B350B99	Y342H72	Q253I61	W311E65	F822G38	M228M28
5	Jan-98	105	477	492	873	424	97	582
6	Feb-98	102	433	528	904	445	111	1149
7	Mar-98	99	591	612	835	553	87	917
8	Apr-98	116	538	546	1143	571	84	898
9	May-98	52	670	573	987	536	97	994
10	Jun-98	97	671	520	720	507	82	1069
11	Jul-98	82	398	501	701	402	95	1170
12	Aug-98	92	559	523	966	388	142	396
13	Sep-98	107	402	432	1161	506	116	881
14	Oct-98	98	419	448	1232	454	116	1138
15	Nov-98	71	562	472	742	620	119	867
16	Dec-98	72	700	531	1109	482	121	1135

The file also contains an Explanation sheet, as shown in Figure 12.2. This summarizes what the exercise is supposed to accomplish. (Similar Explanation sheets will appear in all of the applications in the second part of the book. It is always good to tell the user right away what an application is all about.) The button on this sheet will eventually be attached to a macro that runs the application.

Figure 12.2 Explanation sheet

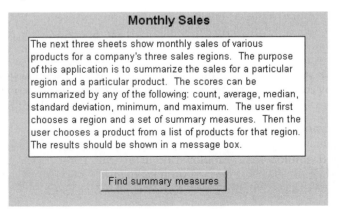

It is easier to show what this application is supposed to do than to explain it in detail. In fact, you can try it out yourself by opening the **SummSalesFinished.xls** file and clicking on the button. The user form in Figure 12.3 is first displayed, where the user must select a region and a set of summary measures. By default, the Atlanta button and the Median and Average boxes should be selected when the user sees this form. The user can then make any desired selections.

Figure 12.3 First user form

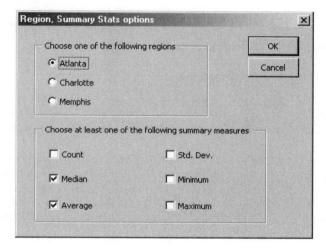

Next, the user sees the user form in Figure 12.4. It contains a message specific to the region chosen and a list of all products sold in that region. (When you write the program, you must find this list of product codes by scanning across row 4 of the region's sales sheet.) By default, the first product code should be selected. The user can then select any product code by scrolling through the list.

Figure 12.4 Second user form

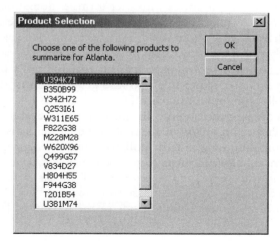

When the user clicks on this OK button, the application should summarize the sales of the product and region chosen, and display the results in a message box. For example, if the user chooses Charlotte, product L769C61, and *all* of the summary measures, the message in Figure 12.5 should appear.

Figure 12.5 Results

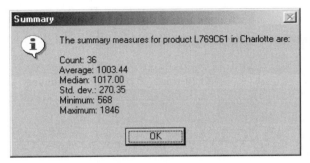

To develop this application, you need to create the two user forms in Figures 12.3 and 12.4, place the appropriate controls on them, give these controls appropriate properties, and write appropriate event code. You also have to insert a module that contains the non-event code. Specifically, this code must "show" the user forms, do any necessary calculations, and display the message box. One hint that will come in handy is the following. To calculate the required summary measures, you can "borrow" any of Excel's worksheet functions: Count, Average, Median, Stdev, Min, or Max. For example, to calculate the average for some range, you can use Application.Average(*range*), where *range* is a reference to the range you want to average.

12.3   Designing User Forms

The first step in developing applications with user forms is designing the forms. This section explains how to do it, but the explanations are purposely kept fairly brief. The more you have to read about designing user forms, the harder you will think it is. It is actually very easy. With a half hour of practice, you can learn how to design user forms. (It will take longer to make them look really professional, but that too is mostly a matter of practice.) So let's get started. As you read this section, you should follow along on your own PC.

First, open a new workbook in Excel, get into the VBE, and make sure the Project Explorer and Properties windows are visible. (If they aren't visible, click on the appropriate buttons on the Standard toolbar or use the appropriate menu items from the View menu.) To add a user form, use the **Insert/UserForm** menu item. A blank user form will appear, and your screen will appear as in Figure 12.6. If it doesn't look exactly like this, you can resize windows and "dock" the Project Explorer and Properties windows at the left side of the screen. In fact, you can move and resize windows any way you like. Also, when you insert the user form, the **Toolbox** at the bottom right should appear. If it ever disappears, you can always redisplay it by selecting the View/Toolbox menu item or clicking on the "hammer and wrench" button on the Standard toolbar.

Figure 12.6 New user form

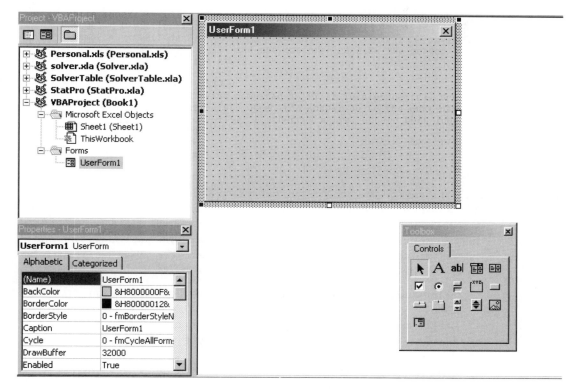

To design user forms, you need to know three things:

1. Which **controls** (also called **ActiveX controls**) are available
2. How to place, resize, and line up controls on a user form
3. How to give controls properties in the **Properties window**

Available Controls

The available controls are those shown in the Toolbox. (See Figure 12.7.) The arrow at the top left is used only for pointing. The rest, starting with the A and going from left to right, have the following generic names:[24]

---

[24] This list uses the technical single-word names for the controls, such as TextBox. Throughout the discussions, we will often revert to less formal names, such as text box.

Figure 12.7 Toolbox

- First row—Label, TextBox, ComboBox, ListBox
- Second row—CheckBox, OptionButton, ToggleButton, Frame, CommandButton
- Third row—TabStrip, MultiPage, ScrollBar, SpinButton, Image
- Fourth row—RefEdit

Each of these controls has a certain behavior built into it. Without going into details, we will simply state that this standard behavior is the behavior you are familiar with from working with dialog boxes in Windows applications. For example, if there are several option ("radio") buttons on a user form and you click on one of them, then the others are automatically unchecked. The following list describes the functionality of the most frequently used controls.

- **CommandButton**—used to run subs (the user clicks on a button and a sub is run)
- **Label**—used mainly for explanations and prompts
- **TextBox**—used to obtain any type of user input (the user types something in the box)
- **ListBox**—used to let the user choose one or more items from a list
- **ComboBox**—similar to a list box, except that the user can type an item that isn't on the list in a box
- **CheckBox**—lets the user check whether an option is desired or not (any or all of a set of check boxes can be checked)
- **OptionButton**—lets the user check which of several options is desired (only one of a set of option buttons can be checked)
- **Frame**—usually used to group a related set of options buttons, but can be used to organize any set of controls into logical groups
- **RefEdit**—similar to a TextBox control, but used specifically to let the user highlight a worksheet range

Adding Controls to a User Form

To add any control to a user form, click on the control in the Toolbox and then drag a shape on the form. That's all there is to it. Try the following step-by-step

Figure 12.8 Controls on practice user form

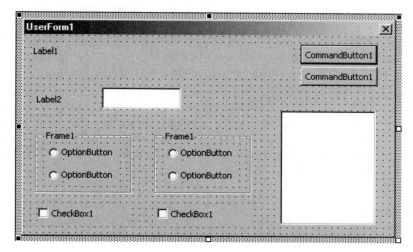

exercise, and don't be afraid to experiment. When you are finished, your user form should appear approximately like the one in Figure 12.8.

Step 1 **Resize form.** Resize the user form (make it considerably wider).

Step 2 **Command button.** Add a command button at the top right. While it is still selected, press the Ctrl key and drag the button down to make a copy. You will know you are copying, not moving, when you see a plus sign as you drag. This is the general way to copy controls—select them and then drag them with your finger on the Ctrl key.

Step 3 **Explanation label.** Add a wide label to the left of the command buttons. This is a good place for explaining what your dialog box does.

Step 4 **Text box and corresponding label.** Add a label (shown as Label2) and a corresponding text box to its right. A text box typically has a corresponding label that acts as a prompt for what the user should enter in the box.

Step 5 **Frame and option buttons.** Add a fairly large frame below the text box. Next, add an option button inside the frame, and make a copy of this option button. Both option buttons should fit entirely within the frame boundary.

Step 6 **Copy frame and option buttons.** Drag over the frame to select it, put your finger on the Ctrl key, and drag the whole thing to the right to make a copy. Note that you get not only a new frame but also a new set of option buttons. The option buttons in a frame are essentially part of the frame, so when you copy the frame, you also copy the option buttons. In addition, the option buttons in any frame are a "logical set," in the sense that only one button *in each frame* can be checked. For example, the top button in the left frame could be checked, *and* the bottom button in the right frame could be checked. If option buttons are not inside frames, then only one option button on the whole user form can be checked.

Step 7   **Check box.** Add a check box at the lower left and make a copy of it to its right.

Step 8   **List box.** Add a list box at the bottom right. It doesn't look like a "list" box yet, because there is no list. This will be added later.

Step 9   **Resize and align.** Resize and align the controls to make the form visually appealing. This is quite easy (if a bit tedious). Just experiment with the menu items under the Format menu. The key is that you can drag over several controls to select them. Then the selected controls are treated as a group for the purpose of aligning and resizing. Also, the *first* one selected is the one the others are aligned or resized with respect to. (It is the one with the white handles; the others have black handles.)

12.4   Setting Properties of Controls

The user form in Figure 12.8 doesn't do anything yet. In fact, it isn't even clear what it is supposed to do. You can fix the latter problem by setting some properties of the controls. You do this in the **Properties** window. Like Excel ranges, worksheets, and workbooks, controls are objects with properties, and many of these are listed in the Properties window. The items in the Properties window change, depending on which control is selected, because different types of controls have different sets of properties. Figure 12.9 shows the Properties window for the user form itself. (To select the user form, click somewhere on it where there are no controls.) The names of the properties are listed on the left and their values are listed on the right.

Microsoft has provided a bewildering number of properties for user forms and controls. Fortunately, you can ignore most properties and concentrate on the few

Figure 12.9   Properties Window for user form

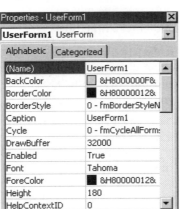

you need to change. For example, you will typically want to change the Name and Caption properties of a user form. The Name property is used in general for referring to the user form (or any control) in VBA code. The default names are generic, such as UserForm1, CommandButton1, and so on. It is typically a good idea to change the Name property only if you plan to refer to the object in VBA code; otherwise, you can let the default name stand. The Caption property is what you see on the screen. For a user form, the caption appears in the title bar of the user form. For now, go through the following steps to change certain properties. (See Figure 12.10 for the finished user form.) For each step, select the control first (click on it), so that the Properties window shows the properties for *that* control.

Figure 12.10 User form with changed properties

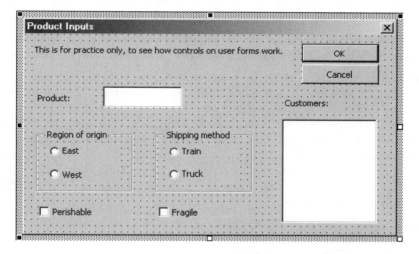

Step 1 **User form.** Change its **Name** property to InputsForm and its **Caption** property to Product Inputs.

Step 2 **Top command button.** Change its **Name** property to OKButton, change its **Caption** property to OK, and change its **Default** property (yes, it is listed as Default in the left pane of the Properties window) to True. This gives the OK button the functionality you expect once the form is operational—namely, you can click on it *or* press the Enter key to accomplish the same thing.

Step 3 **Bottom command button.** Change its **Name** property to CancelButton, change its **Caption** property to Cancel, and change its **Cancel** property to True. The effect of this latter change is to allow the user to press the Esc key instead of clicking on the Cancel button. Again, this is standard behavior in Windows dialog boxes.

Step 4 **Top label.** Usually, the only property you will ever change for a label is its **Caption** property—what appears in the label. You can do this through the Properties window, or you can click on the label once to select it and then again to put a dark border around it.[25] This allows you to type the label "in place." For this label, enter the caption "This is for practice only, to see how controls on user forms work." (Don't include the quotes.)

Step 5 **Label to the left of the text box.** Change its Caption property to Product:.

Step 6 **Text box.** Change the **Name** property to ProductBox.

Step 7 **Frames.** Change their **Caption** properties to Region of origin and Shipping method.

Step 8 **Option buttons.** Change the **Name** properties of the option buttons in the left frame to EastOption and WestOption, and change their **Caption** properties to East and West. (Note that these captions are the "labels" you see next to the buttons.) Similarly, change the Name and Caption properties of the other two option buttons to TrainOption, TruckOption, Train, and Truck.

Step 9 **Check boxes.** These are similar to option buttons. Change their **Name** and **Caption** properties to PerishBox, FragileBox, Perishable, and Fragile.

Step 10 **List box.** Change its **Name** property to CustomerList. A list box does not have a Caption property, so add a label above it with the caption Customers:. Otherwise, the user will not know what the list is all about. There is another property you should be aware of for list boxes: the **MultiSelect** property. Its default value is **0–fmMultiSelectSingle**. This means that the user is allowed to select only one item from the list. Many times you want the user to be able to select *more* than one item from a list. Then you should select option **2–fmMultiSelectExtended**. (See Figure 12.11.) For now, accept the first (default) option. (The middle option is virtually never used.)

Figure 12.11 MultiSelect property for list boxes

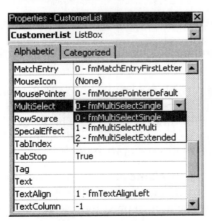

---

[25]If you accidentally double-click on the label or any other controls during the design stage, you will open the event code window, which is discussed later in the chapter. To get back to the user form design, select the View/Object menu item.

Tab Order

There is one final touch you can add to make your user form more professional—the **tab order**. You are probably aware that most dialog boxes allow you to tab from one control to another by pressing the Tab key. To give your user form this functionality, all you need to do is change the **TabIndex** property of each control, using any ordering you like and starting with index 0. There are two things you should know about tabbing:

- Any control with the **TabStop** property set to False cannot be tabbed to. This is typically the case for labels.
- When there is a frame with "embedded" controls such as option buttons, you set the TabIndex for the *frame* relative to the order of the other controls on the form, but the tab order for the controls within the frame is set separately. For example, a frame might have index 6 in the tab order of *all* controls, but its two option buttons would have indexes 0 and 1. Essentially, the user first tabs to the frame and then tabs through the controls inside the frame.

Testing the Form

Now that you have designed the form, you can see how it will look to the user. To do this, make sure the user form, not some control on the form, is selected, and click on the **Run Sub/UserForm** button (the blue triangle button). This displays the user form. It doesn't yet *do* anything, but it should at least look nice. You should note that the **focus** (the cursor location) is set to the control with tab index 0. For example, if you set the tab index of the text box to 0, then the cursor will be in the text box, waiting for the user to type something. You can see how the tab order works by pressing the Tab key repeatedly. To get back to design view, click on the Close button of the form (the X button). Note that you cannot yet close the user form by clicking on the Cancel button, because the Cancel button is not yet "functional." We will make it functional in Section 12.6.

12.5 Creating a User Form Template

If you design a lot of user forms, you will quickly get tired of always having to design the same OK and Cancel buttons required on most forms. This section illustrates a handy shortcut. Open a new workbook and go through the procedure in the previous two sections to design a user form with an OK and a Cancel button, having the properties listed earlier in steps 2 and 3. It should look something like Figure 12.12. Now select the **File/Export File** menu item, and save the form under a name such as **OKCancel.frm** in some convenient folder. Later on, whenever you want a user form with ready-made OK and Cancel buttons, select the **File/Import File** menu item, and open the **OKCancel.frm** file. This can save you a few minutes each time you design a form.

Figure 12.12 User form template

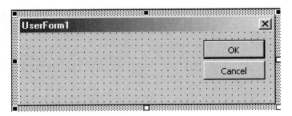

12.6 Writing Event Code for User Forms

Much of Windows programming is built around **events**, where an event occurs whenever the user does something. This could mean clicking on a button, entering text in a text box, clicking on an option button, opening a worksheet, right-clicking on a cell—in short, doing just about anything. Each of these events has a built-in **event handler**. This is a sub that you can add code to so that appropriate actions are taken when the event occurs. These subs are always available—*if* you want the program to respond to certain events. Of course, there are many events that you don't want to bother responding to. For example, you *could* respond to the event where the mouse is dragged over a command button, but you probably have no reason to do so. In this case, you simply ignore that event handler. On the other hand, there are certain events you *do* want to respond to. For these, you have to write the appropriate code. This section illustrates how to do this in the context of user forms.

First, you have to understand where the event handler code (which will be shortened here to **event code**) is placed. Also, you have to understand naming conventions. All of the VBA code to this point has been placed in modules, which are inserted into a project with the Insert/Module menu item. Event code is *not* placed in these modules. Instead, it is placed in a user form's **code window**. To get to a user form's code window, make sure you are viewing the form's design window, and select the **View/Code** menu item. In general, the View/Code and View/Object (or F7 and Shift-F7, if you prefer shortcut keys) toggle between the form's design and its code window.

Another way to get from the design window to the code window is to double-click on a control. (You might already have experienced this by accident.) This not only opens the code window, but it inserts a "stub" for event code. For example, by double-clicking on the OK button in design view, the code window opens and the following stub is inserted:

```
Private Sub OKButton_Click()

End Sub
```

Each control has many such stubs available. The sub names all start with the name of the control, followed by an underscore and an event type. The one you get by double-clicking depends on which event is the *default* event for that control. To understand this better, get into the code window for the user form we created in Section 12.3. You will see two drop-down lists at the top of the window. The one on the left lists all controls on the form, including the form itself, as shown in Figure 12.13. Select any of these and then look at the drop-down list on the right. It lists all events the selected control can respond to. Figure 12.14 illustrates this list for a command button.

Figure 12.13 List of controls

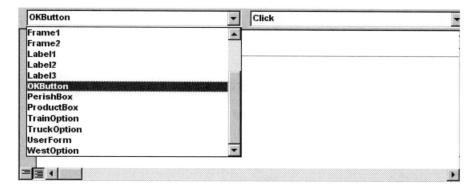

Figure 12.14 List of events for a command button

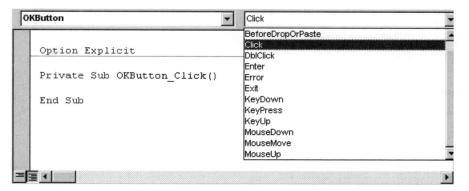

If you double-click on any of the items in the list in Figure 12.14, you get a stub, into which you can write code. For example, if you double-click on the MouseUp item, you will get the following stub:

```
Private Sub OKButton_MouseUp(ByVal Button As Integer, ByVal Shift As Integer, _
    ByVal X As Single, ByVal Y As Single)

End Sub
```

You have no choice over the format of the "sub" line. The sub must be named as shown (control name, underscore, event type), and it must contain any arguments that are given. But how would you ever know what this sub responds to (what is a MouseUp event, anyway?), and how would you know what the arguments are all about? The best way to find out is to consult the **Object Browser**. Try it out. Open the Object Browser and select the **MSForms** library. This library provides help for all objects in user forms. Specifically, it provides a list of controls on the left and their properties, methods, and events on the right, as shown in Figure 12.15. The events are designated by lightning icons. By selecting any of these and clicking on the question mark button, you can get plenty of help. For example, help for the MouseUp and MouseDown events appears in Figure12.16. (You don't need to bother reading this now; just remember how to get to it.)

Figure 12.15 Object Browser

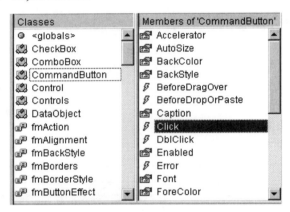

Figure 12.16 Help for MouseUp and MouseDown events

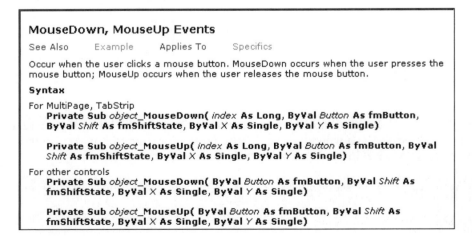

In general, you need to decide which events you want to respond to with code. This chapter will illustrate the ones that are used most often for the applications in later chapters, but you should realize that the floodgates are wide open—you can respond to just about any action the user takes. This can be bewildering at first, but it is the reason Windows programming is so powerful. The following example illustrates some possibilities.

EXAMPLE 12.1

Consider the dialog box in Figure 12.17. It gives the user three choices of where to place results from some analysis—to the right of a data set, on a new worksheet, or in a selected cell. (It is taken from the author's StatPro add-in.) The three option buttons are named ToRightOpt, NewSheetOpt, and CellOpt. If the user chooses the second option, the text box next to this option (named NewSheetBox) is unhidden so that the user can type the name of the new worksheet. Otherwise, this text box is invisible. Similarly, if the user chooses the third option, the ref edit control next to this option (named CellBox) is unhidden so that the user can select the desired cell. Otherwise, this control is invisible.

Figure 12.17 Location dialog box

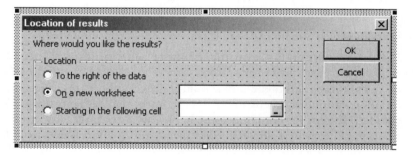

The following three event handlers implement the desired logic. Each responds to the Click event of an option button. They set the Visible property of the NewSheetBox and CellBox controls to True or False, and they use the SetFocus method to place the cursor in the appropriate box. For example, if the user clicks on the NewSheetOpt button, the NewSheetBox appears, with the cursor inside it, and the CellBox is hidden. These subs should give you a taste of the power you have over your applications.

```
Private Sub ToRightOpt_Click()
  NewSheetBox.Visible = False
  CellBox.Visible = False
End Sub
```

```
Private Sub NewSheetOpt_Click()
    With NewSheetBox
        .Visible = True
        .SetFocus
    End With
    CellBox.Visible = False
End Sub

Private Sub CellOpt_Click()
    NewSheetBox.Visible = False
    With CellBox
        .Visible = True
        .SetFocus
    End With
End Sub
```

EXAMPLE 12.2

This example illustrates event code for the user form we created in Sections 12.3 and 12.4. (The completed version is in the file **PracticeForm.xls**.) It is typical of the forms you will see in later chapters. There are three event handlers: **UserForm_Initialize**, **OKButton_Click**, and **CancelButton_Click**. The first determines how the user form will look when the user first sees it, and the latter two determine what occurs when the user clicks on the OK and Cancel buttons.[26]

UserForm_Initialize Code

For this application, we want the following behavior when the user form initially appears: the East and Truck buttons should be checked, the Perishable box should be unchecked, the Fragile box should be checked, and the CustomerList should be filled with a list of customers. (Of course, the developer gets to make these choices.) Except for the last requirement, this is easy. Each control has properties that can be set with VBA code. Also, each type of control has a default property.[27] If you want to set the default property, you don't even have to list the property's name. For example, the **Value** property is the default property of an option button and a check box. It is True or False, depending on whether the control is checked or not. To set this property, you can write

```
EastOption.Value = True
```

or you can use the shortened version

```
EastOption = True
```

---

[26]Unlike what you might expect, the initialize sub is called UserForm_Initialize, not InputsForm_Initialize. It always has this generic name, regardless of how you name the form.

[27]The default property for a control has a small blue dot above it in the Object Browser. For example, if you select OptionButton in the Object Browser and scan its list of properties, you will see a blue dot above the Value property.

Similarly, the **Value** property is the default property of a text box control. It indicates the value, treated as a string, in the box. For example, to make a text box blank, you can write

```
ProductBox.Value = ""
```

or

```
ProductBox = ""
```

List boxes are a bit trickier. You can populate them in several ways. Two methods are illustrated here. For both, we assume that there is a worksheet with a list of customers in a range named Customers. This list might appear as in Figure 12.18, where the Customers range is A2:A28.

Figure 12.18 Customer list on a worksheet

	A	B
1	Customer list	
2	Adobe	
3	Altaire	
4	Canon	
5	Compaq	
6	Diamond	
7	Epson	
25	Symantec	
26	Toshiba	
27	Visioneer	
28	Xerox	

Then the **AddItem** method of the list box can be used inside a For loop to add the customers to the list box, one at a time. The only required argument of the AddItem method is the name of the item to be added.

The completed UserForm_Initialize code appears below.

```
Private Sub UserForm_Initialize()
    Dim cell As Range
    ProductBox = ""
    EastOption = True
    TruckOption = True
    PerishBox = False
    FragileBox = True

' If the RowSource property of the CustomerList list box is set to
' Customers, the following For Each loop can be omitted.
    For Each cell In Range("Customers")
        CustomerList.AddItem cell.Value
    Next
End Sub
```

Alternatively, the **RowSource** property of the list box can be set to Customers at design time (through the Properties window). This tells VBA to populate the list box with the list in the Customers range. Then the For Each loop in the above code would not be necessary.

When the user form is shown initially, it will appear as in Figure 12.19. Of course, the user is then free to change the settings.

Figure 12.19 Initialized user form

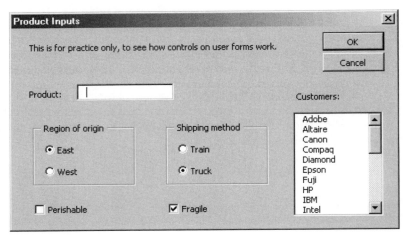

CancelButton_Click Code

There is usually not much you want to happen when the user clicks on the Cancel button. This is the user's way of saying she doesn't want to continue, so the typical CancelButton_Click code is as follows.

```
Private Sub CancelButton_Click()
   Unload Me
   End
End Sub
```

The first line says to unload the user form (which can be referred to with the keyword **Me**). This makes the form disappear. The second line says to end the program.

OKButton_Click Code

This is usually the lengthiest part of the event code. This is where you capture the user's inputs. Typically, they are stored in public variables, declared in a module, so that they can be used by the module code later on, but are also recognized by the event code. Also, as will be explained in more detail in the next chapter, this code generally performs some error checking to ensure that the user provides "valid" inputs. For the user form used here, the only things the user could do wrong are (1) leave the product box blank, (2) enter an invalid product in the product box, or (3) fail to select a customer in the list box. For illustration, we will assume that the company's products are indexed from 1 to 1000. Any number not in this range, or any nonnumeric value, will not be accepted in the product box. Then the following event code will do the job.

```
Private Sub OKButton_Click()
' Capture the value of ProductBox, but make sure it is from 1 to 1000.
    With ProductBox
        If .Value = "" Or Not IsNumeric(.Value) Then
            MsgBox "Enter a product number from 1 to 1000."
            .SetFocus
            Exit Sub
        End If
        ProductIndex = ProductBox
        If ProductIndex < 1 Or ProductIndex > 1000 Then
            MsgBox "Enter a product number from 1 to 1000."
            .SetFocus
            Exit Sub
        End If
    End With
' Capture region (in a string variable).
    If EastOption = True Then
        Region = "East"
    Else
        Region = "West"
    End If
' Capture shipping method (in a string variable).
    If TruckOption = True Then
        Shipping = "Truck"
    Else
        Shipping = "Train"
    End If
' Capture check box settings (in Boolean variables).
    IsPerishable = PerishBox
    IsFragile = FragileBox
' Capture customer (in a string variable).
    With CustomerList
        If .ListIndex <> -1 Then
            Customer = CustomerList.Value
        Else
            MsgBox "Select a customer from the list."
            .SetFocus
            Exit Sub
        End If
    End With
' Unload the form.
    Unload Me
End Sub
```

Most of this code is straightforward, but you should note the following.

- The user inputs are captured in the variables ProductIndex, Region, Shipping, IsPerishable, IsFragile, and Customer. These must be declared as **public** variables at the top of the module where they will be used, as illustrated below. The idea is that the values of these variables are captured in the user form event code. Then they are used later on in the module code.

```
' Public variables captured from the user form.
Public ProductIndex As Integer, Region As String, Shipping As String, _
    IsPerishable As Boolean, IsFragile As Boolean, Customer As String
```

- The first error check made on ProductBox uses VBA's **IsNumeric** function to check whether an input is numeric. This and the **IsDate** function are very handy for error checking.
- If an error check is not passed, a message box displays an error message, the focus is set to the offending control, and the sub is exited immediately with the **Exit Sub** statement, *without* unloading the user form. This last part is important. It guarantees that the user form does not disappear and that the user has to try again.
- Default properties are not shown explicitly. For example, we use the line IsFragile = FragileBox rather than IsFragile = FragileBox.Value. Both versions work equally well.
- The **Value** property of a list box indicates the item selected—in this case, the name of the customer. The **ListIndex** property indicates the position in the list of the selected item, starting with 0. For example, it returns 3 if the fourth item is chosen. If no item is selected, ListIndex is –1. This explains the error check. We want to ensure that *some* item has been selected.

You have to remember to unload the user form at the end of the sub, which is surprisingly easy to forget. If you forget to do this and then test your dialog box by clicking the OK button (in run mode), nothing will happen—the dialog box will just sit there!

12.7 Displaying a User Form

You have probably been wondering how the user form is displayed in the first place. This is easy. Each user form has a **Show** method that displays the form (and runs its **UserForm_Initialize** event code). To illustrate, the **PracticeForm.xls** file from the previous example has a module containing the following Main sub, which is attached to a button on a worksheet. When the user clicks on the button, the Main sub runs. The **InputsForm.Show** line displays the user form. Execution of the Main sub is then suspended until the user is finished entering inputs and clicks on the OK button or the Cancel button. If the user clicks on Cancel, the program simply ends. If the user clicks on OK, the Main sub resumes and displays the user's inputs in a message box, as in Figure 12.20. Of course, a real application would then use these inputs in some further analysis. That is, there would be further code in the module.

```
Sub Main()
    InputsForm.Show
    MsgBox "The user chose the following:" & vbCrLf _
        & "Product index: " & ProductIndex & vbCrLf _
        & "Region of origin: " & Region & vbCrLf _
```

```
            & "Shipping method: " & Shipping & vbCrLf _
            & "Perishable? " & IsPerishable & vbCrLf _
            & "Fragile? " & IsFragile & vbCrLf _
            & "Customer: " & Customer, vbInformation, "User inputs"
    ' The rest of the program would then act on the user's inputs.
    End Sub
```

Figure 12.20 Display of user's inputs

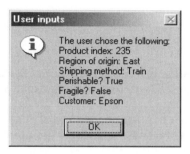

12.8 Looping Through the Controls on a User Form

There are many times when you place several related controls on a user form and would then like to loop through them to perform some action. For example, you might have a group of check boxes, one for each region of the country, and you would like to use event code to see which of them are checked. The easiest way to do this would be to form an *array* of controls and then go through the array elements with a For loop. Unfortunately, however, VBA does not allow you to form arrays of controls.[28] An alternative method that *is* possible is to use a For Each loop to loop through the **Controls** collection on the user form. This will loop through *all* controls—the text boxes, the labels, the command buttons, and so on. If you want to perform some action only on a particular type of control such as the text boxes, you can use the **TypeName** function, as illustrated in the following code.

```
Dim ctl As Control
For Each ctl In Me.Controls
    If TypeName(ctl) = "TextBox" Then
        If ctl.Value = "" Or Not IsDate(ctl) Then
            MsgBox "Enter valid dates in the text boxes.", _
                vbInformation, "Invalid entry"
            ctl.SetFocus
            Exit Sub
        End If
    End If
Next
```

---

[28] This *is* possible in Visual Basic 6.0, but for some reason it has not yet been implemented in VBA.

Note that ctl is declared as a generic control. The For Each loop goes through all controls in the collection Me.Controls (where Me is a reference to the user form). Then the **If TypeName(ctl) = "TextBox"** statement checks whether the control is a text box. (Note that it requires the formal name, TextBox, spelled exactly as shown.) If it is, certain actions are taken. If it is not, no actions are taken. This looping method is probably not as convenient as being able to loop through an array of controls, but it is the best method available—at least with the current version of VBA.

12.9 Working with List Boxes

List boxes are among the most useful controls for user forms, but they are also among the trickiest to work with. This section explains methods for populating list boxes and capturing users' choices.

First, list boxes come in two basic types: **single** and **multi**. The type is determined by the **MultiSelect** property. A single list box allows the user to select only one item from the list, whereas a multi list box allows the user to select *any* number of items from the list. Of course, the context of the application determines which type to use, but you should know how to work with both.

Single List Boxes

If you want a list box to be of the single type, you do *not* have to change its **MultiSelect** property. By default, a list box is of the single type (the MultiSelect setting is **0 – fmMultiSelectSingle** in the Properties window). There are then two properties you are likely to use: the **Value** property and the **ListIndex** property. These properties were illustrated in Example 12.2. For example, if the user selects Compaq from the list in Figure 12.19, which is the fourth customer in the list, then the Value property is the string "Compaq", and the ListIndex property is 3. (It is 3, not 4, because indexing always starts with 0.) If no item is selected, then ListIndex is –1, which can be used for error checking. (The user is always supposed to select *some* item.)

Multi List Boxes

Multi list boxes are slightly more complex. First, you have to set the **MultiSelect** property appropriately (the correct setting is **2 – fmMultiSelectExtended** in the Properties window) at design time. Second, it would no longer make sense to use Value and ListIndex properties. Instead, you need to know *which* items the user has selected. You do this with the **Selected** property, which acts like a 0-based Boolean array, as we illustrate below. You can also take advantage of the **ListCount** property, which returns the number of items in the list. The following sample code is typical. It uses a public Boolean array variable WasChosen (declared in a module) to capture the user's choices for later use. Because most people prefer 1-based arrays, WasChosen starts with index 1. Unfortunately, it is not possible to make the built-in Selected "array" 1-based; it is always 0-based. This accounts for the difference between the indexes of Selected and WasChosen in the code.

```
For i = 1 To ListBox.ListCount
    WasChosen(i) = ListBox.Selected(i - 1)
Next
```

For example, if there are five items in the list and the user selects the first, second, and fifth, then WasChosen(1), WasChosen(2), and WasChosen(5) will be True, and WasChosen(3) and WasChosen(4) will be False. This information can then be used in the rest of the program.

There is more to say about list boxes. For example, they can have multi-column lists. However, this is enough information for now. Other list box features will be explained as they are needed in later chapters.

12.10   Summary

With the material in this chapter, you can finally start to become a real *Windows* programmer. We have discussed how to design user forms by placing various types of built-in controls on them, and we have illustrated how to write event code that responds to various events triggered by a user's actions. Once you have designed a user form and have made any necessary changes in the Properties window, it is then a matter of writing the appropriate event code in the form's code window. Typically, this means capturing user selections in publicly declared values that can later be analyzed with the code in a module. You will see many examples of how this is done in the second half of the book, most of which use user forms.

PROGRAMMING EXERCISES

1. The file **Receivables.xls** contains data on a company's receivables from its customers. Each row corresponds to a particular customer. It indicates the size of the customer (1 for small, 2 for medium, 3 for large), the number of days the payment has been outstanding, and the amount of the payment due. Develop a user form that has the usual OK and Cancel buttons, plus two sets of option buttons. The first set allows the user to choose the size of the customer (using captions Small, Medium, and Large), and the second set allows the user to choose the Days or the Amount column to summarize. Then write code in a module that takes these choices and displays a message listing the appropriate average. For example, if the user chooses Small and Amount, the message box should display the average amount owed by all small customers.

2. Repeat the preceding exercise, but now use check boxes instead of option buttons. Now a separate message should be displayed for each combination the user checks. For example, if the user checks the Small check box and the Days and Amount

check boxes, one message should display the average of Days for the small customers, and another should display the average of Amount for the small customers.

3. The file **StockReturns.xls** contains stock returns for many large companies. Each sheet contains the returns over a 5-year period for a certain stock, with the ticker symbol of the stock used as the sheet name. Write a sub that presents the user with a user form. This user form should have the usual OK and Cancel buttons, and it should have a list box with a list of all stocks (actually, their ticker symbols). The user should be allowed to choose only one stock in the list. Then the sub should display a message box that reports the average monthly return for the selected stock.

4. Repeat the previous exercise, but now allow the user to select multiple stocks from the list. Then use a For loop to display a message box for each selected stock separately.

5. The file **ExceptionsFinished.xls** contains monthly sales totals for a number of sales regions. Open the file and click on the button. It allows you to choose two colors and two "cutoff" values. When you click on OK, all sales totals below the minimum cutoff are colored the first color, and all totals above the maximum cutoff are colored the other color. The VBA in this file has been password-protected. Your job is to create this same application, starting with the **Exceptions.xls** file. This file contains only the data. Make sure you do some error checking on the inputs in the user form. Specifically, the text boxes must have numeric values, the minimum cutoff should not exceed the maximum cutoff, and the two chosen colors should not be the same.

6. The file **ScoresFinished.xls** contains scores for various assignments in three courses taught by an instructor. Open the file. You will see an Explanation sheet and a button. Click on the button to run the program. It shows one user form where you can choose a course and any of six summary measures. When you click on OK, you see a second user form where you can choose an assignment for that course. (Note the list of assignments varies from course to course.) When you click on OK, a message box is displayed summarizing the scores on that assignment. The VBA in this file has been password-protected. Your job is to create this same application, starting with the **Scores.xls** file. This file contains only the data.

7. The file **BookRepsFinished.xls** contains data on a number of sales representatives for a publishing company. The data on each rep include last name, first name, gender, region of country, age, years of experience, and performance rating. Open the file and click on the button. It presents two user forms. The first asks for the last name and first name of a rep. After the user enters these, the program searches for a rep with this name. If none is found, a message to this effect is displayed and the program ends. If the rep is found, a second user form is displayed with the rep's characteristics. The user can then change any of these and click on OK. The changes are then reflected in the database. The VBA in this file has been password-protected. Your job is to create this same application, starting with the **BookReps.xls** file. This file contains only the data.

8. Open a new workbook and develop a user form that asks for a beginning date and an ending date in text boxes. It should instruct the user (with an appropriate label) to enter dates from January 1, 1990, and the current date. Then the

OKButton_Click event should perform the following error checks: (1) the date boxes should not be blank, (2) they should contain valid dates (use the **IsDate** function for this), (3) the first date shouldn't be before January 1, 1990, (4) the last date shouldn't be after the current date (use the **Date** function for this), and (5) the first date should be before the ending date. If any of these error checks is not passed, the OKButton_Click sub should be exited *without* unloading the user form, and the focus should be set to the offending text box, so that the user can try again. If all error checks are passed, the dates should be displayed in an appropriate message box. (Alternatively, you could store them in public variables for later use.)

9. Continuing the previous exercise, if you are like us, it will probably take you several tries to get everything, especially the error checking, working properly. Dates are tricky! Once you go to all of this work, you shouldn't have to do it again. The purpose of this exercise, therefore, is to write a Public sub called CheckDates that does the error checking for this type of situation automatically. Then you could use this general sub any time you need it in the future. Structure it as follows. It should take four arguments: TBox1 (a TextBox for the first date), TBox2 (a TextBox for the second date), EarliestDate (a Date, corresponding to the January 1, 1900, date in the previous problem), and NoErrors (a Boolean). This sub should check for all errors. If it finds any, it should set the focus to the offending text box, set NoErrors to False, and return control to the calling sub (which will probably be the OKButton_Click sub). Otherwise, it should set NoErrors to True and return control to the calling sub. Then the calling sub can check the value of NoErrors passed back to see whether to exit without unloading the form or capture the user's *valid* dates. Write this CheckDates sub, which should be placed in a *module*, and then use it to solve the previous exercise.

10. This chapter has explained only the most frequently used controls: command buttons, labels, text boxes, option buttons, check boxes, and frames. However, there are a few others you might want to use. This exercise and the next one let you explore two of these controls. In this exercise, you can explore the SpinButton control. Open a new workbook, get into the VBE, add a user form, and place a spin button on the form. You can probably guess the functionality this button should have. If the user clicks on the up arrow, a counter should increase. If the user clicks on the down arrow, the counter should decrease. To operationalize the button, set its Min, Max, and SmallChange properties to 1, 10, and 1 in the Properties window. This will allow the user to change the counter from 1 to 10 in increments of 1. But how would a user know the value of the counter? The trick is to put a text box right next to the spin button and make the text box's Value property equal to the spin button's Value property (which is the counter). To keep them in sync, write a line of code in the spin button's Change event code that sets the text box's value equal to the spin button's value. Try it out by running the form (by clicking on the blue triangle "run" button). How can you make sure that the two controls *start* in sync when the form is first displayed?

11. Continuing the previous exercise, put a spin button to work on the **CarLoan.xls** file. This file contains a template for calculating the monthly payment on a car loan, given the amount financed, the annual interest rate, and the term of the loan

(the number of months to pay). Develop an application around this template that does the following: (1) It has a button on the sheet to run a Sensitivity1 sub in a module, (2) the Sensitivity1 sub "shows" a user form with the usual OK and Cancel buttons, a spin button and corresponding text box, and appropriate label(s) that allows the user to choose a term for the loan (allow only multiples of 12, up to 60), and (3) the Sensitivity1 sub then places the user's choice of term in cell B5, which automatically updates the monthly payment.

12. This exercise continues the previous two exercises, but it now asks you to explore the ScrollBar control. Open a new workbook, get into the VBE, add a user form, and place a scroll bar on the form. (You can make it vertical or horizontal. Take your choice.) As you can probably guess, the scroll bar's Value property indicates the position of the "slider." It can go from the Min value to the Max value. The SmallChange property indicates the change in the slider when the user clicks on one of the arrows. The LargeChange property indicates the change when the user clicks somewhere inside the scroll bar. You could proceed as with spin buttons to place a text box next to the scroll bar that shows the current value of the scroll bar. Here, however, you will try another possibility. You will place *labels* at the ends of the scroll bar and around the middle, as illustrated in Figure 12.21. These should provide plenty of guidance for the user. Now try all of this out on a variation of the previous exercise, using the same **CarLoan.xls** file. Write a Sensitivity2 sub that "shows" a user form with a scroll bar. The Min, Max, SmallChange, and LargeChange properties of the scroll bar should be 10000, 50000, 500, and 2000 (by using the Properties window at design time). The goal is the same as in the previous exercise, except that now the sensitivity analysis is on the amount financed.

Figure 12.21 Scroll bar with informational labels

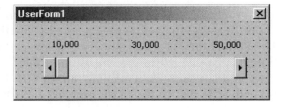

Debugging and Error Handling

13.1 Introduction

It is not very uplifting to write an entire chapter about errors, but it is unfortunately a topic that a book on computer programming cannot ignore. Everyone who writes computer programs makes errors—this author does, the geniuses at Microsoft do, and you certainly will—so methods are required for detecting errors and fixing them. This chapter illustrates some of the techniques for doing this, that is, for **debugging**, in the VBA environment. It is not as painful a process as you might expect. Unfortunately, there is more to the topic than fixing your *own* errors. The applications you will be developing are typically interactive. An application displays one or more dialog boxes for the user to fill in, and it then responds to the user's inputs with appropriate actions. But what if the user is asked to enter a percentage as a decimal between 0 and 1, and she enters 25? Or what if a user is asked for a date and he enters 13/35/99? Your code must check for these types of errors that a *user* might make. VBA will not do it automatically for you. It is up to you to include the appropriate "error-trapping" logic.

13.2 Exercise

One of the best ways to become proficient at debugging is to try fixing someone *else's* buggy code. This exercise gives you a chance to do so.

Exercise 13.1   Debugging Code

This exercise builds on Exercise 12.1 from the previous chapter. As before, the purpose of the application is to ask the user for a region, several summary measures, and *at least* one product sold in the region, and then display summary statistics for the chosen region and products in a sequence of message boxes, one for each product selected. The only change from the exercise in the previous chapter is that the user can now select *several* products, not just one, to summarize.

The file **Debugging.xls** contains the required user forms and code. However, it has a number of errors, as you will discover when you try to run it. These are not "obscure" errors that have been created just to trick you. They are all fairly common errors. Your task is to locate them and fix them. If you get stuck, or if you want to check your work, the file **DebuggingFinished.xls** has the corrected code. Also, at the top of its module, it contains comments listing the errors in the

Debugging.xls file. As usual, however, try not to look at this list until you have done some detective work on your own. The tools in this chapter should make your search considerably easier.

13.3 Debugging

We begin with the errors that *you* as the programmer make, and how you can debug your programs to fix these errors. The first step is to categorize the possible types of errors. There are three basic types: **syntax** errors, **runtime** errors, and **logic** errors.

Syntax Errors

Syntax errors are usually the easiest to spot and fix. They occur when you spell something wrong, omit a keyword, or commit various other "grammatical" errors. They are easy to spot because the VBE detects them immediately, colors the offending code red, and displays a warning in a message box.[29] You have probably already experienced this behavior numerous times, but in case you haven't, type the following line of code and press the Enter key:

```
If FirstNumber > SecondNumber
```

You will be reminded immediately that this line contains a syntax error: the keyword Then is missing. Sometimes the resulting error message will tell you in clear terms what the error is, and other times it will be more mysterious. But at least you know there is something wrong with your syntax, you know approximately where the error is, and you have a chance to fix it right away. There is no excuse for not fixing these types of errors immediately. If you are not sure of the correct syntax, you can look it up in online help.

Runtime Errors

Runtime errors are more difficult to spot and fix. They occur when there is something wrong with your code, but the error is not discovered until you run your program. The following lines illustrate a typical example.

```
Option Explicit
Option Base 1

Sub Test()
    Dim MyArray(10) As Integer, i As Integer, NReps As Integer
    NReps = InputBox("Enter the number of replications.")
    For i = 1 To NReps
```

---

[29]This is the default behavior of the VBE, and you should probably leave it in place. However, if you get tired of the warnings, you can use VBE's Tools/Options menu item and uncheck the Auto Syntax Check under the Editor tab.

```
        MyArray(i) = 20 * i
    Next
End Sub
```

This code has no syntax errors, but it is likely to produce a runtime error. The user is asked to enter a number of replications, which is stored in the variable NReps. If the user enters a value less than or equal to 10, the program will run fine. However, if the user enters a number greater than 10, the program will try to fill the array with more values than it is dimensioned for. If you run this program and enter 15 in the input box, you will get the error dialog box in Figure 13.1. It is one of Microsoft's cryptic error messages that you will come to despise, both because it means that *you* made an error and because you can't make any sense out of the message.

Figure 13.1 Error dialog box

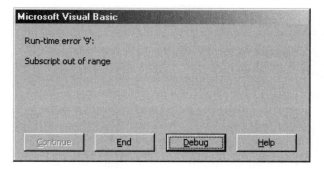

At this point, you have the three options indicated by the enabled buttons: (1) you can ask for help, which is usually not very helpful; (2) you can end the program, which doesn't do anything to solve the problem; or (3) you can click on Debug. This latter option displays the offending line of code colored in yellow. If you then move the cursor over variables, you can see their current values, which might provide just the clue you need. Figure 13.2 shows what happens if you click on Debug and then put the cursor over the variable i in the offending line. Its current value is 11, and the array is dimensioned for only 10 elements.

Figure 13.2 Code after clicking on Debug

```
(General)                                          ▼  Test

    Option Explicit

    Option Base 1
    Sub Test()
        Dim MyArray(10) As Integer, i As Integer, NReps As Integer
        NReps = InputBox("Enter the number of replications.")
        For i = 1 To NReps
⇨           MyArray(i) = 20 * i
        Next|      i = 11
    End Sub
```

This is the clue you need to fix the program, as shown below. The trick is to redimension the array *after* discovering the value of NReps.

```
Sub Test()
    Dim MyArray() As Integer, i As Integer, NReps As Integer
    NReps = InputBox("Enter the number of replications.")
    ReDim MyArray(NReps)
    For i = 1 To NReps
        MyArray(i) = 20 * i
    Next
End Sub
```

The problem with runtime errors is that there is an infinite variety of them, and the error messages provided by Microsoft can be quite misleading. Consider the following sub, which purposely violates the cardinal rule of indenting to mask the error in the program. Can you spot it?

```
Sub Test()
Dim cell As Range
For Each cell In Range("A1:D10")
If cell.Value > 10 Then
With cell.Font
.Bold = True
.Italic = True
End If
Next
End Sub
```

The properly indented version listed below clearly indicates the problem—the With construction is missing an End With.

```
Sub Test()
    Dim cell As Range
    For Each cell In Range("A1:D10")
        If cell.Value > 10 Then
            With cell.Font
                .Bold = True
                .Italic = True
        End If
    Next
End Sub
```

However, if you run this program (either version), you will get the error message in Figure 13.3, and the End If line of the sub will be highlighted in yellow! As you can imagine, this type of misleading information can drive a programmer crazy. Of course, some snooping around indicates that the problem is *not* with the If–End If construction but is instead with the With–End With, but an unsuspecting programmer could be led down a time-consuming blind alley searching for the error. Therefore, it is best to interpret runtime error messages with caution. They typically point you in the general *neighborhood* of the offending code, but they do not always pinpoint the problem. And, as you can probably guess, the Help button in this case will not be of any help at all.

Figure 13.3 Misleading error message

When you get any of these runtime error messages, your program goes into **break mode**, which essentially means that it is "on hold." You always know a program is in break mode when a line of code is highlighted in yellow. Sometimes you can fix a line of code while in break mode and then click on the **Run Sub/Userform** button on the VBE Standard toolbar to let the program finish. (See Figure 13.4.) Other times, it is impossible to continue. You need to click on the **Reset** button, fix the error, and then rerun the program. It is usually best to do the latter. If you ever get a message to the effect that something can't be done because the program is in break mode, get back into the VBE and click on the Reset button.

Figure 13.4 VBE Standard toolbar

Logic Errors

The third general type of error, a logic error, is the most insidious of the three, because you frequently don't even know that you *have* an error. You run the program, it produces some results, and you congratulate yourself that your work is finished. However, if your program contains any logic errors, even a single "tiny" error, the results can be totally wrong! You might or might not get an error message to tip you off.

Here is a typical example. We want to average the numbers in column A (through row 10) in Figure 13.5 and display the average in a message box. The correct average, calculated with Excel's Average function, appears in cell A12.

The AverageScores sub listed below contains no syntax errors and no runtime errors.[30] If you run it, it will display the message box in Figure 13.6—with the *wrong* average! Can you spot the problem?

---

[30]Of course, you would never write such complex code to perform such a simple task. It is done here only to illustrate a point.

Figure 13.5 Scores to average

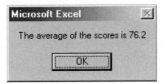

	A	B
1	Scores	
2	87	
3	78	
4	98	
5	82	
6	77	
7	99	
8	80	
9	85	
10	76	
11		
12	84.67	

```
Sub AverageScores()
    Dim ScoreRange As Range, cell As Range, Sum As Single
    With Range("A1")
        Set ScoreRange = Range(.Offset(0, 0), .End(xlDown))
    End With
    For Each cell In ScoreRange
        If IsNumeric(cell.Value) Then Sum = Sum + cell.Value
    Next
    MsgBox "The average of the scores is " & _
        Sum / ScoreRange.Cells.Count
End Sub
```

Figure 13.6 Display of incorrect average

Microsoft Excel

The average of the scores is 76.2

OK

There are actually two problems. The first problem, and probably the more important one, is that if the correct average had not been calculated separately in cell A12, the programmer would probably have accepted the answer in the message box as being correct. In fact, just stop and think about it—how many programs out there have errors that no one is even aware of? Is it possible, for example, that there are errors in the gigantic programs used by the IRS to check your tax returns? It is a scary thought.

However, assuming that you are suspicious of the answer in the message box, the second problem is to find the error and fix it. Fortunately, the VBE has some powerful tools for debugging your programs. One of the most useful methods is to **step through** a program one line at a time, possibly keeping a **watch** on one or more key variables. VBE's **Debug** toolbar is very handy for doing this. (See Figure 13.7.) Equivalently, you can use menu items and shortcut keys to perform the same tasks.

Figure 13.7 VBE Debug toolbar

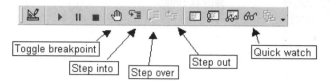

Let's use this method to find the faulty logic in the average example. To do this (and you should follow along at your own PC), get into the VBE and put a watch on the key variable Sum. The easiest way to do this is to put the cursor anywhere on the Sum variable (any place it appears in the code) and click on the **Quick watch** button. The **Watch window** then opens, as shown in Figure 13.8. It allows you to watch the contents of Sum as the program executes. In general, you can put watches on as many variables as you like.

Figure 13.8 Watch window

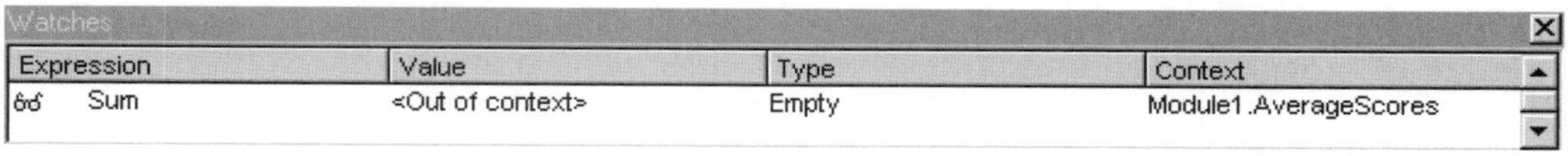

Expression	Value	Type	Context
∂∂ Sum	<Out of context>	Empty	Module1.AverageScores

At this point, Sum has not yet been defined, so its value is listed as "out of context." But it changes as you step through the program. To do this, put the cursor anywhere in the AverageScores sub, and repeatedly click on the **Step into** button. (Alternatively, press the **F8** key repeatedly.) This executes a line of code at a time. If the line changes the value of Sum, the updated value will appear in the Watch window. By the time the For Each loop is finished, the Watch window appears as in Figure 13.9.

Figure 13.9 Watch window after For Each loop

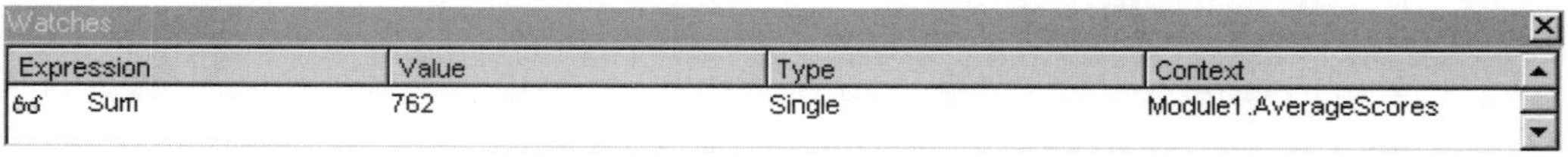

Expression	Value	Type	Context
∂∂ Sum	762	Single	Module1.AverageScores

If you sum the numbers in the range A2:A10 of Figure 13.5, you will find that the sum is indeed 762. This means that the problem is *not* with the logic for calculating Sum. The only other possible problem is with the number Sum is divided by to obtain the average. (Now do you see the error?) A careful look at the code shows that the ScoreRange includes the label in cell A1. Therefore, **ScoreRange .Cells.Count** returns 10, not 9. The correct average is 762/9, not 762/10.

The general point made by this example is that stepping through a program, together with a careful use of the Watch window, can localize a problem and enable you to fix it. You can also employ some other debugging tools to fine-tune your search for bugs. This is particularly important if you have a large program with several subs and you are confident that most of them are bug-free. Then you can use the following tools.

- **Set breakpoints.** Put the cursor on any line of code and click on the **Toggle breakpoint** button. This puts a red dot in the left-hand margin of the code window (or it removes the red dot if one was already there). If you now run the program, it will execute until it encounters this line of code, at which time it goes into break mode. Then you can examine values of variables or step through the program from there on. In general, whenever you click on the Run Sub/Userform button, the program will always advance to the *next* breakpoint. (If there isn't another breakpoint, the program will run to completion.)
- **Step over subs.** As you are stepping through a program, you might get to a line that calls another sub. If you do not want to step through that sub line by line (because you are confident it is bug-free), click on the **Step over** button. It will execute the sub all at once, without stepping through it.
- **Step out of subs.** Similarly, if you are stepping through a sub and decide there is no point in stepping through the rest of it, click on the **Step out** button. The rest of the sub will be executed all at once and control will pass back to the calling sub, which you can then continue to step through.

These tools are great for debugging, but they are not magic bullets. Incorrect logic creeps into almost all programs of any reasonable size, and it is the programmer's task to find them. This requires a thorough knowledge of the program, a lot of detective work, and perseverance. The easy way out is to seek immediate help from someone else (your instructor?) as soon as something goes wrong. However, you should try to find the bugs yourself, using the tools described here. It is probably the most effective way to become a good programmer. You will undoubtedly learn at least as much from your errors as from any programming manuals.

13.4 Error Handling

To this point, we have discussed the errors made by *you*, the programmer. This section discusses methods for trapping errors made by a user. Despite your best efforts to provide clear explanations to users, you can never be sure that they will respond appropriately. Of course, inappropriate user inputs can lead to nonsense results, even though your program is doing exactly what it is supposed to do. Part of your job as a programmer—and it is becoming an increasingly important part with today's interactive programs—is to anticipate possible user "errors" and handle them appropriately.

On Error Statement

One way to do this is with the **On Error** statement. There are several forms of this statement. They all essentially watch for errors and then respond in some way. The following lines provide a simple example.

```
On Error Resume Next
Application.DisplayAlerts = False
Worksheets("Results").Delete
MsgBox "Now the program can continue."
```

The objective here is to delete the Results sheet. However, there might not *be* a Results sheet, in which case the Delete line will cause a runtime error. The **On Error Resume Next** statement says, "If an error is encountered, just ignore it and go on to the next statement." In this case, if there is no Results sheet, no error message will be displayed, and the MsgBox statement will be executed.

A variation of this is listed below. If an error is encountered, control still passes to the next statement, but the default **Number** property of the built-in **Err** object will have a *nonzero* value that an If statement can check for. Actually, each specific type of error has a particular error code that is stored in the Err object. For example, this particular error (trying to delete a worksheet that doesn't exist) returns error code 9. You can discover this by running the following code to obtain the message box in Figure 13.10. However, unless you plan to do a *lot* of programming, you don't need to learn these error codes. Just remember that Err is nonzero if an error occurs, and it is 0 otherwise.

```
On Error Resume Next
Application.DisplayAlerts = False
Worksheets("Results").Delete
If Err <> 0 Then MsgBox "The Results worksheet couldn't be deleted because it " _
   & "doesn't exist. This is error code " & Err
```

Figure 13.10 Error code message

The **On Error Resume Next** statement is useful when you want to ignore an "unimportant" error. However, there are some errors that you definitely do *not* want to ignore. The following code illustrates a typical method that programmers use to handle errors.

```
Sub TryToOpen()
    On Error GoTo ErrorHandling
    Workbooks.Open "C:\VBABook\Ranges.xls"
    Statements
    Exit Sub
ErrorHandling:
    MsgBox "The Ranges.xls file could not be found."
    End
End Sub
```

The purpose of this sub is to open the Ranges.xls file, located in the VBABook folder of the C drive and then perform some actions on this file (designated by the

Statements line). However, there is always the possibility that this file does not exist, at least not in the specified location. The On Error GoTo ErrorHandling line handles this possibility. It says, "Watch for an error. If an error is encountered, go to the ErrorHandling **label** farther down in the sub. Otherwise, continue with the normal sequence of statements." You can have any number of labels in a sub, each followed by a colon, and you can give them any names you like. Each label acts like a bookmark that you can "GoTo."

Note that the **Exit Sub** statement is necessary in case there *is* no error. Without it, the Ranges.xls file would be opened and the *Statements* lines would be executed—so far, so good. But then the MsgBox statement would be executed, and the program would end—not exactly what the programmer has in mind.

If you have an **On Error GoTo** statement somewhere in a sub, it is "active" throughout the entire sub, always monitoring for errors. If you want to turn off this monitoring, you can use the **On Error GoTo 0** statement. This disables any error checking.

Doing Your Own Error Checking

In addition to On Error statements, you can check explicitly for invalid user inputs. This is done in most of the OKButton_Click subs in later chapters to check that the user has entered appropriate values in a user form. A typical example of this is the following. The dialog box in Figure 13.11 contains two text boxes that the user must fill in. They are named Date1Box and Date2Box. There are several inappropriate inputs that could be given: the boxes could be left blank, the entries could be invalid dates (or not dates at all), or the beginning date could be *after* the ending date. Hopefully, the user will not provide any such invalid inputs, but the programmer should not trust to luck.

Figure 13.11 Dialog box for dates

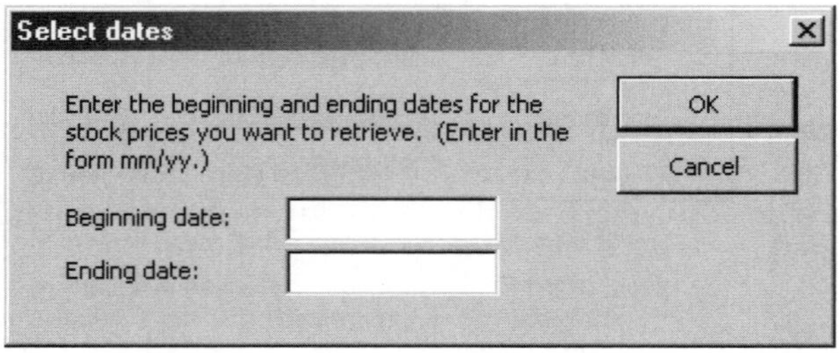

The following sub uses no error checking. It simply captures the user's inputs in the public variables BegDate and EndDate and hopes for the best. If invalid dates are supplied, there is no telling what might go wrong in the rest of the program.

```
Private Sub OKButton_Click()
    BegDate = Date1Box
```

```
        EndDate = Date2Box
        Unload Me
    End Sub
```

A much better way is to check for possible invalid dates, as illustrated in the code below. It goes through all of the controls on the user form and checks whether they are text boxes. For the text boxes, it checks whether they are blank or contain invalid dates (with VBA's *very* handy **IsDate** function). In either case, an error message is displayed, focus is set to the offending text box, and the sub is exited *without* unloading the user form. That is, the user has to try again. If these error checks are passed, a later error check is performed to see if the beginning date is after the ending date. If it is, another error message is displayed, the focus is set to the first date box, and the sub is again exited without unloading the user form. By the time this user form is eventually unloaded, the programmer can be sure that BegDate and EndDate contain valid dates.

```
Private Sub OKButton_Click()
    Dim ctl As Control
    For Each ctl In Me.Controls
        If TypeName(ctl) = "TextBox" Then
            If ctl.Value = "" Or Not IsDate(ctl) Then
                MsgBox "Enter valid dates in the text boxes.", vbInformation, _
                    "Invalid entry"
                ctl.SetFocus
                Exit Sub
            End If
        End If
    Next
    BegDate = Date1Box
    EndDate = Date2Box

    If BegDate >= EndDate Then
        MsgBox "The beginning date should be before the ending date.", _
            vbInformation, "Invalid dates"
        Date1Box.SetFocus
        Exit Sub
    End If
    Unload Me
End Sub
```

Writing this error checking code is not a lot of fun, but it is mandatory for any program that claims to be professional and "bullet proof." It not only prevents the program from accepting invalid inputs and then proceeding blindly, but it also provides users with "helpful" error messages so that they can change their responses appropriately. You will probably never be able to check for *all* conceivable errors, but you should attempt to anticipate the most likely ones.

13.5 Summary

Debugging and error handling are probably no one's favorite programming topics, but they are necessary evils if you want to consider yourself a professional programmer. There are actually two skills we have discussed in this chapter. The first has to do with finding and fixing errors in your own code. If these are syntax errors, the job is easy, but if they are runtime errors or logical errors, a good bit of detective work is sometimes necessary to locate them. Fortunately, the debugging tools in the VBE make the job much easier. The second skill deals with error handling—writing code that deals appropriately with invalid input data. Here you try to anticipate things that could go wrong and "trap" for them. Again, it isn't always fun, but in today's programming world, it is expected.

PROGRAMMING EXERCISES

1. Open a new workbook and make sure it has two sheets in it named Sheet1 and Sheet2. Then write a sub that has three lines. The first should be **Application .DisplayAlerts = False**. (See Section 4.9 to recall what this does.) The second line should delete Sheet2, and the third should delete Sheet3. What happens? Change your code so that if it tries to delete a sheet that doesn't exist, nothing happens—and no error message is given.

2. Open a new workbook and make sure it has two sheets in it named Sheet1 and Sheet2. Then write a sub that has three lines. The first should be **Application .DisplayAlerts = False**. (See Section 4.9 to recall what this does.) The second line should delete Sheet2, and the third should delete Sheet1. What happens? The problem is that Excel won't allow you to delete a sheet if it's the only sheet left. Restore Sheet2. Then add an appropriate **On Error GoTo** line and an associated label in your sub to trap for the error and take an appropriate action when it occurs. Use a message box to learn the code for this error (from the **Number** property of the built-in **Err** object).

3. Open a new workbook, insert a module, and write a sub that does the following: (1) It uses an input box to ask the user for the path and name of an Excel file to open, and (2) it then tries to open the file. Run this sub and enter the name of a file that you know to exist. It should open the file with no problem. Then run it again and enter a file that you know does not exist. What happens? Rewrite the sub with the appropriate error handling capability to take care of this possibility—and present a "nice" message to the user in either case.

4. The file **StateSales.xls** lists sales in a number of states by some company. Each state has its own sheet, with the name of the state used as the sheet name. There is a module that contains the sub ListStates. The purpose of this sub is to display a message that lists all of the states. Unfortunately, it has a few bugs. Find them and correct them.

5. Continuing the previous exercise, the module in **StateSales.xls** contains the subs StateSearch and FindState. The StateSearch sub should get the name of a state from the user, call the FindState sub, and then display a message saying whether that state is one of the sheets in the workbook. The FindState sub searches for the state passed to it and returns the Boolean variable Found, which should be True if the state is found and False otherwise. Again, these subs have bugs. Find them and correct them.

6. Continuing Exercise 4 once more, the module in **StateSales.xls** contains the sub CountSales. The purpose of this sub is to ask the user for a state and a sales rep. Then it should count the number of sales by this sales rep in this state and report the result in a message box. An On Error statement is supposed to trap for the error that the given state is not one of the states in the workbook. As you can see, this sub is in bad shape. The red lines indicate syntax errors. Find and fix all of the errors, syntax and otherwise.

7. Continuing Exercise 4 once more, the module in **StateSales.xls** contains the sub TotalSales1. The purpose of the sub is to ask the user for a date. Then the total of all sales in all states up to (and including) this date should be found and displayed in a message box, with the date and the total suitably formatted. Again, this sub is full of bugs, including syntax errors. Find and fix all of the errors, syntax and otherwise.

8. Continuing Exercise 4 one *last* time, the module in **StateSales.xls** contains a sub TotalSales2. There is also a user form called InputsForm. The purpose of these is to let the user choose a state and a sales rep from list boxes on the user form. Then the TotalSales2 sub should calculate the total of all sales made by this sales rep in the selected state and display it in a message box. Before showing the user form, the TotalSales2 sub creates an array of all states and an array of all sales reps (in all sheets). It uses these to populate the list boxes. The logic in the TotalSales2 sub and the event code for the user form is basically correct, but there are numerous "small" errors that keep the program from running correctly. Find all of them and fix them. Whenever you think you have everything fixed and running correctly, check your total sales (for some state and some rep) manually, just to make *sure* you have it correct!

9. The file **Shaq.xls** contains hypothetical data on Shaquille O'Neal's success from the free throw line. For each of several games, it lists the number of free throws attempted and the number made. Then it divides the number made by the number attempted to get his free throw percentage for that game. Unfortunately, this results in a #DIV/0! error in games where he didn't take any free throws. The question explored here is how you can recognize and react to this cell error in VBA code. There is already a DisplayPcts sub in this file that goes through each cell in the Pct Made column and displays the cell's value in a message box. Run the sub and watch how it bombs. Now try to rewrite the code so that if this error ever occurs, a message is displayed to the effect that no percentage can be reported because no free throws were attempted—and no nasty error messages are displayed. Do this by checking only the cell in column D; don't check the cell in column B. (*Hint*: One solution uses VBA's **IsError** function. Another possibility might take advantage of the following information. When the error first occurs, if you click on the Debug button and put your cursor over cell.Value in the offending yellow line, you will see that this error has code 2007. If you find a way to use this code, please e-mail the author, who tried unsuccessfully to use it!)

10. Open a new workbook, get into the VBE, insert a user form, add a text box named LastNameBox, and add a Last Name label to its left. This text box is supposed to capture a person's last name. Therefore, it should contain alphabetical characters only. You could perform an error check in the OKButton_Click sub,

but you might want to check for non-alphabetical characters at the same time the user is typing the name. You can do this with the **Change** event for a text box. In this case, the sub's name would be **LastNameBox_Change**. This event "fires" each time any change occurs to the contents of the text box, including the insertion of a new character. Write appropriate event code for this sub. It should check whether the *last* character is alphabetical. If not, it should display an appropriate message box telling the user to type alphabetical characters only, set the focus to the text box, and exit the sub. For example, if the user types Smi7, it should recognize that the fourth character is non-alphabetical and respond accordingly.

11. The file **CountryForm.xls** contains the user form shown in Figure 13.12. The user can click on any of the option buttons, named USAOpt, CanadaOpt, and EuropeOpt. When any of these is selected, the labels and text boxes should change appropriately. Specifically, if the USA button is clicked, the caption of the top label, named LocationLabel, should change to State, and the bottom label and text box, named LangLabel and LangBox, should be invisible. (Presumably, English is the common language in the USA.) If the user chooses the Canada option, the LangLabel and LangBox should be visible, and the caption of the LocationLabel should change to Province. Similarly, if the user chooses the Europe option, the LangLabel and LangBox should be visible, and the caption of the LocationLabel should change to Country. Write event code for the Click event of the option buttons to guarantee this behavior. Try it out by "running" the user form.

Figure 13.12 User form for Exercise 11

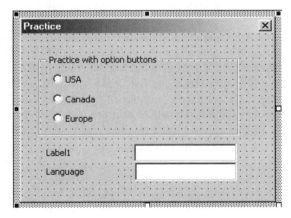

Part II

VBA Applications for Management Science

This part of the book builds upon the VBA fundamentals in the first 13 chapters by presenting a series of management science applications. We have two objectives in this part of the book. First, we have attempted to present applications that are interesting and useful in the business world. Most of these are derived from similar models in our *Practical Management Science* book. Even if readers want to ignore the VBA code in these applications completely, they can still benefit from the applications themselves. For example, they can use the network flow application in Chapter 19 to solve practically any single-product network flow model, they can use the queuing simulation in Chapter 24 to simulate a wide variety of multiple-server queues, they can use the option model in Chapter 25 to price European and American options, they can use the portfolio application in Chapter 27 to find the efficient frontier for any group of stocks, using *live* stock data from the Web, and they can use the AHP application in Chapter 29 to make a job decision.

The second objective in this part of the book is to illustrate a number of ways VBA can be used to convert a spreadsheet model into a decision support application. This is not always easy. Businesses want *powerful* applications, and power is not always easy to achieve. However, the VBA techniques used in these applications are within the grasp of anyone who is armed with the VBA fundamentals from the earlier chapters and is willing to make the effort. This effort should pay off handsomely in the job market.

The chapters in this part of the book can be read in practically any order, depending on the reader's interests. The only exception is Chapter 14, which should be read first. It presents a number of guidelines for application development, and it illustrates these guidelines in a reasonably straightforward car loan application.

Basic Ideas for Application
Development with VBA

14

14.1 Introduction

It is now time to start using the elements of VBA from the first part of the book to develop modeling applications. This chapter will establish some guidelines for application development, and it will also introduce a relatively simple car loan application to illustrate some of these guidelines. The guidelines discussed here leave much room for creativity. There are many ways to develop a successful application. From the user's standpoint, the main criteria for a successful application are that it be useful, clear, and, of course, correct. Beyond this, users like an application that has the familiar look and feel of a Windows application. As later chapters will illustrate, this leaves the door wide open for many possibilities, but it still provides some useful guidance.

14.2 Guidelines for Application Development

The topic of software application development is a huge one, and whole courses are devoted to discussions of it. If you are a software developer in a large or even a small company, there are important issues you must be aware of, and there are important procedures you must adhere to. You are typically *not* the only person who is, or ever will be, working on any particular application. Other programmers are usually working with you, and future programmers might need to update your code to meet new requirements. Therefore, your programs must be understandable by other programmers. Also, whenever possible, you should program with future extensions in mind. If new functionality is required of the program you write, another programmer should not have to start from scratch to incorporate this new functionality. In short, you need to write programs that are readable and reasonably easy to maintain.

This section is certainly not a complete treatise on the application development process; this is well beyond the scope of the book. However, there are several simple guidelines provided here—and illustrated later on—that will help you write programs that are readable and maintainable. They are as follows.

1. **Decide clearly what you want the application to accomplish.** This is probably the single most important guideline. It is particularly important if you are developing the application for a client, but it is important even if you are working only for yourself. Application development can be a lengthy process,

and you certainly do not want to spend that time going in the wrong direction. Decide ahead of time exactly what functionality your application should have and how you plan to implement it. For example, where will the input data come from—dialog boxes, worksheets, text files, or database files? What information will be reported? Will it be reported in tables or charts, or in both? Programming is always challenging, but if you don't even know which direction you are heading toward, it is impossible.

2. **Communicate clearly to the user what the application does and how it works.** You can't assume that the user will know what your application does and how it works. After all, the user has not been working on this application for several days (or weeks) as you have. The user needs a road map. In real applications, this is often done through printed materials and/or online help. Because the applications in this book are somewhat limited, their explanations are provided in an Explanation sheet that the user sees *first* upon opening the Excel files. If more explanation is required later on, it is provided, for example, in dialog box labels. The user might have no idea what is going on behind the scenes—the technical part—but the explanations should leave no doubt about the *objectives* of the application and what the user needs to do to make it work.

3. **Provide plenty of comments.** The best way to document your programs is to insert plenty of comments. It is a natural human tendency to want to plow through the coding process as quickly as possible and get the program to work, thereby omitting the comments until the last minute (or all together). Try to fight this impulse. Comments are useful not only to the next programmer who will have to read and maintain your work, but they are also useful to you as you are writing your code. They remind you of the logical thought process you should be following. Besides that, they are invaluable when you revisit your own program in a week or a month. It might be crystal clear to you—at the time you are writing—why you have done something in a certain way, but it is often a complete mystery a month later. And if it is a mystery to you, the programmer, think how mysterious it will be to another programmer (or your instructor). So when there is any possibility for confusion, add comments. Of course, you can overdo it. As an example, the comment in the following lines is a waste of typing.

```
' Add 1 to the counter.
Counter = Counter + 1
```

4. **Use meaningful names for variables, subs, and other programming elements.** There are unfortunately many existing programs that *consistently* use variable names such as i, j, k, n, and nn. They tend to be completely unreadable. Fortunately, programmers are becoming increasingly fussy about using meaningful names for variables and other programming elements. Names such as UnitCost and TotalProfit tend to make a program self-documenting. You can look at the names and figure out exactly what is going on. There is even a movement among professional programmers to use prefixes to indicate variable types. For example, they use "str" in strFirstName to indicate that this is

a string variable, whereas they use "int" in intCounter to indicate that this is an integer variable. For beginning programmers this is probably asking too much, and the code in this book does not use this convention, but don't be surprised if you are required to use a similar naming convention in your eventual job. It is just one more way to make your programs readable.

As with comments, you can overdo naming. For example, if you want a variable name for the price paid by the first customer to enter your store, you could use PriceForFirstCustomerToEnterStore. Unless you love to type, you will probably want to shorten this name to something like PriceCust1 or Price1.

5. **Use a modular approach with multiple short subs instead of one long sub.** Beginning programmers tend to write one long sub to do everything. As discussed in Chapter 10, this is a bad habit for at least two reasons. First, it is hard to read one long sub that goes on and on, even if it is well documented with comments. It is much easier to read short subs, especially when each of them has a very specific objective. Second, programs are much easier to maintain, extend, and debug when they are written in a modular fashion. For example, suppose you have written a program that creates a sensitivity table of some type. Later on, you decide to accompany this with a chart. If your program has a "Main" sub that calls several other subs to do the work, then all you need to do is create a "CreateChart" sub that has the specific objective of creating the chart and then call CreateChart from the Main sub. The rest of your program, if written properly, should not be affected at all.

6. **Borrow from other programs that you or others have developed.** The concept of "shared" code is becoming an increasingly important issue among programmers. The idea is that there is no need to reinvent the wheel each time you write a program. There are almost certainly elements of any program you write that are common to other programs you have written. Sometimes entire subs can be copied and pasted from one program to another. If this is not possible, it is still probably possible to copy and paste specific lines of code. As for "borrowing" code written by others, this is a gray area from a legal/ethical standpoint. You should certainly not borrow a whole program or significant portions of a program written by someone else and claim it as your own. However, many programmers make much of their code available for others to use—with no strings attached.[31] If you know that this is the case, then you can feel free to borrow (and adapt) that code for your own purposes, possibly with a comment or two to acknowledge the original programmer.

7. **Decide how to obtain the required input data.** Almost every application you write (and almost all of the ones in this book) require input data. For example, the car loan application illustrated later in this chapter requires four inputs: the price of the car, the down payment, the annual interest rate, and the term of the loan. The question is how the data should be obtained by the

---

[31]If programmers really want to keep other users from borrowing their code, they will probably password-protect it. This can be done easily with the Protection tab under the Tools/VBA Project menu item in the VBE.

application. Perhaps the most natural way is to use one or more dialog boxes. This method is especially convenient when there are just a few data inputs, such as in the car loan application. However, there are times when it would be impractical to ask the user to type *numerous* inputs into a bulky dialog box. For example, the minimum cost network flow model discussed in Chapter 19 can have literally hundreds of input values. The dialog box approach makes no sense in this case.

When there is a lot of input data, the chances are that the data are stored in some type of database. Several possibilities are illustrated in later chapters. Each represents a different database format, and each must be handled in a particular way by the VBA code. The possible data locations include (1) a "data" worksheet in the same (or a different) file as the application itself, (2) a text (.txt) file, (3) one or more tables in an Access (or other database) file, and (4) a Web page.

Getting the required data for an application is an extremely important issue, and several applications in later chapters have purposely been included to illustrate some of the possibilities. Of course, you should be aware that in many real applications, you have no control over where the data are located. For example, your company might have the data you require in an Access database file. If this is the case, then you must learn how to retrieve the required Access data into Excel for your application.

8. **Decide what can be done at design time rather than at run time.** This is an extremely important issue for you as a developer. You are probably quite familiar with the Excel interface but still a bit unsure of your VBA skills. Therefore, you should develop as much of your application as possible with the Excel interface at *design* time. Then you can let VBA fill in any other necessary details at *run* time.

To illustrate, suppose you want to develop a linear programming model and then an accompanying report sheet and chart sheet based on the results of the model. It is certainly possible to do *all* of this with VBA code. Before the user runs the application, there would be blank Model, Report, and Chart sheets, and your VBA code would be responsible for filling them completely when the program runs. This is a demanding task! It is much easier for you to develop "templates" for these sheets at design time, using the Excel tools you are familiar with. Of course, you cannot fill in these templates completely because parts of them will depend on the inputs used in any particular run of the application. However, using VBA to fill in the missing pieces of a partially completed template is much easier than having to start from scratch with blank sheets.

This point will be discussed for each of the applications in the following chapters. In each case, we will indicate what can be created at design time—without any VBA.

9. **Decide how to report the results.** The models in this book typically follow a three-step approach: (1) inputs are obtained; (2) a model is created to transform inputs into outputs; and (3) the outputs are reported. There are many ways to implement the third step. The two basic possibilities are to report the

results in tabular and in graphical form. You must decide which is more appropriate for your application. Often you will decide to do both. But even then, you must decide what information to report in the table(s) and what types of charts to create. A reasonable assumption is that many users are nontechnical, so they want the results reported in the most user-friendly, nontechnical manner. A simple table and an accompanying chart frequently do the job, but you must use discretion in each application.

As for charts, there is a tendency among many beginning developers to create the fanciest charts possible—wild colors, three-dimensional design, and other "cool" elements. It is probably a good idea to keep charts as simple as possible. A 3-D chart might look great, but it sometimes portrays the underlying data less clearly than a "boring" 2-D chart. And please, use common sense with color combinations. Red lettering on a purple background might be fine for an art course, but most business users do not appreciate garish color combinations.

A final issue concerning charts is where they should be placed—on the same worksheet as the underlying data or on separate chart sheets. This is entirely a matter of taste. Many developers (including this author) tend to favor separate chart sheets (along with navigational buttons, discussed in the next point) to reduce the clutter. You might disagree. However, if you do decide to place charts on the same worksheets as the underlying data, you must decide whether to let them "cover up" the data. In other words, you will have to decide on proper placement (and sizing) of the charts on the worksheets. This can be tedious—and it might make you decide to place charts on separate chart sheets after all!

10. **Add appropriate finishing touches.** There are a number of finishing touches you can add to make your applications more professional, although some are ultimately a matter of taste. Here are several possibilities.
    - Add navigational buttons. For example, if there is a worksheet with tabular results and a chart sheet that contains a chart of the same results, it is useful to put a button on each sheet that, when clicked, takes the user to the other sheet. The code behind these buttons is simple, with lines such as

```
Sub ViewReportSheet()
  Worksheets("Report").Activate
  Range("A1").Select
End Sub
```

   - Hide sheets until the user really needs to see them. For example, there might be a Report sheet that contains results from a previous run of the application (if any). There is no point in letting the user see this sheet until the application is run and *new* results are obtained. To implement this idea, the following code could be used to hide all sheets except for the Explanation sheet when the application workbook is opened. Then the **Visible** property of the Report sheet could be changed to True at run time, right after the new results are obtained.

```
Private Sub Workbook_Open()
    Dim sht As Object
    Worksheets("Explanation").Activate
    Range("F4").Select
    For Each sht In ActiveWorkbook.Sheets
        If sht.Name <> "Explanation" Then sht.Visible = False
    Next
End Sub
```

- Use the Excel's Tools/Options menu item, with the View tab, to change some of the defaults on selected sheets. For example, it is possible to turn off gridlines, scrollbars, and/or row and column headers. You can even hide the sheet tabs. Some programmers like to do this to make their applications look less like they actually reside in Excel. You might want to experiment with these options.

14.3   A Car Loan Application

This section presents a rather simple application for calculating the monthly payments on a car loan. This calculation is very easy to perform in Excel with the PMT function, but there are undoubtedly Excel users who are unaware of the PMT function. Besides, these users might just want a "point-and-click" application that gets them results with no thinking required. The car loan application does this, and it illustrates many of the guidelines discussed above. In addition, it has purposely been left incomplete. You will have a chance to fill in the missing pieces and thereby practice your VBA skills.

Objectives of the Application

The car loan application has three primary functions:

1. To calculate the monthly payment and total interest paid for any car loan, given four inputs: the price of the car, the down payment, the annual interest rate, and the term (number of monthly payments) of the loan.
2. To perform a sensitivity analysis on any of the four inputs, showing how the monthly payment and total interest paid vary, both in tabular and graphical form.
3. To create an amortization table and accompanying chart showing how the loan payment each month is broken down into principal and interest.

Basic Design of the Application

The application is stored in the file **CarLoan.xls**. (As you read the rest of this section, you should open the file and follow along.) The file consists of four worksheets and two chart sheets. The worksheets are named Explanation, Model, Sensitivity, and Amortization. The two chart sheets are named SensChart and AmortChart. All of these except the Explanation sheet are hidden when the user opens the file. The others (except the Model sheet) are unhidden when necessary. The Explanation sheet, shown in Figure 14.1, describes the application, and it has a button that the user clicks to run the application. (This design is standard in all of the applications in later chapters.)

Figure 14.1 Explanation sheet

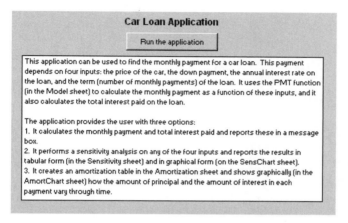

There are three user forms that allow the user to select options or provide inputs. The first, named OptionsForm and shown in Figure 14.2, provides the user with the application's three basic options.

Figure 14.2 OptionsForm

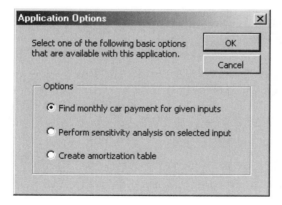

If the user selects the first option, the dialog box in Figure 14.3 appears, requesting the inputs for the car loan. (This user form is named InputsForm.) The initial values in this dialog box are those from the previous run, if any (and come from the hidden Model sheet). Of course, the user can modify any of these inputs. Then the message box in Figure 14.4 displays the monthly payment and total interest paid for this loan.

Figure 14.3 InputsForm

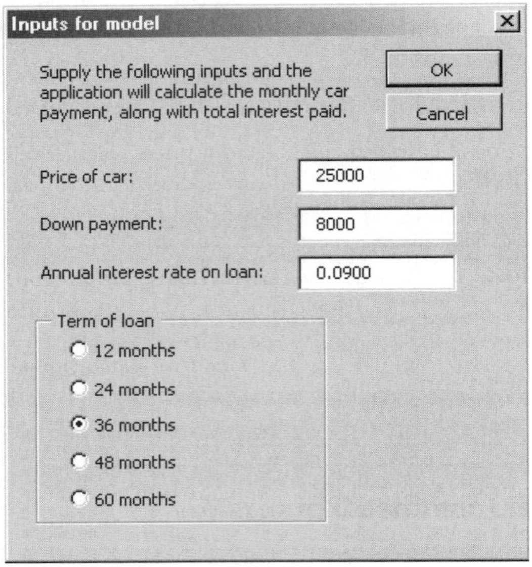

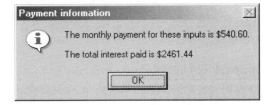

Figure 14.4 Payment information

If the user selects the second basic option, the sensitivity option, the dialog box in Figure 14.5 asks the user to indicate which of the four inputs to vary for the analysis. (This user form is named SensForm.) It then displays the InputsForm shown earlier in Figure 14.3. However, the InputsForm is now slightly different, as shown in Figure 14.6. Specifically, the "explanation" label at the top indicates that these inputs will now be used in a sensitivity analysis. (The labels in dialog boxes should always be as clear as possible, to avoid any user confusion.)

Now that the user has asked to perform a sensitivity analysis on the price of the car, what price range should be used? This is an application design issue. The application could ask the user for this range, or it could choose a default range. This application uses the latter option, primarily to make the application easier to develop. The range chosen is displayed next in an informational message box (see Figure 14.7). Then the results are displayed graphically in the SensChart (see Figure 14.8) and in tabular form in the Sensitivity sheet (see Figure 14.9). Note how the buttons in these figures allow for easy navigation through the application.

Figure 14.5   SensForm

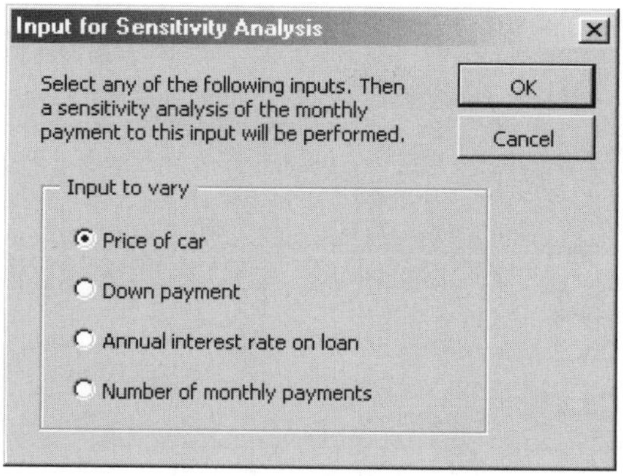

Input for Sensitivity Analysis   ☒

Select any of the following inputs. Then a sensitivity analysis of the monthly payment to this input will be performed.

OK

Cancel

Input to vary

⦿ Price of car

◯ Down payment

◯ Annual interest rate on loan

◯ Number of monthly payments

Figure 14.6   InputsForm with a different label

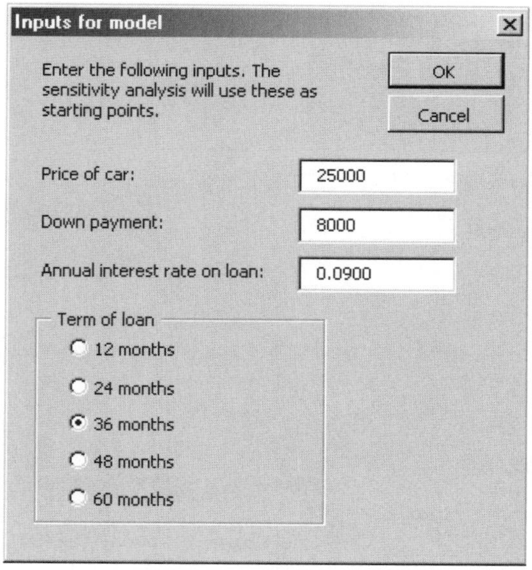

Inputs for model   ☒

Enter the following inputs. The sensitivity analysis will use these as starting points.

OK

Cancel

Price of car: `25000`

Down payment: `8000`

Annual interest rate on loan: `0.0900`

Term of loan

◯ 12 months

◯ 24 months

⦿ 36 months

◯ 48 months

◯ 60 months

Figure 14.7   Information on sensitivity range

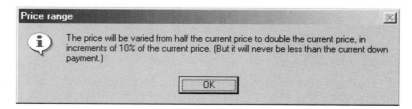

Price range   ☒

ⓘ The price will be varied from half the current price to double the current price, in increments of 10% of the current price. (But it will never be less than the current down payment.)

OK

Figure 14.8 Sensitivity chart

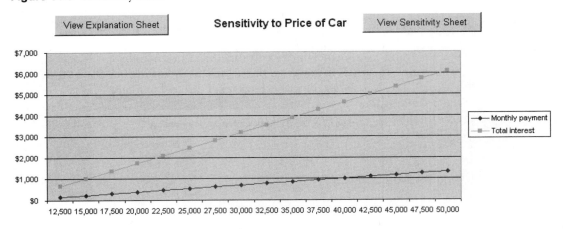

Figure 14.9 Sensitivity table

	A	B	C	D	E
1			Sensitivity analysis		
2					
3		Basic inputs			
4		Price of car	$25,000	View Sensitivity Chart	
5		Down payment	$8,000		
6		Annual interest rate	9.00%	View Explanation Sheet	
7		Term (months to pay)	36		
8					
9		Input to vary	Price		
10					
11		Price	Monthly payment	Total interest	
12		$12,500.00	$143.10	$651.56	
13		$15,000.00	$222.60	$1,013.53	
14		$17,500.00	$302.10	$1,375.51	
15		$20,000.00	$381.60	$1,737.48	
16		$22,500.00	$461.10	$2,099.46	
17		$25,000.00	$540.60	$2,461.44	
18		$27,500.00	$620.09	$2,823.41	
19		$30,000.00	$699.59	$3,185.39	
20		$32,500.00	$779.09	$3,547.36	
21		$35,000.00	$858.59	$3,909.34	
22		$37,500.00	$938.09	$4,271.32	
23		$40,000.00	$1,017.59	$4,633.29	
24		$42,500.00	$1,097.09	$4,995.27	
25		$45,000.00	$1,176.59	$5,357.24	
26		$47,500.00	$1,256.09	$5,719.22	
27		$50,000.00	$1,335.59	$6,081.20	

Finally, if the user selects the application's third option, an amortization table, the InputsForm in Figure 14.3 is again displayed, using a slightly different explanation label appropriate for the amortization objective. (This version of the form is not shown here.) Then the amortization information is shown graphically in the AmortChart sheet (see Figure 14.10) and in tabular form in the Amortization sheet (see Figure 14.11). (The results shown here are for a 24-month loan.)

Figure 14.10 Amortization chart

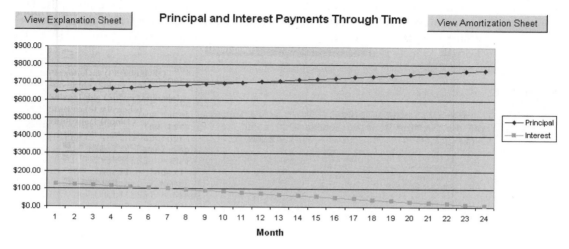

Figure 14.11 Amortization table

	A	B	C	D	E	F	G
1				Amortization schedule			
2							
3		**Basic inputs**					
4		Price of car	$25,000		View Amortization Chart		
5		Down payment	$8,000				
6		Annual interest rate	9.00%		View Explanation Sheet		
7		Term (months to pay)	24				
8							
9		**Month**	**Beginning balance**	**Payment**	**Principal**	**Interest**	**Ending balance**
10		1	$17,000.00	$776.64	$649.14	$127.50	$16,350.86
11		2	$16,350.86	$776.64	$654.01	$122.63	$15,696.85
12		3	$15,696.85	$776.64	$658.91	$117.73	$15,037.94
13		4	$15,037.94	$776.64	$663.86	$112.78	$14,374.08
14		5	$14,374.08	$776.64	$668.84	$107.81	$13,705.24
15		6	$13,705.24	$776.64	$673.85	$102.79	$13,031.39
16		7	$13,031.39	$776.64	$678.91	$97.74	$12,352.49
17		8	$12,352.49	$776.64	$684.00	$92.64	$11,668.49
18		9	$11,668.49	$776.64	$689.13	$87.51	$10,979.36
19		10	$10,979.36	$776.64	$694.30	$82.35	$10,285.07
20		11	$10,285.07	$776.64	$699.50	$77.14	$9,585.57
21		12	$9,585.57	$776.64	$704.75	$71.89	$8,880.82
22		13	$8,880.82	$776.64	$710.03	$66.61	$8,170.78
23		14	$8,170.78	$776.64	$715.36	$61.28	$7,455.42
24		15	$7,455.42	$776.64	$720.72	$55.92	$6,734.70
25		16	$6,734.70	$776.64	$726.13	$50.51	$6,008.57
26		17	$6,008.57	$776.64	$731.58	$45.06	$5,276.99
27		18	$5,276.99	$776.64	$737.06	$39.58	$4,539.93
28		19	$4,539.93	$776.64	$742.59	$34.05	$3,797.34
29		20	$3,797.34	$776.64	$748.16	$28.48	$3,049.18
30		21	$3,049.18	$776.64	$753.77	$22.87	$2,295.41
31		22	$2,295.41	$776.64	$759.43	$17.22	$1,535.98
32		23	$1,535.98	$776.64	$765.12	$11.52	$770.86
33		24	$770.86	$776.64	$770.86	$5.78	$0.00

Design Templates

Most of this application can be set up at design time, using only the Excel interface—no VBA. The Model sheet, shown in Figure 14.12, is never displayed to the user, but it is the key to the application. It can be set up completely at design time, including range names and formulas, using any trial values in the input cells. The key formula in cell B11 is **=PMT(IntRate/12,Term,-Loan)**. (If you want to examine this sheet more closely, you will need to unhide it. To do so, use Excel's Format/Sheet/Unhide menu item.)

Figure 14.12 Model sheet

In addition, templates can be created in the Sensitivity and Amortization sheets, as shown in Figures 14.13 and 14.14. The inputs in both of these sheets are linked to the input cells in the Model sheet. For example, the formula in cell C4 of Figure 14.13 is **=Model!B4**. Therefore, when the user fills in the InputsForm in Figure 14.3, the values are transferred to the Model sheet, and they are then immediately available in the Sensitivity and Amortization sheets. Also, note the partially filled-in section of the Amortization table (rows 10 and 11). It is a good idea to enter the appropriate *formulas* at the top of this table at design time. Then VBA can simply copy them down at run time. As an example, the formula for interest in cell F10 is **=IntRate/12*C10**. (You can examine the **CarLoan.xls** file for more details on the formulas.)

Figure 14.13 Sensitivity template

Figure 14.14 Amortization template

	Month	Beginning balance	Payment	Principal	Interest	Ending balance

Amortization schedule

Basic inputs
Price of car	$25,000
Down payment	$8,000
Annual interest rate	9.00%
Term (months to pay)	24

View Amortization Chart

View Explanation Sheet

Month	Beginning balance	Payment	Principal	Interest	Ending balance
1	$17,000.00	$776.64	$649.14	$127.50	$16,350.86
2	$16,350.86				

We will now examine how the inner details of the application work, starting with the user forms and their event code.

OptionsForm and Event Code

> **Web Help** For more explanation of the code in this application, visit our Web site at http://www.indiana.edu/~mgtsci and download the **Code Explanation - CarLoan.doc** file.

The design of the OptionsForm appears in Figure 14.15. It includes the usual OK and Cancel buttons, an explanation label, a frame for grouping, and three option buttons named PaymentOpt, SensOpt, and AmortOpt. Of course, these controls have to be positioned and named appropriately (through the Properties window) at design time. The **UserForm_Initialize** sub checks the first option by default. The **OKButton_Click** sub captures the user's choice in the public variable AppOpt, which is 1, 2, or 3. The **CancelButton_Click** sub unloads the dialog box and terminates the program. These subs are straightforward and are listed below.

Figure 14.15 OptionsForm design

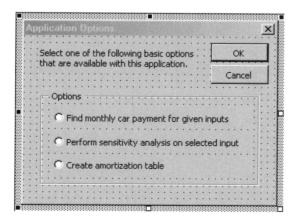

```
Private Sub UserForm_Initialize()
    PaymentOpt = True
End Sub

Private Sub OKButton_Click()
' Capture the option in the public variable AppOpt.
    If PaymentOpt Then
        AppOpt = 1
    ElseIf SensOpt Then
        AppOpt = 2
    Else
        AppOpt = 3
    End If
    Unload Me
End Sub

Private Sub CancelButton_Click()
    Unload Me
    End
End Sub
```

InputsForm Design and Event Code

The design of the InputsForm appears in Figure 14.16. It includes the usual OK and Cancel buttons, a label named ExpLabel at the top, three text boxes named PriceBox, DownPayBox, and IntRateBox (and corresponding labels), a frame for grouping, and five option buttons named Opt12, Opt24, Opt36, Opt48, and Opt60. (Note that it was a *design* decision to limit the term of the loan to multiples of 12 months.) The ExpLabel at the top of the form has a blank caption at design time. The explanation that will be inserted at run time depends on which option the user chooses. (Compare the labels in Figures 14.3 and 14.6, for example.)

Figure 14.16 Design of InputsForm

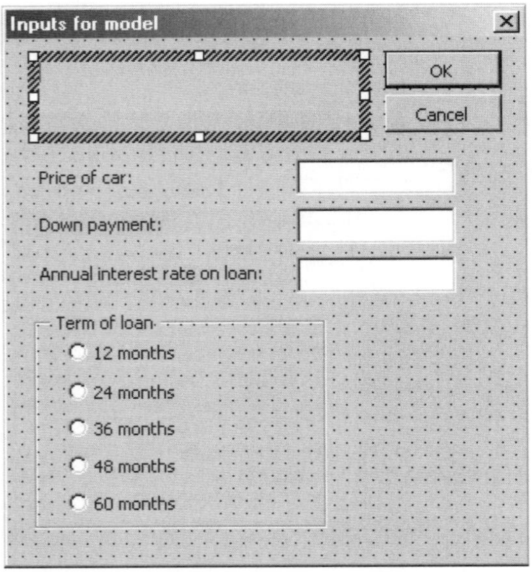

The **UserForm_Initialize** sub for this user form fills the three text boxes with the values currently in the Model sheet. (Alternatively, some programmers might elect to leave these boxes blank.) It also checks the appropriate option button, depending on what term is currently in the Model sheet, and it sets the **Caption** property of ExpLabel to ExpString, a public string variable that has, by this time, been defined in the module code (shown later on).

A note on using colons in statements. VBA allows you to write two or more short statements on a single line, provided that they are separated by colons. This is often done with **Case** statements, as shown below, provided that the statement after each Case is short. The resulting code simply takes up less space.

```vba
Private Sub UserForm_Initialize()
' Enter the values from the Model sheet (from a previous run, if any)
' in the text boxes.
    ExpLabel.Caption = ExpString
    PriceBox = Format(Range("Price"), "0")
    DownPayBox = Format(Range("DownPay"), "0")
    IntRateBox = Format(Range("IntRate"), "0.0000")

' Check the appropriate option button, depending on the Term value
' from the Model sheet.
    Select Case Range("Term")
        Case 12: Opt12 = True
        Case 24: Opt24 = True
        Case 36: Opt36 = True
        Case 48: Opt48 = True
        Case 60: Opt60 = True
        Case Else: Opt36 = True
    End Select
End Sub
```

The **OKButton_Click** sub then goes the other direction, placing the user's choices into the input cells of the Model sheet. (It first performs some error checking for invalid inputs. This error checking actually comprises the majority of the sub and is tedious to write, but it avoids problems later on.) The **Val** function is used several times to ensure that the value in a text box, always considered a *string* by VBA, is converted to a numeric value in a spreadsheet cell. Otherwise, no arithmetic on it would be possible in Excel.

```vba
Private Sub OKButton_Click()
    Dim ctl As Control, Response As Variant
    For Each ctl In Me.Controls
        If TypeName(ctl) = "TextBox" Then
            If ctl = "" Or Not IsNumeric(ctl) Then
                MsgBox "Enter a positive number in each box.", _
                    vbInformation, "Improper input"
                ctl.SetFocus
                Exit Sub
            End If
            If ctl <= 0 Then
                MsgBox "Enter a positive number in each box.", vbInformation, _
                    "Improper input"
                ctl.SetFocus
                Exit Sub
            End If
        End If
    End If
```

```
    Next
    If Val(DownPayBox) > Val(PriceBox) Then
        MsgBox "The down payment can't be greater than the price of the car!", _
            vbInformation, "Improper input"
        DownPayBox.SetFocus
        Exit Sub
    End If
    If Val(IntRateBox) > 0.25 Then
        Response = MsgBox("You entered an annual interest rate greater than 25%. " _
            & "Do you really mean this?", vbYesNo, "Abnormal interest rate")
        If Response = vbNo Then
            IntRateBox.SetFocus
            Exit Sub
        End If
    End If
    Range("Price") = Val(PriceBox)
    Range("DownPay") = Val(DownPayBox)
    Range("IntRate") = Val(IntRateBox)

    If Opt12 Then
        Range("Term") = 12
    ElseIf Opt24 Then
        Range("Term") = 24
    ElseIf Opt36 Then
        Range("Term") = 36
    ElseIf Opt48 Then
        Range("Term") = 48
    Else
        Range("Term") = 60
    End If
    Unload Me
End Sub
```

The **CancelButton_Click** sub unloads the form and terminates the program.

```
Private Sub CancelButton_Click()
    Unload Me
    End
End Sub
```

SensForm Design and Event Code

There are no new concepts in the SensForm, so we will simply display its design in Figure 14.17 and list its code below. Its purpose is to capture the public variable SensOpt, which has possible values 1, 2, 3, 4.

```
Private Sub UserForm_Initialize()
    PriceOpt = True
End Sub

Private Sub OKButton_Click()
    If PriceOpt Then
        SensOpt = 1
    ElseIf DownPayOpt Then
        SensOpt = 2
    ElseIf IntRateOpt Then
        SensOpt = 3
```

```
        Else
            SensOpt = 4
        End If
        Unload Me
End Sub

Private Sub CancelButton_Click()
        Unload Me
        End
End Sub
```

Figure 14.17 Design of SensForm

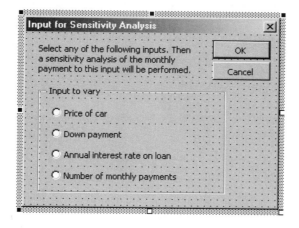

Module Code

The module contains the VBA code that does most of the work. It begins with declaration of a few public variables, along with comments that explain these variables.

```
Option Explicit

'  AppOpt - 1, 2, or 3, depending on which option the user chooses in the OptionsForm
'  SensOpt - 1, 2, 3, or 4, depending on which input the user chooses to vary in the SensForm
'  ExpString - an explanation string that will be used in the InputsForm.
'    It varies depending on the value of AppOpt.

Public AppOpt As Integer, SensOpt As Integer, ExpString As String
```

Main Code

To make the code as modular as possible, a **Main** sub is used as a control center. Its primary purpose is to call the other shorter subs that perform the individual tasks. This Main sub begins by showing the OptionsForm. Based on the user's response, it then uses a Case construct to perform one of three possible actions: (1) show the InputsForm and calculate the monthly payment and total interest paid,

(2) show the SensForm and perform a sensitivity analysis on the selected input, or (3) create an amortization table. Note that the InputsForm is shown in each case, although the explanation string (ExpString) varies slightly. Also, note that for the sensitivity option, there is a nested Case construct that is based on the input variable chosen. (The comments in the code provide further details.)

```
Sub Main()
' See which option of the application the user wants to run.
    OptionsForm.Show
    Select Case AppOpt

  Case 1
' This explanation string will appear at the top of the InputsForm.
      ExpString = "Supply the following inputs and the application " _
          & "will calculate the monthly car payment, along with total " _
          & "interest paid."

' Get the user inputs and display the results in a message box.
      InputsForm.Show
      MsgBox "The monthly payment for these inputs is " _
          & Format(Range("Payment"), "$0.00") & "." & vbCrLf _
          & vbCrLf & "The total interest paid is " _
          & Format(Range("TotInterest"), "$0.00"), vbInformation, "Payment information"

  Case 2
' First, see which input to vary.
      SensForm.Show

' This explanation string will appear at the top of the InputsForm.
      ExpString = "Enter the following inputs. The sensitivity analysis " _
          & "will use these as starting points."

' Get the user's inputs.
      InputsForm.Show

' Perform the sensitivity analysis for the selected input.
      Select Case SensOpt
          Case 1: Call PriceSensitivity
          Case 2: Call DownPaySensitivity
          Case 3: Call IntRateSensitivity
          Case 4: Call TermSensitivity
      End Select

  Case 3
' This explanation string will appear at the top of the InputsForm.
      ExpString = "Enter the following inputs. The amortization table will be based on these."
      InputsForm.Show
      Call Amortization
    End Select
End Sub
```

PriceSensitivity Code

The **PriceSensitivity** sub is called if the user wants a sensitivity analysis on the price of the car. It first unhides and activates the Sensitivity sheet. Next, it clears the contents from the previous run, if any. Then it uses a For loop to cycle through prices as low as half the current price and as high as double the current price. For each of these, it substitutes the price into the Price cell of the Model sheet, captures the monthly payment and total interest paid from the corresponding cells of the Model sheet, and places these values in the Sensitivity sheet. Note how the "counter" variable RowOff (for row offset) keeps track of where to place these values in the Sensitivity sheet. At the end of this loop, it puts the original price back in the Price cell of the Model sheet. Finally, it sets range variables for the ranges of the sensitivity data, and it calls the UpdateSensChart sub with these ranges as arguments.

```vba
Sub PriceSensitivity()
    Dim CurrPrice As Currency, Price As Currency, RowOff As Integer, _
        i As Integer, DataRange As Range, XRange As Range
    With Worksheets("Sensitivity")
        .Visible = True
        .Activate
    End With
' Enter some labels and clear the sensitivity table from a previous run,
' if any.
    Range("C9") = "Price"
    With Range("B11")
        .Value = "Price"
        Range(.Offset(1, 0), .Offset(1, 2).End(xlDown)).ClearContents
    End With
' Capture the current price.
    CurrPrice = Range("Price")
    MsgBox "The price will be varied from half the current price " _
        & "to double the current price, in increments of 10% of the " _
        & "current price. (But it will never be less than the current " _
        & "down payment.)", vbInformation, "Price range"
' For each possible price, enter it in the Price cell (in the Model sheet)
' and then store the corresponding payment and total interest values in
' the sensitivity table.
    RowOff = 0
    With Range("B11")
        For i = -5 To 10
            Price = CurrPrice * (1 + i / 10)
            If Price >= Range("DownPay") Then
                RowOff = RowOff + 1
                Range("Price") = Price
                .Offset(RowOff, 0) = Format(Price, "$0.00")
                .Offset(RowOff, 1) = Format(Range("Payment"), "$0.00")
                .Offset(RowOff, 2) = Format(Range("TotInterest"), "$0.00")
            End If
        Next
    End With
' Restore the current price to the Price range (in the Model sheet).
    Range("Price") = CurrPrice
' Set the ranges for the sensitivity chart and then update the chart.
    With Range("B11")
        Set DataRange = Range(.Offset(1, 1), .Offset(1, 2).End(xlDown))
        Set XRange = Range(.Offset(1, 0), .End(xlDown))
    End With
    Call UpdateSensChart("Price of Car", DataRange, XRange)
End Sub
```

UpdateSensChart Code

The **UpdateSensChart** takes three arguments: a string for chart titles, a range for the source data, and another range for the horizontal axis variable. (Note how Range object variables can be passed as arguments, just like any other variables.) It then updates the already existing SensChart with these arguments. (If you're not sure exactly what part of the chart each of the lines changes, set a breakpoint at the Sub line. Then when you run the application, it will stop here, allowing you to step through the sub with the F8 key and examine the effect of each line.)

```
Sub UpdateSensChart(InputParameter As String, DataRange As Range, XRange As Range)
    With Charts("SensChart")
        .Visible = True
        .Activate
        .SetSourceData DataRange
        .SeriesCollection(1).Name = "Monthly payment"
        .SeriesCollection(2).Name = "Total interest"
        .SeriesCollection(1).XValues = XRange
        .Axes(xlCategory).AxisTitle.Caption = InputParameter
        .ChartTitle.Text = "Sensitivity to " & InputParameter
        .Deselect
    End With
End Sub
```

DownPaySensitivity, IntRateSensitivity, and TermSensitivity Code

The next three subs are analogous to the PriceSensitivity sub. They are relevant for sensitivity analyses on the down payment, the interest rate, and the term, respectively. Their code has purposely *not* been supplied. They are left to you as an exercise. (Right now, they contain only messages that you can delete when you write your code.) Note that you should call the UpdateSensChart sub from each of them, using appropriate arguments in each case.

```
Sub DownPaySensitivity()
    MsgBox "The code for this sensitivity analysis is not yet written. " _
        & "Try writing it on your own.", vbInformation, "Incomplete"
End Sub

Sub IntRateSensitivity()
    MsgBox "The code for this sensitivity analysis is not yet written. " _
        & "Try writing it on your own.", vbInformation, "Incomplete"
End Sub

Sub TermSensitivity()
    MsgBox "The code for this sensitivity analysis is not yet written. " _
        & "Try writing it on your own.", vbInformation, "Incomplete"
End Sub
```

Amortization Code

The **Amortization** sub creates an amortization table. It first unhides and activates the Amortization table and clears the contents of the previous run, if any. Because the amortization table will have as many rows as the term of the loan, the variable

Term is defined to help fill the table. Then the table is built. Its first column, the month number, is filled with the DataSeries method of a Range object. (This is equivalent to Excel's Edit/Fill/Series menu item. You can learn the syntax for the DataSeries line by using this menu item with the recorder on.) The rest of the table is filled by copying the relevant formulas down their respective columns. (These formulas were entered in the template at design time. See rows 10 and 11 of Figure 14.17.) Finally, the sub sets range variables for the ranges of the amortization table, and it calls the UpdateAmortChart sub with these ranges as arguments.

```vba
Sub Amortization()
    Dim Term As Integer, DataRange As Range, XRange As Range
    With Worksheets("Amortization")
        .Visible = True
        .Activate
    End With
' Clear out old table (but leave a few key formulas as is).
    With Range("B10")
        Range(.Offset(2, 0), .Offset(2, 1).End(xlDown)).ClearContents
        Range(.Offset(1, 2), .Offset(1, 5).End(xlDown)).ClearContents
    End With
' Capture the term in a variable. It is the "length" of the amortization table.
    Term = Range("Term")
' Autofill the first column of the table (1,2,3,etc.). Then copy the formulas already
' supplied down the other columns.
    With Range("B10")
        .DataSeries Rowcol:=xlColumns, Step:=1, Stop:=Term
        .Offset(1, 1).Copy Range(.Offset(2, 1), .Offset(Term - 1, 1))
        Range(.Offset(0, 2), .Offset(0, 5)).Copy Range(.Offset(1, 2), .Offset(Term - 1, 5))
    End With
' Set the ranges for the amortization chart and then update the chart.
    With Range("B9")
        Set DataRange = Range(.Offset(1, 3), .Offset(1, 4).End(xlDown))
        Set XRange = Range(.Offset(1, 0), .End(xlDown))
    End With
    Call UpdateAmortChart(DataRange, XRange)
End Sub
```

UpdateAmortChart Code

The **UpdateAmortChart** sub takes two arguments: a range for the source data, and another range for the horizontal axis variable. It then updates the already-existing AmortChart with these arguments.

```vba
Sub UpdateAmortChart(DataRange As Range, XRange As Range)
    With Charts("AmortChart")
        .Visible = True
        .Activate
        .SetSourceData DataRange
        .SeriesCollection(1).Name = "Principal"
        .SeriesCollection(2).Name = "Interest"
        .SeriesCollection(1).XValues = XRange
        .Deselect
    End With
End Sub
```

Navigational Code

The remaining subs are attached to the buttons on the various sheets. They are for navigational purposes only.

```
Sub ViewExplanation()
    Worksheets("Explanation").Activate
    Range("F4").Select
End Sub

Sub ViewSensSheet()
    Worksheets("Sensitivity").Activate
    Range("B1").Select
End Sub

Sub ViewSensChart()
    Charts("SensChart").Activate
End Sub

Sub ViewAmortSheet()
    Worksheets("Amortization").Activate
    Range("B1").Select
End Sub

Sub ViewAmortChart()
    Charts("AmortChart").Activate
End Sub
```

14.4 Summary

This application is not the easiest one you will ever encounter, and there is no way you could develop it in, say, an hour. There are admittedly many details to take care of. As a tactical issue, you might want to try developing this application (on your own) in pieces. For example, you might omit the parts on sensitivity analysis and amortization, along with their charts, and develop only the part that displays the message box for the monthly payment in Figure 14.4. Once you get this working properly, you can try developing the sensitivity analysis part of the application. Then you can tackle the amortization table. The beauty of this approach is that you can work on several small and relatively easy subprojects, rather than one daunting large project, and gain confidence with your successes along the way. In addition, if you keep these small subprojects in separate subs, you can test them independently of one another, thereby eliminating bugs as you proceed.

If you keep this "step-by-step" approach in mind, you will probably agree that there is no single piece of the application that you cannot master with sufficient practice. Many applications in later chapters are like this one. They are somewhat *long*, but they are not *hard*. Just remember the claim in Chapter 1—you can be a successful programmer if you persevere.

PROGRAMMING EXERCISES

1. Complete the DownPaySensitivity, IntRateSensitivity, and TermSensitivity subs that were left incomplete.

2. The charts in the application are currently line charts. Suppose the initial reaction from users is that they would rather see some other chart type such as stacked columns. Make the necessary changes. (Do you need to rewrite any of the code?)

3. Change the application so that the term of the loan can be *any* number of months from 12 to 60. Note that option buttons will no longer be practical. Use a text box instead to capture the term of the loan.

4. Suppose all car loans are for 36 months. Then there is no need to obtain this input from the user, although it would be nice to inform the user of the term in a message box. Change the application appropriately to handle this situation.

5. Suppose a down payment of 20% is required for all car loans. Then there is no need to obtain this input from the user, although it would be nice to inform the user of the down payment in a message box. Change the application appropriately to handle this situation.

6. Change the application so that it is relevant for home loans (mortgages). Assume that the term of the loan can be any number of *years* from 5 to 30 and that a downpayment of *at least* 10% of the price of the home is required. And make sure there are no leftover references to cars!

A Blending Application

15.1 Introduction

This application illustrates how a typical linear programming model, in this case an oil blending model, can be transformed into an impressive decision support system with very little VBA coding. The key to the application is that it is for a *fixed-size* model. Specifically, it works only if there are three types of crude oils blended into three gasoline products. This is certainly a limiting feature of the application. However, the fixed-size property allows the entire application to be set up at design time, without any VBA. The linear programming model can be developed, a report can be created, and several charts can be created. The only VBA tasks are to get the user's inputs for the model and to run the Solver. There are many *Excel* details to take care of at design time, but the finished application is very straightforward, with a minimal amount of VBA code.

New Learning Objectives: VBA

- To see how VBA can be used to develop a complete decision support system around a fixed-size optimization model by supplying input dialog boxes and charts and reports for the results.

New Learning Objectives: Non-VBA

- To develop an understanding of linear programming blending models.

15.2 Functionality of the Application

The application provides the following functionality:

1. The application is based on a typical oil blending model with three crude oils blended into three gasoline products. There are many inputs to the model, including crude oil availabilities, gasoline demands, minimum octane and maximum sulfur percentage requirements on the gasoline products, and others. The user has a chance to view all of these inputs and make any desired changes.

2. The model is developed in a Model sheet and is optimized by the Solver. The key outputs are reported in a Report sheet. Various aspects of the solution are also displayed on several charts. The user can view these charts by clicking on navigational buttons on the Report sheet.

15.3   Running the Application

The application is stored in the file **Blending.xls**. When this file is opened, the Explanation sheet in Figure 15.1 is displayed. When the user clicks on the button on this sheet, the dialog box in Figure 15.2 appears. This indicates that the inputs to the model are grouped into three categories. The user can view (and then change, if desired) the inputs in any of these categories by checking the appropriate boxes. If they are all checked, the dialog boxes in Figures 15.3, 15.4, and 15.5 appear sequentially. The inputs that appear initially in the boxes are those from the previous run of the model (if any). Of course, any of these inputs can be changed.

Figure 15.1 Explanation sheet

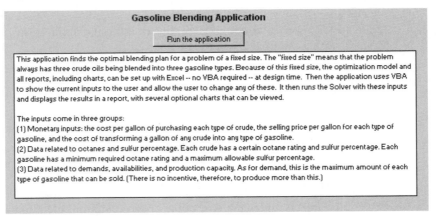

Figure 15.2 Initial dialog box

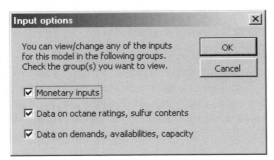

Figure 15.3 Dialog box for monetary inputs

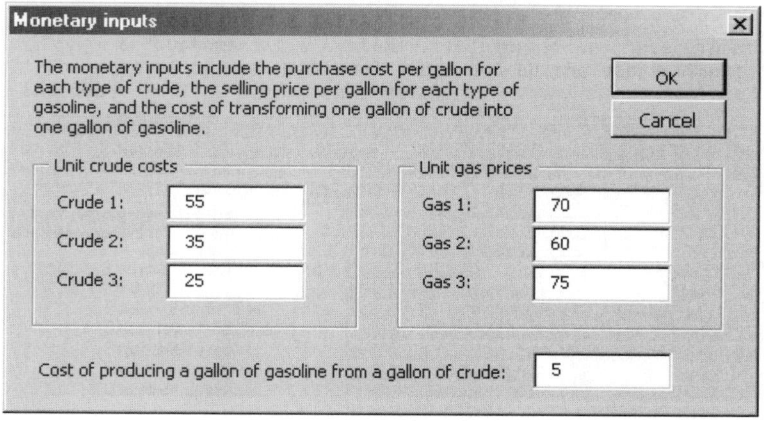

Figure 15.4 Dialog box for octane, sulfur inputs

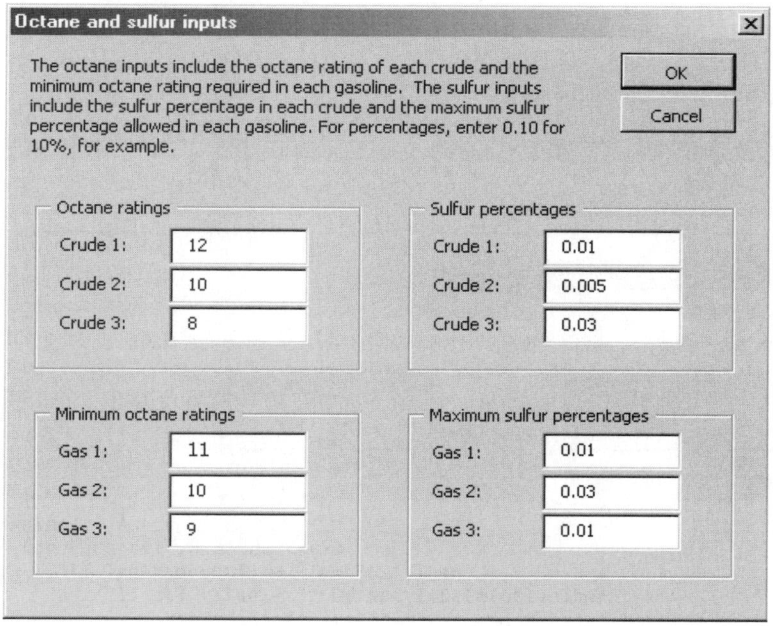

When the user has finished viewing/changing inputs, these inputs are substituted into the model in the (hidden) Model sheet, and it is optimized with the Solver. The important inputs and outputs are displayed in a Report sheet, as shown in Figure 15.6. This sheet contains several buttons for navigating to the various chart sheets and to the Explanation sheet.

Figure 15.5 Dialog box for remaining inputs

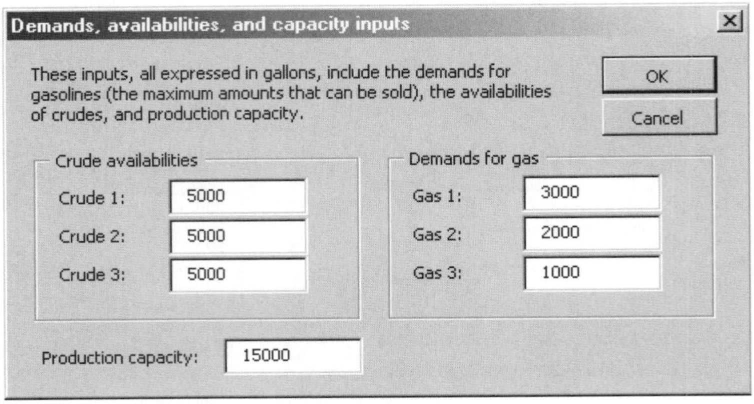

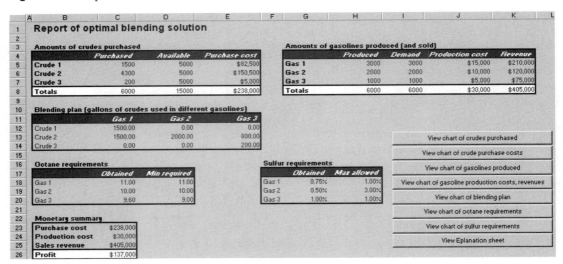

Figure 15.6 Report sheet

Report of optimal blending solution

Amounts of crudes purchased

	Purchased	Available	Purchase cost
Crude 1	1500	5000	$82,500
Crude 2	4300	5000	$150,500
Crude 3	200	5000	$5,000
Totals	6000	15000	$238,000

Amounts of gasolines produced (and sold)

	Produced	Demand	Production cost	Revenue
Gas 1	3000	3000	$15,000	$210,000
Gas 2	2000	2000	$10,000	$120,000
Gas 3	1000	1000	$5,000	$75,000
Totals	6000	6000	$30,000	$405,000

Blending plan (gallons of crudes used in different gasolines)

	Gas 1	Gas 2	Gas 3
Crude 1	1500.00	0.00	0.00
Crude 2	1500.00	2000.00	800.00
Crude 3	0.00	0.00	200.00

Octane requirements

	Obtained	Min required
Gas 1	11.00	11.00
Gas 2	10.00	10.00
Gas 3	9.60	9.00

Sulfur requirements

	Obtained	Max allowed
Gas 1	0.75%	1.00%
Gas 2	0.50%	3.00%
Gas 3	1.00%	1.00%

Monetary summary

Purchase cost	$238,000
Production cost	$30,000
Sales revenue	$405,000
Profit	$137,000

The available charts appear in Figures 15.7 to 15.13. Each of these charts contains a button that navigates back to the Report sheet.

Figure 15.7 Chart of crude oils purchased

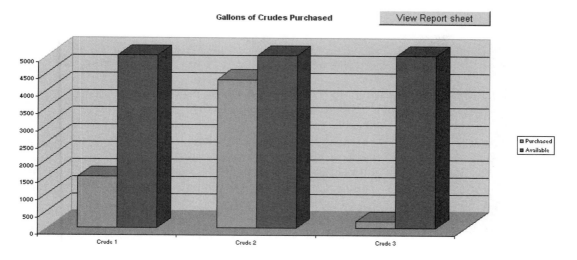

Figure 15.8 Chart of crude oil purchase costs

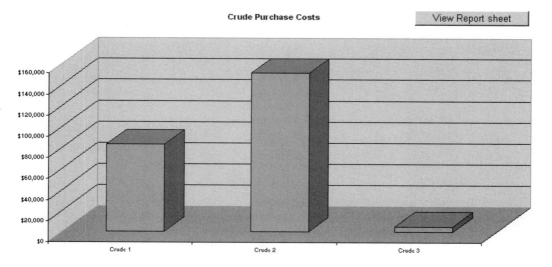

Figure 15.9 Chart of gasolines produced and demands

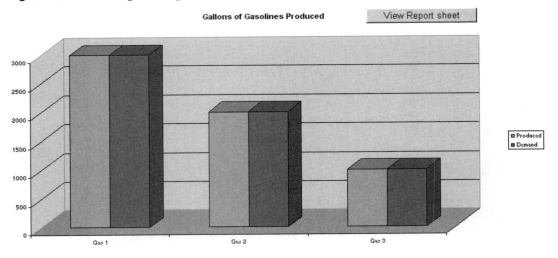

Figure 15.10 Chart of production costs and gasoline revenues

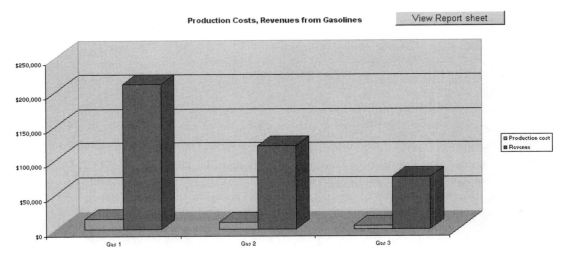

Figure 15.11 Chart of the blending plan

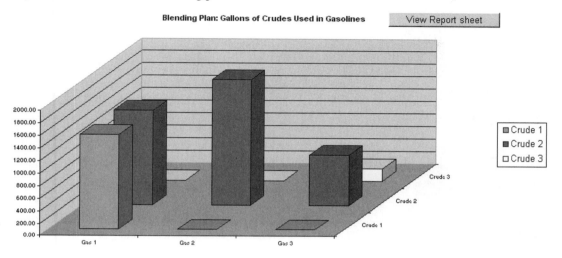

Figure 15.12 Chart of octane requirements

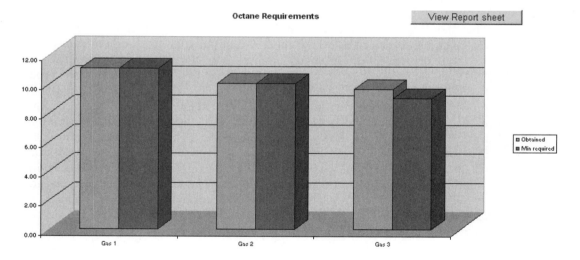

Figure 15.13 Chart of sulfur percentage requirements

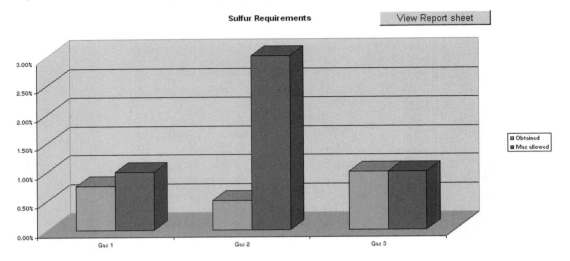

15.4 Setting Up the Excel Sheets

The **Blending.xls** file contains three worksheets and seven chart sheets. *All* of these can be developed at design time, without any VBA. The three worksheets are the Explanation sheet in Figure 15.1, the Model sheet shown below in Figure 15.14, and the Report sheet in Figure 15.6. Because of the fixed size of the problem (always three crude oils and three gasoline products), the structure of the model never changes; the only changes are new input values. Therefore, this model can be developed *completely*, including the Solver dialog box, at design time. Any inputs can be used for testing the model. (The model itself is a straight-forward application of linear programming and is based on a similar model from Chapter 4 of *Practical Management Science*. You can open the **Blending.xls** file, unhide the Model sheet with the Format/Sheet/Unhide menu item, and examine its formulas if you like.) Similarly, the Report sheet can be developed, with links to appropriate cells in the Model sheet, once and for all at design time. Finally, the charts in Figures 15.7 to 15.13 can be developed and linked to appropriate ranges in the Report sheet at design time. After these worksheets and chart sheets are developed, they are ready and waiting for user inputs.

15.5 Getting Started with the VBA

The application includes four user forms, named InputsForm, MonForm, OctForm, and DemForm, a single module, and, because this application will be

Figure 15.14 Blending model

	A	B	C	D	E	F	G
1	**Gas blending model**						
2							
3	Purchase prices per gallon of crude			Sale price per barrel of gasoline			
4	Crude 1	$55			Gas 1	Gas 2	Gas 3
5	Crude 2	$35		$70	$60	$75	
6	Crude 3	$25					
7							
8	Cost to transform one barrel of crude into one barrel of gasoline						
9		$5					
10							
11	Requirements for gasolines						
12		Gas 1	Gas 2	Gas 3			
13	Minimum octane	11	10	9			
14	Maximum sulfur	1%	3%	1%			
15							
16	Octane ratings			Sulfur content			
17	Crude 1	12		Crude 1	1.0%		
18	Crude 2	10		Crude 2	0.5%		
19	Crude 3	8		Crude 3	3.0%		
20							
21	Purchase/production plan						
22		Gas 1	Gas 2	Gas 3	Total purchased		Max Available
23	Crude 1	1500.00	0.00	0.00	1500	<=	5000
24	Crude 2	1500.00	2000.00	800.00	4300	<=	5000
25	Crude 3	0.00	0.00	200.00	200	<=	5000
26							
27	Demand for gasolines						
28		Gas 1	Gas 2	Gas 3			
29	Amount produced	3000	2000	1000			
30		<=	<=	<=			
31	Maximum Demand	3000	2000	1000			
32							
33	Constraint on total production						
34		Total produced		Max Capacity			
35		6000	<=	15000			
36							
37	Octane constraints	Gas 1	Gas 2	Gas 3			
38	Actual total octane	33000	20000	9600			
39		>=	>=	>=			
40	Required	33000	20000	9000			
41							
42	Sulfur constraints	Gas 1	Gas 2	Gas 3			
43	Actual total sulfur	22.5	10	10			
44		<=	<=	<=			
45	Required	30	60	10			
46							
47	Purchase costs	$238,000					
48	Production costs	$30,000					
49	Sales revenue	$405,000					
50							
51	Profit	$137,000					

invoking Solver VBA functions, a reference to the Solver.xla file. (Remember that you set a reference with the Tools/References menu item in the VBE.) Once these items are added, the Project Explorer window will appear as in Figure 15.15.

Figure 15.15 Project Explorer window

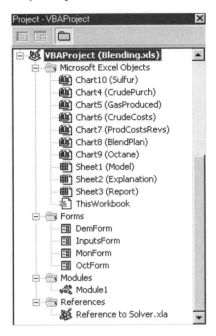

Workbook_Open Code

To guarantee that the Explanation sheet appears when the file is opened, the following code is placed in the **ThisWorkbook** code window. Note that it uses a For Each loop to hide all sheets except the Explanation sheet. (The **Sheets** collection is appropriate here. This collection includes both worksheets and chart sheets. In contrast, the **Worksheets** collection includes only worksheets, and the **Charts** collection includes only chart sheets.)

```
Private Sub Workbook_Open()
    Dim sht As Object
    Worksheets("Explanation").Activate
    Range("F4").Select
    For Each sht In ActiveWorkbook.Sheets
        If sht.Name <> "Explanation" Then sht.Visible = False
    Next
End Sub
```

15.6 Designing the User Forms and Writing Their Event Code

Web Help For more explanation of the code in this application, visit our Web site at http://www.indiana.edu/~mgtsci and download the **Code Explanation - Blending.doc** file.

InputsForm

The design of the InputsForm is shown in Figure 15.16. It contains the usual OK and Cancel buttons, an explanation label, and three check boxes named MonBox, OctBox, and DemBox. We stress that the design of the user forms for this application is completely straightforward. The text boxes must be positioned and named, the labels must be positioned and captioned, and so on—very simple operations. However, we do admit that it takes a bit of time to get everything lined up and looking just the way you want.

Figure 15.16 Design of InputsForm

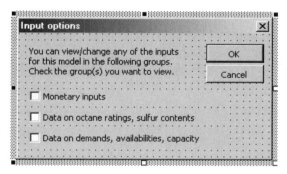

The event code for this user form is listed below. The **Userform_Initialize** sub checks each of the check boxes by default. The **OKButton_Click** event captures the user's entries in the check boxes in the public Boolean variables MonOpt, OctOpt, and DemOpt. The **CancelButton_Click** sub unloads the user form and terminates the program.

Event Code for InputsForm

```
Private Sub Userform_Initialize()
' Have all boxes checked initially.
    MonBox = True
    OctBox = True
    DemBox = True
End Sub

Private Sub OKButton_Click()
' Capture the status of the check boxes in Boolean variables.
    MonOpt = MonBox
    OctOpt = OctBox
    DemOpt = DemBox
    Unload Me
End Sub

Private Sub CancelButton_Click()
    Unload Me
    End
End Sub
```

MonForm

The design of the MonForm is shown in Figure 15.17. It contains OK and Cancel buttons, an explanation label, two frames for grouping inputs, and seven text boxes and corresponding labels. The three text boxes in the Unit crude costs group are named CCost1, CCost2, and CCost3. The three text boxes in the Unit gas prices group are named GPrice1, GPrice2, and GPrice3. Finally, the production cost text box is named PCost.

Figure 15.17 Design of MonForm

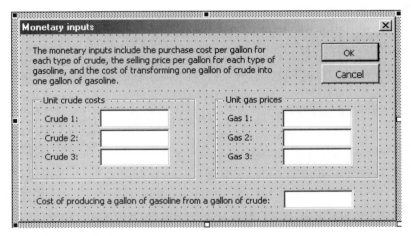

The **Userform_Initialize** sub captures the values in the Model sheet (from a previous run, if any) and enters them in the text boxes. Then the **OKButton_Click** sub takes the user's choices and places them back in the Model sheet. It also performs some error checking on the user's inputs to ensure that they are numeric and positive. It also uses the **Val** function mentioned in the previous chapter to convert a string (which is always the result from a text box) to a numeric value (which is what we want in the worksheet).

Event Code for MonForm

```
Private Sub Userform_Initialize()
' Initialize with the current values in the various ranges from the
' (hidden) Model sheet.
    With Range("PurchCosts")
        CCost1 = .Cells(1)
        CCost2 = .Cells(2)
        CCost3 = .Cells(3)
    End With
    With Range("SellPrices")
        GPrice1 = .Cells(1)
        GPrice2 = .Cells(2)
```

```
                GPrice3 = .Cells(3)
        End With
        PCost = Range("ProdCost")
End Sub


Private Sub OKButton_Click()
    Dim ctl As Control

    For Each ctl In Me.Controls
' Check that the text boxes are not empty, have numeric values, and have
' positive values.
        If TypeName(ctl) = "TextBox" Then
            If ctl.Value = "" Or Not IsNumeric(ctl) Then
                MsgBox "Enter nonnegative numeric values in all boxes.", _
                    vbInformation, "Invalid entry"
                ctl.SetFocus
                Exit Sub
            End If
            If ctl.Value < 0 Then
                MsgBox "Enter nonnegative numeric values in all boxes.", _
                    vbInformation, "Invalid entry"
                ctl.SetFocus
                Exit Sub
            End If
        End If
    Next
' Capture the user inputs in the various ranges in the (hidden) Model sheet.
    With Range("PurchCosts")
        .Cells(1) = Val(CCost1)
        .Cells(2) = Val(CCost2)
        .Cells(3) = Val(CCost3)
    End With
    With Range("SellPrices")
        .Cells(1) = Val(GPrice1)
        .Cells(2) = Val(GPrice2)
        .Cells(3) = Val(GPrice3)
    End With
    Range("ProdCost") = Val(PCost)
    Unload Me
End Sub


Private Sub CancelButton_Click()
    Unload Me
End Sub
```

OctForm and DemForm

The OctForm, shown in Figure 15.4, contains OK and Cancel buttons, an explanation label, four frames for grouping the inputs, and 12 text boxes and corresponding labels. The text boxes in the Octane ratings group are named COct1, COct2, and COct3. The text boxes in the Minimum octane ratings group are named GOct1, GOct2, and GOct3. The text boxes in the Sulfur percentages group are named CSulf1, CSulf2, and CSulf3. Finally, the text boxes in the Maximum sulfur percentages group are named GSulf1, GSulf2, and GSulf3.

The DemForm, shown in Figure 15.5, contains OK and Cancel buttons, an explanation label, a couple of frames for grouping the inputs, and seven text boxes and corresponding labels. The three text boxes in the Crude availabilities group are named Avail1, Avail2, and Avail3. The three text boxes in the Demands for gas group are named Dem1, Dem2, and Dem3. Finally, the production capacity text box is named Cap.

The event code for these two forms is very similar to the code in the MonForm, so it is not listed here.

15.7 The VBA Code in the Module

In most applications, the VBA code in the module does the majority of the work. However, this is not the case here. There is a **Main** module that "shows" the appropriate forms. Recall that the event code for these forms places the user's inputs into the Model sheet. Therefore, all the Main sub needs to do is show the forms and then run the Solver. (Note that it must first unhide the Model sheet. The Solver cannot be run on a model in a hidden sheet.) Other than this, the module contains only "navigational" subs. These are attached to the buttons on the Report sheet and the various chart sheets. There is also a RepositionButtons sub described below.

Option Statement and Public Variables

```
Option Explicit

' These Boolean variables indicate which types of inputs the user wants to
' view/change.

Public MonOpt As Boolean, OctOpt As Boolean, DemOpt As Boolean
```

Main Code

```
Sub Main()
' Find which group(s) of inputs the user wants to view/change.
    InputsForm.Show

' Show the input forms the user has requested.
    If MonOpt Then MonForm.Show
    If OctOpt Then OctForm.Show
    If DemOpt Then DemForm.Show
    Application.ScreenUpdating = False

' Unhide and activate the Model sheet, and run the Solver.
    With Worksheets("Model")
        .Visible = True
        .Activate
    End With

' Call Solver and check for no feasible solutions.
    If SolverSolve(UserFinish:=True) = 5 Then
' There are no feasible solutions, so report this and quit.
        MsgBox "There is no feasible solution to the problem with these " _
            & "inputs. Try again with different inputs.", vbInformation, "Not feasible"
        Worksheets("Model").Visible = False
        Call ViewExplanation

    Else
```

```
' There is a solution, so report it in the Report sheet.
        Worksheets("Model").Visible = False
        With Worksheets("Report")
          .Visible = True
          .Activate
        End With
        Range("A1").Select
     End If
     Application.ScreenUpdating = True
End Sub
```

Navigational Code

The following subs are for navigational purposes. Note that the chart sheets are initially hidden. Each of them has a button that runs the ViewReport sub. When this sub runs, it hides the active chart sheet.

```
Sub ViewReport()
    ActiveChart.Visible = False
    Worksheets("Report").Activate
    Range("A1").Select
End Sub

Sub ViewExplanation()
    Worksheets("Explanation").Activate
    Range("F4").Select
End Sub

Sub ViewCrudePurch()
    With Charts("CrudePurch")
        .Visible = True
        .Activate
    End With
End Sub

Sub ViewCrudeCosts()
    With Charts("CrudeCosts")
        .Visible = True
        .Activate
    End With
End Sub

Sub ViewGasProduced()
    With Charts("GasProduced")
        .Visible = True
        .Activate
    End With
End Sub

Sub ViewProdCostsRevs()
    With Charts("ProdCostsRevs")
        .Visible = True
        .Activate
    End With
End Sub
```

```
Sub ViewBlendPlan()
    With Charts("BlendPlan")
        .Visible = True
        .Activate
    End With
End Sub

Sub ViewOctane()
    With Charts("Octane")
        .Visible = True
        .Activate
    End With
End Sub

Sub ViewSulfur()
    With Charts("Sulfur")
        .Visible = True
        .Activate
    End With
End Sub
```

Repositioning the Buttons

As one final touch, the **RepositionButtons** sub, listed below, ensures that the eight buttons on the Report sheet (see Figure 15.6) are lined up, have the same size, and have the same spacing. (It is difficult to do this manually!) This sub needs to be run only once, at design time. The key to it is that each "shape" floating above a worksheet has **Top, Left, Height**, and **Width** properties. (Buttons are members of the **Shapes** collection. They are the *only* shapes in the Report sheet.) By manipulating these properties, we can position the shapes exactly as desired. Note that measurements for these properties are in **points**, where one point is 1/72 inch.

This sub was run once to line up the 8 buttons on the Report sheet. When this sub was run, the buttons had already been created on the sheet, and the first (top) button was positioned and sized correctly.

```
Sub RepositionButtons()
    Dim i As Integer, t, l, h, w
    With Worksheets("Report")
' Get the coordinates of the top button.
        With .Shapes(1)
            t = .Top
            l = .Left
            h = .Height
            w = .Width
        End With
' Make sure each succeeding button is the same size as the top button and
' is positioned slightly (2/72 inch) below the previous button.
        For i = 2 To 8
            With .Shapes(i)
                .Top = Worksheets("Report").Shapes(i - 1).Top + h + 2
                .Left = l
                .Height = h
                .Width = w
            End With
```

```
        Next
      End With
  End Sub
```

15.8   Summary

This application is a great example of the functionality you can achieve with very little VBA code. Although we don't necessarily encourage you to create all of the applications, from scratch, in the remaining chapters, we urge you to try developing this blending application on your own. There are at least two ways you can proceed. First, you can open a new, blank workbook and create the *entire* application—model, user forms, and code. Alternatively, you can make a copy of the **Blending.xls** file. Then you can delete the user forms and the module from your copy and recreate them on your own, using the explanations in this chapter as a guide. In either case, you will find that there are no *hard* steps in this application; there are just a lot of relatively simple steps. In fact, you will find that many of these steps are rather repetitive. Therefore, you should look for any possible shortcuts, such as copying and pasting, to reduce the development time.

PROGRAMMING EXERCISES

1. All of the charts in this application are types of 3-D column charts. Change the application so that they are different chart types (you can decide which you prefer). Do you need to rewrite any of the VBA code?

2. Continuing Exercise 1, suppose you want to give the *user* the choice of chart types. For example, suppose you want to give the user two choices: the current chart types or some other chart type (you can pick it). Change the application to allow this choice. Now you *will* have to add some new VBA code (along with another user form). However, you will never need to create charts from scratch with VBA; you will only need to modify existing charts.

3. Suppose there is another chemical additive—we'll call it Excron—that is part of each crude oil. We know what percentage of each crude oil is Excron, and we know the *minimum* percentages of each gasoline product that must be Excron. That is, all of these percentages are inputs. Change the optimization model and the application to take Excron into account. (Expand the OctForm to capture the Excron inputs, and make all other necessary modifications.)

4. (More difficult) Changing the size of a model like this one can be quite tedious. Try the following to see what is involved. Assume that the model can have either 2 or 3 crude oils, and it can have either 2 or 3 gasoline products. First, create a new user form called SizeForm to capture these size options. Then modify the rest of the application accordingly. (*Hints*: You can change the **Visible** property of controls on the user forms to hide them or unhide them, depending on whether they are needed. You can change the range names, with VBA, of the parts of the

Model sheet that will appear in the Solver dialog box. As we discussed in Chapter 11, this will make all Solver setups *look* the same, but you will have to do a SolverReset and then respecify all settings because of changes in the physical locations of the ranges. Finally, you might want to remove the autoformatting from the Report sheet (make it less fancy) to make modifications easier.)

16

A Product Mix Application

16.1 Introduction

This application is an example of the product mix mode. As in Chapter 3 of *Practical Management Science*, it is a prototype model often used to introduce linear programming. The products illustrated here are custom-made pieces of wood furniture that require labor hours from senior and junior woodworkers, machine hours, and wood (measured in board feet). There are constraints on the availability of the resources. For some of the products, there are also constraints on the minimum and/or maximum production levels. The objective is to maximize profit: revenues minus costs.

The linear programming model in this application is, if anything, simpler than the blending model in the previous chapter. However, the VBA requirements are considerably more extensive. The model is no longer fixed in size, because the user is allowed to include any number of products in the potential product mix. This means, for example, that the number of changing cells can change from one run to another. From a decision support point of view, this is much more realistic, but it also complicates the VBA. Only a limited amount of the optimization model can be set up at design time. The rest must be developed at run time with VBA code.

New Learning Objectives: VBA

- To see how VBA can be used to get the data inputs from one worksheet and use them to build an optimization model in another worksheet.
- To illustrate how VBA can be used to develop an optimization model of varying size.
- To illustrate how a VBA program that must perform many tasks can be divided into many relatively small subroutines.
- To better understand how VBA can be used to enter formulas into cells.

New Learning Objective: Non-VBA

- To develop an understanding of a prototype linear programming model, the product mix model.

16.2   Functionality of the Application

The application provides the following functionality:

1. It provides a database (on the Data sheet) of all required inputs for the model. Before running the application, the user can change these inputs. In fact, it is possible to manually add/delete products and resources in the list. The VBA code will always capture the current data in the Data sheet when it develops and solves the optimization model in the Model sheet.
2. Given the set of all products listed in the Data sheet, the user can select the products that will be included in the product mix model. If a product is not selected, it will not even be considered in the product mix.
3. Once the user selects the products to be included in the model, a product mix model is developed in the (hidden) Model sheet, and the Solver is invoked to find the optimal product mix. The key results are then listed in a Report sheet.

16.3   Running the Application

The application is in the file **ProductMix.xls**. When this file is opened, the explanation in Figure 16.1 appears.

Figure 16.1   Explanation sheet

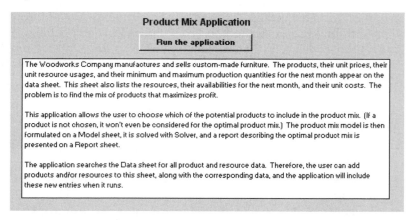

The data for the products and the data for the resources appear in Figures 16.2 and 16.3. The unit costs in column D of Figure 16.2 are actually calculated from formulas: Each is a sum of products of the unit usages in a product row of Figure 16.2 multiplied by the unit resource costs in column N of Figure 16.3. (These ingredients are colored green in the Data sheet.) All other data are given values. The MinUnits and MaxUnits in columns E and F of Figure 16.2 prescribe lower and upper limits on the quantities of the products that can be produced. If a MinUnits value is blank, it is replaced by 0 in the model. If a MaxUnits value is blank, it is replaced by a suitably large value in the model.

Figure 16.2   Data for the products

	A	B	C	D	E	F	G	H	I	J	K
3	**Data on products: unit price, resources required per unit, minimum and maximum units**										
4	Product code	Description	UnitPrice	UnitCost	MinUnits	MaxUnits	SrLaborHrs	JrLaborHrs	MachineHrs	OakFt	CherryFt
5	1243	Oak end table	$190	$130	20	40	0.5	1.3	0.4	2.8	0
6	2243	Cherry end table	$203	$146		30	0.7	1.2	0.4	0	2.8
7	1456	Oak rocking chair	$371	$277	5	20	2.1	2.9	1.2	5.2	0
8	2456	Cherry rocking chair	$407	$308	5	15	2.5	2.7	1.2	0	5.2
9	1372	Oak coffee table	$238	$167	10	30	1.3	1.7	0.6	3.2	0
10	2372	Cherry coffee table	$259	$185		10	1.5	1.5	0.6	0	3.2
11	1531	Oak dining table	$837	$648	5		1.9	3.2	1.7	15.6	0
12	2531	Cherry dining table	$964	$724		10	2.1	2.8	1.6	0	15.6
13	1635	Oak desk	$1,084	$841	5	15	4.3	5.8	3.2	18.2	0
14	2635	Cherry desk	$1,214	$938	5		4.5	5.6	3.5	0	18.2
15	1367	Oak bookshelves	$401	$315	15	30	1.8	2.5	2.1	6.2	0
16	2367	Cherry bookshelves	$455	$349		40	1.9	2.5	2.2	0	6.2

Figure 16.3   Data for the resources

	M	N	O
3	**Data on resources**		
4	Resource	UnitCost	Availability
5	SrLaborHrs	$20	263
6	JrLaborHrs	$12	450
7	MachineHrs	$15	225
8	OakFt	$35	488
9	CherryFt	$40	638

When the user clicks on the button in Figure 16.1, the dialog box in Figure 16.4 appears. This allows the user to select the products that will be included in the model.

Figure 16.4   Dialog box for selecting products in the model

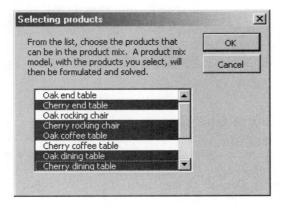

Once the products have been selected, VBA is used to develop the Model sheet. Any results on this sheet from a previous run are cleared. Then a new model is developed, and the Solver is set up and run. Finally, VBA unhides the Report sheet, clears any results from a previous run, and reports the new solution. Typical Model and Report sheets appear in Figures 16.5 and 16.6. We will not spell out the formulas in the Model; it is a straightforward linear programming model. (If you are interested, open the file, run the application once, unhide the Model sheet with the Format/Sheet/Unhide menu item, and examine its formulas.)

Figure 16.5 Model sheet

	A	B	C	D	E	F	G	H	I	J	K	L	M	N
1	Model formulation													
2														
3	Product mix													
4	Product code	2243	2456	1372	1531	2531								
5	Min	0	5	10	5	0								
6		<=	<=	<=	<=	<=								
7	Produced	30	15	30	25	10								
8		<=	<=	<=	<=	<=								
9	Max	30	15	30	31	10								
10														
11	UnitPrice	$203.00	$407.00	$238.00	$837.00	$964.00								
12	UnitCost	$146.40	$308.40	$167.40	$647.90	$723.60								
13	UnitProfit	$56.60	$98.60	$70.60	$189.10	$240.40								
14														
15	Resource usage					Monetary summary			Resources used per unit of products					
16	Resource	Used		Available		Total revenue	$49,900		Resource/Product code	2243	2456	1372	1531	2531
17	SrLaborHrs	166.0	<=	263.0		Total cost	$37,474		SrLaborHrs	0.7	2.5	1.3	1.9	2.1
18	JrLaborHrs	235.5	<=	450.0		Total profit	$12,427		JrLaborHrs	1.2	2.7	1.7	3.2	2.8
19	MachineHrs	106.5	<=	225.0					MachineHrs	0.4	1.2	0.6	1.7	1.6
20	OakFt	486.0	<=	488.0					OakFt	0	0	3.2	15.6	0
21	CherryFt	318.0	<=	638.0					CherryFt	2.8	5.2	0	0	15.6

Figure 16.6 Report sheet

	A	B	C	D	E	F	G	H	I	J	K	L
1												
2	Optimal product mix											
3												
4	Monetary summary											
5	Total revenue		$49,900									
6	Total cost		$37,474									
7	Total profit		$12,427									
8												
9	Product data								Resource data			
10	Product code	Description		Units produced	Revenue	Cost	Profit		Resource	Used	Available	Left over
11	2243	Cherry end table		30	$6,090	$4,392	$1,698		SrLaborHrs	166	263	97
12	2456	Cherry rocking chair		15	$6,105	$4,626	$1,479		JrLaborHrs	235.5	450	214.5
13	1372	Oak coffee table		30	$7,140	$5,022	$2,118		MachineHrs	106.5	225	118.5
14	1531	Oak dining table		25	$20,925	$16,198	$4,728		OakFt	486	488	2
15	2531	Cherry dining table		10	$9,640	$7,236	$2,404		CherryFt	318	638	320

16.4 Setting Up the Excel Sheets

The Model and Report sheets cannot be set up entirely at design time because the number of products and the number of resources could change, depending on the data entered in the Data sheet and the user's choice of potential products from the user form. However, these sheets can be set up partially, and certain cells can be designated as "anchors" (for use in the VBA code) and assigned range names. (It is often convenient to use upper left corner "anchor" cells relative to which everything else is offset.) The names and addresses of the anchor cells for this application are listed here for later reference. Take a look at Figures 16.2, 16.3, 16.5, and 16.6 to familiarize yourself with the locations of these cells.

- ProdAnchor (cell A4 of Data sheet)
- ResAnchor (cell M4 of Data sheet)
- ProdMixAnchor (cell A3 of Model sheet)
- ResUseAnchor (cell A16 of Model sheet)
- MonSummAnchor (cell F15 of Model sheet)
- UnitUseAnchor (cell I16 of Model sheet)
- ProdRepAnchor (cell B10 of Report sheet)
- ResRepAnchor (cell I10 of Report sheet)

The templates for the Model and Report sheets appear in Figures 16.7 and 16.8.

Figure 16.7   Model sheet template

	A	B	C	D	E	F	G	H	I	J	K
1	**Model formulation**										
2											
3	**Product mix**										
4	Product code										
5	Min										
6											
7	Produced										
8											
9	Max										
10											
11	UnitPrice										
12	UnitCost										
13	UnitProfit										
14											
15	**Resource usage**					**Monetary summary**			**Resources used per unit of products**		
16	Resource	Used		Available		Total revenue			Resource/Product code		
17						Total cost					
18						Total profit					
19											

Figure 16.8   Report sheet template

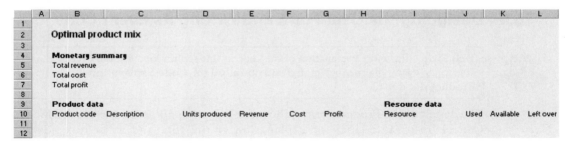

16.5   Getting Started with the VBA

This application requires a user form named ProductForm, a single module, and a reference to the Solver.xla file. Once these items are added, the Project Explorer window will appear as in Figure 16.9.

Figure 16.9 Project Explorer window

Workbook_Open Code

To guarantee that the Explanation sheet appears when the file is opened, the following code is placed in the ThisWorkbook code window. Note that it also hides the Model and Report sheets.

```
Private Sub Workbook_Open()
    Worksheets("Explanation").Activate
    Range("A1").Select
    Worksheets("Model").Visible = False
    Worksheets("Report").Visible = False
End Sub
```

16.6 Designing the User Form and Writing Its Event Code

Web Help   For more explanation of the code in this application, visit our Web site at http://www.indiana.edu/~mgtsci and download the **Code Explanation - ProductMix.doc** file.

The design of the ProductForm is shown in Figure 16.10. It has the usual OK and Cancel buttons, a label for explanation at the top, and a list box named ProductListBox. The MultiSelect property must be changed to option 2 in the Properties window (see Figure 16.11). This enables the user to select *any* number of products from the list, not just a single product.

Once the user form has been designed, the appropriate event code can be written. The **UserForm_Initialize** sub indicates how the form should be presented initially to the user. It fills the list box with the Product array (which will have been created by this time with code in the module), and it selects the first product as the default. (Remember once again that the **Selected** array for a multi-

Figure 16.10   Design of ProductForm

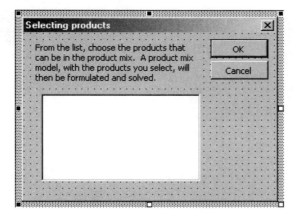

Figure 16.11   Changing the MultiSelect property of the list box

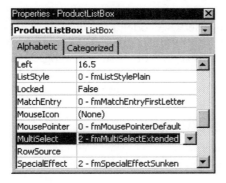

type list box is 0-based. The first item in the list has index 0, the second has index 1, and so on.) The **OKButton_Click** sub captures the user's selections in a public Boolean IsSelected array (1-based) and then unloads the dialog box. The **CancelButton_Click** sub unloads the dialog box and terminates the application.

Event Code for ProductForm

```
Private Sub UserForm_Initialize()
    Dim i As Integer
' Add the product descriptions to the list
    For i = 1 To NProducts
        ProductListBox.AddItem Product(i)
    Next
' Select the first item (so that it will be impossible for the user
' to select no items).
    ProductListBox.Selected(0) = True
End Sub
```

```
Private Sub OKButton_Click()
    Dim i As Integer
' Go through the items in the list box to see which have been selected,
' and use these to form the Boolean IsSelected array. Note that the items
' in a list box always start with index 0, whereas the IsSelected array
' starts with index 1.
    With ProductListBox
        For i = 0 To NProducts - 1
            IsSelected(i + 1) = .Selected(i)
        Next
    End With
    Unload Me
End Sub

Private Sub CancelButton_Click()
    Unload Me
    End
End Sub
```

16.7   The VBA Code in the Module

Most of the work is performed by the VBA code in the module. This code is listed below. The application proceeds in a modular manner. After declaring the public variables at the top, a **Main** sub calls several other subs in a logical order. Some of these subs call other subs. Again, the purpose of dividing the overall program into so many small subs is to make it more readable—and easier to debug.

Option Statements and Public Variables

```
Option Explicit
Option Base 1

' NProducts and NResources indicate the number of products and resources
' listed in the Data sheet, and Product and Resource are arrays of the
' product descriptions and resource names. IsSelected is a Boolean
' array that indicates which products the user selected from the dialog
' box.

Public NProducts As Integer, Product() As String, IsSelected() As Boolean, _
    NResources As Integer, Resource() As String
```

Main Code

The **Main** sub is the control center. It calls all of the other subs that do the real work. The button on the Explanation sheet (see Figure 16.1) has the Main macro assigned to it.

```
Sub Main()
' This macro runs when the user clicks on the button on the
' Explanation sheet.
```

```
        Call GetProducts
        Call GetResources
        Call SelectProducts
        Application.ScreenUpdating = False
        Call SetupModel
        Call RunSolver
        Call CreateReport
End Sub
```

GetProducts, GetResources Code

The **GetProducts** and **GetResources** subs find the numbers of products and resources from the Data sheet, redimension the Product, IsSelected, and Resource arrays appropriately, and fill them with the product and resource names from the Data sheet. Note how the "anchor" cells are used: Everything is offset relative to them. This occurs many times throughout the application.

```
Sub GetProducts()
' Find the number of products and their corresponding data.
    Dim i As Integer
    With Range("ProdAnchor")
        NProducts = Range(.Offset(1, 0), .End(xlDown)).Count
        ReDim Product(NProducts)
        ReDim IsSelected(NProducts)
        For i = 1 To NProducts
            Product(i) = .Offset(i, 1)
        Next
    End With
End Sub

Sub GetResources()
' Find the number of resources and their corresponding data.
    Dim i As Integer
    With Range("ResAnchor")
        NResources = Range(.Offset(1, 0), .End(xlDown)).Count
        ReDim Resource(NResources)
        For i = 1 To NResources
            Resource(i) = .Offset(i, 0)
        Next
    End With
End Sub
```

SelectProducts Code

The **SelectProducts** sub "shows" the ProductForm. This is all it needs to do, because the event code for the ProductForm then takes over and captures the user's selections.

```
Sub SelectProducts()
    ProductForm.Show
End Sub
```

SetupModel Code

The **SetupModel** sub first unhides and activates the Model sheet (which at this point is only a template or contains data from a previous run). Then it calls seven other subs to develop the optimization model.

```
Sub SetupModel()
' Formulate the optimization model through a series of subroutines.
    With Worksheets("Model")
        .Visible = True
        .Activate
    End With
    Call ClearOldModel
    Call EnterProductData
    Call EnterResourceData
    Call EnterUsageData
    Call CalcMaxProduction
    Call CalcResourceUsages
    Call CalcMonetaryValues
End Sub
```

ClearOldModel Code

The **ClearOldModel** sub clears out data, if any, from a previous run to return the Model sheet to its "template" form. Note that it uses the **ClearContents** method. This deletes all values but leaves old formatting in place. Again, note how the "anchor" cells are used with offsetting.

```
Sub ClearOldModel()
' Clear all of the old data from a previous model, if any, but not formatting.
    With Range("ProdMixAnchor")
        Range(.Offset(1, 1), .Offset(10, 1).End(xlToRight)).ClearContents
    End With
    With Range("ResUseAnchor")
        Range(.Offset(1, 0), .Offset(1, 0).End(xlDown).Offset(0, 3)).ClearContents
    End With

    With Range("MonSummAnchor")
        Range(.Offset(1, 1), .Offset(3, 1)).ClearContents
    End With

    With Range("UnitUseAnchor")
        Range(.Offset(0, 0), .End(xlDown).End(xlToRight)).ClearContents
        .Value = "Resource/Product code"
    End With
End Sub
```

EnterProductData Code

The **EnterProductData** sub enters data about the selected products in the Model sheet. It also names a few ranges for later reference.

```
Sub EnterProductData()
' Enter the product data for all products selected in the Product Mix part of the
' Model sheet.
    Dim ProdIndex As Integer, i As Integer, MinVal As Single
' Enter data only for the selected products. ProdIndex is a counter of these.
    ProdIndex = 0
    With Range("ProdMixAnchor")
        For i = 1 To NProducts
            If IsSelected(i) Then
                ProdIndex = ProdIndex + 1
' Enter product code.
                .Offset(1, ProdIndex) = Range("ProdAnchor").Offset(i, 0)
' Enter minimum production level (enter 0 if one wasn't given in the Data sheet).
                If Range("ProdAnchor").Offset(i, 4) = "" Then
                    MinVal = 0
                Else
                    MinVal = Range("ProdAnchor").Offset(i, 4)
                End If
                .Offset(2, ProdIndex) = MinVal
' Set the initial values of the changing cells to 0.
                .Offset(4, ProdIndex) = 0
' Enter labels to identify constraints.
                .Offset(3, ProdIndex) = "<="
                .Offset(5, ProdIndex) = "<="
' Enter unit price and unit cost.
                .Offset(8, ProdIndex) = Range("ProdAnchor").Offset(i, 2)
                .Offset(9, ProdIndex) = Range("ProdAnchor").Offset(i, 3)
' Calculate unit profit.
                .Offset(10, ProdIndex).FormulaR1C1 = "=R[-2]C-R[-1]C"
            End If
        Next
' Name various ranges.
        Range(.Offset(2, 1), .Offset(2, 1).End(xlToRight)).Name = "MinProd"
        Range(.Offset(4, 1), .Offset(4, 1).End(xlToRight)).Name = "Produced"
        Range(.Offset(8, 1), .Offset(8, 1).End(xlToRight)).Name = "UnitRev"
        Range(.Offset(9, 1), .Offset(9, 1).End(xlToRight)).Name = "UnitCost"
        Range(.Offset(10, 1), .Offset(10, 1).End(xlToRight)).Name = "UnitProfit"
    End With
End Sub
```

EnterResourceData Code

The **EnterResourceData** sub enters the resource names and availabilities in the Model sheet and names a couple of ranges for later use.

```
Sub EnterResourceData()
' Enter the resource availabilities in the Resource Usage part of
' the Model sheet.
    Dim i As Integer
    With Range("ResUseAnchor")
        For i = 1 To NResources
' Enter name of resource.
            .Offset(i, 0) = Resource(i)
' Enter label to identify constraint.
            .Offset(i, 2) = "<="
```

```
' Enter resource availability.
            .Offset(i, 3) = Range("ResAnchor").Offset(i, 2)
        Next
' Name resource ranges.
        Range(.Offset(1, 1), .Offset(NResources, 1)).Name = "Used"
        Range(.Offset(1, 3), .Offset(NResources, 3)).Name = "Available"
    End With
End Sub
```

EnterUsageData Code

The **EnterUsageData** sub enters the table of unit resource usages (how much of each resource is used by a unit of each product) in the Model sheet.

```
Sub EnterUsageData()
' Enter the unit usages of resources for selected products in the resource usage
' part of the Model sheet.
    Dim ProdIndex As Integer, i As Integer, j As Integer
    With Range("UnitUseAnchor")
' Enter resource names.
        For i = 1 To NResources
            .Offset(i, 0) = Resource(i)
        Next
' Enter data only for selected products.  ProdIndex is a counter for these.
        ProdIndex = 0
        For j = 1 To NProducts
            If IsSelected(j) Then
                ProdIndex = ProdIndex + 1
' Enter product code.
                .Offset(0, ProdIndex) = Range("ProdAnchor").Offset(j, 0)
' Enter unit usages of all resources used by product j.
                For i = 1 To NResources
                    .Offset(i, ProdIndex) = Range("ProdAnchor").Offset(j, 5 + i)
                Next
            End If
        Next
    End With
End Sub
```

CalcMaxProduction Code

The **CalcMaxProduction** sub finds the maximum limit on production for each selected product and enters it in the Model sheet. If no explicit maximum limit is given for a product in the Data sheet, a suitable maximum limit is calculated in this sub by seeing which of the resources would be most constraining if *all* of the resource were committed to this particular product.

```
Sub CalcMaxProduction()
' Calculate the max production levels for all selected products.
    Dim ProdIndex As Integer, i As Integer, j As Integer, MaxVal As Single, _
        UnitUse As Single, Ratio As Single
' Enter data only for selected products.  ProdIndex is a counter for these.
    ProdIndex = 0
```

```
      With Range("ProdMixAnchor")
          For j = 1 To NProducts
              If IsSelected(j) Then
                  ProdIndex = ProdIndex + 1
                  If Range("ProdAnchor").Offset(j, 5) = "" Then
' No maximum production level was given, so find how much of this product could be
' produced if all of the resources were devoted to it, and use this as a maximum
' production level.
                      MaxVal = 1000000
                      For i = 1 To NResources
                          UnitUse = Range("UnitUseAnchor").Offset(i, ProdIndex)
                          If UnitUse > 0 Then
                              Ratio = Range("Available").Cells(i) / UnitUse
                              If Ratio < MaxVal Then MaxVal = Ratio
                          End If
                      Next
' Enter calculated maximum production level (rounded down to nearest integer).
                      .Offset(6, ProdIndex) = Int(MaxVal)
                  Else
' The maximum production level was given, so enter it.
                      .Offset(6, ProdIndex) = Range("ProdAnchor").Offset(j, 5)
                  End If
              End If
          Next
' Name the range of maximum production levels.
          Range(.Offset(6, 1), .Offset(6, 1).End(xlToRight)).Name = "MaxProd"
      End With
End Sub
```

CalcResourceUsages Code

The **CalcResourceUsages** sub calculates the amount of each resource used by the current product mix and enters it in the Model sheet. Pay particular attention to the following two lines, which are inside the For loop on i.

```
UnitUseAddress = Range(.Offset(i, 1), .Offset(i, 1).End(xlToRight)).Address
Range("Used").Cells(i).Formula = "=Sumproduct(Produced," & UnitUseAddress & ")"
```

We want to enter a formula such as **=Sumproduct(Produced,J17:N17)** in a cell. (For example, if i=1, this would be the formula in cell B17 for the model in Figure 16.5.) To do this, we find the address for the second argument of the Sumproduct function from the first line and store it in the string variable UnitUseAddress. Then we use string concatenation to "build" the formula in the second line. Entering formulas in cells with VBA can be tricky, and it often involves similar string concatenation to piece together a combination of literals and string variables.

```
Sub CalcResourceUsages()
' Calculate the resource usage for each resource by using a Sumproduct function.
' Note how the address of the row of unit usages for resource i is found first, then
' used as part of the formula string.
    Dim i As Integer, UnitUseAddress As String
    With Range("UnitUseAnchor")
        For i = 1 To NResources
```

```
            UnitUseAddress = Range(.Offset(i, 1), .Offset(i, 1).End(xlToRight)).Address
            Range("Used").Cells(i).Formula = "=Sumproduct(Produced," & UnitUseAddress & ")"
        Next
    End With
End Sub
```

CalcMonetaryValues Code

The **CalcMonetaryValues** sub uses Excel's Sumproduct function to calculate the total revenue, total cost, and total profit from the current product mix. It also names the corresponding cells for later reference.

```
Sub CalcMonetaryValues()
    With Range("MonSummAnchor")
        .Offset(1, 1).Formula = "=Sumproduct(Produced,UnitRev)"
        .Offset(2, 1).Formula = "=Sumproduct(Produced,UnitCost)"
        .Offset(3, 1).Formula = "=Sumproduct(Produced,UnitProfit)"
' Name the monetary cells.
        .Offset(1, 1).Name = "TotRev"
        .Offset(2, 1).Name = "TotCost"
        .Offset(3, 1).Name = "TotProfit"
    End With
End Sub
```

RunSolver Code

The **RunSolver** sub sets up the Solver and then runs it.[32] It checks whether there are no feasible solutions. (Remember from Chapter 11 that the numerical code for no feasible solutions in the SolverSolve function is 5.) If the model has no feasible solutions, the Model and Report sheets are hidden, the Explanation sheet is activated, an appropriate message is displayed, and the application is terminated. Note that we impose integer constraints on the changing cells. This, plus the fact that the number of changing cells can change from one run to the next, requires us to repeat the SolverReset and SolverOk lines to get around the Solver bug discussed in Chapter 11. Of course, if you do not want to impose integer constraints, you can delete (or comment out) the appropriate line in this sub.

```
Sub RunSolver()
    Dim Result As Integer
' Reset Solver settings, then set up Solver.
    SolverReset
    SolverOk SetCell:=Range("TotProfit"), MaxMinVal:=1, ByChange:=Range("Produced")
```

---

[32]Even though the Solver setup will always *look* the same—for example, it will always have the constraint Used<=Available—it must be reset and then set up from scratch each time the application is run. If this is not done and the *size* of the model is different from the previous run, the Solver settings will be interpreted incorrectly.

```
' The previous two lines are repeated because of the apparent Solver VBA bug
' (mentioned in Chapter 11) that occurs when there are integer or binary constraints.
    SolverReset
    SolverOk SetCell:=Range("TotProfit"), MaxMinVal:=1, _
        ByChange:=Range("Produced")
' Add constraints.
    SolverAdd CellRef:=Range("Produced"), Relation:=3, _
        FormulaText:=Range("MinProd").Address
    SolverAdd CellRef:=Range("Produced"), Relation:=1, _
        FormulaText:=Range("MaxProd").Address
    SolverAdd CellRef:=Range("Used"), Relation:=1, _
        FormulaText:=Range("Available").Address
' Comment out the next line if you don't want integer constraints on production.
    SolverAdd CellRef:=Range("Produced"), Relation:=4
    SolverOptions AssumeLinear:=True, AssumeNonNeg:=True
' Run Solver and check for infeasibility.
    If SolverSolve(UserFinish:=True) = 5 Then

' There is no feasible solution, so report this, tidy up, and quit.
        MsgBox "This model has no feasible solution. Change the data " _
            & "in the Data sheet and try running it again.", _
            vbInformation, "No feasible solution"
        Worksheets("Explanation").Activate
        Range("A1").Select
        Worksheets("Model").Visible = False
        Worksheets("Report").Visible = False
        End
    End If
End Sub
```

CreateReport Code

The **CreateReport** sub first unhides and activates the Report sheet (which at this point is only a template or contains results from a previous run). It then clears any previous results and transfers the important results from the Model sheet to the appropriate places in the Report sheet through a series of three short subs.

```
Sub CreateReport()
' Fill in the Report sheet, mostly by transferring the results from the Model sheet.
    Dim i As Integer, ProdIndex As Integer
' Hide Model sheet.
    Worksheets("Model").Visible = False
' Unhide and activate Report sheet.
    With Worksheets("Report")
        .Visible = True
        .Activate
    End With
' Enter results in three steps.
    Call EnterMonetaryResults
    Call EnterProductResults
    Call EnterResourceResults
' Make sure columns C and I are wide enough, then select cell A1.
    Columns("C:C").Columns.AutoFit
    Columns("I:I").Columns.AutoFit
    Range("A1").Select
End Sub
```

EnterMonetaryResults, EnterProductResults, and EnterResourceResults Code

These three short subs do exactly what their names imply: They transfer the key results from the Model sheet to the Report sheet.

```
Sub EnterMonetaryResults()
    Dim i As Integer
' Transfer the total revenue, total cost, and total profit.
    With Range("C4")
        For i = 1 To 3
            .Offset(i, 0) = Range("MonSummAnchor").Offset(i, 1)
        Next
    End With
End Sub
```

In addition to transferring the production quantities to the Report sheet, the **EnterProductResults** sub also performs simple calculations to report the revenue, cost, and profit for each product individually.

```
Sub EnterProductResults()
    Dim ProdIndex As Integer, i As Integer
    With Range("ProdRepAnchor")
' Clear old data (if any).
        Range(.Offset(1, 0), .Offset(1, 0).End(xlDown).End(xlToRight)) _
            .ClearContents
' Enter results for selected products only.  ProdIndex is a counter for these.
        ProdIndex = 0
        For i = 1 To NProducts
            If IsSelected(i) Then
                ProdIndex = ProdIndex + 1
' Enter product code, description, and number of units produced.
                .Offset(ProdIndex, 0) = Range("ProdAnchor").Offset(i, 0)
                .Offset(ProdIndex, 1) = Range("ProdAnchor").Offset(i, 1)
                .Offset(ProdIndex, 2) = Range("Produced").Cells(ProdIndex)
' Calculate revenue, cost, and profit for the product.
                .Offset(ProdIndex, 3) = Range("Produced").Cells(ProdIndex) * _
                    Range("UnitRev").Cells(ProdIndex)
                .Offset(ProdIndex, 4) = Range("Produced").Cells(ProdIndex) * _
                    Range("UnitCost").Cells(ProdIndex)
                .Offset(ProdIndex, 5) = Range("Produced").Cells(ProdIndex) * _
                    Range("UnitProfit").Cells(ProdIndex)
            End If
        Next
    End With
End Sub
```

In addition to transferring the resource usages and availabilities to the Report sheet, the **EnterResourceResults** sub also calculates the amount of each resource left over.

```
Sub EnterResourceResults()
    Dim i As Integer
    With Range("ResRepAnchor")
```

```
' Clear old data (if any).
        Range(.Offset(1, 0), .Offset(1, 0).End(xlDown).End(xlToRight)).ClearContents
        For i = 1 To NResources
' Enter resource name, amount used, and amount available.
            .Offset(i, 0) = Range("ResAnchor").Offset(i, 0)
            .Offset(i, 1) = Range("Used").Cells(i)
            .Offset(i, 2) = Range("Available").Cells(i)
' Calculate amount left over.
            .Offset(i, 3).FormulaR1C1 = "=RC[-1]-RC[-2]"
        Next
    End With
End Sub
```

16.8   Summary

We promised in the introduction that this application is considerably more complex from a VBA point of view than the previous chapter's blending application. Although most of it involves Excel manipulations that are easy to do manually, a significant amount of programming is required to perform these same operations with VBA. After all, an entire optimization model must be developed "on the fly" at run time. You can learn a lot of Excel VBA by carefully studying the code in this application. Better yet, open the file, split the screen so that you can see the Excel worksheets on one side and the VBA code on the other, step through the program with the F8 key, and keep watches on a few key variables. This can be *very* instructive. Finally, pay particular attention to how the overall program has been structured as a series of fairly small subs. This, together with a liberal dose of comments, makes the program much easier to read and understand.

PROGRAMMING EXERCISES

1. The application will work with *any* number of products in the Data sheet, provided the data are entered appropriately. Convince yourself of this by adding a few more products to the section shown in Figure 16.2 and then rerunning the application.
2. Continuing the previous exercise, the application will also work for any number of resources, provided that you make space for them in the sections shown in Figures 16.2 and 16.3. Convince yourself of this by adding a new resource (glue, for example). What changes do you have to make to the overall file?
3. As the previous exercise illustrates, it might be inconvenient (and confusing) to the user to have to insert new columns if more resources are added. We thought of putting the resource data in Figure 16.3 *below*, not to the right of, the product data in Figure 16.2, but this could also cause a problem if more products were added. (Then the user might need to insert extra rows.) Try the following alternative approach. Create *two* data sheets, one for the product data in Figure 16.2,

called ProductData, and one for the resource data in Figure 16.3, called ResourceData. Transfer the current data to these two sheets, and make any necessary changes to the application. Now the user will never have to insert any new rows or columns. Do you believe this new design has any drawbacks (from a user's, not a programmer's) point of view? Which design do you like best?

4. Change the application so that the user has no choice of the potential products in the product mix. That is, all products listed in the Data sheet will be in the product mix model, and the user form in Figure 16.4 will no longer be necessary. However, the application should still be written to adapt to any number of products that might be listed in the Data sheet.

5. Continuing the previous exercise, continue to assume that all products in the Data sheet are potential products in the product mix. However, the company now wants, in addition to the current Report sheet, a second report sheet that shows how the optimal profit changes as the availability of all resources increases. Specifically, it should show a table and a corresponding chart such as in Figure 16.12 on a SensReport sheet. This table shows, for example, that when all of the resource availabilities increase by 30%, the new optimal profit is $23,538. Of course, your data might differ, depending on which products are on your Data sheet. (*Hint:* Do as much as you can at design time. Then write VBA code to handle any tasks that must take place at run time.)

Figure 16.12 Sensitivity analysis for Exercise 5

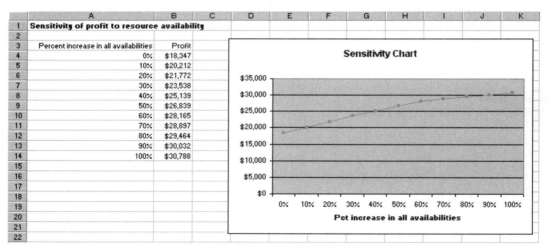

6. This application currently has no charts; it currently displays the outputs in tabular form only. Change the application so that it also displays a column chart (on a separate chart sheet) similar to the one in Figure 16.13, showing the amounts of the various products produced. As part of your changes, create buttons on the Report sheet and the chart sheet, and write navigational subs to attach to them, to

Figure 16.13 Chart of optimal production levels for Exercise 6

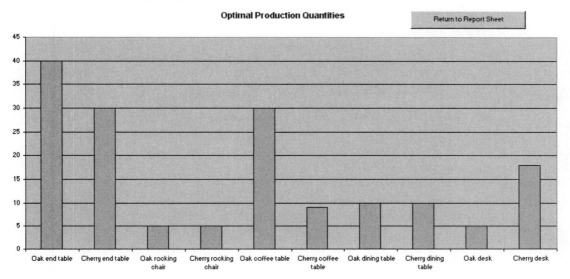

allow the user to go back and forth easily. (*Hint*: Create the chart with the Chart Wizard, not VBA, using representative data from the Report sheet to populate it at design time. Then write VBA code to modify it appropriately at run time.)

An Employee Scheduling Application

17.1 Introduction

This application is based on a model for scheduling workers.[33] A company needs to schedule its workers to meet daily requirements for a 7-day week, and each worker must work 5 days per week. Some of the workers can have nonconsecutive days off. For example, a worker could be assigned to work Monday, Wednesday, Thursday, Friday, and Sunday. This worker's two days off, Tuesday and Saturday, are nonconsecutive. However, there is a constraint that no more than a certain percentage of all workers can be assigned to nonconsecutive days-off shifts, where this maximum percentage is an input to the model. The objective is to minimize the weekly payroll, subject to meeting daily requirements, where the hourly wage rate on weekdays can differ from the wage rate on weekends.

New Learning Objective: VBA

*   To see how VBA can be used to conduct a sensitivity analysis for an optimization model.

New Learning Objective: Non-VBA

*   To learn how employee scheduling can be performed with an optimization model, and how a sensitivity analysis can be formed on a key input parameter.

17.2 Functionality of the Application

This application provides the following functionality:

1. It allows a user to view/change the inputs: daily requirements, weekday and weekend wage rates, and maximum percentage of nonconsecutive days off. Then for these given inputs, it finds the optimal solution to the model and reports it in a user-friendly form.
2. For given daily requirements and wage rates, it performs a sensitivity analysis on the maximum percentage of nonconsecutive days off and displays the results graphically.

---

[33]See Chapter 4 of *Practical Management Science* for a similar scheduling model.

17.3 Running the Application

The application is in the file **Scheduling.xls**. When this file is opened, the explanation and button in Figure 17.1 appear. By clicking on the button, the user can choose one of the two options shown in the dialog box in Figure 17.2.

Figure 17.1 Explanation screen

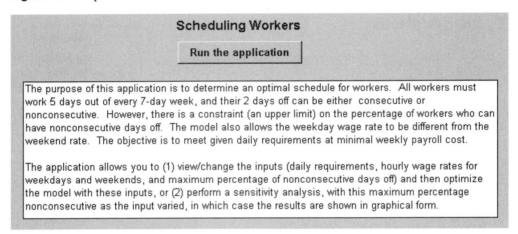

Figure 17.2 Options dialog box

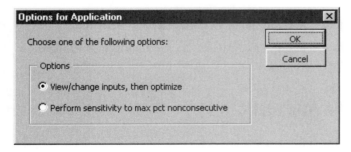

If the first option is chosen, the user sees the dialog box in Figure 17.3. The values in the boxes are from the previous run of the model (if any). Of course, any of these can be changed. When the OK button is clicked, the user's inputs are placed in the appropriate range of the (hidden) Model sheet (see Figure 17.7 below).

Once these inputs are entered and the user clicks on OK, the Solver is invoked and the optimal solution is reported in a Report sheet, as shown in Figure 17.4.

Figure 17.3 Daily requirements dialog box

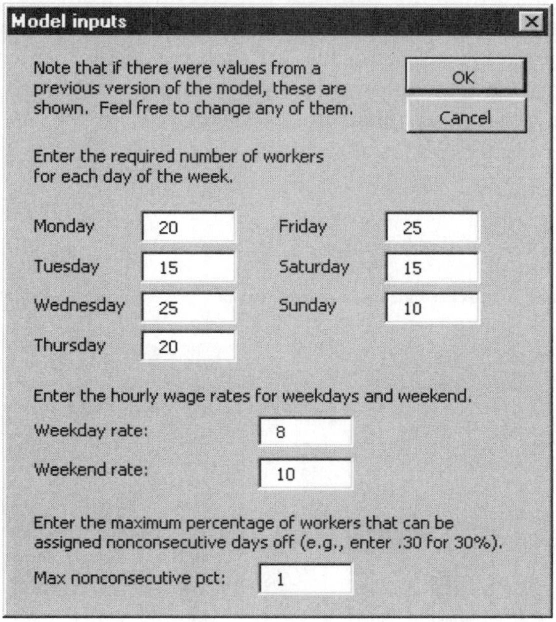

Figure 17.4 Report of optimal solution

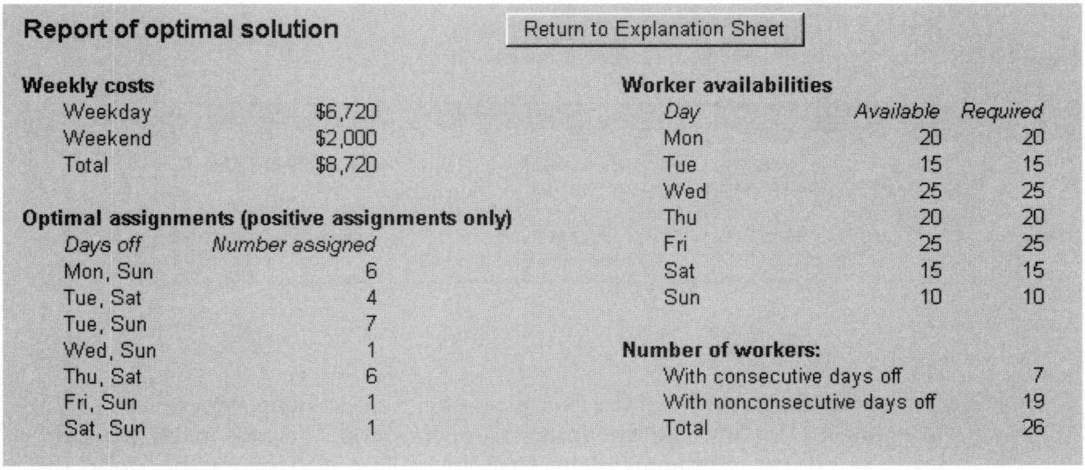

Report of optimal solution [Return to Explanation Sheet]

Weekly costs

Weekday	$6,720
Weekend	$2,000
Total	$8,720

Optimal assignments (positive assignments only)

Days off	*Number assigned*
Mon, Sun	6
Tue, Sat	4
Tue, Sun	7
Wed, Sun	1
Thu, Sat	6
Fri, Sun	1
Sat, Sun	1

Worker availabilities

Day	*Available*	*Required*
Mon	20	20
Tue	15	15
Wed	25	25
Thu	20	20
Fri	25	25
Sat	15	15
Sun	10	10

Number of workers:

With consecutive days off	7
With nonconsecutive days off	19
Total	26

If the second option in Figure 17.2 is chosen, the Solver is invoked several times, once for each maximum nonconsecutive percentage from 0% to 100% in increments of 10%, and important aspects of the optimal solutions appear graphically, as shown in Figure 17.5. Specifically, for each maximum percentage of nonconsecutive days off, the report shows the total number of workers required and the number of these who are assigned nonconsecutive days off. As an aid to the user, the reminder in Figure 17.6 is also displayed.

Figure 17.5 Graphical representation of optimal solutions

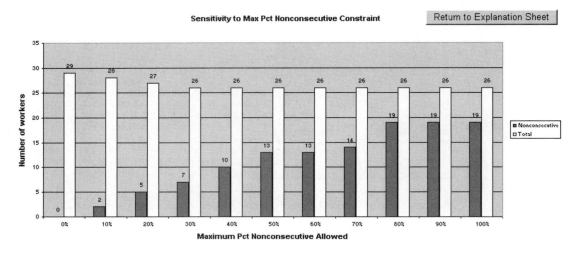

Figure 17.6 Reminder about possible multiple optimal solutions

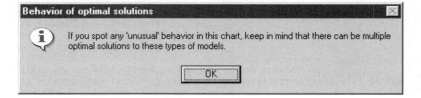

All of these results are based on the prebuilt model in the Model sheet, shown in Figure 17.7. (Although the formulas for this model are reasonably straightforward, you ought to examine them. First, you will need to unhide the Model sheet with the Tools/Sheet/Unhide menu item.)

Figure 17.7 Scheduling model

	A	B	C	D	E	F	G	H
1	Scheduling problem							
2								
3	Maximum percent with nonconsecutive days off					Hourly wage rates		
4		100%				Weekday	$8.00	
5						Weekend	$10.00	
6	Assignment of workers to days off pairs							
7	Days off	Consecutive	Assignments					
8	Mon, Tue	1	0					
9	Mon, Wed	0	0					
10	Mon, Thu	0	0			Return to Explanation Sheet		
11	Mon, Fri	0	0					
12	Mon, Sat	0	0					
13	Mon, Sun	1	6			Note: This model is just like any other		
14	Tue, Wed	1	0			optimization model in this book. Take a look at		
15	Tue, Thu	0	0			the formulas and the Solver setup to see how it		
16	Tue, Fri	0	0			works. You can even run it "manually" just like any		
17	Tue, Sat	0	4			other model (change the value in cell B4 if you like		
18	Tue, Sun	0	7			and use Tools/Solver to solve). Eventually,		
19	Wed, Thu	1	0			however, click on the above button to return to the		
20	Wed, Fri	0	0			Explanation sheet.		
21	Wed, Sat	0	0					
22	Wed, Sun	0	1					
23	Thu, Fri	1	0					
24	Thu, Sat	0	6					
25	Thu, Sun	0	0					
26	Fri, Sat	1	0					
27	Fri, Sun	0	1					
28	Sat, Sun	1	1					
29			26	<-- Total workers				
30	Daily constraints on workers							
31		Mon	Tue	Wed	Thu	Fri	Sat	Sun
32	Available	20	15	25	20	25	15	10
33		>=	>=	>=	>=	>=	>=	>=
34	Required	20	15	25	20	25	15	10
35								
36	Consecutive days off constraint							
37	Number nonconsecutive	19						
38		<=						
39	Maximum	26.00						
40								
41	Payroll							
42	Weekday	$6,720						
43	Weekend	$2,000						
44	Total	$8,720						

17.4 Setting Up the Excel Sheets

This optimization model always has the same size because there are always 7 days in a week. Therefore, most of the application can be developed with the Excel interface—without any VBA. It contains the following four sheets.

1. The Explanation sheet in Figure 17.1 contains an explanation of the application in a text box, and it has a button for running the application.
2. The Model sheet, shown in Figure 17.7, can be set up completely at design time, using any sample input values. Also, the Solver settings can be entered. Again, this is possible because the model itself will never change; only the

inputs to it will change. You can look through the logic of this model in the **Scheduling.xls** file. Most of it is straightforward. Pay particular attention to the formulas for worker availabilities in row 32. For example, the formula in cell E32 is =SUM(AvailThu). Here, AvailThu is the range name used for a set of *non*contiguous cells, namely, those changing cells where Thursday is *not* a day off. Giving range names to noncontiguous ranges is indeed possible and can often be useful.

3. A template for the report shown in Figure 17.4 can be developed in the Report sheet. This template appears in Figure 17.8. The costs section, worker availabilities section, and numbers of workers section have formulas linked to the Model sheet, so they show the results from a previous run, if any. However, the optimal assignments section is left blank. It will contain the *positive* assignments only, and these will not be known until run time. The VBA code will take care of transferring the positive assignments from the Model sheet to this section of the Report sheet.

Figure 17.8 Report template

	A	B	C	D	E	F	G	H	I
1									
2		**Report of optimal solution**				Return to Explanation Sheet			
3									
4		**Weekly costs**					**Worker availabilities**		
5			Weekday	$6,720			*Day*	*Available*	*Required*
6			Weekend	$2,000			Mon	20	20
7			Total	$8,720			Tue	15	15
8							Wed	25	25
9		**Optimal assignments (positive assignments only)**					Thu	20	20
10			*Days off*	*Number assigned*			Fri	25	25
11							Sat	15	15
12							Sun	10	10
13									
14							**Number of workers:**		
15							With consecutive days off		7
16							With nonconsecutive days off		19
17							Total		26

4. The chart in Figure 17.5 is located on a separate Chart sheet. This chart is linked to the data in a remote area of the Model sheet (see Figure 17.9). This area contains the percentages in column AA and the counts from the optimization model in columns AB and AC. Columns AB and AC contain, respectively, the numbers of workers with nonconsecutive days off and the numbers of workers total in the optimal solutions. Any reasonable values can be used in columns AB and AC initially for the purpose of building the chart with Excel's Chart Wizard. They will eventually be replaced with the optimal values by VBA when the sensitivity analysis is run.

Figure 17.9 Data for chart

	AA	AB	AC	AD
1	Sensitivity of solutions to maxpct			
2	MaxPct	Nonconsec	Total	
3	0%	0	70	
4	10%	7	70	
5	20%	14	70	
6	30%	21	70	
7	40%	28	70	
8	50%	15	70	
9	60%	42	70	
10	70%	25	70	
11	80%	25	70	
12	90%	25	70	
13	100%	25	70	

17.5 Getting Started with the VBA

This application requires two user forms, named InputsForm and OptionsForm, a module, and a reference to the Solver.xla file. Once these items are added, the Project Explorer window will appear as in Figure 17.10.

Figure 17.10 Project Explorer window

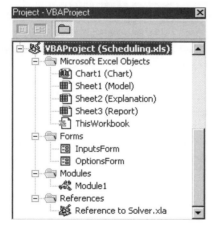

Workbook_Open Code

To guarantee that the Explanation sheet appears when the file is opened, the following code is placed in the ThisWorkbook code window. The **GoToExplanation** sub is actually in the module (see below), but it is perfectly acceptable to call a sub from a module in the Workbook_Open sub.

```
Private Sub Workbook_Open()
    GoToExplanation
End Sub
```

17.6 Designing the User Forms and Writing Their Event Code

> **Web Help**   For more explanation of the code in this application, visit our Web site
> at http://www.indiana.edu/~mgtsci and download the **Code Explanation -
> Scheduling.doc** file.

The design of the OptionsForm appears in Figure 17.11. There are the usual OK
and Cancel buttons, an explanation label, a frame with the caption Options, and
two option buttons inside the frame named Option1 and Option2.

Figure 17.11   Design of OptionsForm

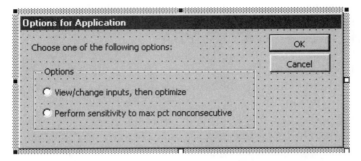

The design of the InputsForm uses 10 text boxes and accompanying labels, as
shown in Figure 17.12, along with the usual OK and Cancel buttons and a couple
of explanation labels to their left. The "day" boxes are named Day1Box to
Day7Box (for Monday to Sunday), the wage rate boxes are named WeekdayBox
and WeekendBox, and the percentage box is named MaxPctBox.

Once the user forms are designed, their event code must be written. For the
OptionsForm, the **UserForm_Initialize** sub specifies that the first option is selected by default. The **OKButton_Click** sub captures the option checked in the
variable Choice. The **CancelButton_Click** sub unloads the user form and ends
the program.

Event Code for OptionsForm

```
Private Sub UserForm_Initialize()
' Make option 1 the default.
    Option1 = True
End Sub

Private Sub OKButton_Click()
' Capture the user's selection in the variable Choice.
    If Option1 = True Then
        Choice = 1
    Else
        Choice = 2
    End If
    Unload Me
End Sub
```

```
Private Sub CancelButton_Click()
    Unload Me
    End
End Sub
```

Figure 17.12　Design of InputsForm

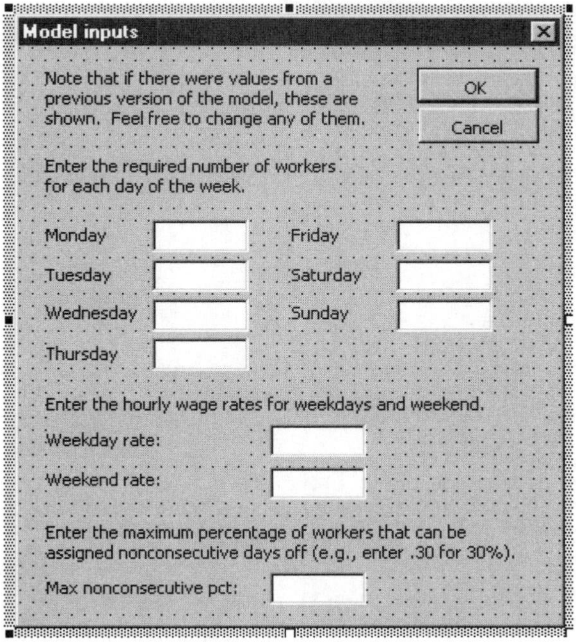

The event code for the InputsForm is somewhat more complex. Now the **UserForm_Initialize** sub captures the existing inputs, if any, from the Model sheet and uses them as starting values in the text boxes. The **OKButton_Click** sub then captures the user's inputs. First, it checks whether the text boxes have appropriate entries. If not, the user sees the same dialog box again, with the focus set to the offending text box. Otherwise, the **Val** function converts user responses (treated as *strings*) to numbers, which are placed in the appropriate cells of the Model sheet. (This Val function would not be needed if the text box values were assigned to *variables* declared as numeric types—Single or Integer, say. However, if the text box values are entered directly into cells, the Val function is required. Otherwise, Excel will treat the cell entries as labels and will disallow any arithmetic on them.)

Event Code for InputsForm

```
Private Sub UserForm_Initialize()
    Dim ctl As Control, DayIndex As Integer
```

```
' Enter values in the text boxes, if any, from the Required, BonusPct, and MaxPct
' ranges.
    For Each ctl In Me.Controls
        If TypeName(ctl) = "TextBox" Then
' Note that the text boxes for Monday through Sunday have been named Day1Box through
' Day7Box. Therefore, the left 3 characters of these names are all "Day", and the
' 4th character goes from 1 to 7.
            If Left(ctl.Name, 3) = "Day" Then
                DayIndex = Mid(ctl.Name, 4, 1)
                ctl.Text = Range("Required").Cells(DayIndex)
            ElseIf ctl.Name = "WeekdayBox" Then
                ctl.Text = Range("WeekdayRate")
            ElseIf ctl.Name = "WeekendBox" Then
                ctl.Text = Range("WeekendRate")
            Else
                ctl.Text = Range("MaxPct")
            End If
        End If
    Next
End Sub


Private Sub OKButton_Click()
    Dim ctl As Control, DayIndex As Integer
' Check for improper entries in the text boxes. If there are any, exit the sub without
' unloading the form.
    For Each ctl In Me.Controls
        If TypeName(ctl) = "TextBox" Then
' Check for empty boxes or nonnumeric values.
            If ctl.Text = "" Or Not IsNumeric(ctl.Text) Then
                MsgBox "Enter a numeric value in each box.", vbInformation, _
                    "Improper entry"
                ctl.SetFocus
                Exit Sub
' Check whether the "Day" boxes have negative values.
            ElseIf Left(ctl.Name, 3) = "Day" And ctl.Text < 0 Then
                MsgBox "Enter a nonnegative integer in each day box.", vbInformation, _
                    "Improper entry"
                ctl.SetFocus
                Exit Sub
' Check whether the wage boxes have nonpositive values.
            ElseIf Left(ctl.Name, 4) = "Week" And ctl.Text <= 0 Then
                MsgBox "Enter a positive wage rate in each wage box.", vbInformation, _
                    "Improper entry"
                ctl.SetFocus
                Exit Sub
' Check whether the percentage box has a value below 0 or above 1.
            ElseIf Left(ctl.Name, 3) = "Max" And (ctl.Text < 0 Or ctl.Text > 1) Then
                MsgBox "Enter a percentage between 0 and 1 in the percentage box.", _
                    vbInformation, "Improper entry"
                ctl.SetFocus
                Exit Sub
            End If
' The entry is OK, so put it in the appropriate cell in the Required range or MaxPct
' range of the Model sheet.  Note that a textbox always returns a string; the Val
' function converts it to a number.
            If Left(ctl.Name, 3) = "Day" Then
                DayIndex = Mid(ctl.Name, 4, 1)
                Range("Required").Cells(DayIndex) = Val(ctl.Text)
            ElseIf ctl.Name = "WeekdayBox" Then
                Range("WeekdayRate") = Val(ctl.Text)
```

```
                ElseIf ctl.Name = "WeekendBox" Then
                    Range("WeekendRate") = Val(ctl.Text)
                Else
                    Range("MaxPct") = Val(ctl.Text)
                End If
            End If
        Next
        Unload Me
End Sub

Private Sub CancelButton_Click()
        Unload Me
        End
End Sub
```

17.7   The VBA Code in the Module

Most of the work in this application is performed by the VBA code in the module. This code is listed below. It proceeds in a modular manner, always a good programming practice. After declaring the public variable Choice, a Main sub calls the other subs in a logical order.

Option Statements and Public variable

```
Option Explicit

    ' Choice is 1 or 2, based on the user's response to the first dialog box.
Public Choice As Integer
```

Main Code

This **Main** sub is the control center and is assigned to the button on the Explanation sheet. It calls other subs to do the real work. The logical progression through this sub is spelled out by the comments.

```
Sub Main()
' This procedure runs when the button on the Explanation sheet is clicked.
' First, show the Options dialog box, and then does the appropriate steps depending on
' the value of Choice.
    OptionsForm.Show
    If Choice = 1 Then
' Show the InputsForm so that the user can enter model inputs.
        InputsForm.Show
' Solve the model and report the results.
        Call RunSolver
        Call CreateReport

    Else
' Run the sensitivity analysis.
        Call Sensitivity
' Activate the Chart sheet, make it visible, and display an informative message.
        Application.ScreenUpdating = True
```

```
        With Sheets("Chart")
            .Visible = True
            .Activate
        End With
        MsgBox "If you spot any 'unusual' behavior in this chart, keep in mind that " _
            & "there can be multiple optimal solutions to these types " _
            & "of models.", vbInformation, "Behavior of optimal solutions"
    End If
End Sub
```

RunSolver Code

The **RunSolver** sub unhides and activates the Model sheet, and then it runs the Solver. Note that the Solver is already set up (this was done at design time), so the SolverSolve function is the only Solver function required. Also, note that there is no need to check for feasibility, because it is always possible to hire enough workers to meet all daily requirements—it might just cost a lot.

```
Sub RunSolver()
    Application.ScreenUpdating = False
    With Worksheets("Model")
        .Visible = True
        .Activate
    End With
    SolverSolve userfinish:=True
End Sub
```

CreateReport Code

This **CreateReport** sub unhides and activates the Report sheet, clears old assignments, if any, from a previous report, and then transfers *positive* assignments from the Model sheet to the appropriate cells (below C10) in the Report sheet.

```
Sub CreateReport()
    Dim i As Integer, Counter As Integer
    Application.ScreenUpdating = False
' Unhide the Report sheet and activate it
    With Worksheets("Report")
        .Visible = True
        .Activate
    End With
' Clear out old assignments from a previous run (the part below C10).
    With Range("C10")
        Range(.Offset(1, 0), .Offset(1, 1).End(xlDown)).ClearContents
    End With
' Transfer the positive assignments from the Model sheet to the Report sheet.
' Counter counts the positive assignments.
    Counter = 0
    With Range("C10")
        For i = 1 To 21
            If Range("Assignments").Cells(i) > 0 Then
                Counter = Counter + 1
```

```
' Record the names of the days off and the number of workers assigned.
                .Offset(Counter, 0) = Range("Assignments").Cells(i).Offset(0, -2)
                .Offset(Counter, 1) = Range("Assignments").Cells(i)
            End If
        Next
    End With
    Range("A1").Select
End Sub
```

Sensitivity Code

The **Sensitivity** sub unhides and activates the Model sheet, and then it runs the Solver 11 times for equally spaced values of the maximum percentage of nonconsecutive days off. The results are stored in cells under cell AA1 (in the Model sheet). Because the prebuilt chart is linked to the data in these cells, the chart updates automatically.

```
Public Sub Sensitivity()
    Dim i As Integer
    Application.ScreenUpdating = False
' Unhide and activate the Model sheet.
    With Worksheets("Model")
        .Visible = True
        .Activate
    End With
' Solve 11 problems for values of the maximum percentage from 0 to 1 in increments
' of 0.1.
    For i = 1 To 11
        Range("MaxPct") = (i - 1) * 0.1
' Enter the maximum percentage of days off, and reset all assignments (changing cells)
' to 0. Then run Solver.
        Range("Assignments") = 0
        SolverSolve userfinish:=True
' Store the results in the range that the existing chart is linked to.
        With Range("AA1")
            .Offset(i, 1) = Range("Nonconsec")
            .Offset(i, 2) = Range("TotalWorkers")
        End With
    Next
End Sub
```

GoToExplanation Code

The **GoToExplanation** sub is for easy navigation. It is attached to the corresponding buttons on the Model, Report, and Chart sheets.

```
Public Sub GoToExplanation()
    Worksheets("Explanation").Activate
    Range("E4").Select
    Worksheets("Model").Visible = False
    Worksheets("Report").Visible = False
    Charts("Chart").Visible = False
End Sub
```

17.8 Summary

This application is similar to the blending optimization model in Chapter 15, in that the size of the model never changes. Therefore, most of the application, including the entire optimization model, can be set up at design time. This decreases the amount of VBA code necessary. Our main objective here has been to show how to build a sensitivity analysis into an application. This has been done here for the maximum percentage of workers with nonconsecutive days off, but in general it can be done for any key input parameters. It is basically just a matter of running the Solver inside a For loop and reporting the results.

PROGRAMMING EXERCISES

1. Change the application so that there is a third option in the OptionsForm. This is the option to perform a sensitivity analysis on the ratio of the weekend wage rate to the weekday wage rate. When you implement this, use the current value of the weekday wage rate from the Model sheet, and let the ratio vary from 1 to 2 in increments of 0.1. In each case, capture the total cost for plotting. Then show the results of this sensitivity analysis (total weekly payroll cost versus the ratio) in graphical form, similar to that shown in Figure 17.5. (You can use the *same* location, starting in column AA of the Model sheet, to store your sensitivity results, and the *same* chart sheet to show the results graphically, or you can create a new location and a new chart sheet for this sensitivity analysis. It should be transparent to the user.)

2. Repeat the previous exercise, but now add a fourth option to the OptionsForm that performs a sensitivity analysis on both parameters simultaneously. That is, it should use a nested pair of For loops to vary the maximum percentage of nonconsecutive days off from 0% to 100%, in increments of 10%, *and* to vary the ratio from the previous problem from 1 to 2, in increments of 0.1. (This will result in $11(11) = 121$ Solver runs.) The total weekly payroll cost from each run should be captured and stored in some remote location of the Model sheet, and a chart based on these results should be created and displayed. You can decide on the most appropriate chart type. One possibility might look like the chart in Figure 17.13.

3. Change the application so that there is no longer a sensitivity option. However, the user should now be allowed to select from approximately 10 different preset patterns of weekly requirements. For example, one pattern might be the weekend-heavy pattern 10, 10, 10, 10, 10, 30, 30 (where these are the requirements for Monday through Sunday), whereas another pattern might be the more stable pattern 15, 15, 15, 15, 20, 20, 15. You can make up any patterns you think might be reasonable. Then allow the user to choose a pattern, along with weekday and weekend wage rates and the maximum percentage of nonconsecutive days off allowed, solve this particular problem, and present the results in a Report sheet.

Figure 17.13 Sensitivity chart for Exercise 2

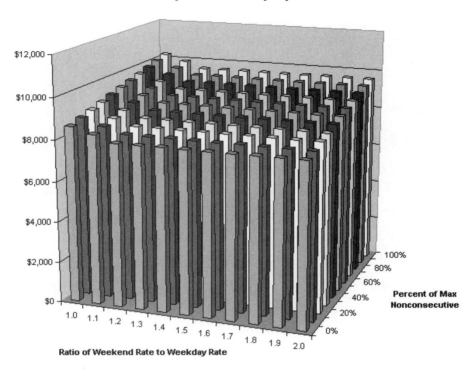

Sensitivity Chart of Weekly Payroll Cost

4. Change the model on the Model sheet, and make any necessary modifications to the application as a whole, when each worker works only four days of the week, not five.

18 A Production Scheduling Application

18.1 Introduction

This application finds an optimal multiperiod production plan for a single product. The objective is to minimize the sum of production and inventory costs, subject to meeting demand on time and not exceeding production and inventory capacities. This model is discussed in all management science textbooks, where the future demands and unit production costs are generally assumed to be known. (See Chapter 3 of *Practical Management Science*, for example.) In reality, these quantities, particularly the demands, must be forecasted from historical data. This application uses exponential smoothing to forecast future demands and unit production costs from historical data. Then it bases the optimal production plan on the forecasted values.

In addition, the user can enter new data, update the forecasts, and then run the optimization model again. This allows the application to implement a rolling planning horizon. For example, it can optimize for January through June, then observe actual data for January, then optimize for February through July, then observe actual data for February, and so on. Because of these powerful features, this application is the most ambitious application discussed so far.

New Learning Objective: VBA

- To learn how an application with several user forms, worksheets, charts, and various user options can be integrated within one relatively large VBA program.

New Learning Objectives: Non-VBA

- To learn how forecasts can be made with exponential smoothing methods and then used as inputs to a production scheduling optimization model.
- To see how a rolling planning horizon can be implemented.

18.2 Functionality of the Application

The application has the following functionality:

1. It finds the optimal production plan for a 3- to 12-month planning horizon, using the data observed to date.

2. It allows the user to view the historical data, along with the exponentially smoothed forecasts, in tabular and graphical form.
3. It allows the user to append new demand and unit production cost data to the end of the historical period and update the forecasts.
4. It allows the user to change any of the smoothing constants and update the forecasts.

The historical data included in the application are fictional monthly data for the years 1995–1999. Demands are seasonal with an upward trend, so it is appropriate to use Winters' exponential smoothing method. Unit production costs are not seasonal but they have an upward trend. Therefore, it is appropriate to use Holt's exponential smoothing method for the cost data. Users can replace these data with their own data (in the Data sheet).

18.3   Running the Application

The application is stored in the file **ProductionPlan.xls**. When the file is opened, the Explanation sheet in Figure 18.1 appears. This explanation indicates two "nonstandard" features of the optimization model. First, the percentage of any month's production that is available to satisfy that month's demand can be *less* than 100%. For example, if this percentage is 70%, then 70% of this month's production can be used to satisfy this month's demand. The other 30% of this month's production is then available for future months' demands. Second, the inventory cost in any month can be based on the ending inventory for the month (the usual assumption), or it can be based on the average of the beginning and ending inventories for the month. Note also that the production and inventory capacities are assumed to be *constant* throughout the planning horizon. This assumption could be relaxed, but it would require additional dialog boxes.

When the button on the Explanation sheet is clicked, the dialog box in Figure 18.2 appears. It indicates the four basic options for the application.

First Option

If the user selects the first option, the dialog box in Figure 18.3 appears. It requests the inputs for the production planning model. It then develops this model on the (hidden) Model sheet, sets up and runs the Solver, and reports the optimal solution in tabular and graphical form, as shown in Figure 18.4.

Second Option

Historical data are stored in the Data sheet. The second option in Figure 18.2 allows the user to view these data, as shown in Figure 18.5 (where several rows have been hidden). Note that the historical data appear in columns B and C, and their exponentially smoothed forecasts appear in columns G and J. The hidden columns

Figure 18.1 Explanation sheet

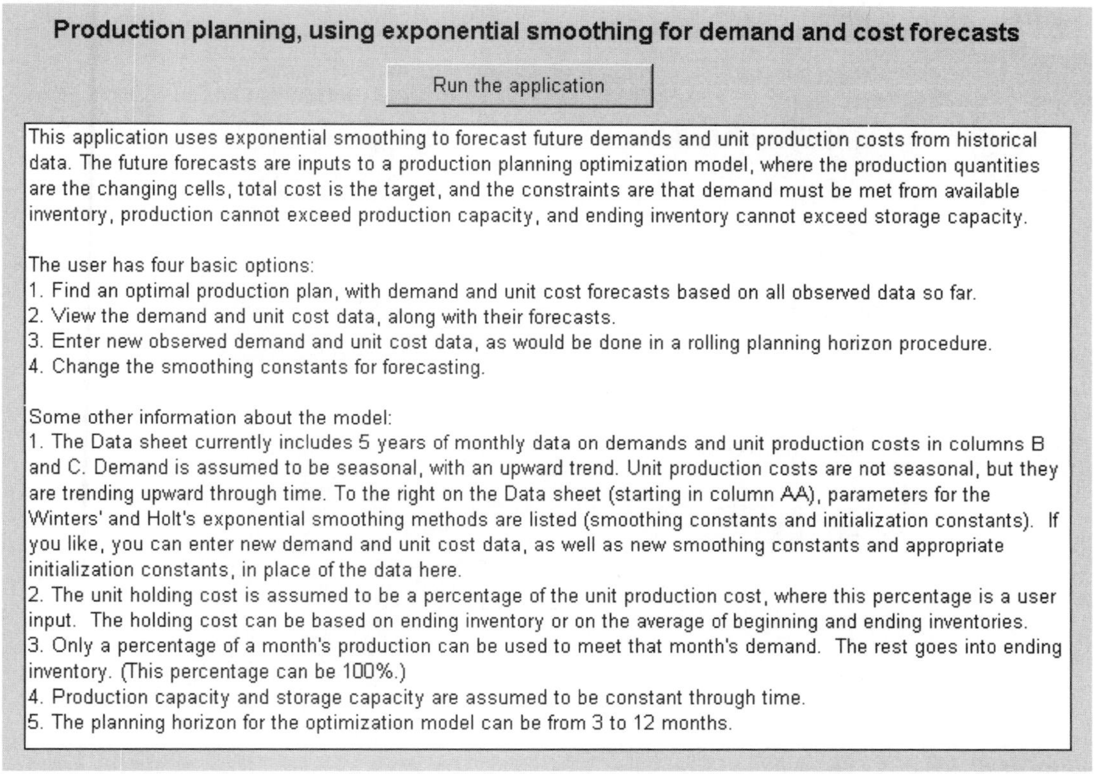

Production planning, using exponential smoothing for demand and cost forecasts

Run the application

This application uses exponential smoothing to forecast future demands and unit production costs from historical data. The future forecasts are inputs to a production planning optimization model, where the production quantities are the changing cells, total cost is the target, and the constraints are that demand must be met from available inventory, production cannot exceed production capacity, and ending inventory cannot exceed storage capacity.

The user has four basic options:
1. Find an optimal production plan, with demand and unit cost forecasts based on all observed data so far.
2. View the demand and unit cost data, along with their forecasts.
3. Enter new observed demand and unit cost data, as would be done in a rolling planning horizon procedure.
4. Change the smoothing constants for forecasting.

Some other information about the model:
1. The Data sheet currently includes 5 years of monthly data on demands and unit production costs in columns B and C. Demand is assumed to be seasonal, with an upward trend. Unit production costs are not seasonal, but they are trending upward through time. To the right on the Data sheet (starting in column AA), parameters for the Winters' and Holt's exponential smoothing methods are listed (smoothing constants and initialization constants). If you like, you can enter new demand and unit cost data, as well as new smoothing constants and appropriate initialization constants, in place of the data here.
2. The unit holding cost is assumed to be a percentage of the unit production cost, where this percentage is a user input. The holding cost can be based on ending inventory or on the average of beginning and ending inventories.
3. Only a percentage of a month's production can be used to meet that month's demand. The rest goes into ending inventory. (This percentage can be 100%.)
4. Production capacity and storage capacity are assumed to be constant through time.
5. The planning horizon for the optimization model can be from 3 to 12 months.

Figure 18.2 Options dialog box

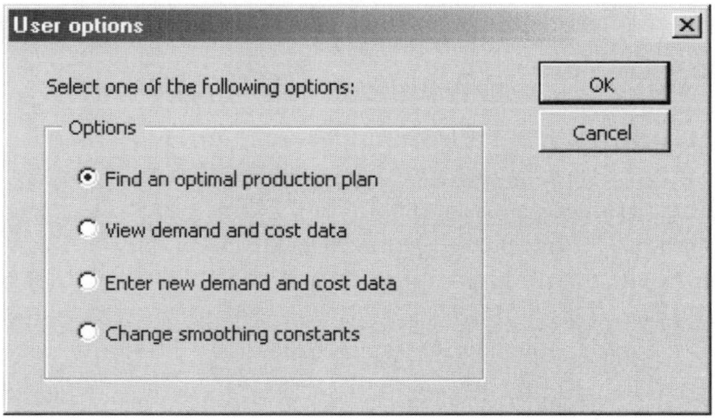

Figure 18.3 Inputs for production planning model

Input data for planning optimization model   ☒

The production planning model will be based on the
following inputs: [OK]

                                                          [Cancel]

Planning horizon (number of months):   [6]

Initial inventory: [500]

Percentage of production in a month
ready to meet demand in that month: [0.80]   E.g. enter .75 for 75%

Unit holding cost percentage (of unit
production cost):   [0.10]   E.g. enter .05 for 5%

┌─ Holding cost options ──────────────────────────────┐
│ ⊙ Based on ending inventory   │
│   │
│ ○ Based on average of beginning and   │
│   ending inventories   │
└──┘

The following are assumed to remain constant through the
entire planning horizon.

Production capacity: [2000]

Storage capacity: [500]

Figure 18.4 Report of optimal production plan

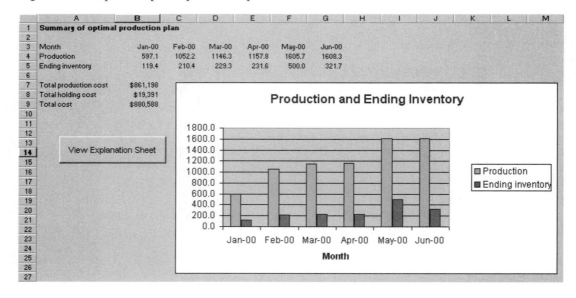

	A	B	C	D	E	F	G	H	I	J	K	L	M
1	**Summary of optimal production plan**												
2													
3	Month	Jan-00	Feb-00	Mar-00	Apr-00	May-00	Jun-00						
4	Production	597.1	1052.2	1146.3	1157.8	1605.7	1608.3						
5	Ending inventory	119.4	210.4	229.3	231.6	500.0	321.7						
6													
7	Total production cost	$861,198											
8	Total holding cost	$19,391											
9	Total cost	$880,588											

in between contain the exponential smoothing calculations. (You can unhide them if you like with the Format/Columns/Unhide menu item.) Note that cell A3 has the range name DataAnchor. This is used later in the VBA code.

Figure 18.5   Data sheet with forecasts

	A	B	C	G	J	M	N	O	P	Q
1	Historical data on demands and unit production costs									
2	View Demand Forecast Chart			View Unit Cost Forecast Chart		View Explanation Sheet		Find Optimal Production Plan		
3	Month	Demand	UnitCost	FCastDemand	FCastUnitCost		MAPE for historical data			
4	Jan-95	376	55.50	366.10	57.20		Demands	10.1%		
5	Feb-95	394	61.00	382.51	58.33		Unit costs	2.6%		
6	Mar-95	416	63.42	458.42	60.38					
7	Apr-95	437	57.17	431.85	62.57		The exponential smoothing calculations and the absolute percentage errors are hidden in columns D-F, H-I, and K-M. Unhide them if you like. Smoothing constants and initialization constants are out in column AA.			
8	May-95	524	62.62	499.21	62.96					
9	Jun-95	672	65.66	706.36	64.36					
10	Jul-95	930	64.18	863.04	66.11					
11	Aug-95	945	69.37	936.41	67.18					
12	Sep-95	719	66.96	706.77	69.11					
13	Oct-95	444	65.87	466.17	70.14					
14	Nov-95	402	62.01	456.85	70.65					
15	Dec-95	870	70.98	833.99	70.12					
16	Jan-96	416	71.72	437.79	71.50					
17	Feb-96	485	71.44	424.19	72.76					
60	Sep-99	1208	115.17	1229.65	112.25					
61	Oct-99	667	114.29	748.06	113.71					
62	Nov-99	760	113.09	722.37	114.72					
63	Dec-99	1885	120.58	1410.45	115.26					

When the left two buttons on the Data sheet are clicked, the charts in Figures 18.6 and 18.7 appear. They show the actual data with the forecasts superimposed.

Figure 18.6   Demand data and forecasts

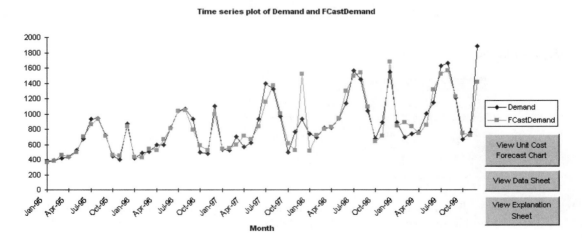

Figure 18.7   Unit production cost data and forecasts

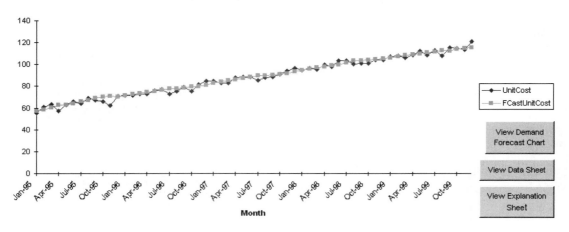

Third Option

If the user selects the third option in Figure 18.2, the dialog box in Figure 18.8 appears. It asks for the number of months of new data. Then the dialog box in Figure 18.9 is shown repeatedly, once for each new month.

Figure 18.8   First new data dialog box

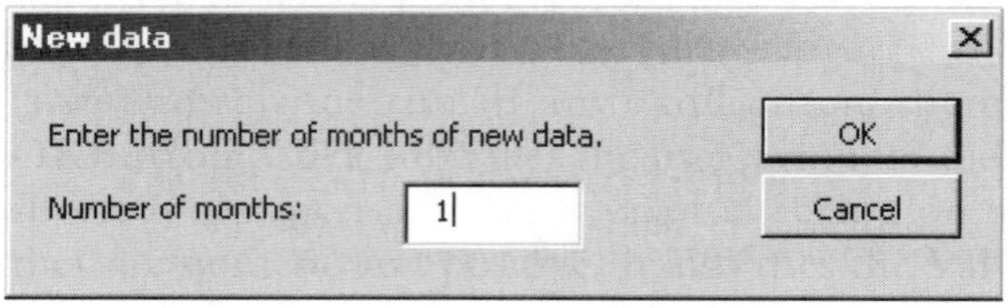

> **New data**
>
> Enter the number of months of new data.   **OK**
>
> Number of months: 1   **Cancel**

Figure 18.9   Second new data dialog box

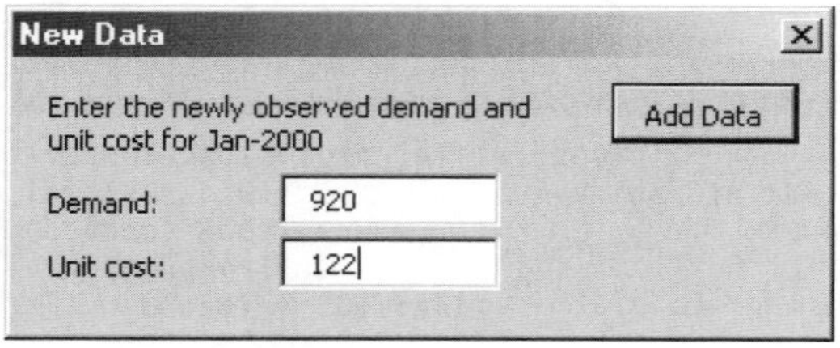

> **New Data**
>
> Enter the newly observed demand and   **Add Data**
> unit cost for Jan-2000
>
> Demand: 920
>
> Unit cost: 122

The new data are automatically appended to the bottom of the historical period in the Data sheet (see Figure 18.10), and the exponential smoothing calculations are extended for this new period. If the user then asks for the new optimal production plan, the planning horizon starts *after* the period of the new data, as illustrated in Figure 18.11.

Figure 18.10 Appended data in data sheet

	A	B	C	G	J
55	Apr-99	767	108.19	743.14	108.66
56	May-99	1003	111.71	852.43	109.47
57	Jun-99	1149	108.53	1316.05	110.87
58	Jul-99	1624	112.37	1521.70	111.30
59	Aug-99	1661	107.38	1564.53	112.44
60	Sep-99	1208	115.17	1229.65	112.25
61	Oct-99	667	114.29	748.06	113.71
62	Nov-99	760	113.09	722.37	114.72
63	Dec-99	1885	120.58	1410.45	115.26
64	Jan-00	920	122	977.72	117.29

Figure 18.11 New production plan report

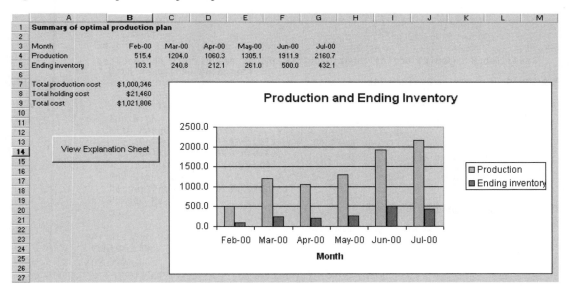

Fourth Option

Finally, if the user selects the fourth option in Figure 18.2, the dialog box in Figure 18.12 appears. It requests new smoothing constants. The updated MAPE (mean absolute percentage error) values are then reported in a message box, as shown in Figure 18.13. The smoothing constants, along with initialization values for Winters' method and Holt's method, are stored in a remote location in the Data sheet, as shown in Figure 18.14.

Figure 18.12 Smoothing constant dialog box

Smoothing constants   [x]

Winters' exponential smoothing method is used to   [OK]
forecast seasonal demand. Enter the three smoothing
constants for this method (all between 0 and 1):   [Cancel]

┌─ Winters' method for Demand ─────────────────┐
│   │
│   Level: [0.8]   │
│   │
│   Trend: [0.1]   │
│   │
│   Seasonality: [0.4]   │
│   │
└───┘

Holt's exponential smoothing method is used to forecast
upward trending unit costs. Enter the three smoothing
constants for this method (all between 0 and 1):

┌─ Holt's method for Unit Cost ────────────────┐
│   │
│   Level: [0.2]   │
│   │
│   Trend: [0.1]   │
│   │
└───┘

Figure 18.13 Updated MAPE values

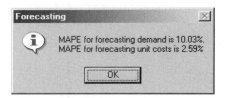

Forecasting   [x]

(i) MAPE for forecasting demand is 10.03%.
     MAPE for forecasting unit costs is 2.59%

         [OK]

Figure 18.14 Exponential smoothing information

	AA	AB	AC	AD	AE	AF	AG
3	Smoothing parameters for exponential smoothing						
4							
5	Winters' method (for demand)			Holt's method (for unit cost)			
6	Level	0.8		Level	0.2		
7	Trend	0.1		Trend	0.1		
8	Seasonality	0.4					
9							
10	Initialization values for Winters' method			Initialization values for Holt's method			
11	Level	512		Level	55.7		
12	Trend	11		Trend	1.5		
13							
14	Seasonal factors						
15	Jan	0.7					
16	Feb	0.7					
17	Mar	0.8					
18	Apr	0.8					
19	May	0.9					
20	Jun	1.2					
21	Jul	1.5					
22	Aug	1.5					
23	Sep	1.1					
24	Oct	0.7					
25	Nov	0.7					
26	Dec	1.4					

Possibility of No Feasible Solutions

There is always the possibility that the production planning model has no feasible solutions. This typically occurs when there is not enough production capacity to meet forecasted demands on time. In this case, the message box in Figure 18.15 is displayed.

Figure 18.15 No feasible solutions message

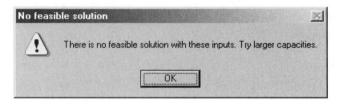

18.4 Setting Up the Excel Sheets

The **ProductionPlan.xls** file contains four worksheets, named Explanation, Data, Model, and Report, and two chart sheets, named DemFCast and CostFCast. The Data sheet can be set up completely at design time, as shown in Figures 18.5 and 18.14. Of course, the hidden columns in Figure 18.5 must contain the exponential smoothing formulas for Winters' and Holt's methods. (See the **ProductionPlan.xls** file for details. If you need a refresher course in exponential smoothing, see Chapter 16 of *Practical Management Science.*)

The Model sheet contains the linear programming production planning model. It must be developed almost entirely at run time. The completed version appears in Figure 18.16 for a 6-month planning horizon (starting in February). Clearly, the number of columns in this model depends on the length of the planning horizon, which is not known until run time. About the only parts that can be entered at design time are the labels in column A. (The formula in cell B34 is the one exception. It is always the sum of cells B32 and B33.)

A template for the Report sheet (shown earlier in Figure 18.4) *can* be developed at design time, as shown in Figure 18.17. In particular, the embedded chart can be created with the Chart Wizard. It can then be linked to the appropriate data in rows 3–5 at run time. Also, formulas in cells B7 to B9 can be entered at design time. These formulas are links to the appropriate Model sheet cells.

Similarly, the chart sheets shown earlier in Figures 18.6 and 18.7 can be created at design time. Then they are linked to the appropriate data from the Data sheet at run time.

Figure 18.16 Completed model sheet

	A	B	C	D	E	F	G
1	**Production planning model**						
2							
3	**Inputs**						
4	Planning horizon	6					
5	Beginning inventory	500					
6	Production pct	80.0%					
7	Holding cost pct	10.0%					
8	Holding cost option	1					
9	Production capacity	2200					
10	Storage capacity	500					
11							
12	**Production plan**						
13	Month	Feb-00	Mar-00	Apr-00	May-00	Jun-00	Jul-00
14	Beginning inventory	500.0	92.3	230.2	201.3	252.0	500.0
15	Production	461.3	1151.0	1006.4	1260.1	1813.1	2080.8
16		<=	<=	<=	<=	<=	<=
17	Production capacity	2200	2200	2200	2200	2200	2200
18							
19	Available to meet demand	869.1	1013.1	1035.3	1209.4	1702.5	2164.6
20		>=	>=	>=	>=	>=	>=
21	Demand	869.1	1013.1	1035.3	1209.4	1565.2	2164.6
22							
23	Ending inventory	92.3	230.2	201.3	252.0	500.0	416.2
24							
25	Storage capacity	500	500	500	500	500	500
26	Average inventory	296.1	161.2	215.7	226.6	376.0	458.1
27							
28	**Cost summary**						
29	Month	Feb-00	Mar-00	Apr-00	May-00	Jun-00	Jul-00
30	Forecasted unit production costs	$120.18	$121.33	$122.48	$123.62	$124.77	$125.92
31							
32	Total production cost	$962,378					
33	Total holding cost	$20,962					
34	Total cost	$983,339					

Figure 18.17 Template for report sheet

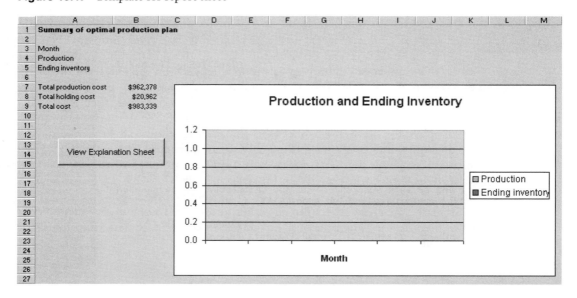

18.5 Getting Started with the VBA

The application includes five user forms, named OptionsForm, InputsForm, NewDataForm1, NewDataForm2, and SmConstForm, a single module, and a reference to the Solver add-in. Once these are inserted, the Project Explorer window will appear as in Figure 18.18.

Figure 18.18 Project Explorer window

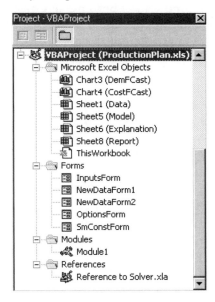

Workbook_Open Code

To guarantee that the Explanation sheet appears when the file is opened, the following code is placed in the ThisWorkbook code window. It also hides all sheets except for the Explanation sheet. (The Sheets collection, not the Worksheets collection, is appropriate here because it includes both worksheets and chart sheets.)

```
Private Sub Workbook_Open()
    Dim sht As Object
    Worksheets("Explanation").Activate
    Range("F4").Select
    For Each sht In ActiveWorkbook.Sheets
        If sht.Name <> "Explanation" Then sht.Visible = False
    Next
End Sub
```

18.6 Designing the User forms and Writing Their Event Code

> **Web Help** For more explanation of the code in this application, visit our Web site at http://www.indiana.edu/~mgtsci and download the **Code Explanation - ProductionPlan.doc** file.

OptionsForm

The OptionsForm has the usual OK and Cancel buttons, an explanation label, a frame for grouping, and four option buttons named OptimizeOpt, ViewDataOpt, NewDataOpt, and SmConstOpt. Its design appears in Figure 18.19.

Figure 18.19 Design of OptionsForm

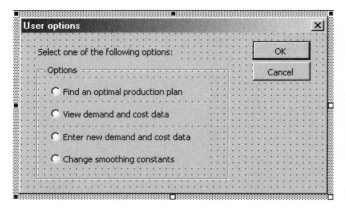

EventCode for OptionsForm

The event code for the OptionsForm is straightforward and is listed below. Its whole purpose is to capture the user's choice in the public variable Choice, which has possible values 1 through 4.

```
Private Sub UserForm_Initialize()
    OptimizeOpt = True
End Sub

Private Sub OKButton_Click()
' Capture the user's choice in the Choice variable.
    If OptimizeOpt Then
        Choice = 1
    ElseIf ViewDataOpt Then
        Choice = 2
    ElseIf NewDataOpt Then
        Choice = 3
    Else
        Choice = 4
```

```
        End If
        Unload Me
    End Sub

    Private Sub CancelButton_Click()
        Unload Me
        End
    End Sub
```

InputsForm

The InputsForm contains the usual OK and Cancel buttons, several explanation labels, a frame that contains two options buttons named HoldOption1 and HoldOption2, and six text boxes, named NMonthsBox, InitInvBox, ProdPctBox, HoldPctBox, ProdCapBox, and InvCapBox. Its design appears in Figure 18.20.

Figure 18.20 Design of InputsForm

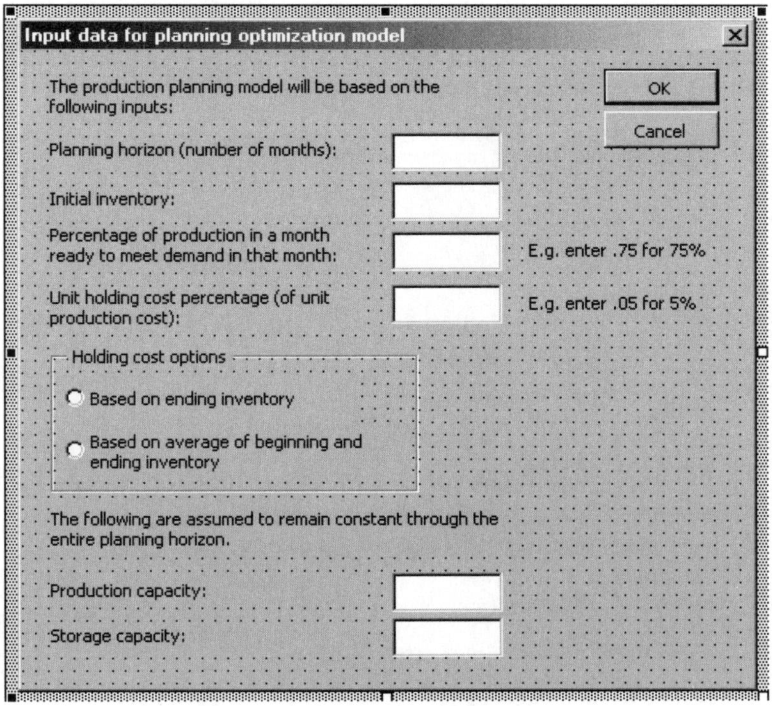

Event Code for InputsForm

The event code for the InputsForm form is rather lengthy, but this is mostly because of error checking for the text boxes. The **UserForm_Initialize** sub fills the dialog box with the previous settings from the Model sheet. Then the

OKButton_Click sub captures the user's settings in public variables (declared in the module), and it enters these values in the appropriate cells of the Model sheet. The **CancelButton_Click** sub unloads the dialog box and terminates the program.

```
Private Sub UserForm_Initialize()
' Use the current values from the Model sheet to initialize the form.
    NMonthsBox = Range("NMonths")
    InitInvBox = Range("InitInv")
    ProdPctBox = Format(Range("ProdPct"), "0.00")
    HoldPctBox = Format(Range("HoldPct"), "0.00")
    If Range("HoldOpt") = 1 Then
        HoldOption1 = True
    Else
        HoldOption2 = True
    End If
    ProdCapBox = Range("ProdCap")
    InvCapBox = Range("InvCap")
End Sub

Private Sub OKButton_Click()
        Dim ctl As Control
' Most of this sub is error checking.
' First check that all of the text boxes are not blank and have numeric values.
    For Each ctl In Me.Controls
        If TypeName(ctl) = "TextBox" Then
            If ctl.Value = "" Or Not IsNumeric(ctl.Value) Then
                MsgBox "Enter a numeric value in each box.", _
                    vbInformation, "Invalid entry"
                ctl.SetFocus
                Exit Sub
            End If
        End If
    Next

' The following If-End If block is typical. It checks whether the NMonthsBox has a
' valid entry (between 3 and 12). If not, the user must try again. If the entry is
' valid, it captures the value in the NMonths variable and puts it in the appropriate
' cell in the Model sheet.
    If NMonthsBox < 3 Or NMonthsBox > 12 Then
        MsgBox "Make the planning horizon at least 3 months " _
            & "and no more than 12 months.", vbInformation, "Invalid entry"
        NMonthsBox.SetFocus
        Exit Sub
    Else
        NMonths = NMonthsBox
        Range("NMonths") = NMonths
    End If

' Initial inventory cannot be negative.
    If InitInvBox < 0 Then
        MsgBox "Enter a nonnegative initial inventory.", vbInformation, "Invalid entry"
        InitInvBox.SetFocus
        Exit Sub
    Else
        InitInv = InitInvBox
        Range("InitInv") = InitInv
    End If
```

```
' The production percentage must be from 0 to 1.
    If ProdPctBox < 0 Or ProdPctBox > 1 Then
        MsgBox "Enter a percentage (in decimal form) between 0 " & "and 1.", _
            vbInformation, "Invalid entry"
        ProdPctBox.SetFocus
        Exit Sub
    Else
        ProdPct = ProdPctBox
        Range("ProdPct") = ProdPct
    End If

' The holding cost percentage must be from 0 to 1.
    If HoldPctBox < 0 Or HoldPctBox > 1 Then
        MsgBox "Enter a percentage (in decimal form) between 0 " & "and 1.", _
            vbInformation, "Invalid entry"
        HoldPctBox.SetFocus
        Exit Sub
    Else
        HoldPct = HoldPctBox
        Range("HoldPct") = HoldPct
    End If

' Store the holding cost option, 1 or 2, in the HoldOpt variable.
    If HoldOption1 Then
        HoldOpt = 1
    Else
        HoldOpt = 2
    End If
    Range("HoldOpt") = HoldOpt

' Production capacity cannot be negative.
    If ProdCapBox < 0 Then
        MsgBox "Enter a nonnegative production capacity.", vbInformation, _
            "Invalid entry"
        ProdCapBox.SetFocus
        Exit Sub
    Else
        ProdCap = ProdCapBox
        Range("ProdCap") = ProdCap
    End If

' Storage capacity cannot be negative.
    If InvCapBox < 0 Then
        MsgBox "Enter a nonnegative storage capacity.", vbInformation, "Invalid entry"
        InvCapBox.SetFocus
        Exit Sub
    Else
        InvCap = InvCapBox
        Range("InvCap") = InvCap
    End If

' Unload the user form. This statement is run only if all user inputs are valid.
    Unload Me
End Sub

Private Sub CancelButton_Click()
    Unload Me
    End
End Sub
```

NewDataForm1 and NewDataForm2

The two user forms for new data, shown earlier in Figures 18.8 and 18.9, are straightforward, so their event code is not listed here. The only new wrinkle is that an Add Data button replaces the usual OK and Cancel buttons on the NewDataForm2 form. Actually, this button has exactly the same functionality as the usual OK button; only its name and caption are different. The Cancel button is purposely omitted. By this time, new data rows have been added to the Data form, so the user *must* enter demand and cost data for them!

SmConstForm

The form for the smoothing constants, shown earlier in Figure 18.12, also contains no new ideas, so its event code is not listed here. It is initialized with the previous smoothing constants from the Model sheet (see Figure 18.14). It then places the user's choice of smoothing constants in these same cells.

18.7   The VBA Code in the Module

The module contains the code that does most of the work. As usual, the button on the Explanation sheet is attached to a Main sub that first shows the OptionsForm and then calls the appropriate sub, depending on the value of the public variable Choice. The public variables and the code for the Main sub are listed below.

Option Statements and Public Variables

```
Option Explicit
Option Base 1

' Definitions of public variables:
'    Choice: 1, 2, or 3, depending on which basic option the user requests
'    NMonthsNew: number of new data entries
'    NMonths: number of months in planning horizon
'    InitInv: initial inventory in first month of planning horizon
'    ProdPct: percentage of a month's production that can be used to meet that
'        month's demand
'    HoldPct: percentage of unit production cost used for unit holding cost
'    HoldOpt: 1 or 2, depending on whether holding cost is based on ending
'        inventory or average of beginning and ending inventories
'    ProdCap: production capacity, assumed constant each month
'    InvCap: storage capacity, assumed constant each month
'    NewMonth: month for new data
'    NewDemand: newly observed demand for NewMonth
'    NewUnitCost: newly observed unit cost for NewMonth

Public Choice As Integer, NMonthsNew As Integer, NMonths As Integer, _
    InitInv As Long, ProdPct As Single, HoldPct As Single, _
    HoldOpt As Integer, ProdCap As Long, InvCap As Long, _
    NewMonth As Date, NewDemand As Long, NewUnitCost As Single
```

Main Code

```
Sub Main()
    OptionsForm.Show
    If Choice = 1 Then
        Call ProdModel
    ElseIf Choice = 2 Then
        Call ViewData
    ElseIf Choice = 3 Then
        Call NewData
    Else
        Call SmConstants
    End If
End Sub
```

ProdModel Code

The **ProdModel** sub "shows" the InputsForm form, activates the Model sheet, clears the contents of any previous model, and calls several subs (**EnterForecasts**, **EnterFormulas**, **RunSolver**, and **CreateReport**) to develop and optimize the production planning model and report the results.

```
Sub ProdModel()
' This sub is run when the user wants to find an optimal production plan,
' based on the historical data observed so far. It calls a sequence of
' subs to do the work.
' First, get the user's inputs.
    InputsForm.Show
    Application.ScreenUpdating = False
' Activate the Model sheet and clear any old model.
    Worksheets("Model").Activate
    Range("B13:M33").ClearContents
' Develop the model and optimize with Solver.
    Call EnterForecasts
    Call EnterFormulas
    Call RunSolver
' Transfer selected results to the Report sheet.
    Call CreateReport
    Application.ScreenUpdating = True
End Sub
```

EnterForecasts Code

The purpose of the **EnterForecasts** sub is to calculate *future* forecasts of demands and unit costs, based on the data in the Data sheet, and then enter these in the Model sheet. Note that the Data sheet contains forecasts for the *historical* period only. Therefore, forecasts for the planning horizon must be calculated in this sub. (Also, remember when reading the code that the DataAnchor cell is cell A3 of the Data sheet, the cell just above the first data entry.)

Unless you thoroughly understand Holt's and Winters' forecasting models, you will probably not understand all of the details in this sub. In that case, it suffices to know that the relevant formulas have *already* been entered in the Data sheet for the historical period. This sub basically copies these formulas down for the planning period.

```
Sub EnterForecasts()
' This sub enters the forecasts of demand and unit cost in the Model sheet. They are
' calculated by Winters' and Holt's exponential smoothing models.
    Dim i As Integer, LevelCell1 As Range, LevelCell2 As Range, Level1 As Single, _
        Trend1 As Single, Level2 As Single, Trend2 As Single, SeasFactor As Single

' The LevelCell1 and LevelCell2 cells are the last values of "smoothed level" for
' demand and unit cost, respectively, in the Data sheet.
    Set LevelCell1 = Range("DataAnchor").Offset(0, 3).End(xlDown)
    Set LevelCell2 = Range("DataAnchor").Offset(0, 7).End(xlDown)

' The next four values are the basis for future forecasts.
    Level1 = LevelCell1
    Trend1 = LevelCell1.Offset(0, 1)
    Level2 = LevelCell2
    Trend2 = LevelCell2.Offset(0, 1)

' Fill up rows 13 and 29 of the Model sheet with the appropriate dates in the planning
' horizon. Dates are tricky to work with, but an easy way to do it here is to
' temporarily put the last historical date in cell A13, then use the AutoFill method
' to fill up the future dates in row 13, then replace the date in A13 with the
' label "Month", then copy row 13 to row 29.
    With Range("A13")
        .Value = Range("DataAnchor").End(xlDown)
        .AutoFill Destination:=Range(.Offset(0, 0), .Offset(0, NMonths)), _
            Type:=xlFillDefault
        .Value = "Month"
        Range(.Offset(0, 1), .Offset(0, NMonths)).Copy Range("B29")
    End With

' For demand forecasts in row 21, project the most recent level upward by i times the
' most recent trend, then multiply by the appropriate seasonal factor. Do the same for
' unit costs in row 30, except that there is no seasonality.
    For i = 1 To NMonths
        SeasFactor = LevelCell1.Offset(i - 12, 2)
        Range("A21").Offset(0, i) = (Level1 + i * Trend1) * SeasFactor
        Range("A30").Offset(0, i) = Level2 + i * Trend2
    Next

' Name some ranges for later use.
    With Range("A13")
        Range(.Offset(0, 1), .Offset(0, NMonths)).Name = "Months"
    End With
    With Range("A21")
        Range(.Offset(0, 1), .Offset(0, NMonths)).Name = "FDemands"
    End With
    With Range("A30")
        Range(.Offset(0, 1), .Offset(0, NMonths)).Name = "FCosts"
    End With
End Sub
```

EnterFormulas Code

The **EnterFormulas** sub is rather lengthy because it has to develop the optimization model "on the fly" at run time. It enters all of the formulas in the Model sheet and names ranges appropriately. The comments spell out the details. (It is helpful to refer to Figure 18.16 when reading this code.)

```
Sub EnterFormulas()
' This sub enters all of the formulas for the production planning model. It uses the
' Formula or FormulaR1C1 property, depending on which is more natural.
    Dim i As Integer
    For i = 1 To NMonths

' Calculate beginning inventories in row 14. Other than the first, these equal the
' previous ending inventory (9 rows below).
        If i = 1 Then
            Range("A14").Offset(0, i).Formula = "=InitInv"
        Else
            Range("A14").Offset(0, i).FormulaR1C1 = "=R[9]C[-1]"
        End If

' Row 15 contains the production quantities, the changing cells. Enter 0's initially.
        Range("A15").Offset(0, i) = 0

' Enter <= labels in row 16 to denote constraints.
        Range("A16").Offset(0, i) = "<="

' Enter a link to the ProdCap cell throughout row 17.
        Range("A17").Offset(0, i).Formula = "=ProdCap"

' Calculate onhand inventory (available to meet demand) in row 19 as beginning
' inventory (5 rows above) plus the production percentage times production (4 rows up).
        Range("A19").Offset(0, i).FormulaR1C1 = "=R[-5]C+ProdPct*R[-4]C"

' Enter >= labels in row 20 to denote constraints.
        Range("A20").Offset(0, i) = ">="

' Calculate ending inventory in row 23 as the difference between onhand inventory
' (4 rows up) and demand (2 rows up), plus (1 minus the production percentage) times
' the production (8 rows up).
        Range("A23").Offset(0, i).FormulaR1C1 = "=R[-4]C-R[-2]C+(1-ProdPct)*R[-8]C"

' Enter a link to the InvCap cel throughout row 25.
        Range("A25").Offset(0, i).Formula = "=InvCap"

' Calculate the average of beginning inventory (12 rows up) and ending inventory
' (3 rows up) in row 26.
        Range("A26").Offset(0, i).FormulaR1C1 = "=(R[-12]C+R[-3]C)/2"
    Next

' Name some ranges for later use.
    With Range("A15")
        Range(.Offset(0, 1), .Offset(0, NMonths)).Name = "Production"
    End With
    With Range("A17")
        Range(.Offset(0, 1), .Offset(0, NMonths)).Name = "ProdCaps"
    End With
    With Range("A19")
        Range(.Offset(0, 1), .Offset(0, NMonths)).Name = "Onhand"
    End With
    With Range("A23")
        Range(.Offset(0, 1), .Offset(0, NMonths)).Name = "EndInv"
    End With
```

```
    With Range("A25")
        Range(.Offset(0, 1), .Offset(0, NMonths)).Name = "InvCaps"
    End With
    With Range("A26")
        Range(.Offset(0, 1), .Offset(0, NMonths)).Name = "AvgInv"
    End With

' Calculate the total production cost.
    Range("B32").Formula = "=Sumproduct(Production,FCosts)"

' Calculate the total holding cost.
    If HoldOpt = 1 Then
        Range("B33").Formula = "=Sumproduct(EndInv,HoldPct*FCosts)"
    Else
        Range("B33").Formula = "=Sumproduct(AvgInv,HoldPct*FCosts)"
    End If

' The total cost in cell B34 already has a formula in it, which never changes.
End Sub
```

RunSolver Code

The **RunSolver** sub resets the Solver dialog box, sets it up appropriately, and runs the Solver. A check is made for feasibility. If there are no feasible solutions, a message to this effect is displayed and the program is terminated.

```
Sub RunSolver()
' Reset Solver, then set up the Solver.
    SolverReset
    SolverOK SetCell:=Range("TotalCost"), MaxMinVal:=2, ByChange:=Range("Production")
    SolverAdd CellRef:=Range("Production"), Relation:=1, FormulaText:="ProdCaps"
    SolverAdd CellRef:=Range("OnHand"), Relation:=3, FormulaText:="FDemands"
    SolverAdd CellRef:=Range("EndInv"), Relation:=1, FormulaText:="InvCaps"
    SolverOptions AssumeLinear:=True, AssumeNonNeg:=True

' Run the Solver. If the result code is 5, this means there is no feasible solution,
' so display a message to that effect and quit.
    If SolverSolve(UserFinish:="True") = 5 Then
        MsgBox "There is no feasible solution with these inputs. Try " _
            & "larger capacities.", vbExclamation, "No feasible solution"
        Call ViewExplanation
        End
    End If
End Sub
```

CreateReport Code

The **CreateReport** sub copies the data on months, production quantities, and ending inventory levels from the Model sheet to the Report sheet. In the case of ending inventory levels, the Model sheet contains formulas, so these are pasted as *values* in the Report sheet. Finally, this sub updates the embedded chart on the Report sheet with the new data.

```
Sub CreateReport()
' The Report sheet is already set up (at design time), so just copy (with PasteSpecial/
' Values when formulas are involved) selected quantities to the Report sheet.
    Dim i As Integer
' Unhide and activate the Report sheet.
    With Worksheets("Report")
        .Visible = True
        .Activate
    End With
' Clear old values.
    Range("B3:M5").ClearContents
' Copy results to rows 3-5.
    Range("Months").Copy Range("B3")
    Range("Production").Copy Range("B4")
    Range("EndInv").Copy
    Range("B5").PasteSpecial xlPasteValues

' Name some ranges for later use.
    With Range("A3")
        Range(.Offset(0, 1), .Offset(0, NMonths)).Name = "RepMonths"
        Range(.Offset(1, 0), .Offset(1, NMonths)).Name = "RepProd"
        Range(.Offset(2, 0), .Offset(2, NMonths)).Name = "RepEndInv"
    End With
' Update the embedded chart on the Report sheet.
    With ActiveSheet.ChartObjects(1).Chart
        .SetSourceData Source:=Union(Range("RepProd"), Range("RepEndInv"))
        .SeriesCollection(1).XValues = Range("RepMonths")
    End With
' Color the whole sheet blue.
    ActiveSheet.Cells.Interior.ColorIndex = 37
    Range("B14").Select
End Sub
```

NewData Code

The **NewData** sub "shows" the NewDataForm1 and NewDataForm2 and appends the new data to the bottom of the historical data range in the Data sheet. It then copies the exponential smoothing formulas down to these new rows, and it renames ranges to include the new rows. Finally, it calls the UpdateCharts sub to update the two chart sheets that show historical data with superimposed forecasts.

```
Sub NewData()
' This sub allows the user to enter newly observed demand and unit cost data.
    Dim i As Integer, LastMonth As Date
' Unhide and activate the Data sheet.
    With Worksheets("Data")
        .Visible = True
        .Activate
    End With
' Get the number of new data values from the user.
    NewDataForm1.Show
    With Range("DataAnchor").End(xlDown)
' Enter new dates in column A with the AutoFill method.
        .AutoFill Range(.Offset(0, 0), .Offset(NMonthsNew, 0))
' Get demand and unit cost data for new months and enter them below old data.
        For i = 1 To NMonthsNew
            NewMonth = .Offset(i, 0)
```

```
            NewDataForm2.Show
            .Offset(i, 1) = NewDemand
            .Offset(i, 2) = NewUnitCost
        Next
    End With
' Copy the formulas in columns D through L of the Data sheet down for the new data.
' These implement the exponential smoothing methods.
    With Range("DataAnchor").Offset(0, 3).End(xlDown)
        Range(.Offset(0, 0), .Offset(0, 8)).Copy Range(.Offset(1, 0), _
            .Offset(NMonthsNew, 8))
    End With
' Rename the ranges for various columns in the Data sheet.
    With Range("DataAnchor")
        Range(.Offset(1, 0), .End(xlDown)).Name = "Month"
        Range(.Offset(0, 1), .Offset(0, 1).End(xlDown)).Name = "Demands"
        Range(.Offset(0, 2), .Offset(0, 2).End(xlDown)).Name = "UnitCosts"
        Range(.Offset(0, 6), .Offset(0, 6).End(xlDown)).Name = "DemFCasts"
        Range(.Offset(0, 9), .Offset(0, 9).End(xlDown)).Name = "CostFCasts"
        Range(.Offset(1, 10), .Offset(1, 10).End(xlDown)).Name = "APE1"
        Range(.Offset(1, 11), .Offset(1, 11).End(xlDown)).Name = "APE2"
    End With
' Update the charts to include all data observed so far.
    Call UpdateCharts
    Range("N9").Select
End Sub
```

UpdateCharts Code

The **UpdateCharts** sub resets the links to the data for the two chart sheets (which were created at design time with the Chart Wizard). This is done to accommodate the new data that were just appended to the historical data range.

```
Sub UpdateCharts()
' This sub updates the source data ranges for the two chart sheets. It is called only
' when the user enters new data.
    With Charts("DemFCast")
        .SetSourceData Source:=Union(Range("Demands"), Range("DemFCasts"))
        .SeriesCollection(1).XValues = Range("Month")
    End With

    With Charts("CostFCast")
        .SetSourceData Source:=Union(Range("UnitCosts"), Range("CostFCasts"))
        .SeriesCollection(1).XValues = Range("Month")
    End With
End Sub
```

SmConstants Code

The **SmConstants** sub "shows" the SmConstForm form and displays a message about the updated MAPE values. (Remember that the event code for the SmConstForm form performs the task of entering the new smoothing constants in the Data sheet.)

```
Sub SmConstants()
' This sub allows the user to change the smoothing constants. After choosing them,
' everything on the Data sheet recalculates automatically, and a message box shows
' the updated MAPE values.
    SmConstForm.Show
    MsgBox "MAPE for forecasting demand is " & Format(Range("MAPE1"), "0.00%") _
        & "." & vbCrLf & "MAPE for forecasting unit costs is " _
        & Format(Range("MAPE2"), "0.00%"), vbInformation, "Forecasting"
End Sub
```

Navigational Code

The rest of the subs listed below are for navigational purposes. They are attached to the buttons on the various sheets.

```
Sub ViewData()
    With Worksheets("Data")
        .Visible = True
        .Activate
    End With
    Range("N9").Select
End Sub

Sub ViewDemFCasts()
    With Charts("DemFCast")
        .Visible = True
        .Activate
    End With
End Sub

Sub ViewCostFCasts()
    With Charts("CostFCast")
        .Visible = True
        .Activate
    End With
End Sub

Sub ViewExplanation()
    Dim sht As Object
    Worksheets("Explanation").Activate
    Range("F4").Select
    For Each sht In ActiveWorkbook.Sheets
        If sht.Name <> "Explanation" Then sht.Visible = False
    Next
End Sub

Sub ViewReport()
    Worksheets("Report").Activate
    Range("B14").Select
    Charts("DemFCast").Visible = False
    Charts("CostFCast").Visible = False
End Sub
```

18.8 Summary

The forecasting/optimization application is admittedly fairly long and complex, but this is the price to be paid for accomplishing so much. The application combines two traditional areas of management science. First, it implements exponential smoothing forecasting methods. Second, it uses the exponential smoothed forecasts as inputs to a production scheduling optimization model. In this way, the application can be used to implement a rolling planning horizon used by many organizations.

PROGRAMMING EXERCISES

1. The application currently creates a column chart of production quantities and ending inventories on the Report sheet. (See Figure 18.4.) Change it so that two *separate* charts are created on the Report sheet: one of production quantities and one of ending inventories. Also, make each of them *line* charts.

2. The planning horizon can currently be any number of months from 3 to 12. Suppose the company involved insists on a 6-month planning horizon—no more, no less. Would this make your job as a programmer easier or harder? Explain in words what basic changes you would make to the application.

3. Some programmers might object to our EnterFormulas sub, arguing that it is too long and should be broken up into smaller subs. Try doing this. You can decide how many smaller subs to use and what specific task each should have. Then test the application with your new code. It should still work correctly!

4. We have used our own (fictional) historical data to illustrate the application. Try using your own. Specifically, enter your own data in columns A, B, and C of the Data sheet (see Figure 18.5), and make sure the columns next to them (D–J) have the same number of rows as your new data. (Delete rows or copy down if necessary.) You'll also have to enter "reasonable" initialization values for the smoothing methods. (See Figure 18.14 for the cells involved.) Now run the application. Does it work correctly? It should!

5. The third basic option in the application allows the user to enter *any* number of new observations. Change this so that only *one* new observation (of demand and unit cost) can be added on a given run. In this case, you won't need NewDataForm1.

6. (More difficult, and only for those familiar with exponential smoothing) The fourth basic option in the application allows the user to enter *any* smoothing constants from 0 to 1. Delete this option. Instead, have the application choose the smoothing constants to minimize the "root mean square error," which is defined as the square root of the sum of squared differences between observations and forecasts. You will need to write code to set up and run Solver for this minimization. Write this as two subs, one for the demands and one for the unit costs (since each has its own set of smoothing constants). Then decide when these subs should be called, and update other subs accordingly.

7. (More difficult, and only for those familiar with exponential smoothing) The application is written for a product with seasonal demand. This is the reason for using Winters' method. Change the application so that the user can choose (in an extra user form) which of three exponential smoothing methods to use for forecasting demand: simple, Holt's, or Winters'. Then the appropriate formulas should be used. (*Hint*: There are probably fewer required modifications than you might expect, because the formulas for simple exponential smoothing and Holt's methods are *special cases* of the built-in Winters' method.)

A Minimum-Cost Network Flow Application

19.1 Introduction

This application solves a fairly general minimum-cost network flow model, where a company needs to ship a product from various suppliers to various customers, possibly through various transshipment points. There can be as many as 200 arcs in the network (only because this is the maximum number of changing cells allowed by the Solver), each of which has a unit shipping cost and possibly a minimum required flow and a maximum allowed flow. The suppliers have capacities and the customers have demands that must be satisfied. The objective is to ship the products from suppliers to customers at minimal cost.

This problem requires extensive input data, including node data (names of suppliers and customers, as well as capacities and demands) and arc data (existing arcs in the network, unit costs, minimum flows, and maximum flows). The data for a real problem of this type would probably reside on a database, not within Excel, so this possibility is illustrated here. The data are in two tables (Nodes and Arcs) of an Access database. This application shows how the Access data can be imported into an Excel worksheet to create a Solver model, which can then be solved in the usual way. To do so, it uses Microsoft's new **ActiveX Data Objects** (**ADO**) object model.[34] This enables us to use VBA to import data from external databases into Excel. We do not even need to own the database package, such as Access, to make it work. Fortunately, ADO is quite easy to implement in VBA, as this chapter will illustrate. This gives the developers of decision support systems a whole new level of power—the ability to access external databases from Excel.

New Learning Objective: VBA

- To learn how to import data from Access or other database files into Excel applications by using the ADO object model.

New Learning Objective: Non-VBA

- To learn about minimum-cost network flow models and how they can be optimized with the Solver.

---

[34]It is so new that this application will not work in Excel 97, which has no knowledge of ADO. It will work only in Excel 2000 (or later).

19.2 Functionality of the Application

The application performs the following functions:

1. It uses the ADO object model, through VBA, to retrieve the data from the Nodes and Arcs tables of an Access database called **NetworkFlow.mdb**. This database file must be in the same directory as the Excel application file (named **NetworkFlow.xls**). The Access file contains two tables, Nodes and Arcs, which will be discussed in more detail below. The application will work with *any* network data in this Access file, provided the data are structured as shown in these two tables.

2. It uses the node and arc data to set up a minimum-cost network flow model in the (hidden) Model sheet of the Excel file and then uses the Solver to find the minimal-cost set of flows through the network. Finally, it reports the minimum total cost and the flows on all arcs with positive flows in a Report sheet.

19.3 Running the Application

The application is in the Excel file **NetworkFlow.xls**. When this file is opened, the Explanation sheet in Figure 19.1 appears. When the button is clicked, everything happens behind the scenes—the user sees no dialog boxes and makes no choices. The data from the database are imported into the Model sheet, the network flow model is developed, the Solver is set up and run, and the results are transferred to the Report sheet. This Report sheet, shown in Figure 19.2, is the only thing the user sees. The Model sheet, shown in Figure 19.3 (with several hidden rows) is hidden from the user.

Figure 19.1 Explanation sheet

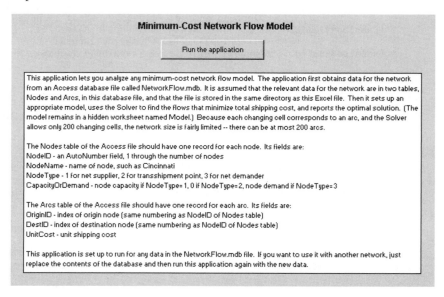

Minimum-Cost Network Flow Model

Run the application

This application lets you analyze any minimum-cost network flow model. The application first obtains data for the network from an Access database file called NetworkFlow.mdb. It is assumed that the relevant data for the network are in two tables, Nodes and Arcs, in this database file, and that the file is stored in the same directory as this Excel file. Then it sets up an appropriate model, uses the Solver to find the flows that minimize total shipping cost, and reports the optimal solution. (The model remains in a hidden worksheet named Model.) Because each changing cell corresponds to an arc, and the Solver allows only 200 changing cells, the network size is fairly limited -- there can be at most 200 arcs.

The Nodes table of the Access file should have one record for each node. Its fields are:
NodeID - an AutoNumber field, 1 through the number of nodes
NodeName - name of node, such as Cincinnati
NodeType - 1 for net supplier, 2 for transshipment point, 3 for net demander
CapacityOrDemand - node capacity if NodeType=1, 0 if NodeType=2, node demand if NodeType=3

The Arcs table of the Access file should have one record for each arc. Its fields are:
OriginID - index of origin node (same numbering as NodeID of Nodes table)
DestID - index of destination node (same numbering as NodeID of Nodes table)
UnitCost - unit shipping cost

This application is set up to run for any data in the NetworkFlow.mdb file. If you want to use it with another network, just replace the contents of the database and then run this application again with the new data.

Figure 19.2 Report of optimal solution

Summary of optimal shipping policy

Total shipping cost:	$14,927

Arcs with positive flows

From	To	Flow	Total cost
Scranton	Syracuse	50	88.5
Memphis	Philadelphia	230	770.5
Wheeling	Philadelphia	50	133
Pittsburgh	Cleveland	340	1037
Scranton	Cleveland	50	273
Memphis	Cleveland	70	210.7
Scranton	Akron	50	178.5
Memphis	Columbus	100	333
Syracuse	Wheeling	240	1176
Scranton	Wheeling	10	39.7
Cleveland	Knoxville	50	84
Scranton	Charlotte	50	185
Pittsburgh	Baltimore	60	227.4
Scranton	New York	200	1214
Columbus	New York	100	316
Charlotte	New York	30	105
Memphis	Boston	50	374
Cleveland	Boston	210	793.8
Pittsburgh	Buffalo	190	1155.2
Memphis	Buffalo	50	381.5
Philadelphia	Buffalo	50	202
Syracuse	Cincinnati	240	1538.4
St. Louis	Cincinnati	20	40.8
Cleveland	Chicago	200	702
Baltimore	Chicago	60	225
Cincinnati	Chicago	50	79
Memphis	Minneapolis	50	416
Wheeling	Minneapolis	200	634
Buffalo	Minneapolis	50	124.5
Pittsburgh	St. Louis	50	366.5
Akron	St. Louis	50	251
Knoxville	St. Louis	50	231
Philadelphia	Atlanta	230	966
Charlotte	Atlanta	20	75.4

19.4   Setting Up the Access Database

The application depends entirely on the Access database. The application currently uses the database with the Nodes and Arcs tables shown in Figures 19.4 and 19.5, but it will work with any similar database, provided that the following requirements are satisfied.

- It should be named **NetworkFlow.mdb**, and it should be located in the *same* folder as the **NetworkFlow.xls** Excel file. Actually, the file name could be changed, but the appropriate lines in the VBA module code, where the name of the file is specified, would have to be changed accordingly.
- It should contain no more than 200 arcs. Actually, this is a Solver requirement. The Excel Solver allows at most 200 changing cells, and each changing cell in the model corresponds to an arc.

Figure 19.3   Model sheet

	A	B	C	D	E	F	G	H	I	J	K
1	**Minimum-cost network flow model**								Total cost	$14,927	
2											
3	Arc data							Node balance constraints			
4	Origins	Destinations	UnitCosts	Flows	MinFlows	MaxFlows		Node	Net inflow/outflow		Required
5	Scranton	Pittsburgh	$2.01	0	0	200		Pittsburgh	640 <=		990
6	Scranton	Syracuse	$1.77	50	50	100		Syracuse	430 <=		460
7	Memphis	Syracuse	$1.90	0	0	200		Scranton	410 <=		410
8	Pittsburgh	Scranton	$2.65	0	0	2410		Memphis	550 <=		550
9	Syracuse	Scranton	$1.96	0	0	2410		Philadelphia	0 =		0
10	Memphis	Scranton	$1.56	0	0	100		Cleveland	0 =		0
11	Pittsburgh	Memphis	$1.75	0	0	100		Akron	0 =		0
12	Pittsburgh	Philadelphia	$4.73	0	0	2410		Columbus	0 =		0
13	Scranton	Philadelphia	$5.45	0	0	2410		Wheeling	0 =		0
14	Memphis	Philadelphia	$3.35	230	0	2410		Knoxville	0 =		0
15	Wheeling	Philadelphia	$2.66	50	50	2410		Charlotte	0 =		0
16	Charlotte	Philadelphia	$2.25	0	0	100		Baltimore	0 =		0
17	Baltimore	Philadelphia	$1.56	0	0	100		New York	330 >=		330
18	Pittsburgh	Cleveland	$3.05	340	0	2410		Boston	260 >=		260
19	Syracuse	Cleveland	$4.32	0	0	2410		Buffalo	240 >=		240
20	Scranton	Cleveland	$5.46	50	50	2410		Cincinnati	210 >=		210
21	Memphis	Cleveland	$3.01	70	0	200		Chicago	310 >=		310
22	Akron	Cleveland	$1.77	0	0	100		Minneapolis	300 >=		300
23	Columbus	Cleveland	$2.34	0	0	2410		St. Louis	130 >=		130
24	Baltimore	Cleveland	$2.30	0	0	2410		Atlanta	250 >=		250
25	Pittsburgh	Akron	$4.61	0	0	100					
26	Syracuse	Akron	$5.19	0	0	2410					
27	Scranton	Akron	$3.57	50	0	200					
28	Memphis	Akron	$5.39	0	0	2410					
29	Baltimore	Akron	$1.55	0	0	2410					
30	Pittsburgh	Columbus	$5.09	0	0	2410					
132	Knoxville	Atlanta	$4.84	0	0	200					
133	Charlotte	Atlanta	$3.77	20	0	200					
134	New York	Atlanta	$2.11	0	0	100					
135	Boston	Atlanta	$2.88	0	0	100					
136	Chicago	Atlanta	$2.64	0	0	2410					

- It should have two tables named Nodes and Arcs.
- The Nodes table should be structured as in Figure 19.4. It should have a record (row) for each node, and it should have four fields (columns) named NodeID, NodeName, NodeType, and SupplyOrDemand. The NodeID field is an "AutoNumber" key field, used to index the nodes. (This means it is automatically populated with consecutive integers.) The NodeName is the name of the node. The NodeType is 1, 2, or 3, depending on whether the node is a net supplier, a transshipment point, or a net demander. The SupplyOrDemand is the node capacity for a net supplier, 0 for a transshipment point, and the demand for a net demander.
- The Arcs table should be structured as in Figure 19.5. It should have a record for each arc, and it should have five fields named OriginID, DestID, UnitCost, MinFlow, and MaxFlow. The OriginID and DestID are indexes of the origin node and destination node for the arc. The UnitCost is the unit shipping cost for the arc. The MinFlow and MaxFlow are the minimum required flow and the maximum allowed flow for the arc. Either of these two can be missing. If MinFlow is missing, the flow on the arc is constrained to be nonnegative. If MaxFlow is missing, the flow on the arc is constrained to be less than or equal to the total capacity of all suppliers (which is no *real* constraint at all).

Figure 19.4 Node data in Access table

NodeID	NodeName	NodeType	SupplyOrDemand
1	Pittsburgh	1	990
2	Syracuse	1	460
3	Scranton	1	410
4	Memphis	1	550
5	Philadelphia	2	0
6	Cleveland	2	0
7	Akron	2	0
8	Columbus	2	0
9	Wheeling	2	0
10	Knoxville	2	0
11	Charlotte	2	0
12	Baltimore	2	0
13	New York	3	330
14	Boston	3	260
15	Buffalo	3	240
16	Cincinnati	3	210
17	Chicago	3	310
18	Minneapolis	3	300
19	St. Louis	3	130
20	Atlanta	3	250

Record: 1 of 20

Figure 19.5 Arc data in Access table

OriginID	DestID	UnitCost	MinFlow	MaxFlow
3	1	$2.01	0	200
3	2	$1.77	50	100
4	2	$1.90	0	200
1	3	$2.65	0	
2	3	$1.96	0	
4	3	$1.56	0	100
1	4	$1.75	0	100
1	5	$4.73	0	
3	5	$5.45	0	
4	5	$3.35	0	
9	5	$2.66	50	
11	5	$2.25	0	100
12	5	$1.56	0	100
1	6	$3.05	0	
2	6	$4.32	0	
3	6	$5.46	50	
4	6	$3.01	0	200
7	6	$1.77	0	100
8	6	$2.34	0	
12	6	$2.30	0	
1	7	$4.61	0	100
2	7	$5.19	0	

Record: 1 of 132

- The database should be relational. Specifically, there should be links from the OriginID and DestID fields of the Arcs table to the NodeID field of the Nodes table. Then index 6, for example, refers to Cleveland in both tables.

19.5   Setting Up the Excel Worksheets

The **NetworkFlow.xls** file contains three worksheets: the Explanation sheet in Figure 19.1, the Model sheet in Figure 19.3, and the Report sheet in Figure 19.2. The Model sheet always has the same type of information in the same columns, but none of the data can be entered until run time. Therefore, the only template that can be formed in the Model sheet at design time is shown in Figure 19.6. Similarly, the only template that can be set up in the Report sheet at design time is shown in Figure 19.7.

Figure 19.6   Template for model sheet

	A	B	C	D	E	F	G	H	I	J	K
1	Minimum-cost network flow model							Total cost			
2											
3	Arc data							Node balance constraints			
4	Origins	Destinations	UnitCosts	Flows	MinFlows	MaxFlows		Node	Net inflow/outflow		Required

Figure 19.7   Template for report sheet

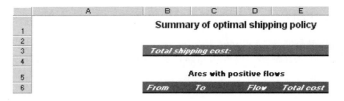

19.6   Getting Started with the VBA

Unlike the applications in previous chapters, this application contains no user forms.[35] Therefore, this application requires only a single module. However, two references must be set. First, because Solver functions are used, a reference must be set to Solver.xla. Then, because the ADO object model is being used, a reference must be set to it. To do so, use the Tools/References menu item in the VBE, scroll down the list for the **Microsoft ActiveX Data Objects 2.1 Library**, and check its box.[36] (See Figure 19.8.) After this is done, the Project Explorer will

---

[35]One possibility would be to allow the user to choose a *subset* of all nodes from the Nodes table, using a dialog box with a list box. Then the network model would be restricted to the nodes from this subset. However, this would make the VBA code considerably more complex.

[36]Version 2.1 is the most recent version at the time of this writing. You should check the box with the most recent version on your PC. Also, remember that ADO is *not* available in Excel 97 or earlier, so you will not see this item on the list—and this application will not work—unless you are using Excel 2000 (or later).

look as in Figure 19.9. Note that there is no reference showing for ADO, only for Solver. Evidently, Microsoft lists only the *non*-Microsoft references in the Project Explorer.

Figure 19.8 References dialog box

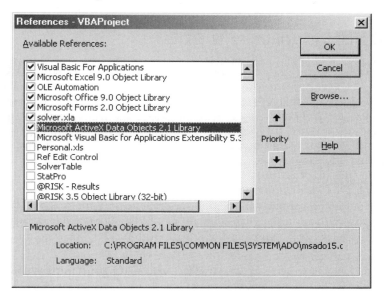

Figure 19.9 Project Explorer window

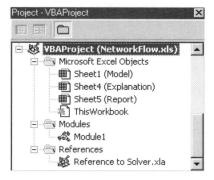

Workbook_Open Code

To guarantee that the Explanation sheet appears when the file is opened, the following code is placed in the ThisWorkbook code window. It also hides the Model and Report sheets.

```
Private Sub Workbook_Open()
    Worksheets("Explanation").Activate
    Range("G4").Select
    Worksheets("Model").Visible = False
    Worksheets("Report").Visible = False
End Sub
```

19.7   A Quick Introduction to ADO

To understand the code listed below, you must first understand something about the way Microsoft allows developers to retrieve data from an external database. Its newest standard is called **OLE DB**. This is a set of code written in a more complex language (C or C++) that essentially retrieves data from practically any type of database and transforms the results into a common row-column (record-field) format. This code is too complex for most programmers to deal with, so **ADO** has been developed as a "go-between." It allows developers to write much simpler code in VBA to retrieve data from an external database, as the code below will illustrate.

To use ADO, the first step is to create a **connection** to the database. This requires, at the very least, a reference to the name and location of the database file and information on the **data provider**.[37] Each type of database has a data provider. A data provider is code stored somewhere on your PC that knows how to deal with a particular type of database. It is analogous to the "drivers" that are provided for various types of printers. There is a provider for Access, Oracle, SQL Server, and other database packages. The provider for Access is called **Microsoft Jet 4.0 OLE DB Provider**.

Once a connection is formed, the next step is usually to open a **recordset** based on the database. A recordset is a temporary database table (temporary in the sense that it resides only in memory, not as a file on a hard drive). It can be an entire table from the database, or it can be the result of a query. In our case, it will be the former.[38]

After the recordset is opened, it is easy to go through its records with a Do loop and retrieve information from any of its fields. A common practice is to use code such as the following:

```
With rs
    Do Until .EOF
        Statements
        .MoveNext
    Loop
End With
```

---

[37] To create a connection to some databases, other information, such as a username and a password, might also be required.

[38] To specify a query, an **SQL string** must be created. It then becomes the first argument of the Open method of a Recordset object. However, SQL statements will not be discussed here.

Here, rs is a **Recordset** object variable. One of its properties is **EOF** (end of file), and one of its methods is **MoveNext**. Very simply, these lines tell the program to go through the records of the recordset, one at a time, taking some actions in the part called *Statements*, and quitting when the end of the file is reached. The MoveNext method moves to the next record. To capture the data in a field named UnitCost, say, a reference to **.Fields("UnitCost")** can be made inside this loop.

How to Open a Connection

To open a connection to a database, you first declare a **Connection** object, as in the following line:

```
Dim cn as ADODB.Connection
```

Here, cn is the name of the Connection object (any generic name could be used), and ADODB indicates that this Connection object comes from a library called ADODB. Second, the line

```
Set cn = New ADODB.Connection
```

creates a new Connection object of the type referenced in the Dim statement. Next, the **ConnectionString** and **Provider** properties and the **Open** method of the Connection object are used to actually open the connection. The next few lines illustrate how to open the connection to the **NetworkFlow.mdb** file. (Note that this code is in the Excel file, so **ThisWorkbook.Path** refers to the folder where the Excel file lives. For the connection to be made, the Access file must be in the *same* folder.)

```
With cn
    .ConnectionString = "Data Source=" & ThisWorkbook.Path & "\NetworkFlow.mdb"
    .Provider = "Microsoft Jet 4.0 OLE DB Provider"
    .Open
End With
```

The **ConnectionString** property in the second line must begin with **"Data Source="** and be followed by the path and name of the database file. The Provider property is the name of the data provider. The Open method opens the connection. (To tidy up, the **Close** method should be used to close the connection once it is no longer needed.)

How to Open a Recordset

Similarly, a new **Recordset** object with a generic name such as rs must be declared and created with the lines

```
Dim rs as ADODB.Recordset
Set rs = New ADODB.Recordset
```

It can then be opened with code such as

```
With rs
    .Open "Nodes", cn, adOpenKeyset, adLockOptimistic
    OtherStatements
End With
```

The first two arguments of the Open method are the table name (or an SQL string) and the Connection object that has already been opened. The last two (or more) arguments are technical and will not be discussed here. As with a Connection object, a Recordset object should be closed with the Close method when it is no longer needed. Then the Close method of the *connection* should be called.

Note that Access does *not* need to be open to do any of this. You don't even need to have Access installed on your PC. All you require is the Access database file and the knowledge of its structure (tables and fields). Of course, if you want to create your own Access database (to replace the one we've provided, for example) you *do* need Access.

On a first reading, this business about connections, recordsets, data providers, and so on, can be intimidating. However, the code varies very little from one application to the next, so there is not as much to learn as you might expect. Besides, the effort required to learn ADO is well worth it, given the power it provides for retrieving external data for your Excel applications.

Relationship Between DAO and ADO

If you look further into the VBA methods for retrieving external data, you will almost surely hear discussions of the **Data Access Objects** (**DAO**) object model. This was Microsoft's original method for retrieving external data. Although DAO itself is rather new, Microsoft is now trying to steer developers away from DAO and toward ADO. Their reasoning is that ADO is a simpler model, and it is capable of dealing with more general data sources. From what we have seen, we tend to agree with both of these arguments. Given the choice of which of these two models to learn, ADO is probably the better bet. However, you should be aware that there are many applications already out there that use DAO in their VBA code, and you might eventually run into one of them.

19.8 The VBA Code in the Module

> **Web Help** For more explanation of the code in this application, visit our Web site at http://www.indiana.edu/~mgtsci and download the **Code Explanation - NetworkFlow.doc** file.

We now see how this is implemented in our network application. The button on the Explanation sheet is attached to a Main sub in the module. This sub calls other subs to retrieve the data from the Access database, develop the network flow model, run the Solver, and report the results.

Option Statements and Public Variables

```
Option Explicit
Option Base 1

' Definition of public variables:
'    NSupNodes: number of net suppliers
'    SupNode: array of supplier names
'    NTransNodes: number of transshipment points
'    TransNode: array of transshipment point names
'    NDemNodes: number of net demanders
'    DemNode: array of demander names
'    NNodes: total number of nodes
'    Node: array of node names
'    NArcs: total number of arcs
'    Capacity: array of capacities for suppliers
'    Demand: array of demands for demanders
'    Origin: array of origin names (for arcs)
'    Dest: array of destination names (for arcs)
'    UnitCost: array of unit costs on arcs
'    MinFlow: array of minimum required flows on arcs
'    MaxFlow: array maximum allowed flows on arcs
'    MaxPossFlow: maximum possible flow on any arc

Public NSupNodes As Integer, NTransNodes As Integer, NDemNodes As Integer, _
    NNodes As Integer, NArcs As Integer, SupNode() As String, _
    TransNode() As String, DemNode() As String, _
    Capacity() As Long, Demand() As Long, Node() As String, _
    Origin() As String, Dest() As String, UnitCost() As Currency, _
    MinFlow() As Long, MaxFlow() As Long, MaxPossFlow As Long
```

Main Code

```
Sub Main()
' Get data on nodes and arcs from the Access database.
    Call GetNodeInfo
    Call GetArcInfo
' Quit if there are more than 200 arcs, because Solver can't handle this many.
    If NArcs > 200 Then
        MsgBox "The Solver can't handle this database because there " _
            & "are more than 200 arcs (Solver's maximum number of changing " _
            & "cells). Try again with a smaller network.", vbInformation, "Too many arcs"
        End
    End If
    Application.ScreenUpdating = False
' Set up the model, solve it, and report the results.
    Call CreateModel
    Call RunSolver
    Call CreateReport
    Application.ScreenUpdating = True
End Sub
```

GetNodeInfo Code

The GetNodeInfo sub gets the data from the Nodes table of the Access database. It uses ADO to create a connection to the **NetworkFlow.mdb** database file, and then it opens a recordset based on the Nodes table. Once this recordset is open, it loops through the records and stores data about the nodes in arrays for later use in the Model sheet.

You should refer to the general discussion of ADO in Section 19.7 as you examine this code. The comments explain it in plenty of detail. However, it is actually very straightforward once you see the big picture. We first create a connection to the database and open a recordset based on one of its tables. Then we move through each record of the recordset and extract data from its fields. For example, we reference **.Fields("NodeName")** to get the value of the NodeName field in the current record. Note that this reference is inside a **With rs** construction, where **rs** is the recordset, which means that the reference is really to **rs.Fields("NodeName")**. Therefore, we see that the familiar "dot" notation used for Excel objects and properties carries over to ADO.

This sub is fairly long because it contains a Case construction. For each node in the network, we must check whether the node corresponds to a supplier, a transshipment point, or a customer. We need to update a counter for each of these categories, and we must also redimension relevant arrays for each of them.

```
Sub GetNodeInfo()
    Dim cn As ADODB.Connection, rs As ADODB.Recordset

' Initialize counters.
    NSupNodes = 0
    NTransNodes = 0
    NDemNodes = 0
    NNodes = 0
    MaxPossFlow = 0

' The Access database must be in the same directory as this workbook.
' Open a connection to the database file.
    Set cn = New ADODB.Connection
    With cn
        .ConnectionString = "Data Source=" & ThisWorkbook.Path & "\NetworkFlow.mdb"
        .Provider = "Microsoft Jet 4.0 OLE DB Provider"
        .Open
    End With

' Open the Nodes table as a recordset.
    Set rs = New ADODB.Recordset
    With rs
        .Open "Nodes", cn, adOpenKeyset, adLockOptimistic

' Loop through the records of the recordset to capture the information on the nodes.
        Do Until .EOF

' Each new record means another node.
            NNodes = NNodes + 1
            ReDim Preserve Node(NNodes)

' Get the node's name from the NodeName field.
            Node(NNodes) = .Fields("NodeName")

' Do three cases, depending on whether the node is a supplier, transshipment point,
' or customer.
            Select Case .Fields("NodeType")
```

```
            Case 1 ' a supplier

' Update the number of suppliers.
                NSupNodes = NSupNodes + 1
                ReDim Preserve SupNode(NSupNodes)
                ReDim Preserve Capacity(NSupNodes)

' Get the supplier's name and capacity from the NodeName and SupplyOrDemand fields.
                SupNode(NSupNodes) = .Fields("NodeName")
                Capacity(NSupNodes) = .Fields("SupplyOrDemand")

' MaxPossFlow is the total capacity of the supplier nodes. No arc could possibly ship
' more than this, so it serves as an upper bound on all arc flows for arcs without a
' given maximum flow requirement.
                MaxPossFlow = MaxPossFlow + Capacity(NSupNodes)

            Case 2            ' a transshipment point

' Update number of transshipment nodes.
                NTransNodes = NTransNodes + 1
                ReDim Preserve TransNode(NTransNodes)

' Get the node's name from the NodeName field.
                TransNode(NTransNodes) = .Fields("NodeName")

            Case 3            ' a customer

' Update the number of customers.
                NDemNodes = NDemNodes + 1
                ReDim Preserve DemNode(NDemNodes)
                ReDim Preserve Demand(NDemNodes)

' Get the customer's name and demand from the NodeName and SupplyOrDemand fields.
                DemNode(NDemNodes) = .Fields("NodeName")
                Demand(NDemNodes) = .Fields("SupplyOrDemand")
        End Select

' Move to the next record.
        .MoveNext
    Loop

' Close the recordset.
        .Close
    End With

' Close the connection to the database.
    cn.Close
End Sub
```

GetArcInfo Code

The **GetArcInfo** sub is very similar. It also opens a connection to the database, and then it opens a recordset based on the Arcs table. Again, the Do loop goes through the arcs and stores data about them in arrays for later use in the Model sheet.

```
Sub GetArcInfo()
    Dim cn As ADODB.Connection, rs As ADODB.Recordset
    Set cn = New ADODB.Connection

' Initialize the counter.
    NArcs = 0

' Open a connection to the database.
    With cn
        .ConnectionString = "Data Source=" & ThisWorkbook.Path & "\NetworkFlow.mdb"
        .Provider = "Microsoft Jet 4.0 OLE DB Provider"
        .Open
    End With

' Open the Arcs table as a recordset.
    Set rs = New ADODB.Recordset
    With rs
        .Open "Arcs", cn, adOpenKeyset, adLockOptimistic

' Loop through the records of the recordset to capture the information on the arcs.
        Do Until .EOF

' Each new record means another arc.
            NArcs = NArcs + 1

' Redimension the arrays appropriately.
            ReDim Preserve Origin(NArcs)
            ReDim Preserve Dest(NArcs)
            ReDim Preserve UnitCost(NArcs)
            ReDim Preserve MinFlow(NArcs)
            ReDim Preserve MaxFlow(NArcs)

' Fill the arrays with data from the current record.
            Origin(NArcs) = Node(.Fields("OriginID"))
            Dest(NArcs) = Node(.Fields("DestID"))
            UnitCost(NArcs) = .Fields("UnitCost")
            If .Fields("MinFlow") <> "" Then
                MinFlow(NArcs) = .Fields("MinFlow")
            Else
                MinFlow(NArcs) = 0
            End If
            If .Fields("MaxFlow") <> "" Then
                MaxFlow(NArcs) = .Fields("MaxFlow")
            Else
                MaxFlow(NArcs) = MaxPossFlow
            End If

' Move to the next record.
            .MoveNext
        Loop

' Close the recordset.
        .Close
    End With

' Close the connection to the database.
    cn.Close
End Sub
```

CreateModel Code

By this time, ADO has done its job and is no longer needed. The required data from the database are now in arrays (Origin, Dest, UnitCost, and so on) that will be used to create the network flow model. The **CreateModel** sub begins by clearing any data in the Model sheet from a previous run, if any. Then it calls three subs, **EnterArcData**, **FormConstraints**, and **CalcCost**, to build the model. As you read the details of these subs, you should refer back to the Model sheet in Figure 19.3.

```
Sub CreateModel()
' Clear any old model, which would be below cells A4 and H4 of the Model sheet.
    With Worksheets("Model")
        .Visible = True
        .Activate
    End With
    With Range("A4")
        Range(.Offset(1, 0), .End(xlDown).Offset(0, 5)).ClearContents
    End With
    With Range("H4")
        Range(.Offset(1, 0), .End(xlDown).Offset(0, 3)).ClearContents
    End With
' The following subroutines do the bulk of the work.
    Call EnterArcData
    Call FormConstraints
    Call CalcCost
End Sub
```

EnterArcData Code

The **EnterArcData** sub transfers the data now in the Origin, Dest, UnitCost, MinFlow, and MaxFlow arrays to the appropriate columns of the Model sheet and then names some ranges for later use.

```
Sub EnterArcData()
' This sub enters data for the arcs, including the changing cells (the flows).
    Dim i As Integer
    With Range("A4")
        For i = 1 To NArcs
            .Offset(i, 0) = Origin(i)
            .Offset(i, 1) = Dest(i)
            .Offset(i, 2) = UnitCost(i)
' Enter initial flows of 0.
            .Offset(i, 3) = 0
            .Offset(i, 4) = MinFlow(i)
            .Offset(i, 5) = MaxFlow(i)
        Next
' Give appropriate range names.
        Range(.Offset(1, 0), .Offset(NArcs, 0)).Name = "Origins"
        Range(.Offset(1, 1), .Offset(NArcs, 1)).Name = "Dests"
        Range(.Offset(1, 2), .Offset(NArcs, 2)).Name = "UnitCosts"
        Range(.Offset(1, 3), .Offset(NArcs, 3)).Name = "Flows"
        Range(.Offset(1, 4), .Offset(NArcs, 4)).Name = "MinFlows"
```

```
            Range(.Offset(1, 5), .Offset(NArcs, 5)).Name = "MaxFlows"
        End With
    End Sub
```

FormConstraints Code

The **FormConstraints** sub is used to enter the left- and right-hand sides of the flow balance constraints for the network model. It does this separately for suppliers, transshipment points, and customers. Each left-hand side uses Excel's SumIf function to find the net inflow or outflow for the node. The right-hand sides are the capacities for the suppliers, 0's for the transshipment points, and the demands for the customers. (For more information on node balance constraints and the use of the SumIf function in this context, see Chapter 5 of *Practical Management Science*, 2nd edition.)

```
Sub FormConstraints()
' This sub creates flow balance constraints for all nodes.  It does so separately for
' suppliers, transshipment points, and customers.
    Dim i As Integer
' Supplier constraints:
    With Range("H4")
        For i = 1 To NSupNodes
            .Offset(i, 0) = SupNode(i)
            .Offset(i, 1).FormulaR1C1 = "=SumIf(Origins,RC[-1],Flows)" _
                & "-SumIf(Dests,RC[-1],Flows)"
            .Offset(i, 2) = "<="
            .Offset(i, 3) = Capacity(i)
        Next
        Range(.Offset(1, 1), .Offset(NSupNodes, 1)).Name = "NetOutflows"
        Range(.Offset(1, 3), .Offset(NSupNodes, 3)).Name = "Capacities"
    End With
' Transshipment constraints:
    With Range("H4").Offset(NSupNodes, 0)
        For i = 1 To NTransNodes
            .Offset(i, 0) = TransNode(i)
            .Offset(i, 1).FormulaR1C1 = "=SumIf(Origins,RC[-1],Flows)" _
                & "-SumIf(Dests,RC[-1],Flows)"
            .Offset(i, 2) = "="
            .Offset(i, 3) = 0
        Next
        Range(.Offset(1, 1), .Offset(NTransNodes, 1)).Name = "NetFlows"
    End With
' Customer constraints:
    With Range("H4").Offset(NSupNodes + NTransNodes, 0)
        For i = 1 To NDemNodes
            .Offset(i, 0) = DemNode(i)
            .Offset(i, 1).FormulaR1C1 = "=SumIf(Dests,RC[-1],Flows)" _
                & "-SumIf(Origins,RC[-1],Flows)"
            .Offset(i, 2) = ">="
            .Offset(i, 3) = Demand(i)
        Next
        Range(.Offset(1, 1), .Offset(NDemNodes, 1)).Name = "NetInflows"
        Range(.Offset(1, 3), .Offset(NDemNodes, 3)).Name = "Demands"
    End With
End Sub
```

CalcCost Code

The **CalcCost** sub calculates the total shipping cost with a SumProduct formula in the Model sheet.

```
Sub CalcCost()
' Calculate the total cost of all flows (the objective to minimize).
    Range("I1").Formula = "=Sumproduct(UnitCosts,Flows)"
End Sub
```

RunSolver Code

The **RunSolver** sub sets up and then runs the Solver. It checks for infeasibility (code 5 of the SolverSolve function). It there are no feasible solutions, a message to that effect is displayed and the program ends.

```
Sub RunSolver()
' Set up and run the Solver.
    SolverReset
    SolverOk SetCell:=Range("TotalCost"), MaxMinVal:=2, ByChange:=Range("Flows")
    SolverAdd Range("Flows"), 1, "MaxFlows"
    SolverAdd Range("Flows"), 3, "MinFlows"
    SolverAdd Range("NetOutflows"), 1, "Capacities"
    SolverAdd Range("NetFlows"), 2, 0
    SolverAdd Range("NetInflows"), 3, "Demands"
    SolverOptions AssumeLinear:=True, AssumeNonNeg:=True
' Check if there is no feasible solution. If there isn't, display an appropriate
' message and quit.
    If SolverSolve(UserFinish:=True) = 5 Then
        Worksheets("Model").Visible = False
        Worksheets("Explanation").Activate
        MsgBox "There is no feasible solution. Evidently, there is not enough " _
            & "capacity in the system to meet the demands.", vbInformation, _
            "No feasible solution"
        End
    Else
' Hide the Model sheet.
        Worksheets("Model").Visible = False
    End If
End Sub
```

CreateReport Code

Finally, the **CreateReport** sub transfers the total shipping cost and the information about all arcs with *positive* flows to the Report sheet. The variable NPos is a counter for the number of positive flows. It indicates the appropriate row offset for placing the next positive flow on the Report sheet.

```
Sub CreateReport()
' Summarize the optimal shipping policy on the Report sheet.
    Dim i As Integer, NPos As Integer
```

```
' Unhide and activate the Report sheet.
    With Worksheets("Report")
        .Visible = True
        .Activate
    End With
' Enter the total cost.
    Range("D3") = Range("TotalCost")
    With Range("B6")
' Clear out old data from any previous run.
        Range(.Offset(1, 0), .Offset(0, 3).End(xlDown)).Clear
' For each arc, check whether there is any positive flow. If so, report its origin and
' destination nodes, its flow, and the total cost of this flow. NPos is a counter for
' the arcs with positive flows.
        NPos = 0
        For i = 1 To NArcs
            If Range("Flows").Cells(i) > 0 Then
                NPos = NPos + 1
                .Offset(NPos, 0) = Range("Origins").Cells(i)
                .Offset(NPos, 1) = Range("Dests").Cells(i)
                .Offset(NPos, 2) = Range("Flows").Cells(i)
' Calculate the cost of this flow.
                .Offset(NPos, 3) = Range("Flows").Cells(i) * _
                    Range("UnitCosts").Cells(i)
            End If
        Next
    End With
' Do some formatting.
    With Range("B6")
        Range(.Offset(0, 0), .End(xlDown).End(xlToRight)).AutoFormat _
            Format:=xlRangeAutoFormatColor2
        Range(.Offset(0, 0), .Offset(0, 1)).HorizontalAlignment = xlLeft
    End With
    Range("D3").Select
End Sub
```

19.9 Summary

Virtually all of the VBA applications you will develop in Excel will require data, and it is very possible that the required data will reside in an external database format such as Access. In this chapter we have demonstrated how to import the data from an Access database into Excel for use in a network flow model. This requires you to learn the basic functionality of a new object model, ADO. However, the effort required to learn this object model is well spent. Knowing how to import data from an external database is an extremely valuable skill in today's business world, and it is likely to become even more valuable in the future.

PROGRAMMING EXERCISES

1. The application currently has no charts. Change it so that the user can view two charts (each on a separate chart sheet) after the Solver has been run. The first should be a column chart showing the total amount shipped and the total capac-

ity for each supplier, something as in Figure 19.10. Similarly, the second chart should show the total amount shipped to each customer and the customer's demand. As always, do as much at design time, and write as little VBA code, as possible.

Figure 19.10   Shipments from suppliers for Exercise 1

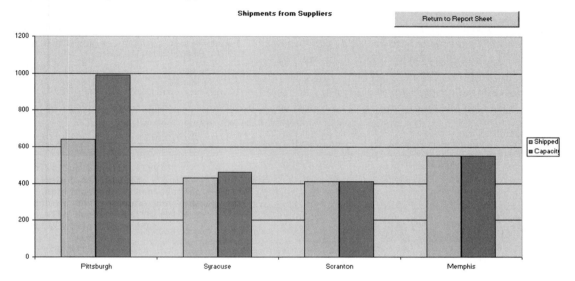

2. We claimed that this application works with any data, provided that the database file is structured properly. Try it out. Open the **NetworkFlows.mdb** file in Access and change its data in some way. (You can change names of suppliers, eliminate arcs, and so on.) Then rerun the application to see if it still works properly.

3. Repeat the previous exercise, but now create a *new* Access file called **MyData.mdb** (stored in the same folder as the Excel application), structured exactly as **NetworkFlows.mdb**, and add some data to it. Then rerun the application to see if it still works properly. (Note that you will have to change the VBA code slightly, so that it references the correct name of your new Access file.)

4. The previous problem indicates a "fix" that no business would ever tolerate—they would never be willing to get into the VBA code to change a file name reference. A much better alternative is to change the VBA code in the first place so that it asks the user for the location and name of the database file. You could do this with an input box (and risk having the user spell something wrong), but Excel provides an easier way—the **GetOpenFilename** method of the **Application** object. This method displays a built-in user form that looks exactly like what you are used to when you use a Windows Open command to open a file. The user can then browse for the desired file in the usual way. The syntax you should use is as follows, where DBFileName is a string variable:

```
DBFileName = Application.GetOpenFilename(Filter:="Access Files (*.mdb),*.mdb", _
    Title:="Database file")
```

This doesn't actually *open* the Access file selected by the user; it just returns the name and the path of the file chosen by the user and stores it in the string variable DBFileName. Use this method to change the application, so that it prompts the user for the name and location of the database file. Actually, you should probably precede the above line with a MsgBox statement so that the user knows she's being asked to select the file with the data. Then try the modified application with your own Access file, stored in a folder *different* from the folder containing the Excel application. (Look up the **GetOpenFilename** method in online help. Its beauty is that it has all of the "open file" functionality you expect built into it— you don't have to *create* this user form!)

A Stock Trading Simulation

20.1 Introduction

In *Practical Management Science*, we illustrate two ways to run spreadsheet simulations. Each method starts with a spreadsheet model that includes random quantities in selected cells. The first method creates a data table to replicate desired outputs. Summary measures and charts can then be obtained manually from this data table. The second method uses a simulation add-in such as @Risk. Once the user designates desired output cells, the add-in runs all of the replications and automatically creates summary measures, including charts, for these outputs. This application illustrates how VBA can be used to automate a simulation model, similar to the way @Risk does it. However, no data tables are created, and no add-ins are required.

The model itself simulates the trading activity of an investor in the stock market over the period of a year (250 trading days). This investor starts with a certain amount of cash and owns several shares of a stock. The investor then uses a "buy low/sell high" trading strategy. The trading strategy implemented in the model is as follows. If the price of the stock increases two days in a row, the investor sells 10% of his shares. If it increases three days in a row, he sells 25% of his shares. In the other direction, if the price decreases two days in a row, the investor buys 10% more shares. For example, if he owns 500 shares, he buys 50 more shares. If the price decreases three days in a row, he buys 25% more shares. The only restriction on buying is that the investor cannot spend more than his current cash. The price of the stock is generated randomly through a common "lognormal" model used by many financial analysts.

The simulation keeps track of five output measures: (1) the investor's cash at the end of the year, (2) the value of the investor's stock at the end of the year, (3) the gain (or loss) from the investor's cash/stock portfolio at the end of the year, relative to what he owned at the beginning of the year, (4) the lowest price of the stock during the year, and (5) the highest price of the stock during the year.

New Learning Objectives: VBA

- To illustrate how to automate a spreadsheet simulation model with VBA.
- To illustrate how the run time of a simulation can be affected by the recalculation mode.
- To show how to use VBA to enter an array function into an Excel range.

New Learning Objective: Non-VBA

- To show how simulation can be used to measure the effectiveness of a stock market trading strategy.

20.2 Functionality of the Application

The application has the following functionality:

1. It allows the user to specify a trading strategy. As written, the user can change the percentages to sell if the stock price increases two or three days in a row, and the similar percentages to buy if the price decreases two or three days in a row. The model could be modified slightly to examine other types of trading strategies (buy high, sell low, for example)—without any changes in the VBA code.
2. The simulation can be run for up to 1000 replications. (This limit could easily be changed.) As it runs, it keeps track of the five outputs listed in the introduction. It then reports summary measures for these outputs (minimum, maximum, average, standard deviation, median, and 5th and 95th percentiles), and it creates histograms of the outputs. The application could be modified fairly easily to incorporate other outputs from the simulation.

20.3 Running the Application

The application is stored in the file **StockTrading.xls**. When this file is opened, the user sees the Explanation sheet in Figure 20.1.

Figure 20.1 Explanation sheet

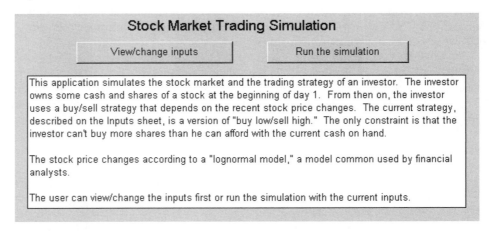

If the user clicks on the left button, the Inputs sheet in Figure 20.2 appears. The various inputs appear in blue borders. The user can change any of these before running the simulation. In particular, a different trading strategy can be examined by changing the percentages in column J. Also, note that the current price (on day 1) and the prices on the three previous days are shown in column E. Because the investor's trading strategy depends on the three previous price changes, these past prices are required for the trading decisions on the first few days.

Figure 20.2 Inputs sheet

	A	B	C	D	E	F	G	H	I	J	K	L
1	Inputs to simulation											
2												
3	Inputs			Recent stock prices				Trading strategy				
4	Initial cash	$75,000		3 days ago	$49.86			Buying: if change is negative				
5	Initial shares owned	500		2 days ago	$49.79			3 days in a row, buy		25%	of current shares	
6				1 day ago	$49.95			2 days in a row, buy		10%	of current shares	
7	Daily growth rate of stock price			Current	$50.00			Selling: if change is positive				
8	Mean	0.01%						3 days in a row, sell		25%	of current shares	
9	StDev	2.0%						2 days in a row, sell		10%	of current shares	
10												
11	Implication for the year (assuming 250 trading days per year)											
12	Mean	2.50%	(average annual growth rate of stock price)									
13	StDev	31.62%	(standard deviation of annual growth rate)									
14												
15												
16					Enter any new inputs in the blue cells. Then click on the							
17					button below to run the simulation with these inputs.							
18												
19												
20					Run the simulation							
21												

When the user clicks on the button in Figure 20.2 (or the right button in Figure 20.1), the input box in Figure 20.3 is displayed. Here the user can choose any number of replications, up to 1000, for the simulation.

Figure 20.3 Input box for the number of replications

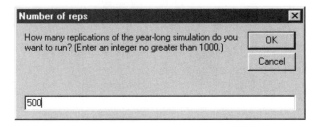

After the user clicks on OK, the simulation runs. It recalculates the random numbers on the (hidden) Model sheet (more about this sheet later) for each replication, stores the outputs on a (hidden) Replications sheet, and calculates summary measures, which are stored on a Summary sheet, as shown in Figure 20.4.

Figure 20.4 Summary results from the simulation

	A	B	C	D	E	F
1	**Summary results from the simulation**					
2						
3		Ending cash	Ending stock value	Cum gain/loss	Min price	Max price
4	Min	$7	$31	($44,665)	$18.26	$50.00
5	Max	$118,875	$106,145	$24,289	$50.00	$155.39
6	Average	$89,601	$10,752	$353	$39.57	$64.47
7	Stdev	$23,779	$20,274	$9,237	$7.06	$13.94
8	Median	$99,923	$1,567	$2,134	$40.64	$60.46
9	5th percentile	$32,038	$51	($20,867)	$26.78	$50.03
10	95th percentile	$107,478	$61,763	$10,816	$49.39	$92.19
11						
12						
13		For further results, take a look at any of the "Hist" sheets.				
14		They show histograms of the various output measures.				
15						

This can take quite a while, so a replication counter, placed on the Explanation sheet, shows the progress. (This counter is in no way necessary for the proper running of the simulation, but it is a nice touch for the user.)

Each output has a corresponding histogram on a chart sheet and a corresponding data sheet that contains the ingredients for the histogram. These are created at design time, and they are then updated at the end of the simulation. As an example, the histogram for the cumulative gain/loss output appears in Figure 20.5.

Figure 20.5 Histogram for cumulative gain/loss

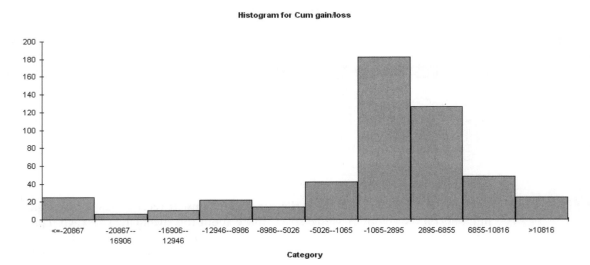

If the user then returns to the Explanation sheet and runs the simulation again, the results will differ, even if the same inputs are used, because *new* random numbers will be used in the simulation.

20.4 Setting Up the Excel Sheets

The **StockTrading.xls** file contains ten worksheets and five chart sheets. The worksheets are named Explanation, Inputs, Model, Replications, Summary, and DataHist1 through DataHist5. The chart sheets are named Hist1 through Hist5.

The Model Sheet

The Model sheet, shown in Figure 20.6 (with many hidden rows), can be set up *completely* at design time.

Figure 20.6 Simulation model and outputs

	A	B	C	D	E	F	G	H	I	J	K	L
1	**Stock Market Simulation**											
2												
3	**Outputs from one year-long simulation**											
4	Ending cash	$104,697										
5	Ending value of stock owned	$1,726										
6	Cumulative gain/loss	$6,423										
7	Lowest stock price	$41.44										
8	Highest stock price	$60.74										
9												
10	**Simulation**											
11		**Stock price**		**Trading activity**				**Value of stock/cash portfolio**				
12		Day	Beginning price	Change from previous day	Beginning shares	Shares sold	Shares purchased	Ending shares	Beginning cash	Change in cash	Ending cash	Worth of shares	Cumulative gain/loss
13			$49.86										
14			$49.79	-$0.07									
15			$49.95	$0.16									
16		1	$50.00	$0.05	500	50	0	450	$75,000	$2,500	$77,500	$22,500	$0
17		2	$48.96	-$1.04	450	0	0	450	$77,500	$0	$77,500	$22,032	($468)
18		3	$49.02	$0.06	450	0	0	450	$77,500	$0	$77,500	$22,059	($441)
19		4	$49.14	$0.12	450	45	0	405	$77,500	$2,211	$79,711	$19,302	($387)
20		5	$47.42	-$1.72	405	0	0	405	$79,711	$0	$79,711	$19,205	($1,084)
262		247	$54.89	$0.29	36	0	0	36	$104,481	$0	$104,481	$1,976	$6,457
263		248	$53.18	-$1.71	36	0	0	36	$104,481	$0	$104,481	$1,914	$6,396
264		249	$53.53	$0.35	36	0	0	36	$104,481	$0	$104,481	$1,927	$6,408
265		250	$53.95	$0.42	36	4	0	32	$104,481	$216	$104,697	$1,726	$6,423

From row 10 down, this sheet models the trading activity for a 250-day period. We will discuss a few of the formulas in this sheet; you can open the file and examine the rest. First, the stock prices in column B are determined from the well-known lognormal stock price model. Specifically, the formula in cell B17, which is copied down column B, is

=ROUND(B16*EXP((GrMean-0.5*GrStdev^2)
+GrStdev*NORMINV(RAND(),0,1)),2)

This formula uses the daily mean growth rate and standard deviation of growth rate (GrMean and GrStdev, from cells B8 and B9 of the Inputs sheet), along with a standard normal random number—from **NORMINV(RAND(),0,1)**—to generate the day's price from the previous day's price in cell B16.

Second, the trading strategy is implemented in columns E and F with rather complex IF functions. For example, the number of shares bought in cell F16 uses the formula

=IF(AND(C14<0,C15<0,C16<0),MIN(ROUND(BuyPct3*D16,0),
INT(H16/B16)),IF(AND(C15<0,C16<0),
MIN(ROUND(BuyPct2*D16,0),INT(H16/B16)),0))

Here, BuyPct3 and BuyPct2 are 25% and 10%, respectively, from cells J5 and J6 of the Inputs sheet. The formula first checks whether the price has decreased three days in a row. If it has, the investor buys the smaller of two quantities—the number of shares he would like to buy (25% of what he owns), and the number of shares he has cash for (his cash divided by the current stock price, rounded down to the nearest integer). If the price has not decreased three days in a row, then the formula checks whether it has decreased two days in a row. If it has, the investor again purchases the smaller of two quantities. If it hasn't, the investor buys nothing.

Finally, the cumulative gain/loss in column L is the current value of the cash/stock portfolio minus the initial value on day 1. For example, the formula for the last day in cell L265 is

=(J265+K265)-(InitCash+InitShares*InitPrice)

where InitCash, InitShares, and InitPrice refer to cells B4, B5, and E7 of the Inputs sheet.

Once the 250-day model has been developed, the outputs in rows 4–8 can be calculated easily. For example, the formulas in cells B6 and B7 are **=L265** and **=MIN(B16:B265)**. Note that these outputs summarize a *single* 250-day replication.

The Replication Sheet

When the simulation runs for, say, 500 replications, the VBA code forces the model to recalculate 500 times, each time producing new random numbers and therefore new outputs in the Model sheet. It captures these outputs and stores them in the (hidden) Replications sheet, as shown in Figure 20.7 (with many hidden rows). These outputs are then summarized in the Summary sheet at the end of the simulation. Note that the Replications sheet and the Summary sheet (in Figure 20.4) have only labels, no numbers, at design time.

Data Sheets for Histograms

The histogram for each output is formed from a column of data in Figure 20.7 and from information on categories (usually called "bins"). The individual data, such as ending cash amounts, are placed into these bins and are then counted to obtain the histogram. We have used 10 bins for each histogram. The first bin extends up to the 5th percentile for the output, the last extends beyond the 95th

Figure 20.7 Replications sheet

	A	B	C	D	E	F
1	Results of individual replications					
2						
3	Replication	Ending cash	Ending stock value	Cum gain/loss	Min price	Max price
4	1	$100,061	$76	$137	42.29	78.82
5	2	$101,587	$60	$1,647	43.41	60.7
6	3	$101,801	$726	$2,526	38.24	54.75
7	4	$17	$93,141	($6,842)	26.78	56.64
8	5	$19,592	$76,219	($4,188)	29.78	64.92
9	6	$103,400	$305	$3,705	48.15	78.6
10	7	$105,528	$2,372	$7,900	43.99	65.16
11	8	$98,456	$1,495	($49)	37.72	60.47
12	9	$101,084	$43	$1,128	43.32	61.69
13	10	$105,187	$3,322	$8,509	44.58	74.07
499	496	$95,937	$5,303	$1,240	32.65	50.96
500	497	$102,545	$1,137	$3,683	41.74	56.86
501	498	$96,682	$4,462	$1,143	27.31	51.21
502	499	$91,761	$5,301	($2,938)	39.5	69.77
503	500	$104,697	$1,726	$6,424	41.44	60.74

percentile, and the other eight bins are of equal width between the extremes. This information is summarized in a "DataHist" sheet for each output at the end of the simulation. For example, Figure 20.8 shows the DataHist3 sheet for the Cumulative Gain/Loss output. Column A contains the upper limit of each bin (other than the rightmost), column B contains horizontal axis labels, and column C contains the frequencies (obtained with Excel's Frequency function, as discussed below).

Figure 20.8 Data for cumulative gain/loss histogram

	A	B	C
1	Frequency table for Cum gain/loss		
2			
3	Upper limit	Category	Frequency
4	-20867	<=-20867	25
5	-16906	-20867--16906	6
6	-12946	-16906--12946	10
7	-8986	-12946--8986	22
8	-5026	-8986--5026	14
9	-1065	-5026--1065	42
10	2895	-1065-2895	182
11	6855	2895-6855	126
12	10816	6855-10816	48
13		>10816	25

Note that sample data can be placed in these data sheets, and histograms can be created from the sample data, at design time. Then the data sheets can be updated at run time and the histograms will change automatically.

20.5 Getting Started with the VBA

This application includes only a module—no user forms and no references. Once the module is inserted, the Project Explorer window will appear as in Figure 20.9.

Figure 20.9 Project Explorer window

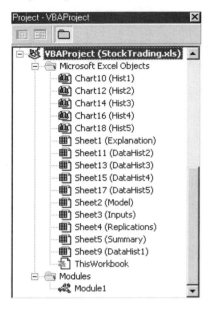

Workbook_Open Code

The following code is placed in the ThisWorkbook code window. It activates the Explanation sheet and hides all other sheets.

```
Private Sub Workbook_Open()
    Dim ws As Object
    Worksheets("Explanation").Activate
    Range("G4").Select
    For Each ws In ActiveWorkbook.Sheets
        If ws.Name <> "Explanation" Then ws.Visible = False
    Next
End Sub
```

20.6 The VBA Code in the Module

Web Help   For more explanation of the code in this application, visit our Web site at http://www.indiana.edu/~mgtsci and download the **Code Explanation - StockTrading.doc** file.

The module contains a **Main** sub, which calls several subs to do most of the work. The Main sub also does some work itself. It gets the number of desired replications from an input box, it clears the contents from the Replications sheet from any previous run, and it places some (temporary) labels in row 18 of the Explanation sheet. These are used to show the progress of the simulation as it runs.[39]

Option Statement and Module-Level Variable

```
Option Explicit

' NReps is the number of replications.
Dim NReps As Integer
```

Main Code

```
Sub Main()
    Dim i As Integer
' Get the number of replications, which cannot be greater than 1000.
    Do
        NReps = InputBox("How many replications of the year-long simulation do " _
            & "want to run? (Enter an integer no greater than 1000.)", "Number of reps")
        If NReps > 1000 Then MsgBox "The number of reps should not exceed 1000.", _
            vbExclamation, "Too many reps"
    Loop Until NReps <= 1000
' Clear previous results.
    With Worksheets("Replications").Range("A3")
        Range(.Offset(1, 0), .Offset(0, 5).End(xlDown)).ClearContents
    End With
' Enter labels for a replication counter on the Explanation sheet.
    Worksheets("Explanation").Activate
    Range("D18") = "Simulating replication"
    Range("G18") = "of"
    Range("H18") = NReps
' Run the simulation and collect the stats.
    Call RunSim
    Call CollectStats
' Delete the replication counter on the Explanation sheet.
    Range("D18:H18").ClearContents
' Update the histogram data.
    Call UpdateHistograms

' Show the results.
    With Worksheets("Summary")
        .Visible = True
        .Activate
        .Range("A2").Select
    End With
' Unhide the histogram chart sheets.
    For i = 1 To 5
        Charts("Hist" & i).Visible = True
    Next
End Sub
```

---

[39]We intended to put this "progress report" in Excel's status bar, but Excel claims the status bar for its own message, as you will see when you run the simulation.

RunSim Code

The **RunSim** sub runs the simulation the desired number of replications and stores the outputs in the Replications sheet for later summarization. The key to this sub is the **Calculate** method of the **Application** object (which is Excel). Each time this method is called, it forces a recalculation of the workbook, the effect of which is to use new random numbers in the simulation model. It's that simple!

A note on recalculation. Each workbook recalculation takes a fraction of a second, but these fractions add up. The recalculations take place each time the Calculate method is called from VBA code, but also each time any change is made to the workbook. This means, for example, that each of the Offset lines below causes a recalculation—each time through the loop! The effect is that the simulation runs rather slowly. Fortunately, we can change Excel's recalculation mode from Automatic, the default mode, to Manual. (This is done through Excel's Tools/Options menu item, using the Calculation tab.) In Manual mode, recalculations take place only when the Calculate method is called from VBA (or the F9 key is pressed). We originally ran the simulation in Automatic mode. However, when we converted to Manual mode, the run time decreased dramatically (from about 220 seconds to 30 seconds for a 500-replication run). Try it yourself.

```
Sub RunSim()
    Dim i As Integer
' Loop over the replications.
    For i = 1 To NReps
' Show the current replication number on the Explanation sheet.
        Range("RepNumber") = i
' Force a recalculation.
        Application.Calculate
' Record outputs on the Replication sheet.
        With Worksheets("Replications").Range("A3")
            .Offset(i, 0) = i
            .Offset(i, 1) = Range("EndCash")
            .Offset(i, 2) = Range("EndStockVal")
            .Offset(i, 3) = Range("CumGainLoss")
            .Offset(i, 4) = Range("MinPrice")
            .Offset(i, 5) = Range("MaxPrice")
        End With
    Next
End Sub
```

CollectStats Code

The **CollectStats** sub uses a For loop to go through the simulation outputs, one at a time. For each, it "sets" the RepRange object variable to the range of data in the Replications sheet to be summarized. Then it uses Excel functions to calculate the summary measures and places them in the Summary sheet. For example, **Application.Average(RepRange)** uses Excel's Average function to calculate the average of the data in the RepRange.

```
Sub CollectStats()
    Dim i As Integer, RepRange As Range
```

```
' Loop over the output measures.
   For i = 1 To 5
' RepRange is the range on the Replications sheet to summarize.
      With Worksheets("Replications").Range("A3")
         Set RepRange = Range(.Offset(1, i), .Offset(NReps, i))
      End With
' Use Excel's functions to calculate summary measures, and put them on the
' Summary sheet.
      With Worksheets("Summary").Range("A3")
         .Offset(1, i) = Application.Min(RepRange)
         .Offset(2, i) = Application.Max(RepRange)
         .Offset(3, i) = Application.Average(RepRange)
         .Offset(4, i) = Application.StDev(RepRange)
         .Offset(5, i) = Application.Median(RepRange)
         .Offset(6, i) = Application.Percentile(RepRange, 0.05)
         .Offset(7, i) = Application.Percentile(RepRange, 0.95)
      End With
   Next
End Sub
```

UpdateHistograms Code

The **UpdateHistograms** sub also loops over the simulation outputs. For each, it updates the appropriate DataHist sheet (see Figure 20.8), using the results from the simulation.

   A note on array functions. Pay particular attention to the line

```
Range(.Offset(1, 2), .Offset(10, 2)).FormulaArray = _
   "=Frequency(Replications!" & RepRange.Address & "," & BinRange.Address & ")"
```

Excel's **Frequency** function is called an **array function**. To enter it manually in a worksheet, you need to highlight the range where the frequencies will be placed, type the formula, and press Ctrl-Shift-Enter. To do this in VBA, you specify the range where it will be entered and then use the **FormulaArray** property. Two other points about this formula are worth noting. First, it is not enough to specify RepRange.Address in the first argument. Because this range is on a *different* worksheet from where the formula is entered, its worksheet name and an exclamation point must precede its address. Second, the bin range required in the second argument is the range of upper limits for the bins. These are the values in column A of the relevant DataHist sheet.

```
Sub UpdateHistograms()
   Dim i As Integer, j As Integer, Pct5 As Single, Pct95 As Single, _
      Increment As Single, RepRange As Range, BinRange As Range
' Loop over the output measures.
   For i = 1 To 5
' The histograms each have 10 "bins". The lowest extends up to the 5th percentile, the
' last extends beyond the 95th percentile, and the remaining ones are equal-width
' beyond these extremes.
      Pct5 = Worksheets("Summary").Range("A9").Offset(0, i)
      Pct95 = Worksheets("Summary").Range("A10").Offset(0, i)
      Increment = (Pct95 - Pct5) / 8
```

```
' RepRange contains the data for the histogram.
      With Worksheets("Replications").Range("A3")
          Set RepRange = Range(.Offset(1, i), .Offset(NReps, i))
      End With

' The hidden DataHist sheets contain the data for building the histogram. Column A has
' the bins, column B has labels for the horizontal axis, and column C has the
' frequencies (for the heights of the bars).
      With Worksheets("DataHist" & i).Range("A3")
          .Offset(1, 0) = Round(Pct5, 0)
          .Offset(1, 1) = "<=" & .Offset(1, 0)
          For j = 2 To 9
              .Offset(j, 0) = Round(Pct5 + (j - 1) * Increment, 0)
              .Offset(j, 1) = Round(.Offset(j - 1, 0), 0) & "-" _
                  & Round(.Offset(j, 0), 0)
          Next
          .Offset(10, 1) = ">" & Round(.Offset(9, 0), 0)
          Set BinRange = Range(.Offset(1, 0), .Offset(9, 0))

' Excel's Frequency function is an array formula, so the appropriate property is the
' FormulaArray property.
          Range(.Offset(1, 2), .Offset(10, 2)).FormulaArray = _
              "=Frequency(Replications!" & RepRange.Address & "," _
              & BinRange.Address & ")"
      End With
   Next
End Sub
```

ViewChangeInputs Code

The **ViewChangeInputs** sub unhides and activates the Inputs sheet, allowing the user to view the inputs or enter different inputs before running the simulation.

```
Sub ViewChangeInputs()
    With Worksheets("Inputs")
        .Visible = True
        .Activate
    End With
End Sub
```

20.7 Summary

This application illustrates how to run a spreadsheet simulation model with VBA. We first develop a spreadsheet simulation model, including one or more cells with random functions, in a Model sheet. Then to replicate this model, we use a For loop, inside which we call the **Calculate** method of the **Application** object to force a recalculation with new random numbers. The rest is a simple matter of recording selected outputs on a Replications sheet and then summarizing them as desired at the end of the simulation. Because all of this can take a while, especially with many replications of a complex model, we have seen that it is a good idea to set Excel's calculation mode to Manual, rather the Automatic, before running the simulation.

PROGRAMMING EXERCISES

1. Prove to yourself that the simulation runs much faster when Excel's calculation mode is set to Manual. Run the simulation in the current **StockTrading.xls** file for about 250 replications. (This file has calculation mode set to Manual.) Then use the Tools/Options menu item to change the calculation mode to Automatic and run the simulation again. Keep track of the run time for each—you should see a noticeable difference.

2. Experiment with the same basic buy low/sell high trading strategy, but with different percentages in column J of the Inputs sheet. Can you find any strategies that consistently appear to outperform others?

3. Repeat the previous exercise, but now change the basic type of strategy to buy high/sell low. That is, if the price goes up, you buy more shares, whereas if it goes down, you sell. What changes do you need to make to the simulation model? Do you need to make any changes to the VBA code? Do these strategies tend to do better or worse than those in the previous problem?

4. Change the application so that there is no limit on the shares the investor can buy. For example, if his strategy tells him to buy 25% more shares but he doesn't have enough cash to do so, he *borrows* the cash he needs. Now his cash positions in columns H and J of the Model sheet can be negative, indicating that he owes money to the lender. Capture the maximum he ever owes during the year in an extra output cell, and keep track of it and summarize it, just like the other outputs, with your VBA code.

5. Change the application so that if the investor ever gets to a point where his cumulative gain for the year is above some threshold level, he sells his stock and does no more trading for the rest of the year. Your revised application should ask for the threshold with an input box. Also, it should add an extra output cell: the number of days it takes to reach the threshold (which is defined as 251 in case he never gets there). Keep track of this output and summarize it, just like the other outputs, with your VBA code.

21

A Capital Budgeting Application

21.1 Introduction

This application illustrates how VBA can be used to compare an optimal procedure with a good but nonoptimal heuristic procedure. This is done for a capital budgeting problem, where a company must decide which of several projects to undertake. Each project incurs an initial cost and provides a stream of future cash flows, summarized by a net present value (NPV). Each project is an all-or-nothing proposition—it cannot be undertaken part way. Other than that, the only constraint is that the sum of the initial costs of the projects undertaken cannot exceed a given budget. The objective is to find the subset of projects that maximizes the total NPV and stays within the budget.

One solution method is to solve the problem optimally with Excel's Solver, using binary changing cells to decide which projects to undertake. Another possibility is to use an intuitive heuristic procedure that operates as follows. It first ranks the projects in decreasing order of the ratio of NPV to initial cost ("bang for buck"). Then it goes through the list of projects in this order, adding each as long as there is enough money left in the budget. The application compares the total NPVs obtained by these two methods.

New Learning Objectives: VBA

- To illustrate how a simple heuristic can be implemented in VBA with looping and arrays.
- To illustrate how random inputs for a model can be generated by VBA as formulas in a worksheet, and how they can then be "frozen" with the Copy and PasteSpecial methods of Range objects.

New Learning Objectives: Non-VBA

- To compare a simple but reasonable heuristic solution method with an optimal integer programming method.
- To show the effect of the Solver's Tolerance setting in an integer programming model.

21.2 Functionality of the Application

The application has the following functionality:

1. It first asks the user for the total number of projects, which can be any number up to 30. Then it randomly generates the inputs for a model with this many projects—the initial costs, the NPVs, and the budget. It does this so that there is a large enough budget to undertake many, but not all, of the projects.
2. Given the inputs, a capital budgeting model is developed in the (hidden) Model sheet, and it is solved as a 0–1 integer programming model with the Solver. The heuristic procedure is also used to solve the same problem. The outputs from both procedures are shown in the Report sheet, including the heuristic's total NPV as a percentage of the Solver's total NPV.
3. The program can be repeated as often as the user desires, using different random inputs on each run.
4. To show the effect of the Tolerance option in the Solver (which is set to 0 in all of the Solver runs), a sheet named Interesting accompanies the file. It shows one problem where the optimal solution was *not* found by the Solver when the Tolerance setting was set at its default value of 5. (This sheet is not really part of the VBA application, but it illustrates an interesting aspect of the Solver.)

21.3 Running the Application

The application is stored in the **CapBudget.xls** file. Upon opening it, the user sees the Explanation sheet in Figure 21.1. When the button on this sheet is clicked, the dialog box in Figure 21.2 appears and asks the user for a number of projects up to 30. Then it randomly generates the inputs for a capital budgeting model with this many projects in the Model sheet, solves it optimally with the Solver, performs the heuristic on this same problem, and reports the results in the Report sheet.

Figure 21.1 Explanation sheet

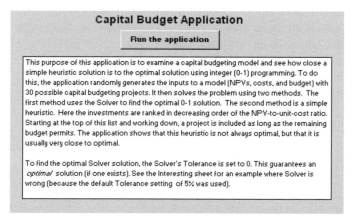

Figure 21.2 Number of projects input box

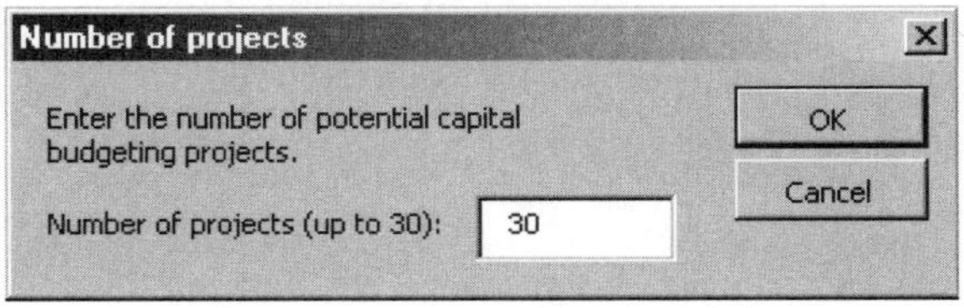

Number of projects	✕
Enter the number of potential capital budgeting projects.	OK
	Cancel
Number of projects (up to 30): 30	

Typical Report sheets from two separate runs of the application appear in Figures 21.3 and 21.4. Each of these problems has 30 potential projects. The first is a case where the heuristic obtains the optimal solution. The second is a case where the heuristic's NPV is 98.16% as large as the optimal NPV. By running the application on many problems of varying sizes, it becomes apparent that the heuristic is very good, often finding the optimal solution and almost always coming within a few percentage points of the optimal solution.

Figure 21.3 An example where the heuristic is optimal

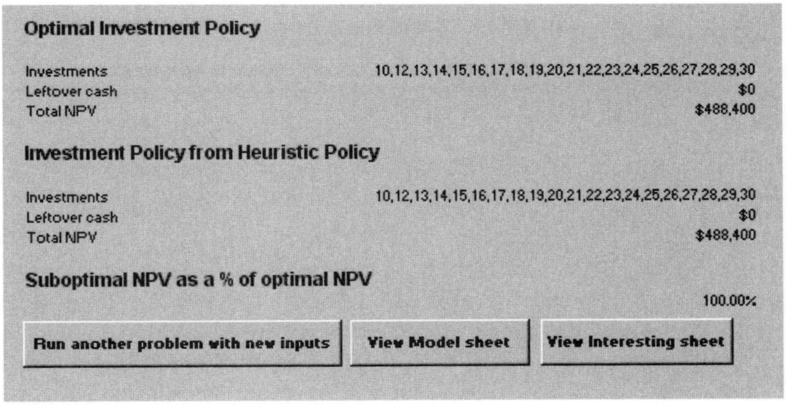

Optimal Investment Policy

Investments	10,12,13,14,15,16,17,18,19,20,21,22,23,24,25,26,27,28,29,30
Leftover cash	$0
Total NPV	$488,400

Investment Policy from Heuristic Policy

Investments	10,12,13,14,15,16,17,18,19,20,21,22,23,24,25,26,27,28,29,30
Leftover cash	$0
Total NPV	$488,400

Suboptimal NPV as a % of optimal NPV

100.00%

| Run another problem with new inputs | View Model sheet | View Interesting sheet |

Figure 21.4 An example where the heuristic is not optimal

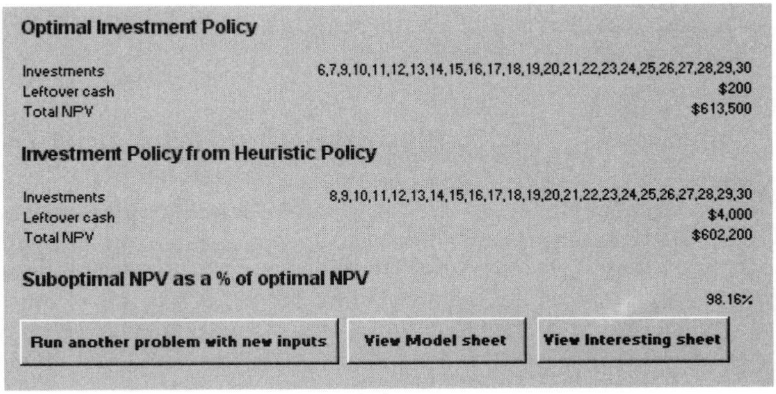

Optimal Investment Policy

Investments	6,7,9,10,11,12,13,14,15,16,17,18,19,20,21,22,23,24,25,26,27,28,29,30
Leftover cash	$200
Total NPV	$613,500

Investment Policy from Heuristic Policy

Investments	8,9,10,11,12,13,14,15,16,17,18,19,20,21,22,23,24,25,26,27,28,29,30
Leftover cash	$4,000
Total NPV	$602,200

Suboptimal NPV as a % of optimal NPV

98.16%

| Run another problem with new inputs | View Model sheet | View Interesting sheet |

The three buttons at the bottom of the Report sheet give the user three options. The user can solve another problem by clicking on the left button. Alternatively, the user can view the (hidden) Model sheet, shown below in Figure 21.5 (with several hidden columns), or the Interesting sheet (not shown here). Each of these sheets has a button that leads back to the Report sheet.

Figure 21.5   Model sheet

	A	B	C	D	E	F	AD	AE
1	**Capital Budgeting Model**							
2								
3	Model							
4	Investment	1	2	3	4	5	29	30
5	Investment level	0	0	0	0	0	1	1
6	NPV	39700	22300	20500	22600	19000	$15,200	30900
7	Investment cost	15400	8500	7300	8000	6600	$2,100	4000
8	Bang-for-buck	$2.58	$2.62	$2.81	$2.83	$2.88	$7.24	$7.73
9								
10	Budget constraint	Spent		Available				
11		$135,900	<=	$136,100				
12								
13	Total NPV	$613,500						
14								
15	Note that the Solver Tolerance has been set to 0.							
16								
17			Return to the Report sheet					
18								

21.4   Setting Up the Excel Sheets

The **CapBudget.xls** file has four worksheets: the Explanation sheet in Figure 21.1, the Report sheet in Figures 21.3 and 21.4, the Model sheet in Figure 21.5, and the Interesting sheet (not shown here, but basically just another version of the Model sheet). The Model and Report sheets cannot be set up completely at design time because they depend on the number of projects. This number determines the number of columns that are necessary in the model. (See rows 4–8 in Figure 21.5.) However, it is possible to develop templates for these sheets. The Model template is shown in Figure 21.6, where the range names that can be created in the Model sheet at design time are shown in a text box.

Figure 21.6   Model sheet template

	A	B	C	D	E
1	**Capital Budgeting Model**				
2					
3	Model		**Range Names at**		
4	Investment		**Design Time:**		
5	Investment level		TotCost - B11		
6	NPV		Budget - D11		
7	Investment cost		TotNPV - B13		
8	Bang-for-buck				
9					
10	Budget constraint	Spent		Available	
11			<=		
12					
13	Total NPV				
14					
15	Note that the Solver Tolerance has been set to 0.				
16					
17			Return to the Report sheet		
18					

The Report sheet template is shown in Figure 21.7, again with the range names used. The highlighted cell, C15, contains the formula =TotNPVHeur/TotNPVOpt. Its current value is undefined (division by 0) because both total NPVs are currently 0, but it will report correctly when the application runs.

Figure 21.7 Report sheet template

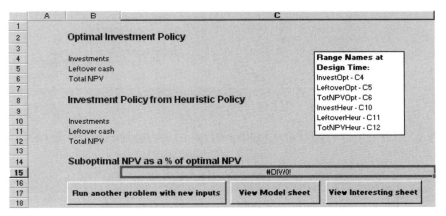

VBA is then used to fill in these templates at run time. (Again, the Interesting sheet is not really an integral part of the application; it is appended only to illustrate the effect of the Solver's Tolerance option. Therefore, it is created at design time and never changes.)

21.5 Getting Started with the VBA

This application requires a user form named ProjectsForm, a module, and a reference to the Solver.xla file. Once these items are added, the Project Explorer window will appear as in Figure 21.8.

Figure 21.8 Project Explorer window

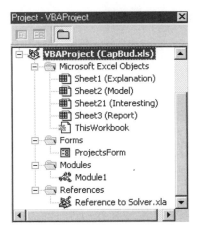

Workbook_Open Code

To guarantee that the Explanation sheet appears when the file is opened, the following code is placed in the ThisWorkbook code window. It uses a For Each loop to hide all sheets except the Explanation sheet.

```
Private Sub Workbook_Open()
    Dim sht As Worksheet
    Worksheets("Explanation").Activate
    Range("F4").Select
    For Each sht In ActiveWorkbook.Worksheets
        If sht.Name <> "Explanation" Then sht.Visible = False
    Next
End Sub
```

21.6 Designing the User Form and Writing Its Event Code

> **Web Help** For more explanation of the code in this application, visit our Web site at http://www.indiana.edu/~mgtsci and download the **Code Explanation - CapBudget.doc** file.

The ProjectsForm design, shown in Figure 21.9, contains the usual OK and Cancel buttons, an explanation label, and a text box named NProjBox and an accompanying label. The event code, listed below, is completely straightforward. The whole purpose is to capture the number of projects in the public variable NProjects, a number that should be no larger than 30.

Figure 21.9 Design of ProjectsForm

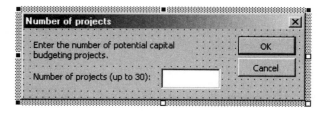

Event Code for ProjectsForm

```
Private Sub UserForm_Initialize()
    NProjBox = ""
End Sub

Private Sub OKButton_Click()
' Make sure the box is not empty and is numeric.
    If NProjBox = "" Or Not IsNumeric(NProjBox) Then
        MsgBox "Enter a positive number of projects.", vbInformation, "Invalid entry"
        NProjBox.SetFocus
        Exit Sub
```

```
    End If
    NProjects = NProjBox
' Check that the number of projects is from 1 to 30, the most allowed in this
' application.
    If NProjects < 1 Or NProjects > 30 Then
        MsgBox "Enter a number from 1 to 30.", vbInformation, "Invalid entry"
        NProjBox.SetFocus
        Exit Sub
    End If
    Unload Me
End Sub

Private Sub CancelButton_Click()
    Unload Me
    End
End Sub
```

21.7   The VBA Code in the Module

The main work is performed by the code in the module. When the user clicks on the button on the Explanation sheet (or the left button on the Report sheet), the **Main** sub is run. It "shows" the ProjectsForm and then calls other subs that perform the individual tasks.

Option Statements and Public Variables

```
Option Explicit
Option Base 1


' Definitions of public variables:
'     NProjects - number of potential projects (<=30)
'     ZeroOne - binary array, indicates which projects are chosen by the heuristic
'     LeftoverHeur - amount of budget left over using heuristic
'     TotNPVHeur - total NPV using heuristic
'     LeftoverOpt - amount of budget left over from the optimal solution
'     TotNPVOpt - total NPV from the optimal solution

Public NProjects As Integer, ZeroOne(30) As Integer, LeftoverHeur As Single, _
    TotNPVHeur As Single, LeftoverOpt As Single, TotNPVOpt As Single
```

Main Code

```
Sub Main()
    Application.ScreenUpdating = False
' Get the number of potential projects.
    ProjectsForm.Show
' Calculate random inputs for the model (NPVs, costs, and budget).
    Call GetInputs
' Sort projects on "bang for buck".
    Call SortProjects
```

```
' Calculate the optimal investments.
    Call RunSolver
' Calculate the investments based on the heuristic.
    Call Heuristic
' Report the results.
    Call CreateReport
End Sub
```

GetInputs Code

The **GetInputs** sub uses the combination of Excel's **Rand** and **NormInv** functions to generate normally distributed values for the budget and for the initial costs and NPVs of the projects. The details are described in the comments below. Actually, this sub enters *formulas* for these random values, and it then "freezes" them with the Copy and PasteSpecial/Values method. (There is no particular reason for using the *normal* distribution here. We simply want to generate "representative" problems randomly, and the normal distribution works as well as any other distribution.) Finally, an initial solution of all 1's is used, so that all projects are initially undertaken. Actually, any other initial solution could be used, and the one used almost certainly overspends the budget.

```
Sub GetInputs()
    Dim i As Integer
' Unhide and activate the Model sheet.
    With Worksheets("Model")
        .Visible = True
        .Activate
    End With
    With Range("A4")
' Clear previous data and name some ranges.
        Range(.Offset(0, 1), .Offset(4, 1).End(xlToRight)).ClearContents
        For i = 1 To NProjects
            .Offset(0, i) = i
        Next
        Range(.Offset(1, 1), .Offset(1, NProjects)).Name = "InvLevel"
        Range(.Offset(2, 1), .Offset(2, NProjects)).Name = "NPV"
        Range(.Offset(3, 1), .Offset(3, NProjects)).Name = "InvCost"
' Calculate the ratio of NPV to investment cost (bang for buck).
        Range(.Offset(4, 1), .Offset(4, NProjects)).FormulaR1C1 = "=R[-2]C/R[-1]C"
    End With
' Randomly generate NPVs, costs, and budget. Use the Round function, with second
' argument -2, to round these to the nearest $100. Each NPV is normal, mean $25000,
' standard deviation $6000.
    Range("NPV").Formula = "=Round(NORMINV(RAND(),25000,6000),-2)"
' Each cost is between 10% and 40% of corresponding NPV.
    Range("InvCost").Formula = "=Round(NPV*(.1+.3*RAND()),-2)"
' The budget is between 30% and 90% of the total cost of all investments.
    Range("Budget").Formula = "=Round(SUM(InvCost)*(.3+.6*RAND()),-2)"
' "Freeze" the random numbers.
    With Union(Range("NPV"), Range("InvCost"))
        .Copy
        .PasteSpecial Paste:=xlValues
    End With
    With Range("Budget")
        .Copy
        .PasteSpecial Paste:=xlValues
    End With
```

```
' Get rid of the dotted line around the copy range.
    Application.CutCopyMode = False
' Use all 1's as an initial solution.
    Range("InvLevel") = 1
' Calculate the total investment cost and the total NPV.
    Range("TotCost").Formula = "=Sumproduct(InvCost,InvLevel)"
    Range("TotNPV").Formula = "=Sumproduct(NPV,InvLevel)"
End Sub
```

SortProjects Code

The **SortProjects** sub sorts the projects according to "bang-for-buck," putting those with the largest ratios of NPV to investment cost to the right. Note that the **Orientation** argument of the **Sort** method must be used, because we are sorting values in a row, not a column.

```
Sub SortProjects()
' Sort the investments in increasing order of "bang-for-buck".
    With Range("A4")
        Range(.Offset(1, 1), .Offset(4, NProjects)).Sort _
            Key1:=Range("B8"), Order1:=xlAscending, Orientation:=xlLeftToRight, Header:=xlNo
    End With
End Sub
```

RunSolver Code

The **RunSolver** sets up and then runs the Solver. It must be reset and then set up each time through, just in case the size of the problem (the number of projects) has changed. Note how the Tolerance is set to 0 in the SolverOptions statement. This guarantees that the Solver will continue to search until it has found the optimal solution. (The nonoptimal solution on the Interesting sheet occurred because the Tolerance was set at its default value of 5.) Also, note the comments about the apparent bug in the Solver's VBA functions. This bug was explained in Chapter 11.

```
Sub RunSolver()
' Set up and run the Solver to find the optimal integer solution.
    SolverReset
    SolverOK SetCell:=Range("TotNPV"), MaxMinVal:=1, ByChange:=Range("InvLevel")
' The two previous lines are repeated because of a bug in the Solver VBA functions
' (mentioned in Chapter 11). If they aren't repeated, the binary constraint might not
' be added!
    SolverReset
    SolverOK SetCell:=Range("TotNPV"), MaxMinVal:=1, ByChange:=Range("InvLevel")
' Add constraints and run the Solver.
    SolverOptions IntTolerance:=0, AssumeLinear:=True
    SolverAdd CellRef:=Range("TotCost"), Relation:=1, FormulaText:="Budget"
    SolverAdd CellRef:=Range("InvLevel"), Relation:=5
    SolverSolve UserFinish:=True
' Capture the optimal total NPV and the amount of the budget left over.
    TotNPVOpt = Range("TotNPV")
    LeftoverOpt = Range("Budget") - Range("TotCost")
End Sub
```

Heuristic Code

The **Heuristic** sub implements the heuristic. It is a perfect example of looping and arrays. The first For loop sets all ZeroOne array elements to 0. Then a single pass through the second For loop checks whether there is enough money left in the budget for each project, where the projects are examined in decreasing order of bang-for-buck. If enough money is left, the project's ZeroOne value is set to 1, its investment cost is subtracted from the remaining budget, and its NPV is added to the total NPV for the heuristic.

```
Sub Heuristic()
' Find the heuristic solution by choosing the investments in decreasing
' order of bang-for-buck.
    Dim i As Integer

' Initialize values so that no projects are currently undertaken and the
' whole budget is available.
    For i = 1 To NProjects
        ZeroOne(i) = 0
    Next
    TotNPVHeur = 0
    LeftoverHeur = Range("Budget")

' Loop through all projects in decreasing order of "bang-for-buck."
' Include the project only if its cost is no more than the remaining
' budget.
    For i = NProjects To 1 Step -1
        If Range("InvCost").Cells(i) <= LeftoverHeur Then
            LeftoverHeur = LeftoverHeur - Range("InvCost").Cells(i)
            TotNPVHeur = TotNPVHeur + Range("NPV").Cells(i)
            ZeroOne(i) = 1
        End If
    Next
End Sub
```

CreateReport Code

The **CreateReport** sub places the results from the Solver and the heuristic in the Report sheet. The main difficulty in doing this is creating *strings* that list the projects undertaken in each solution. (See the lists of investments in Figure 21.3, for example.) To see how this works, suppose the optimal solution undertakes projects 4, 6, 9, and 10. Then the string "4,6,9,10" is created and placed in the InvestOpt cell of the Report sheet. This string and the similar string for the heuristic solution are "built" one step at a time by using string concatenation and the For loop in the middle of the sub. Note that the number of projects undertaken must be known so that the For loop knows when to stop adding a comma to the string. (There is no comma after 10 in the above string.) Therefore, the first For loop in the sub counts the number of projects undertaken by each solution. Then this count variable can be used in an If construction in the second For loop to indicate when to stop adding the comma.

```
Sub CreateReport()
    Dim i As Integer, InvestOpt As String, InvestHeur As String, NOpt As Integer, _
        NHeur As Integer, Counter1 As Integer, Counter2 As Integer

' Hide the Model sheet, then unhide and activate the Report sheet.
    Worksheets("Model").Visible = False
    With Worksheets("Report")
        .Visible = True
        .Activate
    End With
    Range("A1").Select

' Find the number of investments under the optimal plan (NOpt) and under the suboptimal
' plan (NHeur).
    NOpt = 0
    NHeur = 0
    For i = 1 To NProjects
        If Range("InvLevel").Cells(i) = 1 Then
            NOpt = NOpt + 1
        End If
        If ZeroOne(i) = 1 Then
            NHeur = NHeur + 1
        End If
    Next

' Create strings InvestOpt and InvestHeur that list the investments undertaken by the
' two plans. First, initialize strings and counters.
    InvestOpt = ""
    InvestHeur = ""
    Counter1 = 0
    Counter2 = 0

' Loop through all projects.
    For i = 1 To NProjects

' Check whether this project is in the optimal solution.
        If Range("InvLevel").Cells(i) = 1 Then
            Counter1 = Counter1 + 1

' Add a comma to the string only if this investment is not the last one.
            If Counter1 < NOpt Then
                InvestOpt = InvestOpt & i & ","
            Else
                InvestOpt = InvestOpt & i
            End If
        End If

' Check whether this project is selected by the heuristic.
        If ZeroOne(i) = 1 Then
            Counter2 = Counter2 + 1

' Add a comma to the string only if this investment is not the last one.
            If Counter2 < NHeur Then
                InvestHeur = InvestHeur & i & ","
            Else
                InvestHeur = InvestHeur & i
            End If
        End If
    Next
```

```
' Enter the results in the Report sheet, where the range names were created in this
' sheet at design time.
    Range("InvestOpt") = InvestOpt
    Range("InvestHeur") = InvestHeur
    Range("LeftoverOpt") = LeftoverOpt
    Range("TotNPVOpt") = TotNPVOpt
    Range("LeftoverHeur") = LeftoverHeur
    Range("TotNPVHeur") = TotNPVHeur
End Sub
```

Navigation Code

The following subs allow for easy navigation through the application. They are attached to the corresponding buttons on the Model, Interesting, and Report sheets.

```
Sub ViewReport()
    Worksheets("Report").Activate
    Range("A1").Select
End Sub

Sub ViewModel()
    With Worksheets("Model")
        .Visible = True
        .Activate
    End With
    Range("A2").Select
End Sub

Sub ViewInteresting()
    With Worksheets("Interesting")
        .Visible = True
        .Activate
    End With
    Range("A2").Select
End Sub
```

21.8   Summary

This application has illustrated how VBA can be used to generate representative problems of a certain type and then compare the optimal Solver solutions for these problems to heuristic solutions. The context here is capital budgeting, but the same approach could be used to evaluate heuristics to other types of management science problems.

PROGRAMMING EXERCISES

1. The RunSolver sub sets the Tolerance to 0 to ensure that it gets the optimal solution. Change the application so that instead of running the heuristic, the Solver is

run once with the Tolerance at 0, and it is run again with the Tolerance argument omitted in the SolverOptions statement (which will set the Tolerance to its default value). Also, change labels appropriately on the Report sheet. Now the report should compare a solution known to be optimal with one that might not be optimal. Then run the application a few times. Do the two solutions ever differ? (The solution on the Interesting sheet shows that they *can* differ, although it might not happen very often.)

2. The GetInputs sub generates random inputs with statements such as the following:

```
Range("NPV").Formula = "=ROUND(NORMINV(RAND(),25000,6000),-2)"
```

This formula fills the NPV range in the Model sheet with the specified formula. Later, it "freezes" these formulas by copying and then pasting special with the values option. Another possible approach is the following. Inside a For loop that goes over all investments, replace the above line by

```
RandNPV = Round(Application.NormInv(Rnd, 25000, 6000), -2)
```

This line also generates a random NPV and stores it in the variable RandNPV. It does so with the VBA random number generator **Rnd**, not with Excel's Rand function, and it "borrows" Excel's NormInv function to get a normally distributed random NPV. Then it should place the RandNPV value in the appropriate cell of the Model sheet. However, no copying and pasting are necessary now. Change the GetInputs sub to implement this approach for all random inputs. If you want *different* random numbers each time you run the application, you should also insert a **Randomize** line near the top of the Main sub. (This approach is not necessarily better or worse than the formula approach; it is simply an alternative.)

3. Change the heuristic so that it works as follows. First, it orders the investments in increasing order of their investment costs. Then it proceeds as before, scanning from left to right and choosing each investment as long as there is enough budget left to afford it. How does this heuristic compare with the optimal solution? What would you expect?

4. Repeat the previous problem, but now use the heuristic that orders the investments in decreasing order of their NPVs.

5. (More difficult) Change the model so that some investments incur an investment cost right away, some incur an investment cost a year from now, and some incur an investment cost right away *and* a year from now. There are now two budget amounts: the amount available right away and another amount that is allocated for a year from now. A decision on each investment must be made right away—to invest (and gain an NPV) or not to invest. The amount that can be spent a year from now includes the budget set aside for a year from now, plus any of the current budget not used. The following heuristic is proposed. It sorts the investments in decreasing order of the ratio of NPV to the *total* investment cost. It then goes through the investments from left to right and chooses each investment as long as

there is enough money in each year's budget to afford it. (It never considers the possibility of having leftover money from the year 1 budget in year 2.) Develop an application similar to the one in the chapter that implements this new model and compares the heuristic to the optimal Solver solution for randomly generated problems. (If you like, you can use the method described in Exercise 2 to generate the random inputs.)

An Application for Estimating the Relationship Between Two Variables

22

22.1 Introduction

This application estimates the relationship between any two variables, such as demand and price. It begins with data on these two variables. The Data sheet in the **Relationships.xls** file contains sample data that can be used, or the user can supply new data. The application then copies these data to a Report sheet, creates three scatterplots on separate chart sheets, each with a different type of trend line (linear, power, and exponential) superimposed, and calculates the parameters and the mean absolute percentage error (MAPE) for the best-fitting trend line of each type.

New Learning Objectives: VBA

- To illustrate how RefEdit controls can be used in user forms to specify ranges from a worksheet.
- To show how formulas can be entered in cells with the FormulaR1C1 property, using a combination of absolute and relative addresses.

New Learning Objective: Non-VBA

- To illustrate how the relationship between two variables can be estimated by well-known trend curves, and how the fits from these curves can be compared with a measure such as MAPE.

22.2 Functionality of the Application

This application provides the following functionality.

1. The user first selects data for two variables from the Data sheet. (The sample price–demand data can be used, or the user can enter new data. In the latter case, the new data should be entered in the Data sheet *before* running the application.) The data for the two variables should come in pairs (a price and a demand for each of several time periods, for example). One variable is designated as the horizontal axis variable; the other is designated as the vertical axis variable.

2. Three chart sheets named Linear, Power, and Exponential are created. Each chart is a scatterplot of the two variables, with the appropriate trend line (linear, power, or exponential) superimposed.
3. All calculations are performed in a new worksheet named Report. This sheet contains a copy of the data, logarithms of the data (required for the power and exponential curves), formulas for the parameters of the best-fitting trend lines of each type, columns of absolute percentage errors in predicting one variable from the other for each trend line, and the MAPE for each trend line.

22.3 Running the Application

The application is in the file **Relationships.xls**. When this file is opened, the explanation in Figure 22.1 appears. When the user clicks on the button, the Data sheet and the dialog box in Figure 22.2 appear. The user must supply the names of two variables and the ranges for their data. Note that the data set can contain more than two variables, but this application works with only two of them. The only constraint is that the two ranges identified in the dialog box must have equal numbers of cells, because the data (price and demand, for example) must come in pairs.

Figure 22.1 Explanation sheet

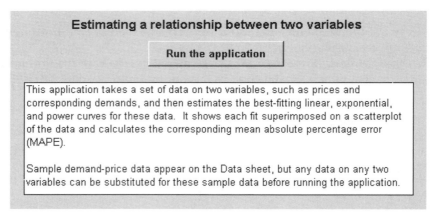

Once the ranges are specified, the application performs calculations on the Report sheet and creates charts on three separate chart sheets named Linear, Power, and Exponential. The completed Report sheet appears in Figure 22.3. It shows the absolute percentage errors for the three fits in columns G, H, and I, and it shows summary measures of the fits in the range C5:E7. (The comments in cells C4 through E4 remind the user what form each trend line takes.) Each chart sheet displays a scatterplot of the data, a superimposed trend line, and the equation of that trend line. For example, Figure 22.4 shows the scatterplot and the power trend line (really a trend *curve*) on the Power chart sheet.

Figure 22.2 Variable names and ranges dialog box

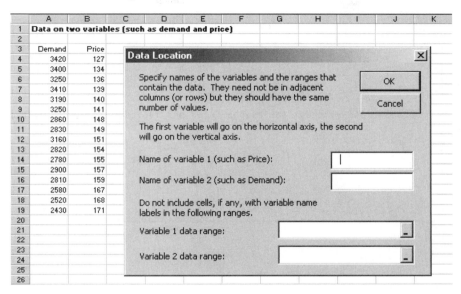

Figure 22.3 Report sheet results

	A	B	C	D	E	F	G	H	I	J	K
1	Calculations and report										
2							The values to the left and below show the parameters of the				
3		Parameters of best-fitting equations					best fits and the corresponding absolute percentage errors				
4			*Linear*	*Power*	*Exponential*		and MAPEs. See the Linear, Power, and Expon sheets for the				
5		a	6532.4110	1195683.7341	9925.9225		corresponding charts.				
6		b	-23.7515	-1.1990	-0.0081						
7		MAPE	2.79%	2.97%	2.87%						
8							Absolute percentage errors				
9		Price	Demand	Log(Price)	Log(Demand)		Linear	Power	Exponential		
10		127	3420	4.844187086	8.13739583		2.81%	4.97%	3.98%		
11		134	3400	4.8978398	8.131530711		1.48%	0.99%	1.16%		
12		136	3250	4.912654886	8.086410275		1.61%	1.75%	1.74%		
13		139	3410	4.934473933	8.13446757		5.25%	5.53%	5.36%		
14		140	3190	4.941642423	8.067776196		0.54%	0.12%	0.36%		
15		141	3250	4.94875989	8.086410275		2.05%	2.56%	2.29%		
16		148	2860	4.997212274	7.958576904		5.50%	4.48%	4.93%		
17		149	2830	5.003946306	7.948031991		5.78%	4.74%	5.18%		
18		151	3160	5.017279837	8.058327307		6.77%	7.69%	7.31%		
19		154	2820	5.036952602	7.944492164		1.94%	1.03%	1.38%		
20		155	2780	5.043425117	7.930206207		2.55%	1.69%	2.01%		
21		157	2900	5.056245805	7.972466016		3.33%	4.00%	3.78%		
22		159	2810	5.068904202	7.940939762		1.92%	2.42%	2.29%		
23		167	2580	5.117993812	7.855544678		0.55%	0.20%	0.25%		
24		168	2520	5.123963979	7.832014181		0.88%	1.86%	1.31%		
25		171	2430	5.141663557	7.795646536		1.68%	3.41%	2.54%		

Figure 22.4 Scatterplot and power trend line

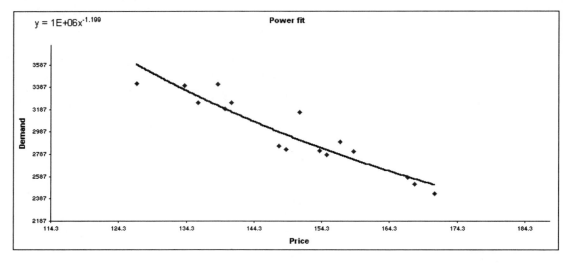

22.4   Setting Up the Excel Sheets

This **Relationships.xls** file contains three worksheets and three chart sheets. The worksheets are the Explanation sheet in Figure 22.1, the Data sheet in Figure 22.2, and the Report sheet in Figure 22.3. The Data sheet must contain data for at least two variables. A template in the Report sheet can be created at design time with *any* sample data, as indicated in Figure 22.5. The application always places

Figure 22.5 Template for Report sheet

	A	B	C	D	E	F	G	H	I	J	K
1		**Calculations and report**									
2							The values to the left and below show the parameters of the				
3		Parameters of best-fitting equations					best fits and the corresponding absolute percentage errors				
4			*Linear*	*Power*	*Exponential*		and MAPEs. See the Linear, Power, and Expon sheets for the				
5		a					corresponding charts.				
6		b									
7		MAPE									
8							Absolute percentage errors				
9		Price	Demand				Linear	Power	Exponential		
10		127	3420								
11		134	3400								
12		136	3250								
13		139	3410								
14		140	3190								
15		141	3250								
16		148	2860								
17		149	2830								
18		151	3160								
19		154	2820								
20		155	2780								
21		157	2900								
22		159	2810								
23		167	2580								
24		168	2520								
25		171	2430								

the data in columns B and C of this sheet, starting in row 10 (with labels in row 9). Then three chart sheets named Linear, Power, and Exponential can be created at design time with Excel's Chart Wizard, using the sample data in columns B and C of the Report sheet template as the source data for XY charts. Also, the trend lines and the associated equations for them can be placed on the charts by using Excel's Chart/Add Trendline menu item. The important point is that these charts can be created, along with any desired formatting, at design time. The only changes required at run time are to their source data, titles, and axis settings.

22.5 Getting Started with the VBA

This application requires a single user form named DataForm and a module. Once they are inserted, the Project Explorer window will appear as in Figure 22.6.

Figure 22.6 Project Explorer window

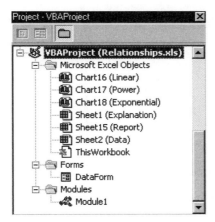

Workbook_Open Code

To guarantee that the Explanation sheet appears when the file is opened, the following code is entered in the ThisWorkbook code window. This code also hides the Report, Linear, Power, and Exponential sheets.

```
Private Sub Workbook_Open()
    Worksheets("Explanation").Activate
    Range("F4").Select
    Worksheets("Report").Visible = False
    Charts("Linear").Visible = False
    Charts("Power").Visible = False
    Charts("Exponential").Visible = False
End Sub
```

22.6   Designing the User Form and Writing Its Event Code

Web Help For more explanation of the code in this application, visit our Web site at http://www.indiana.edu/~mgtsci and download the **Code Explanation - Relationships.doc** file.

The design of the DataForm appears in Figure 22.7. It includes the usual OK and Cancel buttons, several labels, two text boxes named Name1Box and Name2Box for the variable names, and two boxes named Range1Box and Range2Box for the data ranges. These latter two boxes are called **RefEdit** controls. They are controls perfectly suited for allowing a user to select ranges. The RefEdit control is the lower left-hand control in the Control Toolbox in Figure 22.8.

Figure 22.7   Design of DataForm

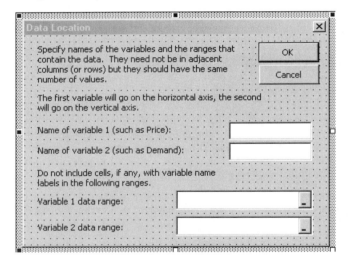

Figure 22.8   Control Toolbox

A note about RefEdit controls. RefEdit controls act somewhat differently than the other controls on the Control Toolbox in Figure 22.8. Specifically, if you use the Object Browser to look for online help on the RefEdit control under the MSForms library, you won't find it. The RefEdit control has its *own* library, which you can open by using the Tools/References menu item in the VBE and checking the Ref Edit Control box. Then you can find the desired online help under the RefEdit library. This brings up another curious point. Do you have to set a reference to the Ref Edit Control to *use* one of these controls on a user form? Fortunately, the answer is "no." As soon as you place a RefEdit control on a user form, the Ref Edit Control box is automatically checked in the list of references!

The event code for the DataForm is listed below. The **UserForm_Initialize** sub clears all name and range boxes. The **OKButton_Click** sub captures the user's inputs and checks for errors. (Other than checking for blank boxes, the only error check we make is to ensure that the two specified ranges have the same number of cells.) The specified variable names and ranges are captured in the public variables Var1Name, Var2Name, Var1Range, and Var2Range. (The latter two must be captured with the keyword Set because they are *object* variables.) The **CancelButton_Click** sub unloads the dialog box, activates the Explanation worksheet, and terminates the program.

Note that the **Value** property of a **RefEdit** control returns the *address* of the designated range as a string. Then a line such as

```
Set Var1Range = Range(Range1Box.Value)
```

can be used to define the Range object variable Var1Range. Actually, because the Value property is the default property, we are allowed to shorten this line to

```
Set Var1Range = Range(Range1Box)
```

Event Code for DataForm

```
Private Sub UserForm_Initialize()
    Name1Box = ""
    Name2Box = ""
    Range1Box = ""
    Range2Box = ""
End Sub

Private Sub OKButton_Click()
    Dim ctl As Control
' Check whether any text box or refedit box is empty.  If so, exit the sub.
    For Each ctl In Me.Controls
        If TypeName(ctl) = "TextBox" Or TypeName(ctl) = "RefEdit" Then
            If ctl.Value = "" Then
                MsgBox "Enter a variable name or a range in each box.", vbInformation, _
                    "Invalid entry"
                ctl.SetFocus
                Exit Sub
            End If
        End If
    Next
```

```
' Capture names and ranges.
    Var1Name = Name1Box
    Var2Name = Name2Box
    Set Var1Range = Range(Range1Box)
    Set Var2Range = Range(Range2Box)
    NObs = Var1Range.Cells.Count
' Check that both ranges are of the same length.
    If Var2Range.Cells.Count <> NObs Then
        MsgBox "Make sure the two ranges have equal numbers of cells", vbExclamation, _
            "Improper selections"
        Range1Box.SetFocus
        Exit Sub
    End If
' Unload the dialog box.  This occurs only if all entries are valid.
    Unload Me
End Sub

Private Sub CancelButton_Click()
    Worksheets("Explanation").Activate
    Range("F4").Select
    Unload Me
    End
End Sub
```

22.7   The VBA Code in the Module

Most of the work is performed by the VBA code in the module. This code is
listed below. The **Main** sub is attached to the button on the Explanation sheet.
In turn, it calls the four subs **GetData**, **TransferData**, **ModifyCharts**, and
DoCalculations. The public variables are listed below. Just remember that index
1 is for the horizontal axis variable, and index 2 is for the vertical axis variable. In
regression terminology, variable 1 is the explanatory (or independent) variable,
and variable 2 is the response (or dependent) variable.

Option Statement and Public variables

```
Option Explicit

' Definitions of public variables
'    NObs - number of observations for each variable
'    Var1Range - range of the data on the horizontal axis
'    Var1Min - smallest observation in Var1Range
'    Var1Max - largest observation in Var1Range
'    Var1LogRange - range of logs of data in Var1Range
'    Var1Name - descriptive name of horizontal axis variable
'    Var2Range, Var2Min, Var2Max, Var2LogRange, Var2Name - similar for vertical axis
'        variable
'    ChartDataRange - range containing both variables for use in the scatterplot

Public Var1Range As Range, Var2Range As Range, NObs As Integer, _
    ChartDataRange As Range, Var1Min As Single, Var1Max As Single, _
    Var2Min As Single, Var2Max As Single, Var1LogRange As Range, _
    Var2LogRange As Range, Var1Name As String, Var2Name As String
```

Main Code

```
Sub Main()
' Specify the data on the Data sheet to be used.
    Call GetData

    Application.ScreenUpdating = False

' Transfer the data to the Report sheet and perform the analysis.
    Call TransferData
    Call ModifyCharts
    Call DoCalculations

    Application.ScreenUpdating = True
End Sub
```

GetData Code

The GetData sub activates the Data sheet and "shows" the DataForm, so that the user can specify the price and demand ranges. If there is no Data sheet, an error message is displayed and the program terminates. Actually, this error check is not necessary, assuming that the user has not deleted or renamed the Data sheet that comes with the file, but we include it here for illustration. Often error checks such as this *are* necessary.

```
Sub GetData()
' Make sure there is a Data sheet. If so, activate it. If not, display an error message
' and quit.
    On Error Resume Next
    Worksheets("Data").Activate
    If Err <> 0 Then
        MsgBox "Make sure there is a Data sheet that contains the " _
            & "data you want to analyze.", vbExclamation, "Data sheet required"
        Worksheets("Explanation").Activate
        Range("F4").Select
        End
    End If

' Show the user input form.
    DataForm.Show
End Sub
```

TransferData Code

The **TransferData** sub copies the selected data in the Data sheet to columns B and C of the Report sheet. When Excel creates a scatterplot (which it calls an XY chart), it automatically places the variable in the leftmost column on the horizontal axis. Therefore, the variable designated as the horizontal axis variable is copied to column B, and the variable designated as the vertical axis variable is copied to column C. Note that the Var1Range and Var2Range object variables are set to the data ranges in columns B and C. Then the ChartDataRange variable is set to their union—both columns B and C—for later use as the source range of the scatterplots.

```
Sub TransferData()
' Unhide and activate the Report sheet.
    With Worksheets("Report")
        .Visible = True
        .Activate
    End With
' Clear any data from a previous run.
    Range("B9").CurrentRegion.ClearContents
    With Range("G9")
        Range(.Offset(1, 0), .End(xlDown).Offset(0, 2)).ClearContents
    End With
' Add and format some labels.
    Range("B9") = Var1Name
    Range("C9") = Var2Name
' Copy the Data from the Data sheet to the Report sheet, with the first variable
' selected in column B and the second variable in column C.
    Var1Range.Copy Range("B10")
    Var2Range.Copy Range("C10")
' Set the pasted ranges and the chart range to Range object variables.
    With Range("B9")
        Set Var1Range = Range(.Offset(1, 0), .Offset(NObs, 0))
        Set Var2Range = Range(.Offset(1, 1), .Offset(NObs, 1))
        Set ChartDataRange = Union(Var1Range, Var2Range)
    End With
' Capture the min and max of the variables for charting purposes later on.
    Var1Min = Application.Min(Var1Range)
    Var1Max = Application.Max(Var1Range)
    Var2Min = Application.Min(Var2Range)
    Var2Max = Application.Max(Var2Range)
End Sub
```

ModifyCharts Code

The **ModifyCharts** sub modifies the properties of the charts that are affected by new data. (Remember that these charts are created at design time.) These properties include the source data, the titles, and the axes. For the latter, the application sets minimum and maximum values for the axes so that the data points fill up most of the chart. Specifically, it ensures that each axis extends from 10% below the smallest observation (on that axis) to 10% above the largest observation.

```
Sub ModifyCharts()
    Dim cht As Chart, ChtIndex As Integer, ChtTitle As String, TrendType As Integer
' Loop through all chart sheets.
    For Each cht In ActiveWorkbook.Charts
' Unhide and activate the chart.
        With cht
            .Visible = True
            .Activate
' Specify the source data for the chart.
            .SetSourceData Source:=ChartDataRange, PlotBy:=xlColumns
' The xlCategory axis is the horizontal axis, and the xlValue axis is the vertical
' axis.
            With .Axes(xlCategory)
                .AxisTitle.Characters.Text = Var1Name
' Set the min and max values on the horizontal axis.
                .MinimumScale = Var1Min * 0.9
```

```
            .MaximumScale = Var1Max * 1.1
        End With
' Set similar properties for the vertical axis, so that the scatterplot takes up most
' of the visible area on the chart
        With .Axes(xlValue)
            .AxisTitle.Characters.Text = Var2Name
            .MinimumScale = Var2Min * 0.9
            .MaximumScale = Var2Max * 1.1
        End With
' Deselect the chart to remove the "handles" around it.
        .Deselect
      End With
   Next
End Sub
```

DoCalculations Code

The **DoCalculations** sub enters formulas in the appropriate ranges of the Report sheet. It first creates logarithms of the data in columns D and E. Next, it uses formulas from regression to calculate the parameters of the best-fitting trend lines in the range C5:E6. Then it calculates the absolute percentage errors in columns G, H, and I. Finally, it calculates the MAPE values in the range C7:E7.

A note on the FormulaR1C1 property. Pay particular attention to how the **FormulaR1C1** property of ranges is used several times to enter formulas with relative and absolute addresses. For example, the *relative* reference RC[-2] refers to the same row and two columns to the left of the cell it is referenced by. If this is called from cell E5, say, it refers to cell C5; if it is called from cell G23, it refers to cell E23; and so on. In contrast, the reference R5C3, without the brackets, is an *absolute* reference to the cell in row 5 and column C. It is essentially equivalent to $C$5. The formulas for calculating absolute percentage errors toward the bottom of this sub use a combination of relative and absolute references. The relative parts are for the actual and estimated values of the variable; the absolute parts are for the parameters of the fitted equation. The FormulaR1C1 property is somewhat more difficult to learn than the Formula property, but it is often more powerful—it enables us to fill an entire range with formulas with a *single* line of code—no loops are required.

```
Sub DoCalculations()
    Dim ParameterRange As Range, APERange As Range, i As Integer
    Worksheets("Report").Activate

' Enter labels for the log variables.
    Range("D9").Value = "Log(" & Var1Name & ")"
    Range("E9").Value = "Log(" & Var2Name & ")"

' Create logarithms of the two variables in columns D and E for later use.
    With Range("D9")
        Range(.Offset(1, 0), .Offset(NObs, 1)).FormulaR1C1 = "=Ln(RC[-2])"
        Set Var1LogRange = Range(.Offset(1, 0), .Offset(NObs, 0))
        Set Var2LogRange = Range(.Offset(1, 1), .Offset(NObs, 1))
    End With
```

```
' Calculate the best-fitting parameters with formulas using Excel's Intercept and Slope
' functions, and place them in the ParameterRange.  (The details won't be clear unless
' you know regression.)
    Set ParameterRange = Range("C5:E6")
    With ParameterRange

' The linear fit uses the original data.
        .Cells(1, 1).Formula = "=Intercept(" & Var2Range.Address & "," _
            & Var1Range.Address & ")"
        .Cells(2, 1).Formula = "=Slope(" & Var2Range.Address & "," & Var1Range.Address _
            & ")"

' The power fit uses the logs of both variables.
        .Cells(1, 2).Formula = "=Exp(Intercept(" & Var2LogRange.Address & "," _
            & Var1LogRange.Address & "))"
        .Cells(2, 2).Formula = "=Slope(" & Var2LogRange.Address & "," _
            & Var1LogRange.Address & ")"

' The exponential fit uses the original variable 1 data and the log of variable 2.
        .Cells(1, 3).Formula = "=Exp(Intercept(" & Var2LogRange.Address & "," _
            & Var1Range.Address & "))"
        .Cells(2, 3).Formula = "=Slope(" & Var2LogRange.Address & "," _
            & Var1Range.Address & ")"
    End With

' Calculate the absolute percentage errors (with formulas) when predicting variable 2
' from the three trend lines.
    With Range("G9")
        Range(.Offset(1, 0), .Offset(NObs, 0)).FormulaR1C1 = _
            "=Abs(RC[-4]-(R5C3+R6C3*RC[-5]))/RC[-4]"
        Range(.Offset(1, 1), .Offset(NObs, 1)).FormulaR1C1 = _
            "=Abs(RC[-5]-R5C4*RC[-6]^R6C4)/RC[-5]"
        Range(.Offset(1, 2), .Offset(NObs, 2)).FormulaR1C1 = _
            "=Abs(RC[-6]-R5C5*Exp(R6C5*RC[-7]))/RC[-6]"
        Set APERange = Range(.Offset(1, 0), .Offset(NObs, 2))
    End With

' Calculate the MAPE values for the three trend lines.
    With Range("B7")
        For i = 1 To 3
            .Offset(0, i).Formula ="=Average(" & APERange.Columns(i).Address & ")"
        Next
    End With
End Sub
```

22.8 Summary

Finding a "trend curve" that relates two variables, or finding the best of several
such trend curves, is an extremely important task in the business world. Excel has
several built-in tools for estimating such curves, including the ability to superim-
pose trend curves and their equations on a scatterplot. This application illustrates
how the whole process can be automated with VBA. The charts indicate visually
how well the trend curves fit the data, and the numerical parameters of the curves
can be used for later forecasting.

PROGRAMMING EXERCISES

1. The application currently calculates the MAPE for each trend curve. Another frequently used measure of the goodness of fit is the mean absolute error (MAE). It is the average of the absolute differences between the actual and predicted values. Change the application so that it reports the MAE for each trend curve rather than the MAPE.

2. Repeat the previous exercise, but now report the root mean square error (RMSE) instead of the MAPE. This is defined as the square root of the average of squared differences between the actual and predicted values. It is another popular measure of the goodness of fit.

3. Change the application so that it reports all three goodness-of-fit measures for each trend curve: the MAPE, the MAE from Exercise 1, and the RMSE from Exercise 2.

4. The application currently shows only the absolute percentage errors in columns G, H, and I of the Report sheet. It doesn't explicitly show the predicted values from the trend equations, although it implicitly uses them in the equations for the absolute percentage errors. Change the application so that it enters the predicted values, with formulas, in columns G, H, and I, and then it enters the absolute percentage errors, again as formulas, in columns J, K, and L. Actually, you should be able to use a *single* FormulaR1C1 property to enter *all* of the errors in columns J, K, and L.

5. This application is typical in the sense that it requires input data. The question from the developer's point of view is where the data are likely to reside. Here we have assumed that the data reside on a Data sheet in the same file as the application. This exercise and the next one explore other possibilities. For this exercise, assume that the data reside in some other worksheet, but in the same file as the application. Change the application so that it can locate the data, wherever they might be. (*Hint*: The RefEdit control allows a user to select a range from *any* sheet.)

6. (More difficult) For this exercise, assume that the data are in another Excel workbook. It will be up to the user to specify the workbook and then the data ranges in that workbook. Change the application so that (1) it informs the user with a message box that he is about to be prompted for the data file, (2) it uses the **GetOpenFilename** method of the **Application** object to get the name of the data file, (3) it opens this file, (4) it uses the same DataForm as in Figure 22.7 to get the names of the variables and the data ranges, (5) it copies the required data to the Report sheet of the application file, (6) it closes the data file, and (7) it proceeds as before to analyze the data. (See Exercise 4 of Chapter 19 for an explanation of the **GetOpenFilename** method. It displays a built-in Excel dialog box for getting the name of a file from a user and is exactly what we need here.)

An Exponential Utility Application

23.1 Introduction

This application illustrates a rather surprising result that can occur when a decision maker is risk averse.[40] Suppose you can enter a risky venture where there will be either a gain of G or a loss of L. The probability of the gain is p and the probability of the loss is $1 - p$. You can have any share s of this venture, where s is a fraction from 0 to 1. Then if there is a gain, you win sG; if there is a loss, you lose sL. You must decide what share you want, given that you are risk averse and have an exponential utility function with risk tolerance parameter R.

The surprising result is that if the gain G increases and all other parameters remain constant, your optimal share s might *decrease*! In other words, you might want a *smaller* share of a better thing. The intuition is that you are risk averse, so you do not like risky ventures. However, as G increases, you can have less exposure to risk by decreasing your share s and still expect to do better in the venture.

In case this argument does not convince you, the application calculates the optimal share s for varying values of G and plots them graphically. The resulting chart shows clearly, at least for some values of the parameters, that the optimal value of s can decrease as G increases.

New Learning Objective: VBA

- To learn how a VBA application, especially one that uses a chart, can illustrate a result that might be very difficult to understand (or believe) in any other way.

New Learning Objective: Non-VBA

- To illustrate the role of risk in decision making under uncertainty.

23.2 Functionality of the Application

The application is slightly more general than explained in the introduction. It does the following:

1. It first gets the inputs G, L, p, and R from the user in a dialog box. This dialog box also asks whether the user wants to vary G or L in a sensitivity analysis,

---

[40] It is based on the article "Too Much of a Good Thing?" by D. Clyman, M. Walls, and J. Dyer, in *Operations Research*, Vol. 47, No. 6 (1999).

and it asks for the range of values for the sensitivity analysis. Although the sensitivity analysis on *G* is of primary interest, it might also be interesting to do a sensitivity analysis on *L*.

2. The user's expected utility from the risky venture, given a share *s*, is calculated in a Model sheet, and then it is maximized with the Solver (as a nonlinear model) several times, once for each value of *G* (or *L*) in the sensitivity analysis.

3. The Solver results are shown graphically in a chart sheet named SensitivityChart.

4. The model and chart show the optimal share *s*. They also show the corresponding certainty equivalent. This is the dollar equivalent of the risky venture, using the optimal share *s*. More specifically, it is the dollar amount such that the decision maker would be indifferent between receiving it for sure and participating in the risky venture. This certainty equivalent should increase as *G* increases, even though *s* might decrease. The chart indicates that this is indeed the case.

23.3 Running the Application

The application is stored in the file **ExpUtility.xls**. When this file is opened, the Explanation sheet in Figure 23.1 is displayed. Clicking on the button on this sheet

Figure 23.1 Explanation sheet

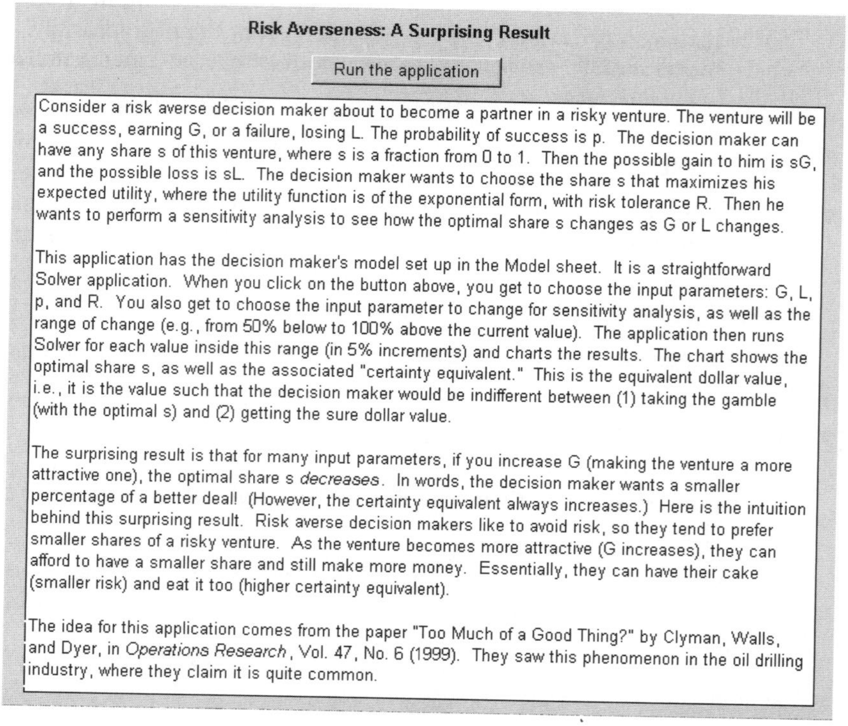

Risk Averseness: A Surprising Result

Run the application

Consider a risk averse decision maker about to become a partner in a risky venture. The venture will be a success, earning G, or a failure, losing L. The probability of success is p. The decision maker can have any share s of this venture, where s is a fraction from 0 to 1. Then the possible gain to him is sG, and the possible loss is sL. The decision maker wants to choose the share s that maximizes his expected utility, where the utility function is of the exponential form, with risk tolerance R. Then he wants to perform a sensitivity analysis to see how the optimal share s changes as G or L changes.

This application has the decision maker's model set up in the Model sheet. It is a straightforward Solver application. When you click on the button above, you get to choose the input parameters: G, L, p, and R. You also get to choose the input parameter to change for sensitivity analysis, as well as the range of change (e.g., from 50% below to 100% above the current value). The application then runs Solver for each value inside this range (in 5% increments) and charts the results. The chart shows the optimal share s, as well as the associated "certainty equivalent." This is the equivalent dollar value, i.e., it is the value such that the decision maker would be indifferent between (1) taking the gamble (with the optimal s) and (2) getting the sure dollar value.

The surprising result is that for many input parameters, if you increase G (making the venture a more attractive one), the optimal share s *decreases*. In words, the decision maker wants a smaller percentage of a better deal! (However, the certainty equivalent always increases.) Here is the intuition behind this surprising result. Risk averse decision makers like to avoid risk, so they tend to prefer smaller shares of a risky venture. As the venture becomes more attractive (G increases), they can afford to have a smaller share and still make more money. Essentially, they can have their cake (smaller risk) and eat it too (higher certainty equivalent).

The idea for this application comes from the paper "Too Much of a Good Thing?" by Clyman, Walls, and Dyer, in *Operations Research*, Vol. 47, No. 6 (1999). They saw this phenomenon in the oil drilling industry, where they claim it is quite common.

produces the dialog box in Figure 23.2. Its top four boxes are filled with parameters from a previous run, if any. (To make things more interesting, think of the monetary amounts as expressed in *millions* of dollars.) The other options are set at chosen default values.

Figure 23.2   User inputs dialog box

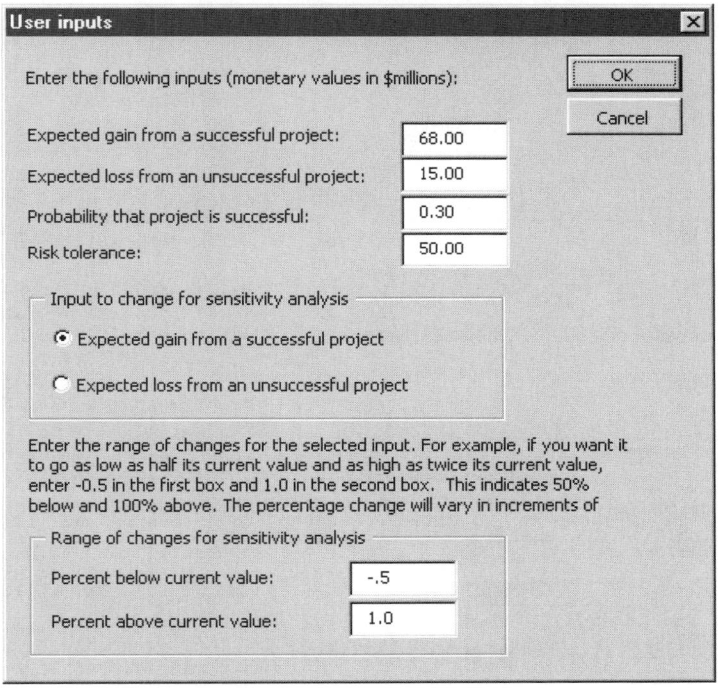

Once the OK button is clicked, the application runs the Solver on a (hidden) Model sheet several times, once for each value in the sensitivity analysis, and reports the results in the SensitivityChart chart sheet. For the parameters in Figure 23.2, the chart appears as in Figure 23.3. This chart shows clearly that the optimal share reaches its maximum of about 0.46 when the gain *G* has increased by about 60% above its original value of $68 million. As *G* increases further, the optimal share *decreases* slightly. However, the certainty equivalent continues to increase. This means that as *G* increases, the decision maker values the risky venture more.

The Model sheet that is the basis for this chart appears in Figure 23.4. It will be discussed further below.

If the second option button in Figure 23.2 is selected, then the sensitivity analysis is performed on the loss *L*, so that *L* varies and all other parameters remain constant. The chart from this analysis appears in Figure 23.5. This chart shows no surprises. As the loss increases, you want a smaller and smaller share of a bad thing, and your certainty equivalent also decreases steadily.

Figure 23.3 Chart for sensitivity analysis on gain *G*

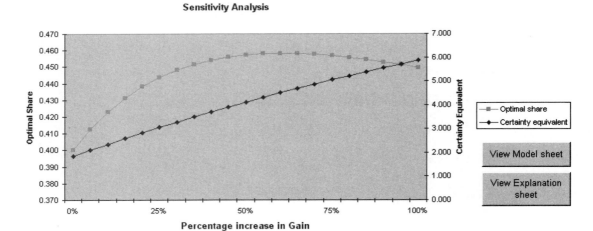

Figure 23.4 Model sheet

	A	B	C	D	E	F
1	**Decision model**					
2						
3	**Inputs**			Original values	Pct change	
4	Gain with success	68.00		68.00	0%	
5	Loss with failure	15.00		15.00	0%	
6	Probability of success	0.300				
7						
8	Risk tolerance	50.00				
9				View Chart		
10	**Decision**					
11	Share of project	0.400		View Explanation		
12	Expected utility	0.037		sheet		
13	Certainty equivalent	1.866				
14						
15	Optimal share and certainty equivalent as a function of percentage change in Gain					
16	Percentage change	Optimal share	Certainty equivalent			
17	0%	0.400	1.866	**Range names used:**		
18	5%	0.413	2.110	Gain: B4		
19	10%	0.423	2.352	Loss: B5		
20	15%	0.431	2.591	PrSuc: B6		
21	20%	0.438	2.824	RiskTol: B8		
22	25%	0.444	3.053	Share: B11		
23	30%	0.448	3.277	ExpUtil: B12		
24	35%	0.451	3.495	CertEquiv: B13		
25	40%	0.454	3.708	OrigGain - D4		
26	45%	0.456	3.915	OrigLoss - D5		
27	50%	0.457	4.117	PctGain - E4		
28	55%	0.458	4.314	PctLoss - E5		
29	60%	0.458	4.505			
30	65%	0.458	4.691			
31	70%	0.457	4.872			
32	75%	0.457	5.048			
33	80%	0.456	5.220			
34	85%	0.454	5.387			
35	90%	0.453	5.549			
36	95%	0.451	5.707			
37	100%	0.449	5.861			

Figure 23.5 Chart for sensitivity analysis on loss L

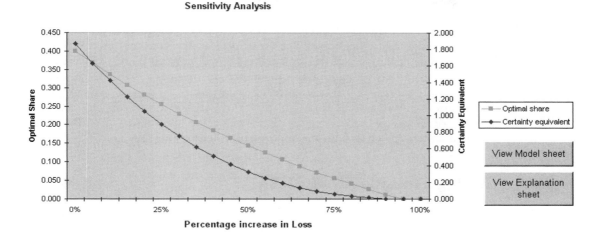

23.4 Setting Up the Excel Sheets

The **ExpUtility.xls** file contains two worksheets: the Explanation sheet in Figure 23.1 and the Model sheet in Figure 23.4. It also contains the SensitivityChart chart sheet. Except for the sensitivity section (from row 17 down), a template for the Model sheet can be formed at design time, as shown in Figure 23.6. (The input cells are shaded with blue borders, and the changing cell has a red border.) The formula in cell B12 calculates the expected utility for any share in cell B11, and the formula in cell B13 calculates the corresponding certainty equivalent. These formulas are

=PrSuc*(1-EXP(-Share*Gain/RiskTol))+(1-PrSuc)
(1-EXP(-Share(-Loss)/RiskTol))

Figure 23.6 Template for Model sheet

	A	B	C	D	E
1	**Decision model**				
2					
3	**Inputs**			Original values	Pct change
4	Gain with success	68.00		68.00	0%
5	Loss with failure	15.00		15.00	0%
6	Probability of success	0.300			
7					
8	Risk tolerance	50.00			
9				View Chart	
10	**Decision**				
11	Share of project	0.400		View Explanation sheet	
12	Expected utility	0.037			
13	Certainty equivalent	1.866			
14					
15					
16	Percentage change	Optimal share	Certainty equivalent		

and

$$=-RiskTol*LN(1-ExpUtil)$$

(See Chapter 9 of *Practical Management Science* for a discussion of expected utility and exponential utility functions.) Then the Solver is set up to maximize cell B12, with the single changing cell B11 constrained to be between 0 and 1. Because of the exponential utility function, this model must be solved as a *nonlinear* model.

The chart sheet can also be created at design time. To do this, we enter *any* trial values in columns A, B, and C of the sensitivity section of the Model sheet (see Figure 23.4) and then create the chart from these trial values. The VBA code will then update the chart with the appropriate values at run time.

23.5 Getting Started with the VBA

This application requires a user form named InputsForm, a module, and a reference to the Solver.xla add-in. Once these items are added, the Project Explorer window will appear as in Figure 23.7.

Figure 23.7 Project Explorer window

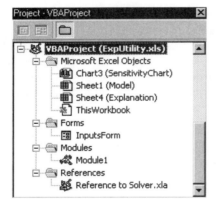

Workbook_Open Code

To guarantee that the Explanation sheet appears when the file is opened, the following code is placed in the ThisWorkbook code window. It also uses a For Each loop to hide all sheets except the Explanation sheet.

```
Private Sub Workbook_Open()
    Dim sht As Object
    Worksheets("Explanation").Activate
    Range("F4").Select
    For Each sht In ActiveWorkbook.Sheets
        If sht.Name <> "Explanation" Then sht.Visible = False
    Next
End Sub
```

23.6 Designing the User Form and Writing Its Event Code

> **Web Help** For more explanation of the code in this application, visit our Web site at http://www.indiana.edu/~mgtsci and download the **Code Explanation - ExpUtility.doc** file.

The design of the InputsForm is shown in Figure 23.8. It includes the usual OK and Cancel buttons, two explanation labels, two frames for grouping controls, two option buttons named GainOpt and LossOpt, and six text boxes with corresponding labels. These text boxes (from top to bottom) are named GainBox, LossBox, ProbBox, RiskTolBox, BelowBox, and AboveBox.

Figure 23.8 Design of InputsForm

User inputs ☒

Enter the following inputs (monetary values in $millions):   [OK]

                                                                    [Cancel]

Expected gain from a successful project: [   ]

Expected loss from an unsuccessful project: [   ]

Probability that project is successful: [   ]

Risk tolerance: [   ]

┌─ Input to change for sensitivity analysis ──────────────────┐
│   ○ Expected gain from a successful project   │
│   │
│   ○ Expected loss from an unsuccessful project   │
└──┘

Enter the range of changes for the selected input. For example, if you want it
to go as low as half its current value and as high as twice its current value,
enter -0.5 in the first box and 1.0 in the second box. This indicates 50%
below and 100% above. The percentage change will vary in increments of

┌─ Range of changes for sensitivity analysis ─────────────────┐
│   Percent below current value: [   ]   │
│   │
│   Percent above current value: [   ]   │
└──┘

The event code for this user form is listed below. Note that the **Userform_Initialize** sub captures the values from the Model sheet from a previous run, if any, and places them in the top four text boxes. It then chooses the first option button by default, and it places the default values 0 and 1 in the bottom two text boxes. (Note how the Format function is used to ensure that the values in the top four text boxes are formatted as numbers with two decimals.) The **OKButton_Click** sub captures the user's inputs in public variables for later use in the module. It also does appropriate error checking for the various user inputs. The **CancelButton_Click** sub unloads the dialog box and terminates the program.

Event Code for InputsForm

```
Private Sub UserForm_Initialize()
' Capture the values from the Model sheet in the first four boxes, and
' use appropriate default values for the others.
    GainBox = Format(Worksheets("Model").Range("Gain"), "0.00")
    LossBox = Format(Worksheets("Model").Range("Loss"), "0.00")
    ProbBox = Format(Worksheets("Model").Range("PrSuc"), "0.00")
    RiskTolBox = Format(Worksheets("Model").Range("RiskTol"), "0.00")
    GainOpt = True
    BelowBox = 0
    AboveBox = 1
End Sub

Private Sub OKButton_Click()
    Dim ctl As Control
' Perform error checking for inputs. Each text box must be nonblank and numeric, the
' BelowBox must not be positive, the ProbBox must be between 0 and 1, and the other
' boxes must not be negative.
    For Each ctl In Me.Controls
        If TypeName(ctl) = "TextBox" Then
            If ctl.Value = "" Or Not IsNumeric(ctl) Then
                MsgBox "Enter numerical values in all of the boxes.", vbInformation, _
                    "Invalid entry"
                ctl.SetFocus
                Exit Sub
            End If
            If ctl.Name = "BelowBox" Then
                If ctl.Value > 0 Then
                    MsgBox "Enter a nonpositive value in this box.", vbInformation, _
                        "Invalid entry"
                    ctl.SetFocus
                    Exit Sub
                End If
            ElseIf ctl.Name = "ProbBox" Then
                If ctl.Value < 0 Or ctl.Value > 1 Then
                    MsgBox "Enter a value between 0 and 1 in this box.", _
                        vbInformation, "Invalid entry"
                    ctl.SetFocus
                    Exit Sub
                End If
            Else
                If ctl.Value < 0 Then
                    MsgBox "Enter a nonnegative value in this box.", vbInformation, _
                        "Invalid entry"
                    ctl.SetFocus
                    Exit Sub
                End If
            End If
        End If
    Next
' Capture the user's inputs in Public variables.
    Gain = GainBox
    Loss = LossBox
```

```
    PrSuc = ProbBox
    RiskTol = RiskTolBox
    If GainOpt Then
        InputToChange = "Gain"
    Else
        InputToChange = "Loss"
    End If
    PctBelow = BelowBox
    PctAbove = AboveBox
' Unload the userform.
    Unload Me
End Sub

Private Sub CancelButton_Click()
    Unload Me
    End
End Sub
```

23.7   The VBA Code in the Module

The module contains a **Main** sub that first "shows" the InputsForm and then calls
several other subs to do the real work. The code is listed below.

Option Statement and Public Variables

```
Option Explicit

' The following variables capture the user's inputs. Note that InputToChange will be
' "Gain" or "Loss".  Also, PctBelow and PctAbove are the extremes in percentage changes
' for the sensitivity analysis.

Public Gain As Single, Loss As Single, PrSuc As Single, _
    RiskTol As Single, InputToChange As String, PctBelow As Single, PctAbove As Single
```

Main Code

The **Main** sub gets the user inputs from the InputsForm, enters these in the
Model sheet, does the sensitivity analysis in the Model sheet, and finally updates
the chart.

```
Sub Main()
' Get the user inputs.
    InputsForm.Show
    Application.ScreenUpdating = False
' Enter the user inputs into the Model sheet.
    Call EnterInputs
' Run the sensitivity analysis in the Model sheet.
    Call DoSensitivity
' Show and update the chart.
    Call UpdateChart

    Application.ScreenUpdating = True
End Sub
```

EnterInputs Code

The **EnterInputs** sub enters the user's inputs from the InputsForm and enters them into prenamed ranges of the Model sheet. (Refer to Figure 23.4.) It enters an initial share of 0.5 in the changing cell, although any other initial share could be entered instead.

```
Sub EnterInputs()
' Unhide and activate the Model sheet.
    With Worksheets("Model")
        .Visible = True
        .Activate
    End With
' Enter the user's inputs into cells (already range-named) in the Model
' sheet.
    Range("OrigGain") = Gain
    Range("OrigLoss") = Loss
    Range("PrSuc") = PrSuc
    Range("RiskTol") = RiskTol
' Set the initial share to 0.5; Solver will find the optimal share.
    Range("Share") = 0.5
End Sub
```

DoSensitivity Code

The **DoSensitivity** sub runs the sensitivity analysis on the chosen input parameter (gain or loss). To do this, it uses a Do loop to run through the various percentage changes for the selected input, and for each setting, it runs the Solver to find the optimal share. As it does this, it records the optimal share and the corresponding expected utility and certainty equivalent in the sensitivity section of the Model sheet. These values are the basis for the chart.

```
Sub DoSensitivity()
    Dim RowOff As Integer, CurrPct As Single
' Enter an appropriate label.
    Range("A15") = "Optimal share and certainty equivalent as a function " _
        & "of percentage change in " & InputToChange
    With Range("A16")
' Clear out old values, if any, from the previous sensitivity table.
    Range(.Offset(1, 0), .Offset(1, 2).End(xlDown)).ClearContents

' RowOff is the current number of rows below row 16, i.e., where the results from the
' current Solver run will be placed. CurrPct is the current percentage change in the
' input being changed.
    RowOff = 1
    CurrPct = PctBelow
' Loop through the percentages to change, incrementing by 5% each time.
    Do
' Enter the current percentage in the sensitivity table and up above (in the PctGain
' or PctLoss cell), which ties it to the model.
        .Offset(RowOff, 0) = CurrPct
        Range("Pct" & InputToChange) = CurrPct
' Run the Solver, which has already been set up.
        SolverSolve UserFinish:=True
```

```
' Enter the Solver results in the sensitivity table.
            .Offset(RowOff, 1) = Range("Share")
            .Offset(RowOff, 2) = Range("CertEquiv")
' Update RowOff and CurrPct for the next time through the loop (if any).
            RowOff = RowOff + 1
            CurrPct = CurrPct + 0.05
' The +0.001 in the next statement handles numerical roundoff. It ensures that the loop
' will be run when CurrPct is equal to PctAbove.
        Loop While CurrPct <= PctAbove + 0.001
' Run Solver one more time, using the original (user's input) values. (This isn't
' really necessary, but the user might want to see the model results with the
' original inputs.)
        Range("Pct" & InputToChange) = 0
        SolverSolve UserFinish:=True
    End With
' Hide the Model sheet.
    ActiveSheet.Visible = False
End Sub
```

UpdateChart Code

Recall that the chart has already been created (and formatted as desired) at design time. Therefore, the only purpose of the **UpdateChart** is to "populate" the chart with the data from the sensitivity analysis. It does this by using the **SetSourceData** method of the active chart. To label the horizontal axis appropriately, it sets the **Text** property of the **Axes(xlCategory).AxisTitle.Characters** object. To set the data range for the horizontal axis, that is, the range of percentage changes, it sets the **XValues** property of the **SeriesCollection(1)** object. (This object refers to the first of the two series plotted in the chart. Because they are both based on the same set of percentage changes, either could be used in this XValues statement.)

```
Sub UpdateChart()
    Dim ChartData As Range, ChartPcts As Range
' Define ranges for the parts of the sensitivity table used for the chart.
    With Worksheets("Model").Range("A16")
        Set ChartData = Range(.Offset(0, 1), .Offset(0, 2).End(xlDown))
        Set ChartPcts = Range(.Offset(1, 0), .End(xlDown))
    End With
' Unhide and activate the chart sheet.
    With Charts("SensitivityChart")
        .Visible = True
        .Activate
    End With
' Update the chart, which was already set up at design time.
    With ActiveChart
        .Axes(xlCategory).AxisTitle.Characters.Text = "Percentage increase in " &
            InputToChange
        .SetSourceData ChartData
        .SeriesCollection(1).XValues = ChartPcts
        .Deselect
    End With
End Sub
```

Navigational Code

The following subs allow for easy navigation through the application. They are attached to the corresponding buttons on the Model and SensitivityChart sheets.

```
Sub ViewModel()
    With Worksheets("Model")
        .Visible = True
        .Activate
    End With
    Range("A2").Select
End Sub

Sub ViewExplanation()
    Worksheets("Explanation").Activate
    Range("F4").Select
    Worksheets("Model").Visible = False
    Charts("SensitivityChart").Visible = False
End Sub

Sub ViewChart()
    Worksheets("Model").Visible = False
    Charts("SensitivityChart").Activate
End Sub
```

23.8 Summary

This chapter has illustrated how a certain type of unexpected behavior can be demonstrated clearly to an unconvinced user. More generally, it has illustrated how a VBA application can perform a sensitivity analysis and present the results in a clear graphical format. This particular application allows the user to run the sensitivity analysis with a variety of inputs to gain insight into the role risk aversion plays in risky ventures.

PROGRAMMING EXERCISES

1. Change the application so that it is possible to perform a sensitivity analysis on the probability p of gain G. In this case, the user should be asked to select the range that p can vary over, in increments of 0.05, where the lower and upper limits of this range must be multiples of 0.05 from 0 to 1. The resulting chart should be like the ones illustrated in the chapter except that the horizontal axis should now show p.
2. Change the application so that it is possible to perform a sensitivity analysis on the risk tolerance parameter R. In this case, the user should be asked to select the range that R can vary over. The resulting chart should be like the ones illustrated in the chapter except that the horizontal axis should now show R.
3. Change the application so that it is possible to perform a sensitivity analysis on both L and G simultaneously. Specifically, the user should be asked for values of

these parameters (as well as p and R). Then it should perform a sensitivity analysis where the possible loss and gain are of the form mL and mG, where m is a multiple that varies from 1 to 10 in increments of 1. The resulting chart should be like the ones illustrated in the chapter except that the horizontal axis should now show m.

4. Change the application so that the risky venture has three possible outcomes: a "large" gain G, a smaller gain g, and a loss L. The associated probabilities should be inputs that sum to 1. The user should now be allowed to perform a sensitivity analysis on G, g, or L. However, g should always be less than G.

Simulation of a Multiserver Queue

24

24.1 Introduction

As we illustrated in Chapter 20, spreadsheet simulation usually means creating a spreadsheet model with random numbers in certain cells and then replicating the model with a data table, an add-in such as @Risk, or VBA. This chapter illustrates a simulation model that is very difficult to model with spreadsheet formulas because of all the timing and bookkeeping involved. A more natural approach is to take care of all the model's logic in VBA and then simply report the results on a worksheet.

The model we consider is a multiserver queueing model. Customers arrive at random times to a service center, such as a bank. There are several identical servers, identical in the sense that they can all serve all customers with the same mean service time. If a customer arrives and all servers are busy, the customer joins the end of a single queue. However, we assume there is a maximum number of customers allowed in the queue. If the queue is already full when a customer arrives, this customer is turned away. At the beginning of the simulation, there are no customers in the system. We then simulate the system for a user-defined length of time. At this time, no further arrivals are allowed to enter the system, but customers already present are served. The simulation terminates when the last customer departs. The model developed here assumes the times between arrivals and the service times are exponentially distributed.

The purpose of the simulation is to simulate the system for the prescribed amount of time and, as it runs, to collect statistics on the system behavior. At the end, we want to display measures such as the average amount of time in queue for a typical customer, the fraction of time a typical server is busy, the fraction of all arriving customers who are turned away, and others.

New Learning Objective: VBA

- To learn how to use VBA to take care of all the timing and bookkeeping details in a queueing simulation.

New Learning Objective: Non-VBA

- To understand the effect of system inputs (arrival rate, mean service time, number of servers) on system outputs (average time in queue, average number in queue, and others) in a typical queueing model.

24.2   Functionality of the Application

The application allows the user to change six inputs to the queueing model: (1) the time unit (minute or hour, say), (2) the customer arrival rate to the system, (3) the mean service time per customer, (4) the number of servers, (5) the maximum number of customers allowed in the system, and (6) the "closing time" (the time when no more customers are allowed to enter the system). The simulation then runs for the specified amount of time and keeps track of many interesting output measures, such as the average amount of time in queue for a typical customer, the fraction of time a typical server is busy, and the fraction of all arriving customers who are turned away. It also tabulates the distribution of the number of customers in the queue and shows this distribution graphically.

24.3   Running the Application

The application is stored in the file **QueueSim.xls**. Upon opening this file, the user sees the Explanation sheet in Figure 24.1. When the button on this form is clicked, the user sees the Report sheet, the top part of which appears in Figure 24.2. This allows the user to change the inputs in the blue border.

Figure 24.1   Explanation sheet

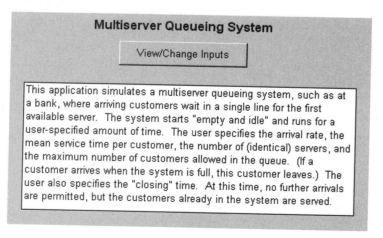

Multiserver Queueing System

View/Change Inputs

This application simulates a multiserver queueing system, such as at a bank, where arriving customers wait in a single line for the first available server. The system starts "empty and idle" and runs for a user-specified amount of time. The user specifies the arrival rate, the mean service time per customer, the number of (identical) servers, and the maximum number of customers allowed in the queue. (If a customer arrives when the system is full, this customer leaves.) The user also specifies the "closing" time. At this time, no further arrivals are permitted, but the customers already in the system are served.

Figure 24.2   Inputs section of Report sheet

	A	B	C	D	E	F	G
1	**Multiple Server Queueing Simulation**						
2							
3	**Inputs**						
4	Time unit	minute		Change any of the inputs in the			
5	Customer arrival rate	1.000	customers/minute	blue cells and then click on the			
6	Mean service time	2.700	minutes	top button to run the simulation.			
7	Number of servers	4					
8	Maximum allowed in queue	15		**Measure of system congestion**			
9	Simulation run time	480	minutes	Traffic intensity	0.675		

A button further down the Report sheet allows the user to run the simulation. It runs for the simulated time shown in cell B9 of Figure 24.2, and then it continues until all customers currently in the system have finished service. When this occurs, statistical measures are calculated and reported in the bottom half of the Report sheet, as in Figure 24.3. The user can then click on the bottom button to show the distribution from row 26 down graphically, as in Figure 24.4. For example, during this 480-minute run, 447 customers arrived, none were turned away, the average time in the queue per customer was half a minute, and the longest time any customer spent in the queue was 4.48 minutes. Also, the typical server was busy 61.8% of the time, and there was no queue at all about 85% of the time. Finally, it took 10.76 minutes to service all customers who were in the system at time 480.

Figure 24.3 Simulation results

	A	B	C	D	E	F	G
11	**Simulation Outputs**						
12	Time last customer leaves	490.76	minutes				
13							
14	Average time in queue per customer	0.30	minutes				
15	Maximum time in queue for any customer	4.48	minutes				
16	Average number of customers in queue	0.27					
17	Maximum number in queue	8					
18							
19	Fraction of time each server is busy	61.8%					
20							
21	Number of customers processed	447					
22	Number of customers turned away	0					
23	Fraction of customers turned away	0.0%					
24							
25	Probability distribution of number in queue						
26	Number in queue	% of time					
27	0	85.03%					
28	1	8.66%					
29	2	3.31%					
30	3	1.61%					
31	4	0.66%					
32	5	0.25%					
33	6	0.11%					
34	7	0.29%					
35	8	0.08%					

Run the simulation

View chart of distribution of number in queue

These results are for a *single* replication of the 480-minute simulation. Clicking repeatedly on the Run button will cause different results to appear. As you will see, these results can differ dramatically, even with the same inputs. Some 480-minute days experience a lot of congestion, and some experience relatively little congestion—just as in real life! It would be possible to embed the current VBA code in a loop over a number of replications. For example, this could simulate 100 480-minute days, each starting empty and idle. Then we could summarize output measures across days. (You will get a chance to do this in an exercise at the end of the chapter.)

Figure 24.4 Distribution of number in queue

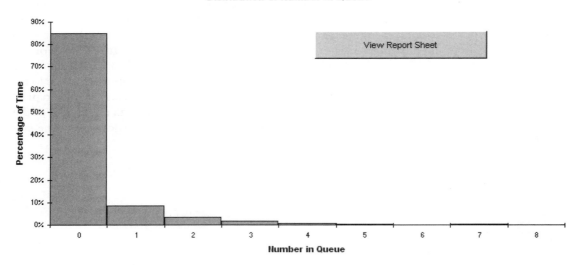

24.4 Setting Up the Excel Sheets

The **QueueSim.xls** file contains two worksheets, named Explanation and Report, and a chart sheet named QChart. The Report sheet can be set up only as a template, with sample inputs in the inputs section and labels only in the outputs section. One measure, called the traffic intensity, can be calculated in cell E9 of the Report sheet (see Figure 24.2) with the formula

=ArriveRate/(NumServers/MeanServeTime)

This is actually the arrival rate divided by the *maximum* service rate of the system (when all servers are busy). If it is greater than 1 or only slightly below 1, the system is likely to experience long waiting times, and many arriving customers are likely to be turned away. However, if the traffic intensity is well less than 1, there will be very little waiting in line, and the servers will tend to have a lot of idle time. Of course, the simulation outputs show exactly what happens on any given run.

The chart sheet can be created at design time with the Chart Wizard, using any sample data in rows 27 down in the Report sheet. Then it can be linked to the actual data at run time.

24.5 Getting Started with the VBA

The application includes only a module—no user forms and no references. Once the module is added, the Project Explorer window will appear as in Figure 24.5.

Figure 24.5 Project Explorer window

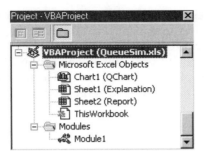

Workbook_Open Code

The Workbook_Open sub guarantees that the Explanation sheet appears when the file is opened, and it hides the Report and QChart sheets.

```
Private Sub Workbook_Open()
    Worksheets("Explanation").Activate
    Range("F4").Select
    Worksheets("Report").Visible = False
    Charts("QChart").Visible = False
End Sub
```

24.6 The Structure of a Queueing Simulation

As we stated in the introduction, there is no "Model" sheet where the logic of the model is captured. Everything is done in memory with VBA. A worksheet is used only as a place to show the inputs and the eventual outputs. Therefore, the VBA code has to take care of all the timing and statistical bookkeeping as the simulation progresses. We explain the general ideas here before looking at the detailed code.

The key idea is one of scheduled events. At any point in time, there is a list of scheduled events of two types. The first type is an arrival. Each time an arrival occurs, the *next* arrival is scheduled at some random time in the future. When it occurs, *another* arrival is scheduled, and so on. The second type of event is a service completion. Each time a customer goes into service (possibly after waiting in the queue), a service completion is scheduled at a random time in the future.

It is important to understand that *nothing happens*, in terms of computer code, between events. There is a simulation "clock" that is updated from one event time to the next. All of the "action" occurs at these event times.

The overall logic of the simulation is placed inside a Do loop, which continues until the clock time is past the closing time and all customers have been cleared from the system. Each pass through the loop deals with a single event—the next (most imminent) event. It is implemented with the following four subroutines.

FindNextEvent Sub

This sub is the key to any queueing simulation. It scans through the list of all scheduled events and finds the most imminent one. For example, it might find that the next event is a departure from server 3 that will occur at clock time 100.47. It would then reset the clock to time 100.47 and return the information about the next event (a service completion from server 3). The next time through, the clock would be reset from 100.47 to the time of the *next* event.

UpdateStatistics Sub

This sub, always called right after the FindNextEvent sub, updates any statistical counters with information since the previous event time. As an example, suppose the clock has just been reset to time 100.47 and that the previous clock time was 99.89. Also, suppose there were 3 customers in the queue from time 99.89 to time 100.47. (Remember that nothing happens between events, so the number in the queue has to remain constant during this time interval.) Then if we have a statistical variable called TotalTimeInQ that accumulates the total customer-minutes spent in the queue, we will add 3 times the difference 100.47 − 99.89 to the previous value of this variable.

Arrival Sub

If the FindNextEvent sub determines that the next event is an arrival, the following logic is played out.

- Schedule the time of the next arrival. If this time is after closing time, disallow the next arrival and don't schedule any future arrivals.
- Check whether the queue is already full. If it is, turn this customer away, and add 1 to the number of customers turned away.
- Check whether all servers are busy. If they are, put this arrival at the end of the queue and keep track of his arrival time to the system (for later statistics). Otherwise, find an idle server, place this customer in service, and schedule a service completion.

Departure Sub

If the FindNextEvent sub determines that the next event is a departure from a particular server, the following logic is played out.

- Increase the number of completed customers by 1.
- Check whether there is anyone in the queue. If there is no queue, decrease the number of busy servers by 1, and do *not* schedule a new departure event for this server. Otherwise, if there is at least one customer in the queue, keep this server busy with the customer at the front of the queue, move all other customers up one space in the queue, and schedule a departure event for this server.

Outputs

Once the clock time is past closing time and all customers have departed, the only thing left to do is report the outputs for the simulation. Some outputs must be calculated first. Other than counters such as the number of customers turned away, the outputs come in two categories: **customer averages** and **time averages**.

A typical customer average is the average time spent in queue per customer. To obtain this average, we keep track of a variable (called SumOfTimesInQ) that sums the queueing times of all customers. Then at the end of the simulation, we divide it by the number of customers who have completed service to obtain the desired average.

A typical time average is the average number of customers in the queue. To obtain this average, we keep track of a variable (called TotalTimeInQ) that sums the total number of customer-minutes spent in the queue. For example, if 6 customers wait in queue for half a minute, this contributes 3 customer-minutes to the total. Then at the end of the simulation, we divide TotalTimeInQ by the final clock time to obtain the desired average. (Can you convince yourself why this gives us what we want?)

Another typical time average is the average server utilization, defined as the fraction of time a typical server is busy. To obtain this average, we keep track of a variable (called TotalTimeBusy) that sums the total number of server-minutes spent serving customers. Then at the end of the simulation, we divide TotalTimeBusy by the final clock time to obtain the average number of servers busy, and we then divide this ratio by the number of servers to obtain the desired server utilization.

The Need for Careful Programming

The logic of most queueing simulations is really quite straightforward—we just "play out" the events as they occur through time. However, the devil is in the details! Queueing simulations are notoriously difficult to get correct. Part of the reason is that there are so many interrelated details. Perhaps an even more important reason is that we don't know what the "answers" ought to be, so it is often not clear whether a queueing simulation is working correctly or not! (We can only imagine how many supposedly correct simulations out there are really wrong.)

Our intent is not to scare you away. Rather, it is to emphasize the need for careful programming. At the very least, variables and subroutines should be named meaningfully. A variable's name should leave little doubt about what it represents. Also, queueing simulations should probably be commented more extensively than any other programs in this book. This clearly helps people who read the program, but it also helps you, the programmer, to understand your own logic.

24.7 The VBA Code in the Module

Web Help   For more explanation of the code in this application, visit our Web site at http://www.indiana.edu/~mgtsci and download the **Code Explanation - QueueSim.doc** file.

Now let's take a look at the code for this application. The following list separates the module-level variables into three categories for ease of interpretation. The system parameters are the user inputs. The system status indicators define the current status of the system at any point in time. The statistical variables are the "bookkeeping" variables that are used eventually to calculate the simulation outputs. You should read these definitions carefully.

Option Statements and Public Variables

```
Option Explicit

' System parameters
'   MeanIATime - mean interarrival time (reciprocal of arrival rate)
'   MeanServeTime - mean service time
'   NumServers - number of servers
'   MaxAllowedInQ - maximum number of customers allowed in the queue
'   CloseTime - clock time when no future arrivals are accepted

Dim MeanIATime As Single, MeanServeTime As Single, NumServers As Integer, _
    MaxAllowedInQ As Integer, CloseTime As Single

' System status indicators
'   NumInQ - number of customers currently in the queue
'   NumBusy - number of servers currently busy
'   ClockTime - current clock time, where the inital clock time is 0
'   TimeOfLastEvent - clock time of previous event
'   EventScheduled(i) - True or False, depending on whether an event of type i is
'       scheduled or not, for i>=0, where i=0 corresponds to arrivals and i from 1 to
'       NumServers corresponds to server i service completions
'   TimeOfNextEvent(i) - the scheduled clock time of the next event of type i (only
'       defined when EventScheduled(i) is True

Dim NumInQ As Integer, NumBusy As Integer, ClockTime As Single, _
    TimeOfLastEvent As Single, EventScheduled() As Boolean, TimeOfNextEvent() As Single

' Statistical variables
'   NumServed - number of customers who have completed service so far
'   NumLost - number of customers who have been turned away (because of a full queue)
'       so far
'   MaxNumInQ - maximum number who have been in the queue at any point in time so far
'   MaxTimeInQ - maximum time any customer has spent in the queue so far
'   TimeOfArrival(i) - arrival time of the customer currently in the i-th place in the
'       queue, for i>=1
'   TotalTimeInQ - total customer-time units spent in the queue so far
'   TotalTimeBusy - total server-time units spent serving customers so far
'   SumOfQTimes - sum of all times in the queue so far, where the sum is over customers
'       who have completed their times in the queue
'   QTimeArray(i) - amount of time there have been exactly i customers in the queue,
'       for i>=0

Dim NumServed As Long, NumLost As Integer, MaxNumInQ As Integer, MaxTimeInQ As Single, _
    TimeOfArrival() As Single, TotalTimeInQ As Single, TotalTimeBusy As Single, _
    SumOfQTimes As Single, QTimeArray() As Single
```

The **Main** sub is attached to the top button on the Report sheet. It runs the simulation. It first calls VBA's **Randomize** function to ensure that *different* random numbers will be used for each simulation, it clears old results from the Report sheet, it captures the inputs from the Model sheet, and it calls the **Initialize** sub to initialize the simulation (see explanation below). Then it enters a Do loop, as explained in the previous section. This loop processes one event after another until the clock time is eventually past closing time and all customers have been cleared from the system. Finally, it calls the **Report** sub to calculate the outputs and place them on the Report sheet.

Main Code

```
Sub Main()
    Dim NextEventType As Integer, FinishedServer As Integer
' Always generate new random numbers.
    Randomize
' Clear previous results, if any, from the Report sheet.
    Call ClearOldResults
' Get inputs from the Report Sheet.
    MeanIATime = 1 / Range("ArriveRate")
    MeanServeTime = Range("MeanServeTime")
    NumServers = Range("NumServers")
    MaxAllowedInQ = Range("MaxAllowedInQ")
    CloseTime = Range("CloseTime")
' The next two arrays have an element for arrivals (element 0) and one for each server.
    ReDim EventScheduled(NumServers + 1)
    ReDim TimeOfNextEvent(NumServers + 1)
' Set counters, status indicators to 0 and schedule first arrival.
    Call Initialize
' Keep simulating until the last customer has left.
    Do
' Find the time and type of the next event, and reset the clock. Capture the index of
' the finished server in case the next event is a service completion.
        Call FindNextEvent(NextEventType, FinishedServer)
' Update statistics since the last event.
        Call UpdateStatistics
' NextEventType is 1 for an arrival, 2 for a departure.
        If NextEventType = 1 Then
            Call Arrival
        Else
            Call Departure(FinishedServer)
        End If
    Loop Until ClockTime > CloseTime And NumBusy = 0
' Report the results.
    Call Report
End Sub
```

ClearOldResults Code

The **ClearOldResults** sub clears all outputs from a previous run from the output section of the Report sheet.

```
Sub ClearOldResults()
    With Worksheets("Report")
        .Range("B12:B23").ClearContents
```

```
        With .Range("A26")
            Range(.Offset(1, 0), .Offset(0, 1).End(xlDown)).ClearContents
        End With
    End With
End Sub
```

Initialize Code

Most of the **Initialize** sub involves setting status indicators and statistical variables to 0. (Remember that the simulation starts at clock time 0 with no customers in the system—empty and idle.) Note in particular how the array QTimeArray is initialized. By the time the simulation has finished, we want an element in this array for each number of customers that have ever been in the queue. At time 0, however, we don't know how long the queue will eventually grow. Therefore, we initialize QTimeArray to have only one element, the 0 element. We will then redimension it appropriately as the queue grows later on.

The Initialize sub also schedules the first event—the time of the first arrival. It does this by setting EventScheduled(0) to True and generating a random time for this event in TimeOfNextEvent(0). However, it sets EventScheduled(i) to False for i from 1 to NumServers. This is because all of the servers are currently idle, so they should not have scheduled service completions.

A note on generating exponential random numbers. The random inter-arrival times and service times in this simulation are all exponentially distributed. (This is an assumption frequently made in queueing models.) If an exponential distribution has mean m, then we can generate a random number from it with the VBA expression

```
- m * Log(Rnd)
```

Here, **Rnd** is VBA's function for generating *uniformly* distributed random numbers from 0 to 1, and **Log** is VBA's natural logarithm function. The minus sign is required because the logarithm of a number between 0 and 1 is *negative*. In general, the program contains several expressions such as

```
TimeOfNextEvent(i) = ClockTime - MeanServeTime * Log(Rnd)
```

This statement schedules the time of the next event (in this case, a service completion) by adding an exponentially distributed random time to the current clock time. (Again, it looks like subtraction, but it is actually *adding* a positive time to the clock time.)

```
Sub Initialize()
    Dim i As Integer
' Initialize system status indicators.
    ClockTime = 0
    NumBusy = 0
    NumInQ = 0
    TimeOfLastEvent = 0
```

```
' Initialize statistical variables.
    NumServed = 0
    NumLost = 0
    SumOfQTimes = 0
    MaxTimeInQ = 0
    TotalTimeInQ = 0
    MaxNumInQ = 0
    TotalTimeBusy = 0
' Redimension the QTimeArray array to have one element (the 0 element, for
' the amount of time when there are 0 customers in the queue).
    ReDim QTimeArray(1)
    QTimeArray(0) = 0

' Schedule an arrival from the exponential distribution.
    EventScheduled(0) = True
    TimeOfNextEvent(0) = -MeanIATime * Log(Rnd)
' Don't schedule any departures because there are no customers initially
' in the system.
    For i = 1 To NumServers
        EventScheduled(i) = False
    Next
End Sub
```

FindNextEvent Code

The **FindNextEvent** sub is the key to the simulation. When it is called, there are typically several events scheduled to occur in the future (such as an arrival and several service completions). The NextEventTime variable captures the minimum of these—the time of the most imminent event. If the most imminent event is an arrival, NextEventType is set to 1. If it is a departure, NextEventType is set to 2, and FinishedServer records the index of the server who just completed service. In either case, ClockTime is reset to NextEventTime. This last operation is crucial. If ClockTime were not updated, the simulation would never end!

```
Sub FindNextEvent(NextEventType As Integer, FinishedServer As Integer)
    Dim i As Integer, NextEventTime As Single
' NextEventTime will be the minimum of the scheduled event times. Start by setting it
' to a large value.
    NextEventTime = 10 * CloseTime
' Find type and time of the next (most imminent) scheduled event. Note that there is a
' potential event scheduled for the next arrival (indexed as 0) and for each server
' completion (indexed as 1 to NumServers).
    For i = 0 To NumServers
        If EventScheduled(i) Then
' If the current event is the most imminent so far, record it.
            If TimeOfNextEvent(i) < NextEventTime Then
                NextEventTime = TimeOfNextEvent(i)
                If i = 0 Then
                    NextEventType = 1
                Else
' For a departure event, also record the index of the server who finished.
                    NextEventType = 2
                    FinishedServer = i
                End If
            End If
        End If
    Next
```

```
' Update the clock to the time of the next event.
    ClockTime = NextEventTime
End Sub
```

UpdateStatistics Code

The **UpdateStatistics** sub first defines TimSinceLastEvent as the elapsed time since the previous event. At the end, it resets TimeOfLastEvent to the current clock time (in anticipation of the *next* time this sub is called). In between, it updates any statistics with what has occurred during the elapsed time. For example, QTimeArray(i) in general is the amount of time exactly i customers have been in the queue. During the time since the previous event, the number in the queue has been NumInQ, so TimeSinceLastEvent is added to the array element QTimeArray(NumInQ). The next two lines add the number of customer-time units in the queue and the number of server-time units being busy, respectively, to the TotalTimeInQ and TotalTimeBusy variables. If there were other outputs we wanted to keep track of, they would probably be updated in this sub.

```
Sub UpdateStatistics()
    Dim TimeSinceLastEvent As Single
' TimeSinceLastEvent is the time since the last update.
    TimeSinceLastEvent = ClockTime - TimeOfLastEvent
' Update statistical variables.
    QTimeArray(NumInQ) = QTimeArray(NumInQ) + TimeSinceLastEvent
    TotalTimeInQ = TotalTimeInQ + NumInQ * TimeSinceLastEvent
    TotalTimeBusy = TotalTimeBusy + NumBusy * TimeSinceLastEvent
' Reset TimeOfLastEvent to the current time.
    TimeOfLastEvent = ClockTime
End Sub
```

Arrival Code

The **Arrival** sub plays out the logic described in the previous section for an arrival event. The comments should clarify the details. Note in particular the case where the arrival must enter the queue. A check is made to see whether this makes the queue length longer than it has ever been before. If it is, the MaxNumInQ variable is updated, and the QTimeArray and TimeOfArrival arrays are redimensioned (to have an extra element). You can think of the TimeOfArrival values as "tags" placed on the customers. Each tag shows when the customer arrived to the system. When a customer eventually goes into service, her tag allows us to calculate how long she has spent in the queue: the current clock time minus her TimeOfArrival value.

```
Sub Arrival()
    Dim i As Integer
' Schedule the next arrival.
    TimeOfNextEvent(0) = ClockTime - MeanIATime * Log(Rnd)
```

```
' Cut off the arrival stream if it is past closing time.
   If TimeOfNextEvent(0) > CloseTime Then
        EventScheduled(0) = False
   End If
' If the queue is already full, this customer is turned away.
   If NumInQ = MaxAllowedInQ Then
        NumLost = NumLost + 1
        Exit Sub
   End If
' Check if all servers are busy.
   If NumBusy = NumServers Then
' All servers are busy, so put this customer at the end of the queue.
        NumInQ = NumInQ + 1
' If the queue is now longer than it has been before, update MaxNumInQ and redimension
' arrays appropriately.
        If NumInQ > MaxNumInQ Then
            MaxNumInQ = NumInQ
' The "+1" in the next line is because QTimeArray is 0-based, so its elements are now
' 0 to MaxNumInQ.
            ReDim Preserve QTimeArray(MaxNumInQ + 1)
' TimeOfArrival is 1-based, with elements 1 to MaxNumInQ.
            ReDim Preserve TimeOfArrival(1 To MaxNumInQ)
        End If
' Keep track of this customer's arrival time (for later stats).
        TimeOfArrival(NumInQ) = ClockTime
   Else
' The customer can go directly into service, so update the number of servers busy.
        NumBusy = NumBusy + 1
' This loop searches for the first idle server and schedules a departure event for
' this server.
        For i = 1 To NumServers
            If Not EventScheduled(i) Then
                EventScheduled(i) = True
                TimeOfNextEvent(i) = ClockTime - MeanServeTime * Log(Rnd)
                Exit For
            End If
        Next
   End If
End Sub
```

Departure Code

The **Departure** sub plays out the logic described in the previous section for a service completion event. It takes one argument to identify the server who just completed service. Again, the comments should clarify the details. The final For loop is important. We want the TimeOfArrival "tags" to remain with the customers as they move up one space in the queue. Therefore, the TimeOfArrival(1) value, the time of arrival of the first person in line becomes TimeOfArrival(2) (since this person used to be second in line), TimeOfArrival(2) becomes TimeOfArrival(3), and so on.

```
Sub Departure(FinishedServer As Integer)
    Dim TimeInQ As Single, i As Integer
' Update number of customers who have finished.
    NumServed = NumServed + 1
```

```
' Check if any customers are waiting in queue.
   If NumInQ = 0 Then
' No one is in the queue, so make the server who just finished idle.
        NumBusy = NumBusy - 1
        EventScheduled(FinishedServer) = False
   Else
' At least one person is in the queue, so take customer from front of queue into
' service.
        NumInQ = NumInQ - 1
' TimeInQ is the time this customer has been waiting in line.
        TimeInQ = ClockTime - TimeOfArrival(1)
' Check if this is a new maximum time in queue.
        If TimeInQ > MaxTimeInQ Then
            MaxTimeInQ = TimeInQ
        End If
' Update the total of all customer queue times so far.
        SumOfQTimes = SumOfQTimes + TimeInQ
' Schedule departure for this customer with the same server who just finished.
        TimeOfNextEvent(FinishedServer) = ClockTime - MeanServeTime * Log(Rnd)
' Move everyone else in line up one space.
        For i = 1 To NumInQ
            TimeOfArrival(i) = TimeOfArrival(i + 1)
        Next
   End If
End Sub
```

Report Code

The **Report** sub, called at the end of the simulation, calculates customer and time averages and then reports the results in prenamed ranges in the Report sheet. It also names a couple of ranges where the distribution of queue length is stored. These are used later for updating the corresponding chart.

```
Sub Report()
    Dim i As Integer, AvgTimeInQ As Single, AvgNumInQ As Single, AvgServersBusy As Single
' Calculate averages.
    AvgTimeInQ = SumOfQTimes / NumServed
    AvgNumInQ = TotalTimeInQ / ClockTime
    AvgServersBusy = TotalTimeBusy / ClockTime
' QTimeArray records, for each value from 0 to MaxNumInQ, the percentage of time that
' many customers were waiting in the queue.
    For i = 0 To MaxNumInQ
        QTimeArray(i) = QTimeArray(i) / ClockTime
    Next
' Enter simulate results in named ranges.
    Range("FinalTime") = ClockTime
    Range("NumServed") = NumServed
    Range("AvgTimeInQ") = AvgTimeInQ
    Range("MaxTimeInQ") = MaxTimeInQ
    Range("AvgNumInQ") = AvgNumInQ
    Range("MaxNumInQ") = MaxNumInQ
    Range("AvgServerUtil") = AvgServersBusy / NumServers
    Range("NumLost") = NumLost
    Range("PctLost").Formula = "=NumLost/(NumLost + NumServed)"
```

```
' Enter the queue length distribution from row 27 down, and name the two columns.
    With Range("A27")
        For i = 0 To MaxNumInQ
            .Offset(i, 0) = i
            .Offset(i, 1) = QTimeArray(i)
        Next
        Range(.Offset(0, 0), .Offset(MaxNumInQ, 0)).Name = "NumInQ"
        Range(.Offset(0, 1), .Offset(MaxNumInQ, 1)).Name = "PctOfTime"
    End With
    Range("A2").Select
End Sub
```

UpdateChart Code

The QChart sheet already contains a chart (built at design time) of the queue length distribution. The **UpdateChart** sub unhides and activates this chart sheet, and it updates the chart with the most recent data in the Report sheet.

```
Sub UpdateChart()
    With Charts("QChart")
        .Visible = True
        .Activate
    End With
    With ActiveChart
        With .SeriesCollection(1)
            .Values = Range("PctOfTime")
            .XValues = Range("NumInQ")
        End With
        .Deselect
    End With
End Sub
```

ViewChangeInputs, ViewReport Code

These last two subs are for navigational purposes. The **ViewChangeInputs** sub is attached to the button on the Explanation sheet. It unhides and activates the Report sheet so that the user can view and change any inputs before running the simulation. It also clears any old outputs from the Report sheet. The **ViewReport** sub simply activates the Report sheet. It is attached to a button on the QChart sheet.

```
Sub ViewChangeInputs()
    Call ClearOldResults
    Call ViewReport
End Sub

Sub ViewReport()
    Worksheets("Report").Activate
    Range("A2").Select
End Sub
```

24.8 Summary

A typical queueing simulation program, as illustrated in this chapter, is considerably different from almost all of the other applications in this book. The reason is that all of the logic must be done behind the scenes in VBA code—there is no spreadsheet model. Although the overall flow of the program is conceptually straightforward, there are a host of timing and bookkeeping details to keep straight, which means that the programmer must be extremely careful. However, we know of no better type of program for sharpening your programming skills. Besides, a successfully completed queueing simulation program can provide many important insights into the system being modeled.

PROGRAMMING EXERCISES

1. Change the simulation so that there is no upper limit on the number allowed in the queue. This means that no customers will be turned away because the system is full. (Make sure you delete any variables that are no longer needed.)
2. Continuing the previous exercise, assume that each customer who arrives to the system looks at the queue (if there is one) and then decides whether to join. Assume the probability that a customer joins the queue is of the form r^n, where r is an input between 0 and 1 (probably close to 1), and n is the current number of customers in the queue. We say that a customer **balks** if she decides not to join. Keep track of the number of customers who balk.
3. Change the simulation so that the servers have different mean service times, so that some tend to be faster than others. Assume that an arrival always chooses the fastest idle server (when more than one are idle). Now report the fraction of time each server is busy.
4. Change the simulation so that all activity stops at closing time—the customers currently in the system are *not* serviced any further. Report the number of customers still in the system at closing time. (Make sure you update statistics from the time of the last event until closing time.)
5. (More difficult) This exercise is based on the "express" lines you see at some service centers. Assume that arriving customers are designated as "regular" or "express" customers when they arrive. The probability that an arrival is an express customer is an input between 0 and 1. Express customers have a relatively small mean service time. The mean service time for regular customers is larger. One of the servers is an "express" server. This server handles only the express customers. The other servers can serve either type of customer. The customers wait (at least conceptually, if not physically) in two separate lines. They are served in first-come-first-served order as servers become available, although the express server cannot serve a regular customer. If an express customer enters, and a regular server and the express server are both idle, assume that the customer goes to the express server. Change the simulation appropriately to handle this situation, and keep

track of separate statistics for express customers and regular customers, as well as for regular servers and the express server.

6. Change the program so that the current simulation is embedded in a For loop from 1 to 100. Each time through the loop, one simulation is run, and its outputs (you can select which ones) are reported on a Replications sheet. After all 100 simulations have run, summarize the selected outputs on a Summary sheet. For each output, use the following summary measures: minimum, maximum, average, standard deviation, median, and 5th and 95th percentiles.

An Application for Pricing European and American Options

25.1 Introduction

This application prices European and American call and put options. A European call option on a certain stock allows the owner of the option to purchase a share of the stock for a certain price, called the exercise (or strike) price, on a certain date in the future, called the exercise date. A put option is the same except that it allows the owner to *sell* a share on the exercise date. An American option is similar, but it can be exercised at *any* time between the current date and the exercise date.

The owner of a call option hopes that the price of the stock will *increase* above the exercise price. Then the option can be exercised and the owner can make the difference by buying the stock at the exercise price and immediately selling it back at the actual price. The opposite is true for a put option. Then the owner hopes that the price of the stock will *decrease* below the exercise price so that he can sell it for a relatively high price and immediately cover his position by buying it back at a cheaper price. The question answered by this application is how much these options are worth.

It is relatively easy to price European options. This is done with the famous Black-Scholes formula. American options are considerably more difficult to price. The usual method is to use a technique called **binomial trees**, as is done in this application. In addition, it can be shown that if no dividends are given, as we assume here, then it is never optimal to exercise an American call option early (before the exercise date). However, this is not true for American put options. For them, there is an **early exercise boundary** that specifies when the put should be exercised. More specifically, this boundary consists of a cutoff price for each date in the future up to the exercise date. If the actual stock price falls below this cutoff price on any particular date, then the put should be exercised at that time. This application calculates the early exercise boundary for American put options (if the user requests it).

New Learning Objectives: VBA

- To gain practice working with dates, including the use of a user-defined function for calculating the number of days between two specified dates, excluding weekends.
- To learn how to manipulate Excel's status bar to indicate the progress of a program.

- To learn how to deal with literal double quotes inside a string.
- To learn how to use Excel's Goal Seek tool with VBA.

New Learning Objective: Non-VBA

- To gain some knowledge of how options work and how they are priced, including the use of the Black-Scholes formula for European options and binomial trees for American options.

25.2 Functionality of the Application

The application has the following functionality:

1. It first asks the user for the inputs required to price any option. These include (1) the current price of the stock, (2) the exercise price, (3) the current date, (4) the exercise date, (5) the annual risk-free rate of interest, (6) the volatility of the stock price (the standard deviation of its annual return), and (7) the type of option (European or American, call or put).
2. It then calculates the price of the option and displays it in a message box.
3. If the option is an American put option, the user can also request the early exercise boundary.

There are two underlying assumptions. First, it is assumed that there are no dividends for the stock. If there were, the calculations would need to be modified. Second, it is assumed that trading days include weekdays but not weekends. This assumption is used to calculate the *duration* of the option, the number of trading days between the current date and the exercise date. It would be possible to exclude some weekdays as trading days (the Fourth of July, for example), but this would add complexity to the application, and it is not done here.

25.3 Running the Application

The application is stored in the file **StockOptions.xls**. Upon opening this file, the user sees the Explanation sheet in Figure 25.1. When the button on this form is clicked, the dialog box in Figure 25.2 appears. The inputs on the left are the current values in the EuroModel sheet (more about it below). Of course, any of these can be changed.

If the user selects any type of option other than an American put, the price of the option is calculated "behind the scenes" in the EuroModel or the AmerModel sheet and is displayed in a message box, as shown in Figure 25.3.

For an American put option, the message box in Figure 25.4 appears. If the user clicks on No, the same type of message as in Figure 25.3 appears. If the user clicks on Yes, then the early exercise boundary is calculated and is reported in the AmerPutReport sheet, as shown in Figure 25.5. This particular example assumes that the current date is June 1, the exercise date is June 30, and the exercise price

Figure 25.1 Explanation sheet

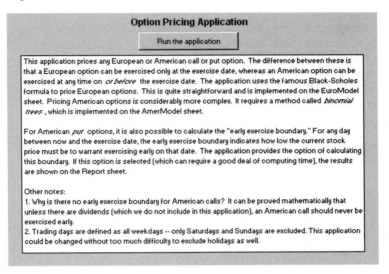

Figure 25.2 User inputs dialog box

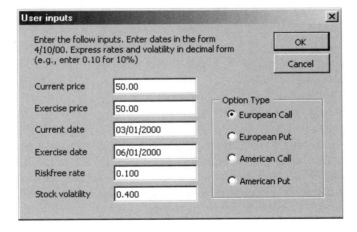

Figure 25.3 Message box display of option price

Figure 25.4   Request for early exercise boundary

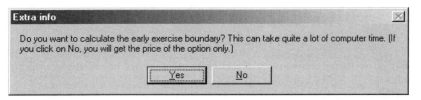

Figure 25.5   Early exercise boundary report

	A	B	C	D	E	F
1	**Option price and early exercise boundary for the American put option**					
2						
3	Price of option	$2.15	View Explanation Sheet			
4						
5	Early exercise boundary: exercise only if stock price on this day is below the value in column B.					
6	Trading date	Boundary price				
7	06/02/00	$41.32				
8	06/05/00	$41.42				
9	06/06/00	$41.61				
10	06/07/00	$41.92				
11	06/08/00	$41.95				
12	06/09/00	$42.29				
13	06/12/00	$42.40				
14	06/13/00	$42.64				
15	06/14/00	$43.07				
16	06/15/00	$43.07				
17	06/16/00	$43.48				
18	06/19/00	$43.77				
19	06/20/00	$43.95				
20	06/21/00	$44.48				
21	06/22/00	$44.80				
22	06/23/00	$45.04				
23	06/26/00	$45.72				
24	06/27/00	$46.64				
25	06/28/00	$47.68				
26	06/29/00	$48.81				
27	06/30/00	$50.00				

is $50. If this were a European put, the owner would wait until June 30 and then exercise the option only if the actual stock price were less than $50. However, the report indicates that the American put should be exercised on, say, June 14 if it hasn't been exercised already and the actual price on June 14 is less than $43.07. By the way, the European put with these same inputs is priced at $2.06. The American option provides more flexibility, so it is priced slightly higher at $2.15.

25.4   Setting Up the Excel Sheets

The **StockOptions.xls** file contains four worksheets: the Explanation sheet, the EuroModel sheet, the AmerModel sheet, and the AmerPutReport sheet. The EuroModel sheet, shown in Figure 25.6, can be set up completely at design time, using any trial values in the input cells. The **duration** of the option (number of trading days until the exercise date) is calculated in cell B12 with a function called

TradeDays written just for this application (see the code at the end of the chapter). The formulas in cells B15, B16, E15, E16, and B18 implement the Black-Scholes formula. (These formulas are rather technical. See the **StockOptions.xls** file for the details.)

Figure 25.6 EuroModel sheet

	A	B	C	D	E	F
1	**Black-Scholes model for pricing European puts, calls**					
2						
3	**Input data**					
4	Type of option (1 for call, 2 for put)	2		**Range names used:**		
5	Stock price	$50.00		EOptType - B4		
6	Exercise price	$50.00		CurrPrice - B5		
7	Today's date	01-Jun-00		ExerPrice - B6		
8	Exercise date	30-Jun-00		CurrDate - B7		
9	Riskfree interest rate	0.100		ExerDate - B8		
10	StDev of annual return	0.400		RFRate - B9		
11				Vol - B10		
12	Duration (trading days)	21		Dur - B12		
13						
14	**Quantities for Black-Scholes formula**					
15	d1	0.12788968		N(d1)	0.449118	
16	d2	0.01420996		N(d2)	0.494331	
17						
18	Option price	$2.06				

The AmerModel sheet sets up a **binomial tree** for calculating the price of an American call or put. A finished version of this sheet appears in Figure 25.7 for a call option with duration 6 days. The binomial tree calculations are performed in the two triangular ranges, which in general have as many rows and columns as the duration (plus 1). Without going into the technical details, we will simply state that the option price is always in the upper left corner of the bottom triangle—in this case, about $1.13.[41] These triangular ranges must be calculated at run time. The only template that can be created at design time appears in Figure 25.8.

Finally, the AmerPutReport sheet, shown earlier in Figure 25.5, must be filled in almost entirely at run time. The only template that can be set up at design time contains labels, as shown in Figure 25.9.

25.5 Getting Started with the VBA

The application includes one user form named InputsForm and a module. The Solver is never used, so no reference to the Solver add-in is necessary. (The Goal Seek tool *is* used, but no reference is necessary for it.) Once these items are added, the Project Explorer window will appear as in Figure 25.10.

---

[41]A good explanation of binomial trees and how they can be implemented in Excel appears in Chapter 56 of Winston, W., *Financial Models Using Simulation and Optimization*, Palisade Corporation, 1998.

Figure 25.7 Finished AmerModel sheet

	A	B	C	D	E	F	G	H
1	**Binomial tree model for pricing American calls, puts**							
2								
3	**Input data**							
4	Type of option (1 for call, 2 for put)	1						
5	Stock price	$50.00						
6	Exercise price	$50.00						
7	Today's date	01-Jun-00						
8	Exercise date	10-Jun-00						
9	Riskfree interest rate	10%						
10	StDev of annual return	40%						
11								
12	Duration (trading days)	6						
13								
14	**Parameters for binomial tree**							
15	Up factor	1.025						
16	Down factor	0.975						
17	Probability of up	0.502						
18	Probability of down	0.498						
19								
20	Future prices	0	1	2	3	4	5	6
21	0	$50.00	51.25586	52.54326	53.863	55.21589	56.60276	58.02446
22	1		48.77491	50	51.25586	52.54326	53.863	55.21589
23	2			47.57984	48.77491	50	51.25586	52.54326
24	3				46.41405	47.57984	48.77491	50
25	4					45.27682	46.41405	47.57984
26	5						44.16746	45.27682
27	6							43.08528
28								
29	Option values	0	1	2	3	4	5	6
30	0	1.12568321	0.528689	0.15189	1.76E-15	0	0	0
31	1		1.725526	0.907426	0.304609	3.53E-15	0	0
32	2			2.547387	1.513295	0.610879	7.09E-15	0
33	3				3.585952	2.420161	1.225089	1.42E-14
34	4					4.723179	3.585952	2.420161
35	5						5.832542	4.723179
36	6							6.914724

Figure 25.8 Template for AmerModel sheet

	A	B	C
1	**Binomial tree model for pricing American calls, puts**		
2			
3	**Input data**		
4	Type of option (1 for call, 2 for put)	1	
5	Stock price	$50.00	
6	Exercise price	$50.00	
7	Today's date	01-Jun-00	
8	Exercise date	10-Jun-00	
9	Riskfree interest rate	10%	
10	StDev of annual return	40%	
11			
12	Duration (trading days)	6	
13			
14	**Parameters for binomial tree**		
15	Up factor	1.025	
16	Down factor	0.975	
17	Probability of up	0.502	
18	Probability of down	0.498	
19			
20	Future prices		

Figure 25.9 Template for AmerPutReport sheet

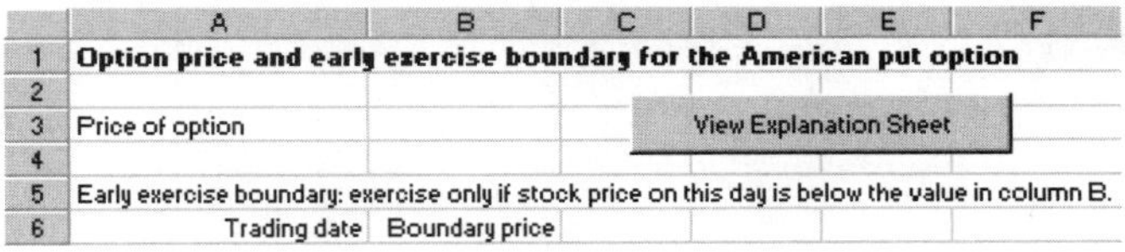

	A	B	C	D	E	F
1	Option price and early exercise boundary for the American put option					
2						
3	Price of option		View Explanation Sheet			
4						
5	Early exercise boundary: exercise only if stock price on this day is below the value in column B.					
6	Trading date	Boundary price				

Figure 25.10 Project Explorer window

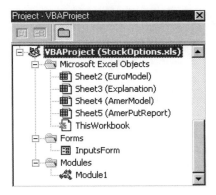

Workbook_Open Code

To guarantee that the Explanation sheet appears when the file is opened, the following code is placed in the ThisWorkbook code window. It also uses a For Each loop to hide all sheets except the Explanation sheet.

```
Private Sub Workbook_Open()
    Dim ws As Worksheet
    Worksheets("Explanation").Activate
    Range("F4").Select
    For Each ws In ActiveWorkbook.Worksheets
        If ws.Name <> "Explanation" Then ws.Visible = False
    Next
End Sub
```

25.6 Designing the User Form and Writing Its Event Code

Web Help   For more explanation of the code in this application, visit our Web site at http://www.indiana.edu/~mgtsci and download the **Code Explanation - StockOptions.doc** file.

The design for the InputsForm, shown in Figure 25.11, contains the usual OK and Cancel buttons, an explanation label, six text boxes and associated labels, and

Figure 25.11 InputsForm design

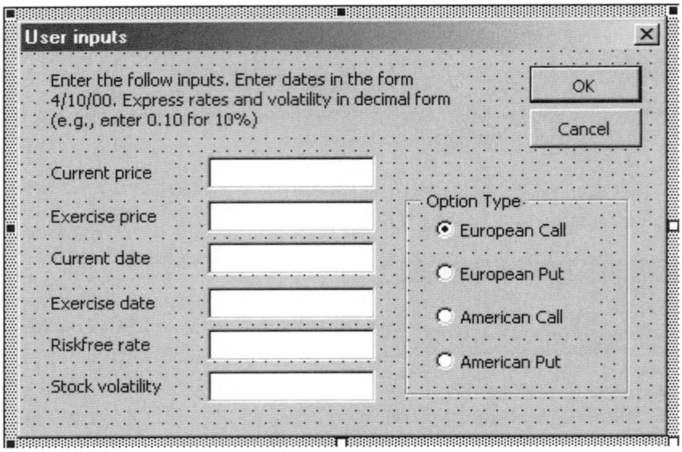

a frame that contains four option buttons. The text boxes are named CPriceBox, EPriceBox, CDateBox, EDateBox, RFRateBox, and VolBox. The option buttons are named ECallOpt, EPutOpt, ACallOpt, and APutOpt.

There are no new ideas in the event code. The **Userform_Initialize** sub loads the input values, if any, from the EuroModel sheet into the text boxes (suitably formatted) and checks the European Call option button by default. The **OKButton_Click** sub does a significant amount of error checking and finally captures the user's choices in a number of public variables for later use. The **CancelButton_Click** sub unloads the form and terminates the program.

A note on dates. Pay particular attention to how VBA's **IsDate** function is used to check for valid dates. This can be very handy. For example, it recognizes that 2/29/96 *is* a valid date, but that 2/29/97 is not! Also, note how an inequality can be used to check whether one date is after another. One date is *after* another if it is *greater* than the other. Finally, note how the dates are formatted with the Format function. The code used here is "mm/dd/yyyy", although a number of other date codes are available.

InputsForm Event Code

```
Private Sub UserForm_Initialize()
' Initialize by checking the European call option and entering the values for the other
' parameters from the corresponding cells on the EuroModel sheet.
    ECallOpt = True
    With Worksheets("EuroModel")
        CPriceBox = Format(.Range("CurrPrice"), "0.00")
        EPriceBox = Format(.Range("ExerPrice"), "0.00")
        CDateBox = Format(.Range("CurrDate"), "mm/dd/yyyy")
        EDateBox = Format(.Range("ExerDate"), "mm/dd/yyyy")
```

```
            RFRateBox = Format(.Range("RFRate"), "0.000")
            VolBox = Format(.Range("Vol"), "0.000")
        End With
End Sub

Private Sub OKButton_Click()
    Dim ctl As Control
' Make sure the non-date boxes have positive numeric values and that the date boxes
' have valid dates.
    For Each ctl In Me.Controls
        If ctl.Name = "CPriceBox" Or ctl.Name = "EPriceBox" Or _
            ctl.Name = "RFRateBox" Or ctl.Name = "VolBox" Then
            If ctl.Value = "" Or Not IsNumeric(ctl) Then
                MsgBox "Enter a positive value in all of the " _
                    & "non-date boxes.", vbInformation, "Invalid entry"
                ctl.SetFocus
                Exit Sub
            End If
            If ctl.Value <= 0 Then
                MsgBox "Enter a positive value in all of the " _
                    & "non-date boxes.", vbInformation, "Invalid entry"
                ctl.SetFocus
                Exit Sub
            End If
        ElseIf ctl.Name = "CDateBox" Or ctl.Name = "EDateBox" Then
            If Not IsDate(ctl) Then
                MsgBox "Enter a valid date in each of the " _
                    & "date boxes.", vbInformation, "Invalid entry"
                ctl.SetFocus
                Exit Sub
            End If
        End If
    Next
' Capture the dates.
    CurrDate = CDateBox
    ExerDate = EDateBox
' Make sure the exercise date is after the current date.
    If CurrDate >= ExerDate Then
        MsgBox "The exercise date must be after the current date.", vbInformation, _
            "Invalid dates"
        CDateBox.SetFocus
        Exit Sub
    End If
' Capture the other inputs and unload the form.
    CurrPrice = CPriceBox
    ExerPrice = EPriceBox
    RFRate = RFRateBox
    Vol = VolBox
    If ECallOpt Then
        OptType = 1
    ElseIf EPutOpt Then
        OptType = 2
    ElseIf ACallOpt Then
        OptType = 3
    Else
        OptType = 4
    End If
    Unload Me
End Sub
```

```
Private Sub CancelButton_Click()
    Unload Me
    End
End Sub
```

25.7 The VBA Code in the Module

The module consists of a **Main** sub that "shows" the InputsForm and then calls the appropriate sub, EuroModel or AmerModel. The **EuroModel** sub is simple because the EuroModel sheet is already set up at design time. However, the **AmerModel** sub is considerably more complex. It has to create all of the formulas for the binomial tree method. In addition, it needs to calculate the early exercise boundary for an American put option. The details in the code will not be spelled out here. They won't make much sense unless you thoroughly understand binomial trees and how they can be used to calculate the option price and the early exercise boundary.[42] We will simply present the code and let the comments speak for themselves.

Option Statements and Public Variables

```
Option Explicit
Option Base 1

' Definitions of public variables:
'    CurrPrice: current stock price
'    ExerPrice: exercise price of option
'    CurrDate: current date (when option is purchased)
'    ExerDate: exercise date of option
'    RFRate: riskfree rate (annual)
'    Vol: volatility of stock
'    OptType: 1 (European call), 2 (European put), 3 (American call), or 4 (American put)
'    Dur: duration of option (in trading days)
'    Cutoff(): an array showing the early exercise boundary for an American put
'    OptPrice: price of the option
'    OptName: "call" or "put"
'    Extra: vbYes or vbNo, indicates whether to calculate the early exercise boundary
'       for an American put
Public CurrPrice As Single, ExerPrice As Single, CurrDate As Date, _
    ExerDate As Date, RFRate As Single, Vol As Single, _
    OptType As Integer, Dur As Integer, Cutoff() As Variant, _
    OptPrice As Single, OptName As String, Extra As Integer
```

Main Code

```
Sub Main()
' Get the user inputs.
    InputsForm.Show
```

---

[42]However, a great exercise is to read the Winston chapter referenced earlier, and then see how the code in this application implements his method.

```
' See whether user wants the early exercise boundary (only for an American put).
    Extra = vbNo
    If OptType = 4 Then
        Extra = MsgBox("Do you want to calculate the early exercise boundary? " _
            & "This can take quite a lot of computer time. (If you click " _
            & "on No, you will get the price of the option only.)", vbYesNo, _
                "Extra info")
    End If
' Define OptName.
    If OptType = 1 Or OptType = 3 Then
        OptName = "call"
    Else
        OptName = "put"
    End If
' Do the appropriate analysis.
    If OptType <= 2 Then
        Call EuroModel
    Else
        Call AmerModel
    End If
End Sub
```

EuroModel Code

The **EuroModel** sub activates the EuroModel sheet, calls the **EnterInputs** sub to enter the user's inputs in the appropriate cells, hides the EuroModel sheet, and displays a message for the option price.

```
Sub EuroModel()
' This sub shows the EuroModel sheet, enters the user inputs in input cells, and
' displays the price of the option.  The formulas for calculating the Black-Scholes
' price are already in the sheet.
    Dim OptPrice As Currency
    Application.ScreenUpdating = False
    With Worksheets("EuroModel")
        .Visible = True
        .Activate
    End With
    EnterInputs
    OptPrice = Range("B18")
' Hide the EuroModel sheet and activate the Explanation sheet.
    Worksheets("EuroModel").Visible = False
    Worksheets("Explanation").Activate
    Range("F4").Select
    Application.ScreenUpdating = True
' Display the results.
    MsgBox "The price of this European " & OptName & " is " _
        & Format(OptPrice, "$0.00"), vbInformation, OptName & " price"
End Sub
```

EnterInputs Code

The **EnterInputs** sub takes the user's inputs and enters them in the input cells of the currently active model sheet. Because the input cells have the same range names in both the EuroModel and the AmerModel sheets, this same code can be called from both the EuroModel and AmerModel subs. This means that it has to be written only *once*. Note that if the duration of the option is extremely long, the range for the binomial tree (for an American option) could extend beyond the right edge of the worksheet. A check is made for this by using **ActiveSheet.Columns.Count**. This returns the number of columns in a worksheet.

```
Sub EnterInputs()
' Enter the user inputs into the appropriate sheet (EuroModel or AmerModel).
    If OptType <= 2 Then
        Range("EOptType") = OptType
    Else
        Range("AOptType") = OptType - 2
    End If
    Range("CurrPrice") = CurrPrice
    Range("ExerPrice") = ExerPrice
    Range("CurrDate") = CurrDate
    Range("ExerDate") = ExerDate
    Range("RFRate") = RFRate
    Range("Vol") = Vol
    Dur = Range("Dur")
' Check whether the duration would take the American model beyond the limits of a
' typical worksheet. If it does, quit.
    If OptType >= 3 And Dur > ActiveSheet.Columns.Count - 2 Then
        MsgBox "Excel cannot accommodate " & Dur & " trading days. Its " _
            & "maximum is " & ActiveSheet.Columns.Count - 2 & ". Try " _
            & "again with less days till the exercise date.", vbInformation, _
                "Too many trading days"
        Worksheets("Explanation").Activate
        End
    End If
' Redim the Cutoff array in case the user wants the early exercise boundary for an
' American put.
    If OptType = 4 And Extra = vbYes Then ReDim Cutoff(Dur)
End Sub
```

AmerModel Code

The **AmerModel** sub implements the American option pricing. It unhides and activates the AmerModel sheet, runs the same **EnterInputs** sub as above, and then calls the **DevelopAmerModel** sub to do most of the work. If the option is an American put and the user wants the early exercise boundary, this sub also calls the **CreateAmerReport** sub to report this information.

```
Sub AmerModel()
' This sub creates the binomial tree model for an American option.
    Application.ScreenUpdating = False
    With Worksheets("AmerModel")
        .Visible = True
        .Activate
    End With
' Enter the user inputs.
    Call EnterInputs
' Develop the model
    Call DevelopAmerModel
```

```
' Display the option price unless it is a put option and the user wants the early
' exercise boundary. In this case, create a report.
    If OptType = 3 Or Extra = vbNo Then
' Hide the AmerModel sheet, activate the Explanation sheet, and display a message about
' the option's price.
        Worksheets("AmerModel").Visible = False
        Worksheets("Explanation").Activate
        Range("F4").Select
        Application.ScreenUpdating = True
        MsgBox "The price of this American " & OptName & " is " _
            & Format(OptPrice, "$0.00"), vbInformation, OptName & " price"
    Else
' This is an American put and the user wants the early exercise boundary, so it must be
' created.
        Worksheets("AmerModel").Visible = False
        With Worksheets("AmerPutReport")
            .Visible = True
            .Activate
        End With
        Call CreateAmerReport
    End If
    Application.ScreenUpdating = True
End Sub
```

DevelopAmerModel Code

The **DevelopAmerModel** sub acts as its own "control center," calling a number of subs (**ErasePrevious**, **CalcFuturePrices**, **CalcValues**, and, in the case of an early exercise boundary, **EraseRowCol** and **RunGoalSeek**) to set up the AmerModel sheet and, if appropriate, calculate the early exercise boundary.

A note on status bar messages. The calculations for the early exercise boundary can take a while, so it is useful to indicate the progress to the user in the status bar at the bottom of the screen. Two properties of the **Application** object are useful here. The **DisplayStatusBar** property is Boolean; it is True if the status bar is visible, and it is False otherwise. The **StatusBar** property returns the message in the status bar. However, this property can also be set to False, which deletes the current message from the status bar.

To illustrate these properties, the next two lines capture whether the status bar was visible (in the Boolean variable OldStatusBar) and then ensure that it *is* visible.

```
OldStatusBar = Application.DisplayStatusBar
Application.DisplayStatusBar = True
```

Then the next line displays a progress indicator on the status bar that keeps changing as the program proceeds through a For loop.

```
Application.StatusBar = "Running Goal Seek on trading day " & Dur - i + 1 & " of " & Dur
```

Finally, the first of the next two lines removes the message, and the second restores the status bar to its original state (visible or not visible).

```
    Application.StatusBar = False
    Application.DisplayStatusBar = OldStatusBar
```

This technique can be very useful if your program takes a long time to run. The user will at least know that something is happening! Try running the program for an American put option with a duration of several months, and you will see what we mean.

Here is the **DevelopAmerModel** sub in its entirety.

```
Sub DevelopAmerModel()
' This sub develops the binomial tree model for an American option.
    Dim i As Integer, OldStatusBar As Boolean
' Get rid of any previous model.
    Call ErasePrevious
' Calculate the possible future stock prices in a triangular range.
    Call CalcFuturePrices
' Calculate the expected cash flows from the option by following an optimal strategy.
    Call CalcValues
' Calculate the early exercise boundary if the user requests it.
    If OptType = 4 And Extra = vbYes Then
' The StatusBar statements allow the user to track the progress of the calculations.
        OldStatusBar = Application.DisplayStatusBar
        Application.DisplayStatusBar = True
' The following loop solves a series of Goal Seek problems. Each finds the early
' exercise cutoff price (exercise only if current price is below this price) for a
' particular trading day. In this loop, i represents the row and column of the binomial
' tree "values" area that will be erased.  This corresponds to trading day Dur-i+1.
        Range("A20").Offset(Dur + 2, 0) = "Goal Seek set cell:"
        For i = Dur To 2 Step -1
            Application.StatusBar = "Running Goal Seek on trading " & "day " & _
                Dur - i + 1 & " of " & Dur
            Call EraseRowCol(i)
            Call RunGoalSeek
            Cutoff(Dur - i + 1) = Range("B21")
        Next
        Application.StatusBar = False
        Application.DisplayStatusBar = OldStatusBar
' The cutoff on the last day requires no calculation — it is the exercise price.
        Cutoff(Dur) = ExerPrice
    End If
End Sub
```

ErasePrevious Code

The **ErasePrevious** sub clears the contents of the triangular ranges in the AmerModel sheet from a previous run, if any.

```
Sub ErasePrevious()
' This sub clears the calculations from any previous model in the AmerModel sheet.
    With Range("A20")
        Range(.Offset(0, 0), _
            .End(xlToRight).End(xlDown).End(xlDown).End(xlDown)).ClearContents
    End With
End Sub
```

CalcFuturePrices Code

The binomial tree method is based on an approximation where the stock price can go up or down on any particular day. The **CalcFuturePrices** sub calculates all possible future prices in the first triangular array in the AmerModel sheet. (Each column corresponds to a particular day in the future.)

```
Sub CalcFuturePrices()
' This sub sets up the possible future stock prices for the binomial tree method in a
' triangular region, starting in cell B21.
    Dim j As Integer
    With Range("A20")
        .Value = "Future prices"
' Enter headings in top row, left column.
        For j = 0 To Dur
            .Offset(j + 1, 0) = j
            .Offset(0, j + 1) = j
        Next
        .Offset(1, 1) = Range("CurrPrice").Value
' Each entry in the top row is just UpFact times the previous entry.
        Range(.Offset(1, 2), .Offset(1, Dur + 1)) _
            .FormulaR1C1 = "=UpFact*RC[-1]"
' Each entry in other rows is (DownFact/UpFact) times the entry right above it.
        Range(.Offset(2, 1), .Offset(Dur + 1, Dur + 1)) _
            .FormulaR1C1 = "=If(RC1<=R20C,(DownFact/UpFact)*R[-1]C,"""")"
    End With
End Sub
```

CalcValues Code

The key to the binomial tree method is that at the beginning of each day, the decision on whether to exercise or not is based on the maximum of two quantities: the value from exercising now, and the expected value from waiting a day and then deciding whether to exercise. This permits a simple recursion that is implemented in the **CalcValues** sub. The FormulaR1C1 line in this sub enters the "same" formula (using relative addressing) in the entire second triangular range of the AmerModel sheet.

A note on double quotes embedded in strings. Suppose you want to use VBA to enter a formula such as =IF(A5<=10,15, "NA") in cell B5. The point is that this formula uses a pair of double quotes to enter a string in the cell B5 if the condition is false. It is tempting to write the following line of code:

```
Range("B5").Formula = "=If(A5<=10,15,"NA")"
```

This line enters the formula literally between the two outer double quotes. However, it will not work correctly! The problem is that VBA will read the formula up through "=If(A5<=10,15," and think it is finished because it has run into a second double quote. We need to indicate that the *inner* two double quotes should be treated as literals, not as double quotes enclosing the string that the formula consists of. In general, if you want a double quote in a string to be treated as a literal and not as one of the double quotes enclosing the string, you need to precede it with *another* double quote. The following line does the job:

```
Range("B5").Formula = "=If(A5<=10,15,""NA"")"
```

The formula toward the bottom of the following sub illustrates how this technique is used. In fact, it can be used for any strings, not just formulas. For example, the following line illustrates how to handle double quotes around the word *strange* in a message box.

```
MsgBox "The results from this run were somewhat ""strange""."
```

Again, any two double quotes in a row inside a string are interpreted as one *literal* double quote.

Here is the **CalcValues** sub in its entirety.

```
Sub CalcValues()
' This sub implements the binomial tree method in another triangular region, right
' below the previous one.  Each formula says that the price of the option at any point
' in time is the maximum of two quantities: the cash flow from exercising now and the
' expected value from waiting a day and then deciding.
    Dim j As Integer
    With Range("A20").Offset(Dur + 3, 0)
        .Value = "Option values"
' Enter headings.
        For j = 0 To Dur
            .Offset(j + 1, 0) = j
            .Offset(0, j + 1) = j
        Next
' Enter the Max formula in all cells of the triangular region.
        Range(.Offset(1, 1), .Offset(Dur + 1, Dur + 1)).FormulaR1C1 = _
            "=If(RC1<=R2OC,Max(ExerPrice-" _
            & "R[-" & Dur + 3 & "]C,(1+RFRate/260)* (PrUp*RC[1]+PrDown*R[1]C[1])),"""")"
' The option price is the top left entry of the region.
        OptPrice = .Offset(1, 1)
    End With
End Sub
```

EraseRowCol and RunGoalSeek Code

The calculation of the early exercise boundary (as explained in the Winston chapter) can be accomplished by a suitable modification of the second triangular range of the AmerModel sheet and a call to Excel's Goal Seek tool. (Goal Seek is used in general to solve one equation in one unknown.) The following two subs implement this method.

```
Sub EraseRowCol(i As Integer)
' A quick way to get the early exercise boundary is to delete the bottom and leftmost
' row and column of the triangular "values" region and then run Goal Seek. This sub
' deletes row i and column i of the region.
```

```
      With Range("A20").Offset(Dur + 3, 0)
         Range(.Offset(i + 1, 1), .Offset(i + 1, i + 1)).ClearContents
         Range(.Offset(1, i + 1), .Offset(i + 1, i + 1)).ClearContents
      End With
End Sub
```

A note on using Goal Seek in VBA. Goal Seek is an Excel tool (found under the Tools menu) for solving one equation in one unknown. It requires you to specify three things: (1) a cell containing a formula that you want to force to some value, (2) the value you want to force it to, and (3) a "changing cell" that can be varied to force the formula to the required value. It is easy to invoke Goal Seek from VBA, using the **GoalSeek** method of a Range object. The following line illustrates how it is done.

```
   Range("B20").GoalSeek 0, Range("B21")
```

This line will force the value in cell B20 to 0, using cell B21 as the changing cell. As this example shows, the GoalSeek method takes two arguments: the value to be forced to and the changing cell. It is to calculate the early exercise boundary in the following **RunGoalSeek** sub.

```
Sub RunGoalSeek()
' This sub runs Goal Seek. (It would also be possible to run Solver, but Goal Seek is
' quicker.) The changing cell is B21, which contains a trial value for the price of the
' stock. Initialize it to a value that is certainly too high: the exercise price.
   With Range("B21")
        .Value = ExerPrice
        .NumberFormat = "General"
   End With
' In between the two triangular regions (in column B), enter a formula: the difference
' between the cash flow from exercising now and the optimal cash flow. Then run Goal
' Seek, trying to drive the value from this formula to 0.
   With Range("A20").Offset(Dur + 2, 1)
        .Formula = "=ExerPrice-B21-" & .Offset(2, 0).Address
        .NumberFormat = "General"
        .GoalSeek 0, Range("B21")
   End With
End Sub
```

CreateAmerReport Code

Finally, the **CreateAmerReport** sub fills in the AmerPutReport sheet with the information (calculated earlier and stored in the Cutoff array) about the early exercise boundary. The most interesting part of this sub is the handling of dates. Note how the report in Figure 25.5 skips dates corresponding to weekend days (non-trading days). This is implemented in the sub with an If construct and Excel's **Weekday** function. This function returns 7 for a Saturday and 1 for a Sunday. Note that the ThisDate variable needs to be declared as a Date variable to make this work properly.

```
Sub CreateAmerReport()
' This sub creates a report of the option price and the early exercise boundary. It is
' done only for an American put and only when the user requests the early exercise
' boundary.
    Dim i As Integer, ThisDate As Date
' Record the option price.
    Range("B3") = OptPrice
' Record the early exercise prices, starting in cell B7. Note that ThisDate captures
' the actual date, but it excludes weekends.
    With Range("A6")
        Range(.Offset(1, 0), .Offset(1, 1).End(xlDown)).ClearContents
        ThisDate = CurrDate
        For i = 1 To Dur
            ThisDate = ThisDate + 1
' If ThisDate is a Saturday, make it the next Monday.
            If Application.Weekday(ThisDate) = 7 Then
                ThisDate = ThisDate + 2
' If ThisDate is a Sunday, make it the next Monday.
            ElseIf Application.Weekday(ThisDate) = 1 Then
                ThisDate = ThisDate + 1
            End If
            .Offset(i, 0) = ThisDate
            .Offset(i, 1) = Cutoff(i)
        Next
    End With
    Range("A2").Select
End Sub
```

ViewExplanation Code

This sub is used for navigational purposes (from the button on the AmerPutReport sheet).

```
Sub ViewExplanation()
    Worksheets("AmerPutReport").Visible = False
    Worksheets("Explanation").Activate
    Range("F4").Select
End Sub
```

TradeDays Function

Two inputs to the option pricing model are the current date and exercise date. The pricing models actually require the **duration** of the option, defined as the number of trading days until the exercise date. To calculate the duration, we created a function specifically for this purpose, with the code listed below. It again uses Excel's **Weekday** function to skip weekends. Then it can be used in an Excel formula in the usual way. For example, the formula in cell B12 of the EuroModel sheet (see Figure 25.6) is

```
=TradeDays(CurrDate,ExerDate)
```

This is a perfect example of *creating* a function to perform a particular task when Excel doesn't have a built-in function to perform it. If you want to use this function in your own workbooks, you should insert a module in your workbook and copy the following code to it.

```
Function TradeDays(FirstDate As Date, LastDate As Date) As Integer
' This function returns the number of trading days between two dates. It excludes
' weekends only, although with extra logic, it could be changed to exclude other days
' (such as Christmas). Note how it uses Excel's Weekday function, which returns 1 for
' Sundays, 7 for Saturdays.
    Dim NDays As Integer, i As Integer, CurrDay As Integer
' Start with the number of days from FirstDate to LastDate
    NDays = LastDate - FirstDate
    TradeDays = NDays
' Now subtract a day for every weekend day.
    For i = 1 To NDays
        CurrDay = Application.Weekday(FirstDate + i)
        If CurrDay = 1 Or CurrDay = 7 Then TradeDays = TradeDays - 1
    Next
End Function
```

25.8 Summary

This application doesn't require a lot of inputs, and it doesn't produce a lot of outputs, but it does perform a number of rather complex calculations in the background to produce some very useful results. Considering that the options business in the financial community is a multimillion-dollar business annually, an application such as this one can be extremely valuable to financial analysts and investors.

PROGRAMMING EXERCISES

1. Develop a message box statement that displays the following message, exactly as it's written here: When you want a literal double quote, ", in a string, you should precede it by another double quote, as in "".

2. Consider the following formula that you want to enter, via VBA, in cell C3: =If(A3="West","Los Angeles",If(A3="East","New York","")). Write a VBA statement to set the Formula property of cell C3 correctly.

3. The file **IRR.xls** contains data on an investment that requires an initial cost at the beginning of year 1 and then receives cash inflows at the ends of years 1 through 10. The net present value (NPV) of this investment is calculated in cell B11 for the discount rate in cell B3. The **internal rate of return** (IRR) of the investment is defined as the discount rate that makes the NPV equal to 0. Write a VBA sub, using the GoalSeek method, to calculate the IRR and display it in a message box, formatted as a percentage with two decimals. (*Note*: Excel has a built-in IRR function. See if you can use it to get the same result as with your VBA sub.)

4. The file **CertEquiv.xls** contains the probability distribution of the monetary outcome for a given investment. Assume that the decision maker is risk averse and has an exponential utility function with the risk tolerance parameter R given in cell B3. Then the **utility** of any monetary outcome x is $e^{-x/R}$, the **expected utility** of an investment is the "sumproduct" of probabilities and utilities of monetary outcomes, and the **certainty equivalent** of the investment is the dollar amount such that its utility is equal to the expected utility of the investment. In words, the certainty equivalent is the monetary value such that the investor would be indifferent between getting it for sure and getting into the risky investment. Write a sub that calculates the expected utility of the investment described from row 7 down and uses the GoalSeek method to calculate the certainty equivalent. Display both of these outputs in a message box. Write the sub so that it will work for *any* probability distribution listed from row 7 down and any risk tolerance given in cell B3.

5. Change the TradeDays function so that it also excludes the *fixed* dates January 1, December 25, and July 4. (In addition, you can exclude any other fixed dates you want to exclude. However, it would be much more difficult to exclude a "floating" holiday like Thanksgiving, so don't worry about these.) Then change the CreateAmerReport sub so that it also excludes these fixed dates.

6. The preceding exercise claimed that it would be difficult to exclude "floating" holidays like Thanksgiving (the fourth Thursday in November). Is this true? Write a function subroutine called Thanksgiving that takes one argument called Year. (For example, this argument will have values like 1999.) It then returns the date that Thanksgiving falls on. Then redo the previous exercise, excluding Thanksgiving as well as the other fixed dates.

7. The file **CitySales.xls** contains sales of 100 products for five cities in California (each on a different sheet) for each day over a 2-year period. Write a sub that fills a 2-dimensional array MaxSale, where MaxSale(i,j) is the maximum sale, over all days, for product j in city i. This will take a while to run, so display a message such as "Analyzing product 17 in San Diego" that shows the current city and product being analyzed. Make sure the message disappears when all cities and products have been analyzed.

An Application for Finding Betas of Stocks

26

26.1 Introduction

The **beta** of a stock is a measure of how the stock's price changes as a market index changes.[43] It is actually the coefficient of the market return when the returns of the stock are regressed on the market returns. If the beta of a stock is greater than 1, then the stock is relatively volatile; if the market changes by a certain percentage, then the stock's price tends to change by a *larger* percentage. The opposite is true when the beta of a stock is less than 1. This application calculates the beta for any company given historical price data on the company's monthly stock prices and a market index. It uses one of four possible criteria to find the best-fitting regression equation.

The application also illustrates another way of getting data from an application—from another Excel file.

New Learning Objectives: VBA

- To illustrate how to capture data from one workbook for use in a VBA application in another workbook.
- To illustrate two new features of list boxes: the use of two columns and the **RowSource** property for populating a list box.
- To illustrate how event code can be written for the Click event of option buttons.

New Learning Objective: Non-VBA

- To learn how nonlinear optimization can be used to estimate the beta of a stock, using any of four possible optimization criteria.

26.2 Functionality of the Application

The application, stored in the file **StockBeta.xls**, gets the required stock return data from another file, **StockData.xls**. The application is written so that these two files must be in the *same* directory. The **StockData.xls** file contains monthly stock

---

[43]More details on estimation of stock betas can be found in Chapter 7 of *Practical Management Science*.

price data for many large U.S. companies for the 1990s. It also contains monthly data on an S&P 500 market index during this same period. The user can choose any of these companies, a period of time containing at least 12 months, such as January 1994 to December 1997, and one of four criteria to minimize: sum of squared errors, weighted sum of squared errors, sum of absolute errors, or maximum absolute error. Then the application uses the company's returns and the market returns for this period, and it estimates the stock's beta using the specified criterion. It does this by estimating a regression equation of the form $Y = a + bX$, where Y is the stock return, X is the market return, and b estimates the stock's beta. It is also possible to view a time series plot of the stock's returns, with the predictions of its returns from the regression equation superimposed on the plot.

Each stock in the **StockData.xls** file has its own worksheet. The user can add more sheets for other stocks, and the application will automatically recognize them. If the user wants to run the application with more recent data (for the year 2000, say) on the included companies or any other companies, only a few changes in the VBA code are necessary. As it stands, however, it expects monthly data from the 1990s.

26.3 Running the Application

When the **StockBeta.xls** file is opened, the Explanation sheet in Figure 26.1 appears. After clicking on the button in this sheet, the user sees the dialog box in Figure 26.2. As it is filled out here, it will find the beta for IBM, based on the returns from January 1996 through December 1999, using the weighted sum of squared errors criterion with a weighting constant of 0.98.

Figure 26.1 Explanation sheet

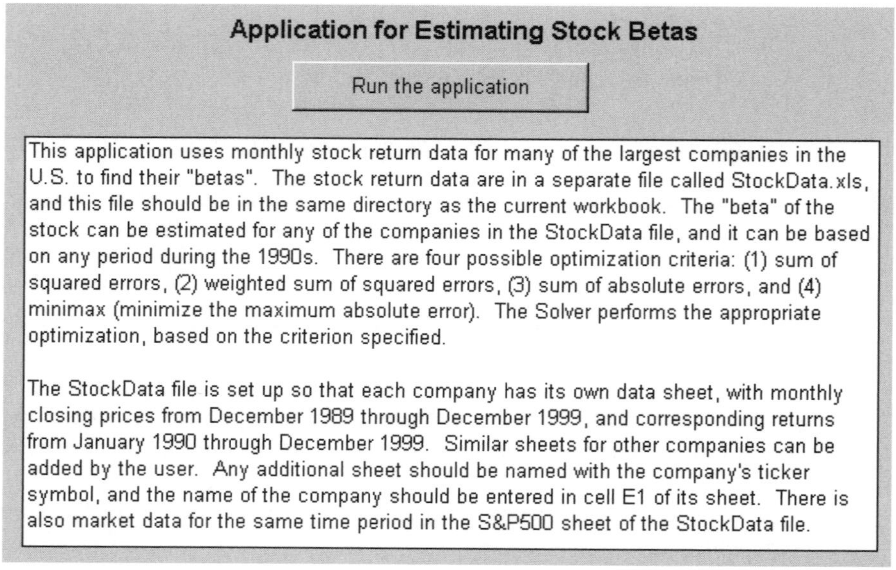

Application for Estimating Stock Betas

> Run the application

This application uses monthly stock return data for many of the largest companies in the U.S. to find their "betas". The stock return data are in a separate file called StockData.xls, and this file should be in the same directory as the current workbook. The "beta" of the stock can be estimated for any of the companies in the StockData file, and it can be based on any period during the 1990s. There are four possible optimization criteria: (1) sum of squared errors, (2) weighted sum of squared errors, (3) sum of absolute errors, and (4) minimax (minimize the maximum absolute error). The Solver performs the appropriate optimization, based on the criterion specified.

The StockData file is set up so that each company has its own data sheet, with monthly closing prices from December 1989 through December 1999, and corresponding returns from January 1990 through December 1999. Similar sheets for other companies can be added by the user. Any additional sheet should be named with the company's ticker symbol, and the name of the company should be entered in cell E1 of its sheet. There is also market data for the same time period in the S&P500 sheet of the StockData file.

Figure 26.2 Inputs dialog box

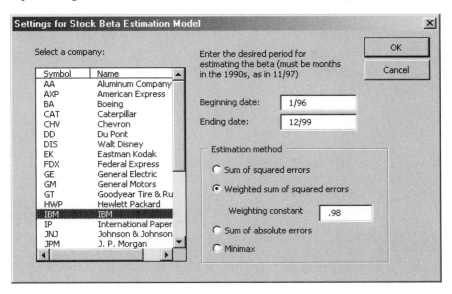

'At this point, the data from the IBM and S&P500 sheets in the **StockData.xls** file are copied to the Model sheet in the **StockBeta.xls** file. Then a Solver model is set up and optimized according to the specified criterion. The resulting beta is displayed in the message box in Figure 26.3, and the full details appear in the Model sheet in Figure 26.4.

Figure 26.3 Beta for IBM

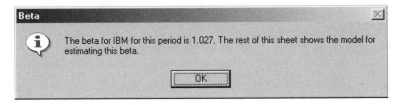

When the left button on the Model sheet is clicked, the chart in Figure 26.5 is displayed. It shows the stock's returns with the predictions from the best-fitting regression equation superimposed.

26.4 Setting Up the Excel Sheets

The **StockBeta.xls** file contains an Explanation sheet, a Model sheet, and a chart sheet named TSChart. The file contains an S&P500 sheet and a separate sheet for each company. These individual company sheets are named by the company's

Figure 26.4 Completed Model sheet for IBM

	A	B	C	D	E	F	G	H	I	J	K
1	Estimation model for IBM: period from 01/96 to 12/99, weighted sum of squared errors estimation method										
2											
3	Parameters										
4	Alpha	0.0157		View Time Series Chart			View Explanation Sheet				
5	Beta	1.0268									
6											
7	Weighting constant	0.98									
8											
9	Optimization model										
10	Date	Mkt return	Stock return	Predicted	Error	SqError	AbsError	Weight		Target for optimization	
11	Dec-99	0.05772	0.04670	0.0749	-0.0282	0.00080	0.0282	1.0000		WSSE	0.208609
12	Nov-99	0.01918	0.05038	0.0354	0.0150	0.00023	0.0150	0.9800			
13	Oct-99	0.06254	-0.18802	0.0799	-0.2679	0.07177	0.2679	0.9604			
14	Sep-99	-0.02855	-0.02860	-0.0136	-0.0150	0.00022	0.0150	0.9412			
15	Aug-99	-0.00625	-0.00798	0.0092	-0.0172	0.00030	0.0172	0.9224			
16	Jul-99	-0.03205	-0.02757	-0.0172	-0.0103	0.00011	0.0103	0.9039			
17	Jun-99	0.05444	0.11423	0.0716	0.0427	0.00182	0.0427	0.8858			
18	May-99	-0.02497	0.11031	-0.0100	0.1203	0.01447	0.1203	0.8681			
19	Apr-99	0.03794	0.18018	0.0546	0.1256	0.01576	0.1256	0.8508			
20	Mar-99	0.03879	0.04418	0.0555	-0.0113	0.00013	0.0113	0.8337			
21	Feb-99	-0.03228	-0.07244	-0.0175	-0.0550	0.00302	0.0550	0.8171			
22	Jan-99	0.04101	-0.00610	0.0578	-0.0639	0.00408	0.0639	0.8007			
51	Aug-96	0.01881	0.06395	0.0350	0.0290	0.00084	0.0290	0.4457			
52	Jul-96	-0.04575	0.08586	-0.0313	0.1172	0.01373	0.1172	0.4368			
53	Jun-96	0.00226	-0.07260	0.0180	-0.0906	0.00821	0.0906	0.4281			
54	May-96	0.02285	-0.00928	0.0391	-0.0484	0.00234	0.0484	0.4195			
55	Apr-96	0.01343	-0.03146	0.0295	-0.0609	0.00371	0.0609	0.4111			
56	Mar-96	0.00792	-0.09276	0.0238	-0.1166	0.01359	0.1166	0.4029			
57	Feb-96	0.00693	0.13018	0.0228	0.1074	0.01153	0.1074	0.3948			
58	Jan-96	0.03262	0.18741	0.0492	0.1383	0.01911	0.1383	0.3869			

Figure 26.5 Time series plot of returns and predictions

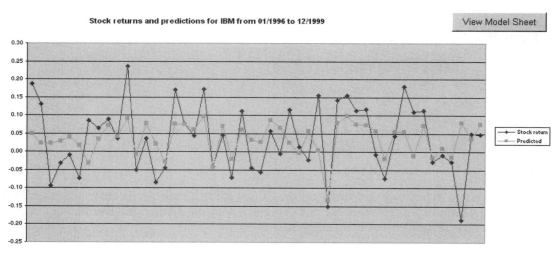

ticker symbol (for example, EK for Eastman Kodak, JNJ for Johnson & Johnson, and so on). A typical company sheet is structured as in Figure 26.6. It contains dates (in reverse chronological order) in column A, monthly closing prices in col-

Figure 26.6 A typical company sheet

	A	B	C	D	E
1	Monthly closing prices and returns for:				IBM
2					
3	Date	Close	Return		
4	Dec-99	107.762	0.04670		
5	Nov-99	102.954	0.05038		
6	Oct-99	98.0162	-0.18802		
7	Sep-99	120.712	-0.02860		
8	Aug-99	124.266	-0.00798		
9	Jul-99	125.266	-0.02757		
10	Jun-99	128.817	0.11423		
11	May-99	115.611	0.11031		
12	Apr-99	104.125	0.18018		
119	May-90	29.782	0.10092		
120	Apr-90	27.052	0.02709		
121	Mar-90	26.3385	0.02166		
122	Feb-90	25.78	0.05323		
123	Jan-90	24.4771	0.04781		
124	Dec-89	23.3603			

umn B, corresponding returns in column C, and the company's name in cell E1. (Note that many rows are hidden in the figure.) The user can add sheets for additional companies in the **StockData.xls** file, but they should all be structured in this way. The S&P500 sheet is structured similarly, as shown in Figure 26.7. Note that the closing prices extend back to December 1989, whereas the returns extend back only to January 1990. This is because each return, being a percentage change, requires the *previous* closing price.

Figure 26.7 The S&P500 sheet

	A	B	C	D	E	F
1	Monthly closing prices and returns				Market index (S&P 500)	
2						
3	Date	Close	Return			
4	Dec-99	1469.25	0.05772			
5	Nov-99	1389.07	0.01918			
6	Oct-99	1362.93	0.06254			
7	Sep-99	1282.71	-0.02855			
8	Aug-99	1320.41	-0.00625			
9	Jul-99	1328.72	-0.03205			
10	Jun-99	1372.71	0.05444			
11	May-99	1301.84	-0.02497			
12	Apr-99	1335.18	0.03794			
119	May-90	361.23	0.09199			
120	Apr-90	330.8	-0.02689			
121	Mar-90	339.94	0.02426			
122	Feb-90	331.89	0.00854			
123	Jan-90	329.08	-0.06882			
124	Dec-89	353.4				

The Model sheet in the **StockBeta.xls** file can be set up at design time as a template, with the labels and range names shown in Figure 26.8. The body of it must be filled in at run time. The TSChart chart sheet can be created with the Chart Wizard at design time, using any trial data. Then it is linked to the actual data on the Model sheet at run time.

Figure 26.8 Template for the Model sheet

	A	B	C	D	E	F	G	H	I	J	K	L
1	Estimation model for Aluminum Company of America: period from 01/90 to 12/99, sum of squared errors estimation method											
2												
3	Parameters											
4	Alpha											
5	Beta			View Time Series Chart			View Explanation Sheet					
6												
7	Weighting constant											
8												
9	Optimization model											
10		Date	Mkt return	Stock return	Predicted		Error	SqError	AbsError			Target for optimization
11												
12												
13			Range names at design time:									
14			Alpha - B4									
15			Beta - B5									
16			AlphaBeta - B4:B5									
17			Weight - B7									
18			Target - K11									
19												

26.5   Getting Started with the VBA

The **StockBeta.xls** file includes a single user form named InputsForm, a module, and a reference to the Solver.xla file. Once these items are added, the Project Explorer window will appear as in Figure 26.9.

Figure 26.9 Project Explorer window

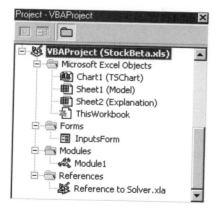

Workbook_Open Code

To guarantee that the Explanation sheet appears when the file is opened, the following code is placed in the ThisWorkbook code window. As usual, it hides all sheets except the Explanation sheet.

```
Private Sub Workbook_Open()
    Worksheets("Explanation").Activate
    Range("E4").Select
    Worksheets("Model").Visible = False
    Charts("TSChart").Visible = False
End Sub
```

26.6 Designing the User Forms and Writing Their Event Code

Web Help For more explanation of the code in this application, visit our Web site at http://www.indiana.edu/~mgtsci and download the **Code Explanation - StockBeta.doc** file.

The design of the InputsForm appears in Figure 26.10. It contains the usual OK and Cancel buttons, two explanation labels, three text boxes and corresponding labels, a frame for grouping, four option buttons, and a list box. The text boxes are named Date1Box, Date2Box, and WtBox, the option buttons are named SSEOpt, WSSEOpt, SAEOpt, and MinMaxOpt, and the list box is named CompanyList.

Figure 26.10 Design of InputsForm

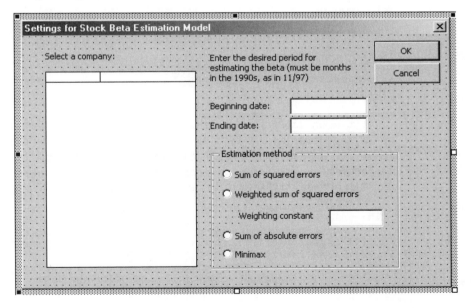

The text boxes and option buttons are standard. However, the list box presents two new features. Specifically, its **ColumnCount** property should be set to 2 at design time. This indicates that the list will contain two columns, one for the ticker symbols and one for the company names. (See Figure 26.2.) The **BoundColumn** property of the list box then specifies which column the **Value** property refers to. For example, if we want to get an item from the list in the first column, we set the BoundColumn property to 1 before accessing the Value property. Finally, the **RowSource** property can be set to a worksheet range at design time (using the Properties window). Then the list box will be populated with the list in this range.

Event Code for InputsForm

The **UserForm_Initialize** event selects the first company in the list box, it enters blanks in the date boxes, it checks the SSE option, and it enters a blank in the weight box and disables it. The **OKButton_Click** does a considerable amount of error checking before finally capturing the user's inputs in a number of public variables. There is also event code for each option button's **Click** event. This enables or disables the weight box, depending on which button has been checked. It makes no sense for the user to enter a value for the weight unless the weighted sum of squares criterion is selected. The **CancelButton_Click** sub unloads the dialog box and terminates the program. It also closes the **StockData.xls** file (which by this time is stored in the public variable DataFile).

```
Private Sub UserForm_Initialize()
    CompanyList.ListIndex = 0
    Date1Box = ""
    Date2Box = ""
    SSEOpt = True
    With WtBox
        .Text = ""
        .Enabled = False
    End With
End Sub
```

A note on dates. The OKButton_Click sub checks that the dates entered are in the range from January 1990 to December 1999. To make a check involving a literal date, the date should be enclosed within pound (#) signs. If you try enclosing them within double quotes, treating them as strings, you won't get an error message, but the checks won't be performed correctly.

```
Private Sub OKButton_Click()
    Dim ctl As Control
' Get the symbol and company name from the user's selection. The BoundColumn of a list
' box indicates which column the Value property refers to.
    With CompanyList
        .BoundColumn = 1
        Symbol = .Value
        .BoundColumn = 2
        Company = .Value
    End With
    For Each ctl In Me.Controls
        If TypeName(ctl) = "TextBox" And ctl.Name <> "WtBox" Then
            If ctl.Value = "" Or Not IsDate(ctl) Then
```

```
                    MsgBox "Enter valid dates in the date boxes.", vbInformation, _
                        "Invalid entry"
                    ctl.SetFocus
                    Exit Sub
                End If
            End If
        Next
' Note how a literal date is enclosed inside pound (#) signs.
        If Date1Box < #1/1/1990# Then
            MsgBox "The beginning date should not be before Jan-1990.", vbInformation, _
                "Invalid date"
            Date1Box.SetFocus
            Exit Sub
        End If
        If Date2Box > #12/31/1999# Then
            MsgBox "The ending date should not be after Dec-1999.", vbInformation, _
                "Invalid date"
            Date2Box.SetFocus
            Exit Sub
        End If
        If Date1Box >= Date2Box Then
            MsgBox "The beginning date should be before the ending date.", vbInformation, _
                "Invalid dates"
            Date1Box.SetFocus
            Exit Sub
        End If
        BegMonth = Date1Box
        EndMonth = Date2Box
' Capture the method to use for optimization.
        If SSEOpt Then
            Method = "SSE"
' If weighted sum of squares is chosen, make sure the weight box is not blank and has a
' numerical value, which must be from 0 to 1.
        ElseIf WSSEOpt Then
            If Not IsNumeric(WtBox) Or WtBox = "" Then
                MsgBox "Enter a numerical weight between 0 and 1.", vbInformation, _
                    "Invalid weight"
                WtBox.SetFocus
                Exit Sub
            ElseIf WtBox < 0 Or WtBox > 1 Then
                MsgBox "Enter a weight between 0 and 1.", vbInformation, "Invalid weight"
                WtBox.SetFocus
                Exit Sub
            End If
            Method = "WSSE"
            Weight = WtBox
        ElseIf SAEOpt Then
            Method = "SAE"
        Else
            Method = "MaxAE"
        End If
        Unload Me
End Sub

Private Sub CancelButton_Click()
    Unload Me
    DataFile.Close
    End
End Sub
```

Event Code for Option Buttons

We usually write event code only for the Initialize event of a user form and the Click events of OK and Cancel buttons. However, remember that event code can be written for numerous events for *any* of the controls on a user form. The following subs illustrate how this works for the Click events of option buttons. Specifically, these subs enable or disable the WtBox text box, depending on which optimization method has been chosen. We want this text box to be enabled when the user clicks on the WSSEOpt button, and we want it to be disabled when the user clicks on any of the other option buttons. (To see the effect, run the application and click on the various option buttons.)

```
Private Sub SSEOpt_Click()
    WtBox.Enabled = False
End Sub

Private Sub WSSEOpt_Click()
    With WtBox
        .Enabled = True
        .SetFocus
    End With
End Sub

Private Sub SAEOpt_Click()
    WtBox.Enabled = False
End Sub

Private Sub MMaxOpt_Click()
    WtBox.Enabled = False
End Sub
```

26.7   The VBA Code in the Module

The **Main** sub is attached to the button on the Explanation sheet. It first creates a list of companies by opening the **StockData.xls** file and looping through its sheets. Then it "shows" the InputsForm to get the user's inputs. Next, it sets up a model and optimizes it, and it updates the chart. It also takes care of closing the **StockData.xls** file when it is no longer needed.

The public variables and the main sub are listed below. Note the use of VBA's **DateDiff** function in the Main sub. It takes three arguments: a time period (for example, "m" for month) and two dates, and it returns the number of time periods between these two dates. For example, it returns 3 if the time period is a month and the dates are March 2000 and June 2000.

Option Statement and Public Variables

```
Option Explicit

'   Symbol - ticker symbol of selected company
'   Company - name of selected company
```

```
'     Method - optimization method used
'     Weight - weighting constant (for weighted least squares only)
'     BegMonth - first month of selected time period
'     LastMonth - last month of selected time period
'     NMonths - number of months in selected time period
'     FirstDateRow - first row of data for estimation period (remember
'          that data are listed in reverse chronological order)
'     DataFile - a workbook object variable for the StockData file
Public Symbol As String, Company As String, Method As String, _
     Weight As Single, BegMonth As Date, EndMonth As Date, _
     NMonths As Integer, FirstDateRow As Integer, DataFile as Workbook
```

Main Code

```
Sub Main()
' Create a list of companies in the Companies range.
    Call CreateCompanyList
' Get user choices.
    InputsForm.Show
' Use VBA DateDiff function to get number of months between two dates - the first
' argument "m" means month, the second and third arguments are the first and last dates
' for the difference. Note that a literal month is again enclosed in pound signs.
    NMonths = DateDiff("m", BegMonth, EndMonth) + 1
    FirstDateRow = DateDiff("m", EndMonth, #1/1/2000#)
    Application.ScreenUpdating = False
' Set up the model in the Model sheet, use the Solver to optimize, and update the
' time series chart.
    Call SetupModel
    Call RunSolver
    Call UpdateChart
    Application.ScreenUpdating = True
' Display the beta in a message box. (More details are displayed to the user in the
' Model sheet.)
    MsgBox "The beta for " & Company & " for this period is " _
        & Format(Range("Beta"), "0.000") & ". The rest of this sheet " _
        & "shows the model for estimating this beta.", vbInformation, "Beta"
End Sub
```

CreateCompanyList Code

The **CreateCompanyList** sub opens the **StockData.xls** workbook and loops through all of its sheets to see which companies are included (other than the S&P 500). As it does this, it creates a list in columns AA and AB of the Model sheet and names the corresponding range Companies. (See Figure 26.11, which has several hidden rows.) This range is the source for the list box in the InputsForm because its **RowSource** property is set to Companies at design time. Note the error handling code. If the **StockData.xls** file cannot be found, control passes to the MissingFile label. At that point, an error message is displayed, and the program ends. However, if there is no error—the file exists—an **Exit Sub** statement ensures that the lines following the label are *not* executed.

```
Sub CreateCompanyList()
' This sub creates a list of companies in the Companies range (in columns AA, AB of the
' Model sheet) for populating the list box in the user form.
    Dim sht As Worksheet, Counter As Integer
```

```
' Clear old list.
    Range("Companies").ClearContents
' Open the StockData file. If it is not in the same directory as the StockBeta file, an
' error occurs, and the program ends.  Otherwise, make StockBeta the active workbook.
    On Error GoTo MissingFile
    Set DataFile = Workbooks.Open(ThisWorkbook.Path & "\StockData.xls")
    Workbooks("StockData.xls").Activate
' Go through all worksheets in the StockData file. If the name is not S&P500, add to
' the list. The sheet name is the ticker symbol, and its cell E1 should contain the
' company name.
    Counter = 0
    With Worksheets("Model").Range("AA1")
        For Each sht In DataFile.Worksheets
            If sht.Name <> "S&P500" Then
                Counter = Counter + 1
                .Offset(Counter, 0) = sht.Name
                .Offset(Counter, 1) = sht.Range("E1")
            End If
        Next
        Range(.Offset(1, 0), .Offset(Counter, 1)).Name = "Companies"
' Sort the list on the ticker symbol.
        .Sort Key1:=.Cells(1, 1)
    End With
    Exit Sub
MissingFile:
    MsgBox "There is no StockData.xls file in the same directory as this " _
        & "workbook, so the application cannot continue.", vbExclamation, _
        "Missing file"
    End
End Sub
```

Figure 26.11 Companies list in Model sheet

	AA	AB	AC	AD
1	Symbol	Name		
2	AA	Aluminum Company of America		
3	AXP	American Express		
4	BA	Boeing		
5	CAT	Caterpillar		
6	CHV	Chevron		
7	DD	Du Pont		
8	DIS	Walt Disney		
9	EK	Eastman Kodak		
24	MSFT	Microsoft		
25	PG	Procter & Gamble		
26	S	Sears Roebuck		
27	T	AT&T		
28	UK	Union Carbide		
29	UTX	United Technologies		
30	WMT	Wal-Mart		

SetupModel Code

The **SetupModel** sub activates the Model sheet and then calls two subs, **CopyData** and **EnterFormulas**, to set up the model for estimating the beta of the stock.

```
Sub SetupModel()
' Unhide and activate the Model sheet, then set up the model by calling
' the CopyData and EnterFormulas subs.
    With Worksheets("Model")
        .Visible = True
        .Activate
    End With
    Call CopyData
    Call EnterFormulas
    Range("A2").Select
End Sub
```

CopyData Code

At this point, the **StockData.xls** file is still open, so the **CopyData** sub copies the data on dates and monthly returns from the selected company sheet and the S&P500 sheet to the Model sheet. It uses the **PasteSpecial** method to paste the monthly return *formulas* as values.

```
Sub CopyData()
' Copy the data from the S&P500 sheet and the sheet for the selected company to the
' Model sheet.
    With Range("A10")
        Range(.Offset(1, 0), .End(xlDown).End(xlToRight)).ClearContents
    End With
' Note how the FirstDateRow is used to designate the appropriate range to copy. Also,
'   because the Returns columns contain formulas, they are pasted special as values in
' the Model sheet.
    With Worksheets("S&P500").Range("A3")
        Range(.Offset(FirstDateRow, 0),.Offset(FirstDateRow + NMonths - 1, 0)).Copy _
            Range("A11")
        Range(.Offset(FirstDateRow, 2),.Offset(FirstDateRow + NMonths - 1, 2)).Copy
        Range("B11").PasteSpecial xlPasteValues
    End With
    With Worksheets(Symbol).Range("A3")
        Range(.Offset(FirstDateRow, 2),.Offset(FirstDateRow + NMonths - 1, 2)).Copy
        Range("C11").PasteSpecial xlPasteValues
    End With
End Sub
```

EnterFormulas Code

The **EnterFormulas** sub is somewhat long, but it is straightforward. It enters the formulas for the optimization model, including the predicted returns, the errors, the squared errors, the absolute errors, the weights for the weighted sum of squares method, and the appropriate objective for the criterion selected. The Case construct is used here to perform different tasks depending on the value of Method.

```
Sub EnterFormulas()
' This sub enters all the required formulas in the Model sheet.
```

```
' First, enter an appropriate label in cell A1.
    Dim MethodName As String
    Select Case Method
        Case "SSE": MethodName = "sum of squared errors"
        Case "WSSE": MethodName = "weighted sum of squared errors"
        Case "SAE": MethodName = "sum of absolute errors"
        Case "MaxAE": MethodName = "minimax"
    End Select
    Range("A1") = "Estimation model for " & Company & ": period from " _
        & Format(BegMonth, "mm/yyyy") & " to " & Format(EndMonth, "mm/yyyy") _
        & ", " & MethodName & " estimation method"
' Enter the weight in the Weight cell (if weighted least squares is selected).
    If Method = "WSSE" Then
        Range("Weight") = Weight
    Else
        Range("Weight") = "NA"
    End If
' Enter the predictions, errors, squared errors, and absolute errors with
' the appropriate formulas in columns D-G.
    With Range("D10")
        Range(.Offset(1, 0), .Offset(NMonths, 0)).FormulaR1C1 = "=Alpha+Beta*RC[-2]"
        Range(.Offset(1, 1), .Offset(NMonths, 1)).FormulaR1C1 = "=RC[-2]-RC[-1]"
        Range(.Offset(1, 2), .Offset(NMonths, 2)).FormulaR1C1 = "=RC[-1]^2"
        Range(.Offset(1, 3), .Offset(NMonths, 3)).FormulaR1C1 = "=Abs(RC[-2])"
        If Method = "WSSE" Then
            .Offset(0, 4) = "Weight"
            .Offset(1, 4) = 1
            Range(.Offset(2, 4), .Offset(NMonths, 4)).FormulaR1C1 = "=Weight*R[-1]C"
        Else
            .Offset(0, 4) = ""
        End If
    End With
' Name the appropriate range and then enter a formula for the appropriate objective in
' the Target cell.
    Select Case Method
    Case "SSE"
        With Range("F10")
            Range(.Offset(1, 0), .Offset(NMonths, 0)).Name = "SqErrs"
        End With
        With Range("Target")
            .Offset(0, -1) = Method
            .Formula = "=Sum(SqErrs)"
        End With
    Case "WSSE"
        With Range("F10")
            Range(.Offset(1, 0), .Offset(NMonths, 0)).Name = "SqErrs"
        End With
        With Range("H10")
            Range(.Offset(1, 0), .Offset(NMonths, 0)).Name = "Weights"
        End With
        With Range("Target")
            .Offset(0, -1) = Method
            .Formula = "=Sumproduct(Weights,SqErrs)"
        End With
    Case "SAE"
        With Range("G10")
            Range(.Offset(1, 0), .Offset(NMonths, 0)).Name = "AbsErrs"
        End With
        With Range("Target")
            .Offset(0, -1) = Method
            .Formula = "=Sum(AbsErrs)"
```

```
            End With
      Case "MaxAE"
          With Range("G10")
              Range(.Offset(1, 0), .Offset(NMonths, 0)).Name = "AbsErrs"
          End With
          With Range("Target")
              .Offset(0, -1) = Method
              .Formula = "=Max(AbsErrs)"
          End With
      End Select
End Sub
```

RunSolver Code

The **RunSolver** sub is particularly simple because the Solver can be set up completely at design time and the *size* of the model never changes. Note that the Solver setup minimizes the Target cell, has the AlphaBeta range as changing cells, and has *no* constraints.

```
Sub RunSolver()
' Run the Solver, which can be set up once and for all at design time.
    SolverSolve UserFinish:=True
End Sub
```

UpdateChart Code

The time series chart is created at design time, so all the **UpdateChart** sub has to do is link the chart to the correct data and modify its title appropriately.

```
Sub UpdateChart()
    Dim SourceData As Range, SourceDates As Range
' Set range variables for the dates and data ranges for the chart.
    With Range("A10")
        Set SourceDates = Range(.Offset(1, 0), .Offset(NMonths, 0))
        Set SourceData = Range(.Offset(0, 2), .Offset(NMonths, 3))
    End With
' Update the chart, including its title.
    With Charts("TSChart")
        .SetSourceData SourceData
        .SeriesCollection(1).XValues = SourceDates
        .ChartTitle.Text = "Stock returns and predictions for " & Company _
            & " from " & Format(BegMonth, "mm/yy") & " to " & Format(EndMonth, "mm/yy")
    End With
End Sub
```

Navigational Subs

The remaining subs are for navigational purposes.

```
Sub ViewExplanation()
    Worksheets("Model").Visible = False
```

```
        With Worksheets("Explanation")
            .Visible = True
            .Activate
        End With
        Range("E4").Select
    End Sub

    Sub ViewModel()
        Charts("TSChart").Visible = False
        With Worksheets("Model")
            .Visible = True
            .Activate
        End With
        Range("A2").Select
    End Sub

    Sub ViewChart()
        Worksheets("Model").Visible = False
        With Charts("TSChart")
            .Visible = True
            .Activate
            .Deselect
        End With
    End Sub
```

26.8 Summary

This application has illustrated another way to obtain data for a VBA application: from another Excel file. If the data are already stored in another Excel file, there is no point in "appending" all of the data to the file that contains the application. Instead, the data file can be opened (and later closed) programmatically, and the necessary data can be copied to the application file. This application has also illustrated four common and useful estimation methods that can be used not only for estimating stock betas but for many other estimation problems.

PROGRAMMING EXERCISES

1. The file **SalesOffices.xls** contains data on a company's sales offices. Each row lists the location of the office (country, state or province, if any, and city) and the sales for the current year. Open another file, and insert a user form and a module in this new file. The user form should contain the usual OK and Cancel buttons and a list box (with an appropriate label above the list box for explanation). The list box should contain three columns: one for country, one for state/province, and one for city. The user should be allowed to choose exactly one item from the list. Then there should be a sub in the module that shows the user form, and then displays a message for the selected location, such as "The yearly sales for the

office in the city of Vancouver in the province of British Columbia in Canada has yearly sales of $987,000." Note that the part about the state/province will be absent for the offices not in the USA or Canada. This sub will also have to open the **SalesOffice.xls** file (and close it at the end) with VBA code.

2. Repeat the previous exercise, but now allow the user to select any number of locations from the list. Then, inside a loop, the sub should display the same type of message for each location selected.

3. Change the application and the data file as follows. For the data file, go to a suitable source (probably the Web), find monthly closing prices for the companies in the file for the year 2000, and add them to the tops of the sheets in the **StockData.xls** file. (You'll also have to find the corresponding market index data.) Feel free to add sheets for other companies as well, if you like. Then make any necessary updates to the **StockBeta.xls** file, including the code, to make it work with the expanded data set.

4. Suppose the **StockData.xls** file has stock price data for different months for different companies. For example, it might have data going back to 1992 for one company and data going back to only 1995 for another company. Rewrite the code in the **StockBeta.xls** file to ensure that it uses only the data available. Should the dialog box in Figure 26.2 be redesigned? Should its event code be changed? These are design issues you can decide. In any case, you can assume that there are plenty of data for the S&P 500 market index—it goes back at least as far as any of the companies—and that the most *recent* closing price date is the same for all companies.

5. The current **StockData.xls** sheets all have stock *returns* calculated in column C. Suppose these are *not* yet calculated—each column C is blank. For example, this might be the case if you downloaded the closing prices from some source, and this source gave only the prices, not the returns. Change the VBA code as necessary.

6. Suppose the stock price data are in some file (in the same format as we have given) in some folder, but the file name is not necessarily **StockData.xls** and the folder is not necessarily the same as the folder where the **StockBeta.xls** file resides. Therefore, you need to give the user a way to locate the data file. You could do this with an input box (and risk having the user spell something wrong), but Excel provides an easier way—the **GetOpenFilename** method of the **Application** object. This method displays a built-in user form that looks exactly like what you are used to when you use a Windows Open command to open a file. The user can then browse for the desired file in the usual way. The syntax you should use is as follows, where DataFileName is a string variable:

```
DataFileName = Application.GetOpenFilename(Filter:="Excel Files " & _
    "(*.xls),*.xls",Title:="Stock price file")
```

This doesn't actually *open* the Excel file selected by the user; it just returns the name and the path of the file chosen by the user and stores it in the string variable DataFileName. Use this method to change the application, so that it prompts the user for the name and location of the data file. Actually, you should probably precede the above line with a MsgBox statement so that the user knows she's being asked to select the file with the data. Then try the modified application with your own Excel file, stored in a folder *different* from the folder containing the Excel application. (Look up the **GetOpenFilename** method in online help. Its beauty is that it has all of the "open file" functionality you expect built into it—you don't have to *create* this user form!)

27

A Portfolio Optimization Application

27.1 Introduction

This application is probably the most ambitious application in the book, and it might also be the most exciting one. There is a Yahoo Web site that contains historical monthly stock price data for most companies during any time period. The application retrieves these data into an Excel file, calculates the summary measures (means, standard deviations, and correlations) for the corresponding stock returns, sets up a portfolio optimization model to minimize the portfolio standard deviation for a given minimum required mean return, and solves this model for several minimum required mean returns to find the efficient frontier, which is shown in tabular and graphical form. The user can select any group of stocks and any time period. All of this is done in "real time," so that an active Web connection is required.

There is a price to pay for anything this powerful—the VBA code is lengthy and sometimes rather difficult. But if you have the perseverance to work through it, you are well on your way to becoming a real—and valuable—programmer.

New Learning Objective: VBA

- To learn how to run Web queries with VBA code.

New Learning Objective: Non-VBA

- To gain some experience with portfolio optimization and efficient frontiers.
- To learn what Web queries are, and how to run them through the Excel interface.

27.2 Functionality of the Application

The application is stored in the **StockQuery.xls** file. At run time, this file contains no data except a list of companies and their stock symbols in a Stocks sheet.[44] The user can add to this list if desired. The application allows the user to select any stocks from the current list and a time period, such as from 1/95 to 12/99. It

---

[44]The file might also contain some leftover data from a previous run, but these data are eventually deleted.

then performs a **Web query**, which opens Yahoo Web pages for the selected stocks and time period, and imports the monthly stock price data back into the **StockQuery.xls** file. From that point, the Web part of the application is finished, and the necessary calculations leading to the efficient frontier described in the introduction are performed.

27.3 Running the Application

The first step is to make sure an Internet connection is open. The user does *not* have to go to the Yahoo Web site; the browser can initially be pointed to *any* site. Next, when the **StockQuery.xls** file is opened, the Explanation sheet in Figure 27.1 appears. When the user clicks on the button on this sheet, the dialog box in Figure 27.2 is displayed, where the user can select any number of stocks from the list. (A portfolio will eventually be formed from the stocks selected.) Then the dialog box in Figure 27.3 appears, where the user can select a time period.

Figure 27.1 Explanation sheet

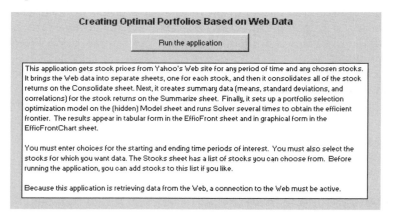

This is the only user involvement. From here, the application does its work in steps. First, it retrieves the data from the Web. A new worksheet for each selected stock is created, named by the stock's ticker symbol, and the Web data are imported into it. A sample appears in Figure 27.4 (with several hidden rows) for Chevron (ticker symbol CHV). The only data on this page that are used in the application are the dates in column A and the adjusted closing prices (adjusted for dividends and stock splits) in column G. The next section discusses Web queries in some detail.

The data from the separate stock sheets such as the one in Figure 27.4 are now analyzed. To do so, the application creates a Consolidate sheet that contains the monthly *returns* (percentage changes in the adjusted closing prices) for all stocks, listed in *increasing* chronological order. (Note that the order is reversed in Figure 27.4. This is how it comes back from the Web.) The finished Consolidate

Figure 27.2 Stock selection dialog box

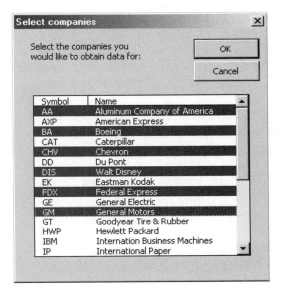

Figure 27.3 Dates selection dialog box

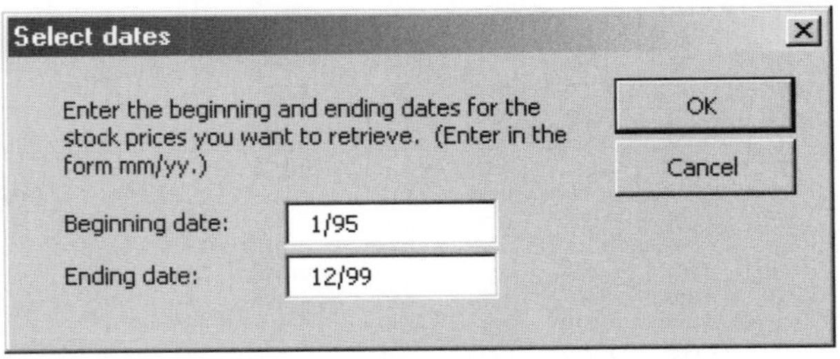

sheet appears in Figure 27.5, again with several hidden rows. Note that the first month, Jan-95, is missing. This is because no percentage change can be calculated for Jan-95 if the stock price for Dec-94 is not given.

The next step is to calculate summary measures (means, standard deviations, and correlations) for these historical returns. This is done in the SummaryMeasures sheet, with the results shown in Figure 27.6.

These summary measures are used as the input data for a portfolio optimization model, which is created in the Model sheet, as shown in Figure 27.7. This optimization model finds the optimal weights (fractions of each dollar invested in the various stocks) that minimize the standard deviation of the portfolio (in cell 19) subject to achieving a minimum required mean return (in cell D16).[45]

---

[45]You might have been taught to minimize the portfolio *variance*. However, this is equivalent to minimizing the portfolio standard deviation.

Figure 27.4 Web data for Chevron

	A	B	C	D	E	F	G
1							
2	Yahoo!						
3	Finance	ome - Yahoo! - Help					
4							
5	**Historical Quotes**	NYSE:CHV					
6							
7		*Month*	*Day*	*Year*	Daily		
8	Start Date:				Weekly		
9	End Date:				Monthly		
10					Dividends	Ticker Symbol:	
11							
12	**Date**	**Open**	**High**	**Low**	**Close**	**Volume**	**Adj.**
13	Dec-99	88.75	92.5	84.75	**86.625**	987,000	85.2977
14	Nov-99	90.5625	92.375	87.1875	**88.563**	1,323,700	87.2055
15	Nov-99			\$0.65 Cash Dividend			
16	Oct-99	88.8125	91.3125	87.4375	**91.313**	1,610,300	89.2896
17	Sep-99	92.75	93	87.3125	**88.75**	1,077,000	86.7838
18	Aug-99	91.3125	93.875	90.9375	**92.313**	1,120,900	90.2674
19	Aug-99			\$0.61 Cash Dividend			
20	Jul-99	96.5	96.9375	91.25	**91.25**	1,226,500	88.6578
21	Jun-99	92.3125	96.4375	89.6875	**95.063**	1,668,800	92.362
22	May-99	99.75	102.5625	92.0625	**92.5**	1,299,400	89.8722
23	May-99			\$0.61 Cash Dividend			
24	Apr-99	88.3125	103.5	86.375	**99.75**	1,313,500	96.2997
91	Feb-95			\$0.46 Cash Dividend			
92	Jan-95	45.25	45.25	44.375	**44.625**	1,110,200	37.3209

Figure 27.5 Consolidate sheet

	A	B	C	D	E	F	G
1	**Consolidated sheet with returns for all stocks**						
2							
3	Date	AA	BA	CHV	DIS	FDX	GM
4	01-Feb-95	-0.008	0.037	0.078	0.049	0.072	0.102
5	01-Mar-95	0.064	0.165	0.008	0.002	0.038	0.032
6	01-Apr-95	0.081	0.023	-0.013	0.037	0.006	0.026
7	01-May-95	0.041	0.070	0.047	0.002	-0.119	0.071
8	01-Jun-95	0.078	0.064	-0.056	0.000	0.015	-0.023
9	01-Jul-95	0.137	0.070	0.065	0.058	0.111	0.040
10	01-Aug-95	0.006	-0.045	-0.010	-0.041	0.063	-0.027
11	01-Sep-95	-0.074	0.066	0.008	0.020	0.157	-0.005
12	01-Oct-95	-0.035	-0.040	-0.041	0.006	-0.011	-0.067
13	01-Nov-95	0.152	0.113	0.067	0.043	-0.093	0.116
14	01-Dec-95	-0.096	0.075	0.061	-0.019	-0.008	0.090
15	01-Jan-96	0.054	-0.011	-0.010	0.091	0.030	-0.005
16	01-Feb-96	0.025	0.047	0.082	0.019	-0.028	-0.019
59	01-Sep-99	-0.039	-0.059	-0.039	-0.063	-0.084	-0.050
60	01-Oct-99	-0.021	0.081	0.029	0.021	0.108	0.119
61	01-Nov-99	0.082	-0.115	-0.023	0.061	-0.020	0.055
62	01-Dec-99	0.267	0.020	-0.022	0.049	-0.030	-0.015

Figure 27.6 SummaryMeasures sheet

	A	B	C	D	E	F	G
1	**Summary measures for stock returns**						
2							
3	**Stock**	AA	BA	CHV	DIS	FDX	GM
4	**Means**	0.0307	0.0139	0.0154	0.0126	0.0222	0.0202
5	**Stdevs**	0.1043	0.0791	0.0524	0.0737	0.1060	0.0761
6							
7	**Correlations**	AA	BA	CHV	DIS	FDX	GM
8	AA	1.000	0.408	0.280	0.249	0.133	0.234
9	BA	0.408	1.000	0.378	0.338	0.108	0.342
10	CHV	0.280	0.378	1.000	0.083	0.224	0.202
11	DIS	0.249	0.338	0.083	1.000	0.301	0.405
12	FDX	0.133	0.108	0.224	0.301	1.000	0.191
13	GM	0.234	0.342	0.202	0.405	0.191	1.000

Figure 27.7 Model sheet

	A	B	C	D	E	F	G	H
1	Portfolio selection model							
2								
3	Stock	AA	BA	CHV	DIS	FDX	GM	Sum
4	Weights	0.266527	0	0.340446	0	0.138824	0.254203	1
5	Means	0.030734	0.013891	0.015429	0.012562	0.022177	0.020161	
6								
7	Covariances	AA	BA	CHV	DIS	FDX	GM	
8	AA	0.010684	0.003308	0.001506	0.001879	0.001443	0.001825	
9	BA	0.003308	0.006144	0.001538	0.001936	0.000887	0.00202	
10	CHV	0.001506	0.001538	0.002701	0.000315	0.001226	0.000791	
11	DIS	0.001879	0.001936	0.000315	0.005342	0.002313	0.002234	
12	FDX	0.001443	0.000887	0.001226	0.002313	0.011049	0.001513	
13	GM	0.001825	0.00202	0.000791	0.002234	0.001513	0.005694	
14								
15	Constraint on mean return							
16		0.021648	>=	0.021648				
17								
18	Portfolio standard deviation							
19		0.051379						

Finally, the application solves this model for 11 equally spaced values of the minimum required mean return in cell D16. These values vary from the minimum return to the maximum return in row 5. This sweeps out the efficient frontier, which is reported in the EfficFront worksheet in Figure 27.8 and the EfficFrontChart chart sheet in Figure 27.9. Note that the EfficFront worksheet also shows the optimal weights for the various portfolios. For example, Chevron gets over half the total weight when a small mean return is required. It is evidently a relatively safe stock. In contrast, American Airlines gets most of the weight when a larger mean return is required. It evidently has higher return—and higher risk.

Figure 27.8 EfficFront sheet

	A	B	C	D	E	F	G	H	I	J
1	Efficient Frontier									
2					Weights for these optimal portfolios					
3		PortStdev	ReqdMean		AA	BA	CHV	DIS	FDX	GM
4		0.0427	0.0126		0.0156	0.0272	0.5713	0.2238	0.0327	0.1294
5		0.0427	0.0144		0.0156	0.0272	0.5713	0.2238	0.0327	0.1294
6		0.0427	0.0162		0.0313	0.0181	0.5629	0.2101	0.0386	0.1390
7		0.0439	0.0180		0.1063	0.0000	0.5053	0.1348	0.0710	0.1826
8		0.0469	0.0198		0.1809	0.0000	0.4367	0.0513	0.1059	0.2250
9		0.0514	0.0216		0.2665	0.0000	0.3404	0.0000	0.1388	0.2542
10		0.0577	0.0235		0.3697	0.0000	0.1996	0.0000	0.1685	0.2621
11		0.0655	0.0253		0.4729	0.0000	0.0588	0.0000	0.1981	0.2701
12		0.0748	0.0271		0.6182	0.0000	0.0000	0.0000	0.1998	0.1821
13		0.0872	0.0289		0.7936	0.0000	0.0000	0.0000	0.1812	0.0252
14		0.1034	0.0307		1.0000	0.0000	0.0000	0.0000	0.0000	0.0000

All of this occurs behind the scenes, and fairly quickly, when the user clicks on the OK button in Figure 27.3. The connection to the Yahoo site is made, the data are returned, the calculations are performed, and, like magic, the user sees the efficient frontier chart.

Figure 27.9 Efficient frontier chart

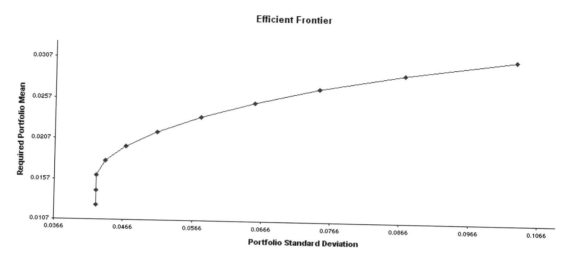

27.4 Web Queries in Excel

To understand this application, you must first understand a bit about Web queries. The application uses VBA to perform a Web query, but a Web query can be performed through the Excel interface, without any VBA. To do this, open a blank sheet in Excel and select the **Data/Get External Data/New Web Query** menu item. This brings up the dialog box in Figure 27.10, although the top box will be blank. The essence of the procedure is that when you type a URL in the top box, the *tables* from the corresponding Web site will be returned to the Excel worksheet.[46]

However, it can be more complicated. Suppose the Web site, like the Yahoo site for this application, asks for parameters—the dates and the stock symbol, as in Figure 27.11. At this point, you could click on the Get Historical Data button on the Web page to see the Chevron data and then click on the Browse button in the New Web Query dialog box. The appropriate URL would automatically appear in the top box, as it does in Figure 27.10. Clicking on OK then automatically imports the Web data into the Excel worksheet. For this particular site, the imported data will appear as in Figure 27.4. You have very little control over what is imported or how it is formatted. This could vary considerably from one Web site to another. But at least you get the data.

---

[46]As we all know, the Web is constantly changing. Therefore, we cannot guarantee that the Yahoo Web site we have used here will continue to exist, in the same form and with the same URL, in the future. If the site changes, appropriate changes might be required in the VBA code for the application.

Figure 27.10 New Web query dialog box

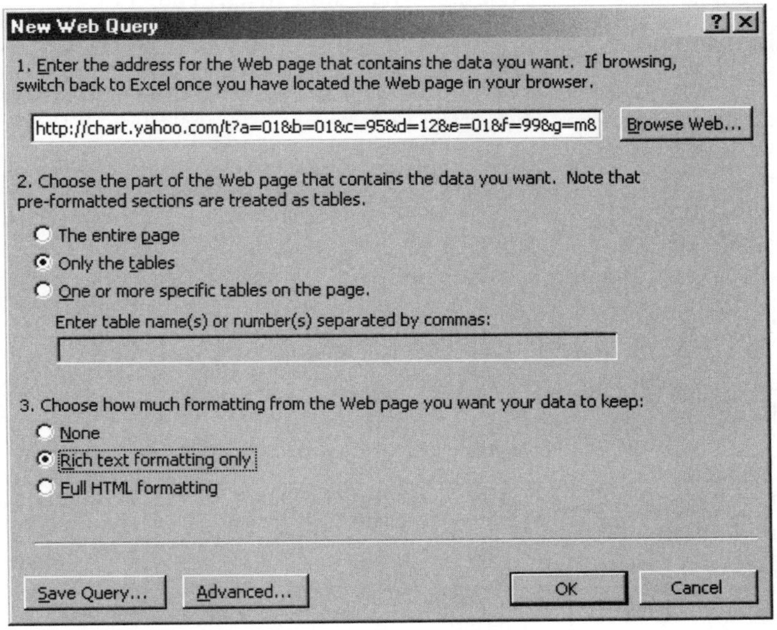

Figure 27.11 Web site request for parameters

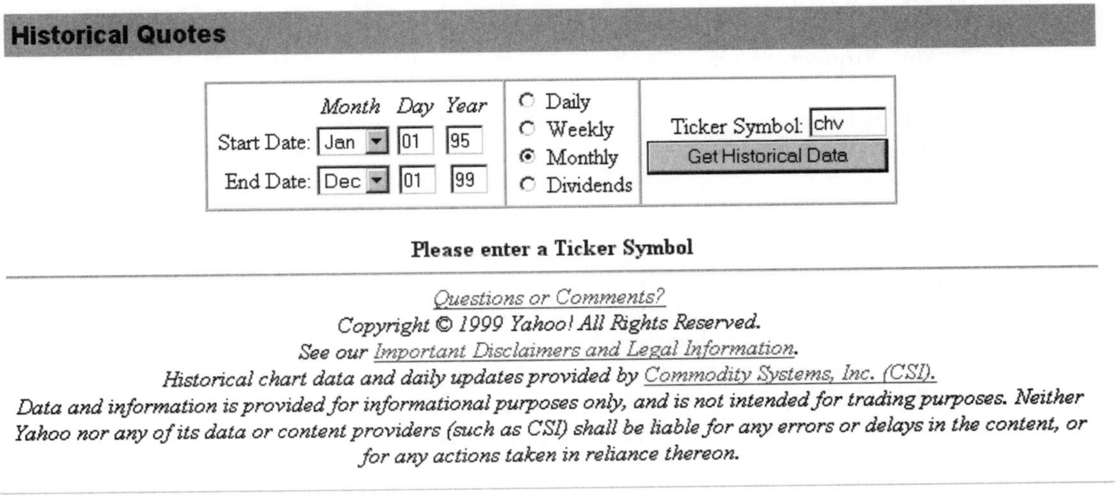

To understand how VBA can take advantage of this great feature, you need to examine the URL in Figure 27.10 in more detail. The full URL in the box is

http://chart.yahoo.com/t?a=01&b=01&c=95&d=12&e=01&f=99&g=m&s=chv

The parts after the question mark are **named parameters** and their values, separated by ampersand characters. For example, f is the name of the ending year parameter, and s is the name of the stock symbol parameter. (These names are chosen by the Web site developers.) Their current values are 99 and chv, respectively. You can find these named parameters for a typical Web site by searching through its HTML source code.[47] For example, we found the following lines (among a lot of other stuff) in the HTML code for the Chevron stock price page:

```
<SELECT NAME="a"><OPTION value=01 selected>Jan
<INPUT NAME="b" TYPE=TEXT VALUE="01" SIZE="2" MAXLENGTH="2">
<INPUT NAME="c" TYPE=TEXT VALUE="95" SIZE="2" MAXLENGTH="2">
<SELECT NAME="d"><OPTION value=01>Jan
<INPUT NAME="e" TYPE=TEXT VALUE="01" SIZE="2" MAXLENGTH="2">
<INPUT NAME="f" TYPE=TEXT VALUE="99" SIZE="2" MAXLENGTH="2">
<INPUT TYPE=RADIO NAME="g" VALUE="m" checked> Monthly
<INPUT TYPE=TEXT VALUE = "chv" SIZE NAME=s>
```

The keyword NAME in these lines is always followed by the parameter names that appear in the URL. The keyword VALUE is followed by possible values for the parameters. Unfortunately, you need to do some of this detective work to call a Web query from VBA code. The reason is that you need a string that is basically the URL but is broken up by values that *you* want to supply. The following line from the application illustrates what this means:

```
ConnectStr = "URL;http://chart.yahoo.com/t?"  & "a=" & BMonth & "&b=01" & "&c=" & BYear & _
    "&d=" & EMonth & "&e=01" & "&f=" & EYear & "&g=m" & "&s=" & StSymbol
```

This **connection string** is the key to the whole process. It specifies where on the Web the data are located and which data from that site you want. Except for the fact that this string starts with **"URL;"**, it is just like the URL in the New Web Query dialog box in Figure 27.10. However, some of the values for the named parameters are literal (as in **"&g=m"**, which means to get *monthly* data), and some are supplied by variable names (as in **"&s=" & StSymbol**, which means to use the stock symbol stored in the *variable* StSymbol). Note the syntax. Some of the ampersands are *inside* double quotes because they are part of the URL string, whereas others concatenate different parts of the string.

This brief introduction gives you a taste of Web queries—how they can be performed through the Excel interface and what is needed to perform them with VBA. This whole topic is in its infancy, and more user-friendly tools for extracting data from the Web into Excel will undoubtedly be developed. Right now, you must typically do some detective work on each Web site you want to query, and

---

[47]In Internet Explorer, use the View/Source menu item to see the HTML source code.

then you must hope for the best. This stock application is not as "bulletproof" as the others discussed in this book, because we cannot guarantee what data the Web is going to return. For example, it crashed when we asked for Sears stock prices before 1995. For some unknown reason, the Web site listed these prices, for example, as 0-0.2889 instead of 28.89. The application imported the data in this form, expecting them to be numbers, but then it could not do arithmetic on them—so it crashed. Sometimes there is a simple fix, but for the problem just described, the only fix we could think of was to omit Sears from the list of stocks!

You might encounter similar problems when you run this application with new stocks or new time periods. In fact, you might experience problems we never even anticipated. Unfortunately, these are the perils of working with the Web.

27.5 Setting Up the Excel Sheets

The **StockQuery.xls** file contains the following sheets at design time: the Explanation, Stocks, Consolidate, SummaryMeasures, and EfficFront worksheets, and the EfficFrontChart chart sheet. (The Model sheet is added at run time.) There is very little that can be done at design time to set up these sheets. The only steps possible are to list the stocks in the Stocks sheet, as shown in Figure 27.12 (with several hidden rows), and to develop an XY chart in the chart sheet from any trial data. The chart will then be populated with the actual data at run time.

Figure 27.12 Stocks sheet

	A	B	C	D	E	F
1	Stock symbols and names to choose from					
2						
3	Symbol	Name				
4	AA	Aluminum Company of America				
5	AXP	American Express				
6	BA	Boeing				
7	CAT	Caterpillar		You can add any other		
8	CHV	Chevron		stocks to this list (or		
9	DD	Du Pont		delete any). If you		
10	DIS	Walt Disney		want to add any, enter		
11	EK	Eastman Kodak		the stock symbol in		
12	FDX	Federal Express		column A, the name in		
13	GE	General Electric		column B.		
14	GM	General Motors				
15	GT	Goodyear Tire & Rubber				
16	HWP	Hewlett Packard				
29	UK	Union Carbide				
30	UTX	United Technologies				
31	WMT	Wal-Mart				

27.6 Getting Started with the VBA

The application requires two user forms, named StocksForm and DatesForm, a module, and a reference to the Solver.xla file. Once these items are added, the Project Explorer window will appear as in Figure 27.13. (Note the wild number-

Figure 27.13 Project Explorer window

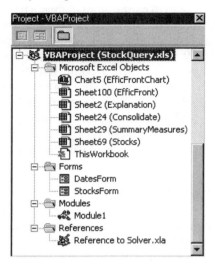

ing of the sheets. By the time we took this screen shot, many stock sheets had been added and subsequently deleted. So the sheet numbering is really meaningless at this point.)

Workbook_Open Code

To guarantee that the Explanation sheet appears when the file is opened, the following code is placed in the ThisWorkbook code window. It also hides all sheets except the Explanation and Stocks sheets.

```
Private Sub Workbook_Open()
    Dim sht As Object
    Worksheets("Explanation").Activate
    Range("F4").Select
    For Each sht In ActiveWorkbook.Sheets
        If sht.Name <> "Explanation" And sht.Name <> "Stocks" Then sht.Visible = False
    Next
End Sub
```

27.7 Designing the User Forms and Writing Their Event Code

Web Help   For more explanation of the code in this application, visit our Web site at http://www.indiana.edu/~mgtsci and download the **Code Explanation - StockQuery.doc** file.

StocksForm

The design for the StocksForm appears in Figure 27.14. It contains the usual OK and Cancel buttons, an explanation label, and a list box named CompanyList. At design time, you should change three of the list box's properties: change the **MultiSelect** property to option 2 (so that multiple companies can be selected), change the **ColumnCount** property to 2, and change the **RowSource** property to Stocks. This is the range name in the Stocks sheet where the list of companies and ticker symbols are located. (See Figure 27.12.)

Figure 27.14 Design of StocksForm

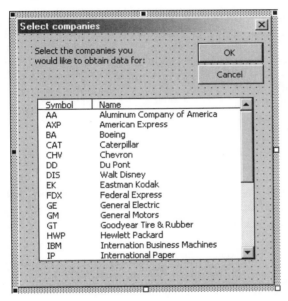

Event Code for StocksForm

The event code for this form is fairly straightforward. The **UserForm_Initialize** sub selects the first company in the list by default. Then the **OKButton_Click** sub uses the **Selected** array property of the list box to capture the names and symbols of the selected stocks in the public arrays StockName and Stock. The **CancelButton_Click** sub unloads the dialog box and terminates the program.

A note on multi-column list boxes. Like the user form from the previous chapter, this list box has two columns. We could use a combination of the **BoundColumn** and **Value** properties to retrieve values from the two columns. (See the previous chapter for details.) Alternatively, we can use the **List** property like a two-dimensional array, which is done here. The first index indicates how far down the list we are (starting with index 0 for the first item in the list), and the second is 0 for the first column and 1 for the second column. With list boxes, there always seems to be more than one way to accomplish the same thing!

```
Private Sub UserForm_Initialize()
    CompanyList.Selected(0) = True
End Sub

Private Sub OKButton_Click()
' Capture the number of stocks selected, their symbols, and their names.
    Dim i As Integer
    NStocks = 0
    For i = 0 To CompanyList.ListCount - 1
        If CompanyList.Selected(i) = True Then
            NStocks = NStocks + 1
            ReDim Preserve Stock(NStocks)
            ReDim Preserve StockName(NStocks)
            Stock(NStocks) = CompanyList.List(i, 0)
            StockName(NStocks) = CompanyList.List(i, 1)
        End If
    Next
    Unload Me
End Sub

Private Sub CancelButton_Click()
    Unload Me
    End
End Sub
```

DatesForm

The DatesForm, with design shown in Figure 27.15, contains OK and Cancel buttons, an explanation label, and two text boxes and corresponding labels. The text boxes are named Date1Box and Date2Box.

Figure 27.15 Design of DatesForm

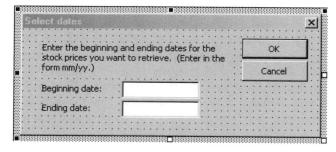

Event Code for DatesForm

The event code for this form, listed below, contains no new ideas. Note how it uses VBA's **IsDate** function to check for valid dates. However, other than checking that the beginning date is before the ending date, it makes no other error checks. You might want to change the code to allow only dates after 1990, for example. If the user requests dates for which the Web site has no data, the program will not work as desired.

```
Private Sub UserForm_Initialize()
    Date1Box = ""
    Date2Box = ""
End Sub

Private Sub OKButton_Click()
    Dim ctl As Control
    For Each ctl In Me.Controls
        If TypeName(ctl) = "TextBox" Then
            If ctl.Value = "" Or Not IsDate(ctl) Then
                MsgBox "Enter valid dates in the text boxes.", _
                    vbInformation, "Invalid entry"
                ctl.SetFocus
                Exit Sub
            End If
        End If
    Next
    BegDate = Date1Box
    EndDate = Date2Box
    If BegDate >= EndDate Then
        MsgBox "The beginning date should be before the ending date.", _
            vbInformation, "Invalid dates"
        Date1Box.SetFocus
        Exit Sub
    End If
    Unload Me
End Sub

Private Sub CancelButton_Click()
    Unload Me
    End
End Sub
```

27.8   The VBA Code in the Module

The module must accomplish a long list of tasks. It starts with the **Main** sub, which is attached to the button on the Explanation sheet. This sub "shows" the two user forms and then calls a number of other subs to accomplish the various tasks. The public variables and the code for the Main sub are listed below.

Option Statements and Public Variables

```
Option Explicit
Option Base 1

'   BegDate: beginning date for data (user input)
'   EndDate: ending date for data (user input)
'   NStocks: number of stocks chosen by user
'   Stock: array of ticker symbols of stocks chosen by user
'   StockName: array of company names for stocks chosen by user
'   BMonth, EMonth: two-digit month strings corresponding to BegMonth, EndMonth
'   BYear, EYear: two-digit year strings corresponding to BegYear, EndYear
'   MinReturn, MaxReturn: the smallest and largest mean historical returns for the
'       chosen stocks
```

```
Public BegDate As Date, EndDate As Date, NStocks As Integer, _
    Stock() As String, StockName() As String, _
    BMonth As String, BYear As String, EMonth As String, EYear As String, _
    MinReturn As Single, MaxReturn As Single
```

Main Code

```
Sub Main()
    Dim StSymbol As String, i As Integer
    With Worksheets("Stocks").Range("A3")
        Range(.Offset(1, 0), .Offset(1, 1).End(xlDown)).Name = "Stocks"
    End With
    StocksForm.Show
    DatesForm.Show
    Call GetDateStrings
    Application.ScreenUpdating = False
' Delete the Model sheet and any sheets for individual stocks, and clear any data from
' the remaining sheets.
    Call ClearOldData
' For each requested stock, add a new sheet and run a query.
    For i = 1 To NStocks
        StSymbol = Stock(i)
        Worksheets.Add.Move After:=Sheets(ActiveWorkbook.Sheets.Count)
        ActiveSheet.Name = StSymbol
        Call RunQuery(StSymbol)
    Next
' Copy closing price data from all stock sheets to a Consolidate sheet and transform
' to returns.
    Call Consolidate
' Calculate summary measures on the SummaryMeasures sheet.
    Call SummaryMeasures
' Create the portfolio optimization model and optimize.
    Call CreateModel
    Call RunSolver
' Create the chart of the efficient frontier and update its chart.
    Call EfficientFrontier
    Call UpdateChart
    Application.ScreenUpdating = True
End Sub
```

GetDateStrings Code

The Web query string eventually wants the months and years to be two-digit strings. For example, it wants "01" instead of "1" for January. (We learned this through trial and error.) The **GetDateStrings** sub builds these two-digit strings. To do this, it uses VBA's **Month** date function and the **Len** and **Right** string functions.

```
Sub GetDateStrings()
' Get the month number with the Month function, and add a 0 if necessary
' to make it a two-character string (e.g., change "1" to "01"). This is
' necessary because the Web query expects dates in this form.
    BMonth = Month(BegDate)
    If Len(BMonth) = 1 Then BMonth = "0" & BMonth
```

```
      EMonth = Month(EndDate)
      If Len(EMonth) = 1 Then EMonth = "0" & EMonth
' Get the last two digits of the year.
      BYear = Right(BegDate, 2)
      EYear = Right(EndDate, 2)
End Sub
```

ClearOldData Code

The **ClearOldData** sub deletes all worksheets except the Explanation, Consolidate, Stocks, SummaryMeasures, and EfficFront sheets. It also deletes all range names except Stocks, and it clears the contents of the Consolidate, SummaryMeasures, and EfficFront sheets. After this sub is executed, the application is practically starting with a blank slate.

```
Sub ClearOldData()
    Dim sht As Worksheet, nm As Variant
    Application.DisplayAlerts = False
' Delete all sheets for individual stocks.
    For Each sht In Worksheets
        If sht.Name <> "Explanation" And sht.Name <> "Consolidate" _
            And sht.Name <> "Stocks" And sht.Name <> "SummaryMeasures" _
            And sht.Name <> "EfficFront" Then sht.Delete
    Next
' Delete all range names except Stocks (on the Stocks sheet).
    For Each nm In ActiveWorkbook.Names
        If nm.Name <> "Stocks" Then nm.Delete
    Next
' Clear contents from the Consolidate, SummaryMeasures, and EfficFront sheets (and
' restore a couple of headings).
    With Worksheets("Consolidate").Range("A3")
        Range(.Offset(0, 0), .End(xlDown).End(xlToRight)).ClearContents
        .Value = "Date"
    End With
    With Worksheets("SummaryMeasures").Range("A3")
        Range(.Offset(0, 1), .Offset(2, 1).End(xlToRight)).ClearContents
    End With
    With Worksheets("SummaryMeasures").Range("A7")
        Range(.Offset(0, 0), .End(xlDown).End(xlToRight)).ClearContents
        .Value = "Correlations"
    End With
    With Worksheets("EfficFront").Range("E2")
        Range(.Offset(1, 0), .Offset(1, 0).End(xlDown).End(xlToRight)).ClearContents
    End With
End Sub
```

RunQuery Code

The **RunQuery** sub is the crucial sub. It creates a **connection string** (stored in the ConnectStr string variable), which is essentially the URL for the Web site, as discussed in Section 27.4. It then adds a **QueryTable** object to the active sheet with the line

```
With ActiveSheet.QueryTables.Add(Connection:=ConnectStr,Destination:=Range("A1"))
```

This is followed by various obscure properties of the QueryTable object. As the comment indicates, we discovered this code by creating the Web query through the Excel menu interface with the recorder on. We do not claim to understand all of the fine details, but it works!

```
Sub RunQuery(StSymbol As String)
' This sets up a new Web query and runs it, placing the Web data into the active sheet.
   Dim ConnectStr As String
' The next line builds a long string that is essentially the URL (preceded by URL;). It
' is used to define the query. Note how it inserts the user's inputs into the string.
' The "input names" (such as a, b, and so on) are found in the HTML source code for
' this Web page.
   ConnectStr = "URL;http://chart.yahoo.com/t?" & "a=" & BMonth & "&b=01" & "&c=" _
        & BYear & "&d=" & EMonth & "&e=01" & "&f=" & EYear & "&g=m" & "&s=" & StSymbol
' The next few lines create a QueryTable object with appropriate properties.  We got
' this code by recording, then deleted parts that appeared unnecessary.
   With ActiveSheet.QueryTables.Add(Connection:=ConnectStr, Destination:=Range("A1"))
        .Name = "StockPrices_" & StSymbol
        .SaveData = True
        .AdjustColumnWidth = True
        .WebSelectionType = xlAllTables
        .WebFormatting = xlWebFormattingAll
        .WebPreFormattedTextToColumns = False
        .WebConsecutiveDelimitersAsOne = True
        .WebSingleBlockTextImport = False
        .WebDisableDateRecognition = False
        .Refresh BackgroundQuery:=False
   End With
End Sub
```

Consolidate Code

The rest of the subs handle the details—and there are a lot of details. We'll let the comments do most of the explaining.

The **Consolidate** sub needs to copy the data below the "Adj." label in each stock sheet (see Figure 27.4) to the appropriate column in the Consolidate sheet. Then it needs to transform them to returns (percentage changes). There are three problems that it encounters, all caused by the form of the imported Web data (over which we have no control). First, some stocks return no data. This was the case for Allied Signal (ALD), for example. Second, there are several blank cells in the data below the "Adj." label because of dividends and stock splits. The VBA code must be written to skip over these blanks. Third, we want the consolidated data to go in *increasing* chronological order, not the opposite. (Remember what we said about programming in Chapter 1. It is a process of getting by one small hurdle after another!)

```
Sub Consolidate()
' At this point, the stock data are in the individual stock sheets.  This sub
' calculates the corresponding returns and puts them in the Consolidate sheet.
```

```
    Dim i As Integer, j As Integer, StSymbol As String, Counter1 As Integer, _
        Counter2 As Integer, DateRange As Range, CloseRange As Range, _
        StartRow As Integer, StartAddress As String, NFound As Integer, _
        FoundCell As Range, FoundStock() As Boolean, NPrices As Integer
    ReDim FoundStock(NStocks)
    With Worksheets("Consolidate")
        .Visible = True
        .Activate
    End With
    NFound = 0
    For i = 1 To NStocks
        StSymbol = Stock(i)
' Initialize counters.
        Counter1 = 1
        Counter2 = 1
' Try to find the label "Adj." in this stock's sheet. This Find method returns a range
' object, which is set to FoundCell. If the Web query couldn't find any data for this
' stock (for whatever reason), this find will be unsuccessful and FoundCell will be
' set to Nothing.
        Set FoundCell = Worksheets(StSymbol).Cells.Find(What:="Adj.")
        If Not FoundCell Is Nothing Then
' FoundStock is a Boolean. Here it is set to true to indicate that the Web query found
' data on this stock.
            FoundStock(i) = True
            NFound = NFound + 1
' The purpose of the next few lines is to transfer the closing prices from this stock's
' sheet to the Consolidate sheet. Unfortunately, the Web query returns a few blank
' cells under the Adj. Close column (because of stock splits and dividends), so the
' program has to go down this column and return only the non-blanks. Counter1 is how
' far down the Consolidate sheet (below A3) we are, whereas Counter2 is how far down
' this stock's sheet (below StartRow) we are.
            With FoundCell
                StartRow = .Row
                StartAddress = .Address
            End With
' The dates (from the Web query) are always in column A.
            Set DateRange = Worksheets(StSymbol).Range("A" & StartRow)
            Set CloseRange = Worksheets(StSymbol).Range(StartAddress)
' Loop through the rows until encountering a blank cell.
            Do While DateRange.Offset(Counter2, 0) <> ""
                If CloseRange.Offset(Counter2, 0) <> "" Then
' Capture the dates and put them in column A of the Consolidate sheet.
                    Range("A3").Offset(Counter1, 0) = DateRange.Offset(Counter2, 0)
' Transfer the closing price to the appropriate row and column of the Consolidate
' sheet.
                    Range("A3").Offset(Counter1, NFound) = CloseRange.Offset(Counter2, 0)
' Update Counter1 after every transfer.
                    Counter1 = Counter1 + 1
                End If
' Update Counter2 whether or not a blank was encountered in the Adj. Close column.
                Counter2 = Counter2 + 1
            Loop
        Else
' Record that no data were found for this stock and delete its sheet.
            MsgBox "No data were returned for " & StockName(i) & ", so this " _
                & "stock will not be included in the analysis.", vbInformation, _
                "No data for stock"
            FoundStock(i) = False
            Application.DisplayAlerts = False
            Worksheets(Stock(i)).Delete
```

```
                  Application.DisplayAlerts = True
            End If
      Next
' In case no data are found for any of the stocks, quit.
      If NFound = 0 Then
            MsgBox "No data were returned for any of the chosen stocks, so " _
                  & "the program cannot continue.", vbInformation, "No data!"
            End
      End If
' Get rid of sheets for stocks not found and update NStocks, Stock, and StockName.
      NFound = 0
      For i = 1 To NStocks
            If FoundStock(i) Then
                  NFound = NFound + 1
                  Stock(NFound) = Stock(i)
                  StockName(NFound) = StockName(i)
            End If
      Next
      NStocks = NFound
      For i = 1 To NStocks
' Enter stock symbols as headings in the Consolidate sheet.
            Range("A3").Offset(0, i) = Stock(i)
      Next
' Sort the data from earliest to latest (the Web query brings it in in the opposite
' order), and give some range names.
      With Range("A3")
            .Sort Key1:=Range("A:A"), Header:=xlYes
            Range(.Offset(1, 0), .End(xlDown)).Name = "Date"
' For the stocks, don't include any possible blank cells in the named ranges.
            For j = 1 To NStocks
                  If .Offset(1, j) = "" Then
                        Range(.Offset(0, j).End(xlDown), _
                              .Offset(0, j).End(xlDown).End(xlDown)).Name = Stock(j)
                  Else
                        Range(.Offset(1, j), .Offset(1, j).End(xlDown)).Name = Stock(j)
                  End If
            Next
      End With
' Replace closing prices by returns (percentage changes).
      For j = 1 To NStocks
            With Range(Stock(j))
                  NPrices = .Cells.Count
                  For i = NPrices To 2 Step -1
                        .Cells(i) = (.Cells(i) - .Cells(i - 1)) / .Cells(i - 1)
                  Next
                  With Range(.Cells(2), .Cells(NPrices))
                        .Name = Stock(j)
                        .NumberFormat = "0.000"
                  End With
            End With
      Next
' There are no returns in row 4 (the first time period), so delete it.
      Rows("4:4").Delete Shift:=xlUp
End Sub
```

SummaryMeasures Code

The **SummaryMeasures** sub uses Excel's Average, Stdev, and Correl functions to summarize the consolidated stock return data in the SummaryMeasures sheet.

```
Sub SummaryMeasures()
    Dim i As Integer, j As Integer
    With Worksheets("SummaryMeasures")
        .Visible = True
        .Activate
    End With
' Enter formulas for averages and standard deviations (using Excel's Average and
' Stdev functions).
    For i = 1 To NStocks
        Range("A3").Offset(0, i) = Stock(i)
        Range("A4").Offset(0, i).Formula = "=Average(" & Stock(i) & ")"
        Range("A5").Offset(0, i).Formula = "=Stdev(" & Stock(i) & ")"
    Next
' Create a table of correlations (using Excel's Correl function).
    With Range("A7")
        For i = 1 To NStocks
            .Offset(i, 0) = Stock(i)
            .Offset(0, i) = Stock(i)
        Next
        For i = 1 To NStocks
            For j = 1 To NStocks
                .Offset(i, j).Formula = "=Correl(" & Stock(i) & "," & Stock(j) & ")"
            Next
        Next
    End With
End Sub
```

CreateModel Code

The **CreateModel** sub uses the summary measures from the previous sub as inputs
to a portfolio optimization model. It starts absolutely from scratch—there is no
Model sheet before this sub is run. It adds this sheet and then develops the model
shown earlier in Figure 27.7.

```
Sub CreateModel()
' Create the portfolio optimization model in the Model sheet.
    Dim i As Integer, j As Integer
' Add a new Model sheet.
    Worksheets.Add After:=Worksheets("SummaryMeasures")
    ActiveSheet.Name = "Model"
' Enter title and headings.
    Range("A1").Value = "Portfolio selection model (solution shown is when " _
        & "required return is halfway between minimum and maximum of stock returns)"
    With Range("A3")
        .Value = "Stock"
        .Offset(1, 0) = "Weights"
        .Offset(2, 0) = "Means"
        For i = 1 To NStocks
            .Offset(0, i) = Stock(i)
' Enter initial equal weights for the portfolio (Solver will find the optimal weights)
' and formulas for the average returns.
            .Offset(1, i) = 1 / NStocks
            .Offset(2, i).Formula = "=Average(" & Stock(i) & ")"
        Next
    End With
' Name ranges.
    With Range("A4")
```

```
            Range(.Offset(0, 1), .Offset(0, 1).End(xlToRight)).Name = "Weights"
            Range(.Offset(1, 1), .Offset(1, 1).End(xlToRight)).Name = "Means"
    End With
' Find the smallest and largest of the average returns, which will be used to create
' the efficient frontier.
    MinReturn = Application.Min(Range("Means"))
    MaxReturn = Application.Max(Range("Means"))
' Calculate the sum of weights (which will be constrained to be 1).
    With Range("A3").Offset(0, NStocks + 1)
        .Value = "Sum"
        .Offset(1, 0).Name = "SumWts"
        .Offset(1, 0).Formula = "=Sum(Weights)"
    End With
' Calculate table of covariances (using Excel's Covar function).
    With Range("A7")
        .Value = "Covariances"
        For i = 1 To NStocks
            .Offset(i, 0) = Stock(i)
            .Offset(0, i) = Stock(i)
        Next
        For i = 1 To NStocks
            For j = 1 To NStocks
                .Offset(i, j).Formula = "=Covar(" & Stock(i) & "," & Stock(j) & ")"
            Next
        Next
        Range(.Offset(1, 1), .Offset(NStocks, NStocks)).Name = "Covar"
    End With
' Form lower bound constraint on mean portfolio return, using an initial lower bound
' halfway between the smallest and largest mean returns.  (This lower bound will be
' varied through the whole range when finding the efficient frontier.)
    With Range("A7").Offset(NStocks + 2, 0)
        .Value = "Constraint on mean return"
        .Offset(1, 1).Formula = "=Sumproduct(Weights,Means)"
        .Offset(1, 2) = ">="
        .Offset(1, 3) = (MinReturn + MaxReturn) / 2
        .Offset(1, 1).Name = "MeanReturn"
        .Offset(1, 3).Name = "ReqdReturn"
' Calculate the standard deviation of the portfolio (using Excel's MMult and Transpose
' matrix functions.)  Note that it uses the FormulaArray property.  This is analogous
' to pressing Ctrl-Shift-Enter.
        .Offset(3, 0) = "Portfolio standard deviation"
        With .Offset(4, 1)
            .FormulaArray = "=Sqrt(MMult(Weights,MMult(Covar,Transpose(Weights))))"
            .Name = "PortStdev"
        End With
    End With
' Adjust width of column A.
    Columns("A:A").ColumnWidth = 11
End Sub
```

RunSolver Code

The **RunSolver** sub is straightforward. It sets up the Solver and then runs it. Note that it does not need to use **SolverReset**. Remember that the Model sheet at this point is brand new, so there is no Solver model to reset.

```
Sub RunSolver()
' Set up and run Solver.
    SolverOk SetCell:=Range("PortStdev"), MaxMinVal:=2, ByChange:=Range("Weights")
    SolverAdd CellRef:=Range("SumWts"), Relation:=2, FormulaText:=1
    SolverAdd CellRef:=Range("MeanReturn"), Relation:=3, FormulaText:="ReqdReturn"
    SolverOptions AssumeNonNeg:=True
    SolverSolve UserFinish:=True
End Sub
```

EfficientFrontier Code

The **EfficientFrontier** sub runs the Solver several times and records the results in the EfficFront sheet. Each run uses a different minimum required mean portfolio return.

```
Sub EfficientFrontier()
' For each of 11 equally spaced values of the required mean portfolio return, run the
' Solver and record the results on the EffFront sheet. Note the Model sheet is still
' the active sheet.  The sheet with the Solver model must be active to run the Solver.
    Dim i As Integer, j As Integer
' Portfolio standard deviations and means are recorded in columns B and C. The
' corresponding portfolio weights are recorded from column E over. First, enter
' headings.
    With Worksheets("EfficFront").Range("E3")
        For i = 1 To NStocks
            .Offset(0, i - 1) = Stock(i)
        Next
    End With
' Run the Solver 11 times and record the results.
    For i = 0 To 10
        Range("ReqdReturn") = MinReturn + i * (MaxReturn - MinReturn) / 10
        SolverSolve UserFinish:=True
        With Worksheets("EfficFront").Range("B4")
            .Offset(i, 0) = Range("PortStdev")
            .Offset(i, 1) = Range("ReqdReturn")
        End With
        With Worksheets("EfficFront").Range("E4")
            For j = 1 To NStocks
                .Offset(i, j - 1) = Range("Weights").Cells(j)
            Next
        End With
    Next
' Hide the Model sheet.
    Worksheets("Model").Visible = False
End Sub
```

UpdateChart Code

The EfficFrontChart already exists as an XY chart (of the type with the dots connected). The **UpdateChart** sub populates it with the newly calculated data in the EfficFront sheet. The sub also ensures that the graph "fills the sheet" by adjusting its axis scales appropriately.

```
Sub UpdateChart()
' Update the efficient frontier chart. Get the source data from the EfficFront
' worksheet.  The part about MinX, MinY, etc. is for scaling the axes appropriately.
    Dim SourceRange As Range, MinX As Single, MaxX As Single, _
        MinY As Single, MaxY As Single, XLength As Single, YLength As Single
    With Worksheets("EfficFront")
        .Visible = True
        Set SourceRange = .Range("B4:C14")
        MinX = .Range("B4")
        MaxX = .Range("B14")
        MinY = .Range("C4")
        MaxY = .Range("C14")
        XLength = MaxX - MinX
        YLength = MaxY - MinY
    End With
    With Charts("EfficFrontChart")
        .Visible = True
        .Activate
        .SetSourceData SourceRange
        With .Axes(xlCategory)
            .MinimumScale = MinX - 0.1 * XLength
            .MaximumScale = MaxX + 0.1 * XLength
        End With
        With .Axes(xlValue)
            .MinimumScale = MinY - 0.1 * YLength
            .MaximumScale = MaxY + 0.1 * YLength
        End With
    End With
    ActiveChart.Deselect
End Sub
```

27.9 Summary

This application has been developed to impress—and to be useful to financial analysts and investors. To achieve anything this ambitious, quite a lot of code must be written, and it is not always straightforward. However, we believe it is well worth the effort. You should pay particular attention to the RunQuery sub, where the data from the Web site are retrieved. In fact, we suspect that many of you will be anxious to make appropriate modifications to this code to obtain data from other Web sites. The ability to get access to the mounds of data available on the Web and then analyze these data with Excel's many tools is indeed a powerful combination.

PROGRAMMING EXERCISES

1. We evidently didn't follow our own guidelines in the Consolidate sub. It is much longer than most professional programmers would advocate. Change it so the Consolidate sub calls several smaller subs. You can decide on the number of smaller subs, but each should have a specific task. You shouldn't have to write very much new code; it is mostly a matter of copying and pasting. However, be very

careful about declaring variables and passing arguments correctly, and test your final product to make sure that it works.

2. Repeat the previous exercise, but now do it for the CreateModel sub. It is also too long!

3. Note that all summary measures are entered as *formulas* in the SummaryMeasures sub. There is no real need to do it this way. Change this sub so that all summary measures are entered as *values*.

4. The Consolidate sub uses the **Find** method to find a cell with some specified value. There is also a **FindNext** method. (Each is a method of a **Range** object.) These can be used in VBA similar to the way they are used in the usual Excel interface to find a piece of information (or the next such piece of information). The file **PianoOrders.xls** contains a list of orders for Steinway pianos. It lists the date of the order and the state where the order was made. Write a sub that searches through the list of states to find each occurrence of California and colors the background of each such cell yellow. (*Hint*: Look up the Find and FindNext methods of the Range object in the Object Browser.)

5. As the application is now written, it automatically retrieves *monthly* data from the Web. See if it is possible to get *weekly* data instead.

6. The following is a list of Web sites that, at least as of the time of this writing, have potentially interesting information. Try doing a Web query on one that interests you. Do it without VBA, using the appropriate menu item from Excel. Then, assuming the search turns up something interesting, write a sub that uses VBA to retrieve the same information.

   a. http://146.142.4.24/cgi-bin/surveymost?eb

   b. http://venus.census.gov/cdrom/lookup

   c. http://wonder.cdc.gov

   d. http://www.econ.ag.gov/db/FATUS/index.asp?Type=XC

   e. http://nces.ed.gov/ipedsearlyrelease/index.html

   f. http://www.bts.gov/ntda/oai/search.html

7. Find a Web site that contains at least one table of data and allows the user to make a choice, such as we did in this application when we got to choose the period of time and the ticker symbol. Then write a sub that retrieves the data specified by a user's choices. These choices can be obtained from an input box or a user form, whichever is more natural for the context. (For example, in this application we got the user's choices from the dialog boxes in Figures 27.2 and 27.3.)

A Data Envelopment
Analysis Application

28

28.1 Introduction

Data Envelopment Analysis (DEA) is a method for comparing the relative efficiency of organizational units such as banks, hospitals, and schools, where efficiency relates to the ability to transform inputs into outputs. For example, DEA could analyze several branch banks, where the inputs for each branch might be labor hours, square feet of space, and supplies used, and the outputs might be the numbers of loan applications, deposits processed, and checks processed during some time period. DEA could then use these data in several linear programming models, one for each branch, to see whether each branch can attach unit costs to its inputs and unit prices to its outputs to make itself appear efficient. By definition, a branch is "efficient" if the total value of its outputs is equal to the total value of its inputs. It is inefficient if the total value of its outputs is *less* than the total value of its inputs.

This application takes data from a text (.txt) file, sets up a Solver model, runs it for each of the organizational units, and reports the results. Among other things, this application illustrates how to import data from a text file into an Excel application.

New Learning Objectives: VBA

- To learn how the data from a comma-delimited text file can be imported into an Excel application.
- To see how a comma-delimited string can be parsed by using appropriate loops and string functions.

New Learning Objective: Non-VBA

- To learn how the DEA procedure can compare various organizational units for efficiency.

28.2 Functionality of the Application

The data for the application are in a file called **DEA.txt**. This is a simple text file that can be created with the Windows NotePad. It lists the names of the inputs and outputs, the names of the organizational units, and the inputs used and

outputs produced by each unit. The application imports these data into the
DEA.xls application file, where they are used as input data for a linear programming model. This model is solved for each organizational unit to see whether the unit is efficient. The results are then reported in a Report sheet.

As the application is currently written, the **DEA.txt** and **DEA.xls** files should be stored in the same folder. The current **DEA.txt** file contains data on four organizational units (departments in a university), each with three inputs and two outputs. However, these data can be replaced with any data, with any numbers of organization units, inputs, and outputs, and the application will respond appropriately. The format for the data in the **DEA.txt** file is discussed below.

28.3   Running the Application

When the **DEA.xls** file is opened, the Explanation sheet in Figure 28.1 appears. When the button on this sheet is clicked, the dialog box in Figure 28.2 requests the size of the problem: the numbers of organizational units, inputs, and outputs. Of course, these should match the data in the **DEA.txt** file.

Figure 28.1   Explanation sheet

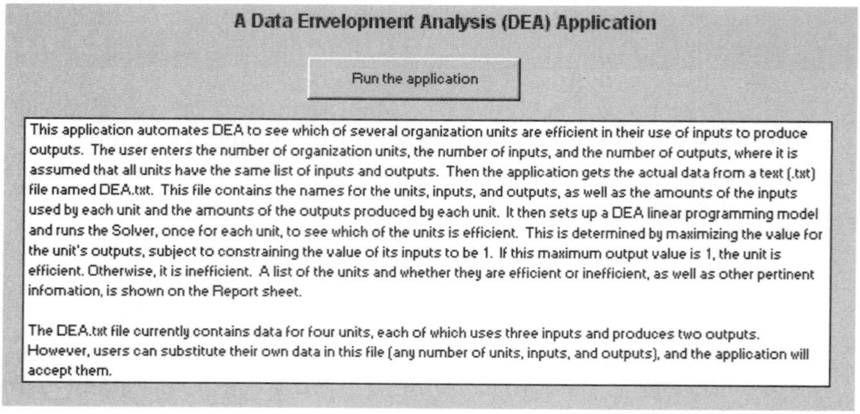

Figure 28.2   Inputs dialog box

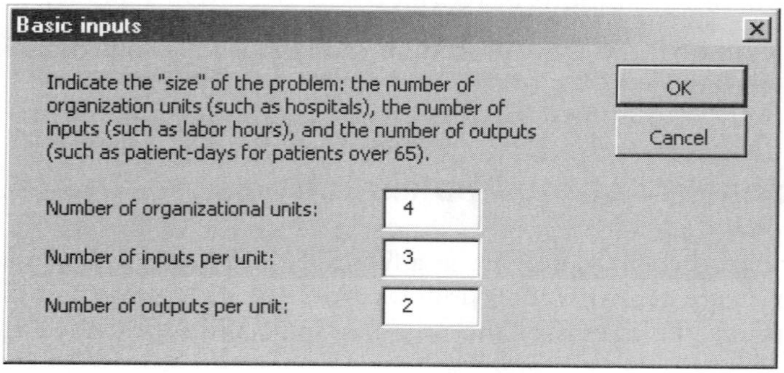

The application then opens the **DEA.txt** file, reads the data and stores them in arrays, sets up a linear programming model in a (hidden) Model sheet, solves it once for each organizational unit, and reports the results in the Report sheet shown in Figure 28.3.

Figure 28.3 Report sheet

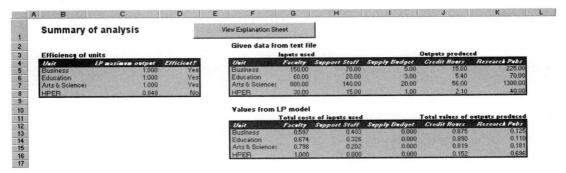

There are three sections in this report. The one on the left indicates whether the units are efficient by reporting the maximum total output value from the linear programming model for each unit. Because the total input values are scaled to be 1, a unit is efficient only if its total output value is 1. For these data, all units are efficient except HPER. The section on the top right reports the original data. It shows the quantities of inputs used and outputs produced for each unit.

Finally, the section on the bottom right indicates input costs and output values from the linear programming model, where input costs are scaled so that they sum to 1 for each unit. For example, Education (internally) assigns *unit* costs to its inputs so that the total values of its faculty and support staff used are 0.674 and 0.326, respectively. It attaches zero value to its supply budget input. Similarly, it attaches *unit* prices to its outputs so that the total values of its credit hours and research pubs produced are 0.890 and 0.110, respectively. With these unit costs and unit prices, Education's total output value is equal to its total input value (both equal 1), which means that it is an efficient unit.

This report is based on the linear programming model shown in Figure 28.4. The version shown here is for checking the efficiency of unit 4 (HPER). For later reference, the following range names are created at run time for the Model sheet. Of course, the actual ranges would change if there were different numbers of organizational units, inputs, or outputs.

Range	*Name*
B6:D9	InputsUsed
G6:H9	OutputsProduced
B11:D11	InputCosts
G11:H11	OutputPrices
B15:B18	InputValues
D15:D18	OutputValues
B21	SelInputValue
B24	SelOutputValue

Figure 28.4 Completed Model sheet

	A	B	C	D	E	F	G	H
1	**DEA model**							
2								
3	Selected unit	4						
4								
5	Inputs used	Faculty	Support Staff	Supply Budget		Outputs used	Credit Hours	Research Pubs
6	Business	150	70	5		Business	15	225
7	Education	60	20	3		Education	5.4	70
8	Arts & Sciences	800	140	20		Arts & Sciences	56	1300
9	HPER	30	15	1		HPER	2.1	40
10								
11	Unit costs	0.033	0	0		Unit prices	0.0725	0.0174
12								
13	Constraints that input costs must cover output values							
14	Unit	Input costs		Output values				
15	1	5	>=	5				
16	2	2	>=	1.609				
17	3	26.667	>=	26.667				
18	4	1	>=	0.848				
19								
20	Constraint that selected unit's input cost must equal a nominal value of 1							
21	Selected unit's input cost	1	=	1				
22								
23	Maximize selected unit's output value (to see if it is 1, hence efficient)							
24	Selected unit's output value	0.848						

The VBA code sets up this model at run time. Then it substitutes the index for each organizational unit (1 to 4 in this example) in cell B3. The formulas in cells B21 and B24 are linked to this value through VLOOKUP functions, so that they update automatically. Then the Solver is run for each possible index in cell B3.

28.4   Setting Up the Excel Sheets and the Text File

The **DEA.xls** file contains three worksheets named Explanation, Model, and Report. However, there are no templates for the Model and Report sheets. At design time, they are blank. The reason is that if the numbers of organizational units, inputs, or outputs change, due to new data in the **DEA.txt** file, the Model and Report setups will change dramatically. Therefore, it is easier to start with a "clean slate" and then fill these sheets completely—values, formulas, headings, and formatting—through VBA code at run time.

The **DEA.txt** file should be structured as a comma-delimited file, as shown in Figure 28.5. The first row should contain the names of the inputs, separated by commas. The second row should contain the names of the outputs, separated by commas. Then there should be three lines for each organizational unit. The first should contain the unit's name, and the second and third should contain its inputs used and outputs produced, respectively, with input values separated by commas and output values separated by commas. There should *not* be any spaces following the commas. If the data are not structured in this way, the application will either crash (with a "nice" error message) or yield misleading results.

Figure 28.5 Structure of DEA.txt file

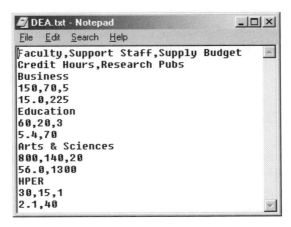

28.5 Getting Started with the VBA

The application contains a single user form named InputsForm, a module, and a reference to the Solver.xla add-in. Once these items are added, the Project Explorer window will appear as in Figure 28.6.

Figure 28.6 Project Explorer window

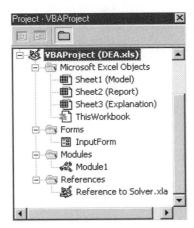

Workbook_Open Code

To guarantee that the Explanation sheet appears when the file is opened, the following code is placed in the ThisWorkbook code window. This sub also hides the Model and Report sheets.

```
Private Sub Workbook_Open()
    Worksheets("Explanation").Activate
    Range("F5").Select
    Worksheets("Report").Visible = False
    Worksheets("Model").Visible = False
End Sub
```

28.6 Designing the User Form and Writing Its Event Code

Web Help   For more explanation of the code in this application, visit our Web site at http://www.indiana.edu/~mgtsci and download the **Code Explanation - DEA.doc** file.

The design of the InputsForm appears in Figure 28.7. It contains the usual OK and Cancel buttons, an explanation label, and three text boxes with corresponding labels. The text boxes are named UnitsBox, InputsBox, and OutputsBox.

Figure 28.7   Design of InputsForm

Basic inputs	✕
Indicate the "size" of the problem: the number of organization units (such as hospitals), the number of inputs (such as labor hours), and the number of outputs (such as patient-days for patients over 65).	OK Cancel
Number of organizational units:	
Number of inputs per unit:	
Number of outputs per unit:	

Event Code for InputsForm

The event code for this form is completely straightforward and is listed below. As usual, the **OKButton_Click** sub does some error checking before finally capturing the user's inputs in public variables.

```
Private Sub UserForm_Initialize()
    UnitsBox = ""
    InputsBox = ""
    OutputsBox = ""
End Sub

Private Sub OKButton_Click()
    Dim ctl As Control
    For Each ctl In Me.Controls
```

```
        If TypeName(ctl) = "TextBox" Then
            If ctl.Value = "" Or Not IsNumeric(ctl) Then
                MsgBox "Enter positive integers in all boxes.", vbInformation, _
                    "Invalid entry"
                ctl.SetFocus
                Exit Sub
            End If
            If ctl.Value < 1 Then
                MsgBox "Enter a positive integer in this box.", vbInformation, _
                    "Invalid entry"
                ctl.SetFocus
                Exit Sub
            End If
        End If
    Next
    NUnits = UnitsBox
    NInputs = InputsBox
    NOutputs = OutputsBox
    Unload Me
End Sub

Private Sub CancelButton_Click()
    Unload Me
    End
End Sub
```

28.7 Getting Data from a Text File

Perhaps the most interesting part of this application, at least from a VBA stand-point, is the way the data from the **DEA.txt** file are obtained. To open the text file, the following line is required:

```
Open ThisWorkbook.Path & "\DEA.txt" For Input As #1
```

The "#1" essentially means that this is the *first* text file opened. (If another were opened in the same session, it would be opened as #2, and so on.) Eventually, the file should be closed with the line

```
Close #1
```

To read a single line from the text file, the following code is required, where DataLine is a string variable:

```
Line Input #1, DataLine
```

Each time this line of code is executed, the next entire line of data is stored as a string in the DataLine variable. Typically, there are several pieces of data in a line of text, separated by commas. The individual pieces must then be **parsed**. Because this parsing operation is required several times, the program contains a **ParseLine** sub that is called whenever it is needed. The ParseLine sub takes three arguments:

the DataLine string, the expected number of pieces of data, and an array (we've named it ReturnArray) to be filled with the individual pieces of data. It then passes the filled ReturnArray array *back* to a **GetData** sub, where its contents are put into public array variables, such as InputName. The details appear in the next section.

Summarizing, the steps required to import data from a text file are: (1) open the file, (2) read an entire line at a time, (3) parse the line into its separate pieces of data, and (4) close the file.

28.8 The VBA Code in the Module

Almost everything is done at run time with the code in the module. The button on the Explanation sheet is attached to the **Main** sub. This sub first shows the InputsForm. Then it captures the data from the **DEA.txt** file in public array variables. Next, it sets up the linear programming model and solves it for each organizational unit. Finally, it creates the report. The public variables and the Main sub are listed below.

Option Statements and Public Variables

```
Option Explicit
Option Base 1

' Definitions of public variables:
'   NUnits: number of organization units
'   UnitName: array of names of units
'   NInputs: number of inputs for each unit
'   InputName: array of names of inputs
'   InputUsed: two-dimensional array of inputs used by units (first
'       dimension is the unit, second is the input)
'   NOutputs: number of outputs for each unit
'   OutputName: array of names of outputs
'   OutputProduced: two-dimensional array of outputs produced by units
'       (first dimension is the unit, second is the output)
'   EffIndex(): an array of maximum outputs from LP model, one for each
'       unit
'   TotalInputCost(): two-dimensional array (first subscript is unit,
'       second is input) - e.g., TotalInputCost(1,3) is the unit cost
'       of input 3 multiplied by the amount of input 3 used by unit 1
'   TotalOUtputValue(): same as TotalInputCost array, except for outputs.
Public NUnits As Integer, UnitName() As String, NInputs As Integer, _
    InputName() As String, InputUsed() As Single, NOutputs As Integer, _
    OutputName() As String, OutputProduced() As Single, _
    EffIndex() As Single, TotalInputCost() As Single, _
    TotalOutputValue() As Single
```

Main Code

```
Sub Main()
' Get the size of the problem: numbers of units, inputs, and outputs
    InputsForm.Show
```

```
' Dimension arrays appropriately.
    ReDim UnitName(NUnits)
    ReDim InputName(NInputs)
    ReDim InputUsed(NUnits, NInputs)
    ReDim OutputName(NOutputs)
    ReDim OutputProduced(NUnits, NOutputs)
    ReDim EffIndex(NUnits)
    ReDim TotalInputCost(NUnits, NInputs)
    ReDim TotalOutputValue(NUnits, NOutputs)
    Application.ScreenUpdating = False
' Get data from the DEA.txt file
    Call GetData
' Create the model in the Model sheet.
    Call CreateModel
' Set up and run the Solver several times, once for each unit.
    Call RunSolver
' Fill in the Report sheet.
    Call CreateReport
    Application.ScreenUpdating = True
End Sub
```

GetData Code

The **GetData** sub is responsible for importing the data from the text file into Excel. First, an attempt is made to open the text file. If there is an error (no such file exists, at least not in the same folder as the application file), an error message is displayed and the program ends. Otherwise, the file is read line by line. If there is ever an error of any type (probably because the text file isn't structured properly), control passes to the BadData label, a message is displayed, and the program ends. Note how the **On Error** statements discussed in Chapter 13 are used here to trap for these errors.

Pay particular attention to the **ParseLine** calls. (The code for the ParseLine sub is listed below.) For example, after the first line of the text file (the one with the names of the inputs) is stored in the DataLine string, the following line is called:

```
Call ParseLine(DataLine, NInputs, ReturnArray)
```

The second argument indicates the number of separate pieces of data that are expected in the DataLine string. This string is then parsed and its pieces are placed in the ReturnArray array (this is done in the ParseLine sub), so that the array is available for the GetData sub.

```
Sub GetData()
    Dim i As Integer, j As Integer, DataLine As String, ReturnArray() As String
    On Error Resume Next
    Open ThisWorkbook.Path & "\DEA.txt" For Input As #1
' Quit if there is no DEA.txt file in the directory of this workbook.
    If Err <> 0 Then
        MsgBox "There is no DEA.txt file in the same directory as " _
            & "this workbook, so the application cannot continue.", vbInformation, _
            "Missing file"
```

```
            End
        End If
 ' Go to the BadData label (and quit) if anything goes wrong reading the file.
        On Error GoTo BadData
 ' The first line contains the names of the inputs.
        Line Input #1, DataLine
        ReDim ReturnArray(NInputs)
        Call ParseLine(DataLine, NInputs, ReturnArray)
 ' Transfer the contents of the ReturnArray array to the InputName array.
        For i = 1 To NInputs
            InputName(i) = ReturnArray(i)
        Next
 ' Do it again, reading the second line for the output names.
        Line Input #1, DataLine
        ReDim ReturnArray(NOutputs)
        Call ParseLine(DataLine, NOutputs, ReturnArray)
        For i = 1 To NOutputs
            OutputName(i) = ReturnArray(i)
        Next
 ' Now go through each organizational unit.
        For i = 1 To NUnits
 ' The unit's name is in the first line - no parsing required.
            Line Input #1, DataLine
            UnitName(i) = DataLine
 ' The unit's inputs used are in the second line.
            Line Input #1, DataLine
            ReDim ReturnArray(NInputs)
            Call ParseLine(DataLine, NInputs, ReturnArray)
            For j = 1 To NInputs
                InputUsed(i, j) = ReturnArray(j)
            Next
 ' The unit's outputs produced are in the third line.
            Line Input #1, DataLine
            ReDim ReturnArray(NOutputs)
            Call ParseLine(DataLine, NOutputs, ReturnArray)
            For j = 1 To NOutputs
                OutputProduced(i, j) = ReturnArray(j)
            Next
        Next
 ' Close the data file.
        Close #1
        Exit Sub
BadData:
        MsgBox "The data file is not set up properly, so the application " _
            & "cannot continue.", vbInformation, "Invalid data"
        End
End Sub
```

ParseLine Code

To parse the DataLine into its individual pieces of data, the **ParseLine** sub uses a For loop to go through the DataLine string one character at a time (from left to right), using the **Mid** function. Specifically, Mid(DataLine, i, 1) returns the character in position i of the string. As it reads these characters, it builds a CurrTxt string. As it progresses, it checks whether each character is a comma or the last character in the DataLine string. In either case, it captures the characters stored in the CurrTxt string as the next element of the ReturnArray and resets CurrTxt to the empty string. If it ever fills the array with the expected number of elements *before* parsing the entire DataLine string, it exits prematurely. (This could be the case if a text line contained more data than is required.)

It is very instructive to step through this sub one line at a time (with the F8 key) and keep a watch on the DataLine and CurrTxt strings in the Watch window. This allows you to see exactly how the strings are parsed.

```
Sub ParseLine(DataLine As String, NVals As Integer, ReturnArray() As String)
    Dim i As Integer, char As String, Counter As Integer, CurrTxt As String
' Counter counts the number of pieces of data in the line.
    Counter = 1
' CurrTxt is any piece of data in the line, where the pieces are separated by commas.
    CurrTxt = ""
    For i = 1 To Len(DataLine)
' Get the character in position i.
        char = Mid(DataLine, i, 1)
' Check if the character is a comma or is the last character in the string.
        If char = "," Or i = Len(DataLine) Then
            If i = Len(DataLine) Then CurrTxt = CurrTxt & char
            ReturnArray(Counter) = CurrTxt
' Stop reading once all NVals values have been read.
            If Counter = NVals Then Exit For
' Get ready for the next piece of data.
            CurrTxt = ""
            Counter = Counter + 1
        Else
' Add this character to the CurrTxt string.
            CurrTxt = CurrTxt & Mid(DataLine, i, 1)
        End If
    Next i
End Sub
```

CreateModel Code

The **CreateModel** sub clears the Model sheet completely by using the ClearContents method of the UsedRange. (The **UsedRange** of a worksheet, discussed briefly in Chapter 6, is basically the area of the worksheet that contains any data.) Then it calls two subs, **EnterInputsOutputs** and **CalcFormulas**, to develop the linear programming model.

```
Sub CreateModel()
' This sub creates the LP model and reports the results. It calls two subs to
' accomplish this. First, unhide and activate the Model sheet and clear all contents.
    With Worksheets("Model")
        .Visible = True
        .Activate
        .UsedRange.ClearContents
    End With
' Enter labels. (Cell B3 will contain the index of the unit currently being analyzed
' for efficiency.)
    Range("A1") = "DEA model"
    Range("A3") = "Selected unit"
```

```
' Enter the user data.
   Call EnterInputsOutputs
' Calculate all required formulas for the model.
   Call CalcFormulas
End Sub
```

EnterInputsOutputs Code

The **EnterInputsOutputs** sub enters the data from the text file, which are by now stored in arrays (from the GetData sub), into the Model sheet. It also enters descriptive headings. Keep in mind that the Model sheet is practically blank when this sub and the next sub are called, so they have a considerable amount of work to do. Refer to Figure 28.4 and the list of range names right above it as you read this code.

```
Sub EnterInputsOutputs()
    Dim i As Integer, j As Integer
' Enter labels and data.
    With Range("A5")
        .Value = "Inputs used"
        For j = 1 To NInputs
            .Offset(0, j) = InputName(j)
        Next
        For i = 1 To NUnits
            .Offset(i, 0) = UnitName(i)
            For j = 1 To NInputs
                .Offset(i, j) = InputUsed(i, j)
            Next
        Next
' Name the range of input amounts. It will be used for formulas in the Model sheet.
        Range(.Offset(1, 1), .Offset(NUnits, NInputs)).Name = "InputsUsed"
' Enter 0's as initial values for the input cost changing cells.
        With .Offset(NUnits + 2, 0)
            .Value = "Unit costs"
            For j = 1 To NInputs
                .Offset(0, j) = 0
            Next
' Name the range of the changing cells for inputs.
            Range(.Offset(0, 1), .Offset(0, NInputs)).Name = "InputCosts"
        End With
    End With
' Do the same for the outputs.
    With Range("A5").Offset(0, NInputs + 2)
        .Value = "Outputs used"
        For j = 1 To NOutputs
            .Offset(0, j) = OutputName(j)
        Next
        For i = 1 To NUnits
            .Offset(i, 0) = UnitName(i)
            For j = 1 To NOutputs
                .Offset(i, j) = OutputProduced(i, j)
            Next
        Next
        Range(.Offset(1, 1), .Offset(NUnits, NOutputs)).Name = "OutputsProduced"
        With .Offset(NUnits + 2, 0)
            .Value = "Unit prices"
```

```
                For j = 1 To NOutputs
                    .Offset(0, j) = 0
                Next
                Range(.Offset(0, 1), .Offset(0, NOutputs)).Name = "OutputPrices"
            End With
        End With
End Sub
```

CalcFormulas Code

The **CalcFormulas** sub continues the model development by entering all required formulas and naming various ranges. Again, refer to Figure 28.4 and the list of range names right above it as you read this code.

```
Sub CalcFormulas()
' This sub calculates formulas for the Model, starting just below the changing cells
' from the previous sub.
    Dim i As Integer
    With Range("A5").Offset(NUnits + 4, 0)
' Set up constraints that input costs incurred must be greater than or equal to output
' values achieved.
        .Value = "Constraints that input costs must cover output values"
        .Offset(1, 0) = "Unit index"
        .Offset(1, 1) = "Input costs"
        .Offset(1, 3) = "Output values"
' There is a constraint for each unit.
        For i = 1 To NUnits
' Labels in column A (1, 2, etc.) are needed for later on, to enable use of VLookup
' function.
            .Offset(1 + i, 0) = i
' The input cost incurred for any unit is the sumproduct of the changing cell range
' (UnitCosts) and the appropriate input data row. The same goes for output value.
' Note how the appropriate row is specified.
            .Offset(1 + i, 1).Formula = _
                "=Sumproduct(InputCosts,"& Range("InputsUsed").Rows(i).Address & ")"
            .Offset(1 + i, 2) = ">="
            .Offset(1 + i, 3).Formula = _
                "=Sumproduct(OutputPrices,"& Range("OutputsProduced").Rows(i).Address & ")"
        Next
' Name appropriate ranges. LTable is for later on with the VLookup function.
        Range(.Offset(2, 1), .Offset(NUnits + 1, 1)).Name = "InputValues"
        Range(.Offset(2, 3), .Offset(NUnits + 1, 3)).Name = "OutputValues"
        Range(.Offset(2, 0), .Offset(NUnits + 1, 3)).Name = "LTable"
    End With
' Set up constraint that the selected unit's total input cost is 1.
    With Range("A5").Offset(2 * NUnits + 7, 0)
        .Value = "Constraint that selected unit's input cost must equal a nominal value of 1"
        .Offset(1, 0) = "Selected unit's input cost"
' Get the selected unit's total input cost with a VLookup.
        With .Offset(1, 1)
            .Formula = "=VLookup(B3,LTable,2)"
            .Name = "SelInputValue"
        End With
        .Offset(1, 2) = "="
        .Offset(1, 3) = 1
        .Offset(3, 0) = "Maximize selected unit's output value (to see if it is 1, " _
            & "hence efficient)"
```

```
            .Offset(4, 0) = "Selected unit's output value"
' Get the selected unit's total output value with a VLookup. It is the target cell
' for maximization.
        With .Offset(4, 1)
            .Formula = "=VLookup(B3,LTable,4)"
            .Name = "SelOutputValue"
        End With
    End With
End Sub
```

RunSolver Code

The **RunSolver** sub uses a For loop to go through each organizational unit and solve the appropriate model. (The particular unit being analyzed depends on the index placed in cell B3.) It then captures the Solver results in the arrays EffIndex, TotalInputCost, and TotalOuputValue for later use in the report.

```
Sub RunSolver()
' Set up and run the Solver once for each unit, first placing its index (1, 2, etc.)
' in cell B3.
    Dim i As Integer, j As Integer
    For i = 1 To NUnits
        Range("B3") = i
        SolverReset
        SolverOk SetCell:=Range("SelOutputValue"), MaxMinVal:=1, _
            ByChange:=Union(Range("InputCosts"), Range("OutputPrices"))
        SolverAdd CellRef:=Range("InputValues"), Relation:=3, _
            FormulaText:="OutputValues"
        SolverAdd CellRef:=Range("SelInputValue"), Relation:=2, FormulaText:=1
        SolverOptions AssumeLinear:=True, AssumeNonNeg:=True
        SolverSolve UserFinish:=True
' Capture the quantities for the report in the TotalInputCost, TotalOutputValue, and
' EffIndex arrays.
        For j = 1 To NInputs
            TotalInputCost(i, j) = Range("InputCosts").Cells(j) * InputUsed(i, j)
        Next
        For j = 1 To NOutputs
            TotalOutputValue(i, j) = Range("OutputPrices").Cells(j) * OutputProduced(i, j)
        Next
        EffIndex(i) = Range("SelOutputValue")
    Next
    Worksheets("Model").Visible = False
End Sub
```

CreateReport Code

To create the report, the current Report sheet is deleted and a new one is added. (Note how **DisplayAlerts** is set to False, so that users are not asked whether they *really* want to delete the sheet.) This provides a fresh start, but it means that all of the data transfers *and* all desired formatting must be done at run time through VBA code. There is nothing difficult about it, but there are a lot of steps. In the spirit of modularizing, the **CreateReport** sub does a few tasks and then calls three subs, **FirstSection**, **SecondSection**, and **ThirdSection**, to do the majority of the work.

A note on adding a button with VBA. Toward the end of this sub, a new button is added to the sheet with the **Add** method of the **Buttons** collection of the **ActiveSheet** object. The resulting **Button** object has an **OnAction** property that is the name of the sub it is attached to. The numbers in the line that adds the button specify the position of the button on the sheet. They are, respectively, the **Left**, **Top**, **Width**, and **Height** properties. (You can discover appropriate numbers by adding a button with the recorder on.)

```
Sub CreateReport()
    Dim i As Integer, j As Integer
' It's easier to start with a brand new Report sheet, so the old one is deleted (with
' DisplayAlerts off), and a new one is added.  Note that the new one automatically
' becomes the active sheet.
    Application.DisplayAlerts = False
    Worksheets("Report").Delete
    Application.DisplayAlerts = True
    Worksheets.Add.Move after:=Worksheets("Explanation")
    ActiveSheet.Name = "Report"
' Zoom to 75% and turn off gridlines.
    With ActiveWindow
        .Zoom = 75
        .DisplayGridlines = False
    End With
' Shrink column width of column A and format the title in cell B2.
    Columns("A:A").ColumnWidth = 3
    With Range("B1")
        .Value = "Summary of analysis"
        .RowHeight = 40
        .VerticalAlignment = xlCenter
        .Font.Bold = True
        .Font.Size = 16
    End With
' Build the rest of the report in three sections with the following three subs.
    Call FirstSection
    Call SecondSection
    Call ThirdSection
' Add a button to run the ViewExplanation sub.
    With ActiveSheet.Buttons.Add(275, 10, 200, 25)
        .OnAction = "ViewExplanation"
        .Characters.Text = "View Explanation Sheet"
    End With
    Range("A1").Select
End Sub
```

FirstSection, SecondSection, ThirdSection Code

Referring to the report in Figure 28.3, the first section is the section on the left, the second section is the top right section, and the third section is the bottom right section. Each of the following subs adds headings and data and then formats its section appropriately.

```
Sub FirstSection()
' This sub enters the efficiencies for the units.
    Dim i As Integer
```

```
' Enter headings.
    With Range("B3")
        .Value = "Efficiency of units"
        .Font.Bold = True
        .Font.Size = 12
    End With
    With Range("B4")
        .Value = "Unit"
        .Offset(0, 1) = "LP maximum output"
        .Offset(0, 2) = "Efficient?"
        For i = 1 To NUnits
            .Offset(i, 0) = UnitName(i)
' Enter target values from the optimization.
            .Offset(i, 1) = EffIndex(i)
' Enter Yes or No depending on whether the target value is 1 or less than 1.
            If EffIndex(i) < 1 Then
                .Offset(i, 2) = "No"
            Else
                .Offset(i, 2) = "Yes"
            End If
        Next
' Format appropriately.
        Range(.Offset(1, 1), .Offset(NUnits, 1)).NumberFormat = "0.000"
        Range(.Offset(0, 0), .Offset(NUnits, 2)).AutoFormat xlRangeAutoFormatClassic3
        .HorizontalAlignment = xlLeft
        Range(.Offset(1, 2), .Offset(NUnits, 2)).HorizontalAlignment = xlRight
    End With
End Sub
```

```
Sub SecondSection()
' This sub enters the given data from the DEA.txt file.
    Dim i As Integer, j As Integer
' Enter headings.
    With Range("F2")
        .Value = "Given data from text file"
        .Font.Bold = True
        .Font.Size = 12
    End With
    With Range("F4")
' Enter more headings.
        .Value = "Unit"
        With .Offset(-1, 1)
            .Value = "Inputs used"
            .Font.Bold = True
        End With
        With .Offset(-1, NInputs + 1)
            .Value = "Outputs produced"
            .Font.Bold = True
        End With
        For i = 1 To NUnits
            .Offset(i, 0) = UnitName(i)
        Next
        For j = 1 To NInputs
            .Offset(0, j) = InputName(j)
        Next
        For j = 1 To NOutputs
            .Offset(0, NInputs + j) = OutputName(j)
        Next
' Enter the inputs used and outputs produced.
```

```
        For i = 1 To NUnits
            For j = 1 To NInputs
                .Offset(i, j) = InputUsed(i, j)
            Next
            For j = 1 To NOutputs
                .Offset(i, NInputs + j) = OutputProduced(i, j)
            Next
        Next
' Format appropriately.
        Range(.Offset(1, 1), .Offset(NUnits, NInputs + NOutputs)).NumberFormat = "0.00"
        Range(.Offset(0, 0), .Offset(NUnits, NInputs + NOutputs)).AutoFormat _
            xlRangeAutoFormatClassic3
        .HorizontalAlignment = xlLeft
    End With
End Sub
```

```
Sub ThirdSection()
' This sub is almost the same as the previous sub, but now the data are total costs of
' inputs used and total values of outputs produced, as calculated from the LP model.
    Dim i As Integer, j As Integer
    With Range("F4").Offset(NUnits + 2, 0)
        .Value = "Values from LP model"
        .Font.Bold = True
        .Font.Size = 12
    End With
    With Range("F4").Offset(NUnits + 4, 0)
        .Value = "Unit"
        With .Offset(-1, 1)
            .Value = "Total costs of inputs used"
            .Font.Bold = True
        End With
        With .Offset(-1, NInputs + 1)
            .Value = "Total values of outputs produced"
            .Font.Bold = True
        End With
        For i = 1 To NUnits
            .Offset(i, 0) = UnitName(i)
        Next
        For j = 1 To NInputs
            .Offset(0, j) = InputName(j)
        Next
        For j = 1 To NOutputs
            .Offset(0, NInputs + j) = OutputName(j)
        Next
' Enter the data from the LP runs.  (These were calculated in the RunSolver sub.)
        For i = 1 To NUnits
            For j = 1 To NInputs
                .Offset(i, j) = TotalInputCost(i, j)
            Next
            For j = 1 To NOutputs
                .Offset(i, NInputs + j) = TotalOutputValue(i, j)
            Next
        Next
        Range(.Offset(1, 1), .Offset(NUnits, NInputs + NOutputs)).NumberFormat _
            = "0.000"
        Range(.Offset(0, 0), .Offset(NUnits, NInputs + NOutputs)).AutoFormat _
            xlRangeAutoFormatClassic3
        .HorizontalAlignment = xlLeft
    End With
End Sub
```

ViewExplanation Code

The **ViewExplanation** sub lets the user navigate back to the Explanation sheet. It also hides the Report sheet.

```
Sub ViewExplanation()
    Worksheets("Report").Visible = False
    Worksheets("Explanation").Activate
    Range("F5").Select
End Sub
```

28.9 Summary

This application has illustrated a very useful method, DEA, for comparing organizational units for relative efficiency. This method has been used in a number of real applications in various industries. (See the references in Chapter 4 of *Practical Management Science.*) In addition, this chapter has illustrated a method for importing data from a comma-delimited text file into Excel. This involves parsing data into its individual pieces, a technique that is very useful in its own right in a number of contexts.

PROGRAMMING EXERCISES

1. If you ever try to open a text (.txt) file in Excel, you'll see that it takes you through a wizard. One of the steps asks for the character delimiter. One choice is the comma (the one used here), and another is the tab character. Rewrite the ParseLine sub so that the separating character is the tab rather than the comma. Then get into Notepad, open the **DEA.txt** file, replace each comma by a tab (highlight the comma and press the Tab key), and rerun the application with your new ParseLine sub. You should get the same results as before. (*Hint*: Open the VBA library in the Object Browser and look under Constants.)

2. Rewrite the ParseLine sub so that it is slightly more general. It should be passed an extra argument called Separator, declared as **String * 1** type. (That is, when you declare this argument, you write **Separator As String * 1**. This means a string of length 1 character.) The Separator is any single character that separates the pieces of the long string being parsed. In our application, the separator was the comma, but it might be another character in other applications.

3. Suppose a line from a text file uses a *single* comma to separate pieces of data, but it uses two *consecutive* commas to indicate a comma is part of a piece of data. For example the line 23,290,21,,200 has three pieces of data: 23, 290, and 21,200. Rewrite the ParseLine sub to parse a typical line with this comma convention.

4. We claimed that this application works with any data, provided that the text file is structured properly. Try it out. Open the **DEA.txt** file in Notepad and change its data in some way. (For example, try adding another academic department and/or

adding an input or an output.) Then rerun the application to see if it still works properly.

5. Repeat the previous exercise, but now create a *new* text file called **MyData.txt** (stored in the same folder as the Excel application), structured exactly as **DEA.txt**, and add some data to it. Then rerun the application to see if it still works properly. (Note that you will have to change the VBA code slightly, so that it references the correct name of your new text file.)

6. The previous problem indicates a "fix" that no business would ever tolerate—they would never be willing to get into the VBA code to change a file name reference. A much better alternative is to change the VBA code in the first place so that it asks the user for the location and name of the database file. You could do this with an input box (and risk having the user spell something wrong), but Excel provides an easier way—the **GetOpenFilename** method of the **Application** object. This method displays a built-in user form that looks exactly like what you are used to when you use a Windows Open command to open a file. The user can then browse for the desired file in the usual way. The syntax you should use is as follows, where DataFileName is a string variable:

```
DataFileName = Application.GetOpenFilename(Filter:="Text Files " & _
    "(*.txt),*.txt",Title:="Data file")
```

This doesn't actually *open* the text file selected by the user; it just returns the name and the path of the file chosen by the user and stores it in the string variable DataFileName. Use this method to change the application, so that it prompts the user for the name and location of the data file. Actually, you should probably precede the above line with a MsgBox statement so that the user knows he's being asked to select the file with the data. Then try the modified application with your own text file, stored in a folder *different* from the folder containing the Excel application. (Look up the **GetOpenFilename** method in online help. Its beauty is that it has all of the "open file" functionality you expect built into it—you don't have to *create* this user form!)

7. Put the ideas from Exercises 2 and 6 together to make the application fairly general. First, create a user form that allows the user to choose the separator character from a list of option buttons. (Make the choices reasonable, such as comma, tab, and semicolon.) Then pass the user's choice to the revised ParseLine sub discussed in Exercise 2 as the Separator argument. Second, let the user select the text file with the data, as discussed in Exercise 6. Now the application should work with any text files with any separator in your list.

An AHP Application for Choosing a Job

29

29.1 Introduction

This application implements the analytical hierarchy process (AHP) in the context of choosing a job. AHP is useful in many multiobjective decision problems.[48] The user lists a number of criteria and a number of possible decision alternatives that meet the criteria to various degrees. In this case, the criteria are salary, nearness to family, benefits, and possibly others, and the decision alternatives are the user's available job offers. The first step in AHP is to compare the criteria—which are the most important to the user? This is discovered through a series of pairwise comparisons. Then the jobs are compared to each other on each criterion, again by making a series of pairwise comparisons. The final result is a score for each job, and the job with the highest score is identified as the preferred job.

New Learning Objectives: VBA

- To learn how online help can be provided on a worksheet by taking advantage of a worksheet's BeforeDoubleClick event.
- To learn several new controls for user forms: scroll bars, combo boxes, and command buttons other than the usual OK/Cancel combination.

New Learning Objective: Non-VBA

- To learn the basics of AHP.

29.2 Functionality of the Application

The application first asks the user to specify the criteria that are relevant for making the job decision. Several criteria, such as salary, location, and benefits, are listed as possibilities, but the user can add other criteria to the list if desired. Next, the user is asked to list the available job offers. Then the user is asked to make a

---

[48]A good reference on AHP can be found in Chapter 9 of *Practical Management Science*. To illustrate that this method can really be used, the author's wife, who teaches 7th grade English, needed to decide whether to stay at her school or move to a new middle school that had just opened. Although she had practically made up her mind to stay, she used this model and was comforted to find that it recommended the same decision.

series of pairwise comparisons, first between pairs of criteria and then between pairs of jobs on each criterion. After all pairwise comparisons have been made, the application performs the necessary calculations for AHP and reports the results on a Report sheet, highlighting the job with the highest score. The scores for the various jobs can also be viewed graphically. Finally, to check whether the user was internally consistent when making the pairwise comparisons, consistency indexes are reported.

After a given AHP analysis, the user can run another analysis with the *same* criteria and jobs (by making new pairwise comparisons). Alternatively, the user can run another analysis with entirely new inputs.

29.3 Running the Application

The application is stored in the file **AHP.xls**. When this file is opened, the Explanation sheet in Figure 29.1 appears. Because AHP is probably not well known to most users, the application provides some help in a text box. This text box is currently hidden, but it can be displayed by double-clicking anywhere in row 1 of the Explanation sheet. The help text box then appears, as in Figure 29.2. It can be hidden by again double-clicking in row 1. The way this online help is accomplished with VBA will be explained later in this chapter.

Figure 29.1 Explanation sheet

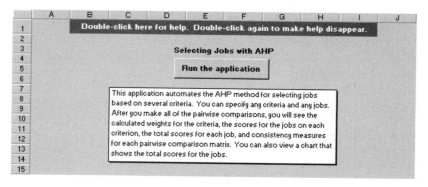

Clicking on the button in Figure 29.1 produces the dialog box in Figure 29.3. It has a combo box with a dropdown list of criteria the user can choose from. Alternatively, the user can type a *new* criterion in the box. After a criterion is entered in the box, the user should click on the Add button to add the criterion to the list that will be used in making the decision.

When all desired criteria have been added, the user should click on the No More button. Then the dialog box in Figure 29.4 appears. It has the same functionality as the first dialog box, except that there is no dropdown list; the user must enter all available jobs, one at a time, in the text box.

Figure 29.2 Help for AHP

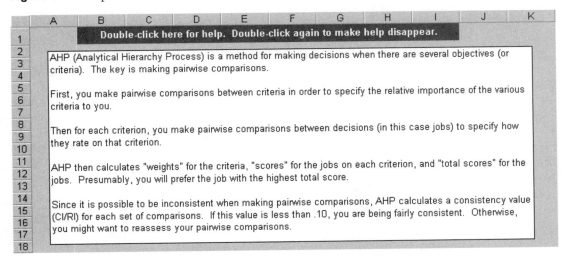

Figure 29.3 Dialog box for criteria

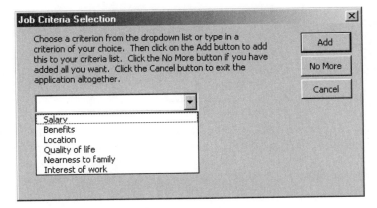

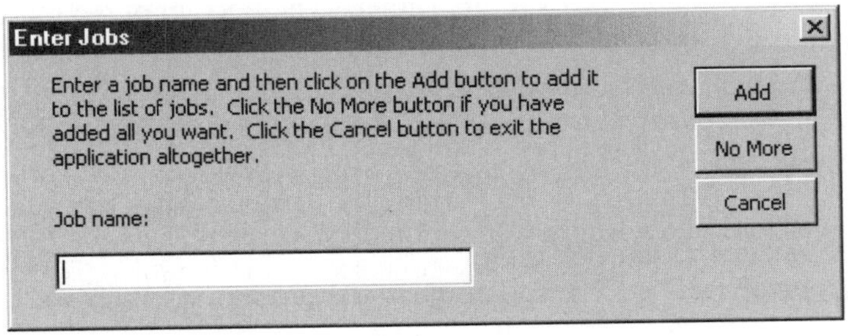

Figure 29.4 Dialog box for available jobs

After all criteria and jobs have been entered, several dialog boxes similar to the one shown in Figure 29.5 appear. Each asks the user to make a pairwise comparison between two of the criteria. This can be done by clicking on the button for the criterion that is considered more important and then using the scroll bar to indicate how much more important it is. (The scroll bar goes in discrete 1-unit steps, from 1 to 9. The labels below the scroll bar attach meanings to the numbers.) Note that there can be quite a few pairwise comparisons to make. For example, if there are four criteria, then there are six such pairwise comparisons (the number of ways two things can be chosen from four things). The counter on the dialog box reminds the user how many more comparisons remain.

Figure 29.5   Pairwise comparison dialog box for criteria

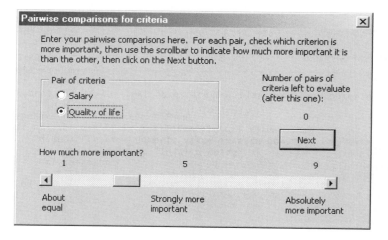

The application then presents a series of dialog boxes similar to the ones shown in Figures 29.6 and 29.7, where the user must make pairwise comparisons between pairs of jobs on the various criteria. Again, if there are quite a few criteria and jobs, the number of required pairwise comparisons will be large.

When all pairwise comparisons have been made, the application does the AHP calculations and reports the results in a Report sheet, as shown in Figure 29.8. This report lists the weights for the criteria, the scores for the jobs on each criterion, and the total scores for the jobs. The job with the highest total score is bold-faced. (In this example, Sears is the winner.) The bottom of the report lists consistency indexes. If the user has to make many pairwise comparisons, there is always the possibility of being inconsistent. This bottom section alerts the user to this possibility. Specifically, if it reports inadequate consistency (as this example does), the user should probably go through the process again and attempt to make more consistent comparisons.

By clicking on the top button on the Report sheet, the user can view the chart in Figure 29.9, which indicates the total scores for the jobs. The other two buttons on the Report sheet allow the user to repeat the analysis with the same criteria and jobs (by making new pairwise comparisons) or with entirely new inputs.

Figure 29.6 Pairwise comparison between jobs on salary criterion

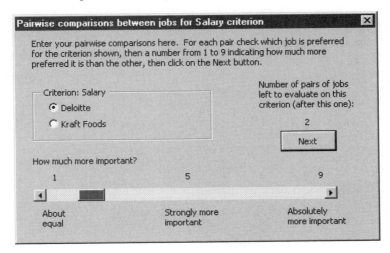

Figure 29.7 Pairwise comparison between jobs on quality of life criterion

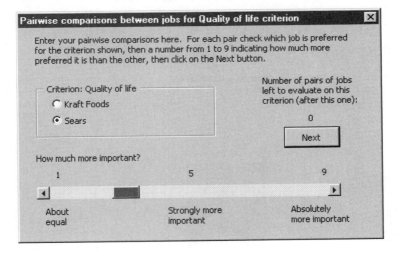

29.4 Setting Up the Excel Sheets

The **AHP.xls** file contains Explanation and Report worksheets and a ScoresChart chart sheet. (Unlike most of the other applications in the book, there is no "Model" sheet where most of the calculations take place. All calculations in this application are done directly in memory with VBA—that is, they are *not* performed through spreadsheet formulas.) The Report sheet, shown earlier in Figure 29.8, must be completed almost entirely at run time. The only template that can

Figure 29.8 Report sheet

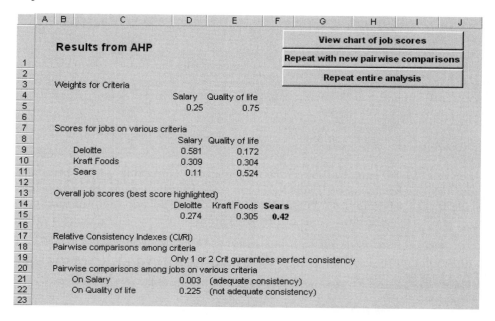

Figure 29.9 Chart of total job scores

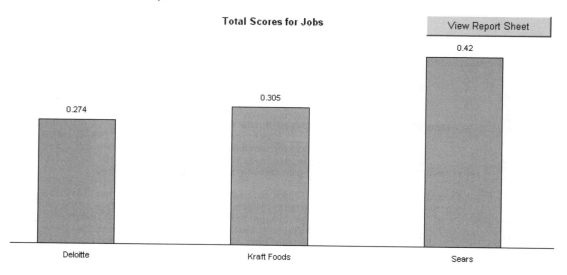

be developed at run time appears in Figure 29.10. However, the chart can be developed with the Chart Wizard at design time, using any set of trial inputs. Then it can be tied to the actual job scores at run time.

Figure 29.10 Template for Report sheet

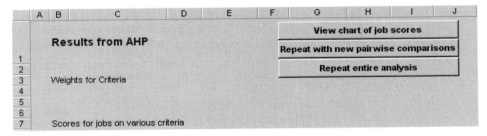

29.5   Getting Started with the VBA

The application contains four user forms named CritForm, JobForm, CritPWForm, and JobPWForm (PW for pairwise) and a single module. Once these are inserted, the Project Explorer window will appear as in Figure 29.11.

Figure 29.11 Project Explorer window

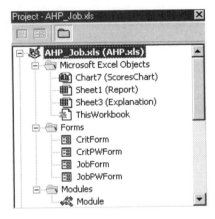

Workbook_Open Code

To guarantee that the Explanation sheet appears when the file is opened, the following code is placed in the ThisWorkbook code window. This code also hides the Report and ScoresChart sheets.

```
Private Sub Workbook_Open()
    Worksheets("Explanation").Activate
    Range("F5").Select
    Worksheets("Report").Visible = False
    Charts("ScoresChart").Visible = False
End Sub
```

Worksheet_BeforeDoubleClick Code

The Workbook_Open sub has been used repeatedly in previous applications. It responds to the Open event of the Workbook object. When the workbook is opened, this code runs. There are many other events that objects can respond to. In each case, it is possible to write code for the event. This can come in very handy. As an example, remember how the user can double-click in row 1 of the Explanation sheet to display or hide a help text box? This is accomplished by the following code for the worksheet's **BeforeDoubleClick** event. The built-in sub for this event comes with an argument called **Target**. This argument is the cell that is double-clicked. Therefore, the If function checks whether **Target.Row** equals 1. If it is, this means that the user double-clicked somewhere in row 1. In this case, the Visible property of the HelpBox (the name of the text box that contains the help) is toggled from True to False or vice versa. Note that the text box is named HelpBox at *design* time. A text box can be named exactly like a range—just select it and then type a name in the name box area in Excel.

```
Private Sub Worksheet_BeforeDoubleClick(ByVal Target As Range, Cancel As Boolean)
' This sub runs when the user double-clicks anywhere in row 1 of the Explanation sheet.
' It toggles a pre-formed text box between visible and not visible.
    Dim HBox As Shape
    If Target.Row = 1 Then
        Set HBox = Worksheets("Explanation").Shapes("HelpBox")
        HBox.Visible = Not HBox.Visible
        Range("F5").Select
    End If
End Sub
```

This code should be stored in the code window for the Explanation sheet. To get to it, double-click on the Explanation sheet item in the Project Explorer window of the VBE. Then in the code window, select Worksheet in the left dropdown list and double-click on the BeforeDoubleClick item in the right dropdown list. (See Figure 29.12.) This inserts a "stub" for the event code, as in the following two lines. You can then enter the code you need in the middle. Note that the Target and Cancel arguments are built in—you have no choice on whether to include them in the first line. However, we use only the Target argument in our code; we ignore the Cancel argument.

```
Private Sub Worksheet_BeforeDoubleClick(ByVal Target As Range, Cancel As Boolean)

End Sub
```

How might you learn about events like this? Probably the best way is to use the Object Browser in the VBE. Figure 29.13 shows where we discovered that a Worksheet has a BeforeDoubleClick event. The online help then describes the details, such as what the Target and Cancel arguments mean.

Figure 29.12 Inserting a sub for BeforeDoubleClick event

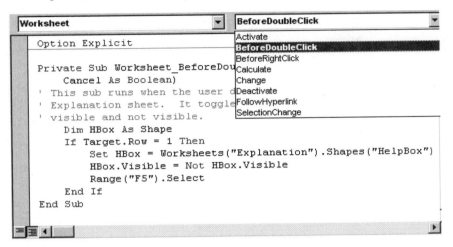

Figure 29.13 Object Browser for BeforeDoubleClick worksheet event

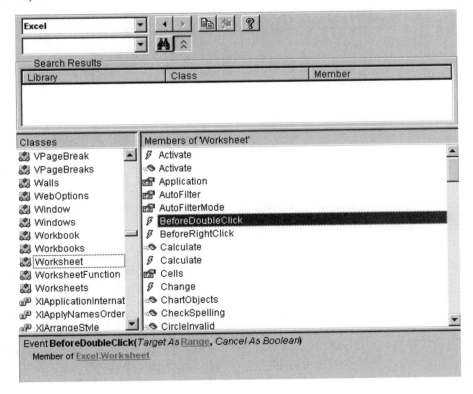

29.6 Designing the User Forms and Writing Their Event Code

> **Web Help** For more explanation of the code in this application, visit our Web site at http://www.indiana.edu/~mgtsci and download the **Code Explanation - AHP.doc** file.

The user forms include some features not seen in previous chapters. The CritForm has a combo box control, the CritPWForm and JobPWForm each have a scroll bar control, and the buttons on the CritForm and JobForm are not the standard OK/Cancel pair. However, this just illustrates the flexibility of the controls available in the Control Toolbox. You can choose the ones that are most appropriate for any particular application.

CritForm

The CritForm has three buttons named AddButton, NoMoreButton, and CancelButton, an explanation label, and a combo box named CritCombo. Its design appears in Figure 29.14.

Figure 29.14 Design of CritForm

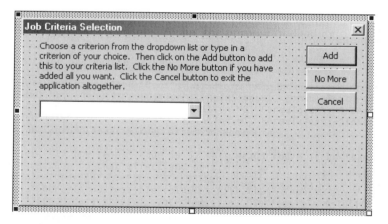

Event Code for CritForm

The **UserForm_Initialize** sub creates an array of criteria that are used to populate the combo box. The **AddButton_Click** sub does some error checking and then adds the newly chosen criterion to the list of criteria in the publicly declared Crit array. The **NoMoreButton_Click** sub simply unloads the form. By this time, the user has entered all desired criteria, so she just wants the dialog box to disappear. The **CancelButton_Click** sub unloads the form and terminates the program.

Note that a **ComboBox** control is essentially a blend of a list box and a text box. Specifically, its **List** property can be set equal to an array to populate the list, and its **Value** property returns the item in the box.

```
Private Sub UserForm_Initialize()
' Define an array of items that make up the "default" list in the combo box. The user
' can add a different item at run time if desired.
    Dim CArray As Variant
    CArray = Array("Salary", "Benefits", "Location", "Quality of life", _
        "Nearness to family", "Interest of work")
' Fill the combo box, but don't select any items by default.
    With CritCombo
        .List = CArray
        .Value = ""
    End With
End Sub

Private Sub AddButton_Click()
    Dim NewItem As String, i As Integer, IsNew As Boolean

' Check that a criterion has been entered and that it is not a criterion that was
' already entered. (If it is, set IsNew to False.)
    With CritCombo
        If .Value = "" Then
            MsgBox "Please make a selection", vbExclamation, "No selection"
            .SetFocus
            Exit Sub
        Else
            NewItem = .Value
            IsNew = True
            If NCrit > 0 Then
                For i = 1 To NCrit
                    If NewItem = Crit(i) Then
                        MsgBox "You already chose this item.", vbExclamation, "Duplicate"
                        IsNew = False
                        Exit For
                    End If
                Next
            End If

' Update the number of criteria in the Crit array only if IsNew is True. (Don't use the
' Preserve option for redimensioning if NCrit is 1. In this case, there is nothing to
' preserve. Besides, it would cause an error if this is not the first time the AHP
' analysis is being run in a session.
            If IsNew Then
                NCrit = NCrit + 1
                If NCrit = 1 Then
                    ReDim Crit(NCrit)
                Else
                    ReDim Preserve Crit(NCrit)
                End If
                Crit(NCrit) = NewItem
            End If

' Get ready for the next criterion.
            .Text = ""
            .SetFocus
        End If
    End With
End Sub

Private Sub NoMoreButton_Click()
    Unload Me
End Sub
```

```
Private Sub CancelButton_Click()
    Unload Me
    End
End Sub
```

JobForm

The JobForm, shown earlier in Figure 29.4, is analogous to the CritForm, so its design and event code are not repeated here. The only difference is that it contains a text box for capturing the job name, not a combo box.

CritPWForm

The design for the CritPWForm appears in Figure 29.15. It has ten labels, a command button named NextButton, a frame that contains two option buttons named FirstChoice and SecondChoice, and a scroll bar named CritScroll. Note that the numbers and descriptions above and below the scroll bar are all *labels*, as is the highlighted number in the figure. This latter label is named NLeft. A **ScrollBar** control has several properties, **Min**, **Max**, **LargeChange**, and **SmallChange**, that can be set at design time. For this application, the SmallChange and LargeChange properties can be left at their default values of 1, but the Min and Max properties should be changed to 1 and 9. (You can probably guess what these properties are all about. See online help on the ScrollBar control for more details.)

Figure 29.15 Design of CritPWForm

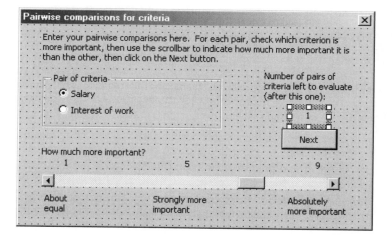

Event Code for CritPWForm

The **UserForm_Initialize** sub uses three public variables, Crit1, Crit2, and NPairsLeft, that have been declared publicly in the module, to initialize the user form. The first two of these are used as captions for the option buttons, and the third (an integer) is used as the caption for the NLeft label. By default, the scroll bar is put at its leftmost position, and the first option button is checked. The **NextButton_Click** sub then captures the option that has been checked and the value of the scroll bar in the public variables FChoice and PWVal. Note that the **Value** property of a **ScrollBar** control is its default property. It is always an integer between the scroll bar's Min and Max, and it is determined by the position of the "slider" on the scroll bar.

```
Private Sub UserForm_Initialize()
' This sub takes advantage of the public variables Crit1, Crit2, and
' NPairsLeft, which have already been defined in the module.
    With FirstChoice
        .Value = True
        .Caption = Crit1
    End With
    SecondChoice.Caption = Crit2
    CritScroll = 1
    NLeft.Caption = NPairsLeft
End Sub

Private Sub NextButton_Click()
' Capture which of the two options is favored (FChoice) and by how
' much (PWVal).
    FChoice = FirstChoice
    PWVal = CritScroll
    Unload Me
End Sub
```

JobPWForm

The JobPWForm, shown earlier in Figures 29.6 and 29.7, is very similar to the CritPWForm, so its design and event code are not repeated here.

29.7 The VBA Code in the Module

The bulk of the work is performed in the module. When the user clicks on the button in the Explanation sheet, the **Main** sub is run. It "shows" the CritForm and JobForm to get the lists of criteria and jobs, redimensions a number of arrays, and then calls the DoCalculations sub to perform the AHP.[49] The list of public variables and the Main code now follow.

---

[49] The RI array at the top of this sub contains the "magic numbers" that are used to check the consistency of any number of pairwise comparisons. For example, 1.12 is the consistency index that would be expected if the user were making *random* pairwise comparisons among a group of five criteria. The users' actual consistency index, CI, is divided by the appropriate RI from the list, and the consistency is deemed "adequate" if this ratio is less than 0.10.

Option Statements and Public Variables

```
Option Explicit
Option Base 1

' Definitions of public variables
'    Crit: array of criteria names
'    NCrit: number of criteria selected
'    PWCrit: two-dimensional array for pairwise comparison matrix among criteria
'    Weight: array of weights for criteria
'    CI: array of consistency indexes for criteria
'    Job: array of job names
'    NJobs: number of jobs selected
'    PWJobs: two-dimensional array for pairwise comparison matrix among jobs
'    Score: array of job scores on any criterion
'    JobCI: array of consistency indexes for jobs
'    RI: list of relative consistency indexes
'    TScore: array of total scores for jobs
'    MaxScore: score attained by best job
'    BestJob: index of best job
'    Crit1, Crit2: current criteria being compared (passed to CritPWForm)
'    NPairsLeft: counter used when doing pairwise comparisons
'    PWVal, FChoice: results of any pairwise comparison (passed back to module)
'    CurrCrit, Job1, Job2: values for job comparison on a criterion (passed to
'        JobPWForm)
Public Crit() As String, NCrit As Integer, PWCrit() As Single, _
    Weight() As Single, CI As Single, Job() As String, NJobs As Integer, _
    PWJobs() As Single, Score() As Single, JobCI() As Single, RI As Variant, _
    TScore() As Single, MaxScore As Single, BestJob As Integer, _
    Crit1 As String, Crit2 As String, NPairsLeft As Integer, _
    PWVal As Integer, FChoice As Boolean, CurrCrit As Integer, _
    Job1 As String, Job2 As String
```

Main Code

```
Sub Main()
' Set up an array for checking consistency indexes.
    RI = Array(0, 0, 0.58, 0.9, 1.12, 1.24, 1.32, 1.41, 1.45, 1.51)
' Initialize.
    NJobs = 0
    NCrit = 0
' Let the user choose criteria.
    CritForm.Show
' Let the user choose the jobs to compare.
    JobForm.Show
' Set the dimensions of the various arrays.
    ReDim Weight(NCrit)
    ReDim PWCrit(NCrit, NCrit)
    ReDim Score(NJobs, NCrit)
    ReDim PWJobs(NJobs, NJobs)
    ReDim JobCI(NCrit)
    ReDim TScore(NJobs)
' Let the user make all pairwise comparisons, then create the report.
    Call DoCalculations
End Sub
```

DoCalculations Code

The **DoCalculations** sub calls a number of other subs to do the individual AHP tasks. This is explained in the comments below.

```
Sub DoCalculations()
' This is a "control center" for all of the calculations that are required.  It calls
' the various subs to take care of the individual tasks.
    Dim i As Integer
' Let the user make pairwise comparisons among criteria.
    Call GetPWCrit
' Calculate the weights for the criteria.
    Call GetWeights
' If there are at least 3 criteria, calculate the consistency index.
    If NCrit > 2 Then Call CritConsistency
' For each criterion, let the user make pairwise comparisons among jobs, then calculate
' the job scores and consistency index.
    For i = 1 To NCrit
        CurrCrit = i
        Call GetPWJobs
        Call GetScores(i)
        If NJobs > 2 Then Call JobConsistency(i)
    Next
' Calculate the results and then report them on a Report sheet.
    Call CalcResults
    Call CreateReport
End Sub
```

GetPWCrit Code

The **GetPWCrit** sub is used to fill the pairwise comparison matrix (the PWCrit array). It does this by repeatedly showing the CritPWForm and capturing the user's choices in the public FChoice and PWVal variables. (The code from here on is actually quite straightforward, but it probably won't make much sense unless you thoroughly understand the AHP method. Again, see Chapter 9 of *Practical Management Science* for further explanation.)

```
Sub GetPWCrit()
' Fill the pairwise comparison matrix among criteria.
    Dim i As Integer, j As Integer
' The diagonals of the pairwise comparison matrix are all 1's.
    For i = 1 To NCrit
        PWCrit(i, i) = 1
    Next
' NPairsLeft is always the number of pairwise comparisons still to be made.
    NPairsLeft = (NCrit * (NCrit - 1)) / 2
' Loop through the pairs of Crit and get each pairwise comparison.
    For i = 1 To NCrit - 1
        For j = i + 1 To NCrit
            Crit1 = Crit(i)
            Crit2 = Crit(j)
            NPairsLeft = NPairsLeft - 1
            CritPWForm.Show
```

```
' Depending on the button selected, the i,j element is either the value from the scroll
' bar or its reciprocal.  In either case, the j,i element is the reciprocal of the i,j
' element.
              If FChoice Then
                    PWCrit(i, j) = PWVal
              Else
                    PWCrit(i, j) = 1 / PWVal
              End If
              PWCrit(j, i) = 1 / PWCrit(i, j)
          Next
     Next
End Sub
```

GetWeights Code

The **GetWeights** sub calculates the weights for the various criteria. These weights sum to 1. The higher the weight for a criterion, the more importance the user attaches to it.

```
Sub GetWeights()
' Calculate the weights for the various criteria.
    Dim i As Integer, j As Integer, Summ() As Single, Norm() As Single
    ReDim Summ(NCrit)
    ReDim Norm(NCrit, NCrit)
' Get the normalized values (so that column sums are 1).
    For j = 1 To NCrit
        Summ(j) = 0
        For i = 1 To NCrit
            Summ(j) = Summ(j) + PWCrit(i, j)
        Next
        For i = 1 To NCrit
            Norm(i, j) = PWCrit(i, j) / Summ(j)
        Next
    Next
' Get the weights (averages of row sums).
    For i = 1 To NCrit
        Weight(i) = 0
        For j = 1 To NCrit
            Weight(i) = Weight(i) + Norm(i, j)
        Next
        Weight(i) = Weight(i) / NCrit
    Next
End Sub
```

GetPWJobs Code

The **GetPWJobs** sub is analogous to the GetPWCrit sub. It shows the JobPWForm repeatedly to get the user's pairwise comparisons between jobs for the various criteria.

```
Sub GetPWJobs()
' For each criterion, get the pairwise comparisons among jobs on that
' criterion.
```

```
    Dim i As Integer, j As Integer
    For i = 1 To NJobs
        PWJobs(i, i) = 1
    Next
    NPairsLeft = (NJobs * (NJobs - 1)) / 2
    For i = 1 To NJobs - 1
        For j = i + 1 To NJobs
            Job1 = Job(i)
            Job2 = Job(j)
            NPairsLeft = NPairsLeft - 1
            JobPWForm.Show
            If FChoice Then
                PWJobs(i, j) = PWVal
            Else
                PWJobs(i, j) = 1 / PWVal
            End If
            PWJobs(j, i) = 1 / PWJobs(i, j)
        Next
    Next
End Sub
```

GetScores Code

The **GetScores** sub is analogous to the GetWeights sub listed earlier. It takes one argument: the criterion currently being analyzed. If you refer back to the DoCalculations sub, you will note that the GetPWJobs and GetScores subs are both called inside a loop over the criteria. Therefore, these subs are run several times, each time with a new criterion. The identity of this criterion (in the Crit variable) is used here for filling the Score array.

```
Sub GetScores(Crit As Integer)
' Get the job scores for each criterion. (The logic is identical to the
' GetWeights sub.)
    Dim i As Integer, j As Integer, Summ() As Single, Norm() As Single
    ReDim Summ(NJobs)
    ReDim Norm(NJobs, NJobs)
    For j = 1 To NJobs
        Summ(j) = 0
        For i = 1 To NJobs
            Summ(j) = Summ(j) + PWJobs(i, j)
        Next
        For i = 1 To NJobs
            Norm(i, j) = PWJobs(i, j) / Summ(j)
        Next
    Next
    For i = 1 To NJobs
        Score(i, Crit) = 0
        For j = 1 To NJobs
            Score(i, Crit) = Score(i, Crit) + Norm(i, j)
        Next
        Score(i, Crit) = Score(i, Crit) / NJobs
    Next
End Sub
```

Consistency Code

The two subs listed below check the consistency of the pairwise comparisons. The first is for criteria; the second is for jobs. Again, the code is fairly straightforward, but it won't make much sense unless you understand the AHP method.

```
Sub CritConsistency()
' Calculate the consistency index for comparisons among criteria.
    Dim i As Integer, j As Integer, Summ() As Single, Ratio() As Single, Avg As Single
    ReDim Summ(NCrit)
    ReDim Ratio(NCrit)
' Calculate the product of the PWCrit matrix and the Weights column. Then calculate
' ratios as this product divided by a weight.
    For i = 1 To NCrit
        Summ(i) = 0
        For j = 1 To NCrit
            Summ(i) = Summ(i) + PWCrit(i, j) * Weight(j)
        Next
        Ratio(i) = Summ(i) / Weight(i)
    Next
' Calculate the consistency index.
    Avg = 0
    For i = 1 To NCrit
        Avg = Avg + Ratio(i)
    Next
    Avg = Avg / NCrit
    CI = (Avg - NCrit) / (NCrit - 1)
End Sub
```

```
Sub JobConsistency(Crit As Integer)
' Calculate the consistency indexes for each pairwise comparison matrix involving jobs.
    Dim i As Integer, j As Integer, Summ() As Single, Ratio() As Single, Avg As Single
    ReDim Summ(NJobs)
    ReDim Ratio(NJobs)
    For i = 1 To NJobs
        Summ(i) = 0
        For j = 1 To NJobs
            Summ(i) = Summ(i) + PWJobs(i, j) * Score(j, Crit)
        Next
        Ratio(i) = Summ(i) / Score(i, Crit)
    Next
    Avg = 0
    For i = 1 To NJobs
        Avg = Avg + Ratio(i)
    Next
    JobCI(Crit) = (Avg / NJobs - NJobs) / (NJobs - 1)
End Sub
```

CalcResults Code

The **CalcResults** sub finishes the AHP calculations. It first uses the criteria weights and the job scores on the criteria to calculate total scores for the jobs. Then it finds the job with the largest total score. Finally, it calculates the consistency ratios used to determine whether the user's pairwise comparisons are reasonably consistent.

```
Sub CalcResults()
    Dim i As Integer, j As Integer, Summ As Single
' Calculate the total score for each job.
    For i = 1 To NJobs
        Summ = 0
        For j = 1 To NCrit
            Summ = Summ + Score(i, j) * Weight(j)
        Next
        TScore(i) = Summ
    Next
' Find the maximum, over all jobs, of the total scores and identify the corresponding
' best job.
    MaxScore = 0
    For i = 1 To NJobs
        If TScore(i) > MaxScore Then
            MaxScore = TScore(i)
            BestJob = i
        End If
    Next
' Calculate the relative consistency indexes.
    If NCrit > 2 Then CI = CI / RI(NCrit)
    If NJobs > 2 Then
        For i = 1 To NCrit
            JobCI(i) = JobCI(i) / RI(NJobs)
        Next
    End If
End Sub
```

CreateReport Code

The **CreateReport** sub fills in the Report sheet. It is fairly long (maybe it should be modularized?), but each part is straightforward, as explained in the comments.

```
Sub CreateReport()
' Create the Report sheet.
    Dim i As Integer, j As Integer, MaxCols As Integer, cell As Range
    Application.ScreenUpdating = False
    With Worksheets("Report")
        .Visible = True
        .Activate
    End With
' Clear any previous report except for a few labels.
    For Each cell In ActiveSheet.UsedRange
        If cell.Address <> "$B$1" And cell.Address <> "$B$3" And cell.Address <> "$B$7" _
            Then cell.Clear
    Next
' Enter the weights for the criteria.
    With Range("C4")
        For i = 1 To NCrit
            .Offset(0, i) = Crit(i)
            .Offset(1, i) = Format(Weight(i), "0.000")
        Next
    End With
' Enter the scores for the jobs on the various criteria, then format.
    With Range("C8")
```

```
                For i = 1 To NJobs
                    .Offset(i, 0) = Job(i)
                Next
                For j = 1 To NCrit
                    .Offset(0, j) = Crit(j)
                Next
                For i = 1 To NJobs
                    For j = 1 To NCrit
                        .Offset(i, j) = Format(Score(i, j), "0.000")
                    Next
                Next
                Range(.Offset(0, 1), .Offset(0, NCrit)).HorizontalAlignment = xlRight
            End With
        With Range("B" & 10 + NJobs)
            .Value = "Overall job scores (best score highlighted)"
' Enter the total scores for the jobs, boldface the best job, and format.
            For i = 1 To NJobs
                .Offset(1, 1 + i) = Job(i)
                .Offset(2, 1 + i) = Format(TScore(i), "0.000")
                If i = BestJob Then Range(.Offset(1, 1 + i), _
                    .Offset(2, 1 + i)).Font.Bold = True
            Next
            Range(.Offset(1, 2), .Offset(1, NJobs + 1)).HorizontalAlignment = xlRight
' Name range for later use in creating chart.
            Range(.Offset(1, 2), .Offset(2, NJobs + 1)).Name = "TotalScores"
        End With
' Expand column widths as necessary.
        If NCrit > NJobs Then
            MaxCols = NCrit + 1
        Else
            MaxCols = NJobs + 1
        End If
        With Range("C1")
            For i = 1 To MaxCols
                .Columns(i).EntireColumn.AutoFit
            Next
        End With
' Enter the results about consistency.
        With Range("B" & 14 + NJobs)
            .Value = "Relative Consistency Indexes (CI/RI)"
            .Offset(1, 0) = "Pairwise comparisons among criteria"
            If NCrit <= 2 Then
                .Offset(2, 2) = "Only 1 or 2 Crit guarantees perfect consistency"
            Else
                .Offset(2, 2) = Format(CI, "0.000")
                If CI < 0.1 Then
                    .Offset(2, 3) = "  (adequate consistency)"
                Else
                    .Offset(2, 3) = "  (not adequate consistency)"
                End If
            End If
            .Offset(3, 0) = "Pairwise comparisons among jobs on various criteria"
            If NJobs <= 2 Then
                .Offset(4, 2) = "Only 1 or 2 jobs guarantees perfect consistency (for all " _
                    & "criteria)"
            Else
                For i = 1 To NCrit
                    .Offset(i + 3, 1) = "On " & Crit(i)
                    .Offset(i + 3, 2) = Format(JobCI(i), "0.000")
                    If JobCI(i) < 0.1 Then
```

```
                        .Offset(i + 3, 3) = "  (adequate consistency)"
                Else
                        .Offset(i + 3, 3) = "  (not adequate consistency)"
                End If
            Next
        End If
    End With
' Color the whole sheet blue.
    ActiveSheet.Cells.Interior.ColorIndex = 37
    Range("H2").Select
    Application.ScreenUpdating = True
End Sub
```

ViewChart Code

The **ViewChart** sub is attached to the top button on the Report sheet (see Figure 29.8). It unhides and activates the ScoresChart sheet and links it to the newly calculated data on total scores.

```
Sub ViewChart()
' Unhide and activate the chart, and "populates" it with the current result data.
    With Charts("ScoresChart")
        .Visible = True
        .Activate
        .SetSourceData Range("TotalScores")
        .Deselect
    End With
End Sub
```

RepeatSame and RecoverData Code

The **RepeatSame** sub is attached to the middle button on the Report sheet (see Figure 29.8). It jumps into the middle of the application, bypassing the CritForm and the JobForm (because the user wants to use the *same* criteria and jobs as before). This is actually a bit tricky. The Crit and Job arrays have to be refilled with their previous values. They are *not* necessarily saved in memory from the previous analysis. For example, the user might run the first analysis, close Excel, and then open it again. Anything previously in memory is then lost. Fortunately, the **RecoverData** sub can recover the Crit and Job arrays from the *labels* in the Report sheet. Then the DoCalculations sub (listed earlier) can be run to get new pairwise comparisons and perform the rest of the AHP analysis.

```
Sub RepeatSame()
' This sub is run when the user clicks on the middle button on the Report sheet.
    Call RecoverData
    Call DoCalculations
End Sub
```

```
Sub RecoverData()
' This sub recovers the numbers and names of the criteria and jobs from the current
' report.  It is run only when the user wants to repeat the AHP with the same criteria
' and jobs but different pairwise comparisons.
```

```
    Dim i As Integer
    RI = Array(0, 0, 0.58, 0.9, 1.12, 1.24, 1.32, 1.41, 1.45, 1.51)
    With Worksheets("Report").Range("C8")
        NCrit = Range(.Offset(0, 1), .Offset(0, 1).End(xlToRight)).Columns.Count
        NJobs = Range(.Offset(1, 0), .Offset(0, 1).End(xlDown)).Rows.Count
        ReDim Crit(NCrit)
        ReDim Job(NJobs)
        ReDim Weight(NCrit)
        ReDim PWCrit(NCrit, NCrit)
        ReDim Score(NJobs, NCrit)
        ReDim PWJobs(NJobs, NJobs)
        ReDim JobCI(NCrit)
        ReDim TScore(NJobs)
        For i = 1 To NCrit
            Crit(i) = .Offset(0, i)
        Next
        For i = 1 To NJobs
            Job(i) = .Offset(i, 0)
        Next
    End With
End Sub
```

RepeatNew Code

The **RepeatNew** sub is attached to the bottom button on the Report sheet (see Figure 29.8). It hides the current report, activates the Explanation sheet, and runs the whole program again by calling the Main sub.

```
Sub RepeatNew()
' This sub runs when the user clicks on the bottom button on the Report
' sheet to run an entirely new analysis.  It first clears the Crit and Job
' arrays (using Redim is an effective way to do this), then hides the
' Report sheet, activates the Explanation sheet, and runs Main.
    ReDim Crit(1)
    ReDim Job(1)
    Worksheets("Report").Visible = False
    Worksheets("Explanation").Activate
    Call Main
End Sub
```

ViewReport Code

The **ViewReport** sub is attached to the button on the ScoresChart sheet. It permits navigation back to the Report sheet (and it hides the chart sheet).

```
Sub ViewReport()
' Hide the chart and activate the Report sheet.
    Charts("ScoresChart").Visible = False
    Worksheets("Report").Activate
    Range("H2").Select
End Sub
```

29.8 Summary

This chapter has presented an application that should be useful for many readers of this book—students who are looking for a job. It is easy to use, and it is realistic. The VBA details are somewhat complex, and they will be mysterious to readers who are not familiar with the inner workings of AHP. However, this is part of the beauty of VBA applications. They can be used by people who are not familiar with what is happening "under the hood."

PROGRAMMING EXERCISES

1. Open a new workbook, make sure the drawing toolbar is visible, and draw an oval on it, positioned and captioned approximately as in Figure 29.16. Then insert a text box, positioned approximately as in the figure, and type some text into it. (Make up anything.) Now write code so that when the user double-clicks on the oval the help appears (if it was invisible) or disappears (if it was visible). (*Hint*: This should happen if the user double-clicks anywhere within the oval, which means it should happen if the user double-clicks on any cell the oval touches.)

Figure 29.16 Online help

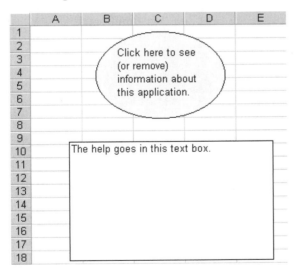

2. The scroll bars used for the pairwise comparison are just one possibility. Another possibility is to use a spinner button and an accompanying text box, as illustrated in Figure 29.17. (See Exercise 10 of Chapter 12 for details on this kind of control.) Change the application so that it uses this approach instead of scroll bars. Make sure the resulting CritPWForm and JobPWForm are laid out nicely and are meaningful for the user.

Figure 29.17 Spinner button and text box

3. Most people who use the AHP method suggest a 1 to 9 scale for making the pairwise comparisons, and this is what we have implemented here. Change the application so that the scale is from 1 to 5. Now the index 5 means what the old index 9 meant. There are simply fewer choices for the user to worry about. From a user's standpoint, which of these two scales would you rather use?

4. Change the application so that it pertains to making a decision on where to go on a vacation. Change the automatic entries in the CritForm's combo box to ones that might be used in this type of decision. Also, replace the text box in the JobForm by a combo box. Place two automatic entries in this combo box: Wife's parents and Husband's parents. (You can assume that these are *always* possible vacation spots, even if they aren't necessarily the preferred ones!)

5. The CreateReport is indeed too long for the taste of most programmers. Rewrite it so that it calls several smaller subs that perform the individual tasks. You can choose the number of smaller subs, but they should make logical sense.

30

A Poker Simulation

30.1 Introduction

This final application is a bit less "serious" than the other applications in the book, but it should be interesting to poker players, and it contains some interesting VBA code. In case you are not a poker player, a player is dealt five cards from a 52-card deck. There are several types of "hands" the player can be dealt, as described in the following list:

- **a pair**: two of some denomination and three of other distinct denominations
- **two pairs**: two of one denomination, two of another denomination, and another card
- **three of a kind**: three of one denomination and two of other distinct denominations
- **a straight**: five denominations in progression, such as 4, 5, 6, 7, 8
- **a flush**: five cards of the same suit, such as five hearts
- **a full house**: three of one denomination and two of another denomination
- **four of a kind**: four of one denomination and another card
- **straight flush**: a straight all of the same suit
- **a bust**: none of the above

Except for a bust, the hands in this list are shown in increasing value, so that, for example, three of a kind beats two pairs. They all beat a bust.

The application simulates 100,000 5-card hands, all from a 52-card deck, and counts the number of each type of hand in the above list. It should be interesting to see whether the likelihoods of the hands go in the opposite order of their values. For example, is a hand with two pairs more likely than three of a kind? The simulation will help answer this question.

New Learning Objectives: VBA

- To illustrate how VBA can perform a simulation completely with code—no spreadsheet model.
- To illustrate how rather complex logic can be accomplished with the use of appropriate If constructs, loops, and arrays.

New Learning Objective: Non-VBA

- To show how simulation can be used to see how a game like poker works and whether its rules are reasonable (do the values of the hands go along with their likelihoods?).

30.2   Functionality of the Application

The only purpose of this application is to repeatedly simulate 5-card hands from a 52-card deck, tally the numbers of hands of each type, and display the relative frequencies in a worksheet.

30.3   Running the Application

The application is stored in the file **Poker.xls**. This file contains a single sheet named Report, shown in Figure 30.1, which the user sees upon opening the file.

Figure 30.1   Report sheet before running the simulation

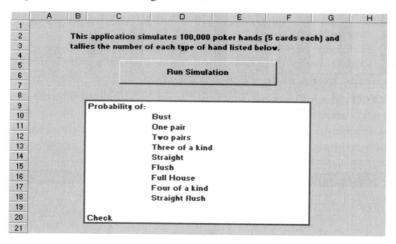

Each time the user clicks on the button, 100,000 *new* 5-card hands are simulated, and the results are displayed in the sheet, as shown in Figure 30.2. (When we ran it, the simulation of 100,000 hands took about 5 seconds.)

We say that 100,000 *new* hands are simulated because each run uses a new set of random numbers for the simulation. Therefore, the results will be slightly different each time the application is run. Figure 30.3 shows results from a different set of 100,000 hands. They are very similar to the results in Figure 30.2, but they are not exactly the same. Of course, this is the nature of simulation. You will undoubtedly get slightly different results when you run it.

Figure 30.2 Results from a simulation run

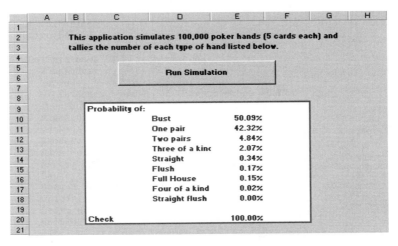

Figure 30.3 Results from another simulation run

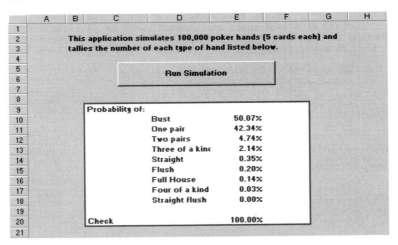

Each of these runs illustrates what can be shown from a formal probability argument—the probabilities of the hands go in reverse order of the values of the hands. A bust is most likely, a pair is next most likely, and so on.[50] And if you are counting on getting four of a kind or a straight flush, dream on!

---

[50]Again, because of the nature of simulation, it is *possible* that you will get results where, for example, there are more flushes than straights.

30.4   Setting Up the Excel Sheets

There is really nothing to set up at design time other than to enter labels and do some formatting in the Report sheet, as shown in Figure 30.1. There is nothing "hidden" here. Other than labels, the sheet is blank, waiting for the simulated results. Furthermore, the simulation occurs completely in VBA code. There is no worksheet where calculations are performed.

30.5   Getting Started with the VBA

The application requires only a module—no user forms or references. After the module is added, the Project Explorer window will appear as in Figure 30.4.

Figure 30.4   Project Explorer window

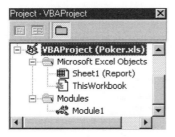

Workbook_Open Code

The following code is placed in the ThisWorkbook code window. It clears results from any previous simulation run.

```
Private Sub Workbook_Open()
    Range("E10:E20").ClearContents
    Range("D6").Select
End Sub
```

30.6   The VBA Code in the Module

> **Web Help**   For more explanation of the code in this application, visit our Web site at http://www.indiana.edu/~mgtsci and download the **Code Explanation - Poker.doc** file.

To this point, it might sound like this application is a cute little exercise for card players. However, the VBA code is far from trivial. It requires some careful logic, and it makes heavy use of arrays. It is an interesting illustration of how humans can easily perceive patterns that computers can discover only with tricky programming. For example, a poker player can look at his hand, without even rearranging the cards, and immediately see that he has a pair, a straight, or whatever. As the code will show, however, it takes considerable computer programming to recognize these patterns.

The module-level variables are listed first. Note that they are declared with the keyword Dim, not with Public. This is perfectly acceptable. The Public keyword makes variables known to other *modules*, including event code modules, but there is only a single module in this application. Still, these module-level variables need to be declared at the top of the module, outside of the subs, so that all of the subs in the module can recognize them.

Option Statements and Module-Level Variables

```
Option Explicit
Option Base 1


' Definitions of module-level variables:
'    NBust - number of hands that results in a bust (with similar definitions for NPair,
'       N2Pair, etc.)
'    Denom - array that indicates which denomination (1 to 13) each card in the deck is
'    Card - array that indicates the cards in the hand - e.g., if Card(3) = 37,
'       this means the third card dealt is the 37th card in the deck
'    NReps - number of simulated hands, in this case 100,000
Dim NBust As Long, NPair As Long, N2Pair As Long, N3ofKind As Long, _
    NFullHouse As Integer, N4ofKind As Integer, NStraight As Integer, _
    NFlush As Integer, NStraightFlush As Integer, _
    Denom(52) As Integer, Card(5) As Integer, NReps As Long
```

Main Code

The **Main** sub runs when the user clicks on the button on the Report sheet. It first calls the **InitStats** sub to set all counters to 0. Next, it calls the **SetupDeck** sub to "define" the cards in the deck. Then it uses a For loop to run the 100,000 replications of the simulation. In each replication it calls the **Deal** sub to deal the cards and the **Evaluate** sub to check what type of hand is obtained. Finally, it calls the **Report** sub to put the results in the Report sheet. VBA's **Randomize** function is placed near the top of the Main sub to ensure that a new set of random numbers will be used each time the simulation is run.

```
Sub Main()
    Dim i As Long
    Randomize
    NReps = 100000
' Set counters to 0.
    Call InitStats
' "Name" the cards in the deck.
    Call SetupDeck
' Deal out NReps poker hands and evaluate each one.
```

```
        For i = 1 To NReps
            Call Deal
            Call Evaluate
        Next
' Report the summary stats from the NReps hands.
        Call Report
        Range("D6").Select
    End Sub
```

InitStats Code

The **InitStats** sets all counters (the number of busts, the number of pairs, and so on) to 0.

```
Sub InitStats()
    NBust = 0
    NPair = 0
    N2Pair = 0
    N3ofKind = 0
    NStraight = 0
    NFlush = 0
    NFullHouse = 0
    N4ofKind = 0
    NStraightFlush = 0
End Sub
```

SetupDeck Code

The **SetupDeck** sub "defines" the deck by filling the Denom array. It does this with two nested For loops. If you follow the logic closely, you will see that Denom(1) through Denom(4) are set to 1 (the "aces"), Denom(5) through Denom(8) are set to 2 (the "deuces"), and so on. You can think of denomination 11 as the Jacks, denomination 12 as the Queens, and denomination 13 as the Kings. Also, there are no explicit hearts, diamonds, clubs, and spades, but you can think of cards 1, 5, 9, and so on as the hearts; cards 2, 6, 10, and so on as the diamonds; cards 3, 7, 11, and so on as the clubs; and cards 4, 8, 12, and so on as the spades.

```
Sub SetupDeck()
    Dim i As Integer, j As Integer
' Give the first 4 cards denomination 1 (aces), the next 4 denomination 2
' (deuces), and so on
    For i = 1 To 13
        For j = 1 To 4
            Denom(4 * (i - 1) + j) = i
        Next
    Next
End Sub
```

Deal Code

The **Deal** sub randomly chooses five cards from the 52-card deck. It is the only sub where any simulation takes place. That is, it is the only code that uses random numbers. It uses VBA's **Rnd** function (which is essentially equivalent to Excel's **Rand** function) to simulate a single random number uniformly distributed between 0 and 1. Then the following line is used to obtain a uniformly distributed *integer* from 1 to 52:

```
CardIndex = Int(Rnd * 52) + 1
```

Note how this works. The quantity **Rnd*52** is uniformly distributed between 0 and 52. Then VBA's **Int** function chops off the decimal, leaving an integer from 0 to 51. Therefore, 1 is added to obtain an integer from 1 to 52.

The Boolean Used array keeps track of which of the 52 cards in the deck have *already* been dealt in the current hand. Essentially, random integers are generated until five *distinct* integers have been obtained. When an integer is generated that is distinct from the previous integers, its Used value is set to True, so that it cannot be used again (in this hand). By the end of this sub, the indexes of the five cards dealt are stored in the Card array. For example, if Card(4) = 47, this means that the fourth card in the hand is the 47th card in the deck (the Queen of clubs).

```
Sub Deal()
    Dim i As Integer, j As Integer
    Dim CardIndex As Integer, Used(52) As Boolean, NewCard As Boolean
' The Used array keeps track of which cards have already been dealt, that is, if
' Used(i)=True, then card i has been dealt (and can't be dealt again).
    For i = 1 To 52
        Used(i) = False
    Next
' NewCard is a flag that remains False until a new card (one that hasn't yet been
' dealt) is generated.
    For i = 1 To 5
        NewCard = 0
        Do
            CardIndex = Int(Rnd * 52) + 1
            If Used(CardIndex) = False Then
                NewCard = True
                Used(CardIndex) = True
            End If
        Loop Until NewCard = True
' Card(i) records the card number of the i-th card dealt in this hand.
        Card(i) = CardIndex
    Next
End Sub
```

Evaluate Code

The most difficult part of the program is the **Evaluate** sub. By this time, the Card array has been generated. It might show that the hand contains the cards 2, 7, 19,

28, and 47. What kind of a hand is this? Is it a bust, a pair, or what? The Evaluate sub goes through the necessary logic to check all possibilities.

The first check is for a straight. It finds the denominations of the five cards and stores them in the CardDenom array. For example, the denomination of the first card is Denom(Card(1)), which is stored in CardDenom(1). These denominations might be out of order, such as 5, 3, 7, 6, 4, so it uses two nested For loops to sort them in increasing order. Then it checks whether the sorted denominations form a progression, such as 3, 4, 5, 6, 7. (If this sounds overly complex, just try doing it any other way.)

The second check is for a flush. For example, the hand with cards 3, 15, 23, 39, 51 is a flush. This is because cards 3, 7, 11, 15, 19, 23, 27, 31, 35, 39, 43, 47, and 51 are the 13 cards of a certain suit (clubs, say). An easy way to check whether *any* five cards are of the same suit is to divide each of them by 4 and see whether the remainders are all equal. (This is the case for 3, 15, 23, 39, and 51. Each has remainder 3.) This can be done with VBA's **Mod** operator. For example, **51 Mod 4** is the remainder when 51 is divided by 4.

The third check is for a straight flush, which will be the case only if the Boolean variables HasStraight and HasFlush are both True.

If the hand is a straight or a flush (or both), then no further checks are necessary. Otherwise, checks for a pair, two of a kind, and the rest are necessary. All of these involve the numbers of like denominations in a hand. For example, a hand with two pairs contains two of some denomination, two of another, and one of another. The Groups array is used to collect this information. A full house has Groups(3) = 1 and Groups(2) = 1, which says that it has one group of size 3 and one group of size 2. Similarly, a bust has Groups(1) = 5, three of a kind has Groups(3) = 1 and Groups(1) = 2, and so on. So by filling the Groups array and checking its contents, the program can discover which type of hand has been dealt. Further details are given in the comments.

See, we told you it is a lot harder than simply *looking* at your cards and knowing immediately what you have!

```
Sub Evaluate()
    Dim i As Integer, Count(13) As Integer, Groups(4) As Integer, j As Integer, _
        HasStraight As Boolean, _
        HasFlush As Boolean, CardDenom(5) As Integer, Temp As Integer
' First, check for a straight.
    HasStraight = False
    For i = 1 To 5
        CardDenom(i) = Denom(Card(i))
    Next
' Sort the denominations in increasing order.
    For i = 1 To 4
        For j = i + 1 To 5
            If CardDenom(j) < CardDenom(i) Then
                Temp = CardDenom(j)
                CardDenom(j) = CardDenom(i)
                CardDenom(i) = Temp
            End If
        Next
    Next
```

```
' Check if they are in a progression, like 4, 5, 6, 7, 8.
    If CardDenom(2) = CardDenom(1) + 1 And _
        CardDenom(3) = CardDenom(2) + 1 And _
        CardDenom(4) = CardDenom(3) + 1 And _
        CardDenom(5) = CardDenom(4) + 1 Then
        HasStraight = True
        NStraight = NStraight + 1
    End If
' Next, check for a flush.
    HasFlush = False
    If Card(1) Mod 4 = Card(2) Mod 4 And Card(2) Mod 4 = Card(3) Mod 4 _
        And Card(3) Mod 4 = Card(4) Mod 4 And Card(4) Mod 4 = Card(5) Mod 4 Then
        HasFlush = True
        NFlush = NFlush + 1
    End If
' Next, check for a straight flush.
    If HasStraight And HasFlush Then
        NStraightFlush = NStraightFlush + 1
        NStraight = NStraight - 1
        NFlush = NFlush - 1
    End If
' There's no need to check the rest if the hand is a straight or a flush (or both).
    If HasStraight Or HasFlush Then Exit Sub
' Otherwise, check all the other possibilities. Count(i) will be the number of cards of
' denomination i in the hand.
    For i = 1 To 13
        Count(i) = 0
    Next
    For i = 1 To 5
        Count(Denom(Card(i))) = Count(Denom(Card(i))) + 1
    Next
' Groups(i) will be the number of "groups" of size i. For example, if Groups(2) = 1,
' then there is one group of size 2, that is, one pair (of some denomination).
    For i = 1 To 4
        Groups(i) = 0
    Next
    For i = 1 To 13
        If Count(i) > 0 Then Groups(Count(i)) = Groups(Count(i)) + 1
    Next
' Now go through all of the possibilities.
    If Groups(1) = 5 Then
        NBust = NBust + 1
    ElseIf Groups(1) = 3 And Groups(2) = 1 Then
        NPair = NPair + 1
    ElseIf Groups(1) = 1 And Groups(2) = 2 Then
        N2Pair = N2Pair + 1
    ElseIf Groups(1) = 2 And Groups(3) = 1 Then
        N3ofKind = N3ofKind + 1
    ElseIf Groups(2) = 1 And Groups(3) = 1 Then
        NFullHouse = NFullHouse + 1
    Else
        N4ofKind = N4ofKind + 1
    End If
End Sub
```

Report Code

The **Report** sub lists the results in the Report sheet. Note that it reports the relative frequencies, such as the number of busts divided by the total number of replications. The formula in cell E20 is not really necessary, but it provides a comforting check that the relative frequencies sum to 1, as they should. If a number other than 1 appeared in cell E20, this would indicate a bug in the program.

```
Sub Report()
    Range("E10") = NBust / NReps
    Range("E11") = NPair / NReps
    Range("E12") = N2Pair / NReps
    Range("E13") = N3ofKind / NReps
    Range("E14") = NStraight / NReps
    Range("E15") = NFlush / NReps
    Range("E16") = NFullHouse / NReps
    Range("E17") = N4ofKind / NReps
    Range("E18") = NStraightFlush / NReps
    Range("E20").Formula = "=Sum(E10:E18)"
End Sub
```

30.7 Summary

The application in this chapter is not earth-shaking, except perhaps to avid poker players, but it does illustrate an interesting and certainly nontrivial use of logic, loops, and arrays. In addition, the results of the simulation agree with our intuition about the game of poker itself. They show that as hands become more valuable, they become less likely. And if you always thought you were unlucky because you got a lot of busts, you now realize that this happens about 50% of the time.

PROGRAMMING EXERCISES

1. Change the application so that it contains a chart sheet displaying the frequencies of the various types of hands, as in Figure 30.5. Put a button on the Report sheet to navigate to this chart sheet. (Do you need to write any code to update the chart after each run?)

2. There are many versions of poker. Change the application so that it works for a version where the player is dealt six cards and then gets to discard any one of them. Assume that the player will discard the card that makes the remaining hand as valuable as possible. (*Hint:* Run the Evaluate sub on each of the possible 5-card hands with one of the six cards omitted, and take the best.)

3. A more realistic version of the previous problem is that the player is dealt five cards. Then he can discard as many as four of these and request replacements from the remaining deck. The problem with simulating this version is that we have to know the player's strategy—depending on what he's dealt, what will he discard? Simulate the following strategy. (*Hint:* Run the Evaluate sub on the original hand to see what he should discard. Then run it again on the final hand.)

   • If dealt a bust, discard all but a single card. (Normally, a player would keep the highest card, but it doesn't make any difference here.)

Figure 30.5 Chart sheet for Exercise 1

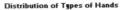

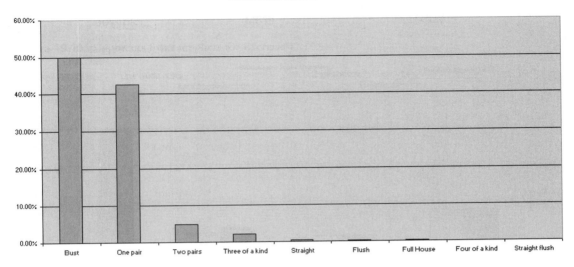

Distribution of Types of Hands

- If dealt a pair, keep the pair and discard the other three cards.
- If dealt two pairs, keep the pairs and discard the other card.
- If dealt three of a kind, keep these three and discard the other two cards.
- If dealt any other type of hand, keep it and discard nothing.

4. (More difficult) In the preceding exercise, the player never tries to "fill in" partial straights or flushes. For example, if he has a 4, 5, 6, 7, and 10, he doesn't discard the 10, hoping to fill the straight with a 3 or an 8. Similarly, if he has four hearts and a spade, he doesn't discard the spade, hoping to fill the flush with another heart. Simulate such a strategy. Specifically, assume he first checks for a bust. If he has a bust, then he checks whether he has a partial straight that could be completed on either end. (This means, for example, 4, 5, 6, 7, but not 1, 2, 3, 4. Trying to complete this latter straight is too risky because only a 5 will do it.) If he has such a partial "inside" straight, he discards the other card. Otherwise, still assuming he has a bust, he checks whether he has four cards of one suit. If so, he discards the other card. Otherwise, he discards any four cards from the bust. The rest of his strategy is the same as the last four bulleted points in the previous exercise. In other words, he tries to complete a straight or a flush only when he has a bust. Based on your simulation results, is this strategy better or worse than the strategy in the previous exercise?

5. In the game of bridge, each of four players is dealt 13 cards from a 52-card deck. Concentrate for now on a particular player. Develop a simulation similar to the poker simulation that finds the distribution of the number of aces the player is dealt. (*Note*: Since you're concentrating on one player only, you need to simulate 13 cards only; you can ignore what the other three players get.)

6. Continuing the previous exercise, again concentrate on a single player and simulate the distribution of the maximum number of any suit the player is dealt. For example, if the hand has 5 hearts, 3 diamonds, 3 clubs, and 2 spades, this maximum number is 5. How likely is it that a player will get at least 11 cards of some suit?

Index

IMPORTANT!

If the CD-ROM Packaging has been opened, the purchaser cannot return the book for a refund! The CD-ROM is subject to this agreement.

LICENSING AND WARRANTY AGREEMENT

Notice to Users: Do not install or use the CD-ROM until you have read and agreed to this agreement. You will be bound by the terms of this agreement if you install or use the CD-ROM or otherwise signify acceptance of this agreement. If you do not agree to the terms contained in this agreement, do not install or use any portion of this CD-ROM.

License: The material in the CD-ROM (the "Software") is copyrighted and is protected by United States copyright laws and international treaty provisions. All rights are reserved to the respective copyright holders. No part of the Software may be reproduced, stored in a retrieval system, distributed (including but not limited to over the www/Internet), decompiled, reverse engineered, reconfigured, transmitted, or transcribed, in any form or by any means—electronic, mechanical, photocopying, recording, or otherwise—without the prior written permission of Duxbury (the "Publisher"). Adopters of Albright's *VBA for Modelers* may place the Software on the adopting school's network during the specific period of adoption for classroom purposes only in support of that text. The Software may not, under any circumstances, be reproduced and/or downloaded for sale. For further permission and information, contact Duxbury, 511 Forest Lodge Road, Pacific Grove, California 93950.

Limited Warranty: The warranty for the media on which the Software is provided is for ninety (90) days from the original purchase and valid only if the packaging for the Software was purchased unopened. If, during that time, you find defects in the workmanship or material, the Publisher will replace the defective media. The Publisher provides no other warranties, expressed or implied, including the implied warranties of merchantability or fitness for a particular purpose, and shall not be liable for any damages, including direct, special, indirect, incidental, consequential, or otherwise.

For Technical Support:
Voice: 1-800-423-0563
Fax: 1-859-647-5045
E-mail: support@kdc.com